# Henry Constable: The Complete Poems

Elizabethan poet Henry Constable (1562–1613), a Protestant-born Catholic convert, is a fascinating case study in how religious and political preoccupations could drive the learned across the unstable confessional divide. He threw over an early career of government service to work towards the return of England to the Catholic fold, and this dramatic change of course was accompanied by a turn to spiritual matters in his poetry. Under the weight of the Protestant-Whig narrative of English history, Constable was long dismissed as a minor poet, a Catholic traitor, or both, and his achievements have tended to be overlooked. His writings illustrate a journey through the confessional spectrum, revealing unresolved tensions between the public and the private, hope and disillusion, the secular and the religious.

This book provides a new comprehensive critical edition of Constable's sonnets that returns to the primary sources – some of them newly discovered. It rests on extensive first-hand collation, a concern with material aspects and the circumstances of textual production and transmission, and a sound grasp of the intellectual and cultural contexts. It offers readable, uncluttered texts alongside a complete textual apparatus and notes. Along with an updated biography and a study of the sonnet collections, the introduction provides an authoritative revision of the canon of Constable's poetry and an overview of its critical reception.

This volume will be of interest not only to literary scholars but also to political and cultural historians working on early modern England and France and on the growing area of transnational English Catholicism.

*Studies and Texts* 232

CATHOLIC AND RECUSANT TEXTS
OF THE LATE MEDIEVAL
& EARLY MODERN PERIODS 5

Edited by
ANN M. HUTCHISON, *York University and PIMS*
MICHAEL QUESTIER, *University of Durham*
ALISON SHELL, *University College London*

The Pontifical Institute of Mediaeval Studies acknowledges the support of the late JOSEPH and CLAUDINE POPE, who generously helped initiate the publication of Catholic and Recusant Texts of the Late Medieval and Early Modern Periods.

# HENRY CONSTABLE

# The Complete Poems

*Edited by*

MARÍA JESÚS PÉREZ-JÁUREGUI

*Toronto*
**PIMS**
PONTIFICAL INSTITUTE OF MEDIAEVAL STUDIES

*Acknowledgement*

The publication of this volume was made possible by funds generously provided by Ann M. Hutchison, James P. Carley, and the Janet E. Hutchison Foundation, Toronto.

*Library and Archives Canada Cataloguing in Publication*

Title: The complete poems / Henry Constable ; edited by María Jesús Pérez-Jáuregui.
Other titles: Poems
Names: Constable, Henry, 1562–1613, author. | Pérez-Jáuregui, María Jesús, editor. | Pontifical Institute of Mediaeval Studies, publisher.
Series: Studies and texts (Pontifical Institute of Mediaeval Studies) ; 232. | Catholic and recusant texts of the late medieval & early modern periods ; 5.
Description: Series statement: Studies and texts ; 232 | Catholic and recusant texts of the late medieval & early modern periods ; 5 | Includes bibliographical references and indexes.
Identifiers: Canadiana (print) 2023047263X | Canadiana (ebook) 20230472672 | ISBN 9780888442321 (hardcover) | ISBN 9781771104319 (PDF)
Subjects: LCSH: Constable, Henry, 1562–1613. | LCSH: Sonnets, English.
Classification: LCC PR2235.C5 A18 2023 | DDC 821/.3–dc23

© Pontifical Institute of Mediaeval Studies 2023

Pontifical Institute of Mediaeval Studies
59 Queen's Park Crescent East
Toronto, Ontario M5S 2C4
Canada
pims.ca

PRINTED IN CANADA

*For my mentor,*
*María José Mora-Sena*

# Contents

*Illustrations* • ix
*Tables* • xi
*Abbreviations, Sigla, and Notes* • xiii

*Preface* • xix

CHAPTER ONE
Henry Constable: A Biographical Account • 1

CHAPTER TWO
The Amatory and Dedicatory Sonnets • 32

CHAPTER THREE
The *Spiritual Sonnets* • 92

CHAPTER FOUR
Henry Constable and the Sonnet Form • 105

CHAPTER FIVE
The Critical Reception of Constable's Poetry • 131

CHAPTER SIX
The Present Edition • 147

HENRY CONSTABLE
The Poems • 155
Explanatory Notes • 248
Bibliographical Description of Main Textual Sources • 364

Appendix A: Two Anonymous Sonnets from *T* Dedicated to Constable • 384
Appendix B: Arrangement of the Secular Sonnets in All Sources • 388
Appendix C: Headings and Arrangement of the *Spiritual Sonnets* in the
    Two Manuscripts • 398

*Bibliography* • 400
*Index of Manuscripts* • 431
*Index of First Lines with Regularized Spelling* • 433
*General Index* • 436

# Illustrations

*Sources of all illustrations are indicated below. Every effort has been made to ensure that owners and photographic sources are accurately credited; if there are any errors or omissions, please bring them to the attention of the Pontifical Institute of Mediaeval Studies, so that appropriate corrections may be made in any future edition.*

## Figures

| | |
|---|---|
| Figure 1 | A genealogical chart showing Constable's connections with noble families • 2 |
| Figure 2 | Transmission hypothesis; stemma with dates of compilation or printing • 75 |
| Figure 3 | Transmission of sonnet 15 • 78 |
| Figure 4 | Transmission of sonnet 60 • 80 |
| Figure 5 | Transmission of sonnet 32 • 82 |
| Figure 6 | Transmission of sonnet 25 • 83 |
| Figure 7 | Transmission of sonnet 27 • 84 |
| Figure 8 | Transmission of sonnet 52 • 85 |
| Figure 9 | Authorial ascription in all sources • 89 |
| Figure 10 | Constable's signature as found in a letter to Cecil, CP 188/108. Reproduced with permission of the Marquess of Salisbury, Hatfield House • 97 |
| Figure 11 | Archetypes and transmission of the *Spiritual Sonnets* • 98 |

## Plates

*Plates are located after page 154.*

| | |
|---|---|
| Plate 1 | Dublin, Marsh's Library MS Z3.5.21 (*M*), fol. 25r. By permission of the Governors and Guardians of Marsh's Library. © Marsh's Library. |

Plate 2   Arundel, Arundel Castle, MSS, Harrington MS. Temp. Eliz., the "Arundel Harington MS" (*H*), fol. 148r, showing Sir John Harington's hand. By permission of the Duke of Norfolk, Arundel Castle Archives.

Plate 3   London, National Art Library, Victoria and Albert Museum, MS Dyce 44 (*T*), fol. 42v. © Victoria and Albert Museum, London.

Plate 4   New Haven, Yale University, Beinecke Library, MS 621 (*Bn*), fol. 14v. © Beinecke Rare Book and Manuscript Library, Yale University.

Plate 5   San Marino, Huntington Library, RB 58467: title page of the 1592 edition of *Diana* (*D92*). Reproduced by permission of the Huntington Library.

Plate 6   London, British Library, C.39.a.60: title page of the 1594 edition of *Diana*, first printing (*D94a*). © British Library Board.

Plate 7   London, British Library, Harley MS 7553 (*HA*), fol. 40r. © British Library Board.

Plate 8   Berkeley, Gloucs., Berkeley Castle, Select Books 85 (*BE*), p. 12. By kind permission of Berkeley Castle.

# Tables

Table 1    Order of the sonnets in *M* • 37
Table 2    Order of the sonnets in *H* and *D92* • 42
Table 3    Order of the sonnets in *E* and other sources • 51
Table 4    Order of the sonnets in *A* and other sources • 55
Table 5    Order of the sonnets in *H* and *D94* • 66
Table 6    Errors in sonnets 1–66 • 72
Table 7    The *Spiritual Sonnets* in the two manuscripts • 95
Table 8    Errors in sonnets 67–87 • 101

# Abbreviations, Sigla, and Notes

## Abbreviations

*Archives and Libraries*

ASV   Archivio Segreto Vaticano, Vatican City
BAV   Biblioteca Apostolica Vaticana, Vatican City
BL   British Library, London
Bodl.   Bodleian Library, Oxford
CP   The Cecil Papers at Hatfield House
SP   State Papers
SSF   Segretaria di Stato, Francia
TNA   The National Archives, Kew

*Printed Sources*

Aquinas, *ST* • *The Summa Theologiæ of St. Thomas Aquinas*, trans. Fathers of the English Dominican Province (London, 1920), http://www.newadvent.org/summa/index.html.

Arber • Edward Arber, *A Transcript of the Registers of the Company of Stationers of London, 1554–1640, A.D.*, 5 vols. (London, 1875–1894).

Barnes, *Divine Centurie* • Barnabe Barnes, *A divine centurie of spirituall sonnets* (London, 1595), RSTC 1467.

Barnes, *P&P* • Barnabe Barnes, *Parthenophil and Parthenophe* (London, 1593), RSTC 1469.

Barnfield, *Cynthia* • Richard Barnfield, *Cynthia: With certaine sonnets, and the legend of Cassandra* (London, 1595), RSTC 1484.

Beal, *Dictionary* • Peter Beal, *A Dictionary of English Manuscript Terminology, 1450–2000* (Oxford, 2008).

Briquet • Charles-Moïse Briquet, *Les filigranes: Dictionnaire historique des marques du papier des leur apparition vers 1282 jusqu'en 1600, avec figures dans le texte et 16, 112 facsimilés de filigranes*, 2nd ed, 4 vols. (Leipzig, 1923).

CELM • Peter Beal, *Catalogue of English Literary Manuscripts*, http://www.celm-ms.org.uk.
Craig, *Amorose Songes* • Alexander Craig, *The amorose songes, sonets, and elegies* (London, 1606), RSTC 5956.
CSPD • *Calendar of State Papers Domestic: Edward VI, Mary, Elizabeth, and James I*, ed. R. Lemon and Everett Green, 12 vols. (London, 1856–1872).
CSPSc • *Calendar of State Papers relating to Scotland and Mary Queen of Scots, 1547–1603*, ed. Joseph Bain et al., 13 vols. (Edinburgh, 1898–1969).
CSPSp • *Calendar of Letters and State Papers Relating to English Affairs Preserved Principally in the Archives of Simancas*, ed. Martin A.S. Hume, 4 vols. (London, 1892–1899).
CSPV • *Calendar of State Papers and Manuscripts Relating to English Affairs, Existing in the Archives and Collections of Venice, and in Other Libraries of Northern Italy*, ed. Rawdon Brown et al., 38 vols. in 40, (London, 1864–1947).
Daniel, *Delia* • Samuel Daniel, *Delia and Rosamond augmented. Cleopatra* (London, 1594), RSTC 6243.4.
Desportes, *Cleonice* • Philippe Desportes, *Cleonice*, in *Œuvres de Philippe Desportes*, ed. Alfred Michiels (Paris, 1858), 180–225.
Desportes, *Diane 1* • Philippe Desportes, *Diane*, book 1, in *Œuvres*, ed. Michiels, 13–67.
Desportes, *Diane 2* • Philippe Desportes, *Diane*, book 2, in *Œuvres*, ed. Michiels, 67–114.
Desportes, *Diverses amours* • Philippe Desportes, *Diverses amours*, in *Œuvres*, ed. Michiels, 368–430.
Desportes, *Hippolyte* • Philippe Desportes, *Hippolyte*, in *Œuvres*, ed. Michiels, 116–177.
Donne, *HS* • John Donne, *Holy Sonnets*, in *The Complete Poems*, ed. Robin Robbins (Edinburgh, 2010).
Drayton, *Idea* • Michael Drayton, *Idea*, in *Poems: By Michaell Draiton Esquire* (London, 1605), sig. Bb1r–Cc8v, RSTC 7216.
Drayton, *Ideas mirrour* • Michael Drayton, *Ideas mirrour: Amours in quatorzains* (London, 1594), RSTC 7203.
Du Bellay, *L'Olive* • Pierre Du Bellay, *L'Olive*, ed. Ernesta Caldarini (Geneva, 1974).
EEBO • *Early English Books Online*, ProQuest, https://eebo.chadwyck.com/home.
EH • *England's Helicon* (London, 1600), RSTC 3191.
Fletcher, *Licia* • Giles Fletcher, *Licia, or Poemes of love* (London, 1593), RSTC 11055.
GL • Jacobus de Voragine, *The Golden Legend or Lives of the Saints*, trans. William Caxton, ed. Frederick S. Ellis, 7 vols. (London, 1900–1931).

Gray • *The Poems & Sonnets of Henry Constable*, ed. John Gray (London, 1897).
Griffin, *Fidessa* • Bartholomew Griffin, *Fidessa, more chaste then kinde* (London, 1596), RSTC 12367.
Grundy • *The Poems of Henry Constable*, ed. Joan Grundy (Liverpool, 1960).
Hazlitt • *Diana: The Sonnets and Other Poems of Henry Constable*, ed. William C. Hazlitt (London, 1859).
HMC *Rutland* • Historical Manuscripts Commission, *The Manuscripts of His Grace the Duke of Rutland, G.C.B., Preserved at Belvoir Castle*, 4 vols. (London, 1888–1905).
HMC *Salisbury* • Historical Manuscripts Commission, *Calendar of the manuscripts of the Most Hon. the Marquis of Salisbury, K.G., preserved at Hatfield House, Hertfordshire*, 24 vols. (London, 1883–1976).
Hughey • Ruth Hughey, ed., *The Arundel Harington Manuscript of Tudor Poetry*, 2 vols. (Columbus, 1960).
ODNB • *Oxford Dictionary of National Biography*, ed. H.C.G. Matthew and Brian Harrison; online edition, ed. Lawrence Goldman (2004–), https://www.oxforddnb.com.
OED • *Oxford English Dictionary*, Oxford University Press (2014–), http://www.oed.com.
Park, *Heliconia* • Thomas Park, ed., *Heliconia: Comprising a Selection of English Poetry of the Elizabethan Age*, 3 vols. (London, 1815).
Park, *THM* • Thomas Park, ed., *The Harleian Miscellany*, vol. 9 (London, 1812).
Parker • Tom W.N. Parker, *Proportional Form in the Sonnets of the Sidney Circle: Loving in Truth* (Oxford, 1998).
Petrarch, *Rime* • Francesco Petrarca, *Petrarch: The Canzoniere, or Rerum Vulgarium Fragmenta*, trans. Mark Musa (Bloomington, IN, 1999).
Ronsard, *Amours* • Pierre de Ronsard, *Les amours*, in *Œuvres complètes*, ed. Jean Céard, Daniel Ménager, and Michel Simonin, vol. 1 (Paris, 1993–1994), 25–162.
RSTC • *A Short-Title Catalogue of Books Printed in England, Scotland, & Ireland and of English Books Printed Abroad 1475–1640*, first comp. by A. W. Pollard and G. R. Redgrave, 2nd ed., rev. W. A. Jackson, F. S. Ferguson, and Katharine F. Pantzer, 3 vols. (London, 1976–1991).
Scève, *Délie* • Maurice Scève, *Délie: Object de plus haulte vertu*, ed. Françoise Joukovsky (Paris, 1996).
Scott, *Sonnets* • Janet G. Scott, *Les sonnets élisabéthains: Les sources et l'apport personnel* (Paris, 1929).
Shakespeare, *R&J* • William Shakespeare, *Romeo and Juliet*, in *The Oxford Shakespeare: The Complete Works*, ed. Stanley Wells and Gary Taylor (New York, 1986), 378–412.

Shakespeare, *Sonnets* • William Shakespeare, *Shakespeare's Sonnets*, ed. Katherine Duncan-Jones (London, 2010).

Sidney, *A&S* • Sir Philip Sidney, *Astrophil and Stella*, in *The Major Works*, ed. Katherine Duncan-Jones (New York, 2008), 153–211.

Spenser, *Amoretti* • Edmund Spenser, *Amoretti and Epithalamion* (London, 1595), RSTC 23076.

Spenser, *FH* • Edmund Spenser, *Fowre Hymnes* (London, 1596), RSTC 23086.

SS • Henry Constable, *Spiritual Sonnets* (as a collection).

TF • T.W., *The tears of fancie: Or, Love disdained* (London, 1593), RSTC 25122.

Venn • John Venn and J.A. Venn, *Alumni Cantabrigienses: A Biographical List of All Known Students, Graduates and Holders of Office at the University of Cambridge, from the Earliest Times to 1900*. 2 parts in 10 vols. (Cambridge, 1922–1954).

Watson, *Hekatompathia* • Thomas Watson, *The hekatompathia or Passionate centurie of love* (London, 1582), RSTC 25118a.

Wickes, *Bio* • George Wickes, "Henry Constable, Poet and Courtier, 1562–1613," *Biographical Studies* 2 (1954): 272–300.

Wickes, *Courtier* • George Wickes, "Henry Constable: Courtier Poet," in *Renaissance Papers: A Selection of Papers Presented at the Renaissance Meeting in the Southeastern States* (Columbia, SC, 1956), 102–107.

Wickes, *Sonnets* • George Wickes, "Henry Constable's Spiritual Sonnets," *Month* 18 (1957): 30–40.

Williams, *Edition* • Claire B. Williams, "An Edition of National Art Library (Great Britain) MS Dyce 44," 2 vols. (PhD diss., University of Sheffield, 2012).

Woudhuysen, *Circulation* • Henry Woudhuysen, *Sir Philip Sidney and the Circulation of Manuscripts, 1558–1640* (Oxford, 1996).

# Sigla

*Textual Archetypes*

Secular Sonnets
X    Lost holograph, compiled by 1588
Y    Lost holograph, compiled by 1589
Z    Lost holograph, compiled in 1590

Spiritual Sonnets
α    Lost holograph, compiled ca. 1595
β    Lost holograph, compiled by 1603

*Manuscripts*

| | |
|---|---|
| A | Oxford, Bodleian Library, MS Ashmole 38 |
| BE | Berkeley, Gloucs., Berkeley Castle, Select Books 85 |
| Bn | New Haven, Yale University, Beinecke Library, MS 621 |
| E | Edinburgh, Edinburgh University Library, MS H.-P. Coll. 401 |
| H | Arundel, Arundel Castle, The Arundel Harington MS |
| HA | London, British Library, Harley MS 7553 |
| M | Dublin, Marsh's Library, MS Z3.5.21 |
| OBL | London, British Library, Additional MSS 18920 |
| T | London, National Art Library, MS Dyce 44, also known as the Todd MS |

*Printed Works*

| | |
|---|---|
| AP | Sir Philip Sidney, *An apologie for poetrie* (London, 1595), RSTC 22534. |
| CM | Henry Constable, *The Catholike moderator: Or a moderate examination of the doctrine of the Protestants*, trans. W.W. (London, 1623), RSTC 5636.2. |
| D92 | Henry Constable, *Diana: The praises of his Mistres, in certaine sweete sonnets* (London, 1592), RSTC 5637. |
| D94 | Henry Constable, *Diana: The excellent conceitful sonnets of H.C. augmented with divers quatorzains of honorable and lerned personages* (London, 1594?). |
| D94a | Earliest printing, British Library, RSTC 5638. |
| D94b | Second printing, Bodleian Library and Huntington Library, RSTC 5638.3. |
| Discovery | [Henry Constable?], *A discoverye of a counterfecte conference helde at a counterfecte place, by counterfecte travellers, for thadvancement of a counterfecte tytle, and invented, printed, and published by one (person) that dare not avowe his name* (Paris?, 1600), RSTC 5638.5. |
| DP | John Donne, *Poems* (London, 1635), RSTC 7046. |
| Examen | Henry Constable, *Examen pacifique de la doctrine des Huguenots* (London, 1589), RSTC 5638.7. |
| O91 | Sir John Harington, *Orlando furioso in English heroical verse* (London, 1591), RSTC 746. |
| PE | James VI and I, *His Majesties poeticall exercises at vacant houres* (Edinburgh, 1591), RSTC 14379. |

*PR1*         Francis Davison, ed., *A poetical rapsody*, 1st ed. (London, 1602), RSTC 6373.
*PR2*         Francis Davison, ed., *A poetical rapsodie*, 2nd ed. (London, 1608), RSTC 6374.

## Editorial Symbols and Abbreviations

^         omitted punctuation mark
*om*      omitted word
Ɛ         a variant that is deemed an error in the stemma of transmission

## Biblical Citations

All biblical citations are to the King James Bible (1611), which, despite being completed after Constable's sonnets were written, was based on previous translations with which he would have been familiar.

# Preface

This volume is the culmination of the research I began as a graduate student in 2008. The scope of this research has widened over time; it evolved from a preliminary study of Henry Constable's sonnets dedicated to prospective patrons into my PhD thesis – a conservative edition based on archival work – and further still into the present critical edition.

Under the weight of the Protestant-Whig narrative of English history, Constable was long dismissed as a minor poet, a Catholic traitor, or both, and his achievements have tended to be overlooked. He has been the target of disparaging comments – one critic remarked that "few hearts would leap with joy at the discovery of a previously lost manuscript of sonnets" by him.[1] He has also fallen victim to fanciful speculation, of which the best example is perhaps Elaine Scarry's volume on Constable and Shakespeare's purported romance.[2] Even his twentieth-century editor, Joan Grundy, was content not to vindicate her book, and often engages with the poet's shortcomings rather than his accomplishments.[3]

The present work is fundamentally aimed at restitution. It seeks to give Constable his due as a writer of secular verse showing rich Continental and English influences. His sonnets, endowed with some freshness of conceit and diction, did indeed contribute to the Elizabethan sonnet vogue at its very outset. To the amatory and dedicatory sonnets that gave him fame among his contemporaries must be added his more personal and lesser-known religious – distinctly Catholic – sonnets, which confirm Constable as a pioneering religious poet writing before Donne and Herbert. As a Protestant-born convert, his writings illustrate a journey through the confessional spectrum and reveal unresolved tensions between the public and the private, hope and disillusion, and the secular and the religious. Amorous conceits, political ambition, and the drive for patronage interweave with a personal quest for the true faith and salvation, infusing vitality into his oeuvre.

1. Heather Dubrow, *Echoes of Desire: English Petrarchism and Its Counterdiscourses* (Ithaca, NY, 1995), 57.
2. Elaine Scarry, *Naming Thy Name: Cross Talk in Shakespeare's Sonnets* (New York, 2016).
3. *The Poems of Henry Constable*, ed. Joan Grundy (Liverpool, 1960).

This seems like the right time to reassess Constable's career and works, considering the exciting directions taken in the study of Catholic history and cultural manifestations, and the renewed interest in manuscript transmission and the materiality of texts. Inspired by the seminal scholarship of Marotti, Beal, Woudhuysen, May, and others, my edition rests on extensive firsthand examination of primary sources scattered around two continents, some of which I had the joy of rediscovering and collating for the first time. It provides an account of the circumstances of production and transmission of Constable's sonnets, and how he and other agents revised them to suit shifting circumstances. At the same time, it does not lose sight of the intellectual and cultural context surrounding his poetry. I am driven by a desire for transparency in the exercise of editorial judgement, so that readers may be able to benefit from clear, uncluttered texts of the sonnets while having a thorough textual apparatus and notes at their disposal.

Above everything else, this book is the scholarly manifestation of a personal ambition, that Constable's sonnets may be more widely read and fully understood.

It would be impossible to complete a project such as this without incurring a debt with countless institutions and individuals.

Research towards the publication of this volume has been partially funded by the Universidad de Sevilla, which awarded me graduate and postdoctoral fellowships as well as short-term study-abroad grants;[4] the Junta de Andalucía, through the research group "Estudios Medievales y Renacentistas Ingleses" (HUM-322); and the Universidad de Córdoba, which gave me financial support for a one-month research leave in the United Kingdom.[5]

Staff working at countless libraries and archives have gone out of their way to facilitate my research whether in person or by correspondence. Special thanks are due to the former archivist at Berkeley Castle, David Smith; Peter Foden, archivist at Belvoir Castle; Danielle Spittle at the Centre for Research Collections, Edinburgh University Library; and the curators at Arundel Castle, Marsh's Library, the Beinecke Rare Book and Manuscript Library, the Huntington Library, the National Art Library, the Rare Books and Music and Manuscripts rooms at the British Library, the Corpus Christi College Library in Oxford, and the Bodleian Library.

---

4. The "Beca de Personal Investigador en Formación," within the "III Plan Propio de Investigación," had a duration of four years.

5. "Plan Propio de Fomento de la Investigación" (2018).

I am grateful to colleagues and specialists who have aided me in more ways than I can count. Claire Loffman (née Williams) was generous enough to share her PhD thesis on MS Dyce 44 with me. Paulina Kewes and Hayley Morris enabled me to access resources at Oxford for an extended period of time. James Freeman, medieval manuscripts curator at Cambridge University, undertook some research at the Huntington Library on my behalf. Paul Murray, James Kelly, and Theresa Phillips warmly welcomed me to the Centre for Catholic Studies at Durham University. During a conference on Renaissance manuscripts in Sheffield I met Arthur Marotti, Steve May, Henry Woudhuysen, and other specialists who have been very supportive of my project. The Catholic Record Society invited me to speak at their 2017 annual conference, where I received invaluable encouragement and feedback.

To Peter Beal I owe a debt of gratitude, as he alerted me to the existence of the Berkeley Castle manuscript of Constable's *Spiritual Sonnets*. This book is heavily indebted to his *Catalogue of English Literary Manuscripts* (*CELM*) and seminal publications on scribal practices and hopes to do justice to his work. George Wickes, who wrote his dissertation on Constable in the 1950s, kindly sent me copies of the resulting publications and gave me a very sound piece of advice – to look into the religious sonnets – at a very early stage.

Among the scholars who have offered comments and assistance regarding my written work, I must mention David Norbrook and Reid Barbour, who kindly read my MA and PhD theses respectively; the members of my doctoral committee, Leticia Álvarez-Recio, Maria de Jesus Crespo Candeias Velez Relvas, Francisco Alonso-Almeida, and Jordi Sánchez-Martí; Manuel J. Gómez-Lara – president of that committee – and Zenón Luis-Martínez, who have read the commentary to this edition attentively, and Rafael Vélez-Núñez, who answered a query about early modern music.

Warm thanks to Alison Shell, who believed in this project as soon as she learnt of it and encouraged me to send a proposal. She has been a supportive and unfailingly kind editor and guide over the last years. Ann Hutchison, Fred Unwalla, and the editors at the Pontifical Institute of Mediaeval Studies have been forthcoming with their assistance and exceedingly patient. The insightful comments by two anonymous readers and the thorough copyediting by Jonathan Brent have helped give the manuscript its final, improved shape.

To my doctoral advisor, mentor, and friend María José Mora-Sena I dedicate this book, as it would simply not exist without her. I first heard the name Henry Constable from her lips, and she has been a beacon in the dark through my entire academic career and adult life in more ways than I could express. Thank you.

I would also like to thank my longtime colleagues and friends at the Universidad de Sevilla and former colleagues at the Universidad de Córdoba, who have cheered me on and asked me the most dreaded question of all – "How is the book going?" – out of genuine interest and affection.

Special thanks go to the close friends who have put up with my long absences and silences and always welcomed me back with open arms. Last but not least, none of this would have been possible without my patient, loving family, especially my parents, my sister, my significant other, and our supportive cats. Thank you for letting Henry Constable sit at our dinner table.

CHAPTER ONE

# Henry Constable: A Biographical Account

Henry Constable came from a prominent Yorkshire family whose members had traditionally combined military service and public office, strengthening connections with the nobility and seeking royal favour. His great-great-grandfather, Sir Marmaduke Constable of Flamborough (ca. 1456–1518), served four different kings from Edward IV to Henry VIII.[1] His daughter Eleanor married into the Berkeley family and was grandmother to the notorious recusant Thomas Throckmorton.[2] Sir Robert Constable of Flamborough (1478?–1537), Sir Marmaduke's eldest son, provides early evidence of the Catholic connections of the family. He became one of the leaders of the Pilgrimage of Grace and was executed in 1537.[3] His younger brother – Henry Constable's ancestor – was Sir Marmaduke Constable of Everingham. He was knighted at Flodden, fought in various Scottish campaigns, served as MP for Yorkshire and accompanied Henry VIII to his meetings with the French and the Spanish monarchs.[4]

Sir Robert Constable of Everingham (b. 1495–1558), the poet's grandfather, married Katherine Manners, sister to Thomas Manners, the first earl of Rutland (see figure 1).[5] Their second son was Sir Robert Constable (ca. 1522–1591),

---

1. Sir Marmaduke was sheriff of Staffordshire and Yorkshire, and Knight of the Body to Richard III and Henry VII. As a young man, he served under Henry Percy, fourth earl of Northumberland. After the earl's death in the rebellion of 1489, Marmaduke became associated with Thomas Howard, earl of Surrey, and fought under him at Flodden in 1513. See Rosemary Horrox, "Constable, Sir Marmaduke (1456/7?–1518)," in *ODNB*, and *Testamenta eboracensia: A Selection of Wills from the Registry at York* (Durham, 1836–1902), 5: 88–93.

2. Eleanor married Thomas Berkeley, fifth Baron Berkeley, and their eldest son Thomas became the sixth baron. See John Smyth, *The Berkeley Manuscripts: The Lives of the Berkeleys, Lords of the Honour, Castle, and Manor of Berkeley in the County of Gloucester from 1066 to 1618*, ed. Sir John MacLean (Gloucester, 1883–1885), 2: 230–231.

3. Christine Newman, "Constable, Sir Robert (1478?–1537), rebel," in *ODNB*.

4. Horrox, "Constable, Sir Marmaduke."

5. Given the complexity of the network of family relations, only those connections that are of relevance are included in the family tree. The protection of the Rutlands, in particular, would be of the utmost importance in Henry Constable's life.

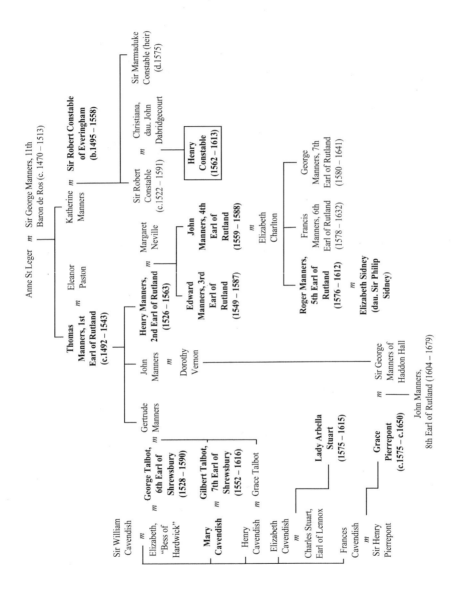

Figure 1. A genealogical chart showing Constable's connections with noble families.

who settled in Newark-upon-Trent, Nottinghamshire, with his wife Christiana, the daughter of John Dabridgecourt of Langon Hall.[6] Sir Robert was knighted on the battlefield in Scotland and held various offices in service of the crown, including that of marshal of Berwick and Lieutenant of the Ordnance. He visited King James of Scotland at Stirling and was included in a 1583 list of "the principal officers of the army," together with Sir Philip Sidney, Lord Grey, and others.[7] He kissed Queen Elizabeth's hand and received royal commendation after a successful tournament he organized at Greenwich in her honour.[8] Throughout his life, Sir Robert's efforts were rewarded with grants of lands, and a number of letters illustrate his good relations with his kinsman Rutland, Sir Francis Walsingham, and William Cecil, Lord Burghley.[9] There is no evidence that his Protestantism was ever in doubt.

Sir Robert had paved the way for Henry, his only son and heir, born on 6 March 1562.[10] Henry attended St John's College, Cambridge, where he matriculated as fellow-commoner in 1578 and obtained his BA two years later.[11] His name is listed in the cast of the Latin play *Richardus tertius*, performed at the bachelors' commencement feast in March 1579; he played Lord Strange, a non-speaking role, in the third act.[12] His friendship with Sir John Harington, who stood in the audience, probably dates from their time in Cambridge. Constable's name appears in the admission register of Lincoln's Inn for February 1583,[13] but a few months later he left to begin his diplomatic career.

---

6. On Sir Robert Constable, see Wickes, *Bio*, 272; and Ceri Sullivan, "Constable, Henry (1562–1613)," in *ODNB*.

7. TNA, SP 12/165, fol. 124r.

8. "Constable, Sir Robert (c.1522–91), of the Spittal, Newark, Notts. and the Minories, London," in *The History of Parliament: the House of Commons 1558–1603* (London, 1981), http://www.historyofparliamentonline.org/volume/1558-1603/member/constable-sir-robert-1522-91.

9. Wickes, *Bio*, 272. Some of the grants are mentioned in TNA, SP 12/60, fol. 153; SP 12/126, fol. 29. The former is a letter by Edward Clinton, earl of Lincoln, to Cecil recommending Sir Robert for the lease of an estate. It was thanks to Rutland that Sir Robert secured the friendship of Walsingham; he said as much in a letter to his kinsman in 1575 – see HMC *Rutland*, 1: 107.

10. During a visitation in 1575 Henry was reported to be twelve years old; see Charles H. Hunter Blair, ed., *Visitations of the North, Part 4: Visitations of Yorkshire and Northumberland* (Durham, 1932), 5. See notes to sonnet 78.

11. See Venn, 1: 380.

12. Martin Wiggins and Catherine Richardson, eds., *British Drama 1533–1642: A Catalogue* (Oxford, 2011–), 1: 235.

13. Lincoln's Inn Society, *Records of the Honorable Society of Lincoln's Inn* (London, 1896), 1: 97.

As a member of Walsingham's retinue, Henry travelled to Scotland on what Budiansky has described as a "hopeless mission," an ill-timed attempt to secure James's friendly disposition towards England and prevent his turning to France.[14] Henry wrote to Sir Robert to let him know about the "somwhat strange" welcome and "entertaynment" the secretary was given.[15] Constable may have made the acquaintance of poets Alexander Montgomerie and Henry Keir at that time.[16] In December he went to Paris, where he delivered intelligence concerning the Catholics Charles Arundell and Charles Paget to the English ambassador Sir Edward Stafford.[17] Henry's indignation at the publication of an anonymous "trayterous libell" slandering Elizabeth for her "just proceedinges" about Catholics evidences his commitment to the Protestant cause at the outset of his career.[18] He was singled out as a potential candidate to be sent to "comfort" Henri of Navarre "in his religion," and he was recommended to reformed theologian Theodore Beza.[19]

From July 1584, when he reported to Walsingham that he was about to set off, he went on various journeys around Europe, intermittently returning to France to await further instructions.[20] He travelled to Poland – as reported in sonnet 23 – Italy, and Heidelberg, where he responded to the libel that had so incensed him the year before. Evidence survives in a document titled "A note of such slanders as be dispersed in a libell against her majesties made by Thomas Throgmorton 1583 and answered by M. Constable at Heydelberge 1585 in May."[21] Thomas Throgmorton (or Throckmorton) was brother to the more famous conspirator Francis, and was then living in Paris. According to this summarised account, Thomas criticized the queen's imprisonment of Mary, Queen of Scots, whom he called "the Lawfull Queene" of Scotland, her interference in Scottish and French affairs – to the point of "nourishinge civill warres" there –

---

14. Stephen Budiansky, *Her Majesty's Spymaster: Elizabeth I, Sir Francis Walsingham, and the Birth of Modern Espionage* (New York, 2005), 126.

15. HMC *Rutland*, 1: 168. After a series of diplomatic affronts, Walsingham was received by the young king on 9 September.

16. Roderick J. Lyall, "'Thrie Truer Hairts'": Alexander Montgomerie, Henry Constable, Henry Keir and Cultural Politics in Renaissance Britain," *The Innes Review* 54 (2003): 186–215, at 197–198.

17. Stafford and Constable were related through the poet's great-great-grandmother, Joyce Stafford. See TNA, SP 78/10, 108 and 113.

18. HMC *Rutland*, 1: 158.

19. TNA, SP 78/11, 118; SP 15/29, 13.

20. TNA, SP 15/28/2, 82.

21. Oxford, Bodleian Library, Tanner MS 169, fols. 197v–198r. The authorship of the libel must have become known after Constable told Rutland about it.

and her intention to assist the Low Countries in their struggle against Spanish rule.[22] Constable's refutation of his arguments has not survived; it has been erroneously identified with the "booke he wrote in an answer to certayne objections against her [Elizabeth's] proceedings in the Low countryes" mentioned in the heading to sonnet 23.[23]

Henry did have a continued interest in Dutch affairs, probably due to his connections with the Walsingham-Leicester circle. His sonnets to Louise de Coligny, princess of Orange, have made his biographers wonder when, if ever, he set foot in the Netherlands, and if he could have been a member of the retinue of Robert Dudley, the earl of Leicester, there.[24] The first piece of evidence supporting the latter belief is a letter from Leicester himself to William Cecil, dated 7 November 1587, in which he regrets not having found the way to favour Henry; it provides the earliest portrayal of Constable's character: "I have made choyce of your old honest servant Constable to cary this paquett to hir majesty & my lords; I wold god ther had bin occasion to hav placed him hear; he is worthy for he is forward honest & painfull."[25] A second, less precise piece of information is the fact that the son and namesake of Dutch statesman and poet Janus Dousa translated one sonnet by Constable which he could only have obtained in manuscript; this points to a Dutch connection, however indirect.[26]

Besides these biographical leads, a long prose treatise written in the second half of 1587 reveals the depth of Henry's commitment to the Crown and the circle of the earl of Leicester, as well as his anti-Catholic stance. A summary of its contents in Marsh's Library, Dublin, has long been known, but the original manuscript was thought lost.[27] However, I have identified it within a volume in New

---

22. Bodl. Tanner MS 169, fol. 197v.

23. Wickes, *Bio*, 274; Grundy, 22. Grundy notes that Constable's answer must have taken "the form of an oral disputation."

24. Grundy, 24. Van Dorsten argues that Constable was not a member of Leicester's retinue because his name does not appear in any of the surviving lists, as his social status would have warranted; see Jan van Dorsten, *Poets, Patrons, and Professors: Sir Philip Sidney, Daniel Rogers, and the Leiden Humanists* (Leiden, 1962), 83–84. However, I have found Sir Robert Constable's name listed as one of four colonels in a memorandum from spring 1587, alongside better-known names such as Sir John Norris; see TNA, SP 84/19, 337.

25. TNA, SP 84/19, 34. Other letters written at that time manifest Leicester's despair at the state of affairs in the Low Countries. Excerpts of letters and primary sources in English in general are transcribed following the conventions of this edition.

26. See notes to sonnet 4, "Thyne eye, the glasse where I behold my hearte," for Dousa's version.

27. Dublin, Marsh's Library, MS Z3.5.21 (henceforth *M*), fols. 93v–109v. See Edward Dowden, "An Elizabethan MS Collection: Henry Constable," *The Modern Quarterly of Language and Literature* 1 (1898): 3–4; Grundy, 24. The heading is "A short vew of a large

Haven, Yale University, Beinecke Library, MS 621, fols. 15r–43r, catalogued as anonymous. It is titled *A Commentarie or explication of a letter written by Cardinall Allen in defence of Sir William Stanleys act of Betrayinge of Deventer* and is an early scribal copy bearing corrections in Constable's hand. It is no coincidence that the treatise was bound immediately after a separate item containing a copy of sonnet 25 headed "To the Queen."[28] In the long, neatly structured prose work Constable engages with William Allen's written defence of Stanley and York's surrender of Deventer and Zutphen to Spain, and painstakingly counters the Cardinal's every argument.[29]

By deploying his knowledge of history, scripture, and politics, plus his familiarity with very recent events, Constable attempts to tackle a man whom he saw as one of the heads of rebellious, militant Catholicism, a formidable adversary who could not go unchallenged. The tract also bears witness to Henry's early self-fashioning as a Protestant loyal to the queen and as her enemies' enemy, and can be read as his defence of what Roger B. Manning defines as "militant Protestant activism," even though he probably never wielded the sword himself.[30] It was not published, but it appears to have circulated in manuscript and had some repercussions, if the Jesuits' anxious reaction is anything to judge by. Robert Southwell reported on it to their superior general Claudio Acquaviva:

---

examination of Cardinal Allen his trayterous justification of Sir W. Stanley and Yorck, written by Master H. Cons. and this gathered out of his own draught." A version of sonnet 25 to the queen in the same manuscript bears the title "To hir majesty for a preface to his booke" (fol. 26r). Dowden, who wrote the first report of the contents of this commonplace book, expressed his puzzlement that a "Roman Catholic" author had written a work which was "not only loyally English but strongly Protestant in spirit" ("Elizabethan MS," 4).

28. The probability that the two works were put together within a miscellaneous volume by a compiler who did not know of the connection between them is small.

29. The defection to Spain of the Catholic commanders of the English garrisons with most of their army had disastrous consequences. See for instance Paul E.J. Hammer, *Elizabeth's Wars: War, Government, and Society in Tudor England, 1544–1604* (New York, 2003), 133–134. Constable cites from the smallest of the two editions of Allen's treatise, William Allen, *A copie of a lettre written by an English Gentleman, out of the campe of the low contryes, unto the Reverend, Master Doctor Allain, towching the act of rendring the Towne of Deventer and other places, unto the Cathol. King and his answerre and resolution unto the same* (Antwerp, 1587), RSTC 370.5. In this work Allen encourages English soldiers to disobey a "heritike" and excommunicate queen whose troops fight "for the dishonerable defense of rebelles, pyrates, and infidels," and to help restore to the king of Spain what is his by right (27, 43). Allen seasons his argumentation with biblical references and mentions both past and present wars in his attempt to prove that God "fighteth ... generally for all Catholike armies" (39).

30. Roger B. Manning, *An Apprenticeship in Arms: The Origins of the British Army 1585–1702* (Oxford, 2006), 27.

Certain pamphlets have appeared, not printed but written out. ... The other replies to a pamphlet by the Most Illustrious William, Cardinal Allen to clarify or approve the action of Mr William Stanley. Many applaud this rejoinder but, in my judgement, the pamphlet is quite insipid enough in itself and thoroughly alien to any sense of Christian justice insofar as in the book a certain courtier, either an atheist or a person of dubious faith plays the theologian, and makes examples of war the foundations of his axioms.[31]

The treatise was finished in autumn 1587 and, while no evidence that he presented a copy to the queen survives, he was certainly favoured and allowed to stay at court for the next two years.[32]

Many of Constable's amatory and dedicatory sonnets are intimately connected with events that took place and acquaintances he met during his time in England. It is no surprise that a young man who had started out as Walsingham's, and later Leicester's, protégé should reach out to members of the Sidney-Essex circle as well as to his own powerful relatives, especially the Talbot-Cavendish family.[33] Constable's elegies on Sir Philip Sidney (1554–1586) and his sonnets to Sidney's sister, his widow, and – more significantly – his "Stella," Penelope Rich, reveal his desire to be seen as one of Sidney's successors. He was uniquely positioned at the intersection of three groups: that formed by what Steven W. May has called Sidney's rightful "literary heirs," Mary, countess of Pembroke, Fulke Greville, and Robert Sidney; the courtier poets – Sir Walter Ralegh, Sir Arthur Gorges, and Sir John Harington – who "acknowledged Sidney's achievement without permitting it to influence their own poetic careers ... with respect to the genres and forms they employed"; and the poets who furthered the son-

---

31. Printed in Thomas M. McCoog, *And Touching our Society: Fashioning Jesuit Identity in Elizabethan England* (Toronto, 2013), 167. McCoog does not mention that the reference is to Constable's tract.

32. The time of composition is inferred from a reference to the Battle of Coutras, which Constable reports to have taken place "the other day." This battle was fought on 20 October 1587. This is consistent with the fact that the edition of Allen's *Lettre* Constable refers to was published bearing the date 20 July 1587. On the evidence available to her at the time, Grundy conjectured it must have been written in early 1588; see Grundy, 24.

33. Gertrude, daughter to Thomas Manners, the first earl of Rutland, and first cousin to Sir Robert Constable, married Sir George Talbot, sixth earl of Shrewsbury (ca. 1522–1590). Later, in 1568, Shrewsbury married Elizabeth, Bess of Hardwick (ca. 1527–1608), widow of Sir William Cavendish; the dynastic alliance was strengthened through the double marriage of Elizabeth's children Mary and Henry Cavendish to Shrewsbury's children Gilbert and Grace Talbot. See Elizabeth Goldring, "Talbot [née Hardwick], Elizabeth [Bess] [called Bess of Hardwick], countess of Shrewsbury," in *ODNB*.

net vogue of the 1590s and at some point hoped to attract the favour of Sidney's relatives – Samuel Daniel and Edmund Spenser, to name but two.[34]

No correspondence between Constable and Sidney survives, so the nature of their relationship must remain conjectural. However, Sidney appears to be the connection shared by the princess of Orange, the Dutch poets, the earl of Leicester, and the earl's secretary, the French Huguenot Jean Hotman (1552–1636). G.H.M. Meyjes makes a case for Hotman's and Constable's early acquaintance: they might have met "at the beginning of the eighties either in France or in England," from which moment their paths kept crossing.[35] Louise de Coligny, princess of Orange (1555–1620), held Sidney in great esteem. She had spent time in his company in Middleburgh and Flushing and often used Hotman as intermediary in their communications.[36] All were devastated at Sidney's untimely death.[37] Their shared friends aside, Henry Woudhuysen has thrown light on Constable's participation in the manuscript culture surrounding Sidney. He was among the group of men "who first betrayed Sidney's poems to print, or at least allowed their writings to appear in the same company as his."[38] He also joined in the collective mourning, writing a total of three elegies in Sidney's memory, sonnets 52 to 54.

Constable tried to make the most of his time in England. Leicester had asked Lord Burghley to favour Henry if he could, and in December 1587 Constable was striving to obtain an official appointment.[39] John Chamberlain was probably referring to a clerkship at the Privy Council when he reported, "I guess that Constable aspires to yt, for I se him much at court and in great formality."[40] In March

34. The first two groups are contrasted in Steven W. May, *The Elizabethan Courtier Poets: The Poems and their Contexts* (Columbia, 1991), 166. An in-depth study of the literary response to Sidney is Gavin Alexander, *Writing after Sidney: The Literary Response to Sir Philip Sidney, 1586–1640* (Oxford, 2006).

35. G.H.M. Posthumus Meyjes, *Jean Hotman's English Connection* (Amsterdam, 1990), 36–39, at 37. Meyjes highlights Hotman's role in the circulation of Constable's sonnets and one of his prose works.

36. John Buxton, *Sir Philip Sidney and the English Renaissance* (Basingstoke, 1987), 170. Hotman had first met Sidney in 1582 and was ever thankful to him for the recommendation that made Leicester take him into his service. Meyjes, *Jean Hotman*, 22–24.

37. Van Dorsten, *Poets, Patrons, and Professors*, 155. Sidney died in October 1586 from a wound received at the siege of Zutphen; he was given a lavish funeral, and scholars and poets mourned him throughout Europe. See Henry R. Woudhuysen, "Sidney, Sir Philip (1554–1586)," in *ODNB*.

38. Henry R. Woudhuysen, *Sir Philip Sidney and the Circulation of Manuscripts, 1558–1640* (Oxford, 1996), 220.

39. TNA, SP 84/19, 34.

40. J.W. Stoye, "An Early Letter from John Chamberlain," *The English Historical Review* 62 (1947): 522–532, at 531.

1588 Henry attended the funeral of John Manners, the fourth earl of Rutland, in which his father Sir Robert was a chief mourner.[41] The majority of that year and the following he spent establishing or renewing connections with powerful acquaintances and prospective patrons. He tried to make himself useful both to Henri of Navarre and to King James, and seems to have played a role in the delivery of some of James's letters, entrusted to him by a supporter of Navarre, Claude De l'Isle, within the context of marriage negotiations between the Scottish king and Navarre's sister Catherine de Bourbon. The Frenchman describes Constable as James's "affectionate servant."[42] At home, he wrote sonnets to curry favour, and many of his friends also participated in the manuscript circulation of his works. Such is the case of Sir John Harington, who had literary ambitions of his own and who refers to Constable as a "well learned Gentleman" and his "very good frend" in his translation of *Orlando furioso*.[43] Harington compiled twenty-one of Constable's sonnets in a volume now known as The Arundel Harington Manuscript (henceforth *H*), under a heading that both ascribes them unequivocally to Constable and points at Lady Penelope Rich as the poetic mistress.

Penelope Rich (1563–1607) was sister to Robert Devereux, the second earl of Essex. An educated, beautiful, and influential lady, she became the focus of extensive praise and many literary dedications. Recent criticism has looked beyond her identification as Sidney's "Stella." Chris Laoutaris emphasizes her role "in a culture of encryption and espionage": she "had a direct line of communication to Elizabeth I; conducted a secret correspondence with James VI of Scotland; courted some of the most notorious spies and intelligence operatives in Europe; and cultivated an identity as political advisor to royalty."[44] Sally Varlow notes that by becoming acquainted with Penelope and addressing her in writing, Constable might have been imitating Sidney, and Sylvia Freedman believes that he was in love with her on the grounds of a letter that Penelope sent to Hotman wishing – in jest or in earnest – that Constable would

---

41. HMC *Rutland*, 1: 245.

42. My translation. The letter, in French, is transcribed in Annie I. Cameron, ed., *The Warrender Papers* (Edinburgh, 1932), 2: 86.

43. Sir John Harington, *Orlando furioso in English heroical verse* (London, 1591), 288.

44. Chris Laoutaris, "'Toucht with bolt of Treason': The Earl of Essex and Lady Penelope Rich," in *Essex: The Cultural Impact of an Elizabethan Courtier*, ed. Annaliese F. Connolly and Lisa Hopkins (Manchester, 2013), 201–236, at 201. Her intelligence and skill for languages have also been emphasized; see Katherine Duncan-Jones, *Sir Philip Sidney: Courtier Poet* (New Haven, 1991), 189.

"stop being amorous."⁴⁵ She may have seen the sonnets. In the *T* collection, two – 35 and 36 – are explicitly dedicated to her, whereas 42, 43, and 55 praise her under some pretext, and an even greater number contain puns on her name. Ascertaining the authenticity of Henry's feelings for Penelope is both impossible and immaterial; Marotti's observation that for courtier poets "poems were an extension of artful, polite behaviour and, at the same time, ways of formulating actual or wished-for social transactions" certainly holds.⁴⁶

Penelope appears to have been the mastermind behind an intrigue that sent both Hotman and Constable to Scotland in 1589. It has been called the "Rialta affair" due to the codename she used in her correspondence.⁴⁷ The goal was to assure James of the support of the Essex circle in the event of Elizabeth's death. Hotman was the first messenger; he arrived in Edinburgh in late summer bearing letters from Penelope and her brother Essex and met the king in person.⁴⁸

On 20 October "young Constable" was reported to be at the Scottish court, and to have had "secret conference sundry times" with the king.⁴⁹ Constable had brought James messages from Essex, Lady and Lord Rich, and the countesses of Warwick and Cumberland, supposedly congratulating him on his marriage to Anne of Denmark. More intriguingly, he had borne with him "Rialta's picture," a lost miniature of Penelope painted by Nicholas Hilliard – whose craft Constable celebrates in sonnet 43 – and, probably, a picture of the countesses, which he accompanied with sonnet 32b. From Lady Mary Talbot, the wife of his cousin Gilbert, Constable brought "a special commission" which was all the more significant because of the Talbots' family connection with Arbella Stuart, another

---

45. Sally Varlow, *The Lady Penelope: The Lost Tale of Love and Politics in the Court of Elizabeth I* (London, 2007), 168; Sylvia Freedman, *Poor Penelope: Lady Penelope Rich, an Elizabethan Woman* (Abbotsbrook, 1983), 82; the translation is hers. Penelope's original French reads, "Qu'il ne soit plus amoureux." The letter is published in P.J. Blok, *Correspondance inédite de Robert Dudley, comte de Leycester, et de François et Jean Hotman* (Haarlem, 1911), 256. Hotman enjoyed Penelope's trust because he had married one of her ladies-in-waiting, Jeanne de Saint-Martin; see David Baird Smith, "Jean de Villiers Hotman," *Scottish Historical Review* 14 (1917): 147–166, at 152.

46. Arthur F. Marotti, *Manuscript, Print, and the English Renaissance Lyric* (Ithaca, 1995), 9.

47. For fuller accounts of this intrigue, see Laoutaris, "'Toucht with Bolt of Treason,'" 202–209; and Varlow, *Lady Penelope*, 112–115. The Rialta affair has been viewed as evidence of Penelope's participation in politics and her active role in her brother's affairs.

48. Details of the intrigue are known from reports by Thomas Fowler, Lord Burghley's agent in Scotland, to his master. See HMC *Salisbury*, 3: 426 and 435; see also Lyall, "'Thrie Truer Hairts,'" 207.

49. See Fowler to Burghley, Edinburgh, 20 November 1589, CP 18/55; transcribed in HMC *Salisbury*, 3: 438.

potential candidate for the English throne.[50] The poet himself was said to have been "in the company" and "near allied" to Arbella, and dedicated sonnets 33 and 34 to her.[51] He minimised this supposed loyalty to Arbella in order to assure James of his support, which provides an early example of Henry's tendency to engage in double-dealing.

With his participation in this intrigue Constable furthered the hidden agenda of the English gentry and his own. He courted James's favour in verse and was apparently let into the king's literary circle, as his four sonnets to the monarch and the evidence of his connection with Scottish poets reveal.[52] Although they were treading on dangerous ground by meddling in the banned issue of Elizabeth's succession, there were no serious consequences for those involved in the Rialta affair. On 8 November, Thomas Fowler, Lord Burghley's agent in Scotland, reported that "Victor" – codename for James – did not care much for their "offers," and that "the instruments are worst rewarded of all that ever came here of that nation."[53] Constable was one of these "instruments," and a letter from Richard Douglas, who had facilitated access to the king, hints at some unnamed slight the poet received right before James departed for Denmark to fetch his bride, which may simply have been the lack of immediate reward.[54] However, Douglas assured Henry of James's esteem "as your virtues and good parts deserve."[55] There was reason to hope for future favour, and James would indeed remember the messenger-poet upon his accession.

Exactly how good Constable's prospects were in late 1589 is made clear by George Wickes's insightful observation:

50. Arbella was Mary Talbot's niece. A descendant of Margaret, Henry VIII's elder sister, her claims to the throne were strong on account of her English birth and upbringing. See Sarah Gristwood, *Arbella: England's Lost Queen* (London, 2003); P.M. Handover, *Arbella Stuart, Royal Lady of Hardwick and Cousin to King James* (London, 1957); Ruth Norrington, *In the Shadow of the Throne: The Lady Arbella Stuart* (London, 2002).

51. HMC *Salisbury*, 3: 438. He would later dedicate the whole collection in Z to her.

52. He even had access to the king's poems circulating only in manuscript at the time. See notes to sonnets 26 through 29 for the individual circumstances surrounding the composition of each.

53. HMC *Salisbury*, 3: 443.

54. See "X" [R. Douglas] to Constable, Edinburgh, November 1589, CP 167/4; transcribed in HMC *Salisbury*, 3: 442. Douglas also provides one of the first statements regarding the reception of Constable's works by referring to a book of his that he received from Hotman.

55. Ibid. Lyall conjectures that Constable must have visited Scotland again in the winter of 1589–1590, which would explain sonnet 29 complaining about the king's delay in Denmark; see Lyall, "'Thrie Truer Hairts'," 209–210. However, there is no documentary evidence of this visit other than the sonnet.

At this point the future must have looked bright for Henry Constable. He had received the best preparation possible for a career at court, had excellent family connections and powerful acquaintance, and he was not lacking in wit. Evidently he attached his hopes to the rising star of Essex and counted on the favour of a King who was confidently expected to succeed shortly to the English throne.[56]

However, there were early signs that his career would be jeopardised by his religion. The Protestant faith that had informed Constable's treatise about the Low Countries was wavering by the second half of 1589, although he probably maintained a solid façade before members of his circle. Some of his secular sonnets are fraught with religious imagery and anxiety, but it is a prose work, *Examen pacifique de la doctrine des Huguenots*, which intensifies the sense of crisis. Written in French, it bears a false Paris imprint on the title page, and the date "Octob. 1589." It was actually entered in the Stationers' Register by the printer John Wolfe on 26 August, "to be prynted both in Frenche and Englishe," reported to have the approval of ecclesiastical authorities, and shortly after printed in London.[57] A second edition was published a year later in Caen – probably another false imprint. Both editions were published anonymously, which led to its misattribution to Cardinal Davy du Perron, but Constable's authorship is no longer in question.[58] In 1623 an English translation, *The Catholike moderator: Or, a moderate examination of the doctrine of the Protestants*, came out and underwent four editions in a short space of time; the author is identified with the initials "H.C." in the translator's preface.[59]

In the epistle to the reader, the author makes it clear that his intention was to engage in the pamphlet wars on the controversy over the succession of a Protestant – Henri of Navarre – to the French throne and the conflicts between Catholics and Huguenots.[60] He also claims to have started drafting the treatise

---

56. Wickes, *Bio*, 275.

57. David Rogers was the first to see through the false imprint, which even Grundy had taken at face value. See David Rogers, "'The Catholic Moderator': A French Reply to Bellarmine and Its English Author, Henry Constable," *Recusant History* 5 (1960), 224–235, at 228; Grundy, 31. No edition in English was printed at the time.

58. See Grundy, 31; John Bossy, "A Propos of Henry Constable," *Recusant History* 6 (1962): 228–237.

59. References here are to the translation, which is mostly faithful to the French text. See Rogers, "'The Catholic Moderator,'" 231.

60. *CM*, n.p. The *Examen* was Constable's response to a French translation of Cardinal Bellarmine's confutation of the *Apologie catholique*, published in French in 1585 to defend Henri of Navarre's right to the throne. Rogers, "'The Catholic Moderator,'" 224–225. Sir John

in 1588 and finished it only after hearing the news of the murder of Henri III in August 1589. More importantly, he identifies himself as a Catholic.[61] Through this puzzling adoption of a Catholic persona, he argues for the reconciliation of the Catholic and Protestant churches, advocating toleration, defending French Huguenots from accusations of heresy, and supporting the cause of Henri of Navarre. After an examination of the major points of contention between the two faiths, he concludes by asserting that Huguenots can be persuaded "that they already beleeve as our Church beleeveth: and consequently, that their Faith is the same, and their Church the same."[62]

There has been disagreement as to whether Constable was still a Protestant or practically a Catholic convert by the time of the *Examen*'s publication.[63] The ambiguity that pervades this work may well have been intentional, and the treatise an exercise in irenism – or irenicism – in its searching for the "shared roots of Catholic and Reformed doctrine."[64] Irenicism has been defined from both political and spiritual standpoints. Alan Haynes emphasises the pragmatic motivation to avoid violent conflicts such as the French wars of religion, whereas Meyjes defines it as an "endeavour to allay or to reconcile tensions or divisions between the confessions in a peaceful way."[65] Humanist thinkers and theologians such as Erasmus, Bucer, and Casaubon were favourable to the idea of reconciliation, but only within the limits of the "established or tolerated churches," and all of them fixated on the notion of a "catholic" church – universal, and

---

Harington quoted extensively from this treatise in one of his own, composed in 1602, and identifies his old friend "Constable in Fraunce" as the author. See John Harington, *A Tracte on the Succession to the Crown*, ed. Clements R. Markham (London, 1880), 64.

61. *CM*, sig. A2r.
62. *CM*, sig. K2r.
63. Wickes reads the *Examen* as a "pro-Catholic treatise"; see Wickes, *Bio*, 275. Bossy contends that it was "written before Constable became a Catholic, and his conversion no doubt entailed the abandonment of some of the opinions expressed in it"; see Bossy, "The Character of Elizabethan Catholicism," *Past and Present* 21 (1962): 39–59, at 55. Rogers sees it as the product of the state of mind of a near convert, and Lyall finds it "Protestant in character." See Rogers, "'The Catholic Moderator,'" 229; Lyall, "'Thrie Truer Hairts,'" 206.
64. Alexandra Gajda, *The Earl of Essex and Late Elizabethan Political Culture* (Oxford, 2012), 123.
65. Alan Haynes, *The White Bear: Robert Dudley, the Elizabethan Earl of Leicester* (London, 1987), 78; G.H.M. Posthumus Meyjes, "Protestant Irenicism in the Sixteenth and Seventeenth Centuries," in *The End of Strife: Papers Selected from the Proceedings of the Colloquium of the Commission internationale d'histoire ecclésiastique comparée Held at the University of Durham, 2 to 9 September 1981*, ed. David M. Loades (Edinburgh, 1984), 77–93, at 78.

devoid of heresy.[66] This moderate stance with clear humanistic roots was in line with that of Constable's friends Jean Hotman and Sir John Harington, and Sidney's Flemish correspondent Justus Lipsius, described by Jan van Dorsten as a man who strongly disliked fanaticism.[67] Sidney was interested in – and may have even gravitated towards – this position by the end of his life.[68] Taking into account Constable's Continental connections, the influence of the Leiden circle, with its secularising drive, and French Gallicanism should not be overlooked.[69]

## Conversion

By 1590 Henry Constable had converted to Catholicism. Faced with the inevitable question of why he would do that after having expended time and effort trying to secure some office, four lines of inquiry have yielded some results: his learning and engagement in controversy, the status of his career, disappointment in his personal affairs, and private spiritual motivations. In 1597 a papal legate in Paris, Atilio Amalteo, wrote a letter to Cardinal Aldobrandini discussing Constable's credentials:

> While he was a heretic he was a courtier and a favourite of the Queen. ... Though he seems unassuming on account of his modesty and great humility, he is nevertheless intelligent and knowledgeable, especially in theology, and shows himself well-versed in the controversies with the heretics. He became a Catholic about eight years ago, being first moved to it by God and secondly assisted by his own endeavours through the light gained of the truth

---

66. Meyjes, "Protestant Irenicism," 78–80.
67. Jan van Dorsten, "The Final Year," in *Sir Philip Sidney: 1586 and the Creation of a Legend*, ed. Dominic Baker-Smith, Jan van Dorsten, and Arthur F. Kinney (Leiden, 1986), 16–24, at 23. On Hotman's irenicism, see Meyjes, "Protestant Irenicism," 88–89; and Meyjes, *Jean Hotman*, 11. On Sir John Harington and his refusal to be pigeonholed as a Catholic, Protestant, or Puritan, see Gerard Kilroy, *Edmund Campion: Memory and Transcription* (Aldershot, 2005), 89–120.
68. Van Dorsten, "The Final Year," 23; Dominic Baker-Smith, "'Great Expectation': Sidney's Death and the Poets," in *Sir Philip Sidney: 1586 and the Creation of a Legend*, 83–100, at 99; Haynes, *The White Bear*, 78.
69. For a full study of the former see Mark Somos, *Secularisation and the Leiden Circle* (Leiden, 2011). Irenicism has been associated with the "rhetoric surrounding Henri IV and his supporters." See Katy Gibbons, *English Catholic Exiles in Late Sixteenth-Century Paris* (Suffolk, 2011), 146.

by his study into matters of religion. Thus he resolved for the sake of saving his soul to lose all his patrimony.[70]

In Amalteo's account, Constable's conversion had its origin in divine grace, which the poet accepted and began to work with towards his salvation. Henry's "study" included not only his readings of Scripture and patristics, but also his participation in contemporary religious debates. Michael C. Questier has noted that "conversion to and from Rome was discussed almost exclusively in doctrinal and, indeed, polemical terms." A person changing religion would do so through persuasion that one of the churches was the most likely to be the "true" religion, and hence the "certain path to salvation."[71] As Joshua Rodda has put it: "Religious controversy was an obligation to God and the *beginnings* of persuasion. It was not, indeed, controversy to those who believed, but a presentation of truth, to help prepare the intellect of a reader, listener, or adversary, and move the will to conversion."[72] Constable's interest in polemical writing mirrors that of other converts such as the poet William Alabaster (1568–1640). In his own conversion narrative Alabaster recounts how he underwent a sudden and unexpected change while he was reading a work by the Catholic divine William Rainolds: "I fownde my minde wholie and perfectly Catholic in an instante, and so to be persuaded of all and everie poynt of Catholique religion."[73]

The zeal with which books were written and refuted by members of the opposing party evidences that they were all aware of their potential persuasive power; a pamphlet penned by an enemy could not be left unanswered.[74] Active engagement in controversy has also been read as an act of confirmation, "an expression of one's own faith." In this sense, its function was also spiritual.[75] Constable's penchant for rhetoric and polemics had him joining in a variety of debates on both sides of the religious divide, from his early pro-Protestant Low Countries

---

70. Amalteo to Aldobrandini, Paris, 12 May 1597, ASV, Fondo Borghese III, 73, fol. 123r–v. Translation from the Italian is from Wickes, *Bio*, 296 n23.

71. Michael C. Questier, *Conversion, Politics, and Religion in England, 1580–1625* (Cambridge, 1996), 12.

72. Joshua Rodda, *Public Religious Disputation in England, 1558–1626* (London, 2016), 27.

73. William Alabaster, *Unpublished Works*, ed. Dana Sutton (Salzburg, 1997), 118. On Alabaster and the conversion narrative as a genre not exclusive to Protestant converts, see Molly Murray, "'Now I ame a Catholique': William Alabaster and the Early Modern Catholic Conversion Narrative," in *Catholic Culture in Early Modern England*, ed. Ronald Corthell et al. (Notre Dame, IN, 2007), 189–215.

74. Questier, *Conversion*, 17.

75. Rodda, *Public Religious Disputation*, 23.

treatise, through the grey area of the *Examen*, to later engagements with the banned topic of succession from a Catholic standpoint. He made it clear that he would discuss religion with anyone who was willing to listen.

Issues related to a man's career and patronage or lack thereof must always have influenced an individual's decision to change religion. Disappointment with worldly politics and the royal court pervades Henry's religious poetry, unspoken past grievances lurking beneath the pious surface. However, John Bossy's argument that Constable's conversion was "a consequence of the failure of his career at the English court" seems ungrounded.[76] By 1590 Sidney, Leicester, and Walsingham were dead, but the Sidneys carried on with the tradition of family patronage, and Robert Devereux, the second earl of Essex, who had just married Sir Philip's widow, was a star on the rise. Constable could also rely on powerful family connections, including the earls of Rutland and Shrewsbury, and he was on good terms with not one but two candidates for the throne – James and Arbella. We might not be seeing the whole picture, but his career seemed to have been headed in the right direction. Benjamin Carier, another notable convert to Catholicism, gave up an ecclesiastical career as King James's chaplain and acknowledged this renunciation in his conversion narrative, expounding his motivations:

> Though I was as ambitious of your Majesty's favour and as desirous of the honours and pleasures of my country as any man that is therein, yet ... if I should for private commodity speak or write or do anything against the honour of Christ his church and against the evidence of my own conscience, I must shortly appear before the same Christ in the presence of the same his church, to give an account thereof. Therefore I neither durst any further pursue my own desire of honour, nor hazard my soul ... .[77]

Henry's renunciation of secular love, which went hand in hand with his conversion, could have had something to do with a sense of disappointment of a more personal nature. Although other female names feature prominently in the sonnets written in the 1580s, the most comprehensive – and latest – collection of secular sonnets (*T*) is dedicated to a lady called "Grace."[78] I agree with Roderick J. Lyall that this must be Grace Pierrepont, daughter to Frances Cavendish

---

76. Bossy, "A Propos," 234.
77. *A treatise, written by M. doctor Carier, wherein hee layeth downe sundry learned and pithy considerations* (n.p., 1614), edited in John Saward et al., eds., *Firmly I Believe and Truly: The Spiritual Tradition of Catholic England* (Oxford, 2011), 180.
78. See the introductory and colophon sonnets, 1 and 63.

and Nottinghamshire MP Sir Henry Pierrepont, and hence Mary Talbot's niece and Arbella's cousin (see figure 1).[79] Grace would have been an unmarried teenager at the time Constable was at court, and their acquaintance was entirely possible due to their shared family connection. If he ever entertained any real hopes of marrying the young lady, they must have soon been thwarted. Plans were underway to expand the excellent connections of the Talbot-Cavendish dynasty through an alliance to the Manners family. In 1593 Grace married Sir George Manners of Haddon Hall, a grandson of the first earl of Rutland and Constable's second cousin. Their issue included the eighth earl.[80]

Beyond these intellectual and external factors, a more personal, spiritual motivation must have existed. Contrary to Protestants' reliance on the power of grace – and grace only – and belief in the powerlessness of human will, Catholics believed in the will, which actively cooperated with divine grace after a first encounter through a process called sanctification.[81] Whereas Protestant conversions relied on the exercise of the intellect, Catholic conversions rested on the exercise of the will.[82] A Catholic convert, Sir Tobie Matthew, pointed out that Catholics who became Protestants lived "notoriously worse than they had done before," while Protestants who became Catholics lived "much better."[83] After all, they placed an emphasis on good works as a means to achieve salvation that was discarded by Protestants. Augustine's conversion provided a model;[84] his rejection of worldly pleasures and turn to God is imitated by Constable, who actively renounced his secular poetry in the prose conclusion to *T* and – although a layman – could have taken some sort of personal religious vows. When he converted, he must have known that he would have to embrace poverty – he lost his

79. Roderick J. Lyall, "Stella's Other Astrophel: Henry Constable's Diana and the Politics of Elizabethan Courtiership," in *Gloriana's Rule: Literature, Religion, and Power in the Age of Elizabeth*, ed. Rui Carvalho Homem and Fátima Vieira (Porto, 2006), 187–205, at 200. Another candidate, Grace Cavendish (née Talbot), daughter to the sixth earl of Shrewsbury, must be ruled out, considering that she had been married to Sir Henry Cavendish since 1568. See Grundy, 219, and Louise Imogen Guiney, *Recusant Poets: With a Selection from their Work* (New York, 1939), 305.

80. G.E. Cokayne et al., eds., *The Complete Peerage of England, Scotland, Ireland, Great Britain and the United Kingdom, Extant, Extinct or Dormant*, 2nd ed. (London, 1910–1998), 11: 263. This marriage was apparently arranged by Elizabeth "Bess" of Hardwick; see Alfred L. Rowse, *Eminent Elizabethans* (London, 1983), 29.

81. Questier, *Conversion*, 59.

82. Ibid., 64–65.

83. Tobie Matthew, *A True Historical Relation of the Conversion of Sir Tobie Matthew to the Holy Catholic Faith*, ed. A.H. Mathew (London, 1904), 164.

84. Arthur F. Marotti, *Religious Ideology and Cultural Fantasy: Catholic and Anti-Catholic Discourses in Early Modern England* (Notre Dame, IN, 2005), 113.

inheritance and had to rely on the goodwill of others – obedience to religious authorities, and chastity. There is no mention of any woman being a part of his life again, and he did not marry.

Bewildering as it could seem in view of everything he lost, Constable's conversion supports Questier's thesis that "flux in religion was the norm rather than the exception in religious experience, actually expected rather than regarded with astonishment."[85] Steadfast Protestants converted into zealous Catholics and performed their conversion in a number of ways, including exile in a Catholic country.[86] The remainder of Constable's life can be read as a continuous performance of conversion, in which his faith was continuously weighed against political and social ambitions.

## Exile: 1591–1598

Henry Constable was a bachelor of twenty-eight when he found himself at a crossroads. In the summer of 1591 he travelled to France as a member of Essex's retinue in order to give aid to Henri IV in his military operations.[87] He had been there for a short time when, according to a secondhand account, he "spake very broad in maintenance of the Popish religion at a supper in Sir Roger Williams' chambers, and ... fearing lest he should be sent back into England, he took his horses the next morning and rode away."[88] What some of his acquaintances must have felt when they had news of his conversion is illustrated by Frenchman Pierre du Moulin, who had been in Constable's service and later became a renowned Protestant theologian:[89]

---

85. Questier, *Conversion*, 206.
86. See Marotti, *Religious Ideology*, 97.
87. Paul E.J. Hammer, "Devereux, Robert, second earl of Essex (1565–1601)," in *ODNB*. Elizabeth, pressing for the siege of Rouen, sent the French king money and – for a limited time – armed forces. In particular, Essex was meant to aid in the suppression of rebels who refused to acknowledge a Huguenot king and the expulsion of Spanish enemies. The earl and his troops landed at Dieppe on 10 and 12 August 1591. They would have eight weeks to give aid to the king. See Nicola M. Sutherland, *Henry IV of France and the Politics of Religion: 1572–1596* (Bristol, 2002), 405–408.
88. See HMC *Salisbury*, 4: 394. This was reported by the clergyman Anthony Tyrrell during his examination in 1593. He had heard it from a "Lieutenant Ferris," who played a role in securing passports for some Englishmen to cross to Dieppe; ibid., 393.
89. Du Moulin met Constable through a French clergyman, Rene Bochart, sieur Du Mesnillet, and entered Henry's service. Even after his exile, Constable's affection for him

I knew already everything you say about Mr. Constable and, though disappointed, am not at all surprised. ... I was always afraid of the way he would turn out. He has killed his father from sorrow, and lost both his reputation and the advancement which the Lord Treasurer would have procured him. He has wrecked his career, and nothing remained but that he should wreck his conscience also. ... I am sorry for him. Though imprudent, he is straightforward, and though unreliable, intelligent.[90]

An anonymous sonnet appended to the collection in the Todd MS reveals the feelings of a friend who lamented Henry's exile. Headed "To H.C. upon occasion of leaving his countrye and sweetnesse of his verse," it metaphorically presents Constable as a "sweete nightingale" that has migrated abroad with his "sister swallowe" (5) – probably Essex – and failed to return with him.[91] The author, who apparently puzzles about Constable's self-imposed exile in "native countryes foe" (3), entreats Constable to return and seek forgiveness: "Come, feare thow not the cage but loyall be / And ten to one thy soveraigne pardons thee" (13–14).[92] In 1592 twenty-three sonnets were taken from the private realm of manuscript circulation and published under the title *Diana: The praises of his Mistres, in certaine sweete sonnets* (henceforth *D92*). Only Constable's initials are given, but the epistle "To the Gentlemen Readers" hints at the fact that the author is in exile: "These insuing Sonnets ... are now by misfortune left as Orphans."[93] The popularity of this book warranted a second edition two years later (*D94*), which included poems by other authors, both known and unknown.

The first years of Constable's exile were spent in Rome and remain mostly obscure, but from later events it can be deduced that he started building a network of connections that included Catholic statesmen and members of the

---

continued and he secured Du Moulin a position as mentor to the young Roger Manners, fifth earl of Rutland, with whom he went to Cambridge. Du Moulin's feelings towards Constable seem to have soured after the latter's conversion. See "Autobiographie de Pierre du Moulin," *Bulletin de la Société de l'histoire du protestantisme français* 71 (1858): 170–182, at 178–179; Johannes van der Meij, "Pierre du Moulin in Leiden, 1592–1598," *Lias* 14 (1987): 15–40, at 15–16.

90. Letter to Bochart from Cambridge, 19 July 1592, quoted in Bossy, "A Propos," 231–232. Bossy translates from the Latin original; see Societe des archives historiques, ed., "Lettre de Pierre Dumoulin au pasteur Bouchard, sieur Du Meuillet," *Archives historiques du déparement de la Gironde* 19 (1879): 535–539, at 535. In Tyrrell's account Constable is also blamed for his father's death; see HMC *Salisbury*, 4: 394.

91. See the full text of the sonnet in appendix A.

92. *T*, fol. 44r.

93. *D92*, sig. A4r.

church of different nationalities. He must have been the "Henricus Constable Eboracensis" who visited the English College in Rome on 3 October 1593 and stayed for ten days.[94] What he clearly did was imbibe the spirit of the Counter-Reformation and the artistic Baroque that inspired him to write his *Spiritual Sonnets*, the first collection of which I have dated around 1595.[95] By August 1595 he was in France, and he would be based in Paris until 1603.[96] He took lodgings at Collège Mignon, which had become one of the English strongholds in Paris, more specifically "a forum for English Catholics who did not seek to overthrow the French or English monarchs" at a time when the city was still controlled by the Catholic League.[97] He was reported to have good "intelligence ... with the papists" in England and abroad, and to have procured "some means of maintenance for the English in Paris."[98] By 1598 he had gained a solid enough foothold in his new community to become one of the petitioners for the creation of an English college in Paris, which ultimately came to nothing.[99]

When considering the effect of exile on Constable, John Bossy's observation on the course of action of those involved in the English "mission" seems pertinent:

> Since no government or faction would be anxious to support them if it had an interest in preserving the *status quo* in England, the protection of the mission implied at least a passive co-operation in attempts to overthrow it. ... They had no access to Parliament; rebellion, in view of the condition and outlook of the Catholic gentry, could never be more than a weak auxiliary; they were therefore forced back on foreign intervention ... .[100]

---

94. Rome, Archivum Venerabilis Collegii Anglorum, liber 282, 31. Wickes believes that the entry on the Pilgrim Book may refer instead to the poet's namesake Sir Henry Constable of Holderness, but this seems unlikely; see Wickes, *Bio*, 278.

95. This is London, British Library, Harley MS 7553 (henceforth *HA*).

96. Cecil was told so in a letter dated 11 August 1595, sent by one of his intelligencers in Rome. See HMC *Salisbury*, 5: 313.

97. The Catholic League had the Spanish-funded Guise family at its heart and the support of the papacy; see Sutherland, *Henry IV*, 45–87. On Collège Mignon, see Gibbons, *English Catholic Exiles*, 145; see also Gibbons, "'A Reserved Place'? English Catholic Exiles and Contested Space in Late-Sixteenth-Century Paris," *French Historical Studies* 32 (2009): 33–62.

98. This is Edward Wilton's report to Essex after meeting Constable in Paris in September 1595, CP 179/156, summarised in HMC *Salisbury*, 5: 386; Historical Manuscripts Commission, *Eleventh Report, Appendix, Part VII* (London, 1887), 265.

99. *CSPD*, 5: 138.

100. Bossy, "Character of Elizabethan Catholicism," 48.

It is no surprise that Constable's activities were followed with interest by the English government and reported by ambassadors. No one expected him to keep a low profile; a former diplomat and controversialist who had chosen exile raised a certain amount of anxiety. Exile entailed loss and renewal, the renegotiation and even reconstruction of one's identity and relations with the world. In the spiritual sphere, the sense of "displacement," as Geert H. Janssen terms it, led to "confessional radicalization."[101]

Constable's multiple allegiances during the first years of his exile paint the picture of a conflicted man to which the "Catholic loyalist poet" label does not apply in a straightforward manner.[102] On the one hand, he still relied on his English connections. For a few years he reached out to the earl of Essex and his secretary, Anthony Bacon; from his letters it can be inferred that Henry was trying to work as an agent in their intelligence network.[103] He repeatedly protested his "love & loyaltye to his Countrey hate to Spayn" and his desire to follow Essex's orders as long as they did not conflict with his new religion.[104] The letters continued until 1597 – although no reply from Essex, if there ever was any, survives. In the last letter Constable not only professes his own loyalty but also writes on behalf of English Catholics in Rome who refuse to support the king of Spain against Elizabeth and oppose "all violent & unlawfull means of proceeding for Religion." He voices his hope that Essex and –through his intercession – the queen may learn to differentiate between Catholics who do and do not wish for the downfall of the current regime; the letter ends with an apology of toleration based on the "union of Religion" which would lead to "the peace of Cristendom" and "quietnes of the state."[105] By this he obviously means the return of England

---

101. Geert H. Janssen, "The Exile Experience," in *The Ashgate Research Companion to the Counter-Reformation*, ed. Alexandra Bamji, Geert H. Janssen, and Mary Laven (Farnham, 2013), 73–90, at 81.

102. Constable is termed as such for instance in Alison Shell, *Catholicism, Controversy, and the English Literary Imagination, 1558–1660* (Cambridge, 1999), 126. On the dominant scholarly trend stressing "the continuing national affinity of Catholic exiles," see Janssen, "Exile Experience," 83–84. Questier considers this loyalism a myth, arguing that no clear-cut distinctions can be made between loyalism and disloyalty as far as English Catholics are concerned; see Michael C. Questier, "Elizabeth and the Catholics," in *Catholics and the "Protestant Nation": Religious Politics and Identity in Early Modern England*, ed. Ethan H. Shagan (Manchester, 2005), 69–94, at 69–71.

103. For an exhaustive account of the way in which Essex's spy network operated, especially in relation to foreign affairs, see the chapter "The Essex, Phelippes and Bacon Intelligence Initiative" in Patrick H. Martin, *Elizabethan Espionage: Plotters and Spies in the Struggle Between Catholicism and the Crown* (Jefferson, NC, 2016), 79–94.

104. HMC *Salisbury*, 5: 386; CP 35/50.

105. CP 175/3.

to the Catholic fold.[106] The letters to Bacon are similar in content, although Constable is bolder in the defence of his own reputation and loyalty, and his desire to improve the lives of his coreligionists. To him he sent a copy of an unpublished work described as "a litle incounter between the ministres of the french gospel and me," which is now lost.[107]

On the other hand, Constable was on good terms with Henri IV, whom he had begun to admire in his Protestant youth when the king had shared his religion. Now a Catholic and relatively safe on the throne, the king granted Constable a pension, apparently through the intercession of the bishop of Évreux, Jacques Davy du Perron, who became a close friend of Constable's.[108] A letter from 1597 reveals this friendship and is the earliest piece of evidence of Constable's plans involving the Scottish monarchs; he is reported to have devised a plan to have James's wife, Queen Anne, converted to Catholicism through French intercession.[109] At this time, Constable also joined the English priests residing in Paris in their petitions for the creation of a "new college or seminary" at Collège Mignon.[110]

Another friend was Christopher Bagshaw, the main actor in the Archpriest Controversy, which fractured English Catholicism. It originated in 1598 when a group of secular priests, known as the Appellants, opposed the pope's appointment of an archpriest over the English clergy.[111] Constable sided with Bagshaw in support of the Appellants and in opposition to the Jesuits – accused of being pro-Spanish and disloyal to the English Crown.[112] This meant a turning point in

---

106. Wickes notes that Constable believed that Catholicism would inevitably follow religious toleration, and that "his countrymen would be won back by the irresistible logic of the Catholic position as soon as free discussion was allowed." See Wickes, *Bio*, 280.

107. This letter was sent from Rouen in January 1596; see London, Lambeth Palace, MS 660, 161. Wickes suggests that it might have been a copy of *Examen pacifique*, but no evidence supports this claim; see Wickes, *Bio*, 281.

108. Du Perron had been the major influence in the conversion of the king; see Sutherland, *Henry IV*, 472–473. Constable saw him as a model of how eloquence and charisma could win over heretics.

109. TNA, SP 77/5, 238.

110. This project did not come to fruition; division between the leaders of the English Catholics was to blame. See Gibbons, *English Catholic Exiles*, 147, 150.

111. See Victor Houliston, *Catholic Resistance in Elizabethan England: Robert Persons's Jesuit Polemic, 1580–1610* (Aldershot, 2007), 121.

112. See Gibbons, *English Catholic Exiles*, 47–49, on the effect of the controversy on English Catholic exiles in France. What on the surface may appear as a clerical dispute concerned the laity and their conflicting views on church government and other controversial topics; see Michael C. Questier, *Catholicism and Community in Early Modern England: Politics, Aristocratic Patronage and Religion, c. 1550–1640* (Cambridge, 2006), 250–253.

his relations with the Jesuit Robert Persons, which had been amicable enough so far: a long letter from Persons dated 31 August 1598 has survived, from which it can be inferred that they agreed on some matters, as they shared some plans concerning a possible appeal to Elizabeth by King Henri that might win Catholics greater toleration. However, mistrust was mounting, and Persons warned Constable to choose his associates wisely.[113]

## Exile: 1598–1603

By 1598, Henry Constable had become a man with a mission: ensuring greater toleration for Catholics in his country and, hopefully, seeing England return to the Roman fold under a converted King James. An intriguing letter in French sent to Essex accuses Constable of being "a double traitor [*un double traitre*], for it is he who hands over, by means of a courier named Jean Symonds, all the letters which come from the Jesuits and other disaffected persons in England."[114] In the eyes of this anonymous intelligencer, Constable was a traitor both to his country and, due to his commitment to the anti-Jesuit faction, to an important part of his fellow Catholics.

Whereas moderate Catholics such as Richard Bristow had tried to reconcile loyalty to a Protestant monarch with their religion and "prayed for the salvation of the sovereign's soul," Constable was not content to pray, but started to actively work for King James's conversion.[115] He saw himself as the right man for the job, since he had made James's acquaintance and written sonnets to him years before. In late 1598, preparations were underway for a journey to Scotland on behalf of the pope.[116] Henry had come to represent the pope's interests abroad because he was backed by the apostolic legate in Paris, Atilio Amalteo, who recommended him to Pope Clement's nephew, Cardinal Pietro Aldobrandini. There is some indication that Constable travelled to Rome himself around this time.[117] Sir Thomas Edmondes, the English diplomat who was *chargé d'affaires* in the embassy in France at the time, wrote to Cecil that Constable was meant "to encourage that King to allow the Catholics there a toleration of religion" and

---

113. Historical Manuscripts Commission, *Eleventh Report, Appendix, Part VII* (London, 1887), 265–266.
114. HMC *Salisbury*, 8: 351. Translated in Wickes, *Bio*, 297 n44.
115. Stefania Tutino, *Law and Conscience: Catholicism in Early Modern England, 1570–1625* (Hampshire, 2007), 57.
116. *CSPD*, 5: 90.
117. ASV, Fondo Borghese III, 73, fol. 123v.

assure him of the loyalty of English Catholics. Because Constable excelled at religious debates, he was expected "to practise on the said Kinges mynde."[118]

He landed at Leith in March 1599. From the combined pieces of intelligence, it can be gathered that he requested an audience with the king. James initially refused saying that he only bore one letter of recommendation, by the duchess of Guise, and that he was "known to be a fugitive and a practiser against his country." Apparently, the king was also aware of Constable's design to convert him. Constable himself claimed to be acting as spokesman for Catholic support of James as the next king of England, which he said was widespread with the exception of "some that were traffickers and practised the course of Spain, whose names in particular he could show his Majesty."[119] Constable managed to remain at court without subscribing to the Articles of Religion. He spoke with the queen and, later, James himself.[120] Apparently, Constable presented James, on behalf of the pope and English Catholics, with the offer of an army and a large sum of money if he declared war on Elizabeth.[121] He also assured him of the support of Catholic princes.

In the end, the mission proved a failure and Henry felt disillusioned when he returned to France in September: he reportedly spoke of James "as little better than an atheist, of no courage nor judgment."[122] Far from giving up, however, he sought the support of his Continental connections in Flanders. The exiles there included Constable's kinsman Charles Neville, earl of Westmorland.[123] They were discontented with the financial support Spain granted them and relished the promise that the French King might secure them some freedom of religion under Elizabeth and, eventually, James.[124] Constable also persuaded some of Henri IV's statesmen and the nuncio in Paris, Gasparo Silingardi, who rec-

118. Thomas Birch, ed., *An Historical View of the Negotiations between the Courts of England, France and Brussels, from the Year 1592 to 1617* (London, 1749), 177.
119. *CSPSc*, 13.1: 421. The king's words are reported by Roger Aston.
120. Ibid., 434. He managed to have a long conversation with the king and was even invited to a hunt; ibid., 461; TNA, SP 77/6, 12–13.
121. Edmund Sawyer, ed., *Memorials of Affairs of State in the Reigns of Q. Elizabeth and K. James I* (London, 1725), 1: 37; Alexandre Teulet, *Relations politiques de la France et de l'Espagne avec l'Ecosse au XVIe siècle* (Paris, 1862), 4: 222–223, translated in Wickes, *Bio*, 297 n55; *CSPSc*, 13.1: 531.
122. *CSPD*, 5: 356.
123. Charles was a grandson of Thomas Manners, first earl of Rutland. He was a Catholic and tended to side with enemies of Elizabeth in exile; see Roger N. McDermott, "Neville, Charles, sixth earl of Westmorland (1542/3–1601)," in *ODNB*.
124. *CSPSp*, 4: 681. This is Robert Persons's report to the Duke of Sessa, Antonio Fernández de Córdoba, who was the Spanish ambassador in Rome at the time. Persons gives more details about Constable's Flemish contacts and his plan.

ommended him to the pope the moment the poet set foot in Rome in 1600. Silingardi wrote that Constable wished to "entrust the remainder of his life" to the pope's protection, and that he should be well treated on account of his many "qualities" and his status as "a very Catholic person and one of great authority" in England.[125]

The Spanish Council of State informed King Philip III that Constable had assured the pope that James's conversion was possible, which would lead to England and Scotland returning to the fold.[126] Clement refused to send him on an official embassy to James, but gave him permission to go if he wished.[127] He did not. During his time in Rome, Constable also used his friendship with Cardinal Frederic Borromeo, archbishop of Milan, to press for the revival of the English Benedictine order, of whose members only one elderly man survived.[128]

The year 1600 also saw the publication of a tract titled *A discoverye of a counterfecte conference*, a response to the polemical *A conference about the next succession to the crowne of Ingland* (Antwerp, 1595), attributed to Robert Persons.[129] Persons had put forth the possibility of a Catholic succession, and his work was generally read as promoting the tenuous claim to the throne of the Spanish infanta, Isabella Clara Eugenia.[130] Printed with a false imprint (probably in Paris), The *Discovery* may have been coauthored, but it all seems to indicate that Constable had a hand in it.[131] Of course, it endorses a Scottish succession: Catholics should respect James's hereditary right and hope for his conversion.[132] Another piece of controversy supposedly cowritten by Constable survives. This is a "defamatory libel" surviving in the Vatican Library in which, according to the duke of Sessa's report, the authors attacked Robert Persons, the Jesuits, and those who supported them in England, "asserting that under colour of religion these

125. ASV, SSF 47, fol. 146r–v; the original is in Italian.
126. On this mission, Constable could have been acting at the behest of Henri IV; see HMC *Salisbury*, 12: 49.
127. *CSPSp*, 4: 682–683.
128. Stephen Marron, "The Second Benedictine Mission to England," *Douai Magazine* 2, no. 3 (1923): 157–165. See also Bossy, "Character of Elizabethan Catholicism," 56–57.
129. The full title is *A discoverye of a counterfecte conference helde at a counterfecte place, by counterfecte travellers, for thadvancement of a counterfecte tytle, and invented, printed, and published by one (person) that dare not avowe his name* (Paris?, 1600).
130. The misinterpretation and true aims of Persons's book are discussed in full in Houliston, *Catholic Resistance*, 74–87.
131. A copy was sent to King James in July that year and Constable was reported to be the author; *CSPSc*, 13.2: 673. Charles Paget was another name connected with the book; see Grundy, 43.
132. On Catholic hopes, see Tutino, *Law and Conscience*, 81.

aimed at nothing else than tyrannously subjecting that kingdom to the crown of Spain against the will of good English Catholics."[133]

Back in Paris, Constable continued to live on King Henri's pension and enjoyed the favour of the bishop of Paris and the new papal nuncio, Innocenzo Del Bufalo. The only description of Constable dates from that time: "a litle man redd face pumpled gray head and a smale beard."[134] He took part in a religious conference in 1602, mainly about the Eucharist, in which he supported Pierre Cayet, whom du Perron had converted to Catholicism, against Pierre du Moulin, Constable's former friend.[135]

Like other exiled countrymen, Constable never abandoned the hope of "a triumphant return" to England.[136] This hope flared upon the succession of James to the English throne. The Elizabethan fines for recusancy had been discontinued in 1603 and, in general, Catholics were hopeful and expected greater toleration from the new king, since they had openly supported his cause.[137] Henry immediately set to finding out if he would be welcomed back despite his religion. He wrote to Scottish friends, Cecil, and the king himself, and begged his kinsman the earl of Rutland to intercede. His letter to Rutland reveals that he had recently lost favour with King Henri because he had got too close to the Guises, now reported to be his "dearest frends" in France, and that Henri would not let him leave without James's approval.[138] To Cecil he promised to "behave ... according to his [i.e., the king's] liking" and to serve in any capacity that James could "with reason require" of him considering his religion.[139]

---

133. Summarised in Leo Hicks, "Sir Robert Cecil, Father Persons and the Succession 1600–1601," *Archivum historicum Societatis Iesu* 24 (1955), 95–139, at 131. The copy of the libel is "Un libello infamatorio pieno di calunnie et false inventioni per infamare l'attioni del Re di Spagna e delli Padri Giesuiti intorno le cose d'Inghilterra fatto per alcuni inglesi inquieti in Roma questo anno 1601," BAV, MS Vat. lat. 6227, 202–204.

134. TNA, SP 15/34, fol. 104r.

135. Sally Anne Wagstaffe, "Forms and Methods of Religious Controversy in Paris: With Special Reference to Pierre du Moulin and his Catholic Opponents" (PhD diss., Durham University, 1990), 146, 150.

136. Gibbons, "'A Reserved Place'?," 48.

137. Michael C. Questier, "Catholic Loyalism in Early Stuart England," *The English Historical Review* 123 (2008), 1132–1165, at 1133.

138. HMC *Rutland*, 1: 391. Henri IV had "inherited the implacable hatred harboured by the Guises – the house of Lorraine – for the Bourbon princes"; see Sutherland, *Henry IV*, 6.

139. From Paris, 11 June 1603, CP 187/71.

## Back in England

In December 1603 Constable arrived in England, perhaps carrying a copy of the *Spiritual Sonnets* with him.[140] His trip was funded by Del Bufalo, who conveyed to the Vatican his belief that Constable's noble connections and his reports would prove him useful to the Church; that is, he was to be a Catholic agent.[141] Apparently he was warmly welcomed at Hampton Court. Queen Anne and old acquaintances such as Penelope Rich were glad to see him back, and he felt so confident that he assured the nuncio that he was in a privileged position to serve the Catholic cause. King James, he reported, was "naturally kind" and "an enemy of persecution," but no more freedom would be granted to Catholics until he were convinced of the good foundations of their faith.[142] The point was that, being a man of reason, he could be persuaded with arguments.

The edict ordering Jesuits and seminary priests to leave the country in February 1604 was a major blow, and Constable stressed the need for the Vatican to act by sending theologians and foreign Catholic noblemen who could speak with the king, representing the interests of the pope and all Catholics.[143] In his letters he gives names and suggests the best candidates, displaying his vast network of acquaintances.[144] Time was ticking by, as Parliament was to convene in March and chances were that it would confirm Elizabeth's law against recusants. Henry came to the conclusion that he had to take action himself, and he undertook to write down the "arguments of the Catholic faith" and "designed a method" which had the approval of his learned friends and those close to the king.[145]

At the beginning of April, Constable's prospects looked bright. He recovered his inheritance and lands, and had a confirmation of arms – those of his

140. See p. 97.
141. Del Bufalo to Aldobrandini, Paris, 14 December 1603, ASV, SSF 48, fols. 232r–233v; the original is in Italian. Del Bufalo took very seriously his role as overseer of English affairs. He had a carefully built diplomatic network, and he constantly received reports from England. See Bernard Barbiche, ed., *Correspondance du nonce en France Innocenzo Del Bufalo, évêque de Camerino, 1601–1604* (Rome: Presses de l'Université grégorienne, 1964), 414.
142. London, 9 January 1604, ASV, SSF 49, fols. 36v–39r. This is a copy of Constable's letter which was forwarded to Aldobrandini in February. The originals of this and other letters to the Nuncio have not been preserved.
143. James was wary of their obedience to foreign authorities, which contested his own absolute power. See W.B. Patterson, *King James VI and I and the Reunion of Christendom* (Cambridge, 1997), 49–50.
144. The names of members of the Guise family stand out. Constable wrote to Charles de Lorraine, duke of Guise, who was James's kinsman. See TNA, SP 78/51, 71–72.
145. London, 26 February 1604, ASV, SSF 49, fols. 62r–66v, at 66v. This is a copy of Constable's letter which was forwarded to Aldobrandini a month later.

father's – drafted by William Segar.[146] He was also reported to be "well esteemed by the king" and frequently discussing religion with him.[147] It must have been Constable's faith in the king's friendship that made him grow bolder and take unnecessary risks. As a mortified Del Bufalo explains, Constable sent letters to France using a courier other than the "usual friend" or courier who was usually entrusted with their secret correspondence, as the man had fallen ill and could not travel.[148] With regard to the content of the letters, according to a secondhand account, "He said that he held it for certain that the King had no religion at all, and that everything he did was governed by political expediency."[149] In a letter dated 14 April, Robert Cecil presents the charges even more emphatically: Constable had "slandered the state" and claimed that, if James converted to Catholicism, the whole Privy Council would follow suit; he had also entreated Del Bufalo to send an emissary who could help further the Catholic cause at court – a dangerous scheme that, Cecil believes, the nuncio would have never dared join. The incendiary content of the letters (they sought to "draw all things into combustion") written by a man who had been welcomed into court had driven the king to "punish him exemplarily" by committing him to the Tower.[150] He was to keep company with Sir Anthony Standen, a fellow Catholic and spy who had also been charged with illicit correspondence.[151]

From the Tower, Constable appealed to Cecil himself, the council, and relatives such as his cousin Gilbert Talbot, earl of Shrewsbury. Of the latter, he asked to let the council know that he wrote "nothing to the prejudice of his Majesty or any of them," although he added: "I willingly and with all humillity aknowledg all other faults in the circonstances of my letters which they shall dislike." He also requested permission to have some relatives visit him in order to sort out "privat affaires" so that he could "make a full conclusion with the world." His tone is one of pious resignation and concern for the loss of his reputation:

> Whether I remayn in prison, or go out, I have lerned to live alone with god, and so I may make up my accompts with the world, in such sort, as nether his Majesty take me for an unduetifull subject nor your Lordship and my other

---

146. A transcription of this document is preserved in London, British Library, Add MS 12225, 59. It must be dated around this time because Segar was appointed as Garter in January 1604; see Anthony R.J.S. Adolph, "Segar, Sir William (c. 1554–1633)," in *ODNB*.

147. Del Bufalo to Aldobrandini, Paris, 6 April 1604, ASV, SSF 49, fols. 86r–87r.

148. As above, 31 May 1604, ASV, SSF 49, fol. 114r–v.

149. Nicolo Molin, Venetian Ambassador in England, to the Doge and Senate, London, 28 April 1604; *CSPV*, 10: 146–147.

150. Cecil to Sir Thomas Parry, London, 14 April 1604, TNA, SP 78/51, 141–142. Parry was the English ambassador in France.

151. See Paul E.J. Hammer, "Standen, Sir Anthony (d. in or after 1615)," in *ODNB*.

honorable frends, that hertofor have favoured me, remayn discontented with me, nor any man els have damage by me, I shall repute my self happy in all other misery.[152]

He was released in July and put under house arrest. His career was essentially over: he lost his inheritance again, and there were rumours that he would be banished.[153] He wrote to Mary, countess of Shrewsbury, hoping that through his relatives' mediation his banishment might be temporary, pending his good behaviour. He also entertained the possibility of going to Spain with the constable of Castile, given that France was no longer an option because of Henri IV's animosity.[154] In the end, he stayed in England, relying on his friends' and kinsmen's financial support. A list on a letter from October 1605 associates him with Henry Goodere, Tobie Matthew, and Sir Edward Baynam, all of whom were suspect Catholics.[155] The discovery of the Gunpowder Plot in November and the 1606 Oath of Allegiance could have only put him in a worse predicament.[156]

In 1607–1608 he embarrassed Gilbert Talbot, who had procured his freedom from a second, undated term in prison on condition that he would not "deale with any person whosoever in matter of Religion" and that he would present himself before the archbishop of Canterbury whenever he was summoned. Despite his promises, Constable failed to appear when requested, and Shrewsbury had to write to the archbishop and Cecil, expressing his astonishment and justifying himself: he had sent for his kinsman and located him easily, for he was not in hiding.[157] Apparently, the king wished to see him and his patience had been exhausted. When Constable appeared, he was sent to Fleet Prison. From there he wrote to the earl and countess of Shrewsbury on 9 February, thanking Mary for her continuous support and sharing his anxiety about the future with Gilbert – he feared that a long term in prison would impover-

152. Constable to the earl of Shrewsbury from the Tower, 6 May 1604; London, Lambeth Palace, MS 708, fol. 125r–v.
153. *CSPV*, 10: 174. A warrant dated 20 May 1605 declared that one of the estates granted to Constable's father, the manor of Chopwell, was not to pass on or be leased to Henry; see *CSPD*, 8: 217.
154. Constable to the Countess of Shrewsbury, London?, undated; London, Lambeth Palace, MS 3205, fol. 92r. Juan Fernández de Velasco, Constable of Castile, led the Spanish delegation whose visit concluded with the Treaty of London in August 1604.
155. Dudley Carleton to Sir Walter Cope, Paris, 14 October 1605, CP 191/54.
156. See Patterson, *King James*, 75–123. It is unknown whether Constable took the oath.
157. Shrewsbury to Cecil, Worksop, 1 February 1608; London, Lambeth Palace, MS 3203, fol. 489v; to Richard Bancroft, Archbishop of Canterbury, Worksop, 1 February 1608; Lambeth MS 3203, fol. 490r.

ish him even more, and leaving the country might well be a more sensible option.[158] To the earl of Rutland he wrote that he did not know what the exact charges against him were, but suspected that religious bigotry was at work: "Every furious puritan that seeth me abroad do in his own imagination forge untruths and then report them for reale acts and I not know what they be nor how to answer for my self."[159]

## Second Exile and Death

Constable left for France in August 1610, three months after Henri IV's death. He bore "a passe ... to depart out of his majesties dominions, and not to returne without speciall directions and warrant in that behalf," and was allowed to take a servant and £100 with him.[160] There are no records of further political activities, although his continuing interest in religious controversy was evidenced by his presence at a theological disputation about the real presence of Christ in the Eucharist held in Paris in September 1612.[161] The following year, Cardinal Du Perron, Constable's longtime friend and personal hero, sent him on his last mission. He was to assist in the conversion to Catholicism of Benjamin Carier, but death overcame him shortly after arriving in Liège, as a Protestant enemy recorded triumphantly: "God blessed not his vaine project, Mr Henrie Constable dying within fortnight after he came from Paris, by Cardinall Perrons appointment, to Leidge, to conferre with him; and himselfe a while after in Paris."[162]

---

158. Ibid., fols. 493r and 495r.
159. Belvoir Castle, Belvoir MSS Additional 1, fol. 105r.
160. London, British Library, Add MS 11402, fol. 159v.
161. The main disputants were Daniel Featly, Protestant chaplain to Sir Thomas Edmondes, the English ambassador in Paris, and Richard Smith, a Roman Catholic priest and controversialist who was a spokesperson for the English secular clergy. The poet Ben Jonson was one of the men present supporting the Protestant side. See Hugh Adlington, "Chaplains to Embassies: Daniel Featley, Anti-Catholic Controversialist Abroad," in *Chaplains in Early Modern England: Patronage, Literature and Religion*, ed. Hugh Adlington, Tom Lockwood, and Gillian Wright (Manchester, 2013), 83–102, at 83; Joseph Bergin, "Smith, Richard (1567–1655)," in *ODNB*. Accounts of this debate were all published in the 1630s and offer contrasting views pertaining to opposed religious stances. See for instance John Lechmere, *The relection of a conference touching the real presence* (Douai, 1635).
162. George Hakewill, *An Answere to a treatise written by Dr. Carier* (London, 1616), 5.

Henry Constable died on 9 October 1613 without issue, as recorded during a herald's visitation to Nottinghamshire.[163] A funeral oration – clearly given by a Catholic friend – preserved in manuscript gives a brief account of his life, emphasising all that he had lost through "his remarkable zeal to spread the Faith": "His successes were noted by the heretics and moved them to anger."[164]

---

163. London, British Library, Harley MS 6953, fol. 16v.
164. The translation is from Wickes, *Bio*, 300. The text he quotes is the final tribute, originally written in Latin in London, Westminster Diocesan Archive, A4/34, 252. Three pages that are also in Latin, faded and illegible in parts, precede it.

CHAPTER TWO

# The Amatory and Dedicatory Sonnets

Constable's secular sonnets survive in manuscript and print collections which will be discussed here with a concern for their contents and their socioliterary history, as the products of networks of transmission whose members obtained exemplars and copied them to share with others – with or without the author's permission.[1] Bibliographic and provenance information can be found in the "Bibliographical Description of Main Textual Sources" (see p. 364).

Constable must have had some agency in the circulation of his sonnets in manuscript at an early stage; meant to secure him patronage or royal favour, his sonnets were shared by friends and relatives, and eventually escaped authorial control. The circumstances surrounding their publication in print are even more obscure, and it seems likely that he was not involved in the publishing process.

## Readers and Transmission of the Sonnets in Manuscript

The manuscript miscellanies in which the largest collections of Constable's sonnets are found are the result of individual or collective compiling efforts.[2] They are particularly significant in that the sonnets seem distinctly alive or, borrow-

---

1. The cultural materialist approach to literary works is well defined in Arthur F. Marotti, "Manuscript, Print and the English Renaissance Lyric," in *New Ways of Looking at Old Texts: Papers of the Renaissance English Text Society, 1985–1991*, ed. William Speed Hill (Binghamton, NY, 1993), 209–222. On the socioliterary approach, see for instance Marotti, "Malleable and Fixed Texts: Manuscript and Printed Miscellanies and the Transmission of Lyric Poetry in the English Renaissance," in *New Ways*, ed. Hill 159–174; Harold Love, *Scribal Publication in Seventeenth-Century England* (Oxford, 1993); Woudhuysen, *Sir Philip Sidney and the Circulation of Manuscripts, 1558–1640* (Oxford, 1996); Peter Beal, *In Praise of Scribes: Manuscripts and Their Makers in the Seventeenth Century* (Oxford, 1998).

2. A useful overview of manuscript miscellanies and related scholarship is the introduction to Joshua Eckhardt and Daniel Starza Smith, eds., *Manuscript Miscellanies in Early Modern England* (Farnham, 2014), 1–15.

ing Arthur F. Marotti's term, "malleable" in them.[3] They are presented in varying arrangements, with changing headings and intriguing omissions and additions. They are seldom alone in the physical manuscript; Harold Love has noted that the miscellany, and not "the manuscript devoted to the work of a single poet," was "the most characteristic mode through which verse was circulated to its readers" in the early seventeenth century.[4] In these miscellanies, Constable's sonnets are surrounded by prose and verse works or fragments by contemporaries, and the company they keep adds a new layer of meaning that could be missed by looking at poems in isolation.[5] As Mary Hobbs puts it, "without using these manuscripts [i.e., miscellanies], any edition of a single poet is liable to distortion."[6]

Although the names of the compilers and the particulars of some of these collections remain elusive, a brief account of their provenance and an overview of their contents can throw some light on the inclusion of Constable's verse in them. This section will also cover the peculiarities of his verse as presented in each miscellany, and their relationship with the lost authorial manuscripts. The terms "collection" or "cluster" tend to be favoured over "sequence" here because the groups of sonnets as they appear in some of the primary sources can hardly be said to have a thematic unity or form a sequential narrative in the manner of Petrarch or Sidney. However, *H* fits Michael Spiller's working definition of "sequence" as "a collection of poems, dominantly sonnets, linked together intentionally by something other than single authorship."[7] Constable perceived the text later represented in *T* as a definite compilation due to its careful arrangement and the presence of prefatory and concluding pieces, and it might be termed the most authoritative sequence of his secular sonnets. Two manuscripts containing a single sonnet by Constable, *Bn* and *OBL*, hint at the possibility that his sonnets may also have been circulating separately in the early, authorially supervised stages of transmission, an idea which is strengthened by the translations made by acquaintances abroad.

3. Marotti, "Malleable and Fixed Texts."
4. Love, *Scribal Publication*, 5.
5. Neil Fraistat, *Poems in Their Place: The Intertextuality and Order of Poetic Collections* (Chapel Hill, NC, 1986), 8. Fraistat termed it "contexture," defined as "the contextuality provided for each poem by the larger frame within which it is placed, the intertextuality among poems so placed, and the resultant texture of resonance and meanings" (3).
6. Mary Hobbs, *Early Seventeenth-Century Verse Miscellany Manuscripts* (Aldershot, 1992), 144.
7. Michael R.G. Spiller, *The Sonnet Sequence: A Study of Its Strategies* (Farmington Hills, MI, 1997), 16–17.

## Marsh's Library MS Z3.5.21 (M)

The Marsh manuscript (M), held in the collections of Marsh's Library, Dublin, is an octavo-size volume of miscellaneous Elizabethan verse and prose. It originated in the same university environment as other contemporary poetic miscellanies; it shares thirteen English poems with Oxford, Bodleian Library, Rawlinson Poetry 85, and ten with London, British Library, Harley MS 7392.[8] As in the case of the Rawlinson manuscript, the compilation of M can be traced back to St John's College, Cambridge, where a group of teenaged amateur scribes were involved in the circulation and copying of texts by elite, lesser-known, and anonymous authors. The anti-Catholic sentiment that characterizes its contents is coherent with St John's Puritanism and northern connections.[9]

The contents in M are dated roughly between 1570 and 1615.[10] Fifteen of Constable's sonnets form the most significant cluster by a single author. Of the remaining forty-six poems in English, five are by Sir Philip Sidney; three by Sir Walter Raleigh; three by Edward de Vere, earl of Oxford; and two by Sir Edward Dyer.[11] Single poems by William Hunnis, Humphrey Coningsby, Sir Henry Goodere, Francis Kinwelmarsh, Thomas Buckley, and James Reshoulde are also included, together with some which bear only initials such as "T.B." or "H.A.,"

---

8. On Rawlinson Poetry 85, see Randall L. Anderson, "'The Merit of a Manuscript Poem': The Case for Bodleian MS Rawlinson Poet. 85," in *Print, Manuscript & Performance: The Changing Relations of the Media in Early Modern England*, ed. Arthur F. Marotti and Michael D. Bristol (Columbus, 2000), 127–171, at 134; Laurence Cummings, "John Finet's Miscellany" (PhD diss., Washington University, 1960), 45–46. On the Harley miscellany and its two possible compilers, see Woudhuysen, *Circulation*, 278–280; Bernard M. Wagner, "New Poems by Sir Edward Dyer," *The Review of English Studies* 11 (1935): 466–471, at 466 n3; L.G. Black, "Studies in Some Related Manuscript Poetic Miscellanies of the 1580s" (PhD diss., Oxford University, 1970), 1: 47–54.

9. Victor Morgan points out that "Sidney Sussex, and St John's in the earlier part of Elizabeth's reign, were essentially puritan seminaries and both had strong connections with the north fostered by the acquisition of scholarships tied to schools in the northern counties." These grammar schools were founded to counteract Catholicism in areas that mostly held on to it. See Victor Morgan, *A History of the University of Cambridge, Vol. 2: 1546–1750* (Cambridge, 2004), 190.

10. Contents can be dated based on allusions to contemporary people and events – as they have a strong occasional character – and their inclusion in other printed or manuscript miscellanies whose date is certain. Topical allusions which allow dating include references to the duke of Norfolk's trial and execution in 1572; to the earl of Oxford's affair with Anne Vavasour, discovered in 1581; and to the rise of the earl of Essex in the late 1580s, among others.

11. These are catalogued in *CELM*, http://www.celm-ms.org.uk/repositories/marshs-library-dublin.html#marshs-library-dublin_id694004.

and eight anonymous poems.[12] Of the latter group, "Dy Dy desire and bid delight adeue" (fol. 23r–v) enjoyed considerable popularity and circulated widely, whereas others are solely preserved in this collection.

The actual copying of the items began in the second half of the 1580s. An interest in the figure of Mary, Queen of Scots, executed in 1587, shows throughout the volume.[13] Other prose texts clustered together evidence a preoccupation with the succession to the throne, which was on everyone's minds in the 1580s and, especially, the 1590s.[14] Two texts by Constable provide some of the most reliable clues as to when the miscellany was being compiled. "A short vew of a large examination of Cardinal Allen his trayterous justification of Sr W. Stanley and Yorck, written by Master H. Cons. and this gathered out of his own draught" is the heading given to a summary of his treatise on Dutch affairs, written in response to William Allen's commendation of the deserting officers.[15] The treatise was drafted in the second half of 1587, given that in *Bn* Constable refers to the Battle of Coutras as having taken place "the other day" (fol. 41v).[16] The summary in *M*, written in a hand other than that responsible for Constable's sonnets, was included in 1588, given that this time reference is changed to "this other year" (fol. 108v), and it begins halfway through part 2 of the original. Constable's sonnets point to the same year. The heading of an occasional piece on the birth of Penelope Rich's daughter, number 42 in this edition, refers to "this yeare. 1588."

---

12. Some of the contributors were students at St John's. James Reshoulde obtained his BA from St John's in 1586–1587; Sir Henry Goodere's nephew and namesake matriculated as a fellow-commoner there in 1587, and may be responsible for the inclusion of a poem by his uncle.

13. This is noted in George Martin, "Marsh's Library MS z3.5.21: An Edition of the English Poems" (master's thesis, University of Waterloo, 1971), 175, 39. A long prose item in Latin bears the heading "Letera Regina Scotorum ad Elizabeth" and the date "1587" (fols. 183v–190r). The Latin couplet known as the Buxton distich, attributed to Mary, begins a verse dialogue on fol. 22v.

14. One, "Peter Wentworth in the parliament for an heir apparant" (fols. 167r–176r), is derived from Wentworth's tract on the matter, written in 1587 but not published until 1598. The pro-Jacobean tract was printed in Scotland with the title *A pithie exhortation to her Maiestie for establishing her successor to the crowne* (Edinburgh, 1598). See Susan Doran and Paulina Kewes, *Doubtful and Dangerous: The Question of Succession in Late Elizabethan England* (Manchester, 2014), 48–50.

15. The full version – deemed lost for a long time – is preserved in New Haven, Yale University, Beinecke Library, MS 621 (*Bn*), fols. 15r–43r. The pamphlet that Constable answers is William Allen, *A copie of a lettre written by an English Gentleman, out of the campe of the low contryes* (Antwerp, 1587).

16. This battle was fought on 20 October 1587.

Constable had been at St John's from 1578 to 1580.[17] His friends at that time included Sir John Harington, Abraham Fraunce, and John Palmer.[18] His early sonnets, however, were drafted later, when his diplomatic and courtly career began, and they must have been coveted by younger students, who viewed him as unambiguously Protestant. The scribe who copied his sonnets onto the miscellany (scribe B) could have either been associated with Constable or shared an acquaintance with him. Possible candidates who might have supplied the sonnets include his kinsman Roger Manners, the young earl of Rutland, who was at Cambridge from 1587 to 1595, and the earl's older companion at Corpus Christi, French Huguenot Pierre du Moulin.[19] The fact that Constable's name was well-known at the college may explain why his initials, "H.C.," and not his full name, follow the last of his fifteen sonnets. Members of a social group would not have needed more than that to identify the author. Alternatively, the use of initials could be meant to obscure the authorial ascription if the miscellany was intended only for the eyes and exclusive use of a close-knit coterie who wished to withhold that piece of information from everyone else.[20]

M is invaluable because it preserves what can safely be assumed to be the earliest collection of Constable's sonnets that has survived. It derives from arche-

17. The Constables' connection to St John's went far back. Sir Marmaduke, Henry's great-great-grandfather, and his brother John created the Constable scholarship or foundation through generous gifts; Sir Marmaduke's wishes were that "the people of his own county might be occasionally instructed by a learned divine, his fellow shall always be a Yorkshire priest." See Richard Rex, "The Sixteenth Century," in *St John's College, Cambridge: A History*, ed. Peter Linehan (Woodbridge, 2011), 5–93, at 14–15; J.E.B. Mayor, ed., *Early Statutes of the College of St. John the Evangelist* (Cambridge, 1859), 405.

18. Palmer, a fellow of the college at that time, played Richard in the Latin play *Richardus tertius*, performed at the Bachelors Commencement Feast in March 1579. Fraunce and Constable had minor roles in that play, and Harington was a member of the audience. See Martin Wiggins and Catherine Richardson, eds., *British Drama 1533–1642: A Catalogue* (Oxford, 2012–), 1: 224–235; on this play and other pensioners, see Rex, "The Sixteenth Century," 76–77.

19. The fifth earl attended Queen's College and Corpus Christi College, where he became MA in February 1595; see Paul E. J. Hammer, "Manners, Roger, fifth earl of Rutland (1576–1612)," in *ODNB*. At the time of his exile, Constable secured Du Moulin a position in the service of Rutland. See "Autobiographie de Pierre du Moulin," *Bulletin de la Société de l'histoire du protestantisme français* 71 (1858): 170–182, at 178–179. Du Moulin is listed as Peter Molineus in Venn, 3: 197.

20. Different reasons why full, partial (in the form of initials), or no authorial ascriptions were included in manuscript texts by their copyists are discussed in Marcy L. North, *The Anonymous Renaissance: Cultures of Discretion in Tudor-Stuart England* (Chicago, 2003); see esp. 67–71.

Table 1. Order of the sonnets in *M*

| *M* | Edition | *M* | Edition |
|---|---|---|---|
| 1 | [64] | 9 | [35] |
| 2 | [6] | 10 | [26] |
| 3 | [10] | 11 | [18] |
| 4 | [60b] | 12 | [17] |
| 5 | [25] | 13 | [16] |
| 6 | [32b] | 14 | [58] |
| 7 | [65] | 15 | [42] |
| 8 | [15b] | | |

type *X*, either an authorial holograph or fair copy produced by 1588.[21] The heading of the sonnet to Penelope Rich's daughter (42) and other more covert allusions to this lady indicate that by this year Constable was an active member of the Sidney-Essex circle and had found a poetic mistress in the deceased hero's "Stella." His sonnet "The love wherewith your vertues chayne my sprite" (25) is the more clearly Protestant, politically correct, and therefore probably the earliest of the three he dedicated to Queen Elizabeth; its heading, "To hir majesty for a preface to his booke," points at the Dutch affairs treatise. Two sonnets to the countesses of Cumberland and Warwick (32b, 65) and one to King James (26) are best understood in the context of the mission that would send Constable to Scotland in 1589. Three sonnets present such significant variants compared to later versions that they are considered different entities in this edition (15b, 32b, 60b). In addition, *M* adds two sonnets to the canon (64, 65).

The fifteen sonnets may rightfully be termed a collection, but they hardly qualify as a sonnet sequence. Nothing in its arrangement indicates whether it mirrors or not the order in *X*, what the organising criteria used by the scribe might have been, or if he decided to exclude some material (see table 1). Nevertheless, two elements give it some sort of cohesion. Firstly, the organising principle seems to be clustering sonnets related to courtly affairs, albeit without the regard for hierarchical order that is apparent in *T*. For instance, the son-

21. See p. 71 below.

net to King James (26) follows one to Penelope Rich (35) instead of that addressed to Queen Elizabeth (25). Secondly, Lady Rich is a pervasive presence throughout the collection, even if she is never mentioned by name in the headings and the sonnets dedicated to her are not arranged consecutively. She is the figure behind the references to "his mistris" in the opening sonnet (64) and "his Ladye" (17, 18). Her famed beauty and conventional disdain are recurrent motifs: "gold" (6) points at her hair; her blond curls are the "golden net" in which the bird-like poet is trapped (18). There are also three puns on her name: "rich" (35), "the riches of her name" (35), and the unique *M* reading "beawtyes ritche treasure" (60). Constable's tribute to her newborn daughter is in fact intended to honour the mother, whom he praises as a nonpareil at whose feet all men have fallen (42).

The amatory sonnets lack narrative continuity beyond the existence of some clusters or thematic subgroups. The sequence begins with "My hope laye gasping on his dying bedd" (64), in which the mistress is said to be sometimes kind, particularly after having been most disdainful. The poet is almost hopeful as he thinks of having his pain eased with another kind word, but the next sonnet (6) is much more pessimistic: he despairs because his heart cannot renounce his love. In the third and fourth sonnets the poet asks the lady for her favour (10) and blames his eyes and their sinfulness for having doomed him to the eternal damnation of the lady's wrath (60b). This notion of condemnation is linked to that in the distinct *M* version of sonnet 15 (15b), in which the punishment of his heart is presented not only in spiritual but also in physical terms through unsettling images of burning. The dark imagery fades away in a sonnet celebrating both the lady's beauty and the poet's role in contributing to her fame by singing her praises (35). The following three (18, 17, 16) form a cluster which is maintained in the *T* sequence; sonnets 18 and 17 praise the lady's hair and hands respectively, whereas the last is "My Ladyes presence makes the roses redd" (16), a blazon in which nature – as described in a garden – borrows its beauty from the strolling lady. All three connect the perfection of her attributes to the hopelessness of the poet's affection. The second to last sonnet is a metaphorical explanation of his falling in love and ends with an image of condemnation that thematically links it to 60b and 15b, so it makes little narrative sense in this placement. The collection concludes with the prediction that Penelope's daughter will become a famed beauty, although her mother cannot possibly be rivalled (42).[22]

---

22. The sonnet on the untimely death of this child (55), preserved in *T*, is missing from *M*.

## The Arundel Harington MS (H)

This miscellany was the work of two generations of the Harington family. A clear distinction can be drawn between contents included under the supervision of John Harington the elder and those copied at the time of his son Sir John Harington. The first group comprises poetry by Sir Thomas Wyatt; Henry Howard, earl of Surrey; Thomas Churchyard; and others, including Harington himself.[23] Before Sir John intervened, the manuscript was planned as an anthology, with its contents carefully arranged by author. Some leaves were left blank throughout the volume and used later by both father and son, and under the supervision of the latter the anthology became more of a miscellany.[24] Sir John added some of his own poems and compositions by Sir Philip Sidney, Edward de Vere, Earl of Oxford, Samuel Daniel, Sir Walter Raleigh, Henry Constable, Fulke Greville, Lord Brooke, Edmund Spenser, Sir Edward Dyer, and others. The composite nature of H manifests the evolution in literary tastes within a single family as mid-Tudor poetry was followed by late Elizabethan, and its importance has been unanimously acknowledged.[25] It reflects the tastes and interests of two men who had insider status in an educated courtly milieu; the social and political content of the poems was as much a criterion for inclusion as their literary quality.[26]

The manuscript reflects Sir John Harington's compiling habits, most notably that of beginning a poem in his own hand only to let a scribe take over shortly after.[27] Scribal labour was time-consuming and generally perceived as hard work.[28] The fact that Sir John copied items himself is assessed by Marcy North

23. For a complete account of the contents, see Hughey, 1: 27–36. Hughey's work remains the most thorough study of this volume to date and includes an annotated edition of all the contents. I have limited this section to what is strictly relevant to provide context for Constable's sonnets.

24. Peter Beal differentiates both types of collection in terms of deliberateness and careful arrangement, although he acknowledges that the lines between them tend to blur; see Beal, *Dictionary*, 18.

25. Woudhuysen states that it is "perhaps the most important of all miscellanies"; see Woudhuysen, *Circulation*, 164.

26. Arthur F. Marotti, *Manuscript, Print, and the English Renaissance Lyric* (Ithaca, 1995), 63.

27. This feature can be observed in the eight miscellanies in which he was involved, as noted by Beal. See Peter Beal, ed., *Index of English Literary Manuscripts, Vol. 1: 1450–1625* (London, 1980), 2: 121.

28. On contemporary opinions about hand copying as inefficient and time-consuming, see Marcy L. North, "Amateur Compilers, Scribal Labour, and the Contents of Early Modern Poetic Miscellanies," *English Manuscript Studies* 16 (2011): 82–111, at 87. Sir John spent a good part of the 1580s writing a translation of Ariosto's *Orlando furioso*, which was published

as evidence of scribal labour in *H* being a "household endeavor," in which it is made clear that Sir John supervised and coordinated the task of the household scribes, who must have been servants – perhaps secretaries – and were "more at the mercy of the collector than other scribes were."[29]

With twenty-one sonnets, Constable is the most widely represented poet in this later collection.[30] His sonnets precede the first and only sonnet of Sidney's *Astrophil and Stella* preserved in *H*, headed "Sonnettes of Sir Phillip Sydneys to the Lady Ritch."[31] Like Sidney's, Constable's sequence was given a remarkable heading: "Master Henry Conestables sonets to the Lady Ritche. 1589" (see plate 2). Not only does Harington identify Penelope as the addressee, but he is also the first manuscript compiler of Constable's secular verse who provides the author's full name instead of his initials.

None of the sonnets in *H* augments the canon of Constable's poetry, since they are also preserved in the 1592 printed *Diana* (*D92*). Both sources derive from authorial archetype *Y*, dated ca. 1589, as their texts often – though not always – agree against other exemplars. Due to the friendship between the two men, Harington could have obtained *Y* from the author. It may be that he borrowed it for a short time only and planned to copy it himself but lacked the time to do so, with the task then given to a household scribe. Harington read and alluded to other works by Constable. He was also interested in the Sidney-Essex circle, and the fact that he decided to begin copying Sidney's sequence almost immediately after Constable's indicates that he made a connection between both poets, based either solely on their literary devotion to Lady Rich or on Constable's not-so-secret wish to emulate Sidney as well. After sonnet 21, Harington left blank the rest of folios 153r and 153v and the whole of folio 154.

---

in 1591. See *The Epigrams of Sir John Harington*, ed. Gerard Kilroy (Aldershot, 2009), 14. This task and his own poetical endeavours would have left him little time to himself copy down the texts that fell into his hands.

29. Marcy L. North, "Household Scribes and the Production of Literary Manuscripts in Early Modern England," *Journal of Early Modern Studies* 4 (2015): 133–157, at 145–146. Woudhuysen points out that, in the case of this and other miscellanies in which the task of copying was shared by Sir John and his scribes, it is extremely difficult to give an exact account of "the division of labour," that is, to identify who copied a particular portion or line; see Woudhuysen, *Circulation*, 107.

30. Hughey, 1: 28.

31. The first sonnet of Sidney's *Astrophil and Stella* derives from a lost manuscript of the sequence called $Z_1$ by Ringler; see *The Poems of Sir Philip Sidney*, ed. William A. Ringler (Oxford, 1962), 541. On other poems by Sidney in *H* and how Harington may have accessed them, see ibid., 541–542; Woudhuysen, *Circulation*, 343–345.

Years later, he used some of that space to copy his translation of an Ovidian elegy.[32] The original blanks indicate that he may have intended to obtain more of Constable's sonnets in due course.

Considered as a whole, and minding that Sir John Harington would have been concerned with accuracy and arrangement and was privy to some first-hand information, *H* seems more of a sequence than *D92*. It represents Constable's organization of the poems, whereas *D92* disrupts it.[33] The discrepancy in order between both (see table 2) allows conjecture as to the original arrangement of *Y*.[34] The sonnets in *H* were printed in *D92* in two groups, the first comprising the even-numbered sonnets in *H* (2 to 22), and the second the odd-numbered sonnets (3 to 21).[35]

The manuscript that served as copy text for both *H* and *D92* could have been a folio or large scroll that had the sonnets arranged in two columns.[36] While the copyists of *H* assumed that the sonnets in the first column had to be copied sequentially before moving to the second, the *D92* printer read across columns, with one sonnet followed by the one opposite. The omission of "Thyne eye, the glasse where I behold my hearte" (4), which would have come fifth, in *H* could be explained as a scribal slip caused by the similarity between the beginning of its first line and that of sonnet 60, "Myne eye with all the deadlie sinnes is fraught."[37] Although Tom W.N. Parker doubts that the missing sonnet was even included in *Y* in the first place, the fact that it reappeared in *D94* in the position that it would have occupied in *D92* adds strength to Kenneth Muir's theory.[38] The inversion in *D92* of the order of the sonnets numbered 21 and 17 in the present edition also needs to be accounted for. Sonnet 17

---

32. Two other autograph copies of this translated poem are extant, one in London, British Library, Add MS 12049, fols. 70r–71r, and another in Washington, DC, The Folger Shakespeare Library, V.a.249, 134–136. Both bear the heading "Ovids confession translated into English for generall Norris 1593". This date makes it clear that the poem was added to *H* later than Constable's sonnets.

33. Lyall agrees on the superiority of the *H* arrangement over that of *D92*; see Roderick J. Lyall, "Stella's Other Astrophel: Henry Constable's Diana and the Politics of Elizabethan Courtiership," in *Gloriana's Rule: Literature, Religion, and Power in the Age of Elizabeth*, ed. Rui Carvalho Homem and Fátima Vieira (Porto, 2006), 187–205, at 193.

34. Credit for this hypothesis goes to Kenneth Muir; see "The Order of Constable's Sonnets," *Notes and Queries* 199 (1954): 424–425.

35. This does not take into account the unique prefatory sonnet in *D92*.

36. Parker's suggestion that it was a presentation manuscript seems sound; see Parker, 154. It could have also been an authorial fair copy in folio size.

37. Muir, "Order of Constable's Sonnets," 424–425.

38. Parker, 153.

Table 2. Order of the sonnets in *H* and *D92*

| Edition | H | D92 | Edition | H | D92 |
|---|---|---|---|---|---|
| -    | -  | 1  | [7]  | 11 | 3  |
| [2]  | 1  | 2  | [22] | 12 | 5  |
| [8]  | 2  | 4  | [48] | 13 | 7  |
| [3]  | 3  | 6  | [61] | 14 | 9  |
| [20] | 4  | 8  | [10] | 15 | 11 |
| [4]  | -  | 10 | [58] | 16 | 13 |
| [60] | 5  | 12 | [45] | 17 | 15 |
| [15] | 6  | 14 | [46] | 18 | 17 |
| [56] | 7  | 16 | [18] | 19 | 19 |
| [16] | 8  | 18 | [21] | 20 | 23 |
| [6]  | 9  | 20 | [17] | 21 | 21 |
| [42] | 10 | 22 |      |    |    |

could have been omitted by mistake and added at the end, or else the last two sonnets were written on a different page in a less obvious order.[39]

The existence of thematic clusters in *H* lends it even greater authority. "Blame not my hearte for flying up so high" (8) is immediately followed by "Fly, love, deare Love; thy sun dost thow not see?" (3). Both share the central image of a soaring heart attracted by a sunlike lady. Sonnets 20 and 60, in which the lady is a goddess who can grant the lover his wish or punish him, appear in fourth and fifth place. In sonnets 16, 6, and 42, which are together in *H*, there is an emphasis on the beauty and the perfect qualities of the lady having sparked hopeless love. The thematic link is even more straightforward in sonnets 45 and 46, seventeenth and eighteenth in *H*, respectively: in both of them the poet is personified as a beggar boy who asks the lady for alms.

39. Muir, "Order of Constable's Sonnets," 425.

## *National Art Library MS Dyce 44 (T)*

This octavo volume at the Victoria and Albert Museum was probably the personal miscellany of Henry Brockman (1573–1630), as Claire B. Williams has proposed. He matriculated from Clare College, Cambridge, in 1587 and was admitted to the Middle Temple in 1592.[40] His Cambridge and Middle Temple connections show throughout the miscellany, and he must have had access to material related to the Inns of Court.[41]

The contents of *T* reflect the individual tastes of Brockman; Williams defines it as "a miscellany of recreation and memorialization" rather than a commonplace book or a poetic miscellany "in the high Petrarchan tradition."[42] Of the 308 separate items, 269 (85 percent) are poems, four of them in Latin with accompanying translations, and the remaining (15 percent) are prose texts.[43] One hundred and forty texts are unique to *T*.[44] Constable's sixty-three sonnets (fols. 12r–44r) are the largest group by a single author. There are also eleven epigrams by Thomas Bastard (fols. 79v–83v), nine poems by Sir John Harington scattered throughout, and seven by Sir John Davies clustered in two groups (fols. 56v–58r, 80r). On folios 77r to 78v the compiler copied two long poems, one of them being "Busie old foole unrulie sunne," and five much shorter epigrams by John Donne. There are also poems by John Taylor, known as "the Water Poet"; four attributed to Sir Walter Raleigh, including the immensely popular "What is oure life? a play of passion" (fol. 70v); and several by a variety of authors such as John Dowland, Thomas Nashe, and King James. Initials are often provided instead of the authors' names, and many items remain unattributed.

Contents copied by Brockman were originally composed between the 1560s and 1616. Among the earliest verse there is a short anonymous poem (fol. 117r) attributed to William Paulet (d. 1572) in another source and dated ca. 1568.[45]

---

40. Venn, 1: 228. For full biographic details on Henry Brockman, see Williams, *Edition*, 1: 14–18.
41. Contemporary Cambridge and Middle Temple students whose works are compiled in *T* include John Marston, Sir John Davies, and Henry Goodere. See Claire B. Williams, "'This and the rest Maisters we all may mende': Reconstructing the Practices and Anxieties of a Manuscript Miscellany's Reader-Compiler," *Huntington Library Quarterly* 80 (2017): 277–292, at 280.
42. Ibid., 279, 288.
43. Williams, *Edition*, 1: 9, 23. My list of the contents does not purport to be comprehensive; refer to Williams, *Edition*, for detail.
44. Ibid., 1: 39.
45. Oxford, Bodleian Library, MS Rawl. Poet. 148. See Black, "Studies in Poetic Miscellanies," 2: 417; Williams, *Edition*, 2: 360.

Sidney's *Certain Sonnets* 19, also in *M*, was composed before 1582. Folio 116v bears a stanza from "If woemen could be fayre and not be fond," possibly by Edward de Vere, earl of Oxford, composed in the first half of the 1580s.[46] Constable's sonnets must date from 1589–1590, as discussed below. The sestet of a sonnet by Samuel Daniel (fol. 107v) derives from the version included in the 1591 edition of Sidney's *Astrophil and Stella*. Also from the 1590s are Thomas Nashe's "The Choise of Valentines" (fols. 2r–4r) and several satirical pieces on the marriage and death of Richard Fletcher, bishop of London (fols. 79r, 66v).[47] Libellous epitaphs on Penelope Rich (fols. 67v, 68v) and her second husband Charles Blount (fol. 66v) date from 1606–1607. The text of two sonnets attributed to Shakespeare seems to derive from the 1612 third edition of *The Passionate Pilgrim*, where they are numbered 7 and 13.[48] A cluster of six poems on folios 97r–99r deal with the scandal surrounding the murder of Sir Thomas Overbury, which brought about the downfall of a favourite of James I's, Robert Carr, in 1615–1616; these libels are the latest dateable items added by Hand A (Brockman's). The actual copying of the items must have taken place between the late 1580s and the 1620s.

A variety of poetic genres are represented in *T*, and their themes are consistent with those in other seventeenth-century collections, as discussed by Hobbs.[49] The collection is loaded with irreverence, epigrams, humour, a concern with the erotic, epitaphs – serious or satirical – and libels regarding contemporary politics, religion, gossip and courtly affairs. As observed by Williams, "a taste for word play and jest" are "unifying features" bringing together a diversity of texts.[50] She also argues that, viewed as a whole, the poems copied by Hand A convey a tone of growing disenchantment and cynicism in the transition from the high Elizabethan to the Jacobean regimes:

46. Steven W. May, "The Poems of Edward DeVere, Seventeenth Earl of Oxford and of Robert Devereux, Second Earl of Essex," *Studies in Philology* 77, no. 5 (1980): 1–132, at 40–41 and 81–82. It was first printed in Nicholas Breton, *Brittons bowre of delights* (London, 1591), sig. O3r.

47. Nashe's pornographic poem is written in substitution cipher devised by the compiler; it was probably in circulation by 1592. See the notes and collation of the manuscript sources in Williams, *Edition*, 2: 9–15. The libels on Fletcher allude to his marriage in 1595 and his death a year later.

48. These are "Fayre is my love but not so fayre as fickle" (fol. 107r) and "Beautie is but a vayne & doubtfull good" (fol. 111r). Shakespeare's authorship has been contested; see James P. Bednarz, "The Passionate Pilgrim and 'The Phoenix and Turtle,'" in *The Cambridge Companion to Shakespeare's Poetry*, ed. Patrick Cheney (Cambridge, 2007), 108–124, at 108–109.

49. Hobbs, *Early Seventeenth-Century Manuscripts*, 26–35.

50. Williams, *Edition*, 1: 44.

The libels, prose anecdotes, and satirical epigrams privilege cynical views about humankind and, while exceptions are made for individuals remembered in sincere elegies and epitaphs, even these (presumably) constituted for their copyist further evidence of goodness passing away. In Dyce 44 there is a sense of something rotten in the state: its pages are peopled with usurers, sexually obliging, pox-ridden women, and unkindly caricatured Puritans.[51]

Against this background, Constable's sixty-three sonnets stand out because they are remnants of a golden age and its taste for Petrarchan courtly love, which the compiler chose to memorialize before the political situation – and his own taste and attitudes – altered. Two anonymous sonnets dedicated to Constable immediately follow (fols. 43v–44r), and three blank pages separate it from the next item.[52]

The collection of Constable's sonnets in *T* is unique in many ways. First and foremost, twenty-five of its sixty-three sonnets are not preserved in any other manuscript or printed source (see appendix B). Secondly, its internal organization seems too carefully planned to be other than authorial; *T* is in fact the most cohesive collection of Constable's secular sonnets and the one that best qualifies as a sequence. They are grouped in three main sections ("of variable affections of love," "the prayse of perticulars," and "tragicall, conteyning only lamentations"), each of them containing three thematic subsections or "arguments," with seven sonnets in each subsection. There are clear signs that sonnets in the different subsections were carefully ordered, as shown in the first group within section two, dedicated to Queen Elizabeth, King James, and other noble personages, where the sonnets are carefully arranged according to decreasing social rank. Thirdly, I agree with previous commentators in that the headings stating the theme or explaining the context of composition of individual sonnets are too specific to have been added by someone other than Constable.[53] It is true that love complaints receive titles that appear conventional, such as "Of the excellencye of his Ladies voyce," which remind readers of Richard Tottel's headings to Wyatt's and Surrey's sonnets in his *Miscellany*.[54] However, occasional and complimentary sonnets are a different matter. Take for instance the heading to sonnet 38, "To the Countesse of Shrewsburye upon occasion of his deare Mistrisse, whoe liv'd

---

51. Williams, "Reconstructing the Practices," 282.
52. Williams notes that blanks are used to separate "some genre-grouped sections"; ibid., 283.
53. See Wickes, *Courtier*, 103–104; Parker, 151.
54. Richard Tottel, *Songes and sonettes, written by the ryght honorable Lorde Henry Haward late Earle of Surrey, and others* (London, 1557).

under her goverment." The addressee could hardly have been identified based on textual clues alone, and the sonnet remains connected to the social milieu in which it originated. Lastly, the presence of an introductory and a colophon sonnet adds to the sense of unity.[55]

Many of these sonnets offer internal evidence that enables dating, as well. In sonnet 52, Constable apologizes for his belatedness in mourning Sidney, who died in October 1586; hence the sonnet must be dated much later, perhaps around 1588, when he was seeking the patronage of members of Sidney's circle. One of the sonnets to King James (26), "whome as yet he had not seene" according to the heading, is also in *M*, so it must be the earliest of the group, whereas the ones that follow (27 to 29) emphasise Constable's inclusion in the monarch's literary coterie in 1589. The sonnet on the birth of Lady Rich's daughter (42), dated 1588, is in *M*, but not the one on the child's death (55), which is obviously later in composition and unique to *T*. Most sonnets to noble ladies have to do with Constable's courtly business or his secret mission to Scotland and can be dated 1588–1589, when Constable spent a longer period of time at the English court. The heading to sonnet 31, "To the Countess of Shrewsbury," explicitly addressed to a "Mary" in the text, was surely added after Mary Cavendish married Gilbert Talbot in 1590.[56] The case of the sonnet to Frances Walsingham seems a bit stranger. The heading reads "To the Countesse of Essex upon occasion of the death of her first husband Sir Philip Sydney" and was surely added in or after October 1590, when she married the earl of Essex and got a second husband. However, the body of the sonnet addresses her merely as Sidney's mourning widow, which seems to be at odds with the title. These headings could have been added by Constable as he revised the sonnets and organized his collection for circulation using both old and new material, in late 1590 or early 1591 – he went into exile in the summer of that year. George Wickes's assessment of the sequence that was copied in *T* as "his literary testament" has been widely accepted.[57] Constable had converted to Catholicism and was ready to leave behind the career, ambitions and acquaintances that pervade the secular sonnets.

55. Spiller refers to the author's "sense of connection" revealed in his or her addition of "one or more sonnets ... often at the beginning or the end, in which the speaker takes an overview ... ." See Spiller, *The Sonnet Sequence*, 16.

56. George Wickes correctly identified this as "the latest datable title." See Wickes, *Courtier*, 106 n4.

57. Ibid., 104. This observation has been accepted by Grundy – who edited the sonnets from *T* – by Hughey, and by Stockard, among others; see Grundy, 33, 85; Hughey, 2: 331; Emily E. Stockard, "Henry Constable, English Poet (1562–1613 )," in *Sixteenth-Century British Nondramatic Writers, Second Series*, ed. David A. Richardson (Detroit, 1994), 45–52.

Two early sonnets preserved in *M*, numbers 64 and 65, were excluded from this final compilation. Sonnet 64 is the opening sonnet in *M*, "My hope laye gasping on his dying bedd." Sonnet 65 is the second sonnet dedicated to the countesses of Cumberland and Warwick, "In Edenn grew many a pleasant springe." The reason why the poet should have discarded these two in particular could be merely structural. The subsection of occasional poetry dedicated "To particular Ladies whome he most honoured" had to contain seven sonnets, and he could have prioritised those to Arbella Stuart and other addressees. If he could only include one to the two sisters, he played it safe by choosing 32, rife with bland innocuous praise, over 65, which insists on the countesses' fruitfulness. The latter would have been inappropriate in 1590 given that Ambrose Dudley, Lady Anne Russell's husband, died in February, and the couple had no issue. As for sonnet 64, whose heading alludes to a particular episode involving his mistress saying "hard & disgratious wordes" to him, it may have been deemed too personal and context dependent, likely to offend the lady in question, and was meant for the eyes of close friends only.

The latest authorial text, archetype *Z* – from which *T* derived – must have included the prose conclusion at the end of the sequence (fol. 42v). In it, the author says that the "vayne poems" that he had written during his "idle houres" amounted to sixty-three, which was considered a "climatericall number," and decided to stop writing foolish love poems. He excluded the introductory and colophon sonnets (1, 63) from this total count; these two may have circulated alongside the original sixty-three in an attempt to rededicate the collection to his later poetic mistress, Grace Pierrepont, and to Grace's cousin Arbella Stuart, framing the rest. The intended sequence of sixty-three is incomplete because two sonnets, the first and the second in the subsection titled "funerall sonets of the death of perticulars," are lost; they must have been on the missing leaf in the sixth gathering, between leaves 36 and 37. The compiler did copy them, so they were in circulation and the possibility of early recantation or self-censorship on the part of the author can be discarded. By 1812, when Park produced his edition based on *T*, they were missing. When or by whom the sonnets were excised must remain a mystery. As to the reason, there is ample room for speculation and no hypotheses have been raised so far. It might have been that the addressee had fallen into disgrace. Bearing in mind Constable's regard for social rank, the deceased surely held a higher position than that of marquess or marchioness.[58] The two possibilities are a royal or a duke. Henry, duke of Guise, was assassinated in December 1588, and a sonnet to him – especially one written after conversion – would be congruous

---

58. A sonnet to Vittoria Colonna, marchioness of Pescara, follows (51).

with Constable's lifelong interest in French affairs, especially in the light of his later activities as an exile. Another exciting possibility is Mary, queen of Scots: her execution was recent and three sonnets on her death and funeral are part of the sequence of the *Spiritual Sonnets*. The inclusion of one or two sonnets to her would have signalled Constable's Catholicism to a far greater degree than anything else in the *T* sequence, and an early reader may have chosen to remove them. In the absence of written evidence, all this must remain conjectural.

The compiler of *T* copied two anonymous sonnets dedicated to Constable immediately following the sequence.[59] The first (fol. 43v) is headed "To H.C. upon occasion of his two former Sonets to the K. of Scots" and is a response to sonnets 26 and 27. The author of the poem seems aware of Constable's spiritual leanings and encourages him to write of divine matters. He hints at the poet's exile, which is made the theme of the second sonnet, "To H.C. upon occasion of leaving his countrye and sweetnesse of his verse" (fol. 44r). In this poem, Constable is exhorted to return to England and prove his loyalty so that the queen may forgive him. Both pieces were probably drafted by the same person, a friend of Constable's who had read his sonnets – as evidenced by his borrowings – and knew about his circumstances.

Brockman's interest in Constable's works is unexplained, but the existence of the Marsh's Library miscellany, *M*, indicates that the sonnets were circulating and coveted well after Constable left St John's.[60] In any case, he obtained a copy of *Z* ($Z_2$), perhaps from the same friend who penned the sonnets dedicated to Constable, and started building his miscellany around the sequence. Late 1591 must be the *terminus a quo* for the copying of Constable's sonnets in *T*, considering the references to the poet's exile.

Brockman includes Constable's initials in his title to the sequence, "H.C. Sonets." His failure to record Constable's full name could be motivated by several reasons. First, he obviously needed no reminders as to who the author whose works he had sought to collect was, nor would his immediate coterie. Alternatively, initials could have been used because Constable, as an exile, had fallen into disgrace: throughout his miscellany, Brockman seems more than aware that other readers might browse through it, which explains his deliberate obscuring of some pieces that could be deemed offensive.[61] If the volume fell into the wrong hands, Constable's identity and Brockman's own reputation would be safe.

59. See appendix A for the full texts.
60. Williams enumerates some possible motivations, including "their rarity" and "their evocation of an earlier phase of the compiler's reading tastes"; see Williams, "Reconstructing the Practices," 282.
61. Brockman's use of cipher when transcribing Nashe's erotic poem is the best example, but not the only one; ibid., 289.

T offers a text that is by no means perfect, as it is at least once removed from a lost authorial manuscript, and texts from sources derived from other Z descendants, when they survive, seem to be superior. Unique variants might be errors or conscious interventions in the text: Williams argues that Brockman is often an unreliable scribe; he "copied with an eye to 'improving' some of his texts," and, whatever his motivations were, his "amending" sometimes blurs stemmatic relations between T and other sources.[62] Scribal errors or changes notwithstanding, this manuscript offers a text that is the most comprehensive descendant of the later family of transmission, portraying Constable's arrangement and motivations at a crucial moment in his life. Its value and use as a copy text is therefore justified.

## Edinburgh University Library H.-P. Coll. 401 (E)

This miscellany preserves copies of eight sonnets by Constable: 16, 17, 26, 29, 30, 32, 36, and 53 in this edition. The compiler can be identified through inscriptions of his name, which appear a total of five times on the original title page (fol. 1r). One is the inscription "Richard Jackson his booke." Another is accompanied by the year "1623." This must be the Richard Jackson (d. 1682) who matriculated from Christ's College, Cambridge, in 1619 and later became rector of Halton, Lancashire (1630–1641), and of Whittington (1641–1680).[63] The other name is that of a John Pecke, probably added around the same time.[64]

Richard Jackson copied a variety of contents in verse and prose over a span of many years. English verse is Elizabethan and Jacobean, and to his selection

---

62. Ibid., 285. Williams estimated an error rate of almost 1.5 words for every hundred words copied, based on comparison of other texts in T to printed editions of the same, which would have entailed no comprehension problems to the scribal eye; she admits that Brockman may have struggled reading his manuscript copy texts. See ibid., 286 n32. In any case, when a sonnet by Constable only exists in T there is no way to know whether the change occurred in archetype Z, the copy of it Brockman perused ($Z_2$), or only in the process of copying the sonnet into T. Even when a sonnet survives in other witnesses, a unique reading may be hard to account for.

63. See Venn, 2: 457; John Peile, ed., *Biographical register of Christ's College, 1505–1905: And of the Earlier Foundation, God's House, 1448–1505; Vol 1., 1448–1665* (Cambridge, 1910), 329.

64. The editors of Robert Herrick read "Perke." See Tom Cain and Ruth Connolly, eds., *The Complete Poetry of Robert Herrick* (Oxford, 2013), 2: 6. There is a John Peck who matriculated from Pembroke in 1619. He was a younger son of William Peck, sheriff of Norwich and lord of Spixworth Hall. However, it is uncertain whether this is the reader of the miscellany. See Venn, 3: 333.

from popular and lesser-known authors Jackson added his own compositions.[65] As a whole, Jackson's compilation has a clear social and topical character, covering contemporary or recent events such as the death of Prince Henry or the assassination of King James's favourite the duke of Buckingham; satire and epitaphs abound, and there is a particular interest in royal affairs: there are poems by and about King James and his son Charles. Sir Walter Raleigh, Sir John Harington, and Constable are among the earliest authors represented, together with Ben Jonson, Francis Quarles, George Wither, Thomas Carew, and Francis Bacon. Although there are references to events in the early seventeenth century such as Elizabeth's death or the Gunpowder Plot, a lot of the datable material covers the years 1624 to 1631.[66]

How Jackson may have come upon a copy of Constable's sonnets in the 1620s is a mystery. Perhaps his Cambridge connections and the fact that Constable's verse did circulate at the university could be credited once more. It is more surprising, however, that he should have wanted to acquire and copy them in the first place. Constable had been in exile and later imprisoned several times on account of his religion; he had ultimately lost King James's favour for good and died abroad in 1613. His sonnets fit awkwardly in a miscellany whose contents on religion are clearly anti-Catholic, with verses "Against the Papists" or "Upon Jesuits." If Jackson's selections reflect his own religious stance, his decision to include some of Constable's sonnets adds weight to the idea that Constable's poetic reputation did survive his conversion and downfall and was alive and well in the early decades of the seventeenth century.

The eight sonnets by Constable are on folios 105v and 106r under the general heading "H. Constables verses."[67] They were all copied in a single scribal stint and with an obvious intention of making the most of the available space. The two sonnets on folio 106r share the page with Thomas Carew's "Upon a flye," written in a different stint and apparently in a greater hurry.[68] Given that Carew's poem was entered later, it seems that Jackson intended to copy more of Constable's sonnets but was unable to; therefore, he began copying with the idea

65. There are many occurrences of his initials, "R.J.," throughout.
66. Cain and Connolly make the latter observation when commenting on the presence of Robert Herrick's verse in this miscellany; see Cain and Connolly, *Poetry of Robert Herrick*, 69.
67. Only the first two, numbers 16 and 17 in this edition, are catalogued in *CELM*. A plausible explanation is that they were printed in *D92* and are the most easily recognizable as his, whereas the other six survive mostly in manuscript.
68. This is the first of two copies of Carrew's poem, known as the "Amorous Fly." See Marcy L. North, "Twice the Effort: Tracing the Practices of Stuart Verse Collectors through Their Redundant Entries," *Huntington Library Quarterly* 77 (2014), 257–285, at 266.

THE AMATORY AND DEDICATORY SONNETS · 51

Table 3. Order of the sonnets in *E* and other sources

| *E* | Edition | Other Sources |
|---|---|---|
| 1 | [16] | T M H D92 D94 |
| 2 | [17] | T M H D92 D94 |
| 3 | [36] | T D94 |
| 4 | [26] | T M |
| 5 | [29] | T |
| 6 | [53] | T AP |
| 7 | [30] | T |
| 8 | [32] | T M PR1 PR2 |

of fitting as many sonnets as he could in the smallest possible space, but his plans were thwarted, most likely because of limited access to the source text.

Although *E* adds no sonnets to the canon, it is a very valuable witness. It bears an ascription before the first sonnet, "H. Constables verses." One sonnet (26) exists in two other manuscripts, *T* and *M*, and two (29, 30) only in *T* (see table 3). Of the five remaining, 16 and 17 were printed in *D92*; 36 was added to *Diana* only in its second edition, *D94*; and two were included in other printed works, the one to Sir Philip Sidney (53) as a prefatory sonnet to *AP* and the one dedicated to the two countesses (32) in *PR1* and *PR2*. The order does not mirror that in *T* or any other collection as a whole but some similar clusters can be identified. The first and second sonnets, "My ladies presence makes the roses red" and "Sweet hand the sweet yet cruell Bowe thou art," also appear together in *T* and *M*; they are sonnets of praise conveying a love complaint. Sonnet 36, in which heraldic devices are employed to honour Penelope Rich, comes third in *E*. It is grouped under the section heading "To particular Ladies" in *T*, as are 30 and 32, which nevertheless do not follow 36 in *E* but are seventh and eighth, respectively. The first three sonnets in *E*, connected by their amatory subject matter, are followed by two sonnets to King James and an elegy on Sir Philip Sidney; therefore, it seems that Jackson gave them precedence and chose to copy the two sonnets to noblewomen last. He disregards Constable's final arrangement when it comes to dedicatory sonnets, reflecting his own interests.

Like *T*, *E* is a descendant from the *Z* family of transmission. Its readings mostly agree with *T* or – in some cases – correct glaring scribal errors in it. *T* and *E* also share very similar headings, which reinforce the idea that these derive from the lost authorial *Z*, considering that, in cases such as sonnet 30 to the princess of Orange, the heading is essential to make sense of an otherwise cryptic text. They avoid the readings of the $Z_1$ family of transmission, so they must derive from a different lost source once removed from *Z*, that is, $Z_2$.

## Yale Beinecke MS 621 (Bn)

The library catalogue lists this folio-sized volume as an "English miscellany on travels, foreign countries, Catholicism and politics."[69] Among its contents, two items directly relate to Constable. His sonnet to Queen Elizabeth, number 25 in the present edition, is on folio 14v. It is followed by his treatise against William Allen's defence of the defection of Sir William Stanley, on folios 15r–43r. The miscellany can be traced back to the Tollemache family, and perhaps to the library of the first baronet, Sir Lionel Tollemache (1562–1612), who collected manuscripts.[70] There are no clues as to its compiler.

The volume is clearly Elizabethan but its contents cover a longer time span.[71] They were probably copied over a long period of time, the process being completed in the early years of James's reign. A clear interest in affairs of state – both domestic and foreign – travel, and religion underlies the compilation of the volume. A letter by Sir Francis Walsingham "to Monsieur Cretoy [i.e., Critoy]" defending Elizabeth's proceedings against Catholics must be dated ca. 1571, in the context of the marriage negotiations with the duke of Anjou.[72] Together with an address by Robert Cecil to Queen Elizabeth "against the Jesuits Schole hostages and league with Spain" (fols. 79v–82r) and Constable's

---

69. See "Orbis: Yale University Library Catalog," Yale University, accessed 10 January 2019, https://orbis.library.yale.edu/vwebv/holdingsInfo?bibId=9612653.

70. Woudhuysen notes that the Tollemaches had "a general interest in books and manuscripts." The library of Sir Lionel contained a "beautifully written and bound" volume with Sidney's *Old Arcadia* and his courtly entertainment *The Lady of May*. See Woudhuysen, *Circulation*, 320–324.

71. May and Ringler date it ca. 1561–1620; see Steven W. May and William A. Ringler, *Elizabethan Poetry: A Bibliography and First-Line Index of Elizabethan Verse, 1559–1603* (London, 2004), 1: 197. In the corresponding entry in *CELM* it is dated in the 1590s.

72. There is another copy in London, British Library, Stowe MS 147, 338.

attack on Allen, it reveals a pervading anti-Catholic and anti-Spanish stance in the volume.[73]

The sonnet "To the Queen" is on a single leaf bound into the volume right before the treatise (see plate 4). This could not have been done by someone who ignored the connection between both items. The sonnet is the only verse item in *Bn* and was intended to act as a preface to the prose work. In *M*, this sonnet bears the more informative heading "To hir majesty for a preface to his booke," and it is no coincidence that a summary of the treatise was also written in that miscellany. The content of the dedicatory sonnet also serves its purpose: the poet bemoans that he can only defend Elizabeth from her enemies in writing, using his pen instead of a sword. The treatise against Allen is nothing if not a loyal, strongly Protestant defence of Elizabeth and English interests abroad.[74]

*Bn* is valuable in that it is a good copy of the earliest lost holograph, archetype *X*; it is most closely related to *M* but, unlike *M*, it is error-free and may actually be identical with the *X* text of this sonnet.[75]

## BL Additional MS 18920 (OBL)

The inclusion of a sonnet by Constable in Sir John Harington's *Orlando furioso* was motivated by their acquaintance, which also led Harington to copy Constable's sonnets in his miscellany (*H*). In the commentary to canto 34, written in his own hand, Harington reflects on literary reputation and fame as a way to outlast time: "[F]ame outlasteth, and owt flyeth all things: as that well learned gentleman, and my very good frend Mr Henry Conestable wrate in his sonnet to the now kyng of Skotland" (fol. 204r). This is followed by sonnet 27 dedicated to King James. The text is reliable, descended from archetype *Z* through $Z_1$, although Harington copied line 6 before the fifth and had to number the lines to compensate for his slip.[76] It was used as copy text by the editor of the printed *Orlando* (*O91*).

---

73. The author of the address is said to be the earl of Salisbury; Robert Cecil held that title from 1605 so it could not have been copied before that year. In *CELM* this address, *A Letter of Advice to the Queen*, is dated 1584 and attributed to Francis Bacon based on other extant copies.

74. The copy of the treatise in *Bn* might have been a middle link in the chain of manuscript transmission of the text, not quite a holograph but authorially modified and supervised prior to its further circulation or copying for presentation. The work was never printed and has remained unidentified so far. A full discussion of it is beyond the scope of the present volume and will be undertaken in due course.

75. See figure 6 below.

76. The lines were printed in the correct order in *O91*.

## Bodleian Library MS Ashmole 38 (A)

This miscellany was compiled by Nicholas Burghe (d. 1670), who became a royalist captain in the Civil War, over a long period spanning from the 1630s to ca. 1660.[77] There is a reference to his name and the date "3d of June 1638" on folios 165r and 166r. Ashmole 38 preserves fourteen sonnets by Constable (see table 4). Burghe selected over four hundred poems by many well-known authors including Donne, Raleigh, Carew, Jonson, and Beaumont, as well as lesser figures, and added some of his own.[78] Constable, Carew, Jonson, and Herrick contribute the largest number of poems. Some genres popular at the time that are represented are libels and political poetry, songs, misogynistic verse, and epitaphs and funeral elegies.[79] Marotti has pointed out that the miscellany evidences a blurring of the lines between the transmission of texts in manuscript and print towards the mid-seventeenth century; some of the poems Burghe copied derive from printed editions.[80]

The sonnets are not ascribed to Constable at all. His name is not mentioned in either the manuscript index or the printed catalogue despite the fact that Burghe was thorough in his attribution of other contents in the miscellany. As Janet W. Starner has pointed out, it may simply be the case that compilers like Burghe "were not much interested in 'authorized' versions of texts or even 'authors'" because they "appropriate texts for their own purposes."[81] The first two sonnets are that

---

77. See references to this manuscript in Marotti, *Manuscript, Print*, 72–73. The compiler was first identified by Peter Beal. Morris and Withington believe that the first 165 pages were transcribed before 1638; see Brian Morris and Eleanor Withington, eds., *Poems of John Cleveland* (Oxford, 1967), lii–liii. For different views on the proliferation of personal miscellanies in the 1630s and their association with the royalist cause, see Hobbs, *Early Seventeenth-Century Manuscripts*, 148–149.

78. A useful, if imperfect, nineteenth-century index of contents is William H. Black, *A Descriptive, Analytical, and Critical Catalogue of the Manuscripts Bequeathed unto the University of Oxford by Elias Ashmole* (Oxford, 1845), 38–61.

79. Marotti, *Manuscript, Print*, 72–73; Harold Love and Arthur F. Marotti, "Manuscript Transmission and Circulation," in *The Cambridge History of Early Modern English Literature*, ed. David Loewenstein and Janel M. Mueller (Cambridge, 2003), 55–80, at 73–74.

80. Arthur F. Marotti, "Manuscript, Print, and the Social History of the Lyric," in *The Cambridge Companion to English Poetry, Donne to Marvell*, ed. Thomas N. Corns (Cambridge, 1993), 52–79, at 74; Love and Marotti, "Manuscript Transmission and Circulation," 74.

81. Janet Wright Starner, "'Jacke on Both Sides': Appropriating Equivocation," in *Anonymity in Early Modern England: What's in a Name?*, ed. Janet W. Starner and Barbara H. Traister (Farnham, 2011), 43–80, at 68. The disappearance of authorial ascription at some point as a text circulated is deemed by Marotti to be the rule rather than the exception; see Arthur F. Marotti, "The Transmission of Lyric Poetry and the Institutionalizing of Literature in the English Renaissance," in *Contending Kingdoms: Historical, Psychological, and Feminist*

Table 4. Order of the sonnets in *A* and other sources

| *A* | Edition | Other Sources |
|---|---|---|
| 1 | [42] | T M H D92 D94 |
| 2 | [32] | T M E PR1 PR2 |
| 3 | [2] | T H D92 D94 |
| 4 | [8] | T H D92 D94 |
| 5 | [20] | T H D92 D94 |
| 6 | [10] | T M H D92 D94 |
| 7 | [46] | T H D92 D94 |
| 8 | [60] | T M H D92 D94 PR1 PR2 |
| 9 | [4] | T D92 D94 |
| 10 | [56] | T H D92 D94 |
| 11 | [57] | T D94 |
| 12 | [36] | T E D94 |
| 13 | [61] | T H D92 D94 |
| 14 | [59] | T D94 |

on the birth of Penelope Rich's daughter (42) and the one to the two countesses (32); they bear separate headings and, after each of these, Burghe wrote the word "finis." The remaining twelve sonnets are clustered together under the general title "To the Fairest that hath bine" and lack individual headings.

The texts of all but one of the sonnets derive from *D94*, whereas sonnet 32 was copied from *PR1* and its heading recovered from the second edition, *PR2*. It is unclear whether Burghe owned or borrowed the printed books, or why he did not copy more sonnets.[82] Seven of the sonnets come from the first "decad" of *D94*, and

---

*Approaches to the Literature of Sixteenth-Century England and France*, ed. Marie-Rose Logan and Peter L. Rudnytsky (Detroit, 1991), 21–41, at 35.

82. Love and Marotti have pointed out that Burghe avoided copying "many poems by any one writer." See "Manuscript Transmission and Circulation," 73.

Burghe – consciously or unconsciously – avoided copying sonnets of doubtful authorship. In order to add the name of the lady to the heading of sonnet 42, which is missing in *D94* ("an honourable Ladies daughter"), Burghe must have consulted another source.[83] This evidences that he made an effort to recover the circumstances of production of the occasional sonnets. The arrangement of the sonnets was most likely Burghe's. As for the texts, they tend to be unreliable, with omissions, unique readings, and glaring errors that often deviate greatly from the earlier sources. They are collated but omitted in the commentary to the present edition.

## Readers and Transmission of the Printed *Dianas*

*Diana* was one of the volumes that helped shape, rather than capitalized on, the 1590s sonnet vogue, and Constable's literary reputation largely rested on it. It was published a year after *Astrophel and Stella*, and in the same year as the first edition of *Delia*.[84] It must have been a popular book, as it warranted a second and third edition (*D94*, *D94b*). Based on the number of times the books were reprinted, Kirk Melnikoff considers the initial popularity of *Diana* on a par with Sidney's sequence, immediately below *Delia*, and above that of the collections of Drayton, Lodge, and Spenser.[85]

### The 1592 Diana (D92)

The first printed collection of Constable's sonnets (STC 5637), including twenty-three, saw the light in 1592. It was entered in the Stationers' Register under the date September 22:

> John Charlewood. Entred for his Copies under th[e h]andes of master watkins and master Stirropp theis thinges followinge ... Item a little Booke intituled. DYANA. the prayses of his mistres in certen sweete Sonnettes &c. vi$^d$.[86]

---

83. Both *H* and *T* identify the baby's mother as Lady Rich.
84. Samuel Daniel's *Delia* was entered in the Stationers' Register on 4 February 1592, just a few months earlier, but it is unclear which edition appeared first. Some of Daniel's sonnets had, of course, come to light in Newman's pirated edition in 1591.
85. See Kirk Melnikoff, *Elizabethan Publishing and the Makings of Literary Culture* (Toronto, 2018), 136, 224 n100.
86. Arber, 2: 292b.

Although it has become a synecdoche for Constable's poetic production, the name "Diana" is most likely not authorial. It is not mentioned in any of the more authoritative manuscripts and there is nothing in the contents of the sequence that warrants its use.[87] Its choice might have been intended to obscure an identification of the poetic mistress with Penelope Rich – Sidney's "Stella" – or make it more subtle through the connection between the moon and the stars, notwithstanding the fact that the lady portrayed in the collection is more of a sunlike figure. The name was conventionally associated with chastity, a Petrarchan attribute, and the educated buyer would have easily guessed that the book would contain a sequence of Petrarchan sonnets on unrequited love by looking at its title. It is also worth bearing in mind that Constable's sonnets are heavily influenced by French poets, especially Philippe Desportes, whose 1573 collection was titled *Les amours de Diane*. In addition, by the mid-1580s Bartholomew Yong had completed his translation of Jorge de Montemayor's *Diana*; it was published in 1598 bearing a dedication to Penelope Rich after years of manuscript circulation.[88]

The unique prefatory sonnet and the address to the readers both clarify and complicate the circumstances of publication of the collection and Constable's involvement in it. "To his absent Diana" (66) emphasises the physical separation between poet and mistress through the use of "sever'd" (66.1), "banisht" (66.2), or the more explicit acknowledgement that the poet's own "fault" has forced him from her "sight" (66.4). The reason he provides for this separation is his "over-weening wit" (66.2): he has been too presumptuous and is punished for it. This could be taken metaphorically, since it was a Petrarchan lover's destiny to moan about separation; as Catherine Bates has argued, absence was a necessity.[89] A farewell sonnet could also be written after some disappointment. On the other hand, the poet's "fault" could have been very real: Constable could have been living in exile when he composed this sonnet, which would account for its absence from earlier manuscripts. Joan Grundy argues that, if this sonnet was specifically written to preface *D92*, Constable must have consented to and played some role in its publication.[90]

87. Williams rightly argues that there is none of the "classical imagery of a moon or huntress that one might expect to find" in a collection bearing that name; see Williams, *Edition*, 2: 72.
88. L.G. Kelly, "Yong, Bartholomew (bap. 1560, d. 1612)," in *ODNB*. On the motivation behind Yong's dedication and the influence of Montemayor's work on Sidney, see Judith M. Kennedy, ed., *A Critical Edition of Yong's Translation of George of Montemayor's Diana and Gil Polo's Enamoured Diana* (Oxford, 1968), xxxiv–xxxviii.
89. Catherine Bates, "Desire, Discontent, Parody: The Love Sonnet in Early Modern England," in *The Cambridge Companion to the Sonnet*, ed. A.D. Cousins and Peter Howarth (Cambridge, 2011), 105–124, at 107. Bates illustrates this idea with Constable's sonnet.
90. Grundy, 93–94.

Parker contends that the subject matter of the sonnet does not imply it was written in exile and it may simply derive from another – lost – source, whereas Wickes deems the sonnet to be "the publisher's contribution."[91] The ambiguity underlying the sonnet is unresolved. Although the poet's final intention is purportedly to present his sonnets to the lady as a literary monument ("my verse still lives to witnes thee devine"), he takes full responsibility for their abandonment in line 9 ("I them forsooke"), which brings this sonnet close to the prose conclusion in *T* as a recantation of amatory poetry.

After this sonnet, there is a short epistle "To the Gentlemen Readers" (sig. A4r), probably by publisher Richard Smith, which makes an intriguing statement about the sonnets being abandoned by their author:

> These insuing Sonnets, (sonnes of no partiall Judge, whose eies were acquainted with Beauties Riches, whose eares frequented to Angelicall sounds, and sense ravished with excellent Science) are now by misfortune left as Orphans: and crave desertfull acceptance of your experienst judgements. … Beeing left desolate, they seeke entertainment … better they desire not, but as you like to use them.

Readers may have picked up the not-so-subtle allusion to Penelope Rich. Smith suggests that he has more inside knowledge that he is willing to share with the reader. The use of Constable's initials, "H.C.," on the title page was – like his epistle – probably a conscious decision on Smith's part to market the book and attract readers' attention; this is consistent with North's notion of the marketability of anonymity, which, well used, could help it compete with names.[92]

Smith was involved in unauthorized publishing: he was responsible for the first edition of George Gascoigne's *A hundreth sundrie flowers* in 1573, which the author claimed was printed while he was abroad, and a sermon by Lancelot Andrewes, *The Wonderful Combat between Christ and Satan*, which seems to have been confiscated.[93] In a recent survey of Richard Smith's publishing practices regarding the *Dianas*, Melnikoff has emphasised the similarities between the title page and authorial ascription of *D92* and Thomas Newman's second edition of Sidney's *Astrophel and Stella*. The latter uses initials instead of a full name, "Sir P.S.," and the adjective "sweete" to describe the poems.[94] The connection is fur-

---

91. Parker, 150; Wickes, *Courtier*, 106 n2.

92. Marcy North, "Ignoto in the Age of Print: The Manipulation of Anonymity in Early Modern England," *Studies in Philology* 91, no. 4 (1994): 390–416, at 413.

93. Melnikoff, *Elizabethan Publishing*, 106–107.

94. Ibid., 126–127.

ther stressed by the fact that John Charlewood (d. 1593) was also the printer of Newman's first – pirated – edition of Sidney's sonnets. Smith's probable disregard for Constable's wishes in the publication of *D92* does not necessarily conflict with the so-called stigma of print, according to which an author worried about his social status would conventionally deny having consented to the publication of his works.[95] The possibility that Constable pretended not to be involved cannot be ruled out entirely.

The individual headings, in Italian, provide no other information than the number of the sonnet in this collection (e.g., "Sonnetto secondo"), with two exceptions. The unique prefatory sonnet (66) bears the heading "To his absent Diana," and the sonnet on the birth of Penelope Rich's daughter (42), printed between the twentieth sonnet and the "Ultimo sonnetto," has a more informative heading than the rest.

Twenty-one of the sonnets in *D92* are shared with one of the manuscripts, *H*. Both derive from archetype *Y* (ca. 1589), and their texts tend to agree despite their different arrangement.[96] In his 1980 edition, Robert F. Fleissner defended his choice of *D92* as his copy text arguing that its text "is the most authoritative mainly because it represents Constable at his spontaneous best" and "was set up from the manuscript the author most probably preferred to see printed."[97] However, there are no grounds for these assertions. The arrangement in *D92* is inferior in that it destroys some of the thematic clusters that seem to give internal coherence to *H*, and Constable's involvement in publication is uncertain at best. Even so, this does not undermine the value of the collection as derived from an authorial manuscript or its importance in its social and literary context. The book was certainly well received, as the publication of a new edition in 1594 evidences.

## The 1594 Diana (D94 and D94b)

The publication of the second edition of *Diana*, also known as the augmented *Diana*, in octavo format, is shrouded in mystery.[98] It is not recorded in the Sta-

---

95. North, "Ignoto in the Age of Print," 409. On authors' anxiety about publication, see for instance Arthur F. Marotti, "Patronage, Poetry, and Print," *The Yearbook of English Studies* 21 (1991): 1–26, at 5–6.

96. See the section on *H* and see table 2 above.

97. Robert F. Fleissner, *Resolved to Love: The 1592 Edition of Henry Constable's Diana* (Salzburg, 1980), iv.

98. Sledd refers to the book as *Diana Augmented* in his article about its dating; see Hassell B. Sledd, "The '1584' Publication of Henry Constable's *Diana Augmented*," *Studies in Bibliography* 23 (1970): 146–148.

tioners' Register, and the date on the title page was cropped in all exemplars. Charlewood, the printer of *D92*, died in 1593, and his widow married a colleague of his, James Roberts. As noted by Grundy, about forty titles were transferred from Charlewood to Roberts on 31 May 1594; although the list does not mention *Diana*, it may have been included in the lot.[99] Considering that Roberts printed works for Richard Smith until 1597, and publisher William Wood held the rights to the work in 1598, the time frame for publication narrows to 1594–1597.[100]

The augmented *Diana* contains a short epistle to the reader and a prefatory sonnet by Richard Smith, followed by seventy-five sonnets organised into eight "decads" (decades) or groups of ten sonnets – with the exception of the eighth, which contains only five plus a colophon sonnet.[101] Organisation of his material into decades or units of ten sonnets must have been Smith's decision. The educated Elizabethan reader would have immediately associated the term with Livy's *Ab urbe condita* (*History of Rome*), traditionally divided into parts consisting of ten books each, known as "decades." Readers were used to navigating and referring to the decades as units, so Smith's decision could have been motivated by an intention to "appeal to buyers as familiar with these sets as discrete units, more interested in interconnected sets of poetry organized around images and themes than in poems arranged in narrative sequences with a single speaker and a single beloved."[102] The use of the comparative is perhaps unwarranted, if the popularity of "single speaker" sequences such as Sidney's or Daniel's is borne in mind. The decade structure is imperfect; the incomplete last decade shows Smith's disregard for structural symmetry – something that might have made Constable wince. However little or much Smith thought of the decade division as a selling strategy, it was not the main one; the marketability of *D94* probably rested on potential buyers' recognition of author "H.C." and the title "Diana" from *D92*, which must have sold rather well.[103]

The very notion of authorship seems to have been consciously blurred by the printer, Richard Smith, to the point that Constable's presence remains only in the initials on the title page.[104] The conspiratorial tone of one who is about to

99. Grundy, 97; Arber, 2: 651–652, 5: 171.
100. Arber, 3: 44.
101. The *OED* defines "decade" as "a division of a literary work, containing ten books or parts; as the decades of Livy" (n. 3) and lists the title page of *D94* as the third recorded instance of use.
102. Melnikoff, *Elizabethan Publishing*, 135.
103. Knight notes that the reconfiguration of books – for instance through enlarging them or annexing other works – worked towards their marketability, and "in contrast to modern conceptions of the book, a lack of fixity was normal and desirable." See Jeffrey T. Knight, *Bound to Read: Compilations, Collections, and the Making of Renaissance Literature* (Philadelphia, 2013), 6.
104. The same observation is made by Melnikoff; see *Elizabethan Publishing*, 129.

divulge courtly secrets so far limited to manuscript circulation, featured in the preface to *D92*, is missing from Smith's short address to the reader in *D94*:

> Obscur'd wonders (gentlemen) visited me in Turnus armor, and I in regard of Aeneas honour, have unclouded them unto the worlde: you are that Universe, you that Aeneas, if you finde Pallas gyrdle, murder them, if not inviron'd [environed] with barbarizme, save them, and eternitie will prayse you.[105]

The emphasis is on the printer's role in releasing the sonnets onto the world, and the appeal to the educated reader to accept or reject them. In the prefatory sonnet "Unto her Majesties sacred honorable Maydes," signed by Smith himself, the ladies are praised in conventional Petrarchan terms and entreated to read "these Orphan poems."[106] This term echoes the epistle to the reader in *D92*, but the allusion to the "misfortune" that occasioned their abandonment and the suggestion of Smith's acquaintance with the circumstances of composition are gone.

Constable's sonnets are mingled with eight of Sidney's *Certain Sonnets* and forty-one by various unidentified authors in this volume. As for those of certain authorship, *D94* includes all the sonnets in *D92* minus "To his absent Diana," most of which – but not all – are within the first and second decades, plus five extra sonnets that derive from a different source; however, none are ascribed to Constable in the edition. Smith did not create author-based divisions like those in the pirated edition of *Astrophel and Stella*, in which the end of the Sidney section and the beginning of that containing "Poems and Sonets of sundrie other Noble men and Gentlemen" (sig. I3v) is clearly marked. Yet his was not an unusual practice. *Brittons bowre of delights* (1591) actually contained only a few poems by Nicholas Breton, but the printer used his name to market the collection.[107]

The inclusion of sonnets by Sidney – which were later published in the 1598 folio edition of Sidney's works – in *D94* has puzzled Henry R. Woudhuysen, who states that "[a] publisher who had eight of Sidney's sonnets then might be expected to make more of them. Yet the poems are not attributed to Sidney, but

105. *D94*, sig. A2r.
106. Ibid., sig. A2v.
107. See Marotti, "The Transmission of Lyric Poetry," 33. An apparently disgruntled Breton voiced a complaint in the preface to *The pilgrimage to paradise*: "I protest it was donne altogether without my consent or knowledge, & many thinges of other mens mingled with few of mine, for except Amoris Lachrima: an epitaphe upon Sir Phillip Sydney, and one or two other toies ... I have no part with any of them." See Nicholas Breton, *The pilgrimage to paradise* (London, 1592), n.p.

silently incorporated within Constable's own work and that of others."[108] He points at the Penelope Rich-Constable link, and the possibility that they had owned manuscripts of Sidney's works, which would have then fallen into someone else's hands. Printer James Roberts is certainly suspect, as he also printed *An apologie for poetrie*, in which four of Constable's sonnets were included. It is possible that Constable himself "might have been supplying Roberts or Smith with Sidney's manuscripts." However, this could have only been possible before Henry's exile in 1591, and I agree with Woudhuysen that an essential clue to this mystery must lie with the unattributed sonnets, and is at present irrecoverable.[109]

Concerning these forty-one sonnets, even some of Constable's contemporaries viewed them as his. In the notes to his translation of *The blazon of jealousie* (1615), Robert Tofte mentions Constable as an old friend and quotes from one of these sonnets, "But beeing Care, thou flyest mee as ill fortune" (D5.7, that is, the seventh sonnet in the fifth decade, sig. D8r).[110] Some early editors and commentators accepted their authenticity.[111] However, Wickes and Grundy have given reasons why they should be discarded. Their metre and rhyme scheme contrast greatly with sonnets undeniably by him; the "haphazard versification" employed includes an array of patterns, at odds with that seen in his manuscript sonnets. These have an Italian octave, with some variation in the sestet, and there are no more than five rhymes. Wickes has called them "the work of a purist" concerned with formal correctness; in contrast, Grundy deems the forty-one sonnets as having been written by one "experimenter" or more.[112] In the Bodleian copy, an anonymous reader has written the initials "H.C." underneath every sonnet that is certainly by Constable, including those new to *D94*, and not any others. It is unclear what source he or she consulted for this attribution.

Both critics agree on the damage that the attribution of these sonnets to Constable has done to his reputation. Wickes laments that it was done "for the sake of convenience" and made him appear as a "careless eclectic who exploited the popularity of the sonnet sequence."[113] Grundy reckons that many of the sonnets are "carelessly written" or even "incoherent in thought and imagery." Nev-

---

108. Woudhuysen, *Circulation*, 290.

109. Ibid., 291.

110. Benedetto Varchi, *The blazon of jealousie*, trans. Robert Tofte (London, 1615), 10. References to sonnets in *D94* throughout this edition are given in abbreviated form with a capital D and the number of the decade followed by the position of the sonnet within it.

111. See Martha F. Crow, *Elizabethan Sonnet Cycles: Delia and Diana* (London, 1896), 86; Scott, *Sonnets*, 130.

112. Wickes, *Courtier*, 104; Grundy, 52.

113. Wickes, *Courtier*, 102.

ertheless, she acknowledges that one or two may be his.[114] The one she is certain about is D7.2, "Fayre Grace of Graces, Muse of Muses all" (sig. E7v), on the grounds that it "puns upon the name Grace in the manner of the opening sonnet of the Todd collection, and has also the formal qualities of Constable's recognised work – balance, logic, control."[115] The sonnet is worth transcribing in full:

> Fayre Grace of Graces, Muse of Muses all,
> thou Paradise, thou onely heaven I know,
> what influence hath bred my hateful woe,
> that I from thee and them am forst to fall?
> Thou falne from mee, from thee I never shall,
> although my fortunes thou hast brought so loe,
> yet shall my faith and service with thee goe,
> for live I doe, on heaven and thee to call.
> Banisht all grace, no Graces with mee dwell,
> compeld to muse, why Muses from mee flye,
> excluded heaven, what can remaine but hell?
> exil'd from Paradise, in hate I lye.
> Cursing my starres, albe I find it true,
> I lost all these when I lost love and you.

The pun on Grace's name is similar to those in sonnets 1 and 38, especially the former, in which the word is used with different meanings. A connection can also be established with the prefatory sonnet in D92, "To his absent Diana" (66), in which the poet describes his "banisht" state. In the above, the allusion to banishment from paradise – the lady's presence – is reinforced through the use of "banisht," "excluded," and even "exil'd," and the poet points a finger at those who have caused his departure through their "influence." The poet is now far, desolate, cursing his luck, aware that he has lost her for good and, with her, his chance at romantic love. Of course, he could also be implying that he is banished from England, imagined as paradise, with no poetic inspiration left, which would make this sonnet a late composition. The tantalising possibility that his "Grace" might have loved him back at one point, glimpsed in line 5 ("Thou falne from mee"), would add to the narrative of Constable and his mistress.

Two other unattributed sonnets are similar in both conceit and language to two popular sonnets of Constable's, 58 and 60, both of which survive in numer-

---

114. Grundy, 52–53.
115. Ibid., 53.

ous sources. They explore the tension between the poet's heart and his eyes in that the latter are blamed for his misfortune, as he fell in love with the lady at first sight. In 58, after trial, "Fortune, sith they by sight my heart betrayd, / From wished sight adjudgd them banishment" (11–12). Sonnet D4.8 in *D94* (sig. D3v) begins as follows:

> Why thus unjustly, say my cruell fate,
> doost thou adjudge my lucklesse eyes and hart?
> The one to live exild from that sweet smart
> where th' other pines, imprisond without date.

The agency of his eyes in letting her eyebeams through is emphasised in 60: "To kill my heart myne eye let in her eye, / And so consent gave to a murther wrought" (7–8). The same happens in 58: "traytoure eyes my hearts death did conspire; / Corrupted with hopes guifts, let in desire / To burne my heart …" (4–6). The octave in D6.7 (sig. E5r) sounds therefore inevitably familiar:

> My hart, mine eye accuseth of his death,
> saying, his wanton sight bred his unrest:
> Mine eye affirmes, my harts unconstant faith
> hath beene his bane, and all his joyes represt.
> My hart avowes mine eye let in the fire,
> which burnes him with an ever-living light,
> mine eye replyes, my greedy harts desire,
> let in those floods which drown him day & night.

Of course, similarity of conceit and diction alone does not suffice to attribute the sonnets to Constable with any degree of certainty, considering that most poets followed the same Petrarchan conventions.[116] The three sonnets discussed are best considered dubia rather than canonical.

As for the remaining sonnets, Melnikoff offers a far more favourable holistic assessment of them:

> Comprised of Petrarchan, Shakespearean, and Spenserian sonnets, the volume affords a range of learned allusions to classical myth and natural history along with poems reminiscent of the Continental verse of Du Bellay and

---

116. The idea of the eye betraying the lover's heart, for instance, may be found also in Raleigh's "Calling to mind, mine eye went long about."

Desportes. It at the same time indicates elite poems, verse readily understood as occasional products from a restricted patrician milieu.[117]

He also identifies common themes that give a degree of cohesion to most of the decades, although the classification is imperfect, with "outliers" here and there, and draws attention to the series of interlinked sonnets, for instance D5.6 to D5.9 (sigs. D7v–D8v), in which the final line of a sonnet becomes the first of the next.[118]

The augmented *Diana* bears no individual headings providing contextual information to Constable's sonnets except for that of the sonnet to Lady Rich's daughter, which comes last in the collection (42). The texts of twenty-two out of the twenty-seven sonnets which are Constable's beyond dispute are based on their *D92* counterparts, that is, they ultimately derive from the *Y* archetype. Their arrangement supports the order in *H*, the manuscript descendant of *Y*, against that in *D92*. The first eight sonnets in *H*, together with "Thyne eye, the glasse where I behold my hearte" (4) and sonnet 36, copied from $Z_1$, constitute the first decade. The sonnets in the second decade are also in sequential order in *H*, although there are some variations in their arrangement (see table 5). Only three sonnets in *H* are moved beyond the first two decades: sonnet 48 is D3.1, 6 is D4.3, and 42 serves as unnumbered colophon to the collection. The five sonnets not in *D92* and *H* (13, 36, 57, 59, 62) derive from $Z_1$, the "better" copy of *Z*, the latest authorial archetype. Sonnet 36 closes the first decade (D1.10), numbers 57, 13, 59 are in the fourth (D4.1, D4.2, D4.6), and 62 in the eighth (D8.5).

Richard Smith might have got hold of $Z_1$ through James Roberts, given that Roberts also worked for Henry Olney in the publication of *AP* and $Z_1$ is the copy text for the four sonnets by Constable in that book. Why he only printed a few sonnets from this manuscript in *D94*, choosing instead to compile a miscellaneous volume, remains a mystery; his source might have been a partial copy.

The rights to *Diana* went to William Wood. An entry dated 6 November 1598 in the Stationers' Register reads "*DIANA. Sonnettes* [by H. Constable]," and the volume is said to be a decimosexto (16°).[119] There is no indication that this new, smaller edition was ever printed.

---

117. Melnikoff, *Elizabethan Publishing*, 130.
118. Ibid., 131–132.
119. Arber, 3: 44.

Table 5. Order of the sonnets in *H* and *D94*

| Edition | H | D94 | Edition | H | D94 |
|---|---|---|---|---|---|
| [2] | 1 | D 1.1 [1] | [7] | 11 | D 2.2 [12] |
| [8] | 2 | D 1.2 [2] | [22] | 12 | D 2.3 [13] |
| [3] | 3 | D 1.3 [3] | [48] | 13 | D 3.1 [21] |
| [20] | 4 | D 1.4 [4] | [61] | 14 | D 2.1 [11] |
| [4] | - | D 1.5 [5] | [10] | 15 | D 2.4 [14] |
| [60] | 5 | D 1.6 [6] | [58] | 16 | D 2.5 [15] |
| [15] | 6 | D 1.7 [7] | [45] | 17 | D 2.6 [16] |
| [56] | 7 | D 1.8 [8] | [46] | 18 | D 2.7 [17] |
| [16] | 8 | D 1.9 [9] | [18] | 19 | D 2.8 [18] |
| [6] | 9 | D 4.3 [33] | [21] | 20 | D 2.10 [20] |
| [42] | 10 | - [76] | [17] | 21 | D 2.9 [19] |

## Readers and Transmission of Sonnets Printed Elsewhere

A few sonnets by Constable survive in other books printed in his lifetime and attest to his reputation. "When others hooded with blind love doe flye" (27) is the first among the dedicatory sonnets prefacing King James's *His Majesties poeticall exercises at vacant houres* (*PE*), published in 1591.[120] This positioning, according to Deirdre Serjeantson, was motivated either by "his reputation as a poet" or "more likely ... his superior social rank" compared to William Fowler, Hadrianus Damman, and Henry Lok, the other contributors.[121] The sonnet is titled "To the King of Scotland" and ascribed to "Henrie Constable" underneath, which makes it the first poem to appear in print bearing Constable's full name. It is a good text, derived from the reliable $Z_1$. The same sonnet is also quoted on sig. Bb3v, page

120. RSTC 14379.
121. Deirdre Serjeantson, "English Bards and Scotch Poetics: Scotland's Literary Influence and Sixteenth-Century English Religious Verse," in *Literature and the Scottish Reformation*, ed. Crawford Gribben and David G. Mullan (Farnham, 2009), 162.

288 of the thirty-fourth book, of the printed *Orlando furioso in English heroical verse* (*O91*), a folio edition of Harington's translation. The sonnet is basically a printed version of the text in the manuscript *OBL*, with lines 5 and 6 in the correct order.

Four sonnets by Constable (52, 51, 54, 53, in that order) are the only introductory material to Henry Olney's quarto edition of Sidney's *An apologie for poetrie* (sig. A3r–v), followed by the printer's address "To the Reader."[122] The book was entered in the Stationers' Register in April 1595 and printed by James Roberts, also responsible for *D94* and perhaps the procurer of the source text of Constable's sonnets, $Z_1$. The rights to publication, however, belonged to William Posonby, who published the work under the title *The defence of poesie*, including no prefatory material, in the same year.[123] Constable's name is printed in full under the fourth sonnet, rightly ascribing the set to him. Sonnet 51 was originally written to the memory of Vittoria Colonna and rededicated to Sidney in this volume. Although they could not have missed the original $Z_1$ heading, which explicitly mentions "the Marquesse of Piscats soule," either Roberts or Olney could have made the connection between her and Sidney as poets with spiritual concerns and accommodated 51 in the minisequence to Sidney. This made sense in practical terms, given that the four sonnets filled two complete pages and thus the leaving of a large blank was avoided. Although the printer seems to be the prime suspect – especially seeing that Constable was abroad by that time – Mary Hobbs's observation regarding the rededication of elegies is worth bearing in mind: they were "frequently reassigned at a later date, to serve for someone else in the compiler's circle of acquaintance."[124] This raises doubts about Constable's possible involvement in the rededication.

Constable's sonnets 60 and 32 are included in the printed miscellany *A poetical rapsody*, first compiled by Francis Davison (1573/1574–d. before 1619), which went through four different editions. His intention was to publish a collection that bore witness to the influence of "a Sidneian poetic tradition," and he even dedicated it to William Herbert, Mary Herbert's son and Sir Philip's nephew. Davison included verse written by himself and his brother Walter, together with poems of Sidney and his sister, Edmund Spenser, and many others, and a variety of genres and forms are represented.[125]

122. RSTC 22534.
123. On the dating and authority of both publications, see Woudhuysen, *Circulation*, 232–234.
124. Hobbs, *Early Seventeenth-Century Manuscripts*, 142.
125. "Poetical Rhapsody," Verse Miscellanies Online, accessed 11 June 2019, http://versemiscellaniesonline.bodleian.ox.ac.uk/texts/poetical-rhapsody.

The first edition, in 1602 (*PR1*) was printed by Valentine Simmes for John Baily.[126] Hyder E. Rollins believes that it "shows signs of rather careful editorial supervision of authors' names or pseudonyms."[127] Constable's sonnets are printed in penultimate place; sonnet 60 (sig. L6v), "Myne eye with all the deadlie sinnes is fraught," is headed "Sonnet," whereas 32 (sig. L7r), to the two countesses, bears a more specific heading that reads "To two most Honorable and Virtuous Ladies, sisters." The initials "H.C." are found under each sonnet. The miscellany was reprinted in 1608, 1611, and 1621 with increasing revisions and additions, but Davison's intervention in publication stopped after 1608. Rollins believes that the text of the poems grew increasingly corrupted.[128] Therefore, only the first two are collated in this edition.

A song included in Martin Peerson's *Private Musick* (1620) bears witness to the popularity of Constable's sonnets in the early seventeenth century; it combines fragments from two different sonnets, numbers 2 and 56, and is accompanied by a musical score (sigs. A3v–A4r).[129] The text seems to derive from the printed *Dianas*, with a few minor variants. As it was customary in the period, the score presents the solo (cantus) part accompanied by the three other voices. The Bassus line runs parallel to the cantus, and the tenor and alto parts appear on the facing page and in different positions. This arrangement allows the musicians to play the song as a lute song, with a single voice accompanied by the lute, or to be performed as a four-part composition. The melody follows the text syllabically; the absence of melismata or complex figurations seems to point at a more declamative – and more faithful to the text – type of song.[130]

## Textual Archetypes, Transmission, and Revision

Constable's secular sonnets were written between 1585 and 1590, the period in which he was active as a courtier and agent abroad. Considering their strong occasional and social character and the ways they were used to sue for patronage and advancement, it is reasonable to suppose he did supervise their copying and circulation at a very early stage. Unfortunately, whereas authors such as John Donne or Henry's friend Sir John Harington left evidence of their roles as – to borrow Harold Love's term – "scribal author-publishers" who oversaw the per-

---

126. RSTC 6373.
127. Hyder E. Rollins, ed. *A Poetical Rhapsody, 1602–1621* (Cambridge, MA, 1932), 2: 39.
128. Ibid., 2: 77–78.
129. The resulting text combines the first four lines of 2 and the whole octave of 56.
130. I am grateful to Dr Rafael Vélez-Núñez for his assistance in describing the score.

sonalisation of presentation copies of their works, no such dedicated fair copies of Constable's sonnets survive.[131] Much like Sir Philip Sidney's, his poems, originally meant for coterie circulation, soon escaped authorial control.[132] The difference is that, in the case of Constable, it happened during his lifetime.[133]

The sonnets made their way into personal miscellanies and successful printed editions; some were copied individually, set to music, and even translated into other languages. All the surviving manuscripts are the products of "user publication," copied by individuals who were well positioned in the currents of manuscript circulation.[134] The agents involved in the process – friends, compilers, scribes, printers – made decisions that had an impact on the sonnets both at the textual and the collection level.[135] Textual variants multiplied; some survive only in their respective copies, while others became fossilised in the print medium. In the collections, sonnets were added, removed or completely revised to suit new circumstances, and headings, attributions, and other material ancillary to the text appeared, disappeared and were transformed. All these features provide information as to how the sonnets circulated in manuscript among Constable's acquaintances and how they were used by printers and publishers.

In his 1999 article, Michael Saenger challenged William A. Ringler's tenet that Newman's first quarto ($Q_1$) of Sidney's *Astrophil and Stella* was a "bad quarto" rife with "scribal distortion" by drawing attention to a number of instances in which the poet revised his texts.[136] He concludes that the sonnet sequence may be, in fact, "a layered creation bearing witness to the rich and unstable world of manuscript circulation."[137] This notion of layered creation is also applicable to the production of Constable's secular sonnets, as sonnets were revised and repurposed by the author; there was no such thing as a single, com-

---

131. Love, *Scribal Publication*, 50, 53.

132. On poets' awareness of the immediate social context of their work, see Arthur F. Marotti, "Manuscript, Print, and the Social History of the Lyric," 52. Saunders's reflection on the loss of authorial control over the process of circulation remains relevant; see J.W. Saunders, "The Stigma of Print: A Note on the Social Bases of Tudor Poetry," *Essays in Criticism* 1 (1951), 139–164, at 153.

133. There is no certainty that the same happened in Sidney's case; see Woudhuysen, *Circulation*, 366.

134. Love, *Scribal Publication*, 79.

135. See Marcy North's discussion of "authoring functions." North, "Ignoto in the Age of Print," 395 n10.

136. Michael Bird Saenger, "Did Sidney Revise *Astrophil and Stella*?" *Studies in Philology* 96, no. 4 (1999): 417–438, at 417–418.

137. Ibid., 438.

prehensive, and perfect authorial manuscript from which all surviving exemplars derived.[138]

Scribal alterations or errors are interwoven with authorial revisions in all the manuscript copies; their nature must be determined and each document must be given its due as witness to a specific stage of transmission.[139] Although Constable's aims may have varied over time in a context of rapidly changing personal and social circumstances, it can be argued that the collection in *T*, used here as copy text, comes closest to presenting his final intentions.[140]

## Variants and Error

Collation of the surviving sources makes it possible to establish relations between texts that point to lost authorial archetypes from which different traditions sprang. Verbal variants are the most genetically indicative, whereas accidentals such as spelling were contingent on individual transcription practices.[141] Sonnet 45 illustrates the latter type. The word "beauty" (45.6) is rendered "bewty" in *H* and "beautie" in *T*; there is no clue as to how Constable might have written the word – it could have been "beawty," for all we know. This would be a "genetically indifferent" variant according to Love, one that does not provide "adequate basis for textual reasoning."[142] Contrariwise, in sonnet 61, the variant "I lov'd in vayne"

---

138. Ringler, influenced by New Bibliography, viewed "manuscript variability as an unfortunate layer of dust covering texts which properly belong in a unified and fixed printed edition"; see Saenger, "Did Sidney revise *Astrophil and Stella*?" 421. Robert F. Fleissner's disregard for the manuscripts containing Constable's sonnets and his blind reliance on the text of the 1592 *Diana* in his 1980 edition seem consistent with the New Bibliographers' *telos*. The recovery of an imaginary fixed text "purged" of "corruptions," Marotti has noted, is fruitless in the case of authors such as Donne, who consciously chose "the mutable environment of manuscript transmission ... for his writing." Marotti, *Manuscript, Print*, 159.

139. McKenzie's observation that single versions of a revised text have their "own historical identity" and embody "a quite different intention" is relevant in Constable's case. See D.F. McKenzie, *Bibliography and the Sociology of Texts* (Cambridge, 1999), 36–37.

140. On the use of *T* as copy text, see p. 149.

141. Pebworth's terminology in the classification of variants, "verbal" versus "accidental," is here favoured over W.W. Greg's ("substantive" versus "accidental") in order to avoid the connotations of importance attached to Greg's terms. Accidentals can occasionally be considered substantive too. In a more recent work, Hunter favours the term "significant variants" over verbal or substantive. See Ted-Larry Pebworth, "Manuscript Transmission and the Selection of Copy-Text in Renaissance Coterie Poetry," *Text* 7 (1994), 243–261, at 243–244; Michael Hunter, *Editing Early Modern Texts: An Introduction to Principles and Practice* (Basingstoke, 2007), 62.

142. Love, *Scribal Publication*, 331.

(61.4) in *T* is significant because the other sources – *H, D92* and *D94* – have "sigh'd" or "sighd" instead of "lov'd." This is a verbal variant, and it must be explained in terms of either textual corruption or deliberate revision. Nevertheless, in such a tight and cohesive metrical form as the sonnet, some variants that would typically be excluded, such as changing pronouns and determiners (*my/thy*), and changes to the verb form (*doe/doth, hath/had*), are taken into account because the scribe should have been able to prevent alterations to meaning.[143]

Variants are identified as scribal errors or corruptions when the sense, grammar, metre, or rhyme of the line is obviously distorted and they can be explained in terms of a mechanical mistake inadvertently committed by copyists (such as eyeskip), or as the result of attempts to supply missing or obscure words in a less-than-perfect exemplar – an instance of what Ted-Larry Pebworth terms "errors of commission."[144] The table below shows the variants that have been classified as errors during collation of the secular sonnets (1–66), and the sources in which they appear.[145]

In more difficult cases, authorial or scribal improvement originates variants that are semantically and grammatically valid readings. For example, the first line in the *H* text of sonnet 20 reads "A frind of myne pitying my hopeles love," whereas in *T* it becomes "A friend of myne *moaning* my *helplesse* love." The variants in italics fit the context, and revision may have been at work, given that *T* derives from a later authorial text, but any decision as to which variant is better is necessarily subjective. The ambiguity is in some cases best left unresolved.

## *Archetypes and Textual Traditions*

Collation points to the existence of three lost authorial archetypes, either holographs or supervised copies, from which the extant manuscript and printed sources are descended.[146] Regardless of the corruptions in its descendants, each

---

143. The larger group of indifferent variants has been tested against the hypotheses generated by collation of genetically indicative ones, although they have been excluded from the apparatus to this edition to avoid clutter.

144. Pebworth, "Manuscript Transmission," 253–254. On errors, see Beal, *Dictionary*, 360–361.

145. Note that unique readings in *A* which do not agree with other sources have been excluded.

146. This hypothesis agrees with Williams's in the basic identification and transmission families, although it has significant variations. First, *E* was not known to Williams and is therefore not included. Secondly, Williams argues for the existence of an intermediate $\Sigma$ collection, a presentation manuscript given to Lady Rich, derived from *Y* and from which *H* and *D92* descended. This theory is based on the existence of two errors shared by *H* and *D92* that did

## Table 6. Errors in sonnets 1–66

| Sonnet.Line | Correct Reading | Error | Sources with Error |
| --- | --- | --- | --- |
| 2.14 | thyne | your | H D92 D94 A |
| 2.14 | the | my | D92 D94 A |
| 3.1 | lowe | love | T |
| 3.6 | And so | And | T |
| 4.3 | my | thyne | T |
| 4.11 | water | matter | T |
| 4.12 | doe | doth | D94 A |
| 6.1 | thoughts | thought | T |
| 6.10 | heapes | heape | T |
| 6.13 | oute | not | D92 D94 |
| 6.13 | love | gold | H |
| 7.3 | my | thy | D94a |
| 7.14 | thy hearte | my hart | D92 D94 |
| 8.4 | become | begin; begun | D92; D94 A |
| 8.12 | drawth | doth draw | T |
| 10.5 | Nor when on | When on poore | D92 |
| 13.3 | hearts | eyes | D94 |
| 16.4 | her | *omitted* | H |
| 16.12 | quickeneth | quickneth | T |
| 17.4 | in | in my; my | M; H D92 D94 |
| 17.14 | shrine | shine | T |
| 18.7 | flee | see | T |
| 18.10 | tame | tane | D92 D94 |
| 20.2 | love | hope | D92 |
| 21.13 | dothe | doe | T |

not later make it into Z. The Z family is only said to have one intermediate source, Φ, and its descendants are distributed differently. Finally, PR is shown to descend from D94, but that does not account for the one sonnet not in that printed edition. See Williams, *Edition*, 2: 69.

THE AMATORY AND DEDICATORY SONNETS · 73

Table 6 – *continued*

| Sonnet.Line | Correct Reading | Error | Sources with Error |
|---|---|---|---|
| 21.14 | be | is | D92 D94 |
| 22.4 | be | he | T |
| 22.14 | light | heate | T |
| 23.13 | a | *omitted* | T |
| 24.6 | An | And | T |
| 25.6 | sweet | *omitted* | T |
| 25.7 | of | yf | M |
| 25.14 | make | makes | M T |
| 26.12 | song | throne | T |
| 27.9 | worldlye | wodly | OBL |
| 27.9 | wings | things | T |
| 27.13 | flee | flye | T |
| 29.5–8 |  | *lines missing* | E |
| 29.7 | hir | his | T |
| 30.2 | yow | the | E |
| 32.8 | other | others | T |
| 32.11 | you | one | PR2 |
| 36.3 | three | things | E |
| 36.4 | of | a | D94 E A |
| 36.12 | the coate the starrs declare | might by the starres appeare | D94 A |
| 36.14 | beares | weareth | D94 A |
| 41.8 | hold | held | T |
| 42.2 | on | in | T |
| 42.3 | planet | *omitted* | H |
| 42.14 | do | doth | T |
| 45.6 | that | *omitted* | H |
| 46.4 | thence | *omitted* | T |

Table 6 – *continued*

| Sonnet.Line | Correct Reading | Error | Sources with Error |
|---|---|---|---|
| 46.8 | need | meed | T |
| 48.8 | thoughts | wrongs | H D92 D94 |
| 48.13 | rewarded | revenged | H D92 D94 |
| 48.14 | more | poore | D94 |
| 50.11 | be | *omitted* | T |
| 50.14 | dye | denye | T |
| 51.6 | fayre, and | *omitted* | T |
| 52.2 | importune | importund | AP |
| 52.3 | thow | now | T |
| 52.5 | slow | bold | T |
| 54.3 | part of | *omitted* | T |
| 56.13 | youre ... my | my ... youre | T |
| 57.6 |  | *line missing* | T |
| 57.11 | thee, but | beautie | T |
| 58.1 | My | *omitted* | M |
| 58.12 | wished | wicked | M |
| 59.7 | which by the | the which by | D94 A |
| 60.3 | made | *omitted* | H |
| 60.5 | my | by | D94 PR1 |
| 60.8 | consent gave | was accessarie | T |
| 60.11–12 |  | *order inverted* | D92 D94 A PR1 PR2 |
| 61.8 | sight | praise | D94 A |
| 62.1 | sometymes I | somtime in verse I | D94 |
| 62.7 | flame | fire | D94 |
| 62.9 | paine | follie | T |
| 62.9 | lesse | more | D94 |
| 62.12 | Still blameth | skillesse blames | D94 |

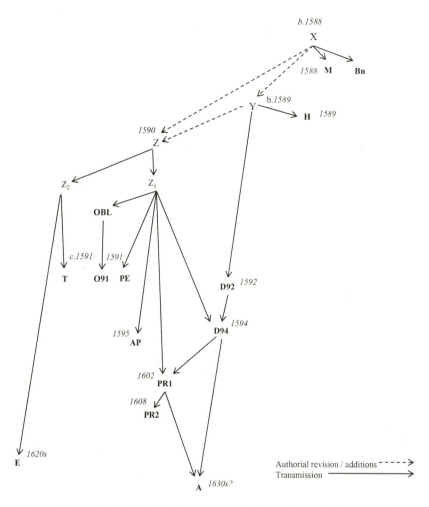

Figure 2. Transmission hypothesis; stemma with dates of compilation or printing.

archetype would have been a good text for the author and his immediate circle at the moment of composition or revision. They have been assigned the sigla *X*, *Y*, and *Z* in chronological order (see figure 2). All of the sonnets in the earliest, *X*, were written by 1588. One was copied into *Bn*, a separate – a physically independent unit – containing only that sonnet, and fifteen in *M*; all but two of these underwent further transmission.[147]

147. It is unclear whether *X* contained more sonnets.

The sonnets in *H* and the first *Diana*, *D92*, derive from another authoritative compilation, *Y*, put together by 1589. *Y* fell into the hands of Sir John Harington and the people involved in the printing of *D92*. The second edition, *D94*, was built upon the first. Some of its sonnets, which after Constable's departure were certainly beyond authorial control, had their readings increasingly corrupted as they were included in *PR1* and *PR2*. Decades later, the compiler of *A* made extensive use of *D94* as a source.[148]

The third archetype is *Z*, a collection put together by Constable by the end of 1590, containing the largest number of sonnets and important revisions of the *X*- and *Y*-derived texts. *Z* must have circulated more widely than the others, given that its descendants are at least twice removed from it. They derive from two different copies of it, $Z_1$ and $Z_2$, which tend to agree against earlier witnesses but present some significant variants. All the sonnets in *AP*, one in *PR1*, the one shared by *PE* and Harington's *Orlando* in its manuscript (*OBL*) and printed (*O91*) versions, and five sonnets in *D94* which were not in *D92* derive from the intermediate $Z_1$. The collection of sixty-five sonnets in *T*, dated around 1591, and the eight in *E*, copied much later, descend from $Z_2$.

The three sonnets which have served as case studies to construct the stemma, numbers 15, 32, and 60, not only survive in copies belonging to all three families of transmission but also present such different readings that they can be deemed to exist in two separate versions, the second being the result of a process of authorial revision motivated by personal, stylistic, or social reasons.

The first, sonnet 15, underwent two such revisions, a major one as the text made its way from *X* to *Y* and a minor one as it became part of *Z* (see figure 3). The version in *M*, "False the report, & unjust is the blame" (15b) is radically different from the other copies; therefore, only the lines that can be collated (9–12) are included in the diagram below. The poet draws a comparison between the obstinacy of his enamoured heart and the steadfastness of Protestant martyrs burnt at the stake. The first revision expunged the central elements that gave cohesion to the sonnet – the image of the lady as a saint, the charge of heresy brought against the lover, and the threat of punishment by fire. The single references to the poet's pen, tongue, and heart, which stand accused of worshipping the lady too much, scattered throughout the *M* sonnet, are brought together in *H* to introduce the conceit that is to be developed: "ffalslie dothe envie of your

---

148. *A* is an extreme example of how mid-seventeenth-century miscellany compilers appropriated texts to such an extent that their "tastes, interests, and habits" prevailed over notions of "textual integrity." Woudhuysen, *Circulation*, 163. The texts in *A* are rife with corruptions and modifications, perhaps by Nicholas Burghe himself, and its variants offer little information about the archetypes from which the sonnets ultimately derive, or about their early circulation.

THE AMATORY AND DEDICATORY SONNETS · 77

prayses blame / my toung my penn my hart of flatterie" (1–2). The poet then reviews the accusations levelled against each element in the triad in an attempt to give structural cohesion to the new version of the sonnet, and there is repetition throughout:

> becawse I sayd there was no sunn but thee
> yt calld my toung the partiall troump of fame
> and sayth my penn hath flattered thy name
> becawse my penn did to my tounge agree,
> and that my hart must needs a flatterer be
> which taught both tounge and penn to say the same. (3–8)

The agreement between the *H* and *D92* texts makes it possible to recover the *Y* readings. Only lines 9–12 made their way from *X* to *Y* in a basically unchanged manner; the poet claims that it is the sun he flatters when he compares the lady to it. The ending was rewritten as well. The early version of sonnet 15 in *M* brings the theme of punishment and burning to a conclusion; the lover's heart has been consumed by the fire of love so it cannot be burnt further: "And thoghe I erd, my hart cannot for this / be burnt, for it already burned is" (13–14). The same lines in *H* seem remarkably weaker: "witnes myne eyes I say the truth in this / they have seen thee and knowe that so yt ys."

*T* contains small improvements on the *Y* text of the sonnet, and its lack of obvious scribal errors means that it remained stable during the later stage of transmission. All the verbs in lines 4 and 5 are changed to the past tense: "call'd," "sayd," "had flattered." Other alterations seem driven by a desire to enhance cohesion by eliminating empty function words. In line 7 the conjunction "that" is avoided by reversing word order. Other such transpositions are found in lines 9, 11, and 14. The somewhat abrupt line in the *H* version of line 10, "the sunn: sith that the sunn was never suche," becomes in *T* "The sun, sith sun in world was never such" through the addition of a lexical item.

Considering that the *M* version could rightfully be deemed a richer and far more intriguing text, why would a poet revise one of his sonnets to turn it into a weaker, more conventional piece?[149] The suppressed image was heavily loaded

---

149. Constable's editors to date have not discussed the revision of this sonnet in depth. Williams notes that the *M* text must represent an earlier draft; Fleissner ignores *M* and collates *H*, *D92*, *D94*, and *T*, arguing that "the variant readings seem relatively inconsequential." Grundy transcribes lines 1–8 in *M* in the apparatus to the sonnet and merely points out that *M* "has a different version." Hughey states that "lines 7 and 10" in *T* "suggest a reviser's hand," and quotes *M* in full in her notes; see Williams, *Edition*, 2: 69; Fleissner, *Resolved to Love*, 33, 64; Grundy, 129; Hughey, 2: 339.

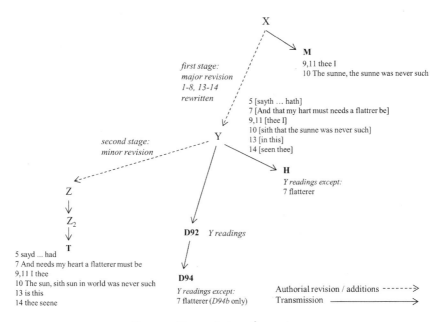

Figure 3. Transmission of sonnet 15.

religiously and politically. It resonates with the horrors of the persecutions during the reign of Mary Tudor and was written from a Protestant stance at a time when anti-Catholic hysteria was mounting. However, by 1589, when *H* was copied from *Y*, Constable was facing a major crisis and had already published his *Examen*, advocating religious moderation. Both his conversion and the *Z* sequence were complete by the end of 1590. The sonnet therefore underwent a transformation commensurate with his own.

Another sonnet that maps authorial and editorial revision is "Myne eye with all the deadlie sinnes is fraught" (60), of which no less than eight copies survive. It is one of the best examples of stylistic revision on Constable's part: he preserved his original conceit but produced a more internally cohesive and perfected version (see figure 4). The poet's enumeration of the seven deadly sins which his eyes have committed is accompanied by numbers added on the margin in all texts but *M* and *H*. The *M* text (60b) can be considered a first draft. It contains a number of function words that were later replaced with lexical items to improve the structure of the line. Lines 2–4 in *M* feel cluttered with empty words and two instances of enjambment: "first Prowde, because it is cause that so highe / my love presumd, & Slothfull is for why / save only gaze about it, it doth naught."

These lines were revised in *Y* and all later texts agree with *T*:[150] "1. First proud, sith it presum'd to looke so hye; / A watchman being made, stood gazing by / 2. And, idle, tooke no heed till I was caught." More obtrusive relative and personal pronouns were removed in the rewriting of lines 5, 9, and 11. In some cases this helped clarify meaning. In *M*, line 7 bears the subject pronoun "it" referring back to "myne eye" (line 1): "it hath let in hir eye." The later texts replace the pronoun with "myne eye" and do away with the auxiliary "hath." The revision of line 14 added more lexical content and eliminated the ill-sounding anaphora in lines 13 and 14 of *M* ("and therefore"). There is also visible improvement in the rewriting of "& therefore I am dampnd in Love his fire" as "Wherefore my heart is damn'd in loves sweet fire" (*T*). *H* omits "sweet" but the spelling of "damned" as a two-syllable word compensates for the loss in terms of metre; this alteration is found also in *A*, which stands at the end of its line of transmission and is generally unreliable. The agreement seems coincidental.

Other revisions to the *X* text were motivated by more personal reasons. The reference to covetousness in lines 9–10 includes a pun on Lady Penelope's name in *M*: "And covetous, whose only god is this, / beawtyes ritche treasure hourded in my hart." The allusion became subtler in all later versions; her last name was replaced with the more conventional reference to her famous blond hair, as seen in the *T* version: "5. And covetouse, it never would remove / From her fayre hayre, gold so doth please his sight." A similar revision occurs in line 5 of sonnet 58, in which the *M* reading "ritch hope" becomes "hopes guifts" in later texts. Both can be understood as an attempt to mask Penelope's identity for a wider readership, even though friends like Sir John Harington identified this lady as the addressee of the whole *Y* sequence. Later texts resolve another ambiguity that may have given offence. Lines 12–13 in *M* read as follows: "and all these sinns shew how Unchast thou art. / And therefore thou deservst a Goddesse ire." Considering that the poet has referred to his eyes using third-person pronouns so far, the shift could prove confusing, and was avoided in the revision, as seen in *T*: "7. Unchast, a baude between my hearte and love. / These sins procured have a goddesse ire."

Inversion of the order of lines 11 and 12, containing the sins of gluttony and lechery, yields two different arrangements (see figure 4). In the manuscripts, lechery comes last and is therefore highlighted; this can be considered the original or authorial order. In all the printed versions, which derive from *D92*, gluttony is the seventh sin. The authorial order yields a CDDC rhyme scheme, whereas the inverted order yields CDCD. The transposition of the two lines

---

150. The *H* text has "made" omitted by scribal error, so the line is one syllable too short.

80 • CHAPTER TWO

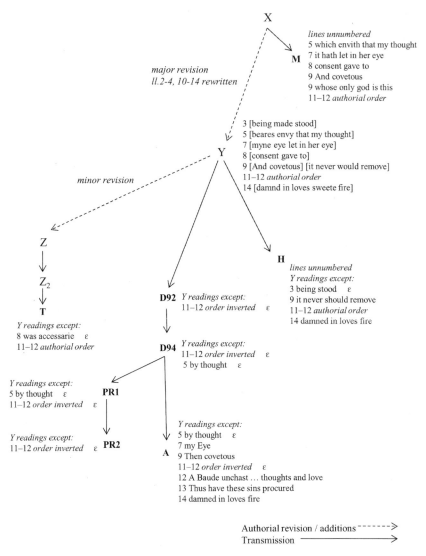

Figure 4. Transmission of sonnet 60.

became fossilised in the print medium. It later made its way into *A*, which is therefore proven to have been copied from *D94*.

The only major change in *T*, as compared to the *Y* witnesses, is the replacement of "consent gave to a murder wrought" with "was accessarie to a murder wrought" in line 8. The new adjective seems semantically cohesive with the murder motif. However, the resulting line is metrically corrupted, and the change may be an example of creative revision on the part of the *T* scribe. This practice has been noted by Williams and may explain at least some of the corruptions in the *T* texts of the sonnets.[151]

The revision of sonnet 32, a dedicatory piece addressed to two sisters, the countesses of Cumberland and Warwick, was motivated by reasons different to those mentioned so far. This sonnet survives only in sources derived from the earliest and latest authorial archetypes; like other sonnets to noble personages other than Penelope, it is missing from the *Y* witnesses, *H* and *D92*. It is also the one sonnet that the editor of *PR1* must have copied from $Z_1$ (see figure 5). The changes to the *M* (32b) version are more noticeable in the last six lines, which were completely rewritten as a result of the loss of the occasional character of the sonnet in changing social circumstances. This revision resulted in two different sonnets.

Collation of lines 1–8 reveals that the three manuscript sources, *M*, *T*, and *E*, tend to agree against the printed *PR* texts, although some variants identify *T* and *E* as descended from the latest archetype. Some of these changes regularise metre or avoid ambiguity. Line 1 in *M*, "That I two sisters with yow nine compare," becomes a perfect iambic pentameter through the insertion of an auxiliary; *T* and *E* read "That I two sisters doe with nyne compare." Lines 3 and 4 praise the countesses as surpassing the muses in virtue. Given that the purpose was to flatter both ladies in equal measure, the *M* reading "one of these" (3) is altered to "eyther of these" in the later manuscripts. In line 4, the repetition of "yow Muses" (*M*) is avoided through the insertion of a periphrasis, so that the line in *T* and *E* reads "In vertue is, then all the heavenly nyne." In the manuscript texts, the poet praises the beauty of the ladies by calling them "more cleare then clerest starr" (*M*) or "as cleare as clearest star" (*T*, *E*). The replacement of this comparison with the more common collocation with "bright" in *PR1* is but one example of the many liberties that the editor took; his changes are reflected in the later *A*.

The last six lines in *M* reveal that the sonnet was originally meant to accompany a portrait or miniature of the countesses. Lines 9 and 10 refer to "this table" and "two pictures," respectively, and the use of the second-person pronoun in "yow see" is perhaps intended to refer to the muses and also to the beholder – or receiver – of the gift portrait. This must be understood in the context of the intrigue that sent Constable to Scotland in 1589, in which the countesses and other courtiers were involved.[152] These lines lost their occasional character as

---

151. Williams, "Reconstructing the Practices," 285.
152. See p. 10.

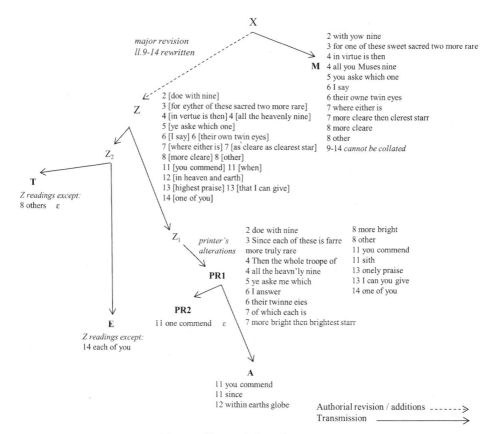

Figure 5. Transmission of sonnet 32.

the sonnet was revised; in the later version, praise of the two sisters is rounded out by adding references to their spotless reputation. The conclusion is neither innovative nor surprising; the sonnet ends with a couplet condensing his eulogy of the ladies. By 1590, when the *Z* collection was put together, Constable's visit to Scotland was a thing of the past and his sights were set on the English court; therefore, his dedicatory sonnet had to be rewritten in order to be as effective and lasting as possible.

The sonnets discussed test the transmission hypothesis as a whole, but some issues pertaining to specific branches of the stemma need to be considered. With regard to the first family of transmission, an important issue is the reliability of *M* and *Bn* as witnesses of the lost *X* (see figure 6). There are two errors in *M* which are avoided in *Bn*. Lines 7–8 in *Bn* read, "And of my pen, my swoord doth envi-

THE AMATORY AND DEDICATORY SONNETS · 83

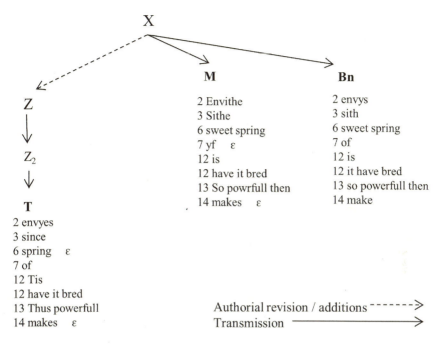

Figure 6. Transmission of sonnet 25.

ous grow / That pen befor my swoord your foes should smite." The word "doth" is an instance of scribal emendation, written above the line. In *M* "yf" replaces "of," introducing a nonexistent conditional clause. The better *Bn* reading is found also in *T*. The final couplet in *M* presents a verbal disagreement between "virtues" and "makes": "So powrfull then your sacred virtues be / Which vice it selfe a vertue makes in me." In *Bn* the scribe crossed out the final *s*, rendering it "make." The error could have originated in *X* and been fixed in *Bn* but not in *M*. The later *T* shares the *M* variant. Line 13 provides another instance in which *Bn* and *M* agree against *T*, as "So" becomes "Thus" in the later source. This line is missing the word "then" in *T*, but in this case the spelling of "powerfull" indicates that it was to be read as a three-syllable word, so the metre is not disrupted and it could have been a later revision. *T* is again missing one word in "which spring" (line 6), and *Bn* and *M* both supply the missing adjective "sweet." Due to *Bn* containing only one sonnet, it is difficult to make any conjectures beyond the fact that it seems to have been copied together with the prose treatise it prefaces; in any case, it seems to be very close to the archetype, and thus an authoritative text bearing witness to the first stage of transmission.

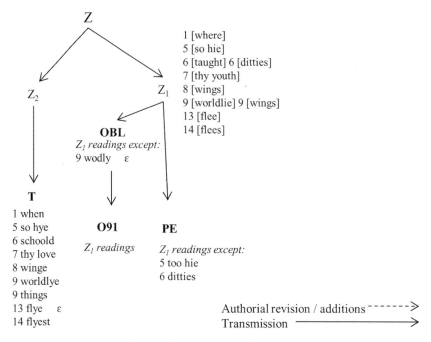

Figure 7. Transmission of sonnet 27.

The two *Y*-derived witnesses, *H* and *D92*, often share readings that are different from *T*; for instance, in sonnet 45, line 9 has "poor orphans" in *H* and *D92*, but "yonge orphans" in *T*. Both are consistent with the image of the poet's personified love as a begging boy. However, reconstructing the readings of the lost *Y* is a more complex matter when *H* and *D92* disagree on their verbal variants as a result of the scribe's or the compositor's lapse or misreading of a letter or word. In sonnet 7, an error had disastrous consequences when it destroyed the climactic image of the sonnet in the *D92* text and was then passed on to *D94*. Developing a complex conceit of picture magic and witchcraft, the poet comes to the conclusion that Love shoots his arrows at the poet's heart only in order to hit the picture of the lady painted on it and make her requite his love (lines 9–14). The last line in *H* and *T* reads "And through thy pictures side might wound thy hearte." *D92* and *D94* have "my hearte" instead, and the misprint indicates that the whole point of the poem must have been lost on the compositor or editor. Different readings in *H* are attributable to either Sir John Harington or his scribe. An instance of the former is found in the first line of sonnet 3, which in *D92* begins "fly low, deare Love," whereas *H* has "fly low, my Love." Considering that *T* also

## THE AMATORY AND DEDICATORY SONNETS • 85

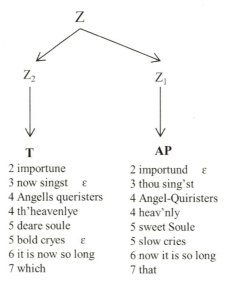

Figure 8. Transmission of sonnet 52.

has "deare," and that this seems to be the more authoritative variant, Harington could have seen fit to alter the line, as scribes – especially those who were poets themselves – often did.

The existence of two different copies of archetype $Z$ is revealed by the collation of sonnets shared by $T$ and a group of sources that can be considered to be from the same family of transmission. Sonnet 27 survives in $T$ and in three copies descended from $Z_1$, namely $PE$, $OBL$, and $O91$ (see figure 7). The readings of the latter group tend to agree when compared to $T$. For instance, they share the variant "age taught by tyme" (line 6), whereas $T$ has "age schoold by tyme." The two words are similar in meaning but would have hardly been confused by a scribe, so the change is either a conscious act of revision or an instance of corruption as $Z$ made it to the $Z_1$ family or to $T$ as a descendant of $Z_2$. Both variants seem equally appropriate.[153] The last word in line 13, "flye," in $T$ destroys the rhyme with "thee," so the other sources share the correct reading, "flee."

Collation of the sonnets in $T$ which were printed prefacing Sidney's $AP$ also supports the notion that as a whole the $Z_1$ readings were more reliable than their

153. The $Z_1$ reading has perhaps more authority considering that it survives in Harington's copy of the sonnet ($OBL$) and it is easy to imagine that he would have had access to a good manuscript of his friend's sonnets other than $Y$. The scribe of $T$, Brockman, could have made a deliberate alteration, but the question must remain unsolved.

$Z_2$ counterparts as witnessed by $T$, or else that the $T$ scribe was responsible for some textual corruptions. In sonnet 51, $T$ omits one foot, which results in a metrically faulty line: "Long tyme before thy glittering rayes." *AP* supplies "fayre, and," which may have been the original $Z$ reading. The same happens in sonnet 54, written in alexandrines. In *AP*, line 2 reads "So every vertue now for part of thee doth sue." However, "part of" is missing in $T$. A more complex textual crux is that of sonnet 52 (see figure 8). Line 5 reads "Give pardon eke, deare soule, to my bold cryes" in $T$; the last four words are a repetition of the ending of the first line and, were this reading authorial, it would be unique in the sequence, given that Constable avoids repeating whole phrases in final position. *AP* has "to my slow cryes" in line 5. Previous editors have emended to "slow eyes," which would be cohesive with the rest of the quatrain, especially "I saw thee" in line 6. If their guess is correct, the *AP* text only helps to recover the original in part. Some $Z$ readings, therefore, remain irrecoverable except for educated guesswork.

Even *D94* is valuable as a witness of $Z$, given that it has five sonnets that must derive from it rather than from *D92*; these are 13, 36, 57, 59, and 62. The text of sonnet 57 in *D94* helps reconstruct an entire line that is missing in $T$: "Love is not in my hart, no Lady no." The variants which arise from collation of *D94* and $T$ point to two different copy texts. In some cases it is uncertain which is the correct reading, as in sonnet 62, which survives only in these two sources. In line 7, both the $T$ reading, "flame," and that in *D94*, "fire," make sense, fit the metre, and could have been in $Z$; "fire" is repeated in the next line, however. "More follie lesse follie have" (line 9) in $T$ is "more paine more folly" in *D94*. The former reading disrupts the metre and the latter makes little sense, so a combination of both, "more paine less follie," must have been the original reading. Other variants seem to be printer's slips or revisions in *D94*. In line 12, he prints "skillesse blames" instead of "still blameth." More dramatic is the change of order of lines 9–10 and 13–14, which results in the sonnet having a different ending.[154] In the case of sonnet 36 the existence of another manuscript version, *E*, lends authority to the $T$ variants against *D94*, and lays out the many liberties taken by the printer. The most noticeable is the rewriting of line 11, which in $T$ and *E* reads "How glittering was the coate the starrs declare," and in *D94* "how glittering twas, might by the starres appeare." The latter adds more function words and creates a repetition, as line 13 ends with "appeareth."

---

154. See notes to this sonnet for a transcription of the last six lines in *D94*.

## Changing Headings and Ascriptions

The readers, copyists, and editors who received and helped circulate Constable's sonnets supplied or erased information that helped recontextualise or decontextualise sonnets which had originated as occasional pieces, composed within a specific context and for a specific purpose and audience.[155] Once no actual dialogue was possible "between the poet and the lyric audience," Ilona Bell argues, the poem was "published."[156] The new readers would often be ignorant of the particulars surrounding the composition of a sonnet. A comparison of the headings that some of them bear in different sources throws light on how the information that readers would receive was manipulated by agents other than the author.

In sonnet 32 "sisters" seems to be the key word for understanding the comparison of the two countesses to the muses, and it is included in all the headings. The *M* heading reads "To the most honorable Ladyes the Countesses of Comb. & War. sisters." The use of abbreviations is consistent with the fact that the scribe made a copy of the sonnet in a miscellany that originated and was circulating among individuals familiar with the context of production; a degree of closeness of the collectors to the courtly milieu is implied. In the other manuscript sources, *E* and *T*, the ladies' titles are given in full and the honorific is dropped, so that may have been the case in the lost *Z*. *T* has "To the Countesses of Cumberland and Warwicke, sisters," whereas *E* inverts the order, naming Warwick first. Francis Davison, the editor of *PR1*, decontextualised the heading, printing instead "To two most Honorable and Virtuous Ladies, sisters." This alteration excludes the buyer of the printed miscellany from the high-class coterie in which manuscripts circulated. It is not clear to what extent Davison was involved in the second edition, *PR2*.[157] Either he or someone else supplied the missing information, including the honorific, the ladies' full names, and their titles, thus recovering as much of the context as possible. The compiler of *A*, Nicholas Burghe, copied the text of the sonnet from *PR1* but had to consult *PR2* in order to include the identification of the ladies in his heading, "To the two Sisters Margarett Countess of Cumberland and Anne Countess of Warwicke." *A* was copied decades after the composition of the sonnet, and any potential readers would have valued the information.

---

155. On poems transcending the environment in which they were first produced and received, see Marotti, "The Transmission of Lyric Poetry," 10; and Marotti, "Manuscript, Print, and the Social History of the Lyric," 52.
156. Ilona Bell, *Elizabethan Women and the Poetry of Courtship* (Cambridge, 1998), 25.
157. Rollins, ed., *A Poetical Rhapsody, 1602–1621*, 2: 76.

The sonnet on the birth of Penelope Rich's daughter, number 42, also presents an array of variations in its heading. The *M* scribe provides invaluable information that helps date the collection as a whole: "A sonet in manner of a calculation on the nativitye of a yonge Ladye borne on a friday, in this yeare. 1588." However, he withholds the identity of the child's mother. In light of the accurateness of his identification of the other addressees in *M*, there might have been other reasons to conceal the name of Penelope, which seems surprising in a collection that contains puns on her name throughout. It is uncertain whether the lost *Y* contained such identification because *H* and *D92* disagree. The author himself could have omitted it, as it would be consistent with other acts of revision by which direct allusions to her were removed.[158] Members of his circle, however, knew it well, and Harington added it to the heading in *H*: "The Calculation of the nativity of the daughter of my Lady Rich borne on a fryday Anno do: 1588." The form of polite address is perhaps intended to underline his own acquaintance with Penelope at the same time that he reveals himself as privy to the circumstances of composition. The printers of *D92* gave the sonnet a much more general title that focuses on the newborn rather than her mother: "A calculation upon the birth of an honourable Ladies daughter, borne in the yeare, 1588, & on a Friday." Penelope's name reappears in *T*, which adds that 1588 was "the yeare of wonder," providing some more contextual information. However, it was the *D92* heading that passed on to *D94*. Burghe's recovery of the missing information in his heading "A Calculation uppon the birth of the Ladye Riches Daughter, borne Anno 1588, & on A Friday" is significant because it means that he must have consulted another source although *D94* was his copy text. The other sonnets he copied were amatory instead of dedicatory, so no further evidence of Burghe's contextualising efforts survives.

The two sources that agree most closely on their headings are *T* and *E*. Whereas the heading of an amatory sonnet such as "Of his Mistrisse upon occasion of her walking in a garden" (16) could be reconstructed from the conceit, the correspondence between the headings of the dedicatory sonnets deserves further commentary. Sonnet 26 is headed "To the Kinge of Scotts" in *M*, but *T* and *E* throw more light on its circumstances. *T* adds "whome as yet he had not seene," and *E* includes the King's name, "James 6th," after his title, followed by "one king whom as yet he had not seene." The heading of sonnet 29 tells an even longer story. In *T* it reads "To the K. of Scots upon occasion of his longe stay in Den-

158. See sonnets 58 and 60b. Lyall comments that "in creating the 22-sonnet sequence, Constable wished to avoid any allusion which would tie his passion too explicitly to Penelope Rich." He adds that this may be why sonnet 35, "O, that my songe like to a ship might be," was left out of this sequence. See Lyall, "Stella's Other Astrophel," 194–195.

# THE AMATORY AND DEDICATORY SONNETS • 89

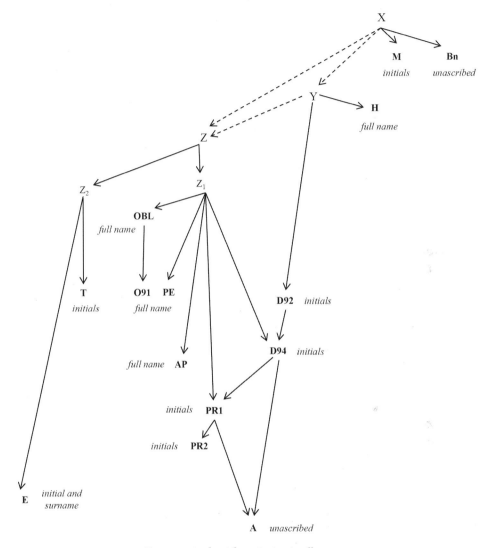

Figure 9. Authorial ascription in all sources.

marke by reason of the coldnesse of the winter and freezing of the sea." Given that both sonnets to James are grouped together in *E*, the heading there is "To the same King upon occasion of his long aboad in Denmarke by reason of the coldnes of the winter & the frezing of the sea." The dedication of sonnet 30 to Louise de Coligny would be irrecoverable without the heading "To the princes of Orange," identical but for the spelling in *T* and *E*. All this lends authority to the hypothesis that they descended from the same source, $Z_2$, which contained the authorial Z headings.

The textual rationale used to describe the transmission of the sonnets themselves does not explain the inclusion or omission of an authorial ascription. Two sources (*Bn*, *A*) bear no ascription whatsoever (see figure 9).[159] Six have the poet's initials, "H.C.," and the same number bear his full name. *E* has the initial "H" followed by his full surname. Any guesses as to the presence or absence of an ascription in the lost archetypes would be conjectural.

## Constable in Translation

Although there is no evidence of a direct relationship between Constable and the son and namesake of Dutch statesman and poet Janus Dousa, it seems plausible that the link between them was the French Huguenot Jean Hotman, whose father was friends with Dousa the Elder.[160] Hotman, then secretary to Robert Dudley, earl of Leicester, had followed the earl to the Low Countries in 1585 and was acquainted with leading humanists and diplomats at Leiden, including the Dousas.[161] The younger Dousa translated two poems by Constable. His Latin rendition of sonnet 8, "Blame not my heart for flying up so high," saw the light in his 1591 Ἐρωτοπαίγνιον (*Erotopaignion*) under the heading "Adumbratum de Anglico Henrici Conestabilis."[162] The Ἐρωτοπαίγνιον antedates the publication of *Diana* and contains works written years earlier, so there is little doubt that Dousa somehow obtained and read a manuscript copy of the sonnet sometime between 1586 and 1588.[163] If this was an early sonnet, it may have circulated sep-

---

159. The authorially revised prose manuscript that *Bn* accompanies is also anonymous.
160. Jan Van Dorsten, *Poets, Patrons, and Professors: Sir Philip Sidney, Daniel Rogers, and the Leiden Humanists* (Leiden, 1962), 84.
161. G.H.M. Posthumus Meyjes, *Jean Hotman's English Connection* (Amsterdam, 1990), 31–33.
162. Janus Dousa the Younger, *Poemata*, ed. Gulielmo Rabo (Rotterdam, 1704), 156–157. See the full text of his translation below, in the notes to sonnet 8.
163. The fact that the younger Dousa was interested in English letters in 1586, combined with his connection with Sidney's literary circle via Hotman, could have rendered a sonnet born in that background appealing to him; see Van Dorsten, *Poets*, 87. Van Dorsten's assumption that the manuscript Dousa used as his source must have contained more sonnets is ungrounded. See also Roderick Lyall, "'Thrie Truer Hairts': Alexander Montgomerie, Henry Constable, Henry Keir and Cultural Politics in Renaissance Britain," *The Innes Review* 54 (2003): 186–215, at 199.

arately, which would help explain its absence from *M*, and it was not derived from the later *Y* archetype, either. Dousa also translated sonnet 4, "Thyne eye, the glasse where I behold my hearte," into Dutch ("U Oog is een glas, daar mijn hart is ingegreven"); this sonnet opens the section "Epigrammata quaedam belgico idiomate" in his *Poemata*.[164] The *Poemata* itself was published in 1607, which means that he could have used the printed editions, and not a manuscript, as his source this time.

The Scottish poet Alexander Montgomerie translated sonnet 4 into Scots, reinforcing the idea that it enjoyed some popularity and had a wide circulation abroad. Constable and Montgomerie must have met during Henry's first visit to the Scottish court in 1583, and then again when Constable spent more time within the King's literary circle six years later. The autumn of 1589 seems a likely time for Constable to be showing some of his compositions to his fellow poet.[165] Montgomerie's version shows some variations in the sestet which result in a different rhyme scheme. He "avoids Constable's *rime riche (come/become)*, a device [King] James condemns" in his *Reulis and Cautelis*.[166]

---

164. Dousa, *Poemata*, 163.

165. Parker mentions Montgomerie's translation of sonnet 4 as evidence that "it could have been circulated on its own." See Parker, 153.

166. Alexander Montgomerie, *Poems*, ed. David J. Parkinson (Edinburgh, 2000), 1: 120, 2: 106. See the full text of his translation below, in the notes to sonnet 4.

CHAPTER THREE

# The *Spiritual Sonnets*

## The Manuscripts

The *SS* exist in a textual tradition that is totally separate from that of Constable's amatory and dedicatory sonnets. They were never printed, and their manuscript circulation was probably very limited in comparison; as a result, no contemporary mention of them survives and they went unnoticed for centuries. It was not until 1815 that Thomas Park, who had already edited the secular sonnets from *T*, used a British Library manuscript (henceforth *HA*) to edit sixteen of its seventeen sonnets.[1] For two centuries after Park published his collection of Elizabethan poetry, known as the *Heliconia*, *HA* was considered the only source of the *SS*. The existence of a second manuscript in Berkeley Castle (henceforth *BE*) has been unknown to editors of Constable and largely ignored (see table 7). *BE* was included in *CELM* in 2013 and its examination greatly contributes to a better understanding of the *SS* as a proper sequence, closely monitored by the author, which may have been intended to play a role in the restitution of Constable's career.

## *BL MS Harley 7553 (HA)*

The Harley manuscript is a quarto-sized composite made of various textually and physically independent units, with materials ranging from the middle ages to the seventeenth century. The seven items it now contains relate to religious matters, so the compilation may have been grounded in theme. There were a total of ten items, but the first three were removed in 1897 and are now in the British

---

1. Park excluded the last sonnet to St Mary Magdalene, number 84 in this edition, arguing that it might offend some readers' sensibilities due to the "latitude of expression" the poet employed in writing about spiritual matters using the language of love. See "Advertisement," in Park, *Heliconia*, 2: n.p.

Library's Department of Oriental Printed Books and Manuscripts, as they contain texts in Hebrew and Arabic.[2] Item 4, the first remaining, comprises twelve leaves of vellum with fragments of divinity in a textura hand; it is followed by an assortment of texts on paper catalogued as "various irregular memorandums" with notes and commentaries in Latin and English and references to scripture. Name allusions point at various dates of composition throughout the seventeenth century.[3] Item 6 is a prose treatise titled "Of the Rosary," in English, written from a devout Catholic perspective in what looks like an early seventeenth-century hand. The seventh and eighth items are a fragment of a sermon in English with an emphasis on the themes of happiness and holy living, and part of a treatise on the Trinity, in Latin. Constable's *SS* are item 9. They are followed by a forty-two line devotional poem in secretary hand whose first line reads "Unless we whollie doe depend," and another poem made of two ten-line stanzas, a paraphrase of Psalm 122 ascribed to royalist composer Henry Cooke; it begins "Come lett us pray and god will heere."

*HA* was compiled as a separate booklet made of paper whose watermark points at a 1590s Venetian origin.[4] This piece of material evidence hints at the circumstances of production of the manuscript. Constable spent the first years of his exile in Italy; he could have acquired a ream of Venetian paper or had a copy made by a scribe who supplied his own, as was often the case. It seems likely that the *SS* were composed and copied by 1595.[5] The title page reads "Spirituall Sonnettes / To the honour of God: and hys Sayntes. / by H: C."

Before the rediscovery of a second manuscript at Berkeley Castle (*BE*), *HA* was the only known copy of Constable's *SS*. In *HA* the sonnets appear in the same order as in *BE*, although four are missing, and their arrangement is not quite as carefully planned (see appendix C). They all bear individual titles; the three consecutive sonnets to the Virgin (79–81), for instance, are titled "To our blessed Lady." There are no headings grouping sonnets to the same addressee together

---

2. See *Catalogue of the Harleian Manuscripts in the British Museum* (London, 1808–1812), 3: 535.

3. One text contains allusions to an anti-Catholic author of polemical treatises named Bidell, who could be the Church of Ireland's bishop of Kilmore, William Bedell (bap. 1572–1642). Another mentions Sir Richard Gipps, who was Master of the Revels to Charles II.

4. See the "Bibliographical Description of Main Textual Sources" (below, p. 364) for information about the provenance and codicological and palaeographical features of the two manuscripts described.

5. Lee dated them to "about 1593" but failed to provide any arguments. Wickes does not attempt to date the *SS* but links them to Constable's stay in Italy and "the influence of Italian Counter-Reformation verse." See Sidney Lee, *A Life of William Shakespeare* (London, 1901), 440; Wickes, *Bio*, 278.

94 • CHAPTER THREE

or establishing divisions in the sequence. Considering Constable's preoccupation with organisation and symmetrical patterns, a collection with seventeen sonnets seems inferior to that containing twenty-one; however, seventeen does not lack biblical symbolism and is often shown to be a sign of spiritual victory in both testaments.[6]

With regard to authorial ascription, *HA* bears initials instead of the poet's full name in its title. *HA* must have had a limited circulation while Constable was living abroad, and he probably kept his religious sequence close at that early stage. If his readers were acquainted with him and knew the sonnets to be his, there would have been little need to include his name in the authorial manuscript from which *HA* derived, *a*. Either it bore no name or only his initials were included and passed on to *HA*.

## *Berkeley Castle Select Books 85 (BE)*

This manuscript is a single booklet in quarto size that was never rebound into a miscellany. The collection of Constable's *SS* which it preserves is of paramount importance for various reasons. First and foremost, it adds four sonnets (78, 85–87) to the canon of his poetry. The neatness of the handwriting, the variety of scripts used, and the absence of corrections reveal that this was a copy produced by a professional scribe based on a fair authorial text, with a great deal of care and focus on the final result and not on speed or time. The sonnets also form a true sequence whose arrangement is so carefully planned that it can be nothing but authorial.

Constable's regard for rank and hierarchy, which informs the organisation of the secular sonnets in *T*, underlies this collection as well. The arrangement is first mentioned in the title to the sequence, "Certen Spirituall Sonnets to the honner of God and his Sainctes: withe Nyne other directed by particuler devotion to 3 blessed Maryes." There are two clear sections (see appendix C). The first groups three sonnets to the three persons of the Trinity, respectively, one to the Blessed Sacrament, one to the Virgin Mary, and seven to different saints. Within, sonnets 67–74 are arranged according to the position of their addressees in the Confiteor in the Tridentine Mass.[7] For instance, the sonnet to John the Baptist (73) is placed between number 72 to St Michael and 74 to St Peter and St Paul. Given

---

6. To give but one instance of its appearance, in Romans 8:35–39 St Paul enumerates seven disasters that might separate the believer "from the love of Christ," and lists ten obstacles that could not perform this separation.

7. "Confiteor Deo omnipotenti, beatæ Mariæ semper Virgini, beato Michaeli Archangelo, beato Ioanni Baptistæ, sanctis Apostolis Petro et Paulo, omnibus Sanctis ... ."

Table 7. The *Spiritual Sonnets* in the two manuscripts

| Edition | First Line | BE | HA |
|---|---|---|---|
| [67] | Greate god, within whose simple essence wee | [1] 3 | [1] 32r |
| [68] | Younge Prince of heaven, begotten of that Kinge | [2] 3 | [2] 32v |
| [69] | Eternall sprite, which arte in heaven, the love | [3] 4 | [3] 33r |
| [70] | When thee, o holy sacrificed Lambe | [4] 4 | [4] 33v |
| [71] | In that, Oh Queene of Queens, thy birth was free | [5] 5 | [5] 34r |
| [72] | When as the Prince of Anngelles, puft with pryde | [6] 5 | [6] 34v |
| [73] | As Anne, longe barren, mother did become | [7] 6 | [7] 35r |
| [74] | He that for feare his Maister did deny | [8] 6 | [8] 35v |
| [75] | For few nightes sollace in delitious bedd | [9] 7 | [9] 36r |
| [76] | Because thou was the Daughter of A kinge | [10] 7 | [10] 36v |
| [77] | Fayre Amazon of heaven, which took'st in hande | [11] 8 | [11] 37r |
| [78] | This day, oh blessed virgine, is the daye | [12] 8 | - |
| [79] | Soveraigne of Queens, yf vayne ambition move | [13] 9 | [12] 37v |
| [80] | Whie should I any love, oh Queene, but thee? | [14] 9 | [13] 38r |
| [81] | Sweete Queene, althoughe thy beauty rayse up me | [15] 10 | [14] 38v |
| [82] | Blessed offender, which thy self haste tri'd | [16] 10 | [15] 39r |
| [83] | Suche as, retir'd from sight of men like thee | [17] 11 | [16] 39v |
| [84] | Sweete sainct, thou better can'st declare to me | [18] 11 | [17] 40r |
| [85] | I write of tears and blud at on time shedd | [19] 12 | - |
| [86] | It is not pompe of solemne funerall | [20] 12 | - |
| [87] | I doe the wronge, o Queene, in that I saye | [21] 13 | - |

her importance in the Counter-Reformation, it is not surprising that St Mary Magdalene should be the first addressee in the group of sonnets to female saints that follows. The much-venerated St Catherine and St Margaret come immediately after, and the placement of the sonnet to St Colette (78) – exclusive to *BE* – at the end of this section is hardly random because, being a fourteenth-century saint, her status could not compete with the virgin martyrs and she was a lesser-known figure. The second section opens with a general heading that repeats part of the title, "Nyne other sonnetts directed by particuler Devotion unto 3 blessed Maryes." The three women named Mary are also ordered by rank, and each triad of sonnets bears a title clearly stating the addressee, which renders individual sonnet headings unnecessary.

Numbers 3 and 7 play a prominent role in the organisation of *BE*, much as they do in *T*.[8] Besides the triads to the three "Maryes," the first twelve sonnets can also be divided into groups of three. The Trinity gets three sonnets; the next three deal with God as present in the Eucharist, as the spouse and son of Mary, and as the vanquisher of the devil through St Michael. Three more meditate on the lives of Christ's apostles or disciples, St John, St Peter and St Paul – together – and the Magdalene; and three are dedicated to female saints, St Catherine, St Margaret, and St Colette. The total number of sonnets is twenty-one, which equals three times seven. Compared to *HA*, the *BE* arrangement seems superior. *BE* also resembles *T* in the initial authorial statement, which in *T* is a prose introduction and in *BE* a general title to the sequence written on the first page. Both provide some information about the contents and internal organization of the collections. Headings and crossheadings then repeat some of this information in order to mark the internal arrangement of the sequence more clearly.

The authorial ascription in *BE* is also important. Out of the two manuscripts of the *SS*, only *BE* gives the name of the author practically in full in the inscription "By Hen. Conestable Esquire." This inscription bears a remarkable similarity to the poet's own signature as it appears in at least nine holographic letters, with three letters of his first name followed by his surname spelled out in full (see figure 10). The scribe seems to be imitating Constable's signature to the best of his ability, down to the slant and shape of the initial *h*. It may be safely assumed that this fair copy was derived from a now lost holographic text ($\beta$), signed by the author himself. This effort to advertise, instead of concealing, the authorship of a collection of potentially inflammatory Catholic sonnets must have suited Constable's purposes at the time.

    8. The sonnets in *T* are grouped into three main sections containing further subdivisions in groups of seven. Both three and seven are considered perfect, or sacred, numbers, and appear throughout the Bible.

Figure 10. Constable's signature as found in a letter to Cecil, CP 188/108.

The circumstances surrounding Constable's return to England in 1603 after a long exile, together with the provenance of the manuscript, make it possible to at least hypothesise how *BE* came to be. It was part of the collections of Elizabeth Berkeley, née Carey (1576–1635). Queen Elizabeth had been her godmother and, when she married Thomas Berkeley, the couple enjoyed royal favour. Upon James I's coronation, Thomas was created Knight of the Bath, and his wife was among the ladies who paid homage to Queen Anne in July 1603 and dined with the monarchs at Windsor Castle.[9] The group also included the countesses of Shrewsbury and Pembroke and Penelope Rich, all of whom had been addressed in sonnets by Constable in the late 1580s.[10] By the poet's own account, when he arrived in England in December 1603, Penelope and other ladies informed him that his return had pleased the queen greatly and she was eager to converse with him, but was busy with preparations for a masque at that moment.[11] Constable's reputation probably rested upon his early career and secular sonnets, but he could have also been welcomed back as a Catholic gentleman by Anne and her ladies.[12]

The possibility that Constable could have sent *BE* or its copy text ($\beta$) from France while he was living in exile and Elizabeth I was still queen, which would have been risky and pointless considering that he had set his hopes on the smooth succession of James, must be ruled out. The manuscript is a fair copy without a dedication, which contrasts with Constable's use of personalised and dedicatory sonnets in the past. *BE* was perhaps copied abroad, brought with him in 1603, and meant to be shown to a number of people. Its excellent condition, however, reveals that it did not go from hand to hand. Alternatively, it could have been

9. On Sir Thomas Berkeley, see Joseph Foster, *Alumni Oxonienses: the Members of the University of Oxford, 1500–1714* (Oxford, 1891–1892), 1: 114.

10. John Nichols, *The Progresses, Processions, and Magnificent Festivities, of King James the First, His Royal Consort, Family and Court* (London, 1828), 1: 195.

11. London, 9 January 1604, ASV, SSF 49, fol. 36v.

12. An ambassador at court reported, "She [the Queen] endeavours to place in office as many Catholic nobles as possible, as the King is extremely attached to her she succeeds in all she attempts." See *CSPV*, 10: 68. Constable must have been well aware of this and tried to get to James through his wife.

## CHAPTER THREE

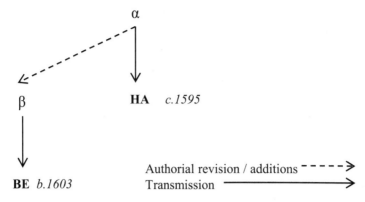

Figure 11. Archetypes and transmission of the *Spiritual Sonnets*.

produced in England, with someone in the entourage of Queen Anne commissioning a scribal copy. Both Elizabeth Berkeley herself and her childhood tutor and friend Henry Stanford, who was an active participant in manuscript circulation across a number of noble households, are strong candidates.[13] The Berkeleys and Stanford were constantly suspected of Catholicism.[14] Stanford may have had some agency in the copying of Constable's sonnets, but the manuscript is not written in his hand, which is too idiosyncratic to miss.[15]

Regardless of the exact circumstances of production, it is clear that the *SS* would have been of more use to Constable upon his return to England. Proof of this is that *BE* contains three elegies on the king's mother, Mary, Queen of Scots, which could have been written at a later date than the remaining *SS*, or else withheld from circulation altogether up to that moment (see plate 8). These elegies complete the sequence to numerical and structural perfection. All things considered, *BE* is the more perfect witness of the *SS*, directly descended from β, the latest authorial text (see figure 11).

13. See Steven W. May, "Stanford, Henry (c. 1552–1616)," in *ODNB*.
14. The Berkeleys had family connections with Surrey, Norfolk, and Arundel. Before working at the Hunsdon-Carey household, Stanford had been employed by the Catholic Paget family, and his connections rendered him suspect even though he was an ordained Anglican priest. He compiled an anthology of Elizabethan and Jacobean verse and another miscellany containing mostly prose, the latter of which is also held at Berkeley Castle, together with some of his other books and letters. See Steven W. May, "Henry Stanford's 'God Knows What,'" in *English Manuscript Studies 1100–1700*, ed. Richard Beadle and Colin Burrow (London, 2011), 70–82.
15. I have consulted a holographic letter by Stanford (Berkeley, Gloucs., Berkeley Castle, GL 5/129) and have found no similarity to the handwriting in *BE*.

## Revision and (Mis)attribution

The most obvious differences between both manuscripts have to do with the number and arrangement of sonnets. Unlike the secular sonnets, the text of the *SS* is relatively stable, and collation reveals a smaller number of verbal variants. Nevertheless, evidence of authorial revision and the presence or absence of scribal errors prove *HA* to be the earliest collection, a good copy derived from a first authorial manuscript, whereas *BE* is a later, revised collection, a fair copy that represents the final authorial arrangement of the *SS*.

### Collation

Idiosyncratic scribal practices account for some variants. The scribe of *BE* consistently favours the use of "which" as the relative pronoun with human antecedent throughout the collection, for instance in sonnet 70, "like our fore fathers, which in Limbo were" (11), and in 73, "the kinge which god did take" (9). The *HA* scribe, however, consistently writes "who," as in 70 ("who in Lymbo were"), or "whom," as in 73 ("whom God dyd take"). It is impossible to determine which was Constable's choice of pronoun in his drafts. The word "spirit" is rendered "spright" in *HA* and "sprite" in *BE*, as in 67 or 69. The former spelling may be authorial, considering that this term appears in sonnet 25 and both *Bn* and *M* have "spright." In any case, spelling must be considered an accidental feature prone to scribal erasure and replacement.

Some verbal variants were caused by the misreading of certain words and are not genetically indicative whether or not they alter the meaning of the line. The variation between "than" and "thou" in line 6 of sonnet 69 ("in fiery tonnges than cam'st downe unto his") could be due to their similar spelling but does not destroy meaning. In line 9 of the same, the plural noun in "true loves springes" looks like an error in *BE* that is avoided in *HA* (see table 8). Adding an *s* in final position was a common scribal slip, especially when the next word began with that letter. Scribal misreading may have also originated the variation between "still" in *BE* and "shall" in *HA* in sonnet 81: "And still new loves and new delightes distill" (12). Both words fit the line, although "still" creates an internal rhyme with the final word and "shall" recurs three more times in the sonnet. Confusion of final *e*, *s*, and *es* was common enough and must be behind an agreement error in the *BE* text of sonnet 83: "finde" (7) does not agree with the subject "she" (6), and *HA* has the correct reading, "findes." Similar errors in concord are the variant "doste" (3) in the *BE* text of 67, which is not consistent with the past verb forms in the next line; *HA* has the archaic second-person past form "dydd'st." In 76, it is *HA* that seems to be in error in line 7, since "haith," a third-person singular form, does not agree with "these graces," the subject in line 5.

Another small group of variants affects the metre. In 83, the verb in *BE* "lamenteth" has one more syllable than *HA* "laments" and line 6 is too long. The opposite also happens. The spelling "Magdalene" in *HA* is one syllable longer than its *BE* counterpart "Mawdlin" in line 10 of sonnet 82, and the latter fits the metre better. One of the most conspicuous errors in *HA* is the omission of a word in sonnet 80. Line 6 reads "thou all in perfections doest exceede" and is one syllable too short. Previous editors who noticed the error emended the line by inserting "thy" before "perfections." However, *BE* reveals that the missing word is "all": "thou all in all perfections dost exceede."

The variants above must be considered in the light of others which cannot easily be explained unless they are viewed as the products of authorial revision. On three occasions one word is replaced with another. "All pleasure" (81.10) in *HA* becomes "all sweetnes" in *BE*; the former may well be a scribal repetition of the word in the previous line, or else "pleasure" could have been used in an early version of the poem and then altered to eliminate repetition. The change in the initial apostrophe of sonnet 68, which in *HA* reads "Great Prince" and in *BE* "Younge Prince," is certainly not an accident. Like every first word in the sonnets in *BE*, "Younge" is carefully penned in gothic script, a task which demanded the scribe's full attention. Given that sonnet 67 ("To God the Father") begins with the apostrophe "Greate god," Constable may have wanted to avoid a repetition that would have stood out on the page. Finally, in sonnet 70 the poet presents his own body as the funerary monument in which Christ – embodied in the Communion bread and wine – is to be placed (7–8). The beginning of line 9 in *BE*, "intomb'd in me," seems an improvement on the *HA* reading "buryed in me" because it is more semantically cohesive, and it is surely the product of stylistic revision.

Whole phrases were also revised. In the *HA* text of sonnet 82 to St Mary Magdalene, the poet asks the saint, "No longer let my synfull sowle abyde / in feaver of thy fyrst desyres faynte" (5–6). In *BE* "former passions" replaces "fyrst desyres." The two variants are metrically and semantically sound. The same sonnet presents the clearest instance of rewriting in the collection. In *HA*, the poet's request that the Magdalene should weep with him is followed with a commonplace allusion to the saint crying beside Christ's tomb: "while I sighe for that grave, for which thow cry'd" (4). In *BE*, the image of the weeping Magdalene is replaced with an increased focus on the poet as penitent and Christ's salvation of mankind: "and pittye hym for whome thy Maister dy'd."

Another act of revision that seems to have been performed by either the author or the scribe at a later stage is metrical standardisation. This helps explain the change in sonnet 72, in which the fallen angels defeated by St Michael are referred to as "vanquish't in battayle" (6) in *HA* and "in battell vanquisht" in *BE*; the latter is more regular in its use of iambic feet only. In 70 the poet describes his soul as "pryson'd in earth, & bannish't from thy syght" (10) in *HA*; the metre is regularised and the use of the conjunction avoided in *BE*: "in earth imprisoned, bannisht from thy sight."

Although the text of *BE* is not free of error, where collation is possible its verbal variants sanction it as an improvement on *HA*. There are no significant omissions, corrections, or repetitions due to scribal carelessness. Some facts surrounding the history of production and transmission of the manuscripts also support the notion that authorial revision did take place and *BE* is a copy of a final product, the lost $\beta$ (see figure 11 above).

Table 8. Errors in sonnets 67–87

| Sonnet.Line | Correct Reading | Error | Source with Error |
|---|---|---|---|
| 67.3 | dydd'st | doste | *BE* |
| 69.9 | true love | true loves | *BE* |
| 76.7 | have | haith | *HA* |
| 80.6 | all in all | all in | *HA* |
| 81.10 | sweetnes | pleasure | *HA* |
| 82.10 | mawdlin | Magdalen | *HA* |
| 83.6 | laments | Lamenteth | *BE* |
| 83.7 | findes | finde | *BE* |
| 86.12 | serve | sever | *BE* |

## Two Archetypes

Little is known about the origin of *HA* except that it existed as a single booklet containing the *SS* only, and paper evidence points to early 1590s Italy as the time and place in which it was copied from authorial $\alpha$, perhaps shortly after composition. There is nothing in the contents of the sonnets that lends itself to dating. Joan Grundy's contention that the "extreme Catholicism" of the sonnets "suggests that they are the work of an experienced worshipper in that religion rather than of a recent convert" seems ungrounded.[16] William Alabaster's Catholic sonnets were written right after his conversion in 1597, which supports Helen Wilcox's assertion that "the primary function of his writing was to confirm his new-found faith and take personal delight in it."[17] Moreover, Michael Questier provides evidence that steadfast Protestants converted into zealous Catholics.[18] Therefore, the supposed intensity of religious expression cannot help establish the date of composition.

Whether Constable showed the sonnets to his coreligionists abroad is a mystery, but the collection in *HA* could have been copied for that purpose. It is known that during the first years of exile he interacted with other Catholics and became a valuable member of the community in Paris.[19] However, there is no mention of poems in his surviving letters to friends and kinsmen back home, and sending them to England would have been a rather dangerous move – although not a greater risk than others he would take later on. The collection of *SS* was expanded through the addition of four sonnets and reorganised, and *BE* is a fair copy of the later authorial manuscript, $\beta$, and reflects the sequence at its final and perfected stage. Its dating is even more uncertain, but it made its way to England upon Constable's return from exile and was possibly copied within the circle of Elizabeth Berkeley, a member of Queen Anne's entourage, so 1603 could at least be the terminus ad quem.

## The Misattributed Sonnet

One sonnet by Constable dedicated to the Virgin Mary, "In that, Oh Queene of Queens, thy birth was free" (71), was misattributed to John Donne in numerous verse miscellanies and collections of Donne's poetry and made its way into the 1635 edition of his collected *Poems* (henceforth *DP*). This attribution of a "militantly Catholic sonnet" to Donne, Eckhardt states, complicated "Donne's religious politics" further, but was not questioned by collec-

---

16. Grundy, 59.
17. Helen Wilcox, "Sacred Desire, Forms of Belief: The Religious Sonnet in Early Modern Britain," in *The Cambridge Companion to the Sonnet*, ed. A.D. Cousins and Peter Howarth (Cambridge, 2011), 145–165, at 151.
18. Michael C. Questier, *Conversion, Politics, and Religion in England, 1580–1625* (Cambridge, 1996), 79–81.
19. See above, p. 22.

tors of his poems.[20] The relative privacy and lack of circulation of Constable's *SS*, clearly ascribed to him, prolonged this misattribution until the late nineteenth century.[21]

The identity of the person who first removed Constable's sonnet from its original context and copied it separately is unknown, but it was transcribed along with Donne's poetry; in some cases, it followed a number of his religious sonnets, which made it look as if this sonnet were the last item by him.[22] The sonnet was consistently given the heading "On the blessed Virgin Mary." The printer of *DP*, John Marriot, used the O'Flahertie manuscript to expand the first 1633 edition into the second.[23] He printed Constable's sonnet on page 342, after the sixteenth and final sonnet in the group of Donne's "Holy Sonnets," and preceding other poems not written in the sonnet form, starting with "The Crosse."

Although he shifted towards Anglicanism, Donne was deeply influenced by his Catholic background, and remnants of his former faith often colour his religious poetry. Robert S. Miola underlines the residual Marian devotion in "The Litanie," "La Corona," and "Good Friday, 1613. Riding Westward," stating that "the poet reveals a devotion to Mary that the preacher denied, though Dr Donne hung pictures of the Virgin in his deanery."[24] The fifth poem in "The Litanie" is dedicated to the Virgin. The first four lines are confrontational enough in that they emphasise her agency in divine redemption – by giving birth to Christ – and hint at her Immaculate Conception:

For that fair blessed mother-maid –
Whose flesh redeemed us; that she-cherubin
Which unlocked Paradise, and made
One claim for innocence, and disseised sin ... .[25]

---

20. Joshua Eckhardt, "Publication," in *A Handbook of English Renaissance Literary Studies*, ed. John Lee (Hoboken, 2017), 295–307, at 296. Eckhardt provides a detailed history of this misattribution.

21. Interestingly, misattribution continued well past the publication of the *HA* sonnets in Park's *Heliconia*.

22. This is the case in Cambridge, MA, Harvard University, Houghton MS Eng 966.6, dated 1620. The copies of this sonnet are numbered as items CoH 101, 102, and 104–110 in *CELM*.

23. This is Cambridge, MA, Harvard University, Houghton MS Eng 966.5.

24. Robert S. Miola, ed., *Early Modern Catholicism: An Anthology of Primary Sources* (Oxford, 2007), 217.

25. John Donne, *The Complete Poems*, ed. Robin Robbins (Edinburgh, 2010), 501.

The latter belief features even more prominently in the sonnet "The Annunciation" within "La Corona," in which the poet muses on Christ in the Virgin's womb: "Lo, faithful Virgin, yields himsef to lie / In prison, in thy womb; and, though he there / Can take no sin, nor thou give ... " (5–7).[26] The implication is that the Virgin, born without sin, could not have passed it on to the Child.

Considering the above, it is not all that surprising that a compiler would have made a connection between Constable's sonnet and Donne's. In Constable's, the poet also alludes to the Virgin as the mother of God and emphasises the purity of her womb. An important alteration was made to his text, however, which replaced the too-explicit reference to the Immaculate Conception with a subtler one. In *DP*, the beginning of the sonnet reads: "In that, ô Queene of Queenes, thy birth was free / From that which others doth of grace beareave / When in their mothers wombe they life receive." The ambiguous "that" replaces the original reading "guilt."[27] The revision was probably a conscious act of censorship performed by an overanxious Protestant reader who was squeamish about such a militantly Catholic statement. There are other variants worth mentioning. *DP* has "earthly things" (10) instead of "worldly thinges," the *HA* and *BE* reading. This is possibly an error of repetition made during the manuscript transmission of the sonnet given that the same word appears in line 9 ("earthly Crownes") immediately above. A more blatant error is the change of the original "thy spowse" (6) into "his spouse" in *DP*, which destroys the connection between the Holy Spirit and Mary.[28]

---

26. Ibid., 479.
27. This variant is shared with the manuscript versions I have been able to see, which suggests a scribal tradition that was intentionally de-Catholicised.
28. Some manuscript copies do bear the correct possessive.

CHAPTER FOUR

# Henry Constable and the Sonnet Form

Henry Constable made a significant contribution to two different traditions. On one hand, he wrote one of the first amatory sonnet sequences in English, incorporating Continental and national influences and displaying a keen awareness of elite tastes.[1] His collection was, together with Samuel Daniel's, the second to be published after Sir Philip Sidney's *Astrophil and Stella*, but – despite its popularity – a great part of his output remained circumscribed to the manuscript medium, circulating within networks of kinship, friendship, and prospective patronage. In these secular sonnets Petrarchan and Neoplatonic conceits are elegantly reworked or even made to push against the limits of convention in order to praise the addressee and voice the unhappy lover's plight. On the other hand, his *Spiritual Sonnets*, which were never printed and must have been read by a select few, rank among the finest examples of devotional poetry, or sacred parodies, in the late sixteenth century and have attracted even greater critical interest over the last three decades.

Constable's life-changing conversion to Catholicism, which was complete by 1590; the fact that the secular and the religious sonnets never shared physical space; and the unavoidable use of the terms "secular" and "religious" to categorise them may appear to establish a deep divide in his poetic production. Despite the change in subject matter and addressees, however, a clear-cut separation does not hold, and it is possible to analyse all of Constable's poems in terms of the constant struggle and tensions voiced in them, and the worldly and the sacred as inherently permeable categories. First, the sonnet is the locus where the poet-lover, or poet-devotee, negotiates desire – be it erotic or spiritual love. When this profession of love expects reward, the language of suit and recompense comes into play, with patronage and protection as the desired outcome of a dedicatory sonnet, and intercession or salvation that of a religious piece. Even as religious imagery is deployed in the construction of amatory conceits, sometimes with unsettling effects, the *Spiritual Sonnets* are much rifer with erotic lan-

---

1. On the use of the word "sequence" to describe his sonnet collections, see p. 33.

guage than the secular could ever be.[2] The private and the public seem to be perennially at odds; the poet constantly searches for the true faith that might guarantee his salvation, but even in the religious sonnets he does not lose sight of the world: these poems are informed by the poet's circumstances as an exile and his change of allegiances, his purported abandonment of worldly affairs but the sublimation of a strong desire to be welcomed back home.

## Sonnet Forms

The most obvious connection between the two groups of Constable's poems is, of course, the use of the sonnet form. Its Italian origin and popularisation in England in the sixteenth century need little commentary.[3] By the time Constable and his contemporaries were writing, form and genre were closely bound together, so that the choice of the former carried expectations about theme, and the sonnet was predominantly associated with romantic love.[4] Nevertheless, the "conflict between reason and desire" was "a theme capacious enough to embrace political, professional, and philosophical as well as erotic desires."[5] It is no wonder that love and ambition should interweave especially during the reign of a female monarch – mostly unattainable, except for a select few, with an elaborate network comprised of favourites and their supplicants, all of them vying for attention. Sonnets were exchanged as gifts, some heartfelt, most seeking protection or patronage in return.[6]

Besides the fact that the sonnet was an eminently social lyric form, meant to be read aloud or sung in the company of others, and thus suited Constable's purposes as a gentleman-writer, his choice evidences a willingness to partake in a literary trend that was not natively English but European, sustained by the finest

2. Hackett has termed this phenomenon "a continuing cross-fertilisation." See Helen Hackett, *Virgin Mother, Maiden Queen: Elizabeth I and the Cult of the Virgin Mary* (Basingstoke, 1995), 15.

3. See for instance Michael R.G. Spiller, *The Development of the Sonnet: An Introduction* (London, 1992).

4. See Gary Stringer, "Some Sacred and Profane Con-Texts of John Donne's 'Batter my hart,'" in *Sacred and Profane: Secular and Devotional Interplay in Early Modern British Literature*, ed. Helen Wilcox et al. (Amsterdam, 1996), 173–183, at 174.

5. Diana E. Henderson, "The Sonnet, Subjectivity and Gender," in *The Cambridge Companion to the Sonnet*, ed. A. D. Cousins and Peter Howarth (Cambridge, 2011), 46–65, at 48.

6. On Elizabeth I as the focus of courtly literature, see for instance Catherine Bates, *The Rhetoric of Courtship in Elizabethan Language and Literature* (Cambridge, 1992); Ilona Bell, *Elizabeth I: The Voice of a Monarch* (New York, 2010), 19–25.

lyric poets in every country. The education that made Constable qualify as an agent abroad included several languages; he was fluent enough in French to engage in prose writing and correspondence, and he almost certainly knew Latin and Italian; therefore, he was receptive to Continental influences. The imprint of Petrarch and his followers can be traced at specific points throughout the collection, but it is the French sonneteers, and especially Philippe Desportes (1546–1606), to whom Constable is most indebted.[7]

From the vernacular tradition, the impact of Sir Philip Sidney's *Astrophil and Stella*, which Constable read in manuscript, cannot be stressed enough. Constable reworks conceits and borrows images liberally, although no single sonnet can be said to be a close imitation of one of Sidney's. For instance, the theme of the concerned friend in "A friend of myne, moaning my helplesse love" (20) is clearly influenced by Sidney, *A&S* 21, "Your words, my friend, right healthful caustics, blame," but both differ in their development.[8] From Sidney he may have borrowed his favoured rhyme pattern: an Italian octave with two rhymes only and *rima chiusa* (ABBA ABBA), followed by a sestet in varying arrangements which often, but not always, ends with a couplet (EE).[9] Constable also adopted one of Sidney's metrical innovations by writing four sonnets in hexameters or alexandrines (9, 19, 37, 54), which must have been influenced by the six in *A&S*.[10] Constable did not write in the English, or Shakespearean, sonnet form, which is not found in *A&S* either.[11] If Sidney's sonnets were the benchmark by which subsequent sonnet collections were judged, Constable was among his first disciples, and his own sonnets became a model for the sonneteers that followed – Michael Drayton, Barnabe Barnes, and Bartholomew Griffin, among others.

For a poet concerned with formal correctness and order, the sonnet was a ready-made form, with a specific duration and structure, which, Michael R.G.

---

7. Many Italian and, especially, French parallels are identified in Scott, *Sonnets*, and the commentary section in Grundy. Concerning Desportes, Constable must have been familiar with the 1583 edition of *Les premieres oeuvres*, given that he borrows not only from the *Diane* but also from *Cleonice*, a later sequence, among others. On the different editions of Desportes's poetry, see François Rouget, "Philippe Desportes et la logique des recueils poétiques," *Réforme, Humanisme, Renaissance* 62 (2006): 97–108. Parallels and borrowings traced in the commentary to this edition help situate Constable in the pan-European sonneteering tradition.

8. Unless otherwise stated, quotations from *Astrophil and Stella* are from Sir Philip Sidney, *The Major Works*, ed. Katherine Duncan-Jones (New York, 2008).

9. The most recurrent pattern in Constable's sonnets is ABBA ABBA CDCDEE, used in 60 out of the 108 sonnets of Sidney, *A&S*.

10. See Sidney, *Major Works*, 357 n153.

11. Sidney did write a number of English sonnets found elsewhere; see *The Poems of Sir Philip Sidney*, ed. William A. Ringler (Oxford, 1962), 571.

Spiller notes, solved "two problems: proportion and extension."[12] It also conveyed a sense of immediacy, of *now*, with the speaker expressing a present grievance or desire rather than recounting past events.[13] The present tense made it possible to describe events and reactions as if they were unfolding before the reader's eyes. Concerning Constable's development of conceits, Joan Grundy emphasised his "love of analysis and classification" which leads him to break "every image ... into its logical parts; each image becomes a theme for him, and the poem is created by means of amplification and division, and owes more even to the methods of dialectic than to those of rhetoric."[14] A good example of this is sonnet 60, in which the seven deadly sins attributed to the poet's "eye" are analysed one by one in an enumeration leading to the conclusion – the punishment of the poet's heart – which seems logical considering the carefully expounded evidence. Grundy assessed the poems as conventional "confections" devoid of "emotional validity";[15] yet Constable engaged with convention knowingly, manipulating commonplaces – fire and water, Cupid's darts, mirrors, gloves – to achieve his aims as a gentleman writing occasional poetry in a patronage-seeking milieu rather than to express any authentic – by contemporary standards – emotion.[16]

The sonnets also contain some instances of what may be termed metasonneteering, for example in his praise of fellow writers who wrote in the sonnet form. To the Italian poet Vittoria Colonna he writes: "Shall not all poets prayse thy memorie? / And to thy name shall not theyre workes give fame, / Whereas theyre workes be sweetned by thy name?" (51.10–12). The sonnet is the most suitable form to respond to Colonna's poetry. The same happens when Constable feels compelled to offer a response poem to King James. The heading to sonnet 28 begins "To the K. of Scots upon occasion of a sonnet the K. wrote ... ." Beneath the conventional praise bestowed on James and his new bride, this sonnet and its companion (29) are meant to show off Constable's newly gained familiarity with the king, which had allowed him to read James's poems in manuscript and advertise himself as a fellow sonnet writer, skilled enough to join his literary coterie.[17] Con-

---

12. Spiller, *Development of the Sonnet*, 2.
13. Ibid., 5; Catherine Bates, "Desire, Discontent, Parody: The Love Sonnet in Early Modern England," in *Companion to the Sonnet*, 105–124, at 111.
14. Grundy, 73.
15. Ibid., 71.
16. A few sonnets, in particular those to his later mistress, Grace, seem moved by more personal circumstances, which nevertheless can only be hypothesised
17. Marotti states that "answer" verse "foregrounds the social and occasional character of poetic composition, marking poetic discourse less as the product of isolated artistic geniuses than as continuous with other forms of communication." This applies to Constable's perceptions of sonnet writing. See Arthur F. Marotti, *Manuscript, Print, and the English Renaissance Lyric* (Ithaca, NY, 1995), 159–160.

stable also alludes to his own sonnet writing throughout the sequence, for instance in references to his verse attesting to his mistress's beauty (21, 35, 61) or granting her immortality: "But joy in this (though Fates gainst mee repine): / My verse still lives to witnes thee divine" (66.13–14). The word "pen" is a metonym for writing, most often his own, as in sonnets 15, 25, and 62. The renunciation of secular love in 62, titled "Conclusion of the whole," is made all the more dramatic by the declaration that he will stop writing: "Sometymes in verse I prays'd, sometymes I sigh'd; / No more shall pen with love nor beautie mell" (1–2). The sonnet is, therefore, the perfect poetic form to discuss writing, in particular writing within an established tradition.[18]

## Troubling Imagery

In the secular sonnets the poet deploys a wide range of imagery from the natural world (as in 16 and 22), hunting (18), navigation (6), astrology (42, 55), and other semantic fields.[19] Some other elements might have proven a little more disturbing for the Protestant reader and serve as an example that images and beliefs from the Catholic tradition remained part of the "standard furniture of erotic writing" even after they had been declared void within the new Anglican settlement.[20] References to miracles, relics, witchcraft, and images are used to voice a desire to touch the untouchable lady or submit her will to the poet's own. Constable shows an interest in the physicality of holy objects, for example in sonnet 19, which features the notion that adoration must be performed through an image.[21] The poet claims that the lady's "image" should be celebrated; she is the only goddess whom he can "withoute idolatrye adore" (13–14). In sonnet 12 the

---

18. The first sonnet in Sidney, A&S, "Loving in truth, and fain in verse my love to show," is a famous example.

19. A useful monograph on the conceits employed by the sonneteers which refers to Constable throughout is Lisle Cecil John, *The Elizabethan Sonnet Sequences: Studies in Conventional Conceits* (New York, 1966). John quotes from the 1594 *Diana* edition.

20. Helen Hackett, "The Art of Blasphemy? Interfusions of the Erotic and the Sacred in the Poetry of Donne, Barnes, and Constable," *Renaissance and Reformation* 28, no. 3 (2004), 27–53, at 32. Williamson has explored how some religious objects survived, for instance, in drama: the companies took advantage "of audience members' residual interest in the materiality of religion." Elizabeth Williamson, *The Materiality of Religion in Early Modern English Drama* (Farnham, 2009), 5.

21. On the Christian tradition of contact relics, see Christopher Woolgar, "What Makes Things Holy? The Senses and Material Culture in the Later Middle Ages," in *Sensing the Sacred in Medieval and Early Modern Culture*, ed. Robin Macdonald et al. (London, 2018), 60–78.

poet longs to kiss the lady's relic-like hands, lips, and breast, which "worke miracles" as she plays music and sings, and in 17 he fulfils the idolatrous act by envisioning himself kissing her glove, which conceals the hand that has shot the arrows of love and made him bear stigmata in his heart. Worship of relics was demonized by reformers, who assimilated them to "occult practice."[22] In sonnet 7, the poet bears a painting in his heart that is both an instrument of witchcraft and a devotional image, responsible for his suffering but also for the wished-for triumph of his love over the lady.[23]

Excessive love and worship of the goddess-like lady is connected with anxious evocations of religious persecution and related punishments. In the early version of sonnet 15 (15b in the present edition) the poet is accused of heresy and fears that his heart might be liable to death by burning because it is "obstinate" (8) and will not recant its worship of the lady. The unmissable allusion to the burning of Protestant martyrs at the stake during the reign of Mary Tudor was later excised, yielding a more innocuous sonnet of praise.[24] In other sonnets, as Hackett has pointed out, the "imagery ... resonates unsettlingly with the state punishment of Catholicism."[25] In sonnet 50, the poet imagines himself as being subjected to torture at the rack so that he will renounce his love, eventually choosing to remain steadfast and "dye" (14) instead of recanting.[26]

"Exile" is depicted as the only way to alleviate the torments brought about by the lady's rejection in sonnet 59, although death is inevitable. A vivid image of the condemned man's state of mind is painted, and he makes the decision to go away in order not to see her so that he "might take death more patientlye, / Like him

22. Katherine Rowe, *Dead Hands: Fictions of Agency, Renaissance to Modern* (Stanford, 1999), 101.

23. The conceit is built on contemporary beliefs in picture magic as a means of having a physical effect on people's bodies. See Christina Hole, "Some Instances of Image-Magic in Great Britain," in *The Witch Figure: Folklore Essays by a Group of Scholars in England Honouring the 75th Birthday of Katharine M. Briggs*, ed. Venetia Newall (London, 1973), 80–94.

24. An early, extended discussion on the revision of this sonnet is María Jesús Pérez-Jáuregui, "Burning the Heretic: Conscientious Revision in Henry Constable's 'Falslie Doth Enuie of Youre Praises Blame,'" *English Studies* 93 (2012), 897–910.

25. Hackett, "The Art of Blasphemy?" 42.

26. In a contemporary ballad, "Calvarie mount is my delight," a Catholic speaker rejoices in the tortures he will endure for his faith, with similar evocations of the rack. London, British Library, Add MS 15225, fols. 2v–3r, transcribed from Hyder E. Rollins, ed., *Old English Ballads 1553–1625* (Cambridge, 1920), 149–151, with an emendation by Marotti; see Arthur F. Marotti, "Manuscript Transmission and the Catholic Martyrdom Account in Early Modern England," in *Print, Manuscript & Performance: The Changing Relations of the Media in Early Modern England*, ed. Arthur F. Marotti and Michael D. Bristol (Columbus, 2000), 172–199, at 173.

which by the judge condemn'd to dye, / To suffer with lesse feare his eyes doth blinde" (6-8). These lines take on a new layer of meaning when viewed in the context of a process of religious conversion which could bring disastrous consequences for Constable as a newly converted Catholic – punishment or death only avoidable by literal self-exile. Intriguingly, none of this fear of worldly punishment and execution seeped into the SS.[27]

## Secular to Sacred

In writing the SS, Constable carried through the intentions expressed in sonnet 62 and the prose colophon to the T sequence, letting his "follie" die so that he could employ his wit "to other calmer thoughts." When he chose the sonnet form to voice his spiritual preoccupations, he was in fact joining an existing trend. Henderson traces Dante's and Petrarch's leap from fleshly to spiritual yearning after the death of their beloved Beatrice and Laura: "Dying young, they were useful to the poets as means to express the passionate struggle of life in the body and the attempted sublimation of carnal love into Christian spirituality, leading from the lady to the Lord."[28]

The spiritual sonnet can be considered a subgenre in its own right; among the first poets to engage in it were Italian churchmen Pietro Bembo and Girolamo Malipiero, the latter of whom notoriously expurgated Petrarch's collection to suit religious purposes.[29] Vittoria Colonna's *Rime*, first published in 1538, adopted the title *Rime spirituali* from 1546 and were avidly read by Constable.[30] The popularity of these Italian works, Virginia Cox notes, "vastly increased during the Counter-Reformation, rising to a peak after around 1580."[31] Among French poets who wrote religious sonnets, Constable would have been familiar with Joachim Du Bellay's thirteen "Sonnets de l'honneste amour" and

---

27. The only poetic indication that Constable may have felt any fear for his life or freedom after converting is given at the end of a sonnet written by an anonymous friend beseeching the poet to return from exile (see appendix A).

28. Henderson, "The Sonnet," 47.

29. Girolamo Malipiero, *Il Petrarca spirituale* (Venice, 1536).

30. On Bembo, Colonna, and other poets who advanced a Reformed spirituality in the sixteenth century, see Abigail Brundin, *Vittoria Colonna and the Spiritual Poetics of the Italian Reformation* (Aldershot, 2008). Although Constable's religious poetry is markedly Catholic, reading Colonna during his Protestant youth had a lasting impact on him.

31. Virginia Cox, *Lyric Poetry by Women of the Italian Renaissance* (Baltimore, 2013), 30.

Desportes's *Sonnets spirituels*; the latter began to appear in the 1575 edition of his works and were gradually expanded until 1598.[32] The fact that the title *Spiritual Sonnets* looks like a literal translation of Desportes is misleading – Constable's religious sonnets owe more to the Italians than to the French.[33] Guillaume de Salluste Du Bartas's poem "L'Uranie" was well-known to Elizabethan authors; in it, the muse bids the poet turn his poetic gift away from secular, and thus sinful, poetry, and towards God.[34]

George Herbert, born around the time Constable's SS were written, complained about the use of the sonnet to deal with profane love only in an address to God: "... Doth Poetry / Wear *Venus* Livery? only serve her turn? / Why are not *Sonnets* made of thee?"[35] Yet there had been English writers who imbued the sonnet form with religious themes and language since 1560, when a sequence titled "A Meditation of a Penitent Sinner," long attributed to Anne Lok, was printed.[36] There had also been voices calling for that shift. Sir Philip Sidney expresses a renunciation of secular love and an intention to focus on the divine only in the last two *Certain Sonnets*, probably written between 1577 and 1581. Number 32 begins, "Leave me, O love which reachest but to dust, / And thou, my mind, aspire to higher things." His farewell comes at the very end: "Then farewell, world; thy uttermost I see; / Eternal love, maintain thy life in me."[37]

On the Catholic front, Robert Southwell sanctioned the use of poetry for religious purposes only: "The vanitie of men, cannot counterpoyse the authoritie of God, who delivering many parts of Scripture in verse, and by his Apostle

32. Joachim Du Bellay, *Les oeuvres* (Paris, 1552); Philippe Desportes, *Les premieres oeuvres* (Paris, 1575). See Guillaume Coatalen, "An English Translation of Desportes' Christian Sonnets Presented to John Scudamour by Edward Ski[...]," *The Review of English Studies* 65 (2014): 619–646.

33. Wickes and Grundy add the names of Erasmo da Valvasone, Torquato Tasso, Angelo Grillo, Ferrante Carrafa, and Girolamo Casio de Medici to the roster of Italian Counter-Reformation writers of *rime spirituali*; however, Grundy's warning that "we cannot point to any definite model" for Constable's SS is worth bearing in mind. See Wickes, *Sonnets*, 35–36; Grundy, 78–79.

34. See Alison Shell, *Catholicism, Controversy, and the English Literary Imagination, 1558–1660* (Cambridge, 1999), 65–66.

35. *The English Poems of George Herbert*, ed. Helen Wilcox (Cambridge, 2007), 4.

36. The sonnets are included in the *Sermons of John Calvin* (London, 1560). Lok's authorship has now been disproved by May, who attributes them to Thomas Norton; see Steven W. May, "Anne Lock and Thomas Norton's *Meditation of a Penitent Sinner*," *Modern Philology* 114 (2017): 793–819.

37. Sidney, *Major Works*, 38. In *The Defence of Poesy*, Sidney had voiced the idea that the "lyrical kind of songs and sonnets" should be employed "in singing the praises of the immortal beauty." See ibid., 246.

willing us to exercise our devotion in Himnes and spirituall Sonnets, warranteth the Arte to bee good, and the use allowable."[38] His own and others' reworkings of Elizabethan love lyric forms to this purpose have been termed sacred parodies.[39]

Out of the poets who wrote religious sonnets in the late Elizabethan period, which would include Barnabe Barnes, Henry Lok, Nicholas Breton, William Alabaster, and Sir Tobie Matthew, the latter two wrote Catholic compositions; Alabaster mostly focuses on repentance and the figure of Christ, whereas Matthew addresses a number of saints.[40] Confessional distinctions can be misleading, however, as Protestant and Catholic verse may draw on the same scriptural material and share other features. For example, Joseph B. Collins grouped Barnes, Constable, and Lok under the label "mystical sonneteers" because they employed the sonnet form "not only in a religious vein, but also definitely in the spirit of Christian mysticism."[41]

Helen Wilcox characterises the religious sonnet as being "an exchange between speaker, listener, reader, and God."[42] In terms of form, poets realised the sonnet's potential to create the effect "of holding the words firmly in place" – by means of locked rhymes in the Italian sonnet form – as the conceit moves from "an arresting opening" to a "strong ending."[43] This is true of Constable's sonnets, the best of which also feature a combination of introspection and apostrophe, emphasising the poet's own plight and reaching out for grace, help, or intercession. In the sonnet to St Margaret (77) the shift happens within a tercet in which the poet compares his soul, trapped in a body assailed by passions, to the legendary dragon that swallowed the saint: "Behoulde my soule shutt in my bod-

---

38. Robert Southwell, *Saint Peters complainte* (London, 1620), sigs. A3v–A4r.

39. See Louis L. Martz, *The Poetry of Meditation: A Study in English Religious Literature of the Seventeenth Century* (New Haven, 1962), 184–193.

40. See *The Sonnets of William Alabaster*, ed. George M. Story and Helen Gardner (Oxford, 1959); *Unpublished Works by William Alabaster* (1568–1640), ed. Dana F. Sutton (Salzburg, 1997); Arthur F. Marotti, *Religious Ideology and Cultural Fantasy: Catholic and Anti-Catholic Discourses in Early Modern England* (Notre Dame, IN, 2005), 98–109. Matthew's sonnets are printed in Anthony G. Petti, "Unknown Sonnets by Sir Toby Matthew," *Recusant History* 9 (1967): 123–158. Cousins contrasts the sonnets by Constable and Alabaster as "related in style to the devotional literary traditions of the Counter-Reformation." See Anthony D. Cousins, *The Catholic Religious Poets from Southwell to Crashaw: A Critical History* (London, 1991), 72–101.

41. Joseph B. Collins, *Christian Mysticism in the Elizabethan Age with Its Background in Mystical Methodology* (Baltimore, 1940), 137.

42. Helen Wilcox, "Sacred Desire, Forms of Belief: The Religious Sonnet in Early Modern Britain," in *The Cambridge Companion to the Sonnet*, 145–165, at 149.

43. Ibid., 149–150.

ies Jayle, / the which the Drake of hell gapes to devoure, / teache me, oh virgin, howe thou did'st prevayle" (9–11).

The metrical patterns employed in the *SS* create a sense of formal continuity. Eleven of them have an Italian octave followed by a sestet ending in a couplet (EE), whereas the remaining ten have a sestet in different configurations – a common one being CDCEDE. The last sonnet (87) contains a metrical innovation: the octave is ABABBABA, a palindromic structure found in Sidney's sonnets as well. This formal departure is perhaps intended to signal the conclusion of the sequence. Unlike in the secular collection, there are no sonnets in alexandrines. Regarding style, the religious sonnet has often been contrasted with the secular in terms of simplicity versus excess. Barnes, who, like Constable, wrote both a secular and a religious sequence, advertised the latter as being "voyde of all colourable varnish."[44] Constable's rhetorical adroitness for parallelism and metaphor combines with the religious plain style that seeks to convey spiritual truth to its audience through "a conversational immediacy of tone and informality of rhythm, a pellucid diction, a virtual lack of ornament (in the guise of the figures of speech) and ... a use of metaphor to crystallize meaning rather than to beautify."[45] This plainness is most evident in the sonnets meditating upon particular biblical passages, as in sonnet 74 to St Peter and St Paul.

The *SS* have been discussed by Gary Kuchar as influenced by affective piety and as proof of the poet's receptiveness to both elements of late-medieval devotion – such as the mystical experience – and Counter-Reformation ideas or devotional modes, of which he performs a "unique synthesis."[46] It was perhaps the use of affective language that led Grundy to voice her astonishment in the introduction to her edition: "What is surprising, after the coldness of the love-sonnets, is the passion of the more personal poems and the imagery chosen to express that passion." She considers the *SS* proto-Metaphysical in their "union of intellect and emotion."[47] George Wickes agrees on their having an "air of sincerity," which according to him "is rare in the secular sonnets."[48] Viewed as prayers or conversations with God and the saints, and considering their reduced audience, there is a sense of privacy in the *Spiritual Sonnets* that is missing from Constable's earlier works – with an important caveat: the outside world is never shunned completely.

---

44. Barnes, *Divine Centurie*, sig. A2v.
45. Cousins, *Catholic Religious Poets*, 8.
46. Gary Kuchar, "Henry Constable and the Question of Catholic Poetics: Affective Piety and Erotic Identification in the Spirituall Sonnettes," *Philological Quarterly* 85 (2006): 69–90, at 70.
47. Grundy, 81, 83.
48. Wickes, *Sonnets*, 33.

In the *SS*, the poet enacts a rejection not only of earthly love and his former mistresses but also of his former career and the personages that he used to honour in writing, commenting on his past on the fringes of the Elizabethan court and the pointlessness of his expectations of material reward and advancement. However, the convert's world continues to be hierarchically organised. The ordinary man is forced to look upwards at the new patron or patroness who may help him achieve the sought-after reward – i.e., salvation – just like the young esquire with a promising future depended on the protection of others. Therefore, he continues to use a rhetoric of suit and recompense, and addresses members of the English and the heavenly court in strikingly similar terms.[49] Donne's commentary on the connection between a person's real-life experience and the terms in which he or she addresses God seems on point:

> As the Prophetts and other Secretaries of the holie Ghost in penning the bookes of scriptures, doe for the most part reteine and express in their wrytings, some ympressions and some ayre of their former professions; Those that had bien bred in courts and Cities ... ever incerting into their wrytings, some phrases, some metaphors, some allusions, taken from that profession which they had exercyzed before.[50]

Michael C. Schoenfeldt uses the term "poetry of supplication" to refer to Donne's and Herbert's poetry, which is informed by an individual's perceptions of a social self and social relationships "as a vehicle for representing his relationship with the divine."[51] This term certainly applies to Constable's religious sonnets as well. In one of his sonnets to the Virgin (80), Constable articulates the reasons why a male courtier may write in praise of a noble lady, looking back on his former quest for patronage from a new perspective and playing on the political and courtly implications of the word "love."[52] One is "favour past" which "a thanckfull love should breede" (2), another is the lady's "wourthe and dignitie" (5), and the last is "hoope of future meede" (7). Upon this enumeration he builds his argument that only the Virgin deserves to be loved, as she provides all three reasons.

49. See Wickes, *Sonnets*, 40.
50. See *The Oxford Edition of the Sermons of John Donne*, vol. 1: *Sermons Preached at the Jacobean Courts, 1615–19*, ed. Peter McCullough (Oxford, 2015), 43.
51. Michael C. Schoenfeldt, "The Poetry of Supplication: Toward a Cultural Poetics of the Religious Lyric," in *New Perspectives on the Seventeenth-Century English Religious Lyric*, ed. John R. Roberts (Columbia, 1994), 75–104, at 85.
52. See Arthur Marotti, "'Love is Not Love': Elizabethan Sonnet Sequences and the Social Order," *English Literary History* 49 (1982): 396–428, at 398.

The other inhabitants of the heavenly court prove superior to their earthly counterparts: "for knightes and Dames, Martirs & virgins stande" (87.11). St Michael the Archangel is presented as the epitome of knighthood and chivalry (72). The "Dames" replace his former female addressees, chosen either because of their connection to the circle of the earl of Leicester, Sir Philip Sidney, and Robert Devereux, earl of Essex, or due to family links. In 76 St Catherine is "the Daughter of A kinge," praised for her wisdom, effectively replacing Arbella Stuart as a lady-scholar.[53] St Margaret is a "fayre Amazon" who suffered under a tyrant and defeated a dragon. It is she whom the poet asks for help in abandoning his earthly passions and obtaining "puritie" in sonnet 77. All in all, the martyrs and virgins of the sequence might grant the poet a favour that far surpasses that bestowed by former patrons: sympathy, intercession, and inspiration to lead a better life.

Different forms of love have an effect on the poet's body and soul. Worldly love causes the usual symptoms of tears, sighs, and sleeplessness, plus physical frustration – as the object of desire is unattainable. In sonnet 2, his sighs are a "sacrifice" in her honour. He makes constant allusions to his tears: the "flowing streames" of his eyes (4.14) shed so much water that it could form "an Ocean sea" (28.5); his eyes are also described as gluttonous, "with teares drunke every night" (60.11), and they are sentenced to death by drowning (58.14). He counts himself among the men who cry out of love for Queen Elizabeth (23); and he is the plaintive mourner who weeps and disrupts Sidney's eternal rest with his "bold cryes" in sonnet 52.[54] Concerning desire, the poet fantasises with the undressed lady after she retires to bed, and he cannot get rid of "the suns heate" even at night (22.12–14). Her naked body is endowed with power, envisioned as capable of subduing men (13.12–14). In 46 he playfully asks the lady for a kiss in vain. Despite the discomfort and despair – so extreme that it is frequently compared to death, as in 59 – the presence of the lady has an uplifting effect on the poet's soul. In sonnet 8, in pure Neoplatonic fashion, his soul rises through contemplation of the divine as reflected in the lady, and he feels driven to renounce erotic love (5–8).

The wish for spiritual upliftment is at the core of the *SS*; the purifying love of divinity is found, for instance, in the sonnet "To God the holy Ghoste" (69), in which the poet's soul longs to be inflamed with His "fyre" and to fly with His

---

53. In sonnet 34, young Arbella's "learning" is emphasised as her most outstanding virtue. In the colophon sonnet in *T* (63), the whole sonnet sequence is rededicated to her – as a potential candidate to the throne – in an explicit appeal for patronage.

54. In other sonnets it is the weeping lady that is evoked; in sonnet 47, for instance, the poet imagines her crying for him.

"winges," becoming an angel-like figure capable of leaving "earthes desire" behind (11–14). Images of ascent ultimately leading to the divine presence recur throughout the sequence.[55] Spiritual love is also presented as physically fulfilling using the affective-erotic language Constable borrows from St Bernard's exegesis of the Song of Songs.[56] Male desire for a female being is transformed into the desire of the female soul for a male God, and this transgender identification follows one of the interpretations for the biblical bride, the perfected soul ready to be married to Christ.[57] In turn, the beloved is given an active role and, unlike the unresponsive, indifferent lady, is all loving and capable of reciprocating affection; God is able to "embrace and kisse" the poet's "enamo'rd soule" (81.10–11). Bernard establishes an analogy between the description of carnal union and mystical union;[58] and Constable, in the same vein, uses erotic imagery to express the religious experiences of his soul, often with shocking explicitness, as when he imagines the "new delightes" that will overrun his soul, heart, and body "to ev'y parte" in sonnet 81.[59] Other images related to human love persist in the religious sonnets in order to clarify meaning and situate this love "as an attractive, infinitely inferior, type of the divine."[60] The courtly idea of the joining of the souls is used to explain the nature of the Trinity and the origin of the Holy Ghost as a result of the perfect union or "kisse" of Father and Son in sonnets 67 and 69. Far removed from the hellish pains of unrequited earthly passion, divine love arises as the most rewarding type, transcending human experience.

55. Gary Kuchar discusses this process of "spiritual ascension," sometimes achieved through contemplation of the Virgin's beauty. See Kuchar, "Henry Constable," 80.

56. See Bernard of Clairvaux, *On The Song of Songs I*, trans. Kilian J. Walsh (Kalamazoo, 1971).

57. Bynum explains the devotee's adoption of the "marked category" of the female as a token of humility and conversion; see Caroline W. Bynum, "'... And Woman His Humanity': Female Imagery in the Religious Writing of the Later Middle Ages," in *Gender and Religion: On the Complexity of Symbols*, ed. Caroline Walker Bynum et al. (Boston, 1986), 257–288, at 273, 269. Cousins discusses the poetic persona's depiction of himself as an "androgyne ... in order to distinguish his spirituality from his gender, to suggest the otherness of the soul." See Cousins, *Catholic Religious Poets*, 83.

58. James Wimsatt, "St. Bernard, the Canticle of Canticles, and Mystical Poetry," in *An Introduction to the Medieval Mystics*, ed. Paul E. Szarmach (Albany, NY, 1984), 77–96, at 80.

59. The comparison between sexual appetite and spiritual longing was exploited by contemporaries such as John Donne. See Donne, *Sermons*, 43. See also Richard Rambuss, *Closet Devotions* (Durham, NC, 1998), 97–98. Although his focus is 17th-century "metaphysical" poetry, Rambuss looks at "a powerful vein in ... English religious writing that ... forthrightly advances religious devotion as a practice of pleasure." Ibid., 85.

60. Cousins, *Catholic Religious Poets*, 75.

The path to everlasting happiness and pleasure, however, is fraught with discomfort and tears. In the sonnet to St Colette (78), the poet muses sadly on his birthday and concludes that he must undergo pain by giving up on earthly passions and suffering physical illness and death before he can leave behind the vale of tears and merit spiritual rebirth.[61] Penance is another focal point in the SS, personified in St Mary Magdalene, who – envisioned as the repentant prostitute – becomes the object of Constable's poetic meditations in no less than four sonnets.[62] By adopting the Magdalene as the model penitent whom he seeks to emulate, the poet simultaneously embraces Counter-Reformation doctrine on the sacrament of penance, with its stages of contrition, confession, and satisfaction, and joins in the tradition of the literature of tears.[63] The carnal pleasures of Mary's past are emphasised in order to add value to her purification; the poet turns to her for inspiration and encouragement as he embarks on the *via penitentiae*, the path of penance. He also identifies with her as a weeping penitent, asking her to cry for him in sonnet 82.

The familiarity of tone with which he addresses the Magdalene points at her being a more comforting model for the poet-devotee than other saints and the Virgin herself. First, as a woman, she was viewed as more prone to sexual desire, and the poet deems this greater capacity for worldly pleasure as conducive to a

---

61. There is a sombre implication of self-mortification in keeping with the suffering experienced by Colette during her life; see Esther Cohen, *The Modulated Scream: Pain in Late Medieval Culture* (Chicago, 2010), 123–124.

62. The term "poetry of meditation" was coined by Martz and, I believe, aptly describes Constable's religious sonnets in that they describe "a particular stage and process in the spiritual life" with a "state of devotion" as goal. See Martz, *The Poetry of Meditation*, 14–15. Constable's exclusion from Martz's anthology *The Meditative Poem: An Anthology of Seventeenth-Century Verse* (New York, 1963) is conspicuous.

63. In the Western tradition, the legend of the Magdalene arose from a conflation of the woman who was freed "of seven devils" and was the first witness of the Resurrection, and different biblical women, and she became identified with the "sinner" in Luke 7:37–50. On her iconography and literary representations, see Michelle Erhardt and Amy M. Morris, eds., *Mary Magdalene: Iconographic Studies from the Middle Ages to the Baroque* (Leiden, 2012). Although her cult had roots in the medieval affective tradition and was also a popular subject of medieval plays, it was a twelfth-century homily that was translated in the sixteenth century as *An Homelie of Mary Magdalene, declaring her fervent love and zele towards Christ* (London, 1555) that greatly influenced the poetry of Southwell, Alabaster, and Constable; see Patricia Badir, *The Maudlin Impression: English Literary Images of Mary Magdalene, 1550–1700* (Notre Dame, IN, 2009), 65–66. Robert Southwell wrote a prose work titled *Marie Magdalens funeral teares* (London, 1591) and a poetic rendering of the same theme, "Marie Magdalens complaint at Christs death," included in *Saint Peters complaint with other poemes* (London, 1595), 37–38. See also Molly Murray, *The Poetics of Conversion in Early Modern English Literature: Verse and Change from Donne to Dryden* (Cambridge, 2009), 56.

greater pleasure of the soul.[64] Secondly, she is a symbol of hope in a way that the Virgin, entirely free from the taint of "other loves" (84.3), could never be. The restoration of lost chastity seems to be the poet's goal, considering that he petitions St Margaret in a similar manner: "give me then puritie" (77.13).[65] The last reason why Constable turns to Mary Magdalene revolves around the concept of seclusion and exile in sonnet 83. Here he describes the penitent saint as "retir'd from sight of men" (1) and stresses that there is happiness to be found in the solitary lives of anchorites who, like her, do penance in order to merit "the Joyes of heaven" (2). With the help of divine grace, he later adds, "I may finde heaven in my retyred harte" (11). The writer of the SS is not only a believer engaged in solitary meditation and prayer, but also, very literally, an exile, and he may be viewing his predicament as a sort of penance in the desert and seeking spiritual comfort for his alienation. His tears, no longer shed out of excessive worldly passions, are meant to wash away his sins so that he may enjoy everlasting happiness in heaven.

Reading both sequences alongside each other, it is possible to trace the change in the poet's romantic priorities and the kind of grace that he hopes to obtain. He concludes the introductory sonnet 1 in *T*, a late piece, pleading with God for the love of his lady or else the total annihilation of his worldly desires: "To him I flye for grace that rules above, / That by my Grace I may live in delight / Or by his grace I never more may love" (12–14). By the "conclusion of the whole" (sonnet 62), he vows not to let his pen concern itself with "love nor beautie" anymore. In the SS, he acknowledges that he is struggling to leave earthly desires behind, but prayer and penance offer him the real possibility of a happy ending, not in this world but the next. This is imagined in joyful language in the last of the sonnets to the Magdalene:

... death shall bringe the night of my delighte
My soule, uncloth'd, shall rest from labours paste
and, clasped in the arms of god, enjoye,
by sweete conjunction, everlastinge Joye. (84.11–14)

64. Katherine L. Jansen, *The Making of the Magdalen: Preaching and Popular Devotion in the Later Middle Ages* (Princeton, 2001), 209–210, 170. The Magdalene is celebrated as a saint "who understands and embraces both sexual and spiritual intimacy." See Kuchar, "Henry Constable," 75.

65. A "harlot saint" was more prone to offer consolation to the sinner than the Virgin Mary: "Her [the Virgin's] unspotted goodness prevents the sinner from identifying with her, and keeps her in the position of the Platonic ideal; but Mary Magdalene holds up a comforting mirror to those who sin again and again, and promises joy to human frailty." See Marina Warner, *Alone of All Her Sex: The Myth and Cult of the Virgin Mary*, 2nd ed. (Oxford, 2013), 239. On the debate about her restored virginity, see Jansen, *Making of the Magdalen*, 240–244.

## Displaced Monarchs

Nowhere else is the deprecation of worldly power that pervades the entirety of Constable's production more apparent than in the sonnets engaging with monarchical rule. The recurrence of this theme creates some remarkable moments of tension. His treatment of the figure of Queen Elizabeth, in particular, has been analysed in terms of her gradual displacement "at the pinnacle of the patronage hierarchy."[66] The earliest sonnet to her must be 25 in the present edition, dated around 1587, which is rife with unequivocal praise, as the poet metaphorically takes up arms – his pen – to defend her from the attacks of her enemies, in a declaration of militant, patriotic Protestantism.[67] In 23, also an early work, he comments on his activities as an undercover agent abroad and the queen's reputation in other nations; she is an agent of preservation due to her effect on her loving subjects and her enemies, as tears – of love and frustration, respectively – keep her island state safe. The safety of Protestant England in times of conspiracy to reinstate Catholicism is viewed as providential, and the sonnet participates in the ongoing construction of Elizabeth as "God's handmaid" and "the mediator (like the Virgin Mary) between God and her people."[68]

A third sonnet, number 24, is more problematic in its depiction of Elizabeth as a cruel fair, the mistress whose beauty causes torment.[69] The poet begins by asking why he should praise a queen who has caused "sin and sorrow" (2), that is, pride and envy, in her subjects and her foreign enemies respectively. As the sonnet progresses, it departs from convention in that these vices are associated with "hell" and "purgatorie" (11–12). Elizabeth is portrayed as an agent of torment for subjects and enemies alike, under whose power men are sent to purgatory. The latter was a concept rejected by Protestants and hotly debated among Catholics.[70] In the context of the poem, the use of such a loaded term seems to invoke the persecution of Catholics under Elizabeth's regime and evidences Con-

---

66. Hackett, *Virgin Mother*, 138.

67. This sonnet was surely written to preface the treatise on Dutch affairs, a copy of which may have been made for presentation to the queen.

68. Kevin Sharpe, *Selling the Tudor Monarchy: Authority and Image in Sixteenth-Century England* (New Haven, 2009), 333.

69. Hackett has observed that the "the cruelty which is deprecated in this sonnet is of a different order, producing a poem strikingly fraught with negative undertones and simmering anxieties within the outward conventions of panegyric." See Hackett, *Virgin Mother*, 137.

70. Hackett, "The Art of Blasphemy?" 45. Constable had addressed the controversy in his *Examen* in similar terms; see the notes to sonnet 24. By the time of the composition of the *SS*, he had accepted the existence of purgatory, as seen in his references to "Limbo" and "purgyng fire" in sonnet 70.

stable's growing anxiety over the figure of the queen, and perhaps his incipient disenchantment with courtly affairs as he leaned towards Catholicism.[71]

At one particular point in the sequence, Elizabeth is conspicuously absent. Sonnet 31 deals with queenship and has been read as an exercise in ambiguity and provocation, most likely written around the time of the poet's conversion.[72] Constable brings in the figure of the Virgin as a paragon of female excellence which he can employ to praise his Catholic relation Mary Talbot, countess of Shrewsbury. He suggests that the Virgin is "meete" to wear a crown in heaven, anticipating later references to the iconography of Mary as Queen of Heaven in his SS. In line 4 he presents the reader with the puzzle of his "creed," which is never solved. Both the Virgin and his cousin are contrasted with namesakes who wore an actual crown and saw atrocities committed in the British isle: "And for the world, this Ile and age shall rue / The bloud and fire was shed and kindled heere / When woemen of youre name the croune did beare" (5–7). The allusion must be to Mary Tudor, associated with the burning of Protestants, and Mary, Queen of Scots. Alison Shell has interpreted these lines as Constable's voiced "regrets" at "the upsurges of militant Protestantism" during both queens' reigns.[73] However, the three sonnets he wrote to the ill-fated Mary Stuart (85–87) add another layer of interpretation to these lines: they are metaphorically drenched in Mary's own blood, spilt at her execution. After complaining that the countess, who merits a crown, cannot have one (8), the ambiguity is driven to an apex in the tercet by leaving the reader to ponder who God's "foes" and "his owne" people, punished and tested respectively, are (9–11).[74] The poet's intent to detach the name of Mary from implications of violence and persecution may also convey the message that other worthy women like Mary Talbot lived according to their faith but avoided direct confrontation with the Elizabethan regime. The sonnet provides a commentary on negative queenship and leaves ample room for discussion. If Mary, Queen of Scots, is one of God's people, it must follow that the monarch who condemned her is to blame – and she will be later in the SS. Although the focus on the name of Mary excludes Elizabeth from a discussion of female rule in which she should have a prominent role, her presence looms large: read alongside sonnet 24,

71. Lilla Grindlay has called this "an extraordinary moment of tension" considering Constable's conversion. See Grindlay, *Queen of Heaven: The Assumption and Coronation of the Virgin in Early Modern English Writing* (Notre Dame, IN, 2018), 137.
72. Shell, *Catholicism*, 124–125; Hackett, "The Art of Blasphemy?" 42–43; Grindlay, *Queen of Heaven*, 138–139.
73. Shell, *Catholicism*, 124.
74. Ibid., 125.

number 31 signals the last step in the process of disenchantment with the queen that culminates in the *SS*.

Royal imagery is employed to refer to the Virgin Mary in the *SS*: she is the "Queene of Queens" (71.1), "soveraigne of Queens" (79.1), and "fairest Queene" (79.13), bountiful and "sweete" (81.1), endowed with every quality that would make subjects love their monarch. The language which the Virgin Queen encouraged from her subjects is "transferred" to Mary.[75] Constable simultaneously voices his Catholic faith and belief in the Virgin as man's mediatrix, his disappointment with earthly monarchs – Elizabeth, in particular – and a measure of self-criticism and commentary on his own misplaced loyalty and ambition.

In sonnet 71, the poet affirms his belief in the Immaculate Conception of the Virgin and extols her "nobilitie" (1–5). Being related to the three persons of the Trinity, her unparalleled high status situates her well above earthly monarchs, whom he collectively addresses in a shocking change of interlocutor in the final lines:

Cease then, Oh Queens which earthly Crownes do weare,
to glory in the pompe of worldly thinges;
yf men suche highe respect unto you beare
Which daughters, wyv's and mothers are of kinges,
what honnor should unto that Queene be donne
which had your god for father, spowse and sonne? (9–14)

Praise of these earthly queens is curtailed and made dependent on their relation to male sovereigns; an attack on Elizabeth's reluctance to marry and lack of issue may be implicit. The Virgin, who fulfils all three roles, is the best equipped to reward service and loyalty within the familiar system of suit and recompense.

The triad of sonnets to the Virgin (79–81) emphasises her role as mediatrix. The poet pleads for her intercession so that he may be able to contemplate God: "shewe me thy sonne in his imperiall place" (79.3). There follows a request to have his love for earthly ladies replaced with a chaste love for the Virgin, the true *donna angelicata*. She in turn ousts the poetic mistress of the secular sonnets, who is a goddess-like figure, sometimes imagined in a classical pantheon, sometimes addressed as an angel in language that is specific to Christianity, or even – more

---

75. Shell, *Catholicism*, 126. On Constable's sonnets to the Virgin, see Hackett, "The Art of Blasphemy?" 45–48, and *Virgin Mother*, 138–139; and Grindlay, *Queen of Heaven*, 133–157. On the iconography invoked in these sonnets, see the notes to the sonnets, below.

intriguingly – in Marian terms.[76] The Virgin is a female paragon: she has a "lovely face / whose beames the Anngelles beauty doe deface" (79.6–7) and surpasses "all in all perfections" (80.6). In the last song of his *Canzoniere* (366), Petrarch recants his love for Laura and turns to the Virgin in a similar way, providing a suitable model.[77] In the thirteenth century, Mariolatry was influenced by the tradition of courtly love, in which she was the object of romantic devotion and in turn played the role of the exalted, jealous lady who demanded exclusive affection from her lover-devotees.[78]

The earthly queen is hence excluded from the poet's affection in a process that could be viewed as a reappropriation of the Protestant misappropriation of Marian imagery in panegyrics to Queen Elizabeth, within the so-called "cult" of the Virgin Queen.[79] The undertone in sonnets 71 and 79 is one of thinly veiled disappointment with Elizabeth, who is no longer in a position to bestow the highest form of grace, or favour, on the poet. In the SS no other lady is as worthy of love as the Virgin; she has already given him, and humanity, the greatest gift in the bringing forth and nursing of Christ and, on a more personal level, she has granted the poet her "succour" (80.4), her comfort in times of need.[80] He then imagines eternal life and contemplation of the Virgin as source of all "pleasure" (80.8) and happiness, the like of which secular love could never provide. In the presence of His mother, the poet-believer will be one step closer to God. The Virgin facilitates the beatific vision, the poet's ultimate wish, in sonnet 81. Her role as mediatrix or intercessor is thus emphasised. God is envisioned as the

---

76. See for instance sonnets 3 and 8, in which the lady's heavenly features are stressed. The overt comparison of the poet's mistress to the Virgin rests on the possibilities for wordplay that her name offered: "Grace, full of grace" (1.1), "Ladie of Ladies" (11.1).

77. See *Petrarch: The Canzoniere, or Rerum Vulgarium Fragmenta*, trans. Mark Musa (Bloomington, IN, 1999), 512.

78. This resulted in Mary being "addressed in erotic terms"; Hackett, *Virgin Mother*, 15–18. Warner sees the blending of Mary, with her "feminine virtues of humility, obedience, modesty, and self-effacement," and the high-class ladies admired by troubadours as a move to subjugate carnal desire to church-endorsed ideas of "sexual chastity and female submission." The Virgin became an epitome of perfection that human women simply could not rival. See Warner, *Alone of All Her Sex*, 150. See also Julia Kristeva, "Stabat Mater," in *The Female Body in Western Culture: Contemporary Perspectives*, ed. Susan R. Suleiman (Cambridge, MA, 1986), 99–118, at 106.

79. See Hackett, *Virgin Mother*, for a thorough examination of overlapping representations of the Virgin and the queen.

80. On Constable's use of the image of Mary as *Virgo lactans*, which is radically Catholic, see Grindlay, *Queen of Heaven*, 149–157. Grindlay notes that "descriptions of Elizabeth as the nursing mother of both the Protestant Church and her subjects amounted almost to a secular appropriation of the *Virgo Lactans* image" (149).

source of all light and all pleasure (5–8), and the poet anticipates the union of his soul with God in heaven, the last stage of mystical experience, described through erotic imagery.[81]

Constable's feelings of exclusion and real and emotional exile from Elizabethan England coexisted with the hope that a new reign might bring Catholics some much-needed toleration. James VI of Scotland was viewed as the right candidate by many, a "prince of hope" (26.5).[82] Constable had gone to great lengths to make James a focus in his quest for patronage, particularly around the year 1589, when he apparently got acquainted with the monarch and his poetic circle, known as the "Castalian Band."[83] In his dedicatory sonnets "To the King of Scots" (26–29), the poet reacts to the monarch's own compositions and commends the king's David-like writing of religious verse despite his youth, an activity which, as in the case of Vittoria Colonna in sonnet 51, confers on him a special quasi-divine status.[84] The evocation of James's "altar throne" in sonnet 26 must also allude to the idea of divinely ordained kingship.

The attributes colouring Constable's poetic portrait of James are transferred to God and his saints in the SS, in which Christ becomes the "younge Prince of heaven" who is "begotten" of a "Kinge" (68.1) and "from kinge Davids roiall stocke" (68.4). God is described as a "highe kynge" (73.11) or "the highest kinge" (79.10). If the Scottish king was, at the time of the writing of Constable's earliest secular sonnets, the one whose hands the poet hoped to kiss (26.1), he is ultimately displaced by the heavenly king, the focus of the longing of the poet's soul (78.11) and the one who will "honnor" his poet-devotee (79.11). Nevertheless, displacement of James cannot be read in the same terms as that of Elizabeth. The latter is effectively left behind in the SS, supplanted with the Virgin. James, on the other hand, could not have disapproved

81. Kuchar's notion of "divine subjection" as a means through which Catholics – unable to move in the social space denied them by Elizabeth's government, especially from the 1580s – could realize themselves as subjects, is very relevant to analyse Constable's sonnets to the Virgin and to the Trinitarian God. Constable found a way to resist "religio-political oppression" by "enacting" his "submission to divine authority." See Gary Kuchar, *Divine Subjection: The Rhetoric of Sacramental Devotion in Early Modern England* (Pittsburgh, 2005), 34–38.

82. See Stefania Tutino, *Law and Conscience: Catholicism in Early Modern England, 1570–1625* (Hampshire, 2007), 81.

83. See Deirdre Serjeantson, "English Bards and Scotch Poetics: Scotland's Literary Influence and Sixteenth-Century English Religious Verse," in *Literature and the Scottish Reformation*, ed. Crawford Gribben and David G. Mullan (Farnham, 2009), 161–190, at 177; Jane Rickard, *Authorship and Authority: The Writings of James VI and I* (Manchester, 2007), 35–45.

84. Colonna is envisioned singing "heavenly songs" (51.1) which she learnt to write well before her death, as her poems reveal.

of the royal imagery employed by Constable to address God. As Constable's political manoeuvres as a Catholic exile demonstrate, the Scottish king was still on the horizon at the time of the *Spiritual Sonnets*' composition: both men knew each other, shared literary interests and a fondness for theological debate, and, if cards were played right, the monarch would welcome the poet back to England one day.

The feelings of complete disenchantment with Elizabeth's reign and hopes for a better future converge in the three sonnets "to the Blessed Martir Marye, Queene of Scotland" (85–87), a poetic locus of uneasiness and outspokenness unmatched in Constable's oeuvre. These sonnets survive in the *BE* sequence only, following two other triads dedicated to the Virgin and St Mary Magdalene, respectively, under a general heading alluding to the poet's "particuler Devotion" to "3 blessed Maryes." The inclusion of the deceased Mary Stuart – mother to another James – in this group points to the process of sanctification which takes place in the sonnets and renders the Scottish queen worthy of "devotion."[85]

The three sonnets form a narrative sequence recounting Mary Stuart's execution, burial, and glorious ascension to heaven to join the ranks of the saints. Countering the official Protestant propaganda presenting Mary as a traitor in political terms, Constable partakes in the Catholic martyrological tradition according to which she was an innocent murdered on account of her religion.[86] In the first sonnet (85), her execution is depicted as a sacrifice that generates immense pathos in the audience, and the poet points an accusing finger at the "Aucthors" of the crime – either Elizabeth or her council – whose reputation abroad will suffer. This can be read as a reversal of Constable's account of foreign praise for Elizabeth, written years earlier, in which he claimed to have heard others talking about "theyre wonder" and the queen's "glorie" (23.3–4). The victim's blood, that on the cheeks of the ashamed executioners, the poet's ink, and his tears intermingle in the poem. The public spectacle of Mary's death leads to her funeral in sonnet 86, a moment of tension between the public and the private,

---

85. For a discussion of these sonnets, including a semidiplomatic transcription, see María Jesús Pérez-Jáuregui, "A Queen in a 'Purple Robe': Henry Constable's Poetic Tribute to Mary, Queen of Scots," *Studies in Philology* 113, no. 3 (2016): 577–594.

86. On eyewitness accounts and written responses to the queen's execution on 8 February 1587, see, inter alia, James Emerson Phillips, *Images of a Queen: Mary Stuart in Sixteenth-Century Literature* (Berkeley, 1964); John D. Staines, *The Tragic Histories of Mary Queen of Scots, 1560–1690: Rhetoric, Passions, and Political Literature* (Aldershot, 2009); Leticia Álvarez-Recio, "Contemporary Visions of Mary Stuart's Execution: Saintliness and Vilification," in *The Rituals and Rhetoric of Queenship: Medieval to Early Modern*, ed. Liz Oakley-Brown and Louise J. Wilkinson (Dublin, 2009), 209–221.

Protestant and Catholic rites.[87] The Catholic poet inveighs against the "schism-rites" used, which desecrate her "sacred boddye" (4–6). He then envisions an alternate ceremony in which the dead queen is honoured by natural elements at night, particularly the stars and the sky (7–12). Thus, she is conferred the dignity that the poet considers her due. Mary's ascension to heaven in the third sonnet (87) is portrayed as her final triumph, the climactic moment in her narrative. In the emphasis on her death without sin, Mary is compared to the Virgin, whose Immaculate Conception is reversed, as Alison Shell has noted.[88] In heaven, she is given a reception fit for a queen and a martyr – a double status symbolized by the purple robe she wears.[89] She becomes a member of the heavenly court, far superior to the earthly courts which she was forced to leave, and occupies a place of honour.

Despite all the elements being set out for a tragedy in the first sonnet, the Queen of Scots's tale is, from a Catholic perspective, one of victory. In the triad of sonnets, she goes through a process of disembodiment: a woman becomes a lamb taken to slaughter, then a corpse that suffers further humiliation at the hands of her enemies but is revered by nature, and she ultimately leaves that body and the material world behind to wear a crown that eclipses the one taken from her. Constable seems to be out for blood when he asserts that he is about to recount her story (85.1), but his angry lyrical voice is almost content toward the end – vengeance is best left to God, and Mary's suffering has been repaid in full.

The decision to culminate the *SS* with a triad to the executed Queen of Scots cannot have been accidental. The shorter *HA* sequence ends with the poet-devotee's soul freed from its bodily prison and ready to enjoy "by sweet conjunction, everlastinge Joye" at the end of the last sonnet to the Magdalene (84.14). Worldly matters are meant to be left behind for good, but in *BE* they are not – Constable's renunciation of the world, its passions, and its corruptions in order to achieve spiritual purification is narrowed to Elizabeth's court, in which a Catholic convert

---

87. On Mary Stuart's burial and funeral, see Jennifer Woodward, *The Theatre of Death: The Ritual Management of Royal Funerals in Renaissance England, 1570–1625* (Woodbridge, 1997), 74–86.

88. Alison Shell, "'I write of tears, and blud': Henry Constable on Mary Stuart" (paper presented at the Annual Meeting of the Renaissance Society of America, Boston, 31 March 2016).

89. Mary Stuart was not canonised by the church, but the validity of her martyrdom would have been accepted in what Clare Copeland has termed a period of "uncertainty" as to how sanctity was defined following the Council of Trent, in which "existing saints, new saints and 'unofficial' saints with reputations for holiness fitted within the same sacred landscape." See Clare Copeland, "Sanctity," in *The Ashgate Research Companion to the Counter-Reformation*, ed. Alexandra Bamji et al. (Farnham, 2013), 225–241, at 226–227.

has no place. The queen is brought down in the universal hierarchy, replaced with the Virgin Mary, and even the woman she viewed as a rival and a threat ranks above her. Constable may have looked at Mary Stuart – the queen who was bereft of her title and her nation and ended up a prisoner in a foreign land – with sympathy, given that he had lost everything himself, as he was forced to leave his country and inheritance behind after his conversion.

Constable's optimism regarding the succession of Mary Stuart's son to the English throne surpassed that of other coreligionists. In a prose treatise that he wrote at least in part, he reinforces the belief that all Catholics should rush in James's support with an allusion to the dead queen: "His most sacred Mother who sealed the same at her death with her bludde for the whiche she is a Martyr, & by the meanes whereof he is a Martyrs sonne, which passeth the dignitiye of a kinge or any other worldly tytle."[90] Being a martyr's son – Constable's logic ran – James could and would be converted; the poet devoted the rest of his life to such an endeavour. Therefore, a more mundane motivation may have driven him to bring a copy of his sequence with him upon his return to England after James's accession.[91] Despite their confessional differences, James valued religious poetry, and the sonnets to his mother could be understood as a further display of loyalty – to pile on the dedicatory secular sonnets, prose works, correspondence, and embassies which Constable had targeted at the king from the beginning of his career. He had not really given up on worldly ambition; he was a man of action, indefatigable in his desire to see a different court and a different England. He envisioned a country ruled by a king who might be willing to retain Constable as a trusted advisor and a poet in his literary coterie.

## The Prayer-Sonnet and Catholic Dogma

Charlotte Clutterbuck's notion of "plea-poems," in which poets "express a desire for an absent God who has not yet answered their pleas ... expressing the need for and the possibility of a change that will occur only with God's help," is relevant to a discussion of Constable's SS.[92] Regardless of the social use he could even-

---

90. *Discovery*, 94.
91. It is also worth remembering that as the 1590s progressed, Constable fell out of favour with Henri IV and became allied with the Guise family, the Queen of Scots' kin on her mother's side. Perhaps the Guises, too, were on his mind when he composed the sonnets.
92. Charlotte Clutterbuck, *Encounters with God in Medieval and Early Modern English Poetry* (London, 2017), 17. Clutterbuck contrasts the notion of the "plea-poem" with that of the "praise-poem."

tually make of them, Constable wrote his *SS* primarily as a private exercise – in that they share a goal with St Ignatius's definition of "spiritual exercise" as "any means of preparing and disposing our soul to rid itself of all its disordered affections and then, after their removal, of seeking and finding God's will in the ordering of our life for the salvation of our soul."[93] In these sonnets he fashions himself as a sinner who is afraid to stand alone in full sight of God until he has been cleansed from guilt. Private reformation and penitence become Constable's main concern, and he petitions God himself for grace, and the Virgin Mary, a number of saints, and martyrs for intercession and assistance – his "plea" encompasses an unusually large number of divine entities.

Most of the *SS* are structured into a reflection on either God or the life of a saint followed by a petition.[94] "Greate god," the direct address that opens the first sonnet, "To God the Father" (67), sets the tone of the sequence, rife with apostrophes that make the sonnets sound like prayers when read aloud. The appeal is not only for his interlocutor to listen, but to exert some influence on the poet's life, as in his meditation on the Eucharist: "Clere thou my thoughtes as thou didst give them light, / and as thou others fred from purgyng fyre, / quench in my harte the flames of bad desire" (70.12–14). Even when invocations are not used, second-person pronouns are employed to establish direct communication with the saint.[95]

Beyond the poet's self-avowed patriotism as a Protestant Englishman, ready to fight for queen and country, there is nothing in the secular sonnets that engages with Reformed dogma. Yet the extent to which the poet embraces the tenets of the Counter-Reformation after his conversion is clear when contrasting his ideas on thorny issues such as the temporal authority of the pope with the statements he had previously made in early prose works. In his treatise on Dutch affairs, he denied the authority of the pope, whom he called "Antechrist" and "the purple whore" from Revelation.[96] Later, in the *Examen*, his pseudo-Catholic persona presented criticism against the pope from the point of view of the Huguenots, mentioning for instance the excessive power of the papacy as a "universall Monarchy."[97] By the

---

93. Ignatius of Loyola, *The Spiritual Exercises and Selected Works*, ed. George E. Ganss (New York, 1991), 121.

94. Exceptions are 68, 71–74, 76, and 85–87. It may be noticed that he never petitions male saints for intercession; sonnets to St Michael, St John the Baptist, and St Peter and St Paul are merely meditative.

95. See for instance sonnet 76 to St Catherine or 86 to Mary Stuart.

96. *A Commentarie or explication of a letter written by Cardinall Allen in defence of Sir William Stanleys act of Betrayinge of Deventer*, in *Bn*, fol. 32r.

97. *CM*, 34.

time he wrote the sonnet "To St Peter & St Paule" (74), he was willing to highlight their connection to Rome and their role in the foundation of the papacy, and to make his acceptance of the pope's temporal authority explicit: "The world and Church were rul'd by one" (14). This acknowledgement is a terminus in his confessional journey, as he engages with a problematic crux for English recusants – especially after the publication of the papal bull excommunicating Elizabeth – and depicts the pope as ruler of the world. The clear implication that the papacy is a monarchy seems aligned with the core tenets of Nicholas Sander's *De visibili monarchia*: in Sander's incendiary work, "the Catholic Church is defined as a 'visible monarchy,' a temporal institution existing in reality."[98]

Another core belief of the Catholic Church against Protestantism, the real presence and sacrifice of Christ in the Eucharist, is the theme of the sonnet "When thee, o holy sacrificed Lambe" (70). The poet presents himself as a communicant beholding the body and blood of Christ in the bread and wine he is about to receive; their consumption is imagined as the physical incorporation of Christ into the poet's own body: "Thou seemest in thy Syndon wrap'd to be / like to a Corse whose monument I am" (7–8). He petitions God to reach his soul through this act of embodiment and to help him improve his spiritual life, particularly by helping him leave earthly passions behind (14). It is the corporeality in this sonnet which marks it as distinctly Catholic: Christ is really present in the sacrament, and it follows that he will enter the communicant's body and potentially have a liberating effect on his soul.[99]

Other features of the sequence of *SS* that embed it in a post-Tridentine tradition include its emphasis on the sacrament of penance. The Protestant doctrine of *sola fide* is rejected by the Catholic convert, who must take an active role in his own salvation.[100] The choice of addressees conforms to Tridentine regu-

---

98. Tutino, *Law and Conscience*, 22. In book 8 he argues that "the ecclesiastical authority was a direct emanation from God, and whoever was granted this authority became a direct representative of God's authority on earth, without intermediary"; ibid., 23. See also Nicholas Sander, *De visibili monarchia ecclesiae libri octo* (Louvain, 1571).

99. The Council of Trent decreed that in the Mass "a true and real sacrifice" is "offered to God"; see Council of Trent, session 22, in *Canons and Decrees of the Council of Trent*, trans. H.J. Schroeder (Rockford, 1978), 149. Cousins quotes this sonnet as one of the poems imagining "unresolved desire" in the sequence: there is a petition, a prayer made "in faith and hope," but no resolution or conclusion. See Cousins, *Catholic Religious Poets*, 73.

100. Mazzaro emphasises Constable's creation of "his own model for recusant sincerity in forgiveness and in his affirmation of the Council of Trent's positions against certain Protestant beliefs ... that intercession and invocation are opposed to the faith and truth which one should have in God alone." See Jerome Mazzaro, "Recusant Sincerity: Henry Constable at Spiritual Sonnets," *Essays in Literature* 17 (1990): 147–159, at 157.

lations on the invocation and veneration of saints. Sonnets 71–74 are even arranged following the order laid out by the Confiteor of the Tridentine Mass.[101] Although the Immaculate Conception of the Virgin Mary was not a dogma until 1854, it was widely accepted among Catholics, promoted by Franciscans and Jesuits, and the Council of Trent explicitly exempted Mary from original sin.[102] During his stays in Italy and France, Constable could not have failed to get acquainted with the artistic manifestations of Marian cults that were promoted in order to counter Protestant attacks on the excessive worship of the Virgin. Therefore, it is not surprising that he should begin sonnet 71 by stating, "Thy birth was free / from guilt, which others doe of grace bereave" (1–2).

## Conclusion: The Porous Sonnets

In her important overview of the religious sonnet subgenre, Helen Wilcox observes that "the boundaries of the early modern religious sonnet are so difficult to pin down that it is not only inappropriate to ally the form exclusively with any particular ecclesiastical allegiance but also virtually impossible to define the borderline of secular and religious sonnets."[103] Constable is the poet whose production illustrates this instability best before John Donne. He did separate his sonnets in two groups; they were never copied together, and readers of his successful *Diana* and the manuscript sequences were most likely ignorant of the existence of the *SS*. Yet the sonnets speak louder when they are viewed as stages in an ongoing narrative, simmering with doubt and a struggle to find the true faith, made all the more dramatic by the interfusion of profane and religious language. The secular seeps into the sacred, and the sacred into the secular, addressees are exalted and replaced, and loyalties transferred. Constable's self-presentation as a lover and a courtier in the secular sonnets is anguished in the face of uncertain reward, much as his humility as a devout, lonely exile in the *SS* is undermined by his latent ambition and his drive to belong. Behind it all there is a poet that exists so long as he desires – whether he desires a lady's love, patronage, intercession, or salvation.

---

101. "Ideo precor beatam Mariam semper Virginem, beatum Michaelem Archangelum, beatum Ioannem Baptistam, sanctos Apostolos Petrum et Paulum, omnes Sanctos ... ."
102. See sessions 5 and 6 in Council of Trent, *Canons and Decrees*, 23, 45.
103. Wilcox, "Sacred Desire," 154.

CHAPTER FIVE

# The Critical Reception of Constable's Poetry

The reputation of Henry Constable as a poet, which seems to have been well established during his lifetime, has waxed and waned across the centuries. Some factors accounting for its fluctuations include his biographers' bewilderment concerning his confessional and political stances, exacerbated by the weight of Protestant-centred scholarship; bouts of scholarly interest and reassessment contrasting with longer periods of neglect; and shifting priorities in the focus of critics and commentators. These have often tended to belittle or ignore the accomplishments of the so-called "minor" poets against those of major figures such as Spenser and Shakespeare, but are now turning to the lesser-known group in light of mounting enthusiasm about the socioliterary history of texts and manuscript studies, together with the revival of Catholic studies.

## The Sweet Poet: Early Reputation

Evidence that Constable was considered a first-rate poet whose sonnets deserved to be read and imitated can be gathered both from the success of the first *Diana* (D92), which warranted a second edition, and from scattered statements by admiring contemporaries. In the third sonnet within the 1599 *Idea*, Michael Drayton raises Constable to the same level as Philip Sidney and Samuel Daniel:

> Many there be excelling in this kind,
> Whose well trick'd rimes with all invention swell
> Let each commend as best shall like his minde,
> Some Sidney, Constable, some Daniell.[1]

Tom W.N. Parker has noted that this statement brings Sidney and Constable together against Daniel, and the separation between two "types" of sonneteer

---

1. Michael Drayton, *Englands heroicall epistles* (London, 1599), sig. P2v.

evidences a polarisation of contemporary taste.[2] Around the same time, Gabriel Harvey included Constable in his enumeration of "florishing metricians" in his handwritten marginalia on a copy of Thomas Speght's edition of Chaucer: "Spencer, Constable, France, Watson, Daniel, Warner, Chapman, Silvester, Shakespeare."[3] Ben Jonson lists poets and their female addressees from the classical tradition to early modern times in one of his odes. Following Petrarch and Pierre de Ronsard, Sidney and Constable are honoured as paragons of English love poetry:

> Hath our great Sydney, Stella set,
> Where never Star shone brighter yet?
> Or Constables Ambrosiack Muse
> Made Dian, not his notes refuse?[4]

More elaborate praise is found in the two sonnets dedicated to Constable copied right after the sequence in *T* (see appendix A). They were probably written by a friend acquainted with the poet's circumstances as a former courtier and exile. In the first the author addresses Constable as "Sweet Muses son, Apollos chief delight" and praises him in very similar terms to those used by Constable in sonnet 27 to King James; in fact, the heading explicitly acknowledges the borrowing, as the sonnet is said to be written "upon occasion of his [Constable's] two former Sonets to the K. of Scots," although the conceit and imagery derive from one. The anonymous author need not have encountered sonnet 27 in manuscript, given that it was also printed in *PE* in 1591. However, Constable is described as "he, which chang'd blind love for love of light" (5), and the reference is to his abandonment of secular poetry for spiritual concerns. This hints at the author being a close acquaintance, perhaps a fellow Catholic, who asks Constable to write about religion ("rest thy Muse upon the Angells winge") and foretells that by doing so, he will merit a place in heaven (13–14). In the second sonnet Constable is called "Englands sweete nightingale" (1) and "the spring" of "English poesie" (12) and is asked to return from exile. This second sonnet contains a further allusion to Constable's poems being "heavenly songs" (4).

    2. Parker, 146.
    3. Geoffrey Chaucer, *The workes of our antient and lerned English poet, Geffrey Chaucer*, ed. Thomas Speght (London, 1598), included in London, British Library, Add MS 42518, fol. 422v. This page contains, among other references, the first recorded allusion to Shakespeare's *Hamlet*.
    4. Ben Jonson, *The Workes of Benjamin Jonson*, vols. 2–3 (London, 1641), 196. Jonson obviously read the sonnets as printed in either *D92* or *D94*.

In the second part of *The Return from Parnassus*, a Cambridge play performed at St John's probably during the Christmas festivities of 1601–1602, a character named Iudicio praises Constable in similar terms: "Sweet Constable doth take the wondering ear, / And lays it up in willing prisonment" (1.2.123–124).[5] Edmund Bolton's praise of Constable in his *Hypercritica* is somewhat more elaborate and grounded on the author's appreciation of literary style: "Noble Henry Constable was a great Master in English Tongue, nor had any Gentleman of our Nation a more pure, quick, or higher Delivery of Conceit; witness among all other, that Sonnet of his before his Majesty's *Lepanto*."[6] Sonnet 27 is once again singled out, which evidences its impact and popularity. Other facts that attest to Constable's good poetic reputation are the setting of some of his verses to music, the imitation of other contemporary poets, and the misattribution of poems by other authors who shared his initials.

## The Poet Dismissed: The Seventeenth Century

Despite Nicholas Burghe's appreciation and inclusion of some of the sonnets in his miscellany (A) sometime between 1630 and 1660, Constable's reputation had waned by the third quarter of the seventeenth century. Edward Phillips refuses to devote an entry to him in his *Theatrum poetarum*. He is grouped with others such as John Markham or Thomas Achelly as a corollary to the entry on Edward Dyer, who is said to have enjoyed "formerly" a good reputation, "being rank't with some of the most noted Poets of Qu. Elizabeth's time."[7] Anthony à Wood discusses Constable in an entry about a John Constable who lived in the early sixteenth century. Of Henry, Wood writes that he was "a noted English Poet," but basically repeats Bolton's and Phillips's assessments, and then refers to sonnet 27 and "several sonnets ... written to Sir Phil. Sidney; some of which are set before the *Apology for Poetry*, written by the said Knight."[8] Other sources such as Davies's *Athenae britannicae* rehash the same information.[9]

---

5. *The Return from Parnassus, or the Scourge of Simony*, ed. Oliphant Smeaton (London, 1905), 13.
6. Joseph Haslewood, ed., *Ancient Critical Essays upon English Poets and Poesy* (London, 1811–1815), 2: 250.
7. Edward Phillips, *Theatrum poetarum, or A compleat collection of the poets, especially the most eminent, of all ages* (London, 1675), 221.
8. Anthony à Wood, *Athenae Oxonienses* (London, 1691), 1: 13.
9. Myles Davies, *Athenae britannicae, or, A critical history of the Oxford and Cambridge writers and writings* (London, 1716), 1: 56.

Thomas Birch's note on Constable, which accompanies the transcription of one of his letters to Anthony Bacon, introduces the idea that the poet was "a zealous Roman Catholic," which became a critical commonplace. He adds that his "religion seems to have occasioned him to live in a state of banishment from England" and mentions his imprisonment in the Tower.[10] Thomas Hawkins, an Anglican priest and literary editor, edited *The Return from Parnassus* in his compilation of early English drama. In the footnotes to Iudicio's allusion to Constable, Hawkins suggests that the poet was mostly unknown to the eighteenth-century reading public. Constable is said to be one of the poets whose "works ... are become obscure," and sonnet 27 is printed in full for the reader to see his "abilities."[11] Thomas Warton, who owned a copy of *D94*, failed to give any substantial information about Constable; he simply states that he was "a noted sonnet-writer of these times."[12] Towards the end of the century, Edmund Lodge printed some of Constable's letters in his *Illustrations of British History*, and included the same pieces of biographical information focusing on the poet's religion and exile.[13] Even more significant than the obscurity surrounding Constable's biography is the fact that none of his sonnets was included in the poetry anthologies of the eighteenth century.

## The Sonnets Rediscovered: The Nineteenth Century

Henry John Todd's discovery of *T* inaugurated a "revival of interest" in Constable, which, in Joan Grundy's words, was "not so much critical as bibliographical."[14] Todd made an effort to retrieve and piece together some early testimonies of Constable's high reputation and the little biographical information available to him. He transcribed the prose introduction to the *T* collection, one of the sonnets dedicated to Constable, and, more surprisingly, sonnet 26 to King James instead of the better-known 27.[15]

Thomas Park was the first editor of Constable. In 1812 he produced the first edition of the secular sonnets in *T* in his *Harleian Miscellany*.[16] His intro-

---

10. Thomas Birch, *Memoirs of the Reign of Queen Elizabeth, from the Year 1581 till her Death* (London, 1754), 1: 302–303.
11. Thomas Hawkins, *The Origin of the English Drama* (London, 1773), 3: 212 n.
12. Thomas Warton, *The History of English Poetry* (London, 1781), 3: 292.
13. Edmund Lodge, *Illustrations of British History* (London, 1791), 3: 79 n.
14. Grundy, 68.
15. Henry J. Todd, ed., *The Poetical Works of John Milton* (London, 1801), 5: 452–455.
16. Park, *THM*, 489–518.

ductory notes flesh out Constable's biography by providing accurate dates and quotes from some of his letters; although Constable's religion continues to be emphasised, Park brings to light the fact that he protested his loyalty to the crown. He also made the first attempt to establish the canon of Constable's poetry, encompassing *T*, "half" of *D94*, the four sonnets in *AP*, and that in *PE*. His reluctance to accept all the sonnets in *D94* as Constable's set an important critical trend. He accurately attributed the seventeen *Spiritual Sonnets* in *HA* to Constable for the first time: "From their regular Italian structure, and the sainted names of those addressed, I am inclined to consider [them] as Constable's: but their complexion would not well assimilate with his lighter amatory strains."[17] Park's critical appraisal of the secular sonnets was scant but still contributed the first original statement in – albeit guarded – praise of Constable since Bolton's *Hypercritica*: "Many of Constable's sonnets, in truth, are full of concetti; though some are ingenious, and a few may be deemed successful efforts."[18] As for the text of his edition, he included the *T* sequence in full and collated those that survive in *D94* too.[19] He observed the old spelling save for his regularisation of *u/v* and *i/j*, expanded contractions, and added editorial punctuation and emendations.

Three years later, Park came to a decision about the *SS* and edited them for the first time in the second volume of *Heliconia*.[20] He excluded one, sonnet 84, fearing that it might offend some readers' sensibilities. In his "Advertisement," he takes the prose conclusion to *T* to be the turning point after which the poet abandoned the "vayne poems" of his past and devoted himself to religious writing, the result of "calmer thought." His brief assessment of the sonnets emphasises Constable's use of erotic imagery with a religious subject matter, and the self-presentation of the poetic voice as female in some of them, both of which he associates with "the Song of Solomon."[21] He followed the same editorial conventions as in his previous edition, but there is no collation – as *BE* was unknown at the time – and he includes a brief section with explanatory notes clarifying obscure allusions after the last sonnet.

The year 1818 saw two facsimile editions of *D94*. Samuel W. Singer used the extant copy of *D94a* as source;[22] signature F, however, was missing and he sup-

17. Ibid., 489–491.
18. Ibid., 491.
19. *D92* was mostly unknown at the time.
20. Park, *Heliconia*, 4–11. Each section in this miscellany bears independent pagination.
21. Park, *Heliconia*, n.p.
22. He must have borrowed the book from Robert Triphook, who owned it at the time.

plied it from *D94b*. He included the erroneous date "1584" on the title page.[23] The Roxburghe Club edition used the Bodleian copy of *D94b*. Its salient feature is that the title page omits the reference to the edition being "augmented," de facto attributing all the sonnets to Constable; this decision would have lasting consequences with regard to later editors' acceptance of the dubia.[24]

Over the next decades, there were several instances of misattribution such as the inclusion of "Let others sing of knights and paladins," a sonnet by Samuel Daniel, as the only sample of Constable's poetry in an anthology compiled by Scottish poet Thomas Campbell.[25] Francis T. Palgrave's influential collection *The Golden Treasury* included "Diaphenia like a daffadowndilly," a pastoral poem first printed in *England's Helicon* (1600) under the initials "H.C.," and ascribed it to "H. Constable" instead of Henry Chettle.[26] Both cases evidence the critical neglect Constable was suffering at this time. His sonnets were obviously of some interest to Alexander Dyce, who acquired and rebound *T*; nevertheless, he remarked that "the pieces of this writer which have descended to our times by no means justify the very high applause bestowed on his poetry by his contemporaries."[27] Concerning the *SS* in this period, sonnet 83 to Mary Magdalene is printed by Robert A. Willmott in his *Lives of Sacred Poets*, but his assessment is far from positive: "Constable occasionally indulges in allusions more applicable to his 'vainer hours,' than these specimens of his 'calmer thought.' The concluding couplet of this sonnet affords an instance of this ill-taste."[28]

In 1859, William C. Hazlitt made the first attempt at publishing a complete edition of Constable's poetry. In it, he provides a fuller critical reassessment of his works, avoiding the usual commonplaces. He commends the "naturalness of sentiment" and "grace of expression" of the sonnets, which bear testimony to a "mind rich in fancy and invention."[29] Unfortunately, he extols a misattributed poem,

23. Henry Constable, *Diana: Or, the excellent conceitful Sonnets of H. C. augmented with diuers quatorzains of honorable and lerned personages; Deuided into viij. decads*, ed. Samuel W. Singer (London, 1818). Only fifty copies of Singer's edition were printed.

24. Henry Constable, *Diana: Or, the excellent conceitful Sonnets of H. C. supposed to have been printed either in 1592 or 1594*, ed. Edward Littledale (London, 1818). This edition had a larger print run.

25. Thomas Campbell, ed., *Specimens of the British Poets* (London, 1819), 2: 321.

26. It is the only poem believed to be by Constable in this collection. Francis T. Palgrave, ed., *The Golden Treasury of the Best Songs and Lyrical Poems in the English Language* (Cambridge, 1861), 9.

27. Alexander Dyce, ed., *Specimens of English Sonnets* (London, 1833), 213, 34–36. He printed sonnet 56 and two of the doubtful sonnets from *D94* in this collection.

28. Robert A. Willmott, *Lives of Sacred Poets* (London, 1834), 19. He also refers to the oft-quoted sonnet 27 as "almost the worst ever written by the author."

29. Hazlitt, v.

"The Sheepheard's Song of Venus and Adonis," as Constable's best work, whereas he dismisses the *SS* as "sacred effusions" that "rarely rise above mediocrity."[30] Despite its shortcomings, Hazlitt's biographical notice was the most complete written to date, and provided an overview of Henry's courtly connections based on some pieces of correspondence; he was the first to underline the good relationship that once existed between Constable and King James, for example, and included Constable's signature as found in manuscript.[31] Hazlitt's edition comprises twenty-eight sonnets from the *Dianas*, thirty-two unique to *T* – which are rearranged but presented with their respective headings – the four in *AP*, four misattributed poems in *EH*, and all seventeen *SS* from *HA*.[32] His text is eclectic, and readings from the printed and manuscript sources are combined in an attempt to eliminate textual corruptions. He preserves the original spelling for the most part and punctuates heavily.

Despite Park's and Hazlitt's rejection of the doubtful sonnets in *D94*, editors and anthologists producing collections of Elizabethan sonnet sequences in the last decades of the nineteenth century turned their attention to the augmented *Diana*.[33] In Edward Arber's *English Garner* all the *D94* sonnets, except for those known to be Sidney's, are presented with modernised spelling.[34] Martha Foote Crow printed *Diana* and Samuel Daniel's *Delia* in the same volume of her collection.[35] Her section on Constable includes the *D94* and some of the *T* sonnets – although her transcription is from Park's edition. The sonnets unique to *T* are grouped separately as "Sonnets from the manuscript edition, not found in that of 1594."[36] She deliberately excluded pieces dedicated to personages. In the case of sonnets preserved in the two sources, she gives them the individual headings they bear in the manuscript, even as she observes their arrangement into decades, which is the organising principle in *D94*. She occasionally adds her own headings when none is available.[37] In her introduction, Crow accepts all the *D94*

    30. Ibid., vi.
    31. Ibid., xxi.
    32. On the four poems in *EH*, see below, p. 147.
    33. Grundy explains this decision as the result of an "interest in the published sequences, rather than in the individual writer." See Grundy, 69.
    34. Edward Arber, ed., *An English Garner* (London, 1879), 2: 225–264. Arber acknowledges that the sonnets are by "H. Constable and others," and written "before 1594," at the top of every page.
    35. Martha Foote Crow, ed., *Elizabethan Sonnet-Cycles: Delia and Diana* (London, 1896), 83–173.
    36. Ibid., 164. These are numbers 5, 9, 11, 12, 14, 19, 44, 47, 49, and 50, presented as a sort of ninth decade.
    37. For instance, sonnet 60 bears no heading in *T* but is here titled "Love's seven deadly sins." Ibid., 101.

sonnets – but Sidney's – arguing that "it seems but fair to leave the *Diana* of 1594 in the hands of Constable" considering that "no more of the sonnets have ... been traced to their sources in the mazes of Elizabethan common-place books."[38] She offers a fresh insight into the *SS*, pointing out that the collection "illustrates an early effort to turn the poetic energy into a new field, to broaden the scope of subject-matter in sonnet-form." Crow is also the first editor to ponder the identity of the lady Constable honours, and, after discussing Penelope Rich and Arbella Stuart as possible candidates, concludes that the "puzzle" must remain "unsolved" because no "special tone of sincerity that leads us to have confidence in our conjecture" is found in the sonnets to both ladies.[39]

In 1897 John Gray produced a luxurious limited edition of Constable's oeuvre, "edited from early editions and manuscripts," and "with wood cut border & decorations executed by Charles Ricketts," the prestigious fin de siècle printer and illustrator.[40] Gray was a member of Oscar Wilde's circle and converted to Catholicism after "a spiritual crisis," which may explain his interest in a literary forebear.[41] The collection begins with the misattributed pastorals from *EH* and is followed by only the undisputed *D94* sonnets, and those unique to *T*. He does not follow the division into decades but observes some of the groupings and headings in the manuscript. The volume concludes with the seventeen *SS*. When editing from manuscript, Gray takes more liberties than Park regarding spelling; however, he often annotates possible emendations instead of inserting them in the text. His book contains no information about Constable's life and career whatsoever.

The last development in the nineteenth century was Edward Dowden's discovery of *M*, another miscellany containing sonnets by Constable. He printed the two sonnets that are unique to *M* (64 and 65) in an article, and described the other contents of the volume briefly.[42] Sir Sidney Lee's influential *Elizabethan Sonnets* is perhaps best referenced here; although published in 1904, it is the product of late-Victorian criticism.[43] For the section on Constable, Lee chose *D94* as his only source, despite admitting that the authorship of many of the sonnets was doubtful.[44] His edition relies on Arber's text, and in his introduction he is intent

38. Ibid., 85.
39. Ibid., 87, 92.
40. John Gray, ed., *The Poems & Sonnets of Henry Constable* (London, 1897).
41. Gray published his own *Spiritual Poems* in 1896; see Karl Beckson, "Gray, John Henry (1866–1934)," in *ODNB*.
42. Edward Dowden, "An Elizabethan MS Collection: Henry Constable," *The Modern Quarterly of Language and Literature* 1 (1898): 3–4.
43. Sidney Lee, ed., *Elizabethan Sonnets* (New York, 1904).
44. Ibid., 1: lxii.

on proving Constable's indebtedness to contemporary French and Italian poets. He reaches the conclusion that "evidence that Shakespeare read Constable's verse and borrowed from it probably gives it its most lasting interest."[45] Lee was also responsible for the entry on Constable in the original *Dictionary of National Biography*, in which he pieced together information from State Papers and letters, mentioning for the first time Constable's early career as a spy under Walsingham and his conversion to Catholicism, and thus denying that he had been a Catholic from the outset. In his critical appraisal of the sonnets, he argues that they are "too full of quaint conceits to be read nowadays with much pleasure, but his vocabulary and imagery often indicate real passion and poetic feeling. The 'Spirituall Sonnetes' breathe genuine religious fervour."[46]

## The Twentieth Century

Lee's judgement of Constable as a minor sonneteer indebted to other writers made its way well into the twentieth century. No edition of his poems was published for sixty years and only a few works of scholarship engage with them at all. L.E. Kastner and Janet Scott focused on drawing parallels between Constable's sonnets and those by the French poets, especially Philippe Desportes, although they relied heavily on the *D94* doubtful sonnets.[47] In 1931 Hyder Rollins made an important contribution by correctly attributing the four pastoral poems in *EH* to Henry Chettle.[48]

The focus of Lisle C. John's *The Elizabethan Sonnet Sequences*, first published in 1938, is the study of conceits, and he often turns to Constable for examples. In his notes, he offers a summary of all the available information concerning the sources of Constable's poems known to that date, and gives *T* its due by stating that the poet's contemporaries probably knew his sonnets as they appeared in manuscript.[49] Louise I. Guiney included a chapter on Constable in her *Recusant Poets* and provided the first comprehensive biography, dating his conversion to 1591 and casting some light on the hitherto obscure circumstances of his impris-

45. Ibid., 1: lxii–lxiii.
46. Sidney Lee, "Constable, Henry (1562–1613), poet," in *The Dictionary of National Biography*, ed. Leslie Smith (London, 1887), 12: 34–35.
47. L.E. Kastner, "The Elizabethan Sonneteers and the French Poets," *The Modern Language Review* 3 (1908): 268–277; Scott, *Sonnets*.
48. Hyder E. Rollins, "England's Helicon and Henry Chettle," *The Times Literary Supplement*, no. 1548 (1931): 749.
49. Lisle C. John, *The Elizabethan Sonnet Sequences: Studies in Conventional Conceits* (New York, 1966), 213–215.

onment. The *M* and *H* collections were unknown to her, although she does allude to a nineteenth-century transcript of the latter.[50] Guiney was the first to mention the presence of some of Constable's sonnets in the miscellany *A poetical rapsody* (1602) and the mid-seventeenth century *A*, plus a doubtful sonnet in Edmund Bolton's *Elements of Armories* (1610). On the other hand, she categorically denied Constable's authorship of *The Catholike Moderator*, the 1623 translation of the *Examen*, claiming that it had been attributed to him "in the hope of thus pressing his name posthumously into Protestant controversy."[51] Guiney's chapter includes a semidiplomatic transcription of seven of the *SS* from *HA*, plus a sonnet in the memory of Sidney from *AP*.[52]

The extensive research conducted by George Wickes in the 1950s saw the light in the form of three articles which became the new cornerstone of Constable studies. His 1954 biographical account rests on firsthand archival research and shows an unprecedented concern for historical accuracy.[53] It covers the different stages in Constable's life, from his beginnings as a prospective courtier writing in order to obtain patronage to his conversion and postconversion activities as an exile and political intriguer. Among his many important statements is the affirmation of Constable's authorship of the *Examen*.[54] In a briefer article published two years later, Wickes makes the crucial point that "it is best to disregard the printed poems and to turn to his poems in manuscript" in order to understand Constable's endeavours as a poet and man of the world.[55] He denies Constable's involvement in the publication of the sonnets and offers a concise description of *H* and *T* as major sources of the secular sonnets, giving preeminence to the latter as

> the closest thing we have to an authoritative text of Constable's verse. For one thing, the poems were collected shortly before his departure from England for a life of exile. For another, Constable took the trouble to assemble the poems he had written over a period of half a dozen years and supplied careful explanatory titles. He also devised an elaborate framework for his poems, organizing them into groups according to the science of numbers.[56]

50. This is London, British Library, Add MS 28635; Louise Imogen Guiney, *Recusant Poets*, ed. Geoffrey Bliss and Louise Imogen Guiney (New York, 1939).
51. Ibid., 316.
52. These are numbers 67, 70, 79, 81, 74, 82, 77, and 51.
53. Wickes, *Bio*, 272–300.
54. Ibid., 275.
55. Wickes, *Courtier*, 103.
56. Ibid., 103–104.

The *SS* are the focus of a third article. Like all other scholars before him, he quotes from *HA*; unlike them, he offers a reassessment of the poet's religious pieces as influenced by the Italian Counter-Reformation.[57]

In 1960 Ruth Hughey completed her monumental edition of the Harington MS, which she had discovered twenty-six years earlier at Arundel Castle.[58] The first volume contains a general introduction and the edited texts, whereas the second has item- or author-based introductions and collations of the texts with other sources. The texts of the twenty-one sonnets by Constable as they appear in *H* were thus made available in print for the first time.[59] Hughey's edition is diplomatic as far as typography allows; she alters neither spelling nor punctuation, leaves contractions unexpanded and reproduces the mise-en-page of the sonnets. Her collation includes *M*, *T*, *D92*, *D94*, and *A*.[60] She is concerned with pointing at the least corrupt or most authoritative text for each sonnet, and she inevitably leans towards *H*. The judgement that "insufficient attention has been given to Constable's work by modern scholars" and that someone ought to "soon undertake a definitive study of Constable and his work" reveals that Hughey was unacquainted with Joan Grundy's edition, published in the same year.[61]

Grundy's *The Poems of Henry Constable* was the most extensive edition of the sonnets so far and has been regularly referenced by commentators. It comprises sonnet 66 ("To his absent Diana") from *D92*, other material prefacing the *Dianas*, the sixty-three sonnets in *T*, the two sonnets unique to *M* (64, 65), and the doubtful sonnet in Edmund Bolton's *Elements of Armories*.[62] After the secular sonnets come the seventeen *SS* in *HA*.[63] A textual apparatus is included in the case of the former group, but not in that of the latter, due to her unacquaintance with *BE*. Two sources containing secular sonnets, *Bn* and *E*, were also unknown

57. Wickes, *Sonnets*, 30–40.
58. A preliminary account had been published in Ruth Hughey, "The Harington MS at Arundel Castle," *Library* 15 (1935), 388–444; Constable's sonnets are mentioned on page 433.
59. Ruth W. Hughey, ed., *The Arundel Harington Manuscript of Tudor Poetry* (Columbus, 1960), 1: 244–252.
60. *M* had been consistently ignored by critics, including Wickes, ever since its discovery by Dowden. Hughey draws attention to it as "the earliest Constable source." Hughey, 2: 332. Years later it became the focus of Martin's thesis and it was one of the miscellanies discussed in Black's dissertation; see George Martin, "Marsh's Library MS z3.5.21: An Edition of the English Poems" (master's thesis, University of Waterloo, 1971); L.G. Black, "Studies in Some Related Manuscript Poetic Miscellanies of the 1580s" (PhD diss., Oxford University, 1970).
61. Hughey, 2: 333–334.
62. Grundy, 109–182.
63. Ibid., 183–192.

to her and remain unaccounted for. The commentary is located at the end of the volume, together with a table showing the arrangement of the sonnets in different sources, and a first-line index. All the doubtful sonnets in *D94* are printed in an appendix but remain undiscussed; this editorial decision clashes with her statement that they must be excluded from the canon, evidencing Grundy's failure to take a stance on the subject of their authorship.[64]

The introduction begins with a biography, a section establishing the canon, in which the *SS* are also discussed, and a survey of the poet's reputation and early reception. A fourth chapter titled "The Poems: Evaluation" can be deemed to have done a disservice to Constable. Grundy's criticism of his shortcomings as a poet is severe, for instance when referring to him as a "dull" poet who fails "to stamp his own individuality upon the convention he is using." She is oblivious of both the specific social context in which the sonnets were produced and their intended audience when she states that "there is no indication of anything in Constable's experience, real or imaginary, to which we can relate them."[65] Grundy's criticism continues for a few pages and only Constable's "diction" comes up for moderate praise as she considers it "his greatest single asset."[66] She then proceeds to analyse the possible literary influences revealed in Constable's secular and religious verse. Her final judgement is that "the best" of the *Spiritual Sonnets* "far surpass the secular ones."[67] In a fifth section, "The Text," she briefly describes the sources for the sonnets – arranged in terms of their presumed importance instead of chronology – and casts some light on their provenance. However, she does not attempt to build stemmata showing their textual relationships; she neither views the sonnets included in miscellanies as parts of a larger whole nor hypothesises on their provenance and compilers. This gives the impression that Constable's sonnets exist in a vacuum, detached from other texts and their social milieu. Furthermore, no connections are drawn between the secular and religious sonnets at all.

Concerning the body of the edition, Grundy's most significant accomplishment is her use of manuscript sources – especially *T* – as copy texts, privileging them over the printed editions. Her transcription is semidiplomatic: she observes the original spelling and, in most cases, the punctuation, and expands abbreviations. The text often incorporates emendations from other sources or her own without an explanation of the criteria at work, and her treatment of variants when it comes to the textual apparatus is just as puzzling: "Variations in spelling and

64. Ibid., 193–217, 51.
65. Ibid., 71.
66. Ibid., 73.
67. Ibid., 80.

punctuation are noted only occasionally. I have emended a few things, but have left certain solecisms unchanged, where the usage seemed likely to be that of the author."[68] As a result, accidental variants are interspersed with verbal ones. There are also significant omissions and errata in the apparatus.[69] Editorial choices regarding the layout of the sonnets remain unexplained; the secular sonnets are presented one per page, imitating the mise-en-page of *T*, whereas the *SS* are clustered together, and often run onto the next page, which makes them look as if they were of lesser importance.

Notwithstanding Grundy's privileging of manuscript sources, other twentieth-century editors opted for *D92* as their copy text. Maurice Evans included twenty-one sonnets from this edition in his influential anthology *Elizabethan Sonnets*.[70] He acknowledges the importance of the longer collection in *T* but argues that his book cannot accommodate all the sonnets, and that *D92* "includes enough sonnets to give an adequate idea of Constable's quality."[71] He does emend his text with readings from *T* when he deems the *Diana* to be corrupt, relying on Grundy's edition, but no textual apparatus accompanies the sonnets. His observation that "Constable's sonnets were more social and political than amatory in their motivation" is sound and has become a critical commonplace.[72] Evans's major contribution to restoring Constable's literary reputation was the positioning of the poet among contemporaries such as Sidney or Daniel, which meant his inclusion in the ranks of sonneteers whose works should be read by students.

In 1980 Robert Fleissner published an edition of Constable's sonnets as they appear in *D92*, a thin volume including collation and commentary. He sought to prove that Hughey's and Grundy's editions were faulty and to give preeminence to the *Diana* text, going as far as to claim that it "represents Constable at his spontaneous best, was set up from the manuscript the author most probably preferred to see printed, and has the fewest eccentric variants."[73] He defers to Park, Hughey, and Grundy for descriptions of the sources, transcriptions, and collations, acknowledging that he has not had "personal access" to any of the three major manuscript collections.[74] The transcription is semidiplomatic and con-

---

68. Ibid., 104.

69. To give but one example, Grundy fails to record the *H* variant "his" in 8.2; ibid., 121.

70. One sonnet is omitted, number 42 on the birth of Lady Rich's daughter, because, according to Evans, it "does not properly belong to the sequence." See Maurice Evans, ed., *Elizabethan Sonnets* (London, 1977), 217. This book has undergone numerous editions.

71. Ibid., 217.

72. Ibid., 218.

73. Robert F. Fleissner, *Resolved to Love: The 1592 edition of Henry Constable's Diana, Critically Considered* (Salzburg, 1980), iv.

74. Ibid., 26 n.

servative in terms of spelling, although punctuation is occasionally amended. In his assessment of variants included in the commentary, he seeks to privilege the printed edition, for instance when he says of sonnet 15 that "the variant readings seem relatively inconsequential," despite the fact that it underwent major revisions that yielded two distinct versions.[75] All in all, there are numerous errors throughout the edition, and Fleissner's original contribution is scant.

## Into the Twenty-First Century

From the 1990s on there have been important contributions to the study of Constable's secular poetry. Some deal with the arrangement of sonnet sequences; others focus on Constable's connections with members of the Sidney circle, or his status as a courtier-poet.[76] The revival of interest in the works by English Catholics, as a result of the so-called "turn to religion" after centuries of Protestant-centred scholarship and neglect, has rendered the SS the object of increasing critical attention.[77] One or more devotional sonnets have been included in anthologies.[78] Anthony D. Cousins offers an in-depth study of Constable's sonnets; his positive appraisal contrasts with earlier assessments such as Toshihiko Kawasaki's.[79] For Alison Shell and Helen Hackett, Constable is a case study of self-professed Catholic loyalism, and they discuss the transference of the poet's allegiance from an earthly to a divine sovereign, quoting from both secular and religious sonnets.[80] Jerome Mazzaro, Gary Kuchar, William Engels, and Helen

---

75. Ibid., 64.

76. See for instance Parker; Woudhuysen, *Circulation*; Steven W. May, *The Elizabethan Courtier Poets: The Poems and their Contexts* (Columbia, 1991), 132. The list of secondary sources in this section is by no means intended to be comprehensive; refer to citations of other important works throughout the present volume.

77. On this trend, see Ken Jackson and Arthur F. Marotti, "The Turn to Religion in Early Modern English Studies," *Criticism* 46 (2004): 167–190.

78. Emrys Jones, ed., *The New Oxford Book of Sixteenth-Century Verse* (Oxford, 1991), 463–467; David Norbrook and Henry R. Woudhuysen, eds., *The Penguin Book of Renaissance Verse* (London, 1993), 254; Robert S. Miola, ed., *Early Modern Catholicism: An Anthology of Primary Sources* (Oxford, 2007), 187–192; John Saward, John S. Morrill, and Michael Tomko, eds., *Firmly I Believe and Truly: The Spiritual Tradition of Catholic England* (Oxford, 2011), 177–179. Jones and Miola also include several secular sonnets.

79. Anthony D. Cousins, *The Catholic Religious Poets from Southwell to Crashaw: A Critical History* (London, 1991), 74–86; Toshihiko Kawasaki, "From Southwell to Donne," *Eibungaku kenkyū* 39 (1963): 11–31, at 21.

80. Alison Shell, *Catholicism, Controversy, and the English Literary Imagination, 1558–1660* (Cambridge, 1999); Helen Hackett, "The Art of Blasphemy? Interfusions of the Erotic

Wilcox have tackled the spiritual dimension of the sonnets, their influences, and the subject of Catholic poetics.[81] More recently, Lilla Grindlay has offered an accomplished analysis of the sonnets to the Virgin Mary, and Robert E. Stillman has discussed Constable as a "peacemaker," "a conciliator and irenicist who espouses a pious cross-confessional identity."[82]

Entries on Constable have recently been updated, as in the case of the *ODNB*, or included in new encyclopaedias and catalogues, for example in *The Encyclopedia of English Renaissance Literature* and in the online *CELM*.[83] The latter contains a list of Constable's works and letters which is incomplete and not always accurate, particularly where his prose treatises are concerned. With a separate item number for each sonnet as it appears in a particular source, it is nevertheless an invaluable research tool.

The most recent edition and commentary of Constable's poetry can be found in Claire Williams's yet-unpublished dissertation in two volumes, an edition of the whole *T* miscellany.[84] The text of the sonnets is found in the first volume.[85] It is a semidiplomatic transcription, conservative with regards to spelling and punctuation, in which abbreviations are expanded but italicised. The mise-en-page of the sonnets is reproduced, and a small textual apparatus containing information about emendations and deletions in the copy text is supplied under each sonnet. The remaining notes, including collation and commentary, are

---

and the Sacred in the Poetry of Donne, Barnes, and Constable," *Renaissance and Reformation* 28, no. 3 (2004): 27–54.

81. Jerome Mazzaro, "Recusant Sincerity: Henry Constable at Spiritual Sonnets," *Essays in Literature* 17 (1990): 147–159; Gary Kuchar, "Henry Constable and the Question of Catholic Poetics: Affective Piety and Erotic Identification in the Spirituall Sonnettes," *Philological Quarterly* 85 (2006): 69–89; William Engels, "Constable's Spirituall Sonnettes and the Three Spiritual Ways," *Medieval and Early Modern English Studies* 14 (2006): 407–430; Helen Wilcox, "Sacred Desire, Forms of Belief: The Religious Sonnet in Early Modern Britain," in *The Cambridge Companion to the Sonnet*, ed. A. D. Cousins and Peter Howarth (Cambridge, 2011), 145–165.

82. Lilla Grindlay, *Queen of Heaven: The Assumption and Coronation of the Virgin in Early Modern English Writing* (Notre Dame, IN, 2018) – see esp. chapter 5; Robert E. Stillman, *Christian Identity, Piety, and Politics in Early Modern England* (Notre Dame, IN, 2021) – see esp. chapter 6.

83. The most recent *Oxford Dictionary of National Biography* entry on Constable is Ceri Sullivan, "Constable, Henry (1562–1613), polemicist and poet," in *ODNB*, dating from 2004 (online ed. 2013). See also Emily E. Stockard, "Constable, Henry," in *The Encyclopedia of English Renaissance Literature*, ed. Garrett A. Sullivan and Alan Stewart (Chichester, 2012), 1: 209–210; *CELM*.

84. Williams, *Edition*.

85. Ibid., 1: 10–75.

located in the second volume, following an introduction to Constable's secular poetry. This opening section includes a biography mostly based on Wickes and the *ODNB*, an account of some internal dating evidence in his sonnets, a chart of rhyme structures in the sonnets in *T*, and a concise description of all the extant manuscript and printed sources containing Constable's secular sonnets – the *SS* are out of Williams's scope. Other tables show the presence or absence of each sonnet in the other sources, their textual accuracy, and their shared errors. These errors serve as basis for her single stemma of transmission, as they are deemed more important than instances of authorial or scribal revision. She does establish some relations between the different sources and raises the hypothesis that there were lost textual archetypes from which the surviving texts derived. Her determination to establish a "best text" for each of the sonnets seems in keeping with that of Hughey and Fleissner. Williams undertakes the first study of the secular sonnets in the context of a manuscript miscellany and attempts to build a stemma.[86] One of her major contributions is the identification of the *T* compiler.[87]

---

86. On differences between her stemma and the one in the present volume, see p. 71 n146.

87. See also Claire B. Williams, "'This and the rest Maisters we all may mende': Reconstructing the Practices and Anxieties of a Manuscript Miscellany's Reader-Compiler," *Huntington Library Quarterly* 80 (2017): 277–292, at 283.

CHAPTER SIX

# The Present Edition

The canon of Henry Constable's poetry comprises ninety sonnets; it has been established on the principles of their transmission in manuscript and the rejection of the misattributed sonnets or works of dubious authorship interspersed with his own. Of the sixty-nine secular and dedicatory sonnets, sixty-three are those constituting the collection in *T*. Three are alternate versions of sonnets in *T* from *M*, an earlier source, all of which are different enough to be considered separate works. These are identified with the sonnet number followed by the letter *b* in this edition. Two, numbers 64 and 65, are early sonnets that only survive in *M*. The final one is the sonnet prefacing *D92*, which exists only in print but is conferred some authority by the facts surrounding publication.

I have excluded four pastoral poems bearing the initials "H.C." in the anthology *England's Helicon,* which were misattributed to Constable for centuries and are in fact the work of Henry Chettle.[1] The introductory sonnet published in Edmund Bolton's *Elements of Armories* in 1610, which also bears the initials "H.C." and does not survive in manuscript, has likewise been rejected. This is quite unlike any other of Constable's sonnets and, were it his own, it would have been written very late in comparison.[2] The most difficult decision in terms of

---

1. This misattribution is found, for instance, in Thomas Warton, *The History of English Poetry* (London, 1781), 3: 292. Hyder Rollins was the first to attribute the sonnets to Chettle, noting that the former identification "was made purely on guesswork." See Hyder E. Rollins, "England's Helicon and Henry Chettle," *The Times Literary Supplement,* no. 1548 (1931): 749.
2. The initials "H.C." were shared by a number of contemporaries including Humfrey Coningsby and Henry Chettle, and heraldry was popular enough among courtiers. Grundy prints this poem in her edition, placing it at the end of the secular sonnets and immediately before the religious sonnets. She justifies her attribution invoking Constable's "known interest in heraldry" and the use of the Italian form; see Grundy, 182, 50. The only connection between the author of this dialogue on heraldic conventions and Constable is the fact that Bolton was a Catholic and that he praised Constable in his later *Hypercritica* (see Joseph Haslewood, ed., *Ancient Critical Essays upon English Poets and Poesy* [London, 1815], 2: 250).

exclusion from the canon pertains to the forty-one unattributed sonnets in *D94*. Their varied metre, character, and literary quality, together with the printer's title page announcement that *Diana* had been "augmented" with "Quatorzains of honorable and lerned personages," and the fact that eight of Sidney's sonnets are also included, have discouraged me from attempting to handpick those sonnets which might indeed be Constable's.[3] My complete agreement with the argument made by previous critics that there is more to be lost than gained from the attribution of these works of doubtful authorship to Constable disinclined me to print them in a section of dubia.[4]

As for the *Spiritual Sonnets*, the canon has been expanded to include twenty-one. The *BE* manuscript, unnoticed for centuries, contains final versions of the seventeen sonnets in *HA* plus four more, one dedicated to St Colette and three elegies on the death and funeral of Mary, Queen of Scots.[5]

## Selection of Copy Texts

Bearing in mind that Constable was a coterie poet whose sonnets circulated among relatives and friends, and that, being in exile, he probably did not oversee their publication, manuscript sources must be privileged.[6] Once this has been established, the editing of his sonnets poses similar problems to those that editors of other early modern poets have to face.[7] The absence of holographs, the

   3. These are nevertheless discussed on pp. 63–64.
   4. See Wickes, *Courtier*, 102, and Grundy, 51–53. Grundy's decision to include the forty-one sonnets as an appendix to her edition, without so much as discussing them in her commentary, seems contradictory.
   5. Park attributed the seventeen sonnets "by H.C." in *HA* to Constable for the first time; see Park, *THM*, 491. An instance of ungrounded misattribution of these sonnets to Henry Cooke is mentioned in Grundy, 53–54. There is little doubt that the extra sonnets in *BE* are also Constable's, considering the manuscript's provenance, the careful arrangement of the sequence, and the heading "by Hen. Conestable, Esquire."
   6. Wickes was the first to confer greater authority to the manuscript sonnets, particularly those in *T*; see Wickes, *Courtier*, 102–103. Grundy also privileges this manuscript as "the most important source" for the secular sonnets; see Grundy, 84.
   7. Constable's case is particularly similar to that of John Donne; Pebworth has discussed the impossibility of putting W.W. Greg's theory of copy-text selection into practice in the case of Donne. See Ted-Larry Pebworth, "Manuscript Transmission and the Selection of Copy-Text in Renaissance Coterie Poetry," *Text* 7 (1994): 243–261, at 244–246. The author of a recent edition of the poems of Surrey has also contended with the absence of holographs and early copies; see Henry Howard, *A Critical Edition of the Complete Poems of Henry Howard, Earl of Surrey*, ed. William McGaw (Lewiston, 2012), lxxxii–lxxxiii.

complex history of transmission resulting in versions that differ in both accidental and verbal variants, and the number of agents intervening in the texts and imposing their own scribal conventions and alterations on them complicate the matter of choosing a copy text that is closest to what Constable wrote.[8]

All sonnets by Constable descend from lost authorial archetypes, and it is collation and stemmatics that reveal the relations between the surviving texts and give proof that the author took part in the process of revision at certain moments in the transmission history. Ideally, collation of the sources based on the verbal variants would enable an editor to select what Ted-Larry Pebworth terms the "least verbally corrupt text" as copy text.[9] In reality, doing so in Constable's case would entail editing his works on a poem by poem basis, selecting the best copy text for each, and creating a patchwork edition devoid of structural integrity.[10] Although some sonnets circulated as separates, Constable was responsible for arranging them into sequences or collections, and this edition abides by his concern with social rank and order. Despite a number of obvious scribal errors and omissions, due to its being twice removed from a holograph (archetype $Z$), the collection in $T$ has been chosen as copy text for the sixty-three sonnets it contains for a number of reasons. First, it is the most comprehensive collection; secondly, it descends from the latest family of transmission; finally, it includes the latest authorial revisions and shows the authorial arrangement of the poems and authorial headings. Therefore, this edition aims to present Constable's final intentions regarding his works as closely as possible.

The other manuscript copy text for the secular sonnets is $M$, derived from the earliest authorial manuscript (archetype $X$), which is the source for 15b, 32b, 60b, 64, and 65. The first three are early versions of sonnets in $T$, and each follows the corresponding $T$ sonnet to facilitate comparison;[11] the latter two are unique

---

8. Pebworth, "Manuscript Transmission," 244–246. I take verbal variants to be those affecting meaning, whereas accidentals depend on varying scribal practices; see below. Textual instability and malleability have been discussed at length in studies by Peter Beal and Arthur Marotti, among others. See Peter Beal, *In Praise of Scribes: Manuscripts and Their Makers in Seventeenth-Century England* (Oxford, 1998) and Arthur Marotti, *Manuscript, Print, and the English Renaissance Lyric* (Ithaca, NY, 1995), inter alia.

9. Pebworth, "Manuscript Transmission," 250.

10. Former editors of Constable, including Ruth Hughey, Robert F. Fleissner, and Claire B. Williams, have tried to establish the best text for the sonnets, often favouring their copy text.

11. On the need to reproduce very different versions of a text separately instead of embedding the variants of one in the apparatus to another, see Michael Hunter, *Editing Early Modern Texts: An Introduction to Principles and Practice* (Basingstoke, 2007), 72–73, and Ted-Larry Pebworth and Ernest W. Sullivan, "Rational Presentation of Multiple Textual Traditions," *The Papers of the Bibliographical Society of America* 83 (1989): 43–60, at 44–45.

to this manuscript. The copy text for sonnet 66, headed "To his absent Diana," is *D92*, as it occurs nowhere else. Headings have been added in order to separate groups of sonnets printed from sources other than *T*, and by doing so preserve the cohesion of the *T* collection.

The case of the religious sonnets is somewhat different. Although there is no certainty as to which accidentals the author himself favoured or whether the scribes simply supplied their own, and no holographs are preserved, both *HA* and *BE* can be considered complete works at their respective stages of transmission, put together for a particular purpose, and once removed from lost authorial originals. With the exception of 71, none of the *Spiritual Sonnets* exist in other copies that might testify to their being immersed in a process of circulation beyond the author's control.[12] *BE* – containing only a few errors – seems to be an accurate scribal transcription of the latest draft and bears witness to the sequence in its final, complete version. Therefore, it has for the first time been used as the copy text for the *Spiritual Sonnets* in the present edition.[13]

## Editorial Conventions

The texts of the sonnets have been edited with a double concern for authenticity and readability. Capitalisation has been retained. Original spelling has been reproduced, with some exceptions made in order to avoid obscuring the text unnecessarily. The use of *u/v* and *i/j* has been modernised, bearing in mind that the usage of these letters was evolving at the time and contingent on individual scribal practices.[14] The double *f* found in *BE* and *M* texts has been rendered as a capital *F* when it appears at the beginning of lines, and a minuscule *f* when it appears in initial position in a word found elsewhere. *BE* also has an instance of a double capital *P*, which has been transcribed as one letter. The ligatures œ and æ ("Phœnix," "æternitye") are rendered *oe* and *ae*. Apostrophes such as those found in some present and past tense verbs (e.g., "desir'd," "dar'st"), which may affect the metre of a line, are considered spelling features and retained.

Tildes over the letters *m* or *n* denoting a double consonant, or those over a vowel indicating that it should be followed by *m* or *n* (e.g., "frō") have been expanded, as have been common abbreviations with superscript letters – such as

12. On the separate circulation of sonnet 71 and its misattribution to Donne, see p. 102.
13. All previous editors of these sonnets have inevitably used *HA* as a copy text.
14. See Hunter, *Editing Early Modern Texts*, 77–78. Quotations from primary texts, manuscript or printed, in the introductory chapters and notes are regularised in this way unless otherwise noted.

$w^{ch}$, $w^{th}$, and $y^t$ – given that speed of composition was the main reason behind their use in handwritten texts.[15] The ambiguous brevigraph $y^u$ in *M* has been transcribed as *thou* because it is consistent with the verb forms used (for instance, "canst" and "art" in 64). Other abbreviations which have been silently expanded include the brevigraphs used for *per*, *pre*, and *par* within a word, the open *c* which denotes an *-es* word ending, the final superscript epsilon for *r* (as in "honnor" in 86.8), and the capital *m* with a superscript epsilon which stands for "Maister" in 74.1.[16] The symbol = has been transcribed as its modern equivalent, the hyphen, when it occurs at the end of a line; in its rare occurrences in medial position (e.g., "hap=ning"), it has been omitted altogether. A period replaces the colon following the abbreviations Q and K for "king" and "queen." The use of the ampersand (&) has been retained due to its intelligibility to contemporary readers. Obvious omissions in the manuscript have been signalled with the use of spaced periods, as in sonnets 43 and 47.

Line numbers have been added for ease of reference. Punctuation is editorial and may or may not mirror that in the copy text. In *T* the scribe has punctuated most sonnets sparingly, whereas others show a larger number of punctuation marks which were probably added later. Bearing in mind that none of the copy texts is a holograph and there is no way to know what the lost authorial sources might have looked like, punctuation has been considered an accidental trait dependent on scribal practices.[17] Instances in which the addition or removal of punctuation may resolve intended ambiguities or entail loss of meaning are explained in the notes.

Regardless of the copy text used and the degree of complexity of the accompanying textual apparatus, one sonnet is presented on each page of this edition in order to avoid overlap between notes. The only exception is sonnet 62, which is followed by a prose text on the same page in *T* and has been reproduced thus. In the case of sonnet 1 and its accompanying prose text, the latter is presented on a different page due to space restrictions. Headings to the sonnets are left-aligned and their line breaks do not mirror those in the copy texts; however, the mise-en-page of the main body of the sonnets has been imitated insofar as indentation and spacing between quatrains and sestets – or couplets – are concerned. Changes in script in the copy texts are not reproduced, and only roman type is used in the body of the sonnets.

15. See Beal, *Dictionary*, 1; and Hunter, *Editing Early Modern Texts*, 76.
16. This spelling is used in line 4 of the same sonnet.
17. See Harold Love, *Scribal Publication in Seventeenth-Century England* (Oxford, 1993), 120.

A degree of editorial intervention has been exercised in the face of scribal errors. Some errors can be traced through the close examination of the transmission history of individual sonnets. In this case, care has been taken to avoid conflating variants from distant textual traditions (e.g., substituting a word stemming from the Z archetype with one from the earlier X) and, whenever possible, errors have been corrected using alternative readings available in descendants from the same textual family – such as emending an error in T with a variant in the printed PE, given that both descend from Z. Manuscript variants, when available, are favoured over printed. Other errors are found in sonnets which have only survived in T and have been emended with even greater caution, with the aim to correct glaring scribal errors or textual corruptions that affect meaning.[18] The collation displays emendations clearly; when the lemma given is a variant from another source, the siglum follows it before the bracket. In sonnets 43 and 47, scribal omissions have not been reconstructed due to the copy text being the only source. All emendations are justified in the notes to each sonnet, and the relations between texts can be seen in the sections on transmission and the stemmata. A concern with what the Donne *variorum* editors have termed "the semiological integrity" of the sonnets as preserved in their early modern sources underlies any exercises of editorial judgement.[19]

## Textual Apparatus

For the sake of clarity, each sonnet is followed by its apparatus. The first line includes a list of sources, with the sigla in italics followed by the folio or page number and a number within brackets indicating the position of the sonnet in relation to the others by Constable in the same source, whether it coincides with the number in the heading or not.

My purpose is to present what David C. Greetham terms a "clear-text" edition.[20] Therefore, alterations and additions to the text by the same scribe, when they exist, are recorded as "miscellaneous features" in the apparatus. Keywords are employed to describe the nature of these changes. The term "superimposed" is used when the letter or word is written over a previous one, transforming it. When a letter or word is added above the line without deleting the previous one, it is said

---

18. On editorial intervention in such cases, see David C. Greetham, *Textual Scholarship: An Introduction* (New York, 1992), 352.

19. John Donne, *The Variorum Edition of the Poetry of John Donne*, ed. Gary A. Stringer and Jeffrey S. Johnson (Bloomington, IN, 2005), 7.1: liii.

20. Greetham, *Textual Scholarship*, 368.

to be "inserted." If there is deletion, it is said to be "replacing" another word "deleted," which may or may not have been rendered illegible. Occasionally a word has been deleted and not replaced with any other because the scribe simply continued penning the line; in this case, the word that follows is described as "replacing" the deleted one. Features that are unique to a sonnet are also recorded in this section, for example the numbers added on the margin in sonnet 60.

The collation makes it possible to reconstruct the texts as they appear in the different sources and to trace editorial intervention. The headings are collated first. The line number in which a variant occurs is given in bold, followed by the lemma – either a single word or a phrase – and a closing square bracket. Variants are separated with a semicolon, and each is followed by the sigla for the source or sources in which it appears. For the purposes of the present edition and to avoid cluttering the apparatus, only verbal variants – those which affect meaning and are not dependent on changing contemporary scribal practices – and other substantive variants are given. The former group includes different word forms (e.g., "doe" and "doth" in 4; "shutes" and "shoote" in 7). The latter includes changes in spelling and punctuation that may affect meaning (e.g., 17.9, in which the position of the parenthesis is relevant).

Variants which have been used as the basis for editorial emendations are always recorded in the collation. For instance, in sonnet 8 line 12 reads "doth draw" and has been emended to "drawth" based on the reading in *H*, which is noted in the collation thus:

12 drawth *H*] doth draw *T*; drawes *D92 D94 A*

This accounts for the reading in *T*, which is deemed inferior to that in *H* because it affects the metre by adding an extra syllable. Occasionally a whole line has been emended according to the reading in another source; line 6 in sonnet 57 reads "Love is not in my heart, no, Lady, no," and is borrowed from *D94* because the scribe omitted it altogether in *T*. Collation records it in the following way:

6 Love ... no *D94 A*] *line missing T*

In the few cases in which its absence or presence alters meaning, punctuation is included in the collation. A small caret (^) marks punctuation that is omitted in the collated source. The abbreviation *om* indicates that a word in the lemma has been omitted, for example in 32:

6 owne] *om PR1 PR2 A*

The abbreviation *om* is also used to indicate that there is no heading in one or more of the sources. When a verbal or substantive variant is listed, alternative spellings are disregarded. Consider sonnet 10:

13 **may**] do *M H D92 D94*; doth *A*

In fact, the first variant is spelled "do" in *M* and *H*, "doo" in *D92*, and "doe" in *D94*, but recording the different spellings would clutter the apparatus and offer no significant information in terms of transmission. As far as longer, multiword variants are concerned, their correspondence at the verbal level is likewise privileged.

The same transcription conventions used throughout the edition have been used to transcribe the variants in the collated sources. Abbreviations are expanded save for the ambiguous $y^u$, which could stand for "you" or "thou." When a variant in a source collated is the product of revision, for example resulting from insertion, only the scribal end product is given in the collation, and any features of interest are noted in the explanatory notes. Marginalia or insertions on the page made in a different hand are dated later and not included in the textual apparatus; they have been recorded within the description of the corresponding manuscript sources.

Beneath the collation, difficult or obscure words are glossed following the line number and the lemma given in bold. These glosses are of two types. First, words or phrases that are listed as rare, archaic, or literary in the *Oxford English Dictionary* (*OED*), and obsolete meanings of current words, whose definition is followed by a parenthetical reference to the corresponding entry. When Constable's use of a word antedates the first recorded use, this is noted in the parenthesis. Secondly, words whose spelling does not make them immediately recognizable to the modern reader are also glossed, e.g., "die" meaning "dye" in sonnet 43, or "nye" for "nigh" in sonnet 60. Where ambiguity could have been intended, the two senses of the word are given, and nuances of meaning are explained in more depth in the notes.

In the explanatory notes, references to sonnets in this edition are given with their number within square brackets.

25

*To his mistris tnt truon hy intertayning*
*hym after hard & disgratious wordes*

My hope layt gasping on his dying bedd
fadne with a word the dart of thy distayut
Another woord breath'd lyfe in it agayne
& stauncht the blood my wounded hert had shed

Sweete tonge then sith y<sup>u</sup> canst reuive y<sup>e</sup> dead
thou easly mayst aswage a sickmans payne
what glory then shall such thy power gayne
woh sicknes, death, both lyfe & death hath bredd

One word hant lyfe: one more can helth restore
ys not? I live but liue as better not
more then speakest not & ys I call for more
more is thy wrath & thy wrath breeds my not

My tonge & thine thus both conspire my smart
myne while I speake, thine refute y<sup>e</sup> silent art

When your refertions to my thoughts appeare
they say amongst them selues, oh happy wee
y<sup>t</sup> euer shall so rare an object see:
But happy hart ys thoughts lesse happy weare

for their delighted huwe tost my hurt full deare
in whome of loue a thousand wishes bee
& each wishe breeds a thousand loues in mee
& each loue more then thousand santz can beare

How can my hart so many loues then hold
w<sup>ch</sup> yet by leapes increase from day to day
but like a shipp thats ouerlargd w<sup>th</sup> gold
must either sinke or hurle y<sup>e</sup> gold away

But sivrle out loue y<sup>u</sup> canst not feeble hart
in thine owne blood y<sup>u</sup> therfore drownd art.

Lady in bewty, & in favour rare
of favour not of but I favour crave
iust not to thee bewty & favour yant
fayre then thou art, & favour y<sup>e</sup> most hart

Mr. Henry Constables sonets to
ye Lady Riche. 1589.

1   Resolvd to love, vnworthye to obtayne
    I doe not favor travel, but humble wyshe
    to thee my syghes in verse I sacryfyse
    Only some pittye and no helpe to gayne.

    Dyer then and ov mynd hart shall ay remayn
    a patient obiect to thy lyghtning eye
    a patient ear vntyll thow be thondryng trye
    fear not the stroke, whyen I the blow sustayne.

    So av thyne ey bred mynd ambitiovs thowght
    I shall thyne eare make prowd my voyst for Joy
    to heer what woonders great by thee be wrowght
    when I but lytle favors doe enioy.

    The voyst yt made the eare for to reioyst
    and yovr ear yevett pleasvre to the voyst.

2   Blame not mynd hart for flying vp to hye
    syth thow art cavst heat yf his flyggst begynne
    for earthly vapovrs drawn vp by the sunne
    Comets become and myst formd in the sky.

    Myne humble hart so wt thyne heavenly eye
    drawn vp alloft all low desyres doth shynne
    tryst thow mee vp av thow myne hart hast donne
    so dwryng myst in heaven remayn may I.

    I say, agayn blame not my hye desyre
    syth of so bote the cavst thereof depends
    In thee doth shyne in mee doth bvrn a fyre
    fyre drawsth vp other and yt selfe ascends.

    thyne ey a fyre a so drawsth vp my love
    My love a fyre and so assends above.

Plate 2. Arundel, Arundel Castle, MSS, Harrington MS. Temp. Eliz., the "Arundel Harington MS" (*H*), fol. 148r, showing Sir John Harington's hand.

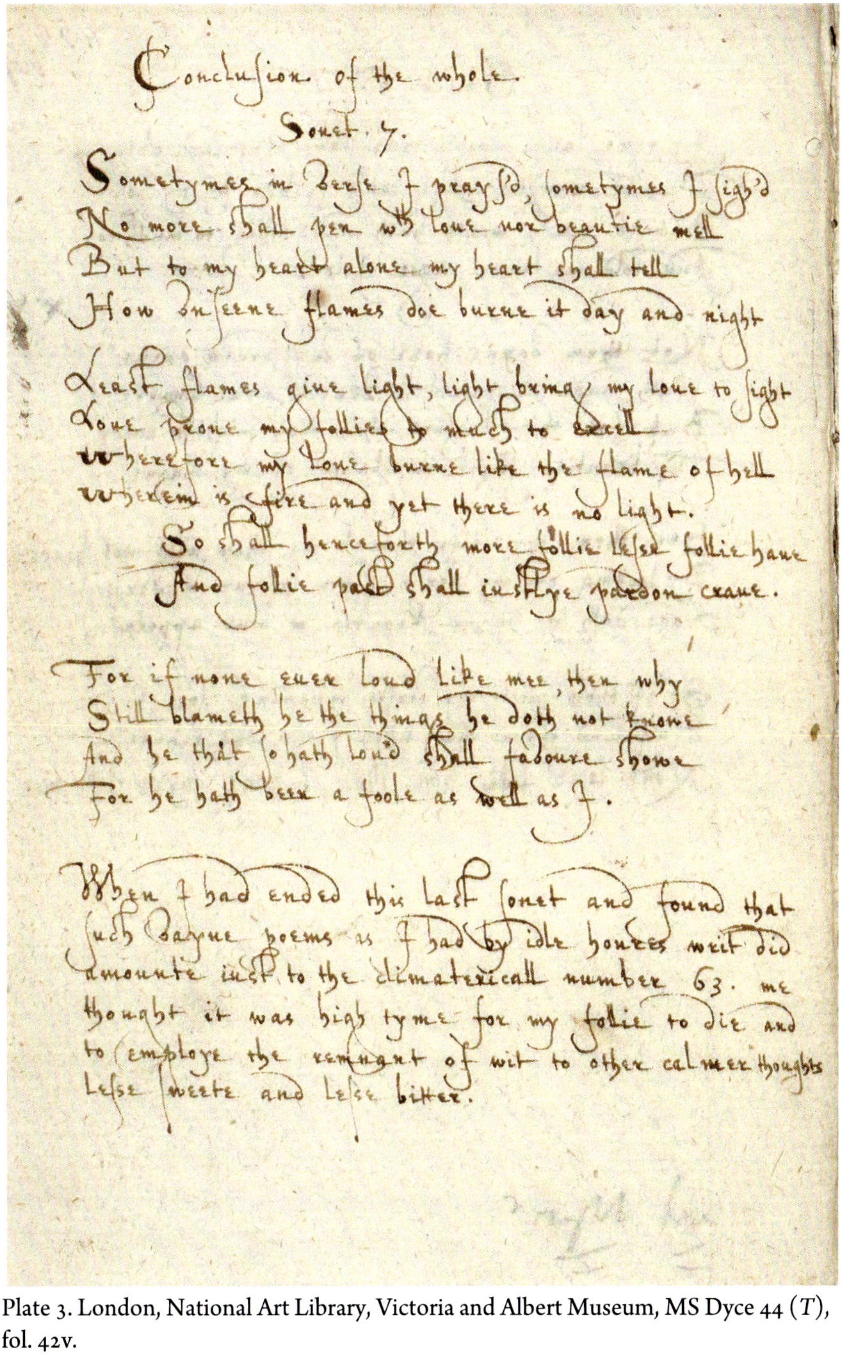

Conclusion of the whole.
   Sonet. 7.
Sometymes in verse I pray'd, sometymes I sigh'd
No more shall pen w<sup>th</sup> loue nor beautie mell
But to my heart alone, my heart shall tell
How vnseene flames doe burne it day and night

Least flames giue light, light bring my loue to sight
Loue prone my follies to much to excell
Wherefore my Loue burne like the flame of hell
Wherein is fire and yet there is no light.
   So shall henceforth more follie lesse follie haue
   And follie past shall iustlye pardon craue.


For if none euer lou'd like mee, then why
Still blameth he the things he doth not knowe
And he that so hath lou'd shall fauoure showe
For he hath been a foole as well as I.


When I had ended this last sonet and found that
such vayne poems as I had by idle houres writ did
amounte iust to the climatericall number 63. me
thought it was high tyme for my folie to die and
to employe the remnant of wit to other calmer thoughts
lesse sweete and lesse bitter.

Plate 3. London, National Art Library, Victoria and Albert Museum, MS Dyce 44 (*T*), fol. 42v.

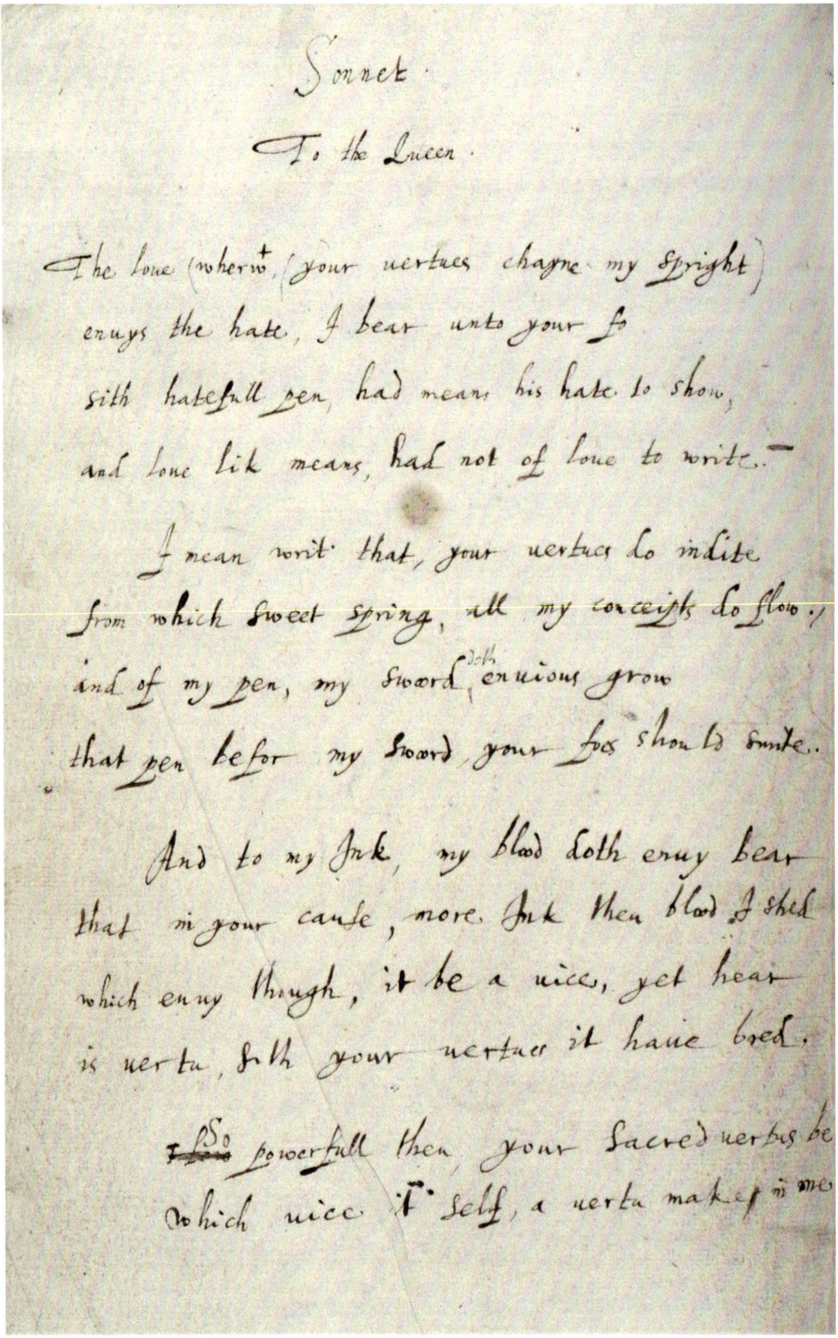

## Sonnet.

### To the Queen.

The loue (wherw.<sup>th</sup> your vertues chayne my Spright)
envyes the hate, I bear vnto your fo
sith hatefull pen, had means his hate to show,
and loue lik means, had not of loue to write.

I mean writ that, your vertues do indite
from which sweet spring, all my conceipts do flow,
ind of my pen, my sword doth envious grow
that pen befor my sword, your foes should smite.

And to my Ink, my blood doth envy bear
that in your cause, more Ink then blood I shed
which envy though, it be a vice, yet hear
is vertu, sith your vertues it haue bred.

~~I~~ So powerfull then, your Sacred vertus be
which vice it' self, a vertu makes in me

Plate 4. New Haven, Yale University, Beinecke Library, MS 621 (*Bn*), fol. 14v.

# DIANA.

The praises of his Mistres,

in certaine sweete Sonnets.

By H. C.

LONDON,
Printed by I. C. for Richard
Smith: and are to be sold at the
VVest doore of Paules.
1592.

Plate 5. San Marino, Huntington Library, RB 58467: title page of the 1592 edition of *Diana* (D92).

# DIANA.

OR,
The excellent conceitful Sonnets
of *H. C.* Augmented with diuers
Quatorzains of honorable and
lerned perfonages.

Deuided into viij. Decads.

*Vincitur a facibus, qui iacet ipfe faces.*

AT LONDON,
Printed by *Iames Roberts* for
Richard Smith.

Plate 6. London, British Library, C.39.a.60: title page of the 1594 edition of *Diana*, first printing (*D94a*).

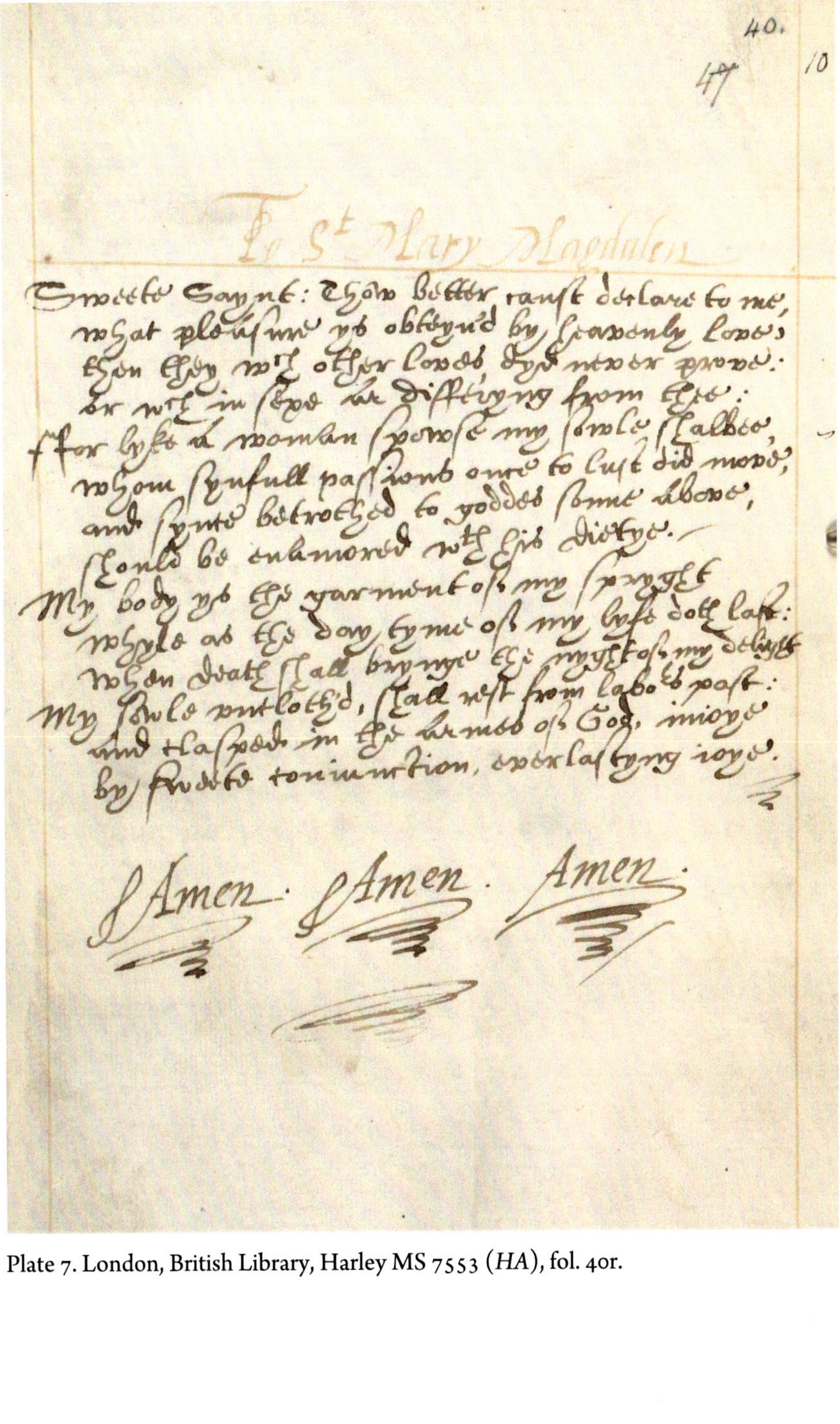

## To St Mary Magdalen

Sweete Saynt: Thow better canst declare to me,
what pleasure ys obteyn'd by heavenly love;
then they wth other loves dyd never prove:
or wth in heav'n are differyng from thee:
ffor lyke a woman whose my soule (albee
whom sensfull passions once to lust did move,
and synce betrothed to goddes sonne above,
showld be enamored wth his dietye.
My body ys the garment of my spryght
whyle as the day, tyme of my buse doth last:
when death shall brynge th' nyght of my delyght
My soule vnclothd, shall rest from labo's past:
and clasped in the armes of God, inioye
by frutefull coniunction, everlastyng ioye.

Amen. Amen. Amen.

Plate 7. London, British Library, Harley MS 7553 (*HA*), fol. 40r.

## To the Blessed Martir Marye
### Queene of Scotland

**I write** of teares, and blud at on time shedd
from one swete bodye and tenne Thowsand eyes
when as a Queene became a sacrifice
like to a Lambe vnto a scaffolde ledd
Vnworthy Alter to be honnored
w<sup>th</sup> so dere off'ring of so highe A price
whose losse no teeres can showe nor words suffice
the Authors shame abroad the worlde to spredd
My ynke euen weepes, & teares y<sup>e</sup> mourning blacke
made Inke againe, striue to recorde this lacke
and that deere bloud w<sup>ch</sup> gusshed from her face
Disdayninge now vppon the grounde to bleede
to theyre face turne w<sup>ch</sup> caus'd this dolefull case
and made them blushe for shame of suche a deede.

**It is** not pompe of solemne funerall
that can excuse the Crime those did commytt
w<sup>ch</sup> after blody sentence did permitt
thy sacred boddye to haue burvall
Nor yett this my ritee turn honnor yt at all
prophane they be, for suche A Corpes vnfitt
nature w<sup>ch</sup> graue all her workes w<sup>ch</sup> it
made all her workes, to honno<sup>r</sup> it w<sup>th</sup> all
earthe the Chest, the heauens the hearse wilbe
when nyght, the Ayre, w<sup>ch</sup> sadd owrs to cuer mye
the skye all hunge w<sup>th</sup> mourninge blacke we see
The starres as lights serue to adorne this hearse
and nowe me thinke the Amyelle dizzies mye
and stoppe my mouth & bidd me end my verse.

Plate 8. Berkeley, Gloucs., Berkeley Castle, Select Books 85 (*BE*), p. 12.

HENRY CONSTABLE

The Poems

## H. C. sonets

[1]

**To his Mistrisse.**

Grace, full of grace, though in these verses heere
My love complaynes of others then of thee,
Yet thee alone I lov'd, and they by mee
(Thow yet unknowne) only mistaken were.
Like him which feeles a heate now heere, now there, 5
Blames now this cause, now that, untill he see
The fire indeed from whence they caused bee,
Which fire I now doe knowe is yow, my deare.
Thus diverse loves dispersed in my verse
In thee alone for ever I unite, 10
But follie unto thee more to rehearse;
To him I flye for grace that rules above,
That by my Grace I may live in delight
Or by his grace I never more may love.

*T* 12r [1]

    **4 Thow** thou; though
    **11 rehearse** recite (a poem, prayer, or other piece of writing), especially before an audience (*OED* v. 4.a)

## The order of the booke.

The sonets following are divided into 3 parts, each parte contayning 3 severall arguments, and every argument 7 sonets.
The first parte is of variable affections of love; wherein the first 7 be of the beginning and byrth of his love; the second 7, of the prayse of his Mistrisse; the thyrd 7, of severall accidents hapning in the tyme of his love.
The second is the prayse of perticulars; wherein the first 7 be of the generall honour of this Ile, through the prayses of the heads thereof, the Q. of England and K. of Scotts; the second 7 celebrate the memory of perticular ladies whoe the author most honoureth; the thyrd 7 be to the honoure of perticulars presented upon severall occasions.
The thyrd parte is tragicall, conteyning only lamentations; wherein the first 7 be complaynts onlye of misfortunes in love; the second 7, funerall sonets of the death of perticulars; the last 7, of the end and death of his love.

*T* 12r

    7 **perticulars** particulars, individuals (*OED* n. 6.a)
    11 **severall** separate, distinct (*OED* adj. 1.a)

**The first 7 only of the byrth and beginning of his love.**

[2]

**Sonet 1**

Resolvd to love, unworthie to obtayne,
I doe no favour crave, but humble wise
To thee my sighes in verse I sacrifice,
Only some pittie and no helpe to gayne.
Heare then and, as my heart shall ay remayne             5
A patient object to thy lightning eyes,
A patient eare bring thow to thundring cryes:
Feare not the cracke when I the blow sustayne.
So as thyne eye bred my ambitiouse thought,
So shall thyne eare make proude my voyce for joy.       10
Loe, deare, what wonders great by thee are wrought
When I but litle favour doe enjoy.
    The voyce is made the eare for to rejoyce,
    And thyne eare giveth pleasure to the voyce.

*T* 12v [2] | *H* 148r [1] | *D92* B1r [2] | *D94* B1r, D1.1 [1] | *A* 52 [3] *The text in A is heavily blotted.*
**Collation: Heading** Master Henry Conestables sonets to the Lady Ritche. 1589 *H*; 1 in l. margin *H*; Sonetto primo. *D92*; The first Decad. / Sonnet I. *D94*; To the fairest that hath bine. 1 *A*
  2 no] not *H*   3 sighes] sightes *A*   5 my] myne *H*   9 thyne eye] thy lookes *A*   my] mine *H D92 D94 A*   10 for] with *A*   11 are] be *H A*   12 favour] favours *H D92 D94 A*   14 thyne] your *H D92 D94 A*   giveth ] bringeth *A*   the] my *D92 D94 A*

  **2 humble wise** humbly (*OED* wise n.¹ 3.b)
  **5 ay** always; at all times (*OED* adv. 1)
  **6 patient** undergoing the action of another; passive (*OED* adj. 2.a)

## [3]

**Of the byrth of his love.**

**Sonet 2**

Fly lowe, deare Love; thy sun dost thow not see?
Take heed, doe not so neare his rayes aspire
Least for thy pride, inflam'd with kindled ire,
It burne thy wings as it hath burned me.

Thow happely sayst thy wings immortall bee     5
And so cannot consumed be with fire:
The one is hope, the other is desire,
And that the heavens bestowed them both on thee.

A Muses words caus'd thee with hope to flye;
An Angells face desire hath begotte;     10
Thy selfe engendred of a goddesse eye.
Yet, for all this, immortall thow art not.
    Of heavenlye eye though thow begotten art,
    Yet thow art borne but of a mortall hearte.

---

T 13r [3] | H 148v [3] | D92 B3r [6] | D94 B2r, D1.3 [3]
**Collation: Heading** om H; 3 in l. margin H; Sonnetto quinto. D92; Sonnet III D94
  1 lowe H D92 D94] love T   deare] my H   3 kindled] wreakfull H D92 D94   6 And so H D92 D94] And T   9 caus'd] made H D92 D94   11 of] by H D92 D94   14 thow art] art thou H D92 D94

    2 **aspire** mount up, soar to (*OED* v. 8)
    3 **least** lest, that ... not (*OED* conj. 1.a)
    5 **happely** haply; perhaps, possibly (*OED* adv. a)

[4]

**Of the conspiracie of his Ladies eyes and his owne to ingender Love.**

**Sonet 3**

Thyne eye, the glasse where I behold my hearte;
Myne eye, the windowe through the which thyne eye
May see my hearte, and there thy selfe espie
In bloudie coloures how thow paynted art.

Thy eye the pike is of a murdering darte;   5
Myne eye, the sight thow takst thy levell by
To hitt my hearte, and never shut'st awrye.
Myne eye thus helpes thyne eye to worke my smarte.

Thyne eye a fire is both in heate and light;
Myne eye of teares a river doth become.   10
O, that the water of myne eye had might
To quench the flames that from thyne eye doe come;
 Or that the fire thats kindled by thine eye
 The flowing streames of myne eye would make drye.

---

*T* 13v [4] | *D92* C1r [10] | *D94* B3r, D1.5 [5] | *A* 54 [9]
**Collation: Heading** Sonnetto nono. *D92*; Sonnet V *D94*; 7 *A*
 3 my *D92 D94 A*] thyne *T* 5 Thy] Thine *D92 D94 A* pike] pyle *D92 D94 A* a] om *A* 7 shut'st] shootes *D92 D94*; shootte *A* 11 water *D92 D94*] matter *T*; waters *A* eye] eyes *D94b A* 12 eye] eyes *D92 D94b A* doe] doth *D94 A* come] runn *A* 13 thats] om *D92 D94*; thus *A* 14 flowing] flaming *A* eye] eyes *D92 D94 A* would] could *D92 D94 A*

 **3 espie** espy, discover (*OED* v. 2.a)
 **5 pike** sharp point; the pointed tip of something (*OED* n.¹ 2.a)
 **6 takst thy level by** you take aim (*OED* n. 9.a) using

## [5]

**Of the suddeyne surprizing of his hearte, and how unawares he was caught.**

**Sonet 4**

Delight in youre bright eyes my death did breede,
As light and glittering weapons babes allure
To play with fire and sworde, and so procure
Them to be burnt and hurt ere they take heed.

Thy beautie so hath made me burne and bleed.  5
Yet shall my ashes and my bloud assure
Thy beauties fame for ever to endure,
For thy fames life from my death doth proceed.

Because my hearte, to ashes burned, giveth
Life to thy fame, thow right a Phoenix art;  10
And like a Pellican thy beautie liveth
By sucking bloud oute of my breast and hearte.
    Loe why with wonder we may thee compare
    Unto the Pelican and Phoenix rare.

*T* 14r [5]
**Miscellaneous features of the copy text:** 5 me] m *superimposed on a vertical stroke meant for* a b

   13 **why** for which reason (*OED* adv. 5.b)

[6]

**Of the discouragement he had to proceed in love through the multitude of his Ladies perfections and his owne lownesse.**

**Sonet 5**

When youre perfections to my thoughts appeare,
They say amonge themselves: O, happie he
Which ever shal so rare an object see!
But happie hearte, if thoughts lesse happie were.

For theyre delights have cost my heart full deare,   5
In whome of love a thowsand causes be;
And each cause breeds a thowsand loves in me,
And each love more then thowsand hearts can beare.

How can my hearte so many loves then hold
Which yet by heapes encrease from day to day?   10
But, like a ship that's overcharg'd with gold,
Must eyther sinke or hurle the gold away.
    But hurle oute love thow canst not, feeble hearte.
    In thyne owne bloud thow therfore drowned arte.

$T$ 14v [6] | $M$ 25r [2] | $H$ 150r [9] | $D$92 D2r [20] | $D$94 D1r, D4.3 [33]
**Collation: Heading** om $M$ $H$; 9 in l. margin $H$; Sonnetto decinove $D$92; Sonnet III $D$94
  1 thoughts $M$ $H$ $D$92 $D$94] thought $T$   2 amonge] emongst $M$   he] wee $M$ $H$ $D$92 $D$94   5 cost] ost $D$94b   deare] d ere $D$94b   10 heapes $H$ $M$ $D$92 $D$94] heape $T$   13 oute] not $D$92 $D$94   love] gold $H$; love: $D$92 $D$94   thow] y$^u$ $M$   14 thow] y$^u$ $M$   drowned $M$ $H$ $D$92 $D$94] damned $T$

  2 **happie** fortunate (*OED* adj. 1.a)

[7]

**How he encouraged himselfe to proceede in love and to hope for favoure in the ende at Loves hands.**

**Sonet 6**
It may be Love doth not my death pretend
Although he shutes at me, but thinkes it fitte
Thus to bewitch thee for my benefitte,
Causing thy will to my wish condescend.
For witches which some murder doe intend                5
Doe make a picture and doe shute at it,
And in that place that they the picture hitt,
The partyes selfe doth languish to the end.
    So Love, to weake by force thy hearte to taynt,
    Within my hearte thy heavenly shape doth paynte,     10
Suffering therein his arrowes to abyde
Only to th'end he might, by witches arte,
Within my hearte pierce through thy pictures side,
And through thy pictures side might wound thy hearte.

*T* 15r [7] | *H* 150v [11] | *D92* B1v [3] | *D94* B6v, D2.2 [12]
**Collation: Heading** om *H*; Sonnetto secondo *D92*; Sonnet II *D94*
  1 doth not my death] my death doth not H D92 D94    2 shutes] shoote H    3 my] thy D94a    7 place that] part where H D92 D94    8 partyes] partie H    the end] his end H D92 D94    13 pictures] picture H    14 pictures] picture H    thy hearte] my hart D92 D94

  1 **pretend** intend (*OED* v. 10.c)
  6 **picture** three-dimensional representation of something, especially as a work of art; a statue, a sculpture (*OED* n. 1.d)
  9 **to weake** too weak   **taynt** attaint; touch (*OED* v. 1)

[8]

**An excuse to his Mistrisse for resolving to love so worthye a creature.**

**Sonet 7**

Blame not my hearte for flying up so high,
Sith thow art cause that it this flight begun,
For earthlye vapoures drawne up by the sun
Comets become and night-suns in the skie.

My humble hearte, so with thy heavenly eye            5
Drawen up alofte, all low desires doth shun.
Rayse thow me up, as thow my heart hast done,
So during night in heaven remayne may I.

Blame not, I say againe, my high desire,
Sith of us both the cause thereof depends:            10
In thee doth shine, in me doth burne a fire,
Fire drawth up others and it selfe ascends.
    Thyne eye a fire, and so drawth up my love;
    My love a fire, and so ascends above.

---

*T* 15v [8] | *H* 148r [2] | *D*92 B2r [4] | *D*94 B1v, D1.2 [2] | *A* 52 [4]
**Collation: Heading** om *H*; 2 *in l. margin H*; Sonneto terzo *D*92; Sonnet II *D*94; 2 *A*
  1 my] myne *H* so] too *H D*92 *D*94 *A* 2 this] his *H* 4 become] begin *D*92; begun *D*94 *A* 5 My] Myne *H D*92 *D*94 *A* thy] thyne *H* 7 Rayse thow] Rayse then *D*92 *D*94 *A* my] myne *H* hast] has *A* 8 may] shall *A* 9 Blame not, I say againe] I say agayn blame not *H D*92 *D*94 *A* 12 drawth *H*] doth draw *T*; drawes *D*92 *D*94 *A* others] other *H D*92 *D*94 *A* 13 and] a *H*

  2 **Sith** since (*OED* conj. 2. a)
  4 **night-suns** mock moons, paraselenes (*OED* n. 1), bright spots in the sky caused by the refraction of moonlight through ice crystals in the atmosphere (*OED* n.)

## The second 7 of his Ladies prayse.

[9]

## An exhortation to the reader to come and see his Mistrisse beautie.

**Sonet 1**

Eyes curiouse to behold what nature can create,
Come see, come see and write what wonder yow doe see,
Causing, by true reporte, oure next posteritye
Curse fortune for that they were borne to late.

Come then, and come ye all, come soon least that 5
The tyme should be to shorte, and men to few should be;
For all be few to write her least parts historie,
Though they should ever write and never write but that.

Millions looke on her eyes, millions thinke on her witte,
Millions speake of her, millions write of her hand. 10
The whole eye or the lip I doe not understand;
Millions to few to prayse but some one parte of it,
    As eyther of her ey or lip or hand to write
      The light or blacke, the tast or red, the soft or white.

---

*T* 16r [9]

    3 **next posteritye** descendants (*OED* n. 1)
    5 **least** lest, that ... not (*OED* conj. 1.a)
    6 **to** too
    7 **her least parts historie** the history of the smallest part of her body
    14 **light** lightness, brightness (*OED* n.² 1)   **blacke** blackness   **tast or red** taste or redness   **soft or white** softness or whiteness

[10]

**Sonet 2**

Ladye in beautye and in favoure rare,
Of favoure, not of due, I favoure crave;
Nature to thee beautye and favoure gave,
Fayre then thow arte, and favoure thow mayst spare.

And when on me bestowed youre favoures are,     5
Lesse favoure in youre face yow shall not have.
If favoure then a wounded soule may save,
Of murders guilte, deare Ladie, then beware.

My losse of life a million fold were lesse
Then the least losse should unto yow befall;     10
Yet grant this guift, which guift when I possesse,
Both I have life and yow no losse at all.
    For by youre favoure only I may live,
    And favoure you may well both keepe and give.

---

T 16v [10] | M 25r–v [3] | H 151v [15] | D92 C1v [11] | D94 B7v, D2.4 [14] | A 53 [6]
**Collation: Heading** *om* M H; Sonnetto decimo. D92; Sonnet IIII. D94; 4 A
    4 thow] y$^u$ M    5 And when on] Nor when on M H D94 A; When on poore D92    8 murders] Murtherers A    deare] great A    9 million] mililon D94b    10 should unto] that myght to A    13 may] do M H D92 D94; doth A

    1 **favoure** appearance, aspect (*OED* n. 9.a)
    2 **Of favoure** out of kindness, goodwill (*OED* n. 2.a)   **due** duty, obligation (*OED* n. 5)
    3 **favoure** attractiveness, comeliness, beauty (*OED* n. 8.)

[11]

**Of the excellencye of his Ladies voyce.**

**Sonet 3**

Ladie of Ladies, the delight alone
For which to heaven earth doth no envie beare;
Seeing and hearing thee, we see and heare
Such voice, such light as never sunge nor shone.

The want of heaven, I grant, yet we may moane: 5
Not for the pleasure of the Angells there,
As though in face or voyce they like thee were,
But that they many bee and thow but one.
    The basest notes which from thy voyce proceed
    The treble of the Angells doe exceed. 10

So that I feare theyre quire to beautefie,
Least thow to soone in heaven shall singe and shine,
Loe (when I heare thee sing), the reason why
Sighes of my breast keepe tyme with notes of thine.

*T* 17r [11]

    **9 basest** lowest in volume, softest (*OED* adj. 3)
    **12 Least** lest, that ... not (*OED* conj. 1.a)

[12]

**Of her excellencye both in singing and instruments.**

**Sonet 4**

Not that thy hand is soft, is sweete, is white,
Thy lipps sweete roses, breast sweet lilye is,
That love esteemes these three the chiefest blisse
Which nature ever made for lipps delight.

But when these three, to shew theyre heavenly might,     5
Such wonders doe, devotion then for this
Commandeth us with humble zeale to kisse
Such thinges as worke miracles in oure sight.

A lute of senselesse wood, by nature dumbe,
Toucht by thy hand, doth speake devinely well,     10
And from thy lips and breast sweet tunes doe come
To my dead hearte, the which new life doe give.
    Of greater wonders heard we never tell
    Then for the dumbe to speak, the dead to live.

*T* 17v [12]

    **9 senselesse** incapable of sensation or perception (*OED* adj. 1.c)

[13]

**Of the prowesse of his Ladie.**

**Sonet 5**

Sweete Soveraigne, sith so many mynds remayne
Obedient subjects at thy beautyes call,
So many thoughts bound in thy hayre as thrall,
So many hearts dye with one lookes disdayne,

Goe seeke that glorie which doth thee pertayne, 5
That the first monarchie may thee befall;
Thow hast such meanes to conquer men withall
As all the world must yeeld, or else be slayne.

To fight thow needst no weapons but thyne eyes,
Thy hayre hath gold enough to pay thy men, 10
And for theyre foode thy beautie will suffice;
For men and armoure, Ladie, care have none:
    For one will soonest yeeld unto thee then,
    When he shall meet thee naked and alone.

*T* 18r [13] | *D94* C8v, D4.2 [32]
**Collation: Heading** Sonnet II. *D94*
   3 thoughts] harts *D94*  hayre] haires *D94*  4 hearts] eyes *D94*  lookes] lookers *D94b*
5 that glorie which] the honour that *D94*  6 first] fift *D94*  10 Thy] thine *D94*  13 soonest] sooner *D94*  14 and] all *D94*

  **1 sith** since (*OED* conj. 2.a)
  **3 thrall** slave, servant (*OED* n.¹ 1.a)
  **5 doth thee pertayne** is your right or privilege (*OED*, s.v. pertain, v. 1.b)
  **6 befall** fall to as one's share or right (*OED* v. 2)

[14]

**Of the envie others beare to his Ladie for the former perfections.**

**Sonet 6**

When beautie to the world vouchsafes this blisse,
To shew the one whose other there is not,
The whitest skinnes red blushing shame doth blot,
And in the reddest cheekes pale envie is.

The fayre and fowle come thus alike by this, 5
For when the sun hath oure Horizon gott,
Venus her selfe doth shine no more, god wot,
Then the least starre that take the light from his.

The poore in beautie thus content remayne
To see theyre jealouse cause reveng'd in thee 10
And theyre fayre foes afflicted with like payne;
Loe, the cleare proofe of thy devinitye;
    For unto god is only dew this prayse,
    The highest to pluck downe, the low to rayse.

*T* 18v [14]

    5 **fowle** foul, ugly (*OED* adj. 11.a)    **come** become (*OED* v. 31.a)
    7 **wot** knows
    8 **starre** in wider use: any celestial object visible in the sky in the day or night (*OED* n.¹ 2)
   10 **reveng'd** punished (*OED* v. 5.b)
   13 **dew** due

[15]

**Of the slander envye gives him for so highlye praysing his Mistrisse.**

**Sonet 7**

Falselye doth envie of youre prayses blame
My tongue, my pen, my heart of flatterye;
Because I sayd there was no sunne but thee,
It call'd my tongue the partiall trumpe of fame.

And sayd my pen had flattered thy name                     5
Because my pen did to my tongue agree,
And needs my heart a flatterer must be
Which taught both tongue and pen to say the same.

No, no, I flatter not when I thee call
The sun, sith sun in world was never such;                 10
But when the sun I thee compar'd withall,
Doubtlesse the sun I flattered to much.
 Witnesse myne eyes I say the truth is this:
 They have thee seene and know that so it is.

T 19r [15] | H 149r [6] | D92 C3r [14] | D94 B4r, D1.7 [7]
See [15b]
**Collation: Heading** om H; 6 in l. margin H; Sonnetto tredeci. D92; Sonnet VII. D94
 **5** sayd] sayth H D92 D94 had] hath H D92 D94 **7** needs] that H D92 D94 a flatterer must be] must needs a flatterer be H D92 (flattrer) D94a (flattrer) D94b **9** I thee] thee I H D92 D94 **10** sun in world] that the sunne H D92 D94 **11** I thee] thee I H D92 D94 **13** is] in H D92 D94 **14** thee seene] seene thee H D92 D94

 **4 trumpe of fame** one that proclaims, celebrates, or summons loudly like a trumpet (*OED*, s.v. trump, n.[1] 4)

[15b]

False the report, & unjust is the blame
that envye of your praise imputes to mee,
when it arreastes my penn of flatterye
for honoringe too much thy sacred name;

And calls my tonge the partiall trompe of fame 5
for saying that ther is no sunne but thee;
and eke would burne my hart for heresye,
sithe obstinate it doth beleve the same.

No, no, I flatter not when thee I call
The sunne, the sunne was never such; 10
but when the sunne the I compared with all,
doubtlesse the sunne I flattered too muche.
    And thoghe I erd, my hart cannot for this
    be burnt, for it already burned is.

*M* 26v [8]

   3 **arreastes** apprehends by legal authority (*OED* v. 11); the meaning of "aret" may be implied: charge, accuse, or indict a person of (*OED* v. 3.a)
   7 **eke** also, too (*OED* adv.)
   8 **sithe** sith, seeing that, since (*OED* conj. 2.a)
  11 **the I** thee I
  13 **erd** should err, go wrong in judgement (*OED* v. 3.a); "sin" may be implied (*OED* v. 4.a)

**The thyrd 7 of severall occasions and accidents happening in the life tyme of his love.**

[16]

**Of his Mistrisse upon occasion of her walking in a garden.**

**Sonet 1**

My Ladies presence makes the roses red,
Because to see her lips they blush for shame;
The lilies leaves for envy pale became,
And her white hands in them this envy bred.

The marygold abroad the leaves did spread                    5
Because the suns and her power is the same;
The violet of purple coloure came
Dy'd with the bloud she made my heart to shed.

In briefe, all flowers from her theyre vertue take,
From her sweet breath theyre sweet smells doe proceed;      10
The living heate which her eybeames doe make
Warmeth the ground and quickeneth the seede.
    The rayne wherewith she watereth these flowers
    Falls from myne eyes, which she dissolves in shewers.

*T* 19v [16] | *M* 27v–28r [13] | *H* 149v [8] | *D*92 D1r [18] | *D*94 B5r, D1.9 [9] | *E* 105v [1]

**Collation: Heading** *om M H*; Sonnetto decisette. *D*92; Sonnet IX. *D*94

4 **her**] *om H*   5 **abroad the leaves**] hir leavs abrode *M*; the leavs abrode *H D*92 *D*94; abroad her leaves *E*   **did**] doth *M H D*92 *D*94   6 **suns**] sunn *H E*   8 **with**] in *D*92 *D*94   9 **theyre**] doe *E*   **vertue**] virtues *M*   11 **living**] lightning *E*   **doe**] doth *D*92 *D*94   12 **quickeneth** *H D*92 *D*94] quickneth *T*   13 **these**] the *H D*92 *D*94

    5 **abroad ... spread** spread abroad, widely, so as to be fully open or outspread (*OED* adv. 1.a)
    11 **eybeames** eye-beams, glances of the eye, imagined as beams of light (*OED* n.)
    12 **quickeneth** quickens, gives life to (*OED* v.¹ 1.b)
    13 **wherewith** by means of which (*OED* adv. 2.a)
    14 **shewers** showers

[17]

**To his Ladies hand upon occasion of her glove which in her absence he kissed.**

**Sonet 2**

Sweet hand, the sweet (yet cruell) bowe thow art
From whence at me five ivorye arrowes flye,
So with five wounds at once I wounded lye,
Bearing in breast the print of every dart.

Saynt Francis had the like, yet felt no smart,⟨5⟩
Where I in living torments never dye;
His wounds were in his hands and feete, where I
All these same helplesse wounds feele in my hearte.

Now, as Saint Francis (if a Saint) am I;
The bow which shotte these shafts a relique is;⟨10⟩
I meane the hand, which is the reason why
So many for devotion thee would kisse.
    And I thy glove kisse as a thinge devine,
    Thy arrowes quiver, and thy reliques shrine.

---

*T* 20r [17] | *M* 27v [12] | *H* 153r [21] | *D92* D2v [21] | *D94* C2r, D2.9 [19] | *E* 105v [2]
**Collation: Heading** To his Ladyes hand *M*; *om H*; Sonnetto vinti. *D92*; Sonnet IX. *D94*.; Upon occasion of his mistris glove which in her absence he kissed. *E*
  1 yet] but *H D92 D94*  2 five] 3 *E*  3 five] 3 *E*  4 in] in my *M*; my *H D92 D94*  6 torments never] torment ever *E*  8 same] five *M H D92 D94*; 3 *E*  9 as Saint Francis] (as Saint Fraunces) *D92 D94*  (if a Saint)] (yf a saynt ^ *M*; ^ yf a Saint ^ *H D92 D94*  10 which] that *M H D92 D94*  shotte] shoot *H*  11 the hand] thy hand *M*  the reason] a reason *M*  12 thee would] would the *E*  13 I] some *M H D92 D94*  14 Thy arrowes] those arrows *M*; this arrowes *H D92 D94*  thy reliques] these relickes *M*; this reliques *H D92 D94 E*  shrine *M H D92 D94 E*] shine *T*

  **8 helplesse** admitting no remedy (*OED* adj. 4)

[18]

**Of his Ladies vayle, wherewith she covered her.**

**Sonet 3**

The fouler hydes, as closely as he may,
The net where caught the sillie byrd should be,
Least that the threatning prison it should see
And so for feare be forst to flye away.

My Ladie so, the while she doth assay 5
In curled knotts fast to entangle me,
Puts on her vayle to th'end I should not flee
The golden net wherein I am a pray.

Alas (most sweete) what need is of a nette
To catch a byrd which is allreadie tame? 10
Sith with youre hand alone yow may it gette,
For it desires to fly into the same.
    What needs such arte my thoughts then to intrap,
    When of them selves they flye into youre lap.

---

T 20v [18] | M 27v [11] | H 152v [19] | D92 D1v [19] | D94 C1v, D2.8 [18]
**Collation: Heading** To his Ladye wearing a vaile over hir heade. *M; om H;* Sonnetto deciotto *D92;* Sonnet VIII. *D94*
   3 Least that] that it *M;* least he *H D92 D94*    it should] should not *M;* should but *H D92 D94*    4 for feare be forst] be forst for feare *M*    7 Puts] put *D94*    flee *M H D92 D94*] see *T*    10 which] that *M H D92 D94*    tame] tane *D92 D94*    11 may it gette] yt may gett *H*    13 needs] neede *M H D92 D94*

   **vayle** veil
   **wherewith** by means of which (*OED* adv. 2.a)
   1 **fouler** fowler, one who hunts wild birds, especially with nets (*OED* n.[1] 1)   **closely** secretly, covertly (*OED* adv. 3)
   2 **sillie** helpless, defenceless (*OED* adj. 2.a)
   3 **least** lest, that ... not (*OED* conj. 1.a)
   5 **doth assay** sets herself (to do something) (*OED* v. 17.a)
   6 **fast** tightly, securely (*OED* adv. 2.a)
   13 **arte** cunning, trickery (*OED* n.[1] 11.a)

[19]

**To his Mistrisse upon occasion of a Petrarch he gave her, shewing her the reason why the Italian Commenters dissent so much in the exposition thereof.**

**Sonet 4**

Miracle of the world, I never will denye
That former poets prayse the beautie of theyre dayes,
But all those beauties were but figures of thy prayse,
And all those poets did of thee but prophecye.

Thy coming to the world hath taught us to descrie  5
What Petrarchs Laura meant (for truth the lips bewrayes),
Loe why th' Italians, yet which never saw thy rayes,
To find oute Petrarchs sence such forged glosses trye.

The beauties which he in a vayle enclosd beheld
But revelations were within his secreat heart,  10
By which in parables thy coming he foretold.
His songes were hymnes of thee, which only now before
    Thy image should be sunge; for thow that goddesse art
    Which onlye we withoute idolatrye adore.

*T* 21r [19]

    3 **figures** emblems, types (*OED* n. 12); related to theological prefiguration, the action of prefiguring or foreshadowing a person or thing by means of a figure or type (*OED* n. 1)
    5 **descrie** descry, announce or proclaim (*OED* v.¹ 4.a)
    6 **bewrayes** reveals, makes known (*OED* v. 4)
    8 **forged** fabricated, invented (*OED* adj. 3)    **trye** try, show or find to be so by test or experience, demonstrate (*OED* v. 13)
    9 **vayle** veil

[20]

**Of his Mistrisse upon occasion of a Friend of his which disswaded him from loving.**

**Sonet 5**

A friend of myne, moaning my helplesse love,
Hoping, by killing hope, my love to slay,
Let not (quoth he) thy hope thy heart betray;
Impossible it is her heart to move.

But sith resolved love cannot remove     5
As longe as thy devine perfections stay,
Thy godhead then he sought to take away;
Deare, seeke revenge, and him a lyer prove.

Gods only doe impossibilityes;
Impossible, sayth he, thy grace to gayne.     10
Shew then the powers of devinityes
By graunting me thy favoure to obtayne.
   So shall thy foe give to himselfe the lye;
   A goddesse thow shalt prove, and happie I.

---

*T* 21v [20] | *H* 148v [4] | *D*92 B4r [8] | *D*94 B2v, D1.4 [4] | *A* 53 [5]
**Collation: Heading** *om H*; 4 *in l. margin H*; Sonnetto settimo. *D*92; Sonnet IIII. *D*94; 3 *A*
  1 moaning] pitying *H D*92 *D*94 *A*   helplesse] hopeles *H D*92 *D*94 *A*   2 love] hope *D*92   4 heart] mynde *A*   5 sith] since *A*   6 As longe] Soe long *A*   stay] sway *A*   9 impossibilityes] impossibillitie *H*   11 the powers] the power *H D*92 *D*94; thy power *A*   devinityes] thy divinitie *H*; thy divinities *D*92 *D*94; Devenytie *A*

  5 **sith** since (*OED* conj. 2.a)   **remove** disappear (*OED* v. 1.d)

  7 **godhead** divine nature, deity (*OED* n. 1.a)

  13 **give to himselfe the lye** prove himself a liar, prove the falsity of his statements (*OED* n.[1] 2.a)

[21]

**Of his Ladies going over earlye to bed, so depriving him to soone of her sight.**

**Sonet 6**

Fayre sun, if yow would have me prayse youre light,
When night approacheth, wherfore doe yow flye?
Tyme is so shorte, beautyes so many be,
That I had need to see them day and night,

That by continuall vew my verses might                     5
Tell all the beames of youre divinitye,
Which prayse to yow and joy should be to me:
Yow living by my verse, I by youre sight.
    I by youre sight, but not yow by my verse;
    Need mortall skill immortall prayse rehearse?     10

No, no, if eyes were blind and verse were dumbe,
Youre beautye should be seene and youre fame knowne.
For by the wind which from my sighes dothe come
Youre prayses rounde about the world be blowne.

---

*T* 22r [21] | *H* 152v [20] | *D92* D3v [23] | *D94* C2v, D2.10 [20]
**Collation: Heading** *om H*; Ultimo Sonnetto. *D92*; Sonnet X. *D94*
    4 That I had] as I have *H D92 D94*    9 but] and *D92 D94*    11 if] though *H D92 D94*
13 dothe *H*] doe *T D92 D94*    14 be] is *D92 D94*

    10 **rehearse** recite (a poem, prayer, or other piece of writing), especially before an audience; read aloud or declaim from memory (*OED* v. 4.a)

[22]

**Of the thoughtes he nourished by night when she was retired to bed.**

**Sonet 7**

The sun his journey ending in the west,
Taking his lodging up in Thetis bed,
Though from oure sightes his beames be banished,
Yet with his light the Antipodes be blest.

Now, when the same tyme brings my sun to rest, 5
Which me so oft of rest hath hindered,
And whiter skin with white sheetes covered,
And softer cheeke doth on softe pillow rest,

Then I, Oh sun of suns, and light of lights,
Wish me with those Antipodes to be, 10
Which see and feele thy beames and heate by night;
Well, though the night both cold and darksome is,
    Yet halfe the dayes delight the night grants me:
    I feel the suns heate though the light I misse.

*T* 22v [22] | *H* 150v [12] | *D*92 B2v [5] | *D*94 B6v, D2.3 [13]
**Collation: Heading** *om H*; Sonnetto quattro. *D*92; Sonnet III. *D*94
   3 sightes] eyes *H D*92 *D*94   4 be *H D*92 *D*94] he *T*   5 same] sunn *H D*92 *D*94   6 so] too *H D*92 *D*94   7 sheetes] sheete *H D*92 *D*94   11 beames] beame *H*   night] nights *D*92 *D*94   14 the suns] my sunns *H D*92 *D*94   though the] though his *H D*92 *D*94   light *H D*92 *D*94] heate *T*

    **6 oft** often (*OED* adv. 1.a)    **of rest hath hindered** has prevented (me) from resting

**The second parte.**
**The first 7 to oure Q. and the K. of Scots.**

[23]

**To the Q. after his returne oute of Italye.**

**Sonet 1**

Not longe agoe in Poland traveiling,
Changing my tongue, my nation and my weede,
Mayne wordes I heard from forreyne mouth proceed,
Theyre wonder and thy glorie witnessing.

How from thy wisdome did those conquests spring     5
Which ruin'd them, thy ruine which decreed;
But such as envyed thee in this agreed:
Thy Ilands seate did thee most succoure bring.

So, if the sea by miracle were drye,
Easie thy foes thy kingdome might invade;     10
Fooles which knowe not the power of thyne eye!
Thine eye hath made a thousand eyes to weepe,
    And every eye a thousand seas hath made,
    And each sea shall thyne Ile in saftie keepe.

*T* 23r [23]
**Miscellaneous features of the copy text: 13** a thousand] a *erased before* thousand
**Emendations of the copy text: 13** a] *om* T

    2 **weede** weed, clothing, apparel (*OED* n.² 2.a)
    3 **Mayne** main, a large number of (*OED* adj.² 1.b, first citation 1609)
    8 **seate** seat, position, situation (*OED* n. 18)
    14 **Ile** isle, island

[24]

**To the Queene touching the cruell effects of her perfections.**

**Sonet 2**

Most sacred prince, why should I thee thus prayse,
Which both of sin and sorrow cawse hast beene?
Proude hast thow made thy land of such a Queene,
Thy neighboures enviouse of thy happie dayes.

Whoe never saw the sunshine of thy rayes      5
An everlasting night his life doth ween;
And he whose eyes thy eyes but once have seene
A thousand signes of burning thoughts bewrayes.

Thus sin thow causd, envye I meane, and pride;
Thus fire and darknesse doe proceed from thee,      10
The very paynes which men in hell abide.

Oh no, not hell, but purgatorie this,
Whose sowles some say by Angells punish'd be,
For thow art shee from whome this torment is.

*T* 23v [24]
**Emendations of the copy text:** 6 An] And *T*

    1 **prince** formerly also applied to a female sovereign (*OED* n. 1.b)
    6 **ween** think, consider (*OED* v. 1)
    8 **bewrayes** bewrays; reveals, shows (*OED* v. 4)

[25]

**To the Q. upon occasion of a booke he wrote in an answer to certayne objections against her proceedings in the Low countryes.**

**Sonet 3**

The love wherewith youre vertues chayne my sprite
Envyes the hate I beare unto youre foe,
Since hatefull pen had meanes his hate to showe,
And love like meanes had not of love to wryte.

I meane, write that youre vertues doe endite,  5
From which sweet spring all my conceyts doe flow;
And of my pen my sword doth enviouse growe
That pen before my sword youre foes should smite.

And to my inke my bloud doth envie beare
That in youre cause more inke then bloud I shed;  10
Which envie, though it be a vice, yet heare
Tis vertue, sith youre vertues have it bred.
    Thus powerfull youre sacred vertues be,
    Which vice it selfe a vertue make in me.

T 24r [25] | Bn 14v | M 26r [5]
Collation: **Heading** To the Queen. *Bn*; To hir majesty for a preface to his booke. *M*
  **2** Envyes] Envithe *M*   **3** Since] sith *Bn M*   **6** sweet *Bn M*] om *T*   **7** of] yf *M*   **12** Tis] is *Bn M*   have it] it have *Bn*   **13** Thus powerfull] So powrfull then *Bn M*   **14** make *Bn*] makes *M T*

    **5 write** writ, writing (*OED* n. 1.a)   **endite** inspire, dictate (*OED* v. 1)
    **8 smite** strike with a sword or spear in order to inflict serious injury or death (*OED* v. 6)
    **12 sith** seeing that, since (*OED* conj. 2.a)

[26]

**To the K. of Scots whome as yet he had not seene.**

**Sonet 4**

Bloome of the rose, I hope those hands to kisse
Which, yonge, a scepter, which, olde, wisdome bore,
And offer up joy-sacrifice before
Thy altar throne, for that receaved blisse.

Yet, prince of hope, suppose not for all this                 5
That I thy place and not thy guifts adore;
Thy scepter, no, thy pen I honoure more:
More deare to me then crowne thy garland is.

That laurell garland which (if hope say true)
To thee for deeds of prowesse shall belong,                  10
And now allreadie unto thee is due,
As to a David for a kinglie song.
    The pen wherewith thow dost so heavenly singe,
    Made of a quill pluckt from an Angells winge.

---

T 24v [26] | M 27r [10] | E 105v [4]
**Collation: Heading** To the Kinge of Scotts. *M*; To the King of Scottes. James 6th. one king whom as yet he had not seene. *E*
    **4** Thy] thine *E*   **8** to me then crowne] then crowne to me *E*   **12** a kinglie] thy kingly *M*   song *M E*] throne *T*

    **3 joy-sacrifice** an offering expressing joy (*OED*, s.v. joy, n. C1.e)
    **6 place** social rank or status (*OED* n.¹ 15. a)   **guifts** gifts, talents (*OED* n.¹ 6. b)
    **8 garland** wreath, crown, etc., worn as a mark of distinction (*OED* n. 3); a collection of short literary pieces, usually poems and ballads (*OED* n. 4)

[27]

**To the K. of Scots touching the subject of his poems dedicated wholie to heavenly matters.**

**Sonet 5**

When others hooded with blind love doe flye
Lowe on the grownd, with buzzard Cupids wings,
A heavenlye love from love of love thee brings,
And makes thy Muse to mount above the skie.

Yonge Muses be not wonte to flye so hye,  5
Age schoold by tyme such sober dittie sings;
But thy love flyes from love of youthful things,
And so the winge of tyme doth overflye.

Thus thow disdainest all worldlye wings as slow,
Because thy Muse with Angells wings doth leave  10
Tymes wings behinde, and Cupids wings below;
But take thow heed, least fames wings thee deceave:
    With all thy speed, from fame thow canst not flee,
    But more thow flyest, the more it followes thee.

---

*T* 25r [27] | *PE* n.p. | *OBL* 204r | *O91* 288
**Collation: Heading** To the King of Scotland. *PE*; om *OBL O91*
  1 When] Where *PE OBL O91*   5 so] too *PE*   6 schoold] taught *PE OBL O91*   dittie] ditties *PE OBL*   7 thy love] thy youth *PE OBL O91*   8 winge] wings *PE OBL O91*
9 worldlye] wodly *OBL*   wings *PE OBL O91*] things *T*   13 flee *PE OBL O91*] flye *T*
14 flyest] flees *PE OBL O91*

  **1 hooded** blindfolded, hoodwinked (*OED* adj. 5.b, first citation 1652); in falconry, the bird's eyes were covered with a hood to prevent distractions.
  **2 buzzard** an inferior kind of hawk, useless for falconry (*OED* n.¹ 1.a); senseless, stupid, blind (*OED* n.¹ C1.b, this line given as first citation)
  **6 dittie** any composition in verse (*OED* n. 2.b)
  **12 least** lest, that ... not (*OED* conj. 1.a)

[28]

**To the K. of Scots upon occasion of a sonnet the K. wrote in complaint of a contrarie winde which hindred the arrival of the Queene oute of Denmark.**

**Sonet 6**

If I durst sigh still as I had begun,
Or durst shed teares in such abundant store,
Yow should have need to blame the sea no more,
Nor call upon the wind as yow have done.

For from myne eyes an Ocean sea should run                     5
Which the desired ships should carrie o're,
And my sighes blowe such winde from northren shore
As soone yow should behold yowre wished sun.

But with those sighes my deare displeased is,
Which should both hast your joy, and slake my payne,           10
Yet, for my good will, O Kinge, grant me this,
When to the winds yow sacrifice agayne:
    Sith I desir'd my sighes should blow for thee,
    Desire thow the winds to sigh for me.

---

*T* 25v [28]

    1 **durst** dared   **still** continually, constantly (*OED* adv. 3.a)
    6 **o're** over
    10 **hast** haste, hasten; cause to move more quickly (*OED* v. 1)   **slake** render less acute or painful, mitigate (*OED* v.¹ 8.a)
    13 **Sith** since (*OED* conj. 2.a)

[29]

**To the K. of Scots upon occasion of his longe stay in Denmarke by reason of the coldnesse of the winter and freezing of the sea.**

**Sonet 7**

If I durst love as heertofore I have,
Or that my heart durst flame as it doth burne,
The ice should not so longe stay youre returne,
My heart should easely thaw the frozen wave.

But when my payne makes me for pittie crave, 5
The blindest see with what just cause I mourne,
So, least my torment to hir blame should turne,
My hearte is forc'd to hide the fire she gave.

But what doth need the sea my heart at all?
Thow and thy spouse be suns, in beautye shee, 10
In wisdome thow; the sun we Phoebus call,
And Phoebus for thy wisdome we call thee.
    Now if the sun can thaw the sea alone,
    Cannot two suns supplie the want of one?

---

T 26r [29] | E 105v [5]
**Collation: Heading** To the same King upon occasion of his long aboad in Denmarke by reason of the coldnes of the winter & the frezing of the sea. *E*
    4 heart] heate *E*    5–8 *lines missing E*    7 hir] his *T*    9 heart] heate *E*

  1 **durst** dared   **heertofore** heretofore, before this time (*OED* adv.)
  3 **stay** hold back, stop, hinder (*OED* v.¹ 20.a)
  4 **wave** sea (*OED* n. 1.c)
  7 **least** lest, that ... not (*OED* conj. 1.a)
  9 **what** for what end or purpose? (*OED* adv. 19)

**The second 7.**
**To particular Ladies whome he most honoured.**

[30]

**To the princes of Orange.**

**Sonet 1**

If nature for her workes proud ever were,
It was for this that she created yow;
Youre sacred head, which wisdome doth indue,
Is only fitte a diademe to weare.

Youre lilie hand, which fayrer doth appeare     5
Then ever eye beheld in shape and hue,
Unto no other use by right is due,
Except it be a scepter for to beare.

Youre cherrie lips by nature framed be
Hearts to commaund; youre eye is only fitte     10
With his wise lookes kingdomes to oversee.

O, happie land whose soveraigne thow hadst beene;
But god on earth full blisse will not permitte,
And this is only cause yow are no Queene.

---

*T* 26v [30] | *E* 106r [7]
**Miscellaneous features of the copy text:** 5 fayrer] r *inserted after* y
**Collation: Heading** To the princesse of orange. *E*
   2 yow] the *E*   4 fitte] meete *E*   11 lookes] looke *E*   14 yow are no] thou art not *E*

    3 **wisdome doth indue** is endowed with wisdom
    9 **framed** created (*OED* v. 7)
    11 **his** its

[31]

**To the Countesse of Shrewsburye.**

**Sonet 2**

Playnlie I write because I will write true:
If ever Marie, but the Virgin, were
Meete in the realme of heaven a crowne to beare,
I as my creed believe that it is yow.

And for the world, this Ile and age shall rue 5
The bloud and fire was shed and kindled heere
When woemen of youre name the croune did beare,
And youre high worth not crownd with honoure due.

But god, which meant for rebell fayth and sin
His foes to punish and his owne to trye, 10
Would not youre sacred name imploy therein.

For good and bad he would should yow adore,
Which never any burnt but with youre eye,
And maketh them yow punish love yow more.

*T* 27r [31]

    3 **Meete** meet, suitable, fit (*OED* adj. 2.a)
    10 **trye** put to the test (*OED* v. 7.a)

190 • HENRY CONSTABLE

[32]

## To the Countesses of Cumberland and Warwicke, sisters.

**Sonet 3**

Yow, sister Muses, doe not ye repine
That I two sisters doe with nyne compare,
For eyther of these sacred two more rare
In vertue is, then all the heavenly nyne.

But if ye aske which one is more devine, 5
I say like to theyre owne twin eyes they are:
Where eyther is as cleare as clearest star,
Yet neyther doth more cleare then other shine.

Sisters of spotlesse fame, of whome alone
Malitiouse tongues take pleasure to speake well, 10
How should I yow commend, when eyther one
All things in heaven and earth so far excell?
    The highest prayse that I can give is this:
    That one of yow like to the other is.

*T* 27v [32] | *PR1* L7r [2] | *PR2* 222 [2] | *E* 106r [8] | *A* 52 [2]
See [32b]

**Collation: Heading** To two most Honorable and Virtuous Ladies, sisters *PR1*; Sonnet. To the most Honorable and vertuous Ladies and Sisters, the Ladie Margaret Countesse of Cumberland, and the Lady Anne Countesse of Warwicke *PR2*; Sonnet. To the Countesse of Warwicke & Cumberland sisters. *E*; To the two Sisters Margarett Countess of Cumberland And Anne Countess of Warwicke *A*

  **1** Yow] Yee *PR1 A PR2*   sister] sisters *E*   ye] you *E A*   **3** For eyther of these sacred two] Since each of these *PR1 PR2 A*   more] is farre more truely *PR1 A*; is farre morely, is farre more ttuly *PR2*   **4** In vertue is, then] Then the whole Troope of *PR1 PR2 A*   **5** ye] you *E A*   aske] aske me *PR1 PR2 A*   one] om *PR1 PR2 A*   **6** say] answer *PR1 PR2 A*   owne] om *PR1 PR2 A*   **7** Where eyther] Of which each *PR1 PR2 A*   as cleare as] more bright than *PR1 PR2 A*   clearest] brightest *PR1 PR2 A*   **8** cleare] bright *PR1 PR2 A*   other *PR1 PR2 E A*] others *T*   **11** yow] one *PR2*   when] sith *PR1 PR2*; since *A*   **12** in heaven and earth] within earths Globe *A*   **13** highest] onely *PR1 PR2 A*   that] om *PR1 PR2 A*   give] you give *PR1 PR2 A*   **14** one] each *E*

    **1 repine** feel or express discontent or dissatisfaction (*OED* v. 1.a)

[32b]

**To the most honorable Ladyes the Countesses of Comb. & War., sisters.**

Yee, sister Muses, doe not ye repine
That I two sisters with yow nine compare,
for one of these sweet sacred two more rare
in virtue is then all yow Muses nine.

But yf yow aske which one is more devine, 5
I say: like to their owne twinn eyes they are,
where either is more cleare then clerest starr,
yet neither doth more cleare then other shine.

So in this table paynted heare yow see
two pictures which do all the world surpasse, 10
for the like to these pearles sisters bee,
whose like in all the world yet never was.
    But like them selves, & unlike to the rest,
    where neyther better is, yet bothe be best.

*M* 26r [6]

  1 **repine** feel or express discontent or dissatisfaction (*OED* v. 1.a)
  9 **table** a board or other flat surface on which a picture is painted, or the picture itself (*OED* n. 3)
  11 **pearles** probably an old spelling of peerless

[33]

**To my Ladye Arbella.**

**Sonet 4**

That worthie Marquesse, pride of Italie,
Whoe for all worth and for her wit and phrase
Both best deserv'd, and best desert could prayse,
Immortall Ladie, is reviv'd in thee.

But thinke not strange that thy divinitie 5
I by some goddesse title doe not blaze,
But through a woemans name thy glorie rayse,
For things unlike of unlike prayses be.

When we prayse men, we call them gods, but when
We speake of gods, we liken them to men; 10
Not them to prayse, but only them to knowe.

Not able thee to prayse, my drift was this:
Some earthlye shadowe of thy worth to showe,
Whose heavenly selfe above worlds reason is.

*T* 28r [33]

    3 **desert** excellence, worth (*OED* n.¹ 1.b)
    6 **blaze** describe, celebrate (*OED* v.² 4.a)
   12 **drift** purpose, intention (*OED* n. 4.a)

[34]

**To the Ladye Arbella.**

**Sonet 5**

Only hope of oure age, that vertues dead
By youre sweet breath should be reviv'd againe;
Learning, discourag'd longe by rude disdaine,
By youre white hands is only cherished.

Thus others worth by yow is honoured; 5
But whoe shall honoure youres? poore wits, in vayne
We seeke to pay the debts which yow pertayne,
Till from youre selfe some wealth be borrowed.

Lend some youre tongues, that every nation may
In his owne heare youre vertuouse prayses blaz'd; 10
Lend them youre wit, youre judgment, memorye,
Least they themselves should not knowe what to say.
And that thow mayst be lov'd as much as prays'd,
My hearte thow mayst lend them, which I gave thee.

*T* 28v [34]
**Miscellaneous features of the copy text: 9 youre**] u *superimposed on* w   10 **vertuouse prayses**] *inserted above* your pr *deleted*

   3 **rude** uneducated (*OED* adj. 3)
   7 **yow pertayne** are your right or privilege (*OED*, s.v. pertain, v. 1.b)
  10 **blaz'd** blazed, described, celebrated (*OED* v.² 4.a)
  12 **Least** lest, that ... not (*OED* conj. 1.a)

[35]

**To my Ladie Rich.**

**Sonet 6**

O, that my songe like to a ship might be,
To beare aboute the world my Ladies fame!
That charged with the riches of her name,
The Indians might oure countryes treasure see.

No treasure, they would say, is rich but she;  5
Of all theyre golden parts they would have shame,
And hap'lye that they might but see the same,
To give theyre gold for nought they would agree.

This wished voyage, though it I begin,
Withoute youre beauties helpe cannot prevayle;  10
For as a ship doth beare the men therein
And yet the men doe make the ship to sayle,
    Youre beauties so, which in my verse apeare,
    Doe move my verse, and it youre beauties beare.

---

*T* 29r [35] | *M* 27r [9]
**Collation: Heading** *om M*
   1 might] cold *M*  6 golden parts] pearles & stones *M*  7 hap'lye] happy *M*  9 it I] I it *M*  13 beauties] beawty *M*  apeare] appeares *M*  14 and it] my verse *M*  beauties beare] beawty beares *M*

  7 **hap'lye** happily; haply (perhaps, possibly) could also be intended (*OED* adv.)
  10 **prevayle** succeed (*OED* v. 2.a)

[36]

**To the Ladie Rich.**

**Sonet** 7

Heralds in armes doe three perfections coate,
To wit: most fayre, most rich, most glittering;
Now when these three concurre within one thing,
Needs must that thing of honoure be of note.

Lately I did behold a rich fayre coate          5
Which wished fortune to myne eyes did bring:
A Lordlye coate, but worthye of a king,
Wherein all these perfections one might note.

A field of lilies roses proper bare,
Two stars in chiefe, the crest was waves of gold;          10
How glittering was the coate the starrs declare,
The lilies made it fayre for to behold.
    And rich it was, as by the gold apeares,
    So happie he which in his armes it beares.

*T* 29v [36] | *D94* B5v, D1.10 [10] | *E* 105v [3] | *A* 54 [12]
**Collation: Heading** Sonnet X. *D94*; to the Lady Rich *E*; *om A*
    1 in] at *D94 A*    doe three] 3 rare *E*    coate] quote *D94 A*    3 Now] So *D94 A*    these] those *D94*    three] things *E*    thing] Coate *A*    4 Needs must that thing] that thing must needes *E*    of note] a note *D94 E A*    5 Lately] Ladye *A*    7 but] yet *D94*; ytt *A*    king] ringe *A*    8 Wherein ... might] in which one might all these perfections *D94*; wherin on myght all thes perfections *A*    11 was] twas *D94 A*    the coate] might by *D94 A*; this coate *E*    declare] appeare *D94 A*    13 apeares] appeareth *D94 A*    14 So] But *D94*; Thryce *A*    which] that *D94 E A*    beares] weareth *D94 A*

    1 **Heralds in armes** heralds of arms; officers recording the names and pedigrees of those entitled to armorial bearings (*OED* n. 1.c)    **coate** quote, observe (*OED* v. 5.a); place in one's coat of arms (*OED* v. 3, first citation 1664)
    3 **concurre** of qualities, to be combined in the same person or thing (*OED* v. 2.f)
    5 **coate** coat of arms (*OED* n. 4)
    9 **proper** in heraldry, represented in natural or realistic colours rather than in conventional tinctures (*OED* adj. 5)    **bare** bore
    10 **in chiefe** in heraldry, borne on or occupying the upper part of the shield (*OED* n. 3)    **crest** in heraldry, a figure or device (originally borne by a knight on his helmet) placed on a wreath, coronet, or chapeau, and borne above the shield and helmet in a coat of arms (*OED* n.[1] 3.a)

**The thyrd 7 to severall persons upon sundrye occasions.**

[37]

**To the princesse of Orange upon occasion of the murther of her father and husband.**

**Sonet 1**

When murdring hands, to quench the thirst of tyrannie,
The worlds most worthye, thy spouse and father, slew,
Wounding thy heart through theyres, a double well they drew:
A well of bloud from them, a well of teares from thee.

So in thyne eyes at once we fire and water see; 5
Fire doth of beautie spring, water of griefe ensue.
Whoe fire and water yet together ever knew,
And neyther water dry'd nor fire quencht to be?

But wonder it is not thy water and thy fyre
Unlike to others be: thy water fire hath bred, 10
And thy fire water makes, for thyne eyes fire hath shed
Teares from a thousand hearts, melted with loves desire.
    And griefe to see such eyes bathed in teares of woes,
    A fire of revenge inflames against thy foes.

*T* 3 or [37]
**Miscellaneous features of the copy text: 2** thy] *replacing* and *deleted*

    3 **well**  copious flow (of tears or blood) (*OED* n.¹ 2.d)
    6 **of grief ensue**  result from grief (*OED* v. 6.a)

[38]

**To the Countesse of Shrewsburye upon occasion of his deare Mistrisse, whoe liv'd under her goverment.**

**Sonet 2**

True worthie dame, if I thee chieftayne call
Of Venus host, let others think no ill.
I graunt that they be fayre, but what prince will
Chuse onlie by the force a generall?

Beauties be but the forces wherewithall 5
Ladies the hearts of private persons kill;
But these fayre forces to conduct with skill,
Venus chose yow, the chiefest of them all.

To yow then, yow, the fayrest of the wise
And wisest of the fayre, I doe appeale: 10
A warrioure of youre campe by force of eyes
Mee pris'ner tooke, and will with rigor deale
  Except yow pity in youre heart will place,
  At whose white hands I only seeke for grace.

*T* 30v [38]

 1 **True** honourable (*OED* adj. 2) **chieftayne** captain, military leader (*OED* n. 2.a)
 2 **Venus host** Venus's army (*OED* n.¹ 1.a)

[39]

**To the Countesse of Pembroke.**

**Sonet 3**

Ladie whome by reporte I only knowe,
Yet knowe so well as I must thee adore;
To honoure thee what need I seeke for more?
Thow art his sister whome I honoured so.

Yet million tongues reporte doth further showe           5
Of thy perfections both such worth and store
As wante of seeing thee paynes me sore,
As sight of others hath procur'd my woe.

All parts of beautie, meeting in one place,
Doe dazle eye, feed love, and ravish witte;              10
Thy perfect shape envies thy princely grace.

Thy minde all say like to thy brother is;
What need I then say more to honoure it?
For I have praysed thyne by praysing his.

*T* 31r [39]

    6 **store** large quantity (*OED* n. 4.a)
    9 **parts** qualities or attributes (*OED* n.¹ 15)
    10 **ravish** entrance, captivate (*OED* v. 4.b)

[40]

**To the Countesse of Essex upon occasion of the death of her first husband, Sir Philip Sydney.**

**Sonet 4**

Sweetest of Ladies, if thy pleasure be
To murther hearts, stay not in England still;
Revenge on Spaine thy husbands death, and kill
His foes, not them that love both him and thee.

O sound revenge that I desire to see! 5
If they be fooles, which wish with theyre owne ill
Hurt to theyre foes, then what be they that will
With theyre owne hurt wish good to enemye?

And thus doe I; and thus ambitiouse Spaine,
Unsatisfied the new-found world to gayne, 10
Two better worlds should have, I meane thyne eyes.

And we oure world, oure world his sun should misse,
Oure sun his heaven; thyne eye oure want supplies:
Oure world, oure sun, oure heaven, oure all it is.

*T* 31v [40]
**Emendations of the copy text: 6** ill] will *T*

    **13 his** its

[41]

**To the Ladie Clinton.**

**Sonet 5**

Since onlye I, sweet Ladie, ye beheld,
Yet then such love I in youre looke did finde,
And such sweet gesses of youre gratiouse mynd,
As never a shorte tyme more happie held.

Forewarning vision which even then foretold 5
Th' eternall cheynes which since my heart did binde,
Even there, where first youre beames into me shin'd,
The fatall prison where my heart I hold.

And how came this? It was thy lovely looke,
Which doth perfume each place it sees with love, 10
As though from yow my deare this sweetnesse tooke.

Because where I saw her, I yow had seen,
Yet every where if any sight me move,
I knowe it is some place where yow have been.

*T* 32r [41]
**Emendations of the copy text: 8** hold] held *T*

   3 **gesses** guesses

[42]

**A calculation of the nativitye of the Ladie Riches daughter, borne upon Friday in the yeare 1588, comonly call'd the yeare of wonder.**

**Sonet 6**

Fayre by inheritance, whome borne we see
Both in the wondrouse yeare, and on the day
Wherin the fayrest planet beareth sway,
The wonders loe of beautyes destinye.

Thow of a world of hearts in tyme shalt be                          5
A monarch great, and with one beautyes ray
So many hosts of hearts thy face shall slay,
As all the rest for love shall yeeld to thee.

But even as Alexander, when he knew
His fathers conquests, wept, least he should leave                  10
No kingdome unto him for to subdue,
Thy mother so shall thee of prayse bereave.
    So many hearts she hath alreadie slayne,
    As few behinde to conquer do remayne.

T 32v [42] | M 28r–v [15] | H 150r [10] | D92 D3r [22] | D94 F6v [76] | A 52 [1]
**Collation: Heading** A sonet in manner of a calculation on the nativitye of a yonge Ladye borne on a friday, in this yeare. 1588. *M*; The Calculation of the nativity of the daughter of my Lady Rich borne on a fryday Anno do: 1588 *H*; A calculation upon the birth of an honourable Ladies daughter, borne in the yeare, 1588, & on a Friday *D92 D94* (yeere, and); A Calculation uppon the birth of the Ladye Riches Daughter, borne Anno 1588, & on A Friday *A*
    **2** and on *M H D92 D94 A*] and in *T*   the day] that day *A*   **3** planet] *om H*  beareth] beare the *H*   **4** The wonders loe] to thee the heavens *M*; the heavens to thee *H D92 D94 A*  of beautyes destinye] this destenye decree *M*; this fortune do decree *H D94*; this fortune doth decree *D92 A*   **7** hosts] hoste *M*  thy face] thyn Eye *A*   **8** As] That *A*  rest] world *A*   **12** Thy mother so shall] so shall thy mother *H D92 D94 A*   **13** she hath alreadie] already she hathe *H D92 D94 A*   **14** As few behinde] That few for the *A*  do *M*] doth *T*; shall *H D92 D94*; will *A*

   **3 beareth sway** rules, exercises influence (*OED*, s.v. sway, n. 7)
   **7 hosts** armies (*OED* n.¹ 1.a)
   **10 least** lest, that ... not (*OED* conj. 1.a)
   **12 bereave** deprive (*OED* v. 2)

[43]

**To Master Hilliard, upon occasion of a picture he made of my Ladie Rich.**

**Sonet 7**

If Michaell the archpainter now did live,
Because that Michaell, he an Angell hight,
As partiall for his fellow Angells, might
To Raphaells skill much prayse and honoure give.

But if in secreat I his judgment shrive, 5
It would confesse that no man knew aright
To give to stones and pearles true die and light,
Till first youre art with orient nature strive.

But thinke not yet yow did that arte devise:
Nay, thanke my Ladie that such skill yow have; 10
For often sprinckling her black sparckling eyes,
Her lips and breast, taught yow the . . . . . . . . . .
    To diamonds, rubies, pearles, the worth of which
    Doth make the jewell which yow paynt seeme rich.

---

*T* 33r [43]
Miscellaneous features of the copy text: 12 *incomplete*

  2 **hight** is called (*OED* v.¹ 4)
  5 **his judgement shrive** hear the confession of his judgement (*OED*, s.v. shrive, v. 1.a)
  7 **die** dye
  8 **orient** pearls of orient (*OED* n. 1.b)  **nature strive** be equal or comparable with nature (*OED*, s.v. strive, v. 6.c)
  11 **sprinckling** scattering or dispersing (liquid, powder, etc.) in small drops or particles (*OED* v.² 1.a)

**The thyrd parte.**

**The first 7 of severall complaynts of misfortune in love onlye.**

[44]

**Sonet 1**

Now, now I love indeed and suffer more
In one day now, then I did in a yeare;
Great flames they be which but small sparkles were,
And wounded now, I was but prickt before.

No mervayle then, though more then heertofore 5
I weepe and sigh: how can great wounds be there
Where moysture runs not oute? And ever, where
The fire is great, of smoke there must be store.

My heart was hetherto but like green wood,
Which must be dry'd before it will burne bright; 10
My former love serv'd but my heart to drye.

Now Cupid for his fire doth find it good,
For now it burneth cleare, and shall give light
For all the world youre beautie to espie.

*T* 33v [44]

1 **Now, now** repeated to stress immediacy or urgency (*OED* adv. 2.b)
3 **sparkles** sparks (*OED* n. 1.a)
5 **No mervayle** no marvel, no wonder (*OED* n.¹ P2)
7 **moysture** the liquid part or constituent of a body (*OED* n.¹ a)
14 **espie** espy, discover (*OED* v. 2.a)

[45]

**Sonet 2**

Wonder it is and pitie tis that she,
In whome all beauties treasure we may find
That may enrich the bodie or the mynd,
Towards the poore should use no charitie.

My love is gone a begging unto thee, 5
And if that beautie had not been more kind
Then pitye, longe ere this I had been pin'd;
But beautie is content his food to be.

O, pitye have when such yonge orphans beg:
Love, naked boy, hath nothing on his backe, 10
And though he wanteth neyther arme nor leg,
Yet maym'd he is, for he his sight doth lacke.
    And yet, though blind, he beautie can behold,
    And yet, though nak'd, he feeles more heate then cold.

---

*T* 34r [45] | *H* 152r [17] | *D*92 C3v [15] | *D*94 B8v, D2.6 [16]
**Collation: Heading** *om H*; Sonnetto quaterdeci *D92*; Sonnet VI *D94*
   1 tis] ys *H*; ist *D92 D94*   3 or] and *D92 D94*   6 that] *om H*   7 I] he *H D92 D94*
9 yonge] poore *H D92 D94*   12 for] sith *H D92 D94*

    **7 Then** than   **pin'd** pined, wasted or exhausted by suffering or hunger (*OED* adj.)

[46]

**Sonet 3**

Pittye refusing my poore love to feed,
A beggar starv'd for want of helpe he lyes
And at youre mouth, the doore of beautie, cryes
That thence some almes of sweet grants may proceed.

But, as he wayteth for some almes deed, 5
A cherrie-tree before the doore he spies;
O deare, quoth he, two cherries may suffice,
Two only life may save in this my need.

But beggars, can they nought but cherries eate?
Pardon my love, he is a goddesse son, 10
And never feedeth but of daintie meate;
Else need he not to pine as he hath done.
    For only the sweet fruite of this sweet tree
    Can give food to my love, and life to me.

---

*T* 34v [46] | *H* 152r [18] | *D*92 C4v [17] | *D*94 C1r, D2.7 [17] | *A* 53 [7]
**Collation: Heading** om *H*; Sonnetto sedeci *D*92; Sonnet VII *D*94; 5 *A*
    2 helpe] food *A*   3 youre] thy *A*   4 thence *H D*92 *D*94 *A*] om *T*   grants] grace *A* may] might *H D*92 *D*94; would *A*   5 But] There *A*   some] an *A*   almes] almouse *H* 7 *line missing A*   8 life may save] may save life *H D*92 *D*94; may give helpe *A*   need *H D*92 *A D*94] meed *T*   10 my love] me (Deare) *A*   11 never feedeth but] onlye feedeth *A*   of] on *H D*92 *D*94; uppon *A*   13 For] And *A*   this] that *A*   14 Can] May *A*

    5 **almes deed** almsdeed, charitable act
    11 **daintie** dainty, luxurious (*OED* adj. 6)   **meate** food (*OED* n. 1.a)
    12 **pine** starve (*OED* v. 3.a)

[47]

**Complaint of his Ladies melancholynes.**

**Sonet 4**

If that one care had oure two hearts possest,
Or yow once . . . what I long suffered,
Then should thy heart accuse, in my hearts stead,
The rigor of it self for myne unrest.

Then should thyne arme upon my shoulder rest,       5
And weight of griefe sway downe thy troubled head;
Then should thy teares upon my sheet be shed,
And then thy heart should pant upon my breast.

But when that other cares thy heart doe seaze,
Alas, what succoure gayne I then by this              10
But double griefe for thine and myne unease?

Yet, when thow seest thy hurts to wound my heart,
And so art taught by me what pitye is,
Perhaps thy heart will learne to feele my smart.

*T* 35r [47]
**Miscellaneous features of the copy text:** 1 two] *inserted after* oure   2 once] *superimposed on an erased illegible word*

   **melancholynes**  melancholiness, a tendency towards melancholy (*OED* n.)
   **3 accuse**  reveal (*OED* v. 4)
   **6 sway downe**  cause to incline or hang down on one side, as from excess of weight (*OED* v. 5.a)
   **9 that**  used with a plural noun or numeral, instead of those (*OED* adj. 1.c)

[48]

**Complaynt of his Ladies sicknesse.**

**Sonet 5**

Uncivill sicknesse, hast thow no regard
But dost presume my dearest to molest?
And, withoute leave, dar'st enter in that breast
Whereto sweet love aproach yet never dar'd?

Spare thow her health, which my life never spar'd, 5
To bitter such revenge of myne unrest;
Although with wrongs my thoughts she hath opprest,
My thoughts seeke not revenge but crave rewarde.

Cease, sicknesse, cease in her for to remayne,
And come and, welcome, harboure thow in me, 10
Whome love long since hath taught to suffer payne.

So she which hath so oft my paynes increast
(O god, if I might so rewarded be)
By my more payne should have her payne releast.

*T* 35v [48] | *H* 151r [13] | *D*92 B3v [7] | *D*94 C3r, D3.1 [21]
**Collation: Heading** om *H*; Sonnetto sesto *D*92; The thyrd Decad. / Sonnet I *D*94
   5 thow] then *H*   never] hath not *H D*92 *D*94   6 myne] my *H D*92 *D*94   7 thoughts] thought *H D*92 *D*94   8 thoughts] wrongs *H D*92 *D*94   but] they *H D*92 *D*94   9 for] then *H D*92 *D*94   12 paynes] paine *H D*92 *D*94   13 if] that *H D*92 *D*94   rewarded] revenged *H D*92 *D*94   14 more] poore *D*94   should] might *D*92 *D*94   her *H D*92 *D*94] my *T*

   1 **regard** respect or deference due to an authority (*OED* n. 1.b)
   2 **molest** afflict or affect, especially recurrently (*OED* v. 1.b)
   4 **Whereto** to which (*OED* adv. 3.a)
   6 **To** too

[49]

**Sonet 6**

Deare, though from me youre gratiouse lookes depart
And of that comfort doe my selfe bereave
Which both I did deserve and did receave;
Triumph not overmuch in this my smarte.

Nay, rather they which now enjoy thy heart 5
For fear just cause of mourning should conceave,
Least thow, inconstant, shouldst theyre trust deceave,
Which like unto the weather changing art.

For in foule weather byrds sing often will,
In hope of fayre, and in fayre tyme will cease, 10
For feare fayre tyme should not continue still.

So they may mourne, which have thy heart possest,
For feare of change; and hope of change may ease
Theyre hearts, whome griefe of change doth now molest.

*T* 36r [49]

    2 **bereave** deprive (*OED* v. 2)
    4 **Triumph** rejoice (*OED* v. 4)
    7 **Least** lest, that ... not (*OED* conj. 1.a)
    14 **molest** afflict or affect, especially recurrently (*OED* v. 1.b)

[50]

**Sonet 7**

If ever any justlye might complayne
Of unrequited service, it is I;
Change is the thanks I have for loyaltye,
And onlye her reward is her disdayne.

So as just spight did allmost me constrayne, 5
Through torment, her due prayses to denye;
For he which vexed is with injurye,
By speaking ill doth ease his heart of payne.

But what, shall tortor make me wrong her name?
No, no, a pris'ner constant thinkes it shame, 10
Though he be rackt, his first truth to gaynsay.

Her true given prayse my first confession is;
Though her disdayne doe rack me night and day,
This I confest and I will dye in this.

*T* 36v [50]
**Emendations of the copy text:** 11 be] *om T*   14 dye] denye *T*

   3 **Change** fickleness (*OED* n. 12.b)
   5 **So as** in such a way that (*OED* conj. 29.a)   **spight** spite
   9 **tortor** torture
   11 **rackt** have one's joints stretched as a punishment or a form of torture (*OED* v.¹ 2.a)
**truth** steadfast allegiance, loyalty (*OED* n. 1)

[51]

**To the Marquesse of Piscats soule, endued in her life tyme with infinite perfections, as her divine poems doe testefie.**

**Sonet 3**

Sweete soule, which now with heavenly songs dost tell
Thy deare redeemers glorie and his prayse,
No mervayle though thy skilfull Muse assayes
The songs of other soules there to excell.

For thow didst learne to sing devinely well 5
Long tyme before thy fayre and glittering rayes
Increast the light of heaven, for even thy layes
Most heavenly were when thow on earth didst dwell.

When thow didst on the earth sing poet-wise,
Angells in heaven prayd for thy companie, 10
And now thow singst with Angells in the skies.
Shall not all poets prayse thy memorie?
    And to thy name shall not theyre workes give fame,
    Whereas theyre workes be sweetned by thy name?

*T* 37r [51] | *AP* A3r [2]
**Collation: Heading** *om AP*
   6 fayre and *AP*] *om T*   14 Whereas] When as *AP*

    3 **assayes** endeavours (*OED* v. 17.b)
    7 **layes** lays, short lyrics intended to be sung (*OED* n⁴ 1.a)

[52]

**To Sir Philip Sydeneyes Soule.**

**Sonet 4**

Give pardon, blessed soule, to my bold cryes
If they, importune, interrupt thy songe,
Which now with joyfull notes thow singst among
The Angells queristers of th' heavenlye skyes.

Give pardon eke, deare soule, to my slow cryes, 5
That since I saw thee it is now so long,
And yet the teares which unto thee belong
To thee as yet they did not sacrifice.

I did not knowe that thow wert dead before;
I did not feele the griefe I did sustayne: 10
The greater stroke astonisheth the more;
Astonishment takes from us sence of payne:
    I stood amaz'd when others teares begun,
    And now begin to weepe, when they have don.

*T* 37v [52] | *AP* A3r [1]
**Collation: Heading** Four Sonnets written by Henrie Constable to Sir Phillip Sidneys soule. *AP*
  2 importune] importund *AP*  3 thow *AP*] now *T*  4 Angells queristers] Angel-Quiristers *AP*  th'heavenlye] heav'nly *AP*  5 deare] sweet *AP*  slow *AP*] bold *T*  6 it is now] now it is *AP*  7 which] that *AP*

  2 **importune** inopportune, untimely (*OED* adj. 3)
  4 **queristers** choristers
  5 **eke** also (*OED* adv.)

[53]

**To Sir Philip Sidneyes soule.**

**Sonet 5**

Great Alexander then did well declare
How great was his united kingdomes might,
When every captayne of his armye might,
After his death, with mightie kings compare.

So now we see, after thy death, how far 5
Thow dost in worth surpasse each other knight,
When we admire him as no mortall wight,
In whome the least of all thy vertues are.

One did of Macedon the king become,
Another sate in the Aegiptian throne, 10
But onlye Alexander selfe had all.

So courteouse some, and some be liberall,
Some wittie, wise, valliant, and learned some;
But Kinge of all the vertues, thow alone.

---

*T* 38r [53] | *AP* A3v [4] | *E* 105v [6]
Collation: Heading *om AP*; To Sir philip sydeneye after his death. *E*
    3 When] Where *E*    11 Alexander] Alexanders *AP E*

    6 **each** every (*OED* adj. 1.a)
    7 **wight** person (*OED* n. 2.a)

[54]

**To Sir Philip Sydneyes soule.**

**Sonet 6**

Even as when great mens heyres cannot agree,
So every vertue now for part of thee doth sue:
Courage proves, by thy death, thy heart to be his due;
Eloquence claymes thy tongue, and so doth courtesie.

Invention knowledge sues, judgment sues memorye;   5
Each sayth thy head is his, and what end shall ensue
Of this strife knowe not I, but this I knowe for true:
That whoesoever gaynes the suite, the losse have we.

Wee, I meane all the world, the losse to all pertayneth;
Yea they which gayne doe loose, and only thy soule gaineth:   10
For loosing of one life, two lives are gained then.

Honoure thy courage moov'd, courage thy death did give;
Death, courage, honoure make thy soule to live,
Thy soule to live in heaven, thy name in tongues of men.

*T* 38v [54] | *AP* A3v [3]
**Collation: Heading** *om AP*
    2 part of *AP*] *om T*   7 not I] I not *AP*   13 make] makes *AP*

    2 **sue** make a legal claim to (*OED* v. 11.a)
    8 **suite** suit, litigation (*OED* n. 7)
    9 **to all pertayneth** is a cause of concern to all (*OED*, s.v. pertain, v. 1.c)

[55]

**On the death of my Ladie Riches daughter, shewing the reason of her untimelye death hindred her effecting these things which by the former calculation of her nativitye he foretold.**

**Sonet 7**

He that by skill of stars doth fates foretell,
If reason give the verdit of his side,
Though by mischance things otherwise betyde
Then he foretold, yet doth he calcule well.

A Phoenix, if she live, must needs excell,　　　　　　　　　　5
And this, by reasons lawes, should not have dy'd;
But thus it chanc't nature cannot abyde
More then one Phoenix in the world to dwell.

Now, as the mother Phoenix death should slay,
Her beauties light did dazle so his eye　　　　　　　　　　　10
As while he, blindfold, let his arrowe flye,
He slew the yonge one, which stood in the way.
　　Thus did the mother scape, and thus did I
　　By good ill hap fayle of my prophecie.

---

*T* 39r [55]

　　2 **verdit** verdict
　　4 **Then** than　　**calcule** calculate, ascertain beforehand the time or circumstances of an event by astrology (*OED* v.¹ 2)
　　5 **Phoenix** a mythical bird; a person of unique excellence or matchless beauty (*OED* n.¹ 1, 2.a)
　　14 **hap** luck (*OED* n.¹ 2)

**The last 7 of the end and death of his love.**

[56]

**Sonet 1**

Much sorrowe in it selfe my love doth move;
More my dispayre, to love a hopelesse blisse;
My follie most, to love where sure to misse;
O helpe me but this last griefe to remove.

All payne, if yow comand it, joy doth prove, 5
And wisdome to seeke joy; then say but this:
Because my pleasure in thy torment is,
I doe command thee withoute hope to love.

So when this thought my sorrowes shall augment,
That myne owne follie did procure my payne, 10
Then shall I say, to give my selfe content,
Obedience only made me love in vayne.
    It was youre will, and not my want of wit;
    I have the payne, beare yow the blame of it.

*T* 39v [56] | *H* 149v [7] | *D92* C4r [16] | *D94* B4v, D1.8 [8] | *A* 54 [10]
**Collation: Heading** *om H*; 7 *in l. margin H*; Sonnetto quindeci *D92*; Sonnet VIII *D94*; 8 *A*
  3 where] whom *H D92 D94 A*    4 this] his *A*    5 payne] paines *D92 D94 A*    doth] shall *H D92 D94 A*    9 sorrowes] sorrowe *H D92 D94*    10 myne] my *D92 D94*    follie] pleasure *A*    11 shall] will *A*    13 youre *H D92 D94 A*] my *T*    and] but *A*    my *H D92 D94 A*] youre *T*

    3 **misse** fail to hit or strike something aimed at, figuratively (*OED* v.¹ 2.c)
    10 **procure** bring (usually something harmful) upon a person (*OED* v. 1.a)

[57]

**Sonet 2**

Needs I must leave and yet needs must I love,
In vayne my witte doth paynt in verse my woe,
Disdaine in thee, dispaire in me, doth showe
How by my witte I doe my follie prove.

All this my heart from love can never move: 5
Love is not in my heart, no, Lady, no,
My heart is love it selfe; till I forgoe
My hearte, I never can my love remove.

How shall I then leave love? I doe entend
Not to crave grace, but yet to wish it still; 10
Not to prayse thee, but beautie to commend,
And so by beauties prayse, prayse thee I will.
    For as my heart is love, love not in me,
    So beautie thow, beautie is not in thee.

---

*T* 4or [57] | *D94* C8r, D4.1 [31] | *A* 54 [11]
**Collation: Heading** The fourth Decad. / Sonet I *D94*; 9 *A*
  1 I must] must I *D94 A*  2 paynt] tell *D94 A*  3 Disdaine in thee] dispayre in me *D94* dispaire in me] disdaine in thee *D94*  6 Love ... no *D94 A*] *line missing T*  7 it selfe] *om A*  till I] I never can *A*  8 hearte] Love *A*  I never can] untill I doe *A*  love] harte *A*  9 shall] can *D94*  leave love] gayne Grace *A*  11 thee, but *D94 A*] beautie *T*  12 thee] he *A*

    7 **forgoe** forsake (*OED* v. 4)
    9 **entend** intend

[58]

**Sonet 3**

My reason, absent, did myne eyes require
To watch and ward, and such foes to descrie
As neare my heart they should approaching spy;
But traytoure eyes my hearts death did conspire;

Corrupted with hopes guifts, let in desire                 5
To burne my heart, and sought no remedie
Though store of water were in eyther eye,
Which well employ'd might well have quencht the fire.

Reason returned, love and fortune made
Judges to judge myne eyes to punishment;                   10
Fortune, sith they by sight my heart betrayd,
From wished sight adjudgd them banishment.
　　Love, sith by fire murdred my hearte was founde,
　　Adjudged them in teares for to be drown'd.

---

*T* 40v [58] | *M* 28r [14] | *H* 151v [16] | *D92* C2v [13] | *D94* B8r, D2.5 [15]
**Collation: Heading** *om M H*; Sonnetto dodeci *D92*; Sonnet V *D94*

　　1 **My**] *om M*　　3 **neare my heart they should**] they should near my hart *M H D92 D94*
5 **hopes guifts**] ritch hope *M*　　6 **and**] yet *M*　　7 **were**] was *M H*　　8 **Which well employ'd might well have quencht**] thoghe not to quenche, yet to asswage *M*　　11 **my**] mine *M*　　12 **wished**] wicked *M*　　13 **sith**] since *M*

> 1 **require** request (*OED* v. 1.a)
> 2 **watch and ward** stand guard (*OED*, s.v. ward, v.¹ 1.a)　　**descrie** reveal (*OED* v.¹ 5.a)
> 7 **store** abundance (*OED* n. 4.b)
> 11 **sith** since (*OED* conj. 2.a)

[59]

**Sonet 4**

Each day new proofes of new dispaire I find,
That is, new death: No mervayle then if I
Make exile my last helpe, to th'end myne eye
Should not behold the death to me assign'd.

Not that from death absence could save my mynde, 5
But that I might take death more patientlye,
Like him which by the judge condemn'd to dye,
To suffer with lesse feare his eyes doth blinde.

Youre lips in skarlet clad my judges be,
Pronouncing sentence of eternall no, 10
Dispaire, the hangman which tormenteth me.

The death I suffer is the life I have,
For onlye life doth make me die in woe,
And onlye death I for my pardon crave.

*T* 41r [59] | *D94* D2v, D4.6 [36] | *A* 55 [14]
**Collation: Heading** Sonnet VI. *D94*; 12 *A*
    2 death] deathes *D94 A*   if] though *D94 A*   5 could] might *D94;* can *A*   6 I] it *D94 A*   7 which by the] the which by *D94 A*   8 lesse feare] more ease *D94 A*   9 Youre] Thy *A*   11 which] that *D94 A*   13 die] live *A*   14 And] An *A*

[60]

**Sonet 5**

Myne eye with all the deadlie sinnes is fraught:
1. First proud, sith it presum'd to looke so hye;
A watchman being made, stood gazing by
2. And, idle, tooke no heed till I was caught.

3. And enviouse, beares envie that my thought        5
Should in his absence be to her so nye;
4. To kill my heart myne eye let in her eye,
And so consent gave to a murther wrought.

5. And covetouse, it never would remove
   From her fayre hayre, gold so doth please his sight;   10
6. A glutton eye, with teares drunke every night,
7. Unchast, a baude between my hearte and love.
   These sins procured have a goddesse ire,
   Wherefore my heart is damn'd in loves sweet fire.

T 41v [60] | H 149r [5] | D92 C2r [12] | D94 B3v, D1.6 [6] | A [8] | PR1 L6v [1] | PR2 211 [1]
See [60b]
**Miscellaneous features of the copy text:** *Numbers added on the left margin*
**Collation: Heading** om H; 5 in l. margin H; Sonnetto undeci. D92; Sonnet VI. D94; 6 A; Sonnet PR1 PR2
   3 made] om H   5 my] by D94 PR1   7 myne] my A   8 consent gave H D92 D94 A PR1 PR2] was accessarie T   9 And] Then A   would] should H   11–12 *lines 12–11* D92 D94 A PR1 PR2   12 Unchast, a baude] A Baude unchast A   hearte] thoughtes A   13 These sins procured have] Thus have thes sinns procured A   14 sweet] om H A

   6 **nye** nigh, near (*OED* adv. 3.a)
   9 **remove** go away from (*OED* v. 1.a)

[60b]

Myne eye with all the deadly sinns is fraught:
first Prowde, because it is cause that so highe
my love presumd, & Slothfull is for why
save only gaze about it, it doth naught.

And Enviouse, which envith that my thoughte 5
Should in his absence be to hir so nighe;
to kill my hart, it hath lett in hir eye
& so consent gave to a murder wrought.

And covetous, whose only god is this,
beawtyes ritche treasure hourded in my hart; 10
A Glutton eye, with teares which drunken is,
and all these sinns shew how Unchast thou art.
    And therefore thou deservst a Goddesse ire,
    & therefore I am dampnd in Love his fire.

*M* 25v [4]
**Miscellaneous features of the copy text: 4** naught] *replacing* not *deleted*
    **14 dampnd** damned

[61]

**Sonet 6**

If true love might true loves reward obtayne,
Dumbe wonder onlye could speake of my joy;
But to much worth hath made thee to much coy
And told me longe agoe I lov'd in vayne.

Not then vayne hope of undeserved gaine 5
Hath made me paint in verses myne annoye,
But for thy pleasure, that thow mightst enjoy
Thy beauties sight in glasses of my payne.

See then thy selfe, though me thow wilt not heare,
By looking on my verse, for payne in verse, 10
Love doth in payne, beautie in love appeare.

So if thow wilt my verses meaning see,
Expound them thus when I my love rehearse:
None loves like him, that is, none fayre like mee.

*T* 42r [61] | *H* 151r [14] | *D*92 B4v [9] | *D*94 B6r, D2.1 [11] | *A* 55 [13]
**Miscellaneous features of the copy text: 14 None ... mee]** *in italic script*
**Collation: Heading** *om H*; Sonnetto ottavo. *D*92; The second Decad. / Sonnet I *D*94; 11 *A*
    2 could] might *D*92 *D*94 *A*    4 lov'd] sigh'd *H D*92 *D*94; sighe *A*    8 sight] praise *D*94 *A*    11 love] loves *A*    12 wilt] wouldst *H D*92 *D*94; wille *A*

    3 **to** too
    8 **glasses** mirrors (*OED* n.¹ 8.a)
    13 **rehearse** recite (a poem, prayer, or other piece of writing), especially before an audience (*OED* v. 4.a)

222 • HENRY CONSTABLE

[62]

**Conclusion of the whole.**

**Sonet 7**

Sometymes in verse I prays'd, sometymes I sigh'd;
No more shall pen with love nor beautie mell,
But to my heart alone my heart shall tell
How unseene flames doe burne it day and night,

Least flames give light, light bring my love to sight,              5
Love prove my follies to much to excell;
Wherefore my love burnes like the flame of hell,
Wherein is fire and yet there is no light.
    So shall henceforth more paine lesse follie have,
    And follie past shall justlye pardon crave.                    10

For if none ever lovd like mee, then why
Still blameth he the things he doth not knowe?
And he that so hath lov'd shall favoure showe,
For he hath been a foole as well as I.

When I had ended this last sonnet and found that such vayne poems as I had by idle houres writ did amount to the climatericall number 63, me thought it was high tyme for my follie to die and to employe the remnant of wit to other calmer thoughts lesse sweete and lesse bitter.

*T* 42v [62] | *D94* F6r, D8.5 [75]
**Collation: Heading** Sonnet V *D94*
   1 sometymes I] somtime in verse I *D94*   2 nor] and *D94*   5 bring] brings *D94*   6 Love] and my love *D94*   follies] follie *D94*   to much] *om D94*   7 burnes *D94*] burne *T*   flame] fire *D94*   9–10 lines 13–14 *D94*   9 So] Thus *D94*   paine *D94*] follie *T*   lesse] more *D94*   10 shall] may *D94*   11–12 lines 9–10 *D94*   11 none ever] one never *D94*   12 Still blameth] skillesse blames *D94*   things] thing *D94*   13 shall] should *D94*   13–14 lines 11–12 *D94*

    2 **mell** concern or busy itself (*OED* v.1 4)
    5 **Least** lest, that ... not (*OED* conj. 1.a)
    6 **excell** exceed (*OED* v. 1.b)

*T* 42v

    **climatericall** constituting a climacteric, any of certain supposedly critical years of human life, when a person was considered to be particularly liable to change in health or fortune (*OED*, s.v. climacteric, n. 2.a)

[63]

**To the divine protection of the Ladie Arbella the author commendeth both his Graces honoure and his Muses aeternitye.**

My Mistrisse worth gave wings unto my Muse,
And my Muse wings did give unto her name;
So, like twin byrds, my Muse bred with her fame,
Together now doe learne theyre wings to use.

And in this booke which heere yow may peruse 5
Abroad they flye, resolv'd to try the same
Adventure in theyre flight; and thee, sweet dame,
Both she and I for oure protectoure chuse.

I by my vow and she by farther right
Under your Phoenix presume to flye, 10
That from all carrion beakes, in saftie, might
By one same wing be shrouded she and I.
    O happie if I might but flitter there,
    Where yow and shee and I should be so neare.

*T* 43r [63]

    **commendeth**  entrusts, commits (*OED* v.1)
    7 **Adventure**  chance, luck (*OED* n. 1.b)
    10 **Phoenix**  a mythical bird; a person of unique excellence or matchless beauty (*OED* n.¹ 1, 2.a)
    12 **shrouded**  protected (*OED* v.¹ 3.a)
    13 **flitter**  flutter, fly with low or short flights (*OED* v. 1.a)

**[Sonnets only in the Marsh MS]**

[64]

**To his mistris curtuously intertayning him after hard & disgratious wordes.**

My hope laye gasping on his dying bedd,
slayne with a word, the dart of thy disdayne;
another woord breathd lyfe in it againe
& stauncht the blood my wounded hope had shed.

Sweete tonge, then, sith thou canst revive the dead       5
thou easely maist aswage a sickmans payne.
What glory then shall such thy power gayne
which sicknes, death, which lyfe & death hast bredd.

One word gave lyfe, one more cann helth restore;
yf noe, I live, but live as better noe.                   10
more thou speakest not &, yf I call for more,
more is thy wrath & thy wrath breeds my woe.

My tonge & thine thus both conspire my smart:
myne while I speake, thine while thou sylent art.

*M* 25r [1]
**Miscellaneous features of the copy text: 9** more] *replacing* word *deleted*

   **disgratious** ungracious, unkind (*OED*, s.v. disgracious, adj. 1, first citation 1598)

[65]

**To the same Ladyes in imitation of Petrarch, riminge only with two wordes in eight significations.**

In Edenn grew many a pleasant springe
of frutefull trees, among which trees wear two
whome god him selfe alotted honour to
more then to all the plantes that there did spring.

No season there was ever but the springe,                    5
whose heate & moysture ay conspired to
preserve these trees both faire & fruitfull toe,
neare unto whome did runn a fowr fould spring.

Eache of these pleasant trees a worthy dame,
these sisters two, these two trees honred soe,               10
the lasting springe, their never withred fame,
the rivers fowr (neare whom these trees do grow),

    The virtues fower wherin they so excell
    as Paradise seemes ech place wher they dwell.


M 26v [7]

    1 **springe** copse or wood consisting of young trees (*OED* n.¹ 22.a)
    6 **ay** always; at all times (*OED* adv. 1)
    8 **fowr fould** fourfold
    10 **honred** honoured

## [A sonnet prefacing the 1592 *Diana*]

[66]

**To his absent Diana.**

Sever'd from sweete Content, my lives sole light,
  Banisht by over-weening wit from my desire,
  This poore acceptance onely I require:
  That, though my fault have forc'd me from thy sight.
Yet that thou wouldst (my sorrowes to requite)        5
  Review these Sonnets, pictures of thy praise,
  Wherein each woe thy wondrous worth doth raise,
  Though first thy worth bereft me of delight.
See them forsaken, for I them forsooke;
  Forsaken first of thee, next of my sence.        10
  And when thou deignst on their blacke teares to looke,
  Shed not one teare my teares to recompence,
     But joy in this (though Fates gainst mee repine):
     My verse still lives to witnes thee divine.

*D92* A3r [1]

  1 **Sever'd** separated (*OED* v. 9.a)
  2 **over-weening** excessive, immoderate (*OED* adj. 2)
  3 **require** request (*OED* v. 1.a)
  6 **Review** look at (*OED* v. 5.a)
  10 **sence** reason, wits (*OED* n. 17.a)
  11 **deignst** condescend (*OED* v. 1.a)
  13 **joy** rejoice (*OED* v. 2.b)    **repine** feel or express discontent or dissatisfaction (*OED* v. 1.a)
  14 **witnes** show forth evidence by faithful speech (*OED* v. 1.e)

Certen Spirituall sonnetts to the honner of God and his Sainctes: withe Nyne other directed by particuler devotion to 3 blessed Maryes. By Hen. Conestable, Esquire

Certayne spirituall sonnetts to the honnor of god and his Sainctes

[67]

### To God the Father

Greate god, within whose simple essence wee
    no thinge but that which is thie self cann fynde;
    when on thy self thou dydd'st reflecte thy mynd,
    thy thought was God, which tooke the forme of thee.
And when this god thus borne thou lov'st, and hee 5
    lov'd thee againe with passion of like kynde,
    as lovers sighes which meete become one wynde,
    bothe breath'd one spright of equall Deitie.
Eternall father, whence these twoe do come,
    and wil'st the title of my father have, 10
    an heavenlie knowledg in my mynde engrave
That it thy sonnes true ymage may become;
    and sence my harte with sighes of holie love
    that it the temple of the sprite may prove.

BE 3 [1] | HA 32r [1]
**Collation:** 3 dydd'st *HA*] doste *BE*

    **honner** honour
    **Certen / Certayne** certain, some; a limited number of (*OED* adj. 7.c)
    8 **spright** spirit (*OED* n.¹ 1.a)
    10 **wil'st** will; desire (*OED* v.¹ 5)
    11 **engrave** fix indelibly (*OED* v. 3.c)
    13 **sence** cense, perfume with odours from burning incense (*OED* v.¹ 1.a)

[68]

**To god the Sonne**

Younge Prince of heaven, begotten of that Kinge
    which rules the kingdome that him self did make,
    and of that Virgin Queene mans shape did take
which from kinge Davids roiall stocke did springe.
No marvell thoughe thie birthe made Anngells singe 5
    and Anngells ditties sheppardes pipes awake,
    and kyngs, like sheppardes, humbled for thy sake
kneele at thie feete and guifts of hommage bringe.
For heaven and erth, the highe and lowe estate,
    as partners of thie birth make equall Clayme: 10
    Anngells, because in heaven god thee begatt,
Sheppards and kings, because thy mother came
    from princelie race, and yet by povertie
    made glorie shine in her humilitye.

*BE* 3 [2] | *HA* 32v [2]
**Miscellaneous features of the copy text:** *A horizontal line made of short strokes of the pen separates lines 4 and 5.*
**Collation: 1** Younge] Greate *HA*    **2** which] who *HA*

[69]

## To God the holy Ghoste

Eternall sprite, which arte in heaven, the love
    with which god and his sonne eache other kisse
    and which, to showe whoe gods beloved is,
    the shape and wings took'st of a lovinge dove.
When Christ ascendinge sente thee from above,           5
    in fiery tonnges than cam'st downe unto his;
    that skill in utt'ring heavenlye misteries
    by heate of zeale bothe faithe & love might move.
True god of love, from whence all true love springes,
    bestowe upon my love thy winges and fyre;           10
    my soule a spirit is and with thy winges
May like an Anngell flye from earthes desire;
    and with thy fyre a harte enflam'd may beare,
    & in thy sight a zeraphyn appeare.

*BE* 4 [3] | *HA* 33r [3]
**Collation: 3** which] who *HA*   **6** than] thow *HA*   **9** whence] whom *HA*   true love *HA*] true loves *BE*

    **6 than** then   **his** those to whom he was closely related (*OED* pron.¹ 4.a)
    **14 zeraphyn** seraphim

[70]

**To the blessed Sacrament**

When thee, o holy sacrificed Lambe,
    in severed signes I, white and liquide, see
    as on thy boddy slayne, I thincke on thee,
    which pale by sheddyng of thy bloud became.
And when againe I doe behould the same                  5
    vayled in white to be receav'd of me,
    thou seemest in thy Syndon wrap'd to be
    like to a Corse whose monument I am.
Intomb'd in me, unto my soule appeare,
    in earth imprisond, bannisht from thy sight,           10
    like our fore fathers, which in Limbo were.
Clere thou my thoughtes as thou didst give them light,
    and as thou others fred from purgyng fyre,
    quench in my harte the flames of bad desire.

*BE* 4 [4] | *HA* 33v [4]
**Collation: 9** Intomb'd] Buryed *HA*   10 in earth imprisond] pryson'd in earth, & *HA*   11 which] who *HA*

    **2 severed** separate (*OED* v. 1.a)
    **7 Syndon** shroud, specifically that in which the body of Christ was wrapped (*OED* n. 2.a)
    **8 Corse** corpse (*OED* n. 2)     **monument** sepulchre (*OED* n. 1)
    **12 Clere** clear, purify (*OED* v. 8)

[71]

**To our Ladye**

In that, Oh Queene of Queens, thy birth was free
    from guilt, which others doe of grace bereave
    when in theyr mothers wombe they life receave,
    god as his sole-borne daughter loved thee.
To matche thee like thy birthes nobilitie,                    5
    he thee his spirit for thy spowse did leave,
    of whome thou did'st his only sonne conceave
    and so wa'st link'd to all the Trinitie.
Cease then, Oh Queens which earthly Crownes do weare,
    to glory in the pompe of worldly thinges;                  10
    yf men suche highe respect unto you beare
Which daughters, wyv's and mothers are of kinges,
    what honnor should unto that Queene be donne
    which had your god for father, spowse and sonne?

BE 5 [5] | HA 34r [5] | DP 342
**Collation: Heading** To our blessed Lady *HA*; On the blessed Virgin Mary *DP*
   2 guilt] that *DP*   doe] doth *DP*   6 thy] his *DP*   7 of] By *DP*   8 wa'st] was *HA*   9 which] who *HA*; that *DP*   10 worldly] earthly *DP*   11 respect] respects *DP*   13 should] can *DP*   14 which] Who *HA DP*

    5 **like** according to (*OED* adv. 3.b)

[72]

## To St Michaell the Arkcaungell

When as the Prince of Anngelles, puft with pryde,
    stird his seditious spirittes to rebell,
    god chose for chiefe his Champion Michaell
    and gave him charge the hoaste of heaven to guide.
And when the Anngells on the rebelles side,      5
    in battell vanquisht, from there glory fell,
    the pride of heaven became the drake of hell
    and in the dungion of dispaire was tyde.
This dragon since lett loose, gods Churche assailde
    and she, by helpe of Michaelles sworde, prevailde;      10
    whoe ever tryde adventures like this knighte,
Which, gennerall of heaven, hell overthrue,
    for suche a Ladye as godes spowse did fighte,
    and suche a monster as the Dyvell subdue?

---

BE 5 [6] | HA 34v [6]
**Collation:** 3 chose] choose HA    5 on] of HA    6 in battell vanquisht] vanquish't in battayle HA

    4 **charge** duty, responsibility (OED n.¹ 12)    **hoaste** host, army (OED n.¹ 1.a)
    7 **drake** dragon, serpent (OED n.¹ 1)
    8 **tyde** tied
    11 **tryde** tried, underwent (OED s.v. try, v. 14)

[73]

**To St John Baptiste**

As Anne, longe barren, mother did become
    of him which last was Judge in Israell,
    thou, last of Prophettes borne, like Samuell
didst from a wombe past hope of yssue come.
His mother, silent, spake, thy father, dombe,             5
    recovering speech, godes wonder did fore tell;
    he after death a prophett was in hell,
and thou, unborne, within thy mothers wombe.
He did annoynt the kinge which god did take
    from charge of sheepe to rule his chosen lande,       10
    but that highe kynge which heaven & earth did make
Receav'd a holier liquor from thy hande
    when god his flocke in humayne shape did feede,
    as Israelles kinge kept his in sheppards weede.

*BE* 6 [7] | *HA* 35r [7]
**Collation:** 2 which] who *HA*   9 which] whom *HA*   11 which] who *HA*

   10 **charge** custody (*OED* n.¹ 13.a)
   12 **liquor** liquid (*OED* n. 1.a)
   14 **weede** weed, clothing, apparel (*OED* n.² 2.a)

[74]

**To St Peter & St Paule**

He that for feare his Maister did deny
    and at a maidens voice amazed stood,
    the mightiest Monarche of the earth withstood
and on his Maisters Crosse rejoyc'd to dye.
Hee whose blinde zeale did rage with crueltie          5
    and help'd to shedd the first of Martirs bloude,
    by light from heaven his blindnes understoode
and with the chieffe Apostle slayne dothe lye.
Oh, thre times happie Twoe, o goulden payre
    which with your bloude did lay the Churches grounde    10
    within the fatall Towne which twynnes did founde,
And setled there the Hebrue fisshers Chayre
    where first the Latyne sheppard ray'sd his throne
    and, since, the world and Church were rul'd by one.

BE 6 [8] | HA 35v [8]
**Collation:** 10 which] who HA

    11 **fatall** destined, fated (*OED* adj. 1)
    12 **fisshers** fisherman's (*OED* n.¹ 1.a)

[75]

## To St Mary Maudlyn

For few nightes sollace in delitious bedd,
    where heate of lust did kindle flames of hell,
    thou nak'd on naked rocke in desart cell
lay thirtie yeares & teares of grieffe did shedd.
But, for that tyme thy harte there sorrowed,           5
    thou now in heaven eternally do'st dwell,
    and, for eache Teare which from thine eyes then fell,
a sea of pleasure now is rendered.
Yf shorte delightes intice my harte to straye,
    let me by thy longe Pennance learne to knowe       10
    how deere I shoulde for trifling pleasures paye.
And if I vertues roughe beginning shunn,
    let thy eternall Joyes unto me showe
    what highe rewarde by litle payne is wonne.

BE 7 [9] | HA 36r [9]
**Collation: Heading** To St Mary Magdalen HA

    3 **desart** desert

[76]

## To St Katheren

Because thou was the Daughter of A kinge,
    whose beautie did all natures wourkes exceede
    and wysedome wonder to the wourlde did breed,
    a muse might rayse it self on Cupids winge.
But sithe these graces which from nature springe 5
    were grac'd by those which from grace did proceed
    & glory have deserv'd, my muse doth neede
    an Angelles feathers when thie prayse I singe.
For all in thee became Anngelicall:
    an Anngell face had Anngelles puritie 10
    and thou an Anngelles tonge did'st speake withall.
Loe whie thy soule sett free by martyrdome
    was Crown'd by god in Angells company
    and Anngelles handes thy bodye did intombe.

BE 7 [10] | HA 36v [10]
**Collation:** 1 was] wast *HA*   7 have] haith *HA*

[77]

**To St Margarett**

Fayre Amazon of heaven, which took'st in hande
    St Michaell and St George to imitate,
    and for a Tyranttes love, transformd to hate,
    wast for thie lilly faith retaynd in bande.
Alone on foote and with thy naked hande 5
    thou did'st like Michaell with his hoste, and that
    for which on horse arm'd George we Celebrate,
    whilst thou like them a Dragon did'st withstand.
Behoulde my soule shutt in my bodies Jayle,
    the which the Drake of hell gapes to devoure, 10
    teache me, oh virgin, howe thou did'st prevayle.
Virginitie, thou sayest, was all thy Ayde:
    give me then puritie, in steed of powre
    and lett my soule, made chaste, passe for a mayde.

*BE* 8 [11] | *HA* 37r [11]
**Collation:** 1 which] who *HA*   6 with] & *HA*

    4 **bande** imprisonment (*OED* n.¹ 1.b)
    6 **hoste** army (*OED* n.¹ 1.a)
   10 **Drake** dragon, serpent (*OED* n.¹ 1)

[78]

**To St Collett on the day of her feaste and his nativitye**

This day, oh blessed virgine, is the daye
    which double lyffe did give to thee and me,
    to thee in heaven lyffe of eternitye
    to me on earth a lyffe that fades awaye.
Yf I to longe in earthes affection staye,                               5
    lett this thy better liffe teache me to see
    howe I muste strive to sett my spiritt free
    before true lyffe and Joye I purchase maye.
When I was borne, I lefte with grieffe and woe
    my mothers wombe, & for to lyve againe                          10
    I muste with payne from my owne bodye goe;
firste from the lustes thereof to live in grace,
    then from it self before I cann obtayne
    a lyfe of glorye in thy dwellinge place.

BE 8 [12]

    5 **to** too   **affection** feeling (as opposed to reason); passion, lust (*OED* n.¹ 1.b)

## Nyne other sonnetts directed by particuler Devotion unto 3 blessed Maryes

## To the blessed Virgin Marye, mother of God

[79]

Soveraigne of Queens, yf vayne ambition move
   my harte to seeke an earthly princes grace,
   shewe me thy sonne in his imperiall place
   whose servants raigne, o're kinges & Queens, above.
And yf alluring passions I doe prove 5
   by pleasing sighs, shewe me thy lovely face
   whose beames the Anngelles beauty doe deface
   and evin inflame the zeraphins with love.
Soe by ambition I shall humble be
   when in the presence of the highest kinge 10
   I serve all his, that he may honnor me.
And love my harte to chaste desires shall bringe
   when fairest Queene lookes on me from her throne
   and, Jelous, biddes me love but her alone.

*BE* 9 [13] | *HA* 37v [12]
**Miscellaneous features of the copy text:** 5 prove] *inserted, replacing an illegible word deleted*
**Collation: Heading** To our blessed Lady *HA*

   4 **o're** over
   5 **prove** evince (*OED* v. 2.a)
   7 **deface** outshine by contrast (*OED* v. 6)

[80]

Whie should I any love, oh Queene, but thee?
    yf favour past a thanckfull love should breede,
    thy wombe did beare, thy brest my saviour feede,
    and thou did'st never cease to succour mee.
Yf love do followe wourthe and dignitie,         5
    thou all in all perfections dost exceede;
    yf love be ledd by hoope of future meede,
    what pleasure more then thee in heaven to see?
An earthly sighte doth onlye please the eye
    and breeds desire, but dothe not satisfie;         10
    thy sight gives us possession of one joye,
And with suche full delightes eache sence shall fill
    as harte shall wyshe but for to see the still
    and, ever seing, ever shall enjoye.

*BE* 9 [14] | *HA* 38r [13]
**Collation: Heading** To our blessed Lady *HA*
    6 all in all] all in *HA*   11 one] all *HA*

    5 **dignitie** desert, merit (*OED* n. 1.b)
    7 **meede** recompense, reward (*OED* n. 1.a)
    12 **eache sence** any of the five senses (*OED*, s.v. sense, n. 12.a)

## [81]

Sweete Queene, althoughe thy beauty rayse up me
    from sight of baser beautyes here belowe,
    yet lett me not reste there, but higher goe
to him which tooke his shape from god and thee.
And if thy forme in him more faire I see,           5
    what pleasure from his deitye shall flowe,
    by whose faire beames his beautye shineth soe,
when I shall it behould eternallie.
Then shall my love of pleasure have his fill,
    when beauty self in whome all sweetnes is           10
    shall my enamo'rd soule embrace and kisse,
And still new loves and new delightes distill
    which from my soule shall gushe into my harte
    and throughe my bodye flowe to ev'y parte.

*BE* 10 [15] | *HA* 38v [14]
**Collation: Heading** To our blessed Lady *HA*
    4 which] who *HA*    10 sweetnes] pleasure *HA*    12 still] shall *HA*

    2 **baser** of a lower or inferior quality or standard (*OED* adj. 7.a)
    10 **self** itself (*OED* pron. 1.a)
    14 **ev'y** every

## To the Blessed sinner St Mary Mawdlyn

[82]

Blessed offender, which thy self haste tri'd
    howe farr a sinner differs from A saincte,
    joine thie wett eyes with teares of my complaint
    and pittye hym for whome thy Maister dy'd.
Noe longer let my sinfull soule abide                                          5
    in feaver of thy former passions fainte,
    but lett that love, which laste thy harte did taynt
    with panges of thy repentance, pearse my side.
Soe shall my soule no foolishe virgin bee
    with emptie Lampe, but like a mawdlin beare                      10
    for oyntment boxe a breste with oyle of grace.
And so the zeale which then shall burne in me
    maye make my harte like to a Lampe appere
    and in my spowses pallace give me place.

BE 10 [16] | HA 39r [15]
**Collation: Heading** To St Mary Magdalen HA
   1 which] who HA    4 and ... dy'd] while I sighe for that grave, for which thow cry'd HA
6 former passions] fyrst desyres HA    10 mawdlin] Magdalen HA

    1 **tri'd** tried, ascertained the truth of a matter (OED v. 5.c)
    6 **fainte** weak, feeble (OED adj. 4.a)
    7 **taynt** attaint, touch (OED v. 1)
    10 **mawdlin** penitent resembling Mary Magdalene (OED n. 1.b)

[83]

Suche as, retir'd from sight of men like thee,
    by pennance seeke the Joyes of heaven to wynne,
    in desarttes make there Paradice begyn
and evin amonge wilde beastes doe Angelles see.
In suche a place my soule doth seeme to bee         5
    when in my boddye she laments her synne
    and non but brutall passions findes therein,
excepte they be sent downe from heaven to me.
Yet if those graces god to me imparte
    which he inspir'd thy blessed brest withall,         10
    I may finde heaven in my retyred harte.
And if thou change the objecte of my love,
    the wing'd affection which men Cupid call
    may gett his sight and like an Angell prove.

BE 11 [17] | HA 39v [16]
**Collation: Heading** To St Mary Magdalen *HA*
  6 laments *HA*] Lamenteth *BE*   7 findes] fyndes *HA*; finde *BE*

  **3 desarttes** deserts
  **7 non** nothing   **brutall** belonging to animals (*OED* adj. 1)
  **14 prove** become (*OED* v. 3.e)

[84]

Sweete sainct, thou better can'st declare to me
    what pleasure is obtaynd by heavenly love
    then they which other loves did never prove
    or which in sex are differinge from thee.
For like a woman-spouse my soule shalbe,         5
    whome sinfull passions once to lust did move
    and since, betrothed to gods sonne above,
    should be enamo'rd with his Deitye.
My boddy is the garment of my sprite
    while as the daye time of my liffe doth laste;       10
    when death shall bringe the night of my delighte
My soule, uncloth'd, shall rest from labours paste
    and, clasped in the arms of god, enjoye,
    by sweete conjunction, everlastinge Joye.

BE 11 [18] | HA 40r [17]
**Collation: Heading** To St Mary Magdalen HA

    **3 prove** taste (*OED* v. 6.c)
    **14 conjunction** union in marriage (*OED* n. 2.a)

## To the Blessed Martir Marye, Queene of Scotland

[85]

I write of tears and blud at on time shedd
    from one sweete bodye and tenne Thowsand eyes,
    when as a Queene became a sacrifice
    like to a Lambe unto a scaffolde ledd.
Unworthy Alter to be honnored 5
    with so dere offring of so highe A price,
    whose losse no teeres can showe nor words suffice
    the Aucthors shame abroad the worlde to spredd.
My yncke even weepes, & teares with mourning blacke
    made Incke againe serve to recorde this lacke, 10
    and that deere bloud which gusshed from her face,
Disdaininge now uppon the grounde to bleede,
    to there face came which cau'sd this dolefull case
    and made them blushe for shame of suche a deede.

BE 12 [19]

    3 **when as** at the time at which (*OED* adv. 1.a)
    10 **againe** in return, in response (*OED* adv. 3.a)
    13 **case** event, occurrence (*OED* n.¹ 2.a)

[86]

It is not pompe of solemne funerall
    that can excuse the Crime those did Comytt
    which, after bloddy sentence, did permitt
    thy sacred boddye to have buryall.
Nor yett schism-rites cann honnor yt at all:           5
    prophane they be, for suche A Corpes unfitt;
    nature, which graced all her workes with it,
    made all her markes to honnor it withall.
The earthe the Cheste, the heavens the hearse wilbe,
    when night, the Ayre with shaddowes coveringe     10
    the skye, all hunge with mourninge blacke we see.
The starres as lightes serve to adorne this hearse;
    and nowe me thinckes the Anngelles dirgies singe
    and stoppe my mouth & bidd me end my verse.

---

BE 12 [20]
**Emendations of the copy text: 12 serve] sever BE**

    5 **schism-rites** schismatic rites
    6 **Corpes** corpse
    9 **Cheste** coffin (OED n.¹ 3)    **hearse** a temple-shaped structure of wood used in royal and noble funerals (OED n. 2.c)
    13 **dirgies** dirges, songs of mourning (OED n. 2)

[87]

I doe the wronge, o Queene, in that I saye
    the Anngelles dargie singe to honnor thee,
    sithe neither men nor angelles use to praye
    for suche as dye from synnes-pollusion free.
Yf any spott in innocence coulde be,                                                         5
    thy blouddy baptisme wasshed it awaye,
    and that which seem'd thy funerall to mee
    was made in heaven thy Coronation daye.
Then in the Courte where god him self is kinge,
    his mother Queene, and by whose princely side                 10
    for knightes and Dames, Martirs & virgins stande,
The anngelles thee unto goddes throne did bringe;
    wherin the purple roobe thy bloud had dide
    thou took'st the Crowne of glory from his hande.

*BE* 13 [21]

    2 **dargie** dirge, song of mourning (*OED* n. 2)
    4 **pollusion** impurity or corruption (*OED* n. 3.a)
    13 **wherin** where in, where wearing    **roobe** robe    **dide** dyed

# Explanatory Notes

## Commentary on the Secular Sonnets

[1] *Grace, full of grace, though in these verses heere*

This sonnet is unique to *T* and serves as an introduction to the sequence; by the poet's own admission, it rededicates a collection addressed to multiple individuals to only one lady, identified in the heading as the poet's mistress. "Grace" must be Grace Pierrepont, daughter to Frances Cavendish, who would have been around eighteen years old and unmarried at the time Constable was at court. They may have been acquainted given his family connections with the Cavendish-Talbots (see p. 16).

1 The opening echoes the Catholic prayer "Hail Mary," in that both his mistress and the Virgin are addressed through an apostrophe and described as "full of grace." It is significant that the lady's name is also the first occurrence of the word "grace," which pervades the sequence and is charged with different layers of meaning.

4 *Thow yet unknowne*] The meaning is ambiguous. This could refer to the lady, whom the poet claims he loved before he even knew her. Cf. John Donne's "Air and Angels" (*The Complete Poems*, ed. Robin Robbins [Edinburgh, 2010], 123): "Twice or thrice had I loved thee / Before I knew thy face or name" (1–2). It may also mean that the poet was not aware of his mistake when he loved other women.

9 The best known of Constable's purported "loves" is Penelope Rich, though many of his dedicatory sonnets are amatory in tone.

11 *follie*] This word could also be an early spelling of "fully." However, "folly" reappears in the sequence in [56] and binds this introductory sonnet to the conclusion [62]. The poet is therefore set on recounting his past foolishness to the lady.

12 The religious undertone comes to the fore in this line and initiates the final wordplay between the lady's name and divine grace: the poet will either gain her favour or dispense with secular love altogether.

## The order of the booke

The arrangement and grouping in three main sections, each of them containing three thematic subsections or "arguments" with seven sonnets, seems too carefully planned to be other than authorial. A concern with narrative structure – from the early stages to the metaphorical "death" of the poet's love – and with social rank informs this arrangement, which is not mirrored in any other sources. The tripartite structure finds its natural continuation in the *Spiritual Sonnets*.

## [2] *Resolvd to love, unworthie to obtayne*

This sonnet can be considered the rightful introduction to the collection, as it opens the sequences proper in *H*, *D92*, and *D94*, derived from archetype *Y*. The heading given to the first group of seven sonnets reinforces this idea.

    3–4 Cf. Daniel, *Delia* 8, in which sighs are also a consequence of suffering, a sacrifice: "Thou poore hart sacrifiz'd unto the fairest, / Hast sent the incens of thy sighes to heaven" (1–2). Cf. also Sidney, *A&S* 1.4: "Knowledge might pity win, and pity grace obtain." The poet-lover in Sidney's sequence seems more optimistic than the one in Constable's, who claims to be aiming for pity only.

    5–7 A similar contrast between the suffering lover's patience and the patience of the lady in hearing his complaints is found in Sidney, *A&S* 56.12–14: "No, patience; if thou wilt my good, then make / Her come and hear with patience my desire, / And then with patience bid me bear my fire."

    6–7 The anaphora links the lady and the poet together in a figurative storm: her eyes are bright as lightning and his complaints loud as thunder.

## [3] *Fly lowe, deare Love; thy sun dost thow not see?*

This sonnet personifies Love as Icarus in the Ovidian myth as depicted in *Ars amatoria* 2.75–76: "iamque nouum delectat iter, positoque timore / Icarus audaci fortius arte uolat" (*Amores: Medicamina faciei femineae; Ars amatoria. Remedia amoris*, ed. E. J. Kenney [Oxford, 1965], 144). Icarus and the poetic subject, whose love flies towards the beloved – the metaphorical sun – at great peril to himself, were linked together in the Italian and French sonnet tradition. The idea of an Icarus-like love that must be warned recurs in Desportes, and it was *Cleonice* 2.1–4 from which Constable probably borrowed. In the first sonnet in Pierre de Ronsard's *Astrée* the poet also envisions himself as an Icarus figure, "feathered with hope" ("emplumé d'esperance"; see Pierre de Ronsard, *Œuvres complètes*, ed. Jean Céard, Daniel Menéger, and Michel Simonin [Paris, 1993–1994], 1: 323). For contemporary renditions of the motif in English, see Alexander Montgomerie's sonnet "Love lent me wings of hope and high desyre" (*Poems*, ed. David J. Parkinson [Edinburgh, 2000], 1: 126); Daniel, *Delia* 31; and Drayton, *Ideas mirrour* 22. In the latter, the Icarian narrative is enacted in full, the destruction of winged love actual instead of envisioned: "Thus soring still, not looking once below, / So neere thyne eyes celestiall sunne aspyred, / That with the rayes his wafting pyneons fired" (9–11).

1 *lowe*] This reading has been favoured because the spelling of *T*'s "loue" is ambiguous and probably a scribal mistake considering that "love" is found elsewhere in the line and both words could have been conflated. Rendering it as "love" would impair the Icarus motif.

3 *kindled*] The variant "wreakful" in *H, D92*, and *D94* offers no grounds for emendation, given that the *T* reading seems semantically cohesive with the idea of burning.

6 *And so cannot*] The absence of "so" in *T* creates a metrical irregularity, which a later reader emended on the margin after comparison with another source.

8 The idea of the divine origin, and hence justification, of love, is a commonplace.

9–11 The passivity of Love is emphasised through the verbs "caus'd," "begotte," and "engendred." All agency is transferred to the beloved, conventionally compared to a muse, an angel, and a goddess. However, Love does not rise out of the contemplation of her beauty alone; her "words" are said to instil hope in the heart of the poet. Cf. Sidney, *A&S* 60.5–8, in which the poet complains that he gets some encouragement from Stella only when he is absent:

> But when the rugged'st step of fortune's race
> Makes me fall from her sight, then sweetly she,
> With words, wherein the muses' treasures be,
> Shewes love and pity to my absent case.

12–14 Immortality is associated with virtue and therefore the virtuous lady is heavenly, as seen in Du Bellay's *Les Regrets* 177, in which virtue is said to be immortal "comme immortelles sont les semences des cieulx [like the seeds of heaven are immortal]" (ed. J. Joliffe and M.A. Screech [Geneva, 1974], 253; my translation).

## [4] *Thyne eye, the glasse where I behold my hearte*

This sonnet survives in *T* and the printed *Dianas*. Its conspicuous absence from *H* may be due to a scribal slip (see p. 41). Contemporary translations evidence its wide circulation; it could have been passed around as a separate. Montgomerie's rendition into Scots (Montgomerie, *Poems*, 1: 120) has a variation in the sestet resulting in a different rhyme scheme:

> Thyne ee the glasse vhare I beheld my hart.
> Myn ee the windo throu the vhilk thyn ee
> May see my hairt, and thair thy self espy
> In bloody colours hou thou painted art.
> Thyne ee the pyle is of a murthereris dart.
> Myn ee the sicht thou taks thy levell by
> To shute my hairt and nevir shute aury.
> Myn ee thus helpis thyn ee to work my smarte.
> Thyn ee consumes me lyk a flamming fyre;
> Myn ee most lyk a flood of teirs do run,
> Oh that the water, in myne ee begun,
> Micht quench the burning fornace of desyre
> Or then the fyr els kindlit by thyn ey
> The flouing teirs of sorou micht mak dry.

Parkinson notes that "Montgomerie avoids Constable's *rime riche* (come/become), a device [King] James condemns," in his *Reulis and Cautelis* (Montgomerie, *Poems*, 2: 106). Janus Dousa the Younger translated the sonnet into Dutch ("U Oog is een glas, daar mijn hart is ingegreven"); it opens the section "Epigrammata quaedam belgico idiomate" in his *Poemata* (ed. Gulielmo Rabo [Rotterdam, 1704], 163).

1–3 The poet plays on the old proverb saying that the eyes are the mirror or window of the soul.

3 *my hearte*] The reading in *T*, "thyne heart," contradicts the point that the poet is making here – that the lady can see right through him and into his heart. The variant selected is backed by the translations of the sonnet: the Dutch version, for example, reads "mijn hart."

4 Two lines in Shakespeare, *Sonnets* 24, convey the same idea of the image of the beloved as painted in the lover's heart: "Mine eye hath played the painter, and hath steeled / Thy beauty's form in table of my heart" (1–2). Other contemporaries seem to be borrowing from Constable when they describe the

"bloody colours" with which the lady is painted in his heart, evoking the lover's suffering. In Griffin, *Fidessa* 19, the poet brings together the mirror and the painting: "She takes the glasse, wherein her selfe she sees / In bloudie colours cruelly depainted" (9–10). The mistress in *TF* 46 makes a similar discovery and sees her face "so sweetlie framed" in the lover's "bleeding brest" (1–2).

5 *pike*] This word and the variant "pyle" are interchangeable in meaning, and the third letter would have been easily misread in a handwritten text. Montgomerie adopts "pyle," and the *OED* quotes this line as the earliest use of "pile" to mean "the pointed head of a dart" (n.¹ 1.c).

5–8 Among the innumerable parallels, cf. Daniel, *Delia* 14, in which the poet describes "those Christall eyes" as "the Dart transpearsing" (4). Constable goes one step further in stressing the part played by the poet's own eye in the murderous act.

11 *water*] The reading "matter" in *T* is an obvious scribal error that destroys semantic cohesion with "quench" in the following line.

## [5] *Delight in youre bright eyes my death did breede*

This sonnet on the poet's metaphorical death brought about by love survives only in *T*.

*Of the suddeyne ... caught*] The heading seems odd in that it covers only the first four lines, ignoring the eternizing conceit at the heart of the sonnet.

2–4 The comparison of the lover to a child who plays with fire or a weapon and gets hurt stresses the dangers of love. Cf. John Cooke's play *Tu quoque* (London, 1614), sigs. B4v–C1r:

> GERALDINE. As little children love to play with fire
> And will not leave till they themselves doe burne,
> So did I fondly dally with Desire ...

10 *Phoenix*] A mythical bird that burnt itself and was reborn out of the ashes. The phoenix is traditionally female and has Christian connotations as a symbol of eternal life. In line 982 of Chaucer's *Book of the Duchess* it is a metaphor for a unique lady: "The solyn fenix of Arabye" (see *The Works of Geoffrey Chaucer*, ed. F.N. Robinson [Boston, 1957], 276). Petrarch's Laura is compared with the immortal phoenix; see for example Petrarch, *Rime* 135 and 185. In the Elizabethan era it also appears as a paragon of beauty or virtue, and the phoenix rising from the ashes is associated with the queen. In Sidney, *A&S* 92.6, the poet refers to the lady using the epithet "Phoenix Stella." See also Daniel, *Delia* 33.11–

14, and Drayton, *Ideas mirrour* 6, "In one whole world is but one Phœnix found" (1); the latter envisions the phoenix-lady's demise by fire as immediately followed by an eternal life that transcends even fame.

11–12 The medieval belief that the pelican feeds its offspring with its own blood is illustrated in a woodcut followed by a short poem in Geffrey Whitney's *A choice of emblemes* (Leiden, 1586), 87: "The Pellican, for to revive her younge, / Doth peirce her brest, and geve them of her blood" (1–2). Pelicans are often associated with generous parents and the redeeming Christ. However, the lady-pelican in Constable's sonnet feeds on the lover's blood in order to keep her beauty alive.

14 Parker suggests that, on their own, the pelican and the phoenix might be used in the conventional praise given to the mistress, but "combined their Christian associations overwhelm more frail conceits" (159). Grundy (222) compares Robert Southwell's poem on "Christs bloody sweate," in which the poet muses on Christ praying in Gethsemane and unites the phoenix and the pelican in one line (see Robert Southwell, *Collected Poems*, ed. Peter Davidson and Anne Sweeney [Manchester, 2007], 17):

> He Pelicans, he Phenix fate doth prove
> Whome flames consume whom streames enforce to die
> How burneth bloud howe bleedeth burninge love
> Can one in flame and streame both bathe and frye (7–10)

[6] *When youre perfections to my thoughts appeare*

This sonnet provides an instance of multiple corrections in *T* owing to its transmission history.

*Of the dicouragement ... lownesse*] The heading seems an odd interpretation of the pessimistic tone of the sonnet, as the ardent lover, though doomed, seldom feels discouraged – not even in the face of death.

1 thoughts] The reading "thought" in *T* destroys grammatical agreement with "they" (2), which seems to agree with "perfections" instead.

9–12 The lover is often associated with a ship on an uncertain voyage, as illustrated in Thomas Wyatt's translation of Petrarch's sonnet 189, "My galley charged with forgetfulness," in which the poetic persona is a ship that cannot navigate in a raging storm because the stars (the lady's eyes) are not visible (see Thomas Wyatt, *Collected Poems*, ed. Joost Daalder [London, 1975], 25). Here, however, the heavy cargo and not the perils of the journey is emphasised. Grundy

(223) compares Desportes, *Cleonice* 23.6–8, in which frightened voyagers throw their dearest riches into the sea. Desportes's sonnet ends rather differently, with the poet-sailor throwing out "l'ame et la liberté" to keep his love afloat (13). The Scottish poet William Drummond borrows the image in "Regrat" (*Poetical Works*, ed. L.E. Kastner [Edinburgh, 1913], 2: 237):

> Hee only saves his barge
> With too much ware who doth it not o'recharge;
> .................................
> Gives what he got with no deploring show,
> And doth againe in seas his burthen throw. (5–10)

Mary Wroth uses imagery similar to Constable's in a sonnet in *Pamphilia to Amphilanthus*, "My paine, still smother'd in my grieved brest," envisioning her soul as burdened with painful love, "Lost, shipwrackt, spoyl'd, debar'd of smallest hope" (9). See Jill Seal Millman and Gillian Wright, eds., *Early Modern Women's Manuscript Poetry* [Manchester, 2005], 39).

11 Although gold is a conventional metaphor for the lady's hair, an allusion to Penelope Rich may be intended; see sonnet [36].

13 Punctuation in this line has been included in the collation because it alters meaning; in *D92* and *D94* there is a mid-line pause so that the first half is read as a command. The variant "not" instead of "oute" makes this command negative. In *T* the line appears as a mere statement that the poet's heart cannot rid itself of love.

13 *love*] The unique variant "gold" in *H* is either a product of scribal revision or an error of repetition considering that this word occurs in previous lines. Since the couplet moves from the ship metaphor to the poet's heart, however, "love" is more cohesive.

14 *drowned*] In *T*, "damned" seems adequate and cannot be ruled out entirely, but it is not as semantically cohesive with the sailing motif, whereas "drowned" points at the cause of death. If the source text was written in secretary hand of less than calligraphic quality, the medial letters could have been misread by the scribe.

## [7] *It may be Love doth not my death pretend*

Thematically linked to [4], which first presented the lover carrying a picture of the lady in his heart, and despite the dark witchcraft-related overtones, this sonnet is imbued with a degree of optimism that is first introduced in the heading.

Scott, *Sonnets* (135) cites Desportes, *Hippolyte* 23 in full in relation with this sonnet, a comparison also borrowed by Grundy (223); however, the only connection seems to be the idea that Love cannot overpower the lady and has to focus on the lover instead. It is an English sonnet that provides the closest parallel, written by Samuel Daniel and included as "Sonnet 10" in Thomas Newman's pirated edition of Philip Sidney's poetry (*Syr P.S. His Astrophel and Stella* [London, 1591], 67):

> The slie Inchanter when to worke his will
> And secret wrong on some forespoken wight,
> Frames waxe, in forme to represent aright
> The poor unwitting wretch he means to kill.
> And prickes the image fram'd by Magicks skill;
> Whereby to vexe the partie day and night (1–6)

In Daniel's sonnet the figure of Cupid disappears, and the lady is herself the witch, making a wax figurine out of his entire body and aiming at his heart. She bewitches him with her eyes, and not with a needle or arrows. The poet does not hope for retribution for the contagion of his love; he is but the passive sufferer of lovesickness. Considering that Constable's sonnet is included in the *H* collection, dated 1589, and its transmission continued while Daniel's was reprinted nowhere else, I agree with Grundy (60) that the debt appears to be Daniel's. Some other well-known parallels are the fifth song in Sidney, *A&S*, and John Donne's "Witchcraft by a Picture" (*Complete Poems*, 281).

1 *doth not my death*] The transposition of words in *H*, *D92*, and *D94* seems equally valid.

3 *bewitch thee for my benefitte*] Pointing at the lady as the victim is a reversal of the trope of the lover's bewitchment at the sight of her beauty.

3 *my*] the variant "thy" in *D94a* alters the meaning; it was emended in the second printing.

5–8 The poet makes use of contemporary beliefs in picture magic, according to which witches could shoot, or prick, a wax or clay figurine representing the person who was to be harmed, on the part of his or her body which was to suffer, and this part of the body would be afflicted. See William Perkins, *A discourse of the damned art of witchcraft* (Cambridge, 1610), 148. Even Queen Elizabeth I became anxious when a wax figure in her shape was discovered with a pin stuck through it in 1578; see Christina Hole, *Witchcraft in England* (Totowa, 1977), 141.

9 The convention of the lady being untouched by Cupid's arrows is exaggerated in Romeo's description of the idealized Rosaline in Shakespeare, *R&J* 1.2.205–208:

... She'll not be hit
With Cupid's arrow; she hath Dian's wit,
And, in strong proof of chastity well armed,
From love's weak childish bow she lives unharmed.

**10** *Within ... paynte*] Love magic begins with the picture in the victim's – the lover's – heart. Heinrich Kramer, the author of the *Malleus maleficarum*, a fifteenth-century antiwitchcraft treatise, describes demons' persuasion of victims towards love or hate by impressing images of the object into their imaginations (trans. Christopher Mackway [Cambridge, 2009], 175–176). Although "picture" could also refer to a figurine, as in line 6, a portrait or painting is meant here; there exist contemporary reports of witches using pictures drawn on pieces of parchment to do harm. See Cecil L'Estrange Ewen, *Witchcraft and Demonianism* (London, 1933), 200–201.

**12–14** Witchcraft was thought to act not only on human bodies but also on passions; the consequence of the lady having her heart wounded is that she will be forced to love him.

On associations of witchcraft with Catholicism in the minds of contemporaries, see Peter Elmer, *Witchcraft, Religion, and the State in Elizabethan and Jacobean England* (Oxford, 2016), 16–17.

**14** *thy hearte*] The printed *Dianas* share the variant "my hart," which destroys the sense completely and must be considered an error.

## [8] *Blame not my heart for flying up so high*

In both *H* and *D92* this sonnet precedes [3] and is thematically linked to it in its flying conceit. This sonnet is not in *M*, so there is no evidence that it was composed before 1589. However, Dutch poet Janus Dousa the Younger translated the poem into Latin, and this version was printed in his 1591 Ἐρωτοπαίγνιον (*Erotopaignion*) under the heading "Adumbratum de Anglico Henrici Conestabilis" (see Janus Dousa the Younger, *Poemata*, ed. Gulielmo Rabo [Rotterdam, 1704], 156–157). Dousa therefore must have seen the poem well before 1591 (see chapter 2, p. 90). Dousa's version runs as follows:

Ne, quod te celso fugiat per inane volatu,
Cor precor ah misero saevius ure mihi.
Culpa tua haec; vestri pennis sublatus Amoris
Mortali ignotas cogitur ire vias.
Ac velut halantes coeli ad confinia fumos

> Cynthius aethereis usque trahit radiis
> Unde trabes flammasque creet, dirosve Cometas,
> Aut crine accendat lampada flammifero;
> Affixam sic ante solo lux enthea mentem
> Sustulit, ut superis inserat ordinibus
> Hic ubi, sacratae radiant velut astra Coronae,
> Fulgurat ardoris sic quoque flamma mei.
> Quin igitur tellure etiam me tollis inerti,
> Ne patiar mentis flebile discidium.
> Sic mihi tu coelum, coeli sic lumine nobis
> Continget totis noctibus usque frui.
> En interum clamo: effectus utriusque caloris
> Expendens, pectus mitus ure meum.
> Idem nos ignis, in te qui fulgurat, urit:
> Secum cuncta trahens ignis, ut attrahitur.
> Ignis more tuum and sese trahit omnia lumen;
> Utque ignis, noster summa petissit amor.

See Jan Van Dorsten, *Poets, Patrons, and Professors: Sir Philip Sidney, Daniel Rogers, and the Leiden Humanists* (Leiden, 1962), 82.

3–4 Constable recounts a contemporary belief rooted in Aristotelian astronomy. Leonard Digges wrote in his astronomical treatise that "a Comete is a flame, workyng in a drie, hote, slymie exhalation, drawen up to the highest part of the ayre" (*A prognostication everlasting of ryght good effecte* [London, 1556], fol. 14r). Pierre de La Primaudaye reflects that comets "are naturally made of an hot exhalation, which attayneth to the supreme region of the aire, where it is enflamed by the element of fire" (*The third volume of the French academie* [London, 1601], 213). Scott (*Sonnets*, 136) points at Desportes, *Diane* 1, "Complainte" as a possible source of inspiration (*Œuvres*, ed. Alfred Michiels [Paris, 1858], 49). Fulke Greville employs a similar image in sonnet 62 in *Caelica* (*Certaine learned and elegant workes* [London, 1633], 207):

> Vapours of earth which to the Sunne aspire,
> As Natures tribute unto heate or light,
> Are frozen in the midst of high desire,
> And melted in sweet beames of selfe-delight (13–16)

The assimilation of the heart to "earthlye vapoures" rests on the Galenic conception of vital spirits, generated from the air in the left ventricle of the heart.

4 *become*] The variants "begin" (*D92*) and "begun" (*D94*) have no manu-

script parallel and may be due to either misreading or conscious alteration; the verb is transitive and used in the sense of "originate" (*OED* v.¹ 3).

**4** *night-suns*] Pliny the Elder described the phenomenon: "A light from the sky by night, the phenomenon usually called 'night-suns,' was seen in the consulship of Gaius Caecilius and Gnaeus Papirius and often on other occasions causing apparent daylight in the night" (see *Natural History* 2.33, ed. and trans. H. Rackham [Cambridge, MA, 1967], 243). A sixteenth-century divine, William Fulke, describes "night sunnes" under the heading "Of many Moones": "They are lykewyse Images of the Moone, represented in an equall cloude, which is watry, smothe, and polyshed, even lyke a glasse. ... they joyned with the light of the true Moone, geve a great shynning light, to dryve awaye the shadowe and darkenes of the nyght" (see *A goodly gallerye* [London, 1563] fols. 42v–43r).

**5–6** Petrarch develops the Neoplatonic idea that the soul rises through contemplation of the divine as reflected in the lady, for instance in Petrarch, *Rime* 13.

**9** *Blame not, I say againe*] The clauses are transposed in *H*, *D92*, and *D94*, and there is no way to tell if the order in *T* may be the product of intentional revision.

**11–12** While the beloved is associated with the divine and endowed with celestial light, the poet-lover burns with passion that is not necessarily identified with physical desire in view of conventional descriptions of divine grace as fire. Henry Church discusses this identification extensively in *Miscellanea philo-theologica* (London, 1637), 259: "Fire hath a constant motion upward: so grace is alwayes aspiring to the things above."

**12** *drawth*] The reading "doth draw" in *T* is an error which results in an overly long line, so it has been amended using *H*, the other manuscript witness.

**13–14** In the sonnet "To the ternall, and aeternall Unitie," printed in the prefatory matter to Thomas Wright's *The passions of the minde in generall* (London, 1604), Hugh Holland seems to be borrowing from Constable, although Holland's poem has a more explicitly religious character: "Kindle my will and heave it up, for why / Even as thy love, like fire, drawes up my love, / Right so my love, like fire, will mount above" (12–14).

[9] *Eyes curiouse to behold what nature can create*

This is the first of four alexandrine sonnets in the *T* sequence and survives nowhere else. Lines 4 and 5 have five feet only; this, together with the irregularity in line 10 and the midphrase caesura in the final line, creates a haphazard effect uncommon in Constable. The sonnet turns out to be an unsuccessful metrical experiment – probably inspired by Sidney's alexandrines in Sidney, *A&S*. It draws on Petrarch, *Rime* 248, although the focus is not on the lady's mortality and possible imminent death, but on the necessity to chronicle and memorialize her physical attributes.

**1–2** *Eyes ... doe see*] The poet-lover in Sidney, *A&S* 71, starts with a similar address to the reader-onlooker:

> Who will in fairest book of nature know
> How virtue may best lodged in beauty be,
> Let him but learn of love to read in thee,
> Stella, those fair lines which true goodness show. (1–4)

The conventional idea of beauty as connected to moral virtues is not explicitly included in Constable's sonnet, however, and the focus seems to be on the act of looking per se rather than in being moved to virtuous action by a quasi-divine sight.

**7–8** Contemplation of the lady must be followed by writing, understood as a collective endeavour because her attributes are too many to be recorded. The lack of a reference to the poet-lover as an individual writer contrasts with Sidney, *A&S* 90.13–14: "Since all my words thy beauty doth endite, / And love doth hold my hand, and makes me write."

**10** *speake of her*] A word seems to be missing after "her," yielding a metrically faulty line. Grundy inserts "lip" (122) which seems coherent because the next lines emphasise the perfection of the lady's hands, lips, and eyes; however, her emendation is conjectural and has no textual basis.

**14** *the light or blacke*] Brightness and the colour black are traits associated with Stella in Sidney, *A&S*, as in the well-known beginning of sonnet 7: "When Nature made her chief work, Stella's eyes, / In colour black why wrapped she beams so bright?" The description points at Penelope Rich as dedicatee, so this sonnet belongs with others not included in *H* but nevertheless addressed to her.

[10] *Ladye in beautye and in favoure rare*

An exercise in antanaclasis, this sonnet praises the lady by using the word "favour" with different meanings.

**5** *And when on me*] All other witnesses read "Nor" instead of "And." *D92* has the unique variant "When on poore me," but the error must have been spotted because it was corrected in *D94*. This case illustrates the contrasting of *D92* and a manuscript source by the *D94* printer.

5–6 Cf. Sidney, *A&S* 100.1–4, in which the poet makes use of antanaclasis and argues that the showing of pity in the form of tears makes the beautiful Stella even more beautiful:

> O tears, no tears, but rain from beauty's skies,
> Making those lilies and those roses grow,
> Which aye most fair, now more than most fair show,
> While graceful pity beauty beautifies

[11] *Ladie of Ladies, the delight alone*

This sonnet survives only in *T*, and is related to [12] in its musical theme.

1–4 Parker notes that the first quatrain "reads like a hymn" to the Virgin Mary (159).

1 *Ladie of Ladies*] The lady is the supreme feminine ideal, a nonpareil. An identical term is used by Walter Raleigh to refer to Queen Elizabeth in his *The Discovery of Guiana* (1596); her virginity is stressed and allows for her association with Mary: "I trust in God, this being true, will suffice, and that he which is king of all kings and Lord of Lords, will put it into her hart which is Lady of Ladies to possesse it" (*The discoverie of the large, rich, and bewtiful empire of Guiana* [London, 1596], 101). In the thirteenth century, Spanish king Alfonso X had referred to the Virgin as "dona das donas" in his *Cantiga* (song) 10 (see Alfonso X the Learned, *Cantigas de Santa Maria: An Anthology*, ed. Stephen Parkinson [Cambridge, 2015], 52).

3 *Seeing and hearing thee*] The pursuit of courtly love was associated with two of the senses, vision and hearing, and not with the more carnal sense of touch, as explained in the fourth book of Baldassare Castiglione's *The Book of the Courtier* (ed. W.E. Henley [London, 1900], 353):

> Let him laye aside therefore the blinde judgemente of the sense, and injoye wyth his eyes the bryghtnesse, the comelynesse, the lovynge sparkles, laughters, gestures and all the other pleasant fournitours of beawty: especially with hearinge the sweetnesse of her voice, the tunablenesse of her woordes, the melodie of her singinge and playinge on instrumentes ... and so shall he with most deintie foode feede the soule through the meanes of these two senses ... .

12 Cf. Petrarch, *Rime* 254, in which the poet expresses a similar fear that the lady may die too soon and be made a star in heaven.

13–14 The poet's sighs and the lady's voice fall into the same rhythm in a synchronized performance.

[12] *Not that thy hand is soft, is sweete, is white*

This sonnet survives only in T, and is related to [11] in its musical theme. The references to the reverence due to relics load it with Catholic undertones.

3 *these three*] Claire B. Williams notes that the lady's "hand, lips and breast" are given a "Trinitarian formulation" (Williams, *Edition*, 2: 83).

5–8 Cf. Shakespeare, *R&J* 1.5.92–105, in which Romeo, after touching Juliet's hand, claims that he must now kiss her hand because pilgrims are bound to kiss a saint's hands.

6–10 A parallel would be Shakespeare, *Sonnets* 128, in which the lover expresses his jealousy of the lute that touches – figuratively kisses – her hand. He states that his lips

> To be so tickled they would change their state
> And situation with those dancing chips,
> O'er whom thy fingers walk with gentle gait,
> Making dead wood more blessed than living lips. (9–12)

7–8 *with ... sight*] Christopher Woolgar notes that "In the cult of relics, there were degrees of holiness, and therefore of effectiveness. Here, proximity or touch came to the fore. There was a long tradition of contact relics: ... Physical contact might come through the kissing of relics... ." (Christopher Woolgar, "What Makes Things Holy? The Senses and Material Culture in the Later Middle Ages," in *Sensing the Sacred in Medieval and Early Modern Culture*, ed. Robin Macdonald et al. [London, 2018], 60–78, at 67). Idolatry and the worship or fetishizing of religious objects were condemned by reformed churches.

9–10 Playing the lute is here described as making an inanimate object speak. This echoes the episode of the dumb man made to speak by Jesus in Mark 7:35.

11–12 Cf. Fletcher, *Licia* 31.1–3: "When as her lute is tuned to her voyce, / The aire growes proude, for honour of that sound: / And rockes doe leape, to shewe howe they rejoyce." In Drayton, *Ideas mirrour* 12, the poet persuades the "unbelieving" that his mistress is divine because she has worked miracles on him:

> Blind were mine eyes, till they were seene of thine,
> And mine eares deafe, by thy fame healed be,
> My vices cur'd, by vertues sprung from thee,
> My hopes reviv'd which long in grave had lyne. (9–12)

On miracles involving the resurrection of Jairus's daughter and Lazarus, see Luke 8:54–55 and John 11:41–44; in both cases, words are instrumental in the miracles. There are also instances of music working wonders in classical myths; Orpheus's voice and his lyre could make even trees and rocks move.

[13] *Sweete Soveraigne, sith so many mynds remayne*

In this sonnet, which survives only in sources derived from the later archetype Z, the lady is portrayed as a queen and a warrior for whom men will gladly fight.

3 The image of the lady's hair as a snare recurs in English sonnet sequences. See for instance Spenser, *Amoretti* 37.5–8:

> Is it that mens frayle eyes, which gaze too bold,
> she may entangle in that golden snare:
> and being caught may craftily enfold,
> theyr weaker harts, which are not wel aware?

Constable's line could be borrowing from a song in book 3 of Philip Sidney's *Old Arcadia* (ed. Jean Robertson [Oxford, 1973], 238): "Her hair fine threads of finest gold / In curled knots man's thought to hold."

5 *that glorie*] The *D94* variant, "the honour," is of dubious authority but cannot be considered an error because it is synonymous.

6 *first monarchie*] The variant "fift" in *D94* is understood as "fifth" by Martha Foote Crow, John Gray, and Grundy and commenters on her text. The *OED* defines the "Fifth monarchy" (n.) as the last of the five great empires referred to in the prophecy of Daniel (Dan. 2:36–44); in the seventeenth century, with the emergence of a Puritan sect known as Fifth Monarchy Men, the fifth monarchy became identified with the millennial reign of Christ predicted to occur at the apocalypse. However, this reading has been discarded because it rests merely on one frequently unreliable printed source. A search for "fifth monarchy" in *EEBO* returns few relevant references before 1600, and I agree with Parker that the allusion would go too far in the identification of the lady with God and would be blasphemous "or transfer a divine status onto the addressee" (Parker, 160). "First" can be understood as related to status or importance (see *OED* adj. 1.a).

13–14 This is a variation on the image of Love or Cupid yielding to the lady, and one of the sauciest sonnet endings in the sequence. Cf. Scève, *Délie* 67.9–10.

[14] *When beautie to the world vouchsafes this blisse*

This sonnet survives only in *T*.

**2** *the one ... is not*] Probably a direct translation from Petrarch, *Rime* 218.2, "costei ch'al mondo non à pare."

**3–4** Shame was commonly associated with blushing and envy with a pale shade of blue or green. Cf. John Studley's translation of Seneca's *Agamemnon*: "ruddy shame with blushing cheekes" (*Seneca his tenne tragedies* [London, 1581], fol. 143r); "pale envy" (fol. 197v). The latter also occurs in Shakespeare, *Titus Andronicus* 2.1.4: "Advanced above pale envy's threat'ning reach" (*The Oxford Shakespeare: The Complete Works*, ed. Stanley Wells and Gary Taylor [New York, 1998], 162). Cf. also Shakespeare, *Sonnets* 99.8–9: "The roses fearfully on thorns did stand, / One blushing shame, another white despair."

**5** *the fayre and fowle*] Both words could also describe an individual's exemplary moral condition or wickedness (see *OED*, s.vv. fair, adj. 12, and foul, adj. 7.a).

**7** *Venus*] This planet is described as "the day starre, messenger of the morning, which alwaies attendeth on the sunne, at his rising and setting: for she riseth every day before him" (see La Primaudaye, *French academie*, 127).

**8** There was an ongoing debate whether planets took the light from the sun or were luminous by themselves.

**14** This line is inspired by the Magnificat, found in Luke 1:52: "He hath put down the mighty from their seats, and exalted them of low degree." Biblical quotations throughout are from the King James Bible.

[15] *Falselye doth envie of youre prayses blame*

This text is the product of a major revision of the eighth sonnet in *M*; see [15b] below. For a longer discussion of this revision as being in accordance with Constable's shift in faith, see pp. 76–77.

**1–8** See Petrarch, *Rime* 247.1–5, in which the poet fends off criticism of his writing in praise of Laura, which others may deem excessive. Cf. also Drayton, *Ideas mirrour* 12.1–4:

> Some Athiest or vile Infidell in love,
> When I doe speake of thy divinitie,

May blaspheme thus, and say, I flatter thee:
And onely write, my skill in verse to prove.

**1** *envie*] The reference to the jealous accusers of the poet links this sonnet to [14].

**2** *My tongue, my pen*] By including it in the enumeration alongside his tongue and his heart, the poet seems to view his pen as a part of his body; the activity of writing feels as natural to him as speaking or being in love.

**4** *the partiall trumpe of fame*] Cf. Spenser, *Amoretti* 85.13: "fame in her shrill trump shal thunder." In the first song in Sidney, *A&S*, Astrophil complains that not even Fame has trumpets that are worthy enough to praise Stella (14).

**7** *needs ... be*] This word order seems preferable to that found in *H* and the printed editions. In *H* and *D94b* the line has one extra syllable.

**9** In Sidney, *A&S* song 1.27–28, the speaker similarly denies that his praise is flattery and untrue: "To you, to you, all song of praise is due; / Only of you the flatterer never lieth." Cf. also Sidney, *A&S* 35.1–2: "What may words say, or what may words not say, / Where truth itself must speake like flattery?"

**10** *sith ... such*] *T* removes "that," which elsewhere creates a rather abrupt effect in the middle of the line, and inserts a new lexical item, "world."

**13** *is*] Grundy amends to "in" following the other witnesses, but there are no grounds to consider this an error.

## [15b] *False the report, & unjust is the blame*

This is the earliest version of [15], which survives in *M* without a heading and is significantly different from the revised text. Laden with images related to religious persecution and trials, it stands as a graphic reminder of Constable's early Protestantism.

**2** *imputes to mee*] The accusation is levelled first and foremost at the poet himself, not at his pen, tongue, and heart personified.

**7–8** In Elizabethan England, the image of the heart, and thus the poet, being liable to the punishment reserved for heretics – burning at the stake – would have evoked the suffering of the Protestant martyrs under Queen Mary, vividly recounted in John Foxe's *Actes and Monuments*.

**8** *obstinate*] According to the Catholic tradition, obstinacy or the unwillingness to recant differentiates heresy from error. Keith Luria explains that "[a]s a result, secular power could be called upon to break the stubborn wills of those who had gone astray" ("The Power of Conscience? Conversion and Confessional

EXPLANATORY NOTES · 265

Boundary Building in Early-Modern France," in *Living with Religious Diversity in Early-Modern Europe*, ed. C. Scott Dixon et al. [Farnham, 2009], 109–125, at 117).

10 This line is one syllable short either due to authorial oversight or scribal error. It was fixed in later revisions of the sonnet; see [15].

13–14 Cf. Spenser, *Amoretti* 22, in which the poet burns his heart as a sacrifice to the lady-goddess: "will builde an altar to appease her yre: / and on the same my hart will sacrifise, / burning in flames of pure and chast desyre" (10–12).

[16] *My Ladies presence makes the roses red*

This is one of Constable's best-known sonnets and is preserved in sources derived from all three archetypes. The conceit fits in a long-standing literary tradition. Possible sources include Petrarch, *Rime* 165, in which Laura's feet on the grass make the flowers grow; Pierre de Ronsard adapted the image in Ronsard, *Amours* 163.5–6. Although Shakespeare's humorous answer to this and other similar sonnets of praise, *Sonnets* 130 ("My mistress' eyes are nothing like the sun"), is well-known, he also seems to be indebted to Constable in sonnet 99, deemed to have been composed ca. 1594–1595 (see William Shakespeare, *The Complete Sonnets and Poems*, ed. Colin Burrow [Oxford, 2002], 105). In it natural elements are given agency and actively steal their attributes from the beloved:

> The lily I condemned for thy hand,
> And buds of marjoram had stol'n thy hair;
> The roses fearfully on thorns did stand,
> One blushing shame, another white despair
> ..................................
> More flowers I noted, yet I none could see,
> But sweet, or colour, it had stol'n from thee. (6–9, 14–15)

Cf. also Griffin, *Fidessa* 37, which also depicts the lady in a natural setting that responds to her presence. A sonnet by Scottish poet Alexander Craig offers an even closer, hitherto unnoted, parallel and deserves to be quoted in full. See Craig, *Amorose Songes*, "To Lithocardia":

> As Marigould did in her Garden walke,
> One day, O ten times happie was that day
> I thitherward to see my Saint, did stalke:
> Where Floraes Imp's joy'd with her feet to play,

And loe unseene behind a Hedge I lay,
Where I beheld the Roses blush for shame,
The Lillies were empald upon the spray,
The Violets were staynd about my Dame:
My Mistris smild for to behold the game,
And sometimes pleasd upon the grasse to sport,
Which canging hew's new cullors did acclaime,
For blythnes of so sweete a Saincts resort,
And from that walke while as away she went,
They weepe with deaw, & I in teares lament.

1 Cf. Persius, *Satires* 2.38: "Quidquid calcaverit hit, rosa fiat" (ed. GG. Ramsay [London, 1928], 338).

1–4 See notes to sonnet [14]. The intermingling of rose red and lily white on the lady's face dates back to the Latin poets. Ovid describes a young woman's face as "rosae fulgent inter sua lilia mixtae" in *Amores* 2.5.37 (ed. Grant Showerman [London, 1914], 396). Cf. Sidney's *New Arcadia* 1: "Then, I say, indeed, methought the lilies grew pale for envy; the roses, methought, blushed to see sweeter roses in her cheeks ... ." (ed. Victor Skretkowicz [Oxford, 1987], 84). Shakespeare's wording in *The Rape of Lucrece*, lines 477–479, is similar to Constable's: "... 'The colour in thy face – / That even for anger makes the lily pale / And the red rose blush at her own disgrace" (see William Shakespeare, *The Complete Sonnets and Poems*, ed. Colin Burrow [Oxford, 2002], 269).

5–6 Early modern herbals noted that marigolds opened and closed in response to the sun. See Vivian Thomas and Nick Faircloth, *Shakespeare's Plants and Gardens: A Dictionary* (London 2014), 222. This flower therefore responds to the sunlike lady. The eyes of sleeping Lucrece are described thus: "Her eyes, like marigolds, had sheathed their light" (line 397; see Shakespeare, *Complete Sonnets*, ed. Burrow, 265).

6 suns] Ruth Hughey argues that the singular form in *H*, "sunn," is "more euphonious ... and quite as logical" (Hughey, 2: 341); it is shared by *E*.

7–8 The violet is dyed with blood from the poet-lover's heart following his metaphorical death. See [84] for a similar image. Ovid tells stories in which flowers spring from a dead body: violets from the blood of Attis, and anemones from that of Adonis. Shakespeare recounts the latter in *Venus and Adonis* (see Shakespeare, *Complete Sonnets*, ed. Burrow, 235):

And in his blood that on the ground lay spilled
A purple flower sprung up, chequered with white,

Resembling well his pale cheeks and the blood
Which in round drops upon their whiteness stood. (1167–1170)

10 Sidney Lee compares Ronsard, *Amours* 143.9–11, in which heaven itself is perfumed with the sweet scent coming from the beautiful garden that stands as a metaphor for the lady (*Elizabethan Sonnets* [New York, 1904], 1: lxii). Grundy (228) quotes Poliziano's elegy *In violas a venere mea dono acceptas*, in which the poet describes the perfume of violets as infused into them by his mistress's sweet breath (see Angelo Ambrogini Poliziano, *Prose volgari inedite e poesie latine e greche*, ed. Isidoro del Lungo [Florence, 1867], 236).

11–12 The *E* variant, "lightning," emphasises the light and heat emitted by the lady's sunlike eyes. Cf. for instance Daniel, *Delia* 6.2: "Her brow shades frownes, although her eyes are sunny." In Sidney, *A&S* 8, Stella's eyes are sunlike and would naturally be expected to have an effect on nature: "Whose fair skin, beamy eyes, like morning sun on snow, / Deceived the quaking boy, who thought from so pure light / Effects of lively heat must needs in nature grow" (9–11). Grundy (228) points out the similarity with the beginning of Lorenzo de' Medici's sonnet 88 (see *Poesie del magnifico Lorenzo De' Medici* [Bergamo, 1763], 77).

12 *quickeneth*] In *T*, *M*, and *E* it is written as a two-syllable word, which creates a metrically shorter line.

13–14 Both lover and mistress, water and sun, are metaphorically united in the act of creating new life. Tears are frequently described as watering either real or metaphorical flowers. In Sidney, *A&S* 100.1–2, the poet describes a weeping Stella and the effect of tears running down her cheeks:

O tears, no tears, but rain from beauty's skies,
Making those lilies and those roses grow ... .

In *The second part of Hero and Leander* (London, 1598), Henry Petowe describes weeping Hero thus: "with downe dropping teares, like liquid sleete, / She watereth the Summer thirstie ground" (352–353).

[17] *Sweet hand, the sweet (yet cruell) bowe thow art*

This sonnet is linked to [12] in that the lady's hand is compared to a relic. The poet's desire to kiss it is now finally enacted, albeit indirectly because he can only kiss her glove – the reliquary.

**1–2** The tradition of praising the lady's hand while at the same time envisioning the pain it exerts on the suffering lover recurs in early modern sequences. It can be traced back to Petrarch, *Rime* 199, in which he addresses Laura's hand in line 1 ("Oh bella man che mi distringi 'l core") and then turns to her glove ("Candido leggiadretto e caro guanto") in line 9. In describing the lady's hand as a bow shooting arrows, Constable is closest to a sonnet by Giovanni Mozzarello (see Girolamo Ruscelli, ed., *I Fiori delle Rime de' Poeti illustri* [Venice, 1586], 170).

**2** *five ivorye arrowes*] One arrow is shot from each of the lady's five fingers. *E* consistently reads "3" instead of "five."

**4** *in breast*] The reading in *M*, "in my breast," makes more sense but disrupts the metre by adding one syllable.

**5** According to Christian tradition, St Francis received the stigmata, five wounds similar to those Christ received at the Crucifixion, in 1224. Most retellings of the event mention physical pain, but not St Bonaventure's *The Life of St. Francis of Assisi*, which Constable could have read, as Grundy suggests (229). In the fourth book of Castiglione's *Book of the Courtier* there is a vivid evocation of "the Aungell that with the fire of love imprinted the five woundes in Saint Francis" (364). There were also many pictorial representations of the legend such as Giotto's *Saint Francis Receiving the Stigmata* (ca. 1300).

**6** Cf. Valentine's question in Shakespeare, *The Two Gentlemen of Verona* 3.1.170: "And why not death rather than living torment?" (*Complete Works*, ed. Wells and Taylor, 14). References to the lover enduring torments pervade Petrarchan poetry. See for instance Petrarch, *Rime* 12 and 356.

**7** Saint Francis received the stigmata in his hands, feet, and side, but Constable makes no mention of the last.

**8** *same helpelesse wounds*] The other witnesses read "five" instead of "same," with the exception of the *E* variant "3." The insistence on three wounds in *E* is at odds with the legend of St Francis but reminiscent of female saints such as St Cecilia or Julian of Norwich. Since all manuscripts tend to agree on the number five throughout the sonnet, it can be assumed that the scribe in *E* took some liberties.

**9** This line presents an interpretive conundrum and punctuation has been considered a substantive variant. In *T*, *M*, and *E*, "if a Saint" is parenthetical and could refer to St Francis or the poet, thus calling into doubt the sanctity of the former – which would conform to the Protestant view on saints – or his own. In the printed *Dianas*, "as Saint Fraunces" is written within parentheses, which resolves the ambiguity.

**9–14** On relics and a parallel in Shakespeare, *R&J* 1.5.92–105, see notes to sonnet [12]. Cf. Spenser, *Amoretti* 22.

13–14 For the comparison of the lady's glove to a reliquary and the lover's urge to kiss it, Scott, *Sonnets* (133–134) contrasts Desportes, *Diverses amours* 18.

14 *shrine*] The variant "shine" in *T* is a scribal error, as collation evidences, and it obscures the meaning of the whole line.

[18] *The fouler hydes, as closely as he may*

This sonnet survives in multiple sources and displays conventional imagery, as illustrated by the numerous parallels.

1–4 Williams links the conceit in these lines with the proverb "He that will take the bird must not scare it" (Williams, *Edition*, 2: 88); Grundy (230) lists some English sonnets with the same conceit.

1 *fouler*] The lover in the Scottish poet William Fowler's *The Tarantula of Love*, sonnet 67, muses on a bird that his mistress has saved and compares its freedom to his own imprisonment. Punning on his own name, he envisions himself as "no Fouler cachting bot a Fouler caught" (10). See *The Works of William Fowler*, ed. Henry W. Meikle (Edinburgh, 1914), 198.

2 *sillie byrd*] Often used to refer to a woodcock because this bird was easy to catch.

5–8 This conventional image can be traced back to Petrarch, *Rime* 59.4–5: "Tra le chiome de l'or nascose il laccio / al qual mi strinse Amore." Cf. also Ariosto, *Rime* 9.1–2 (*Opere minori in versi*, ed. Angelo Solerti [Bologna, 1891], 116), quoted by Grundy (230). Daniel, *Delia* 14, is a direct translation of Du Bellay, *L'Olive* 10: "Those snary locks, are those same nets (my Deere,) / Wherewith my libertie thou didst surprize" (1–2). The variant "amber locks" occurs in the 1592 edition of *Delia*. Daniel's net is not real but figurative. Cf. also Sidney, *A&S* 12.1–2: "Cupid, because thou shin'st in Stella's eyes, / That from her locks, thy day-nets, none 'scapes free." Spenser, *Amoretti* 37, is closest to Constable's sonnet in that the lady wears a headpiece over her hair:

> What guyle is this, that those her golden tresses,
> She doth attyre under a net of gold:
> and with sly skill so cunningly them dresses,
> that which is gold or heare, may scarse be told?
> Is it that mens frayle eyes, which gaze too bold,
> she may entangle in that golden snare (1–6)

The beginning of Griffin, *Fidessa* 26, is similar but it soon takes a darker turn because the poet-bird's death is envisioned:

> The sillie bird that hasts unto the net,
> And flutters to and from till she be taken.
> Doth looke some foode or succour there to get,
> But looseth life, so much is she mistaken (1–4)

    7 *flee*] The *T* reading "see" is an error that may be caused by repetition of the final word in line 3 or else the misreading of an initial long *s*; "flee" is more semantically cohesive with the idea of entrapment.

    10 *tame*] The variant "tane" in the *Dianas* is either a misprint or an acceptable participle form of "take." The latter is less likely because the rhyme with "same" in line 12 is destroyed.

## [19] *Miracle of the world, I never will denye*

This is the second of four alexandrine sonnets in the sequence. It is a clear example of occasional verse that only survives in *T*, with the circumstances of its production – the poet giving a book of Petrarch's verse to his mistress – stated in the heading. The conceit builds on the typological method of scriptural commentary, by which characters and events in the Old Testament prefigure those in the New (Isabel Rivers, *Classical and Christian Ideas in English Renaissance Poetry: A Student's Guide* [London, 1994], 139). The poet argues that every poem written before his lady existed, Petrarch's included, only prophesied her coming and acquire their true meaning when they are read bearing her, a goddess, in mind. The roots of the conceit are found in Petrarch, *Rime* 186, in which the poet argues that if Virgil and Homer had seen Laura, they would have written about her instead of telling the tales of heroes. Petrarch's sonnet served as basis for Ronsard, *Amours* 1.87.

    *the Italian ... thereof*] A reference to the abundance of critical commentaries on Petrarch's verse in Renaissance Italy.

    1–4 Cf. Daniel, *Delia* 50.1–5:

> Let others sing of Knights and Palladines,
> In aged accents, and untimely words:
> Paint shadowes in imaginary lines,
> Which well the reach of their high wits records;
> But I must sing of thee and those faire eyes

In Shakespeare, *Sonnets* 106, the poet muses on how his beloved surpasses anyone who was ever praised for their beauty, using language that is close to Constable's:

> When in the chronicle of wasted time
> I see descriptions of the fairest wights,
> ..................................
> So all their praises are but prophecies
> Of this our time, all you prefiguring (1–2, 9–10)

**5** *Thy coming to the world*] An allusion to the coming of the Messiah, which was anticipated in the Old Testament; see for instance Isaiah 7:14.

**5–6** Laura's Petrarch was but a type of his mistress.

**6** *truth the lips bewrayes*] The voice is meant to reveal the truth.

**7** *thy rayes*] Either the lady's eyes or her beauty, compared to the sun's radiance.

**7–8** Petrarch's *Rime* circulated in editions in which the texts were supplemented by extensive glosses often providing conflicting interpretations. This is also an allusion to biblical exegesis, according to which events in the Old Testament are better understood in the light of the New.

**9** *in a vayle enclosd*] This has a double interpretation. Petrarch first beheld Laura in a church, where she must have been wearing a veil. On the other hand, the God of the Old Testament is reported to be seen as if through a veil until the coming of Christ in 2 Corinthians 3:14: "But their minds were blinded: for until this day remaineth the same vail untaken away in the reading of the old testament; which vail is done away in Christ."

**9–11** Petrarch is compared to a prophet to whom God revealed himself and who anticipated his coming using parables or stories.

**12–14** The mere allusion to an "image" being worshipped would have idolatrous undertones in the eyes of a Protestant reader.

## [20] *A friend of myne, moaning my helplesse love*

Although the development of the conceit is different, the theme of the concerned friend links this occasional sonnet to Sidney, *A&S* 21, "Your words, my friend, right healthful caustics, blame."

**1** *moaning*] Possibly a product of intentional revision, as it improves on "pitying," shared by the other sources.

**1** *helplesse*] Williams prefers the alternative reading "hopeless" based on Constable's use of polyptoton elsewhere (Williams, *Edition*, 2: 90); however, the *T* variant could be the product of revision aimed at eliminating the repetition.

**2** *love*] The variant "hope" in *D92* is a misprint that was corrected in *D94*.

**3–4** These lines open with a single quotation mark that is not closed in *T*.

**5** *resolved*] Read as a two-syllable word.

**11** *powers of devinityes*] "Powers" has to be read as a two-syllable word for the metre to hold. The other witnesses have the singular "power," which would be read as one syllable because "divinitie" (or "divinities," in the *Dianas*) is preceded by "thy."

## [21] *Fayre sun, if yow would have me prayse youre light*

This sonnet on the lady going to bed logically precedes [22] on the same theme.

**1** A rare reference to the lady's willingness to listen to the poet's praise. Grundy (231) compares Costanzo, *Rime* 10 (see *Le Rime d'Angelo di Costanzo* [Padua, 1750], 30).

**4–6** On the poet's need to see the lady day and night and praise her divinity continually, cf. Desportes, *Diane* 1: 43.

**8** *You ... verse*] The trope of the beloved praised and granted immortality in writing recurs in the poetry of the period. Cf. two well-known sonnets, Shakespeare, *Sonnets* 60: "you live in this" (14); and Spenser, *Amoretti* 75: "my verse your vertues rare shall eternize" (11).

**10** A rhetorical question; the question mark is editorial.

**9–10** These lines, and not the final two, are indented to signpost the odd position of the couplet. Only one other sonnet, [62], shows this arrangement.

**13** On the lover's sighs becoming or joining the wind, see for instance Watson, *Hekatompathia* 61: "If Aeole were depriv'd of all his charge, / Yet soon could I restore his winds again, / By sobbing sighs, which forth I blow at large" (13–15).

**13** *dothe*] The *H* reading is correct and differs from that in the *Dianas*. This may be an instance of an error in the initial stages of transmission that was corrected by a particular scribe; the error reappears in *T*.

## [22] *The sun his journey ending in the west*

The arrangement of the sonnets in *T* underscores that this is a companion piece to [21], a logical continuation of the theme of the poetic mistress going to bed.

**1–4** Grundy (231) compares Desportes's epitaph on "Diana de Cosse, Comtesse de Mansfeld" (Desportes, *Œuvres*, 468). See also Sidney, *A&S* 89, which begins by comparing Stella's absence with perpetual darkness:

> Now that of absence the most irksome night
> With darkest shade doth overcome my day;

Since Stella's eyes, wont to give me my day,
Leaving my hemisphere, leave me in night (1–4)

**2** *Thetis bed*] The sea. Thetis was a sea nymph and mother to the Greek hero Achilles. Cf. Thomas Kyd, *The Spanish Tragedy* 1.1.23–24 (ed. David Bevington [Manchester, 1996], 21):

ANDREA
Ere Sol had slept three nights in Thetis' lap
And slaked his smoking chariot in her flood

The image is suggestive because the sunlike beloved is now resting on someone else's bed.

**3** *sightes*] The other witnesses read "eyes," but the variant in *T* seems too different in spelling to be accidental. It is difficult to say whether "sightes" is an error or a product of revision.

**4** *be*] The *T* reading "he" is probably a scribal error considering how similar minuscule *b* and *h* could be. The syntax of this line is meant to mirror that of line 3.

**3–4** Cf. the definition of "Night or Darknes" in a 1598 commonplace book by Nicholas Ling: "Night is ... that part of the day naturall in which the sunne is hidden from us cheering the Antipodes" (Nicholas Ling, *Politeuphuia, wits commonwealth* [London, 1598], 235).

**5** *same tyme*] *H* and the *Dianas* read "sun" with different spellings; the spelling of "sun" and "same" would have been similar to the eye.

**7** *white sheetes*] A symbol of status: the lady sleeps in comfort.

**9–12** He wishes that he could be where she is at night, or the person who sleeps beside her.

**13–14** The effects that the lady has on the poet last at night even if he cannot see her, and this is a small blessing. The last line can be understood in either Neoplatonic or erotic terms.

**14** In Sidney, *A&S* 89.13–14, the same contrast is made between the absence of light and the presence of heat: "That living thus in blackest winter night, / I feel the flames of hottest summer day." Cf. also Fletcher, *Licia* 45.13–14: "Now, never after, soul shall live in dark, / That hath the hap, this western Sun to mark." Constable's line feels less spiritual in comparison. On the continued presence of the beloved in the lover's thoughts, cf. Shakespeare, *Sonnets* 27:

Save that my soul's imaginary sight
Presents thy shadow to my sightless view,
Which like a jewel hung in ghastly night
Makes black night beauteous, and her old face new. (9–12)

In Sidney, A&S 39, the poet addresses sleep and says that it will find the image of his mistress within him when it comes: "... thou shalt in me, / Livelier than elsewhere, Stella's image see" (13–14).

14 *the light*] The repetition of "heate" in T is a glaring error that destroys the meaning of the line.

[23] *Not longe agoe in Poland traveiling*

This is the first of three sonnets dedicated to Queen Elizabeth, preserved in T only, although the unequivocal patriotic feelings expressed point at an earlier date of composition. The heading is very specific and, far from being a summary of the conceit as in the case of the amatory sonnets, it provides additional information about Constable's career.

*after his ... Italye*] Constable's journey to Italy can be dated to 1585. He visited many countries working as an agent or spy under Sir Francis Walsingham's orders for the promotion of the Protestant cause.

1–2 There are no records of Constable's activities either in Italy or in Poland, which is not strange if he went there undercover, adopting a different language, nationality, and apparel.

1 *Poland*] In the early modern period Poland "became a haven for dissenting faiths fleeing generalized religious warfare in Europe" (Jose Casanova, *Public Religions in the Modern World* [Chicago, 1994], 92).

5–6 A number of plots during the 1580s contemplated an invasion of England by Spanish and French forces. I agree with Grundy (231) that it is not the Spanish Armada to which the poet alludes.

7–10 Envious foreigners claimed that England's strategic position as an island was the only reason why her enemies had not been able to invade, with the sea acting as a natural defence. On the providential character of England's insularity, see John of Gaunt's speech in Shakespeare, *Richard II* 2.1.40–49.

11 The poet points directly at the queen, and specifically her eyes, as responsible for England's preservation.

12 The dual power of Elizabeth's eyes is evoked. As a Petrarchan mistress, she has made her (male) subjects cry for love of her; cf. Daniel, *Delia* 29.12: "Th'Ocean of my teares must drowne me burning." As a ruler, she has caused her enemies to shed tears of frustration. Cf. George Gascoigne's "The Vanities of Bewtie," in which the queen's eyes rule over enemies and subjects alike (*The Complete Works of George Gascoigne*, ed. John W. Cunliffe [Cambridge, 1910], 2: 526):

EXPLANATORY NOTES • 275

This is the Queene whose onely looke subdewed,
Her prowdest foes, withowten speare or sheeld
This is the Queene, whome never eye yet viewed,
But streight the hart, was forst thereby to yeelde. (22-25)

13-14 Cf. a poem titled "The substance of all the late entended Treasons," included in Thomas Nelson's *A short discourse: expressing the substaunce of all the late pretended treasons against the Queenes Majestie*, in which the poet emphasises God's protection of the Protestant queen and her country ([London, 1586], sig. A4r-v):

No rebells power can her displace, God will defend her still
True Subjects all will lose their lives, ere Traytors have their will
How many mischiefes are devisde: how many waies are wrought:
How many wilde Conspiracies, against her Grace is fought:
Yet God that doth protect her still, her Grace doth well preserve,
And workes a shame unto her foes, as they doe best deserve. (87-92)

[24] *Most sacred prince, why should I thee thus prayse*

The second sonnet dedicated to Queen Elizabeth survives only in *T* and must be a later composition in view of the negative undertones of the religious imagery the poet invokes and his growing detachment from his addressee, which hint at the inner turmoil of his conversion.

*the cruell ... perfections*] This echoes the motif of the "cruel fair," the mistress whose beauty and qualities cause the poet-lover torment, and who even delights in it. The association of Elizabeth with cruelty is far more dangerous. Mary Villeponteaux explains how the monarch "tried to circumvent a reputation for cruelty" and identification with the biblical Jezebel (see *The Queen's Mercy: Gender and Judgment in Representations of Elizabeth I* [New York, 2014], 22, 12).

3 The sin of pride is attributed to the queen's own subjects.

4 The envy that other nations feel links this sonnet to [23], in which England's enemies marvel at its preservation.

7-8 Anyone who has seen the queen's eyes burns with love. The image of burning is employed to refer to love throughout the sequence. Cf. Sidney, *A&S* 25.12-14: "... for since I her did see, / Virtue's great beauty in that face I prove, / And find the effect, for I do burn in love."

10-11 Elizabeth is depicted as a cause of undoing for enemies and subjects alike by invoking images of hell, described as "a lake of fire burning with brimstone" in Revelation 19:20. Hell has been interpreted to be a dark place based on Job 10:22 and Matt. 8:12.

**12–14** The existence of purgatory was explicitly denied in the Thirty-Nine Articles of 1562: "The Romyshe doctrine concernyng purgatory ... is a fond thyng, vainly fayned, and grounded upon no warrauntie of Scripture, but rather repugnaunt to the word of God" (Church of England, *Articles* [London, 1563], sig. B2v). In his 1589 *Examen* (34–35), Constable addresses the idea of purgatory, emphasising that it is controversial even among Catholics themselves (translated in *CM*, at 17):

> Some of them placing Purgatory here upon earth, others under it; some neither above, nor below, but in the Aire .... Some there be that teach, that the soules are there tormented by Devils; others, by Angels, others by neither or both.

The queen is purportedly praised through comparison to an angel who inflicts torment, using an image laden with Catholic undertones. Anna Riehl has analyzed the association of Elizabeth with angels in visual representations and in poetry (see "'Shine Like an Angel with Thy Starry Crown': Queen Elizabeth the Angelic," in *Queens and Power in Medieval and Early Modern England*, ed. Carole Levin and Robert Bucholz [Lincoln, 2009], 158–186). Cf. Gascoigne's "The Vanities of Bewtie" (*The Complete Works*, 2: 526): "She is so faire, and Angell lyke to see" (18).

## [25] *The love wherewith youre vertues chayne my sprite*

The third sonnet dedicated to Queen Elizabeth may be one of Constable's earliest works, given that it survives not only in *T* but also in *M* and *Bn*, two sources descended from *X*, the earliest authorial archetype. The poet laments his inability to take up arms to protect the queen from slander; he can only write in her defence.

*a booke ... countryes*] The hitherto unidentified tract preserved in New Haven, Yale University, Beinecke Library, MS 621, fols. 15r–43r, which follows this sonnet in *Bn*. In it Constable responds to William Allen's defence of Sir William Stanley's defection to the Spanish army in the Netherlands and defends Elizabeth's intervention in Dutch affairs. Both the treatise and this sonnet had been composed by 1587. A summary of the contents of the treatise survives in *M*, fols. 93v–109v. This heading was previously misconstrued by Grundy (232) and others as referring to Constable's answer to a libel by Thomas Throckmorton.

2 *youre foe*] Cardinal William Allen (1532–1594).

3 *hatefull pen ... showe*] Allen published *A copie of a lettre written by an English Gentleman, out of the campe of the low contryes* (Antwerp, 1587), in which he encourages English subjects to disobey an excommunicate, heretic queen and to serve the King of Spain.

6 *sweet*] Without this adjective, the line in *T* is too short.

7 *of*] *M* has the unique reading "yf," a scribal error introducing a nonexistent conditional clause.

7 *my pen my sword*] Metonymy and personification are employed to draw a contrast between the poet's literary and martial prowess. The pen "is a traditional symbol for the *vita contemplativa* of poets and scholars, which stands in contrast to the *vita activa* of the military or political leader, characterized by the sword" (Heinrich F. Plett, *Rhetoric and Renaissance Culture* [Berlin, 2004], 128).

7–10 Cf. the sonnet "Of Syr Phyllypp Sydney" by Sir Arthur Gorges (*The Poems of Sir Arthur Gorges*, ed. Helen E. Sandison [Oxford, 1953], 117): "For doo the ryght thy sworde shoulde be the penn / thy noble blood the yncke whearwith to wryte" (11–12).

8 *smite*] This verb has religious connotations because it also denotes God's punishment or destruction of his enemies (*OED* v. 4), as in Ezekiel 7:9: "Ye shall know that I am the Lord that smiteth." Connections between the "sword" and the "word" abound in the Bible; to name but one, Psalm 57 alludes to "the sons of men, whose teeth are spears and arrows, and their tongue a sharp sword" (see Jerry C. Nash, "The Fury of the Pen: Crenne, the Bible, and Letter Writing," in *Women Writers in Pre-Revolutionary France: Strategies of Emancipation*, ed. Colette H. Winn and Donna Kuizenga [New York, 1997], 207–226, at 213).

9–10 The shedding of ink in the process of writing is compared to the shedding of blood, and the poet regrets that he can only do the former. Grounding her analysis on Gail Kern Paster's work, Kristen K. Polster argues that "considering that the body was often construed as a vessel of volatile liquids concocted from food, drink, air, and blood, the inkwell and pen could easily have been viewed as extensions of that body." She later adds that "the expulsion of ink could rebalance a system brought to ill health by an excess of any of the four humours," including anger or lust. See Kristen K. Polster, "The Fifth Humor: Ink, Texts, and the Early Modern Body," PhD diss., (University of North Texas, 2012), 9, 11.

11–12 Cf. sonnet [24], in which Elizabeth is said to cause "sin and sorrow" (2). In both sonnets praise of the queen is troubled by references to her effect on her subjects.

12 *have it*] The order is inverted in *Bn*, but revision may be authorial.

13 *Thus powerfull*] *Bn* and *M* share the variant "So powrfull then." In *Bn* "So"

replaces a deleted word, "How." The alternate spelling "powrfull" loses a syllable to compensate for the addition of "then."

**13** *sacred vertues*] The queen is doubly "sacred" as a Petrarchan mistress and as a ruler who is God's representative on earth.

**14** *make*] Bn has the correct reading because it agrees with line 13's plural "vertues."

[26] *Bloome of the rose, I hope those hands to kisse*

This sonnet is the first of four dedicated to James VI of Scotland, later James I of England, and – given that it survives in *M* – probably the earliest. Its presence in *E* points at wider circulation than has hitherto been assumed. The intriguing heading emphasising that Constable had not seen the Scottish king yet narrows the timeline of composition somewhat. Constable first travelled to Scotland in 1583 but he had a minor role as a member of Walsingham's retinue and there is no evidence that he met the King then; moreover, the allusions to James as a royal poet must rest on the publication of *The essayes of a prentise, in the divine art of poesie* in 1584. The sonnet was certainly written before October 1589, when Constable met the king in person, probably much earlier. It exalts James as a poet-king who embodies martial and literary qualities, much like the biblical King David. The desire to greet the king in person and the hopeful tone of the sonnet parallel those in a letter that Sir Philip Sidney sent to George Buchanan, James's mentor, in 1579, transcribed in Scots thus: "I haif nocht bene without desire to see you, and kiss the hand of the young king, in quhome mony have layd thair hoipes" (see Annie I. Cameron, ed., *The Warrender Papers* [Edinburgh, 1931], 1: 146).

**1** *Bloome of the rose*] An allusion to the Tudor rose and the dynastic connection between the Scottish monarch and the English crown. James was great-grandson to Margaret Tudor, Henry VIII's elder sister.

**2** *yonge, a scepter*] James was one year old when he became King of Scotland in 1567.

**3–4** The choice of imagery underlines the sacred character of James's authority. James was a staunch defender of the doctrine of the divine right of kings.

**5** *prince of hope*] James was viewed by many as the rightful successor to Queen Elizabeth.

**8** *garland*] Laurel wreaths were classical symbols of martial victory and literary accomplishment.

**5–8** James was praised for his rank and his literary talent. Ben Jonson may have been influenced by Constable's sonnet, as he praises the king in similar terms in Epigram 4 (*The Complete Poems*, ed. George Parfitt [New Haven, 1975], 36): "How, best of kings, dost thou a sceptre bear! / How, best of poets, dost thou laurel wear!" James's double crown is also alluded to in some verses addressed to the king in Thomas Dekker's pageant *The magnificent entertainment given to King James* ([London, 1604], sig. F1v):

> And doest besides the Red-rose and the white
> With the rich flower of France thy garland dight,
> Wearing above Kings now, or those of olde,
> A double Crowne of Lawrell and of gold (5–8)

9–10 The poet's expectations that James may become a military leader mirror those expressed by the writers of the commendatory sonnets prefacing the *Essayes*. See for instance the sonnet by "T.H.," probably Thomas Hudson (*The Poems of James VI of Scotland*, ed. James Craigie [Edinburgh 1955], 1: 3):

> If Martiall deeds, and practise of the pen
> Have wonne to aunucient Grece a worthie fame:
> ....................................
> Then place this Prince, who well deserves the same:
> Since he is one of Mars and Pallas race (1–2, 5–6)

12 *a kinglie song*] The *T* reading ("a kinglie throne") must be a corruption: it creates an imperfect rhyme, and the implication that James is a king and hence a candidate for succession supersedes the emphasis on his poetry that is supplied by the better *M* and *E* reading ("thy kingly songe"). The latter reading is given greater authority by the fact that the two witnesses belong to different families of transmission.

13 This refers to James's translation of some of the Psalms, one of which was published within the *Essayes* (see James VI, *Poems*, ed. Craigie, 1: 86–88). Others may have been circulating in manuscript at the time.

[27] *When others hooded with blind love doe flye*

This sonnet survives in *T* and in isolation in *PE, OBL*, and *O91*. The version in *PE* was particularly significant in that it prefaced a collection of the king's poetry and bore Constable's name in full, so it helped build his reputation. It derives from the same source as *OBL* and *O91*, the manuscript and printed versions of Sir John Harington's *Orlando*. These texts are free from corruptions that survive in $T$ due to their descent from $Z_1$. The conceit shows Constable's awareness of the king's fondness for hunting.

*his poems ... matters*] James's *Essayes* includes no amatory poems; the works collected there are devoted to classical, rhetorical, and religious matters.

1–2 Buzzards are associated with blindness and an attachment to earthly matters in early modern works. Cf. Samuel Bird's epistle to the reader in *A friendlie communication or dialogue betweene Paule and Damas* (London, 1580): "... as blinde buzzards keepe altogether below: but the learned Christian, like an eagle mounteth up aloft, & useth the creatures as steppes and staires to ascend unto the high God" (sig. A5r). Robert Tofte describes himself as "Beauties Buzzard" after being blinded by Love in sonnet 9 in his sequence *Laura: The toyes of a traveller* (London, 1597).

1–4 Cf. Guillaume de Saluste Du Bartas's sonnet in praise of James, printed as a preface to his French translation of *Lepanto* within *PE*, in which the poet considers himself an earthly or mortal poet as compared to James, a divine one whose talent soars upwards (sig. M2v). Du Bartas met James in 1587 when he visited Scotland and may have begun working on his translation of *Lepanto* then (see Jamie Reid-Baxter, "Scotland will be the Ending of all Empires," in *Kings, Lords and Men in Scotland and Britain, 1300–1625*, ed. Steve Boardman and Julian Goodare [Edinburgh, 2014], 320–340, at 330). The commendatory poem could have been circulating in manuscript well before its publication.

5–6 James engaged with spiritual themes at a young age; he "saw poetry as more fitted for elevating works as a branch of courtly education" (Morna R. Fleming, "The *Amatoria* of James VI: Loving by the *Reulis*," in *Royal Subjects: Essays on the Writings of James VI and I*, ed. Daniel Fischlin and Mark Fortier [Detroit, 2002], 124–148, at 131).

6 *schoold*] The other sources have the variant "taught." The *T* reading adds an extra connotation in that it also meant "to punish" or "to use force to teach a lesson" (*OED*, s.v. school, v.[1] 3.a). It is difficult to say if "schoold" is a later improvement.

8 *winge of tyme*] Time is commonly represented as a winged man in books of emblems.

9 *wings*] *T* has the reading "things," which would not be semantically cohesive with "as slow" unless it were a scribal misreading of "as low." There is no further evidence supporting this reading; Grundy also emended the line using the better variant.

10–11 Cf. Barnes, *Divine Centurie* 1.5–6: "But my Muse fethered with an Angels wing, / Divinely mounts aloft unto the skie."

12 *fames wings*] John Harington observed that "fame outlasteth, and out flyeth all things" right before quoting this sonnet in full in *O91* (288).
13 *flee*] This is the reading in all other witnesses, which preserves the rhyme.


[28] *If I durst sigh still as I had begun*

This occasional sonnet can be dated to the autumn of 1589, after King James received news that storms prevented his bride, Anne of Denmark, from coming to England, and before he sailed to Oslo to meet her in November. Constable was in Scotland at the time, and this sonnet and its companion piece [29] signal his participation in the monarch's literary coterie and his hopes of royal preferment. On James's use of coterie poetry to bestow favour, see Jane Rickard, *Authorship and Authority: The Writings of James VI and I* (Manchester, 2007), 42–43.

*a sonnet ... Denmark*] This double sonnet, made of two quatorzains, is titled "A complaynt against the contrary wyndes that hindered the Queen to com to Scotland from Denmarke," and it is the first in James's *Amatoria*, a sequence of love sonnets that circulated only in manuscript and are preserved in London, British Library, Additional MS 24195.

3–4 *to blame ... done*] This is a direct response to the first sonnet in James's piece (James VI, *Poems*, ed. Craigie, 2: 68):

> From sacred throne in heaven Empyrick hie
> A breathe divine in Poëts brests does blowe
> Wherethrough all things inferiour in degrie
> As vasalls unto them doe hommage showe
> There songs enchants Apollos selfe ye knowe
> And chaste Dianas coache can haste or staye
> Can change the course of Planets high or lowe
> And make the earthe obeye them everie waye
> Make rockes to danse, hugge hills to skippe and playe
> Beasts, foules, and fishe to followe them allwhere
> Though thus the heaven, the sea, and earthe obeye,
> Yett mutins the midde region of the aire.
> What hatefull Juno, Aeolus entiseth
> Wherby contrarious Zephyre thus ariseth.

5–8 The lover's tears and sighs are commonly said to become, or join, the sea and the wind. Cf. Watson, *Hekatompathia* 61:

> My weeping eyes so many tears distill,
> That greater Seas might grow by them alone
> .................................
> If Aeole were depriv'd of all his charge,
> Yet soon could I restore his winds again,
> By sobbing sighs, which forth I blow at large (8–9, 13–15)

*6 the desired ships*] The ships transporting James's bride.

*8 yowre wished sun*] Queen Anne.

*12 sacrifice*] Write a poem and offer it as sacrifice.

13–14 The poet's and the king's wishes on behalf of one another paint a scenario of longed-for camaraderie. As poetry becomes a form of social transaction, the gap between them is bridged in the literary realm.

## [29] *If I durst love as heertofore I have*

This sonnet continues the narrative in [28]. It survives in *T* and *E*, although the *E* text is incomplete. King James travelled to meet Anne of Denmark and spent the whole winter at the Danish court because the weather made his safe return impossible. Constable must have spent part of that winter in Scotland, and this sonnet suggests his frustration at the absence of the monarch whose favour he was striving to gain.

*his longe ... sea*] James departed on 22 October 1589 and returned with his wife on 1 May 1590.

1–4 The poet plays on the commonplace of the lover's fire not thawing the poetic mistress's ice; see for instance Spenser, *Amoretti* 30:

> My love is lyke to yse, and I to fyre;
> how comes it then that this her cold so great
> is not dissolv'd through my so hot desyre,
> but harder growes the more I her intreat? (1–4)

*4 heart*] The variant "heate" in *E* in this line and line 9 also fits the context, and it is uncertain which may be the authorial reading.

*7 hir*] The feminine possessive in *E* is doubtlessly correct.

8 On the lady's eyes as a source of heat and fire, see for instance Spenser, *Amoretti* 7: "That your bright beams of my weak eies admyred, / may kindle living fire within my brest" (11–12).

*11 Phoebus*] A literary name for the sun, and a name for the Greek god Apollo when he was associated with the sun.

**12** Early in his Scottish reign, James was widely praised as a scholar and a poet-king and identified with Apollo, the god of poetry. Cf. Alexander Montgomerie's fourth sonnet "In prais of the Kings Uranie" (Montgomerie, *Poems*, 1: 108).

> As bright Apollo staineth eviry star
> With goldin rayis, vhen he begins to ryse
> ...............................
> So, Quintessenst of Kings, vhen thou Compylis,
> Thou stanis my Versis with thy staitly stylis. (1–2, 13–14)

Kings were commonly associated with the sun in this period, and James consistently became the sun in Jacobean masques. He is presented as the sun, or Phoebus, in Chapman's *The memorable maske* (London, 1613) due to his being a poet and also God's representative on earth; see Donald J. Gordon, "Chapman's *Memorable Masque* (1956)," in *The Renaissance Imagination: Essays and Lectures by D.J. Gordon*, ed. Stephen Orgel (Berkeley, 1975), 194–202, at 199–200.

**14** *two suns*] James and his wife.

## [30] *If nature for her workes proud ever were*

This sonnet survives in *T* and *E*. It is the first sonnet addressed to Louise de Coligny (1555–1620), a French Huguenot noblewoman who was the widow of William the Silent, prince of Orange (see notes to [37]). It must have been written upon Constable meeting Louise in person, when he was in the Low Countries at some point between late 1584 and 1586. Louise cultivated the friendship of Sir Philip Sidney and welcomed Leicester when he arrived in the Netherlands in late 1585.

**2** *yow*] The variant "the" (thee) in *E* must be an error because it destroys the rhyme.

**3** *sacred head*] The Petrarchan lady was often compared to a goddess; this may also allude to the idea that monarchs are appointed by God.

**3** *wisdome*] Louise was considered a woman of great learning and influence. Note that Constable ascribes the same quality to Queen Elizabeth in [23] and King James in [26] and [29].

**4** *fitte*] The *E* reading, "meete," seems equally appropriate.

**12** *soveraigne*] Probably used with the more general meaning of ruler. Under William of Orange, the new Dutch Republic had declared independence from Spain in 1581. William and Louise were married for a year until his assassination in 1584.

**13–14** It is only by God's will that Louise is not a queen, because perfect happiness is reserved for heaven. These lines reinforce the poet's Protestant and anti-Spanish stance towards the Low Countries issue.

[31] *Playnlie I write because I will write true*

This sonnet survives only in *T* and is dedicated to Mary Talbot, née Cavendish (1557–1632), who married Constable's cousin Gilbert Talbot and became countess of Shrewsbury on 10 November 1590. The heading was surely added after that date. Mary was openly Catholic and supported Constable after his conversion. The sonnet is laden with religious elements and ambiguity regarding the poet's own religious stance and political allegiance. Lilla Grindlay points out the "uncanny similarity" between this sonnet and one by Sir John Harington in which he addresses different women named Mary – Mary Herbert, countess of Pembroke, and Mary Talbot, countess of Shrewsbury – including an allusion to his wife, Mary, and perhaps to the Virgin (Lilla Grindlay, *Queen of Heaven: The Assumption and Coronation of the Virgin in Early Modern English Writing* [Notre Dame, 2018], 184–185). For Harington's sonnet, see *The Epigrams of Sir John Harington*, ed. Gerard Kilroy (Farnham, 2009), 227. It opens thus:

> My soule one only Mary doth adore,
> onely one Mary doth inioy my hart,
> yet hath my Muse found out two Maries more,
> that merit endles prayse by dew desart (1–4)

**1** Alison Shell deems this line to be "one of the most disingenuous beginnings ever given to a sonnet," as there is nothing simple about it (*Catholicism, Controversy, and the English Literary Imagination, 1558–1660* [Cambridge, 1999], 124). The poet's self-avowed honesty only raises the stakes in the interpretation of the sonnet.

**2–3** Reformers attacked the glorification of the Virgin Mary by the Roman Catholic Church, and excessive devotion was mistrusted. Protestants would not be prone to envision her as crowned in heaven, but Catholic poets – including Constable himself in his *SS* – allude to her queenship. The Virgin is also invoked as a paragon of female excellence in order to praise Mary Talbot, especially since the countess must have been a devout Marian.

**4** *as my creed*] There is an interplay between the religion of love and the poet-as-devotee convention, and the obscure allusion to the poet's faith.

**5** *this Ile*] Britain.

6–7 The allusion is probably to Mary Tudor and Mary, Queen of Scots. The former was associated with burnings of Protestants in collective memory; that sort of cruelty could be disapproved of by Protestants and Catholics alike. The latter presents a more troubling figure. The allusion to "blood ... shed" could be read as criticism of "the upsurges of militant Protestantism" during her Scottish reign (Shell, *Catholicism*, 124). However, Constable's sonnets to Mary Stuart within the *Spiritual Sonnets* are haunted by images of her spilt blood; a more Catholic reading of these lines is therefore possible.

9–10 The reference to God's plans is deliberately ambiguous, raising the question of who God's enemies and who his chosen people are. A Catholic reading would point at the Protestants burnt at the stake as the "foes" punished "for rebell fayth and sin," whereas Catholics like Mary would be God's martyrs, tested through suffering.

11 God did not want the name of Mary to be associated with violence.

12 *good and bad*] All men, regardless of their righteousness or wickedness.

13–14 Mary Talbot only originates the fire of love instead of any real, physical torments. The masochism latent in Petrarchan convention is foregrounded to deflect attention away from the religious undertones of the sonnet.

[32] *Yow, sister Muses, doe not ye repine*

This dedicatory sonnet survives in three manuscripts (*T, M, E*) and the printed miscellany *A Poetical Rhapsody* (*PR1, PR2*). The last lines in *M* are so different that this version has not been collated and is edited and discussed as [32b].

Lady Anne Russell, countess of Warwick (1548/1549–1604), was the earl of Leicester's sister-in-law and a member of Essex's circle; she was Gentlewoman of the Privy Chamber and had "considerable influence with Elizabeth" (see Paul Hammer, *The Polarisation of Elizabethan Politics: The Political Career of Robert Devereux, 2nd Earl of Essex, 1585–1597* [Cambridge, 1999], 284). Lady Margaret Clifford, countess of Cumberland (1560–1616), was a highly educated lady and literary patroness (see Barbara Lewalski, *Writing Women in Jacobean England* [Cambridge, 1993], 138). On Constable's connections with both ladies, see p. 10.

*To the Countesses ... sisters*] A full discussion on the variations to the heading in different sources and their social implications is given on p. 87.

1–2 The comparison of the two ladies to the goddesses of literature and the arts rests not only on their sisterhood but also on their shared role as patronesses and dedicatees at court.

3 *these sacred two more rare*] The variant readings of this line in *PR1*, *PR2* omit mention of the countesses' divinity, an attempt at the Petrarchan motif of the lady as a saint, and include the verb "is" – perhaps the editor's emendation to avoid enjambment.

4 *In vertue is, then*] The variant "then the whole Troope of" in *PR1*, *PR2* is also editorial; word insertions add little to the meaning of the line.

5 *if ye aske which one*] In *PR1*, *PR2*, the pronoun "me" is added after the verb, making it necessary to omit "one" in order to preserve the metre.

6 *I say*] The replacement of the verb with "answer" in *PR1*, *PR2* adds one syllable to the line, which is compensated for through the omission of "owne."

7 *Where eyther is*] The variant "of which each" in *PR1*, *PR2*, and *A* creates an unpleasant repetition of sounds.

7 *as cleare ... star*] A conventional comparison. Cf. Barnes, *P&P* elegy 21.21–22: "Thou that those cleare eyes (whose light surpasseth a stars light, / Canst make loves flames shoote ... ." In *PR1*, *PR2*, the editor substitutes "bright," choosing a collocation that was more common at the time.

8 *other*] The *T* reading seems inferior because a singular pronoun is needed.

13 *highest prayse*] The variant "onely" in *PR1*, *PR2* detracts from the poet's commendation by implying that he has no other grounds for praising the ladies.

11–14 The ending of the sonnet seems weak and conventional compared to that in *M* (see notes to [32b] below); the particulars of the original circumstances of composition are omitted to suit a more general purpose and audience.

[32b] *Yee, sister Muses, doe not ye repine*

This is the *M* text of sonnet [32]. The first two quatrains are here compared to *T*, as variants can be explained in terms of authorial revision. The last six lines are unique to *M* and reveal its origin as a piece of occasional verse. In *M* this sonnet is followed by another to the same ladies; see [65].

2 *with yow nine*] The deletion of the pronoun and insertion of "doe" before "with" in *T* regularized this line into a perfect iambic pentameter.

3 *for one*] This could be misconstrued as one of the sisters being praised above the other; the reading "eyther" in *T* reinforces their equality.

3 *these sweet sacred*] The adjective "sweet" is omitted in *T* to compensate for the addition of one extra syllable through "eyther."

4 *yow Muses nine*] Repetition of "Muses" is avoided in *T* through the periphrasis "the heavenly nyne."

EXPLANATORY NOTES · 287

*7 more cleare then*] This comparative of superiority is repeated in the next line; in *T* it becomes one of equality ("as cleare as").

9–10 These lines evidence that the sonnet originally belonged together with a portrait of the ladies that could only confirm the poet's praise. Constable and the countesses were some of the players in a 1589 intrigue meant to secure the favour of King James of Scotland, and the poet might have carried the picture with him on his journey. There are contemporary examples both of paintings that incorporate poems and of double portraits, such as this must have been. The "Ditchley Portrait" of Queen Elizabeth (ca. 1592) at the National Portrait Gallery includes a sonnet, now partially illegible; a double portrait (ca. 1581) of the Devereux sisters, Dorothy and Penelope (Lady Rich), hangs at Longleat House. Considering that Constable probably carried the portrait with him, and the fact that he addresses sonnet 43 to Nicholas Hilliard, it could also have been a miniature.

*9 yow see*] The poet is addressing both the muses and the beholder of the gift-portrait, or even King James in particular.

*11 these pearles sisters*] "Pearles" must here be an old spelling of "peerless," in which case "these" must function as a pronoun instead of a determiner.

*13 like*] The numerous repetitions of this word point to the *M* sonnet as an early work which was later authorially revised.

[33] *That worthie Marquesse, pride of Italie*

This is the first of three sonnets dedicated to Arbella Stuart (1575–1615). Unlike her first cousin James VI of Scotland, she had been born in England, which made her a potential candidate to Elizabeth's throne. Constable must have met Arbella through a shared family connection to Mary Talbot, countess of Shrewsbury and Arbella's aunt. They both were at court around the same time in 1588.

*1 That worthie Marquesse*] Vittoria Colonna (1490–1547), marchesana di Pescara, to whom sonnet [51] is addressed.

1–3 In life and after her death, Colonna was considered a paragon of virtue, learning, and literary achievement. In Virginia Cox's words, "Here was a lady of stalwart moral integrity and propriety, yet renowned also for her erudition and poetic genius: a living reproach to the popular prejudice that associated learning in women with a propensity to sexual misconduct." Colonna became a "model ideal of femininity" (see Virginia Cox, "The Exemplary Vittoria Colonna," in *A Companion to Vittoria Colonna*, ed. Abigail Brundin et al. [Leiden, 2016], 467–472, at 468–469).

*2 her wit and phrase*] Her learning and her literary skill.

3 *best deserv'd ... prayse*] She was at the same time dedicatee and poet.

5–7 A reference to his own love poetry, in which he frequently compares his mistress to a goddess; see for instance sonnets [20] and [60]. Arbella is compared to an excellent mortal woman instead.

8 This emphasis on difference may imply that Arbella is not his mistress, so he is not employing the usual conventions to honour her. The same separation between his poetic mistress and potential patroness can be seen in colophon sonnet [63].

9–10 *when ... to men*] For instance in classical mythology.

13 *earthlye shadowe*] An allusion to the Platonic view that there is an ideal world of which we see but reflections or shadows.

14 *heavenly selfe*] Arbella could be envisioned here as future queen, God's representative on Earth, considering that the poet does the same in his portrayal of Queen Elizabeth as "sacred" in sonnet [25].

## [34] *Only hope of oure age, that vertues dead*

This is the second sonnet to Arbella Stuart (1575–1615); see [33]. Here the poet commends the young lady for her learning, subtly drawing a connection between him and his addressee grounded on their shared skills and interests. Biographers agree that Arbella received an education fit for a queen. Her uncle, Charles Cavendish, wrote in a letter that "Lord Burghley had spoken to Sir Walter Ralegh 'greatly in hir commendation,' saying that she could speak Italian and French, played instruments, danced and sewed beautifully" (Sarah J. Steen, ed., *The Letters of Lady Arbella Stuart* [Oxford, 1994], 20). Other contemporaries such as Sir John Harington praised her education, her musical taste, her skill for languages, and the contrasting "sobriety in her fashion of apparel and behaviour" (Sarah Gristwood, *Arbella: England's Lost Queen* [London, 2003], 74).

1 *Only hope of oure age*] Because she was a candidate to succeed Elizabeth. Note that Constable addresses King James of Scotland in very similar terms in [26]: "prince of hope" (5).

3–4 It is implied that Arbella holds books in her conventionally white hands.

4 *only*] The placement of this word is ambiguous; it may mean that the lady does not care about material or earthly affairs but only about her studies.

5 *others worth*] That of authors or scholars.

6–8 Written praise, which requires literary talent, is depicted as a form of currency. Poets like himself have none when compared to Arbella, so in order to honour her as she deserves they must borrow some of her own talent. The motif seems appropriate in the sense that written dedications were instrumental in social exchange.

13–14 This is the only instance of amatory language in the sonnets addressed to Arbella, and it must be considered part of the poet's quest for female patronage and therefore conventional.

## [35] *O, that my songe like to a ship might be*

This sonnet is dedicated to Penelope Rich (1563–1607), née Devereux, who was Sidney's "Stella" and one of the most influential ladies at court. She has been identified as the addressee of Constable's amatory sonnets, although only a handful are unambiguously dedicated to her. This sonnet circulated in manuscript only but it is conspicuously absent from the collection in *H*, which bears a general dedication to Lady Rich.

3 *riches*] A pun on Penelope's married name. Cf. Sidney, *A&S* 37.5–6: "Towards Aurora's court a nymph doth dwell, / Rich in all beauties which man's eye can see." Alexander Craig does the same when dedicating sonnets to Penelope; see Craig, *Amorose Songes*, "I Serve a Mistris infinitely faire": "If curious heades to know her name do crave, / Shee is a Lady Rich ..." (9–10).

4 *Indians*] The inhabitants of the New World, who were a source of fascination for contemporary readers of travel accounts.

6 The poet alludes to the contemporary belief that America was full of gold for the taking, made popular by works such as the translation of Francisco López de Gómara's *The pleasant historie of the conquest of the Weast India* (London, 1578). This line may be echoing Sidney, *A&S* 32.10–13, in which Morpheus answers the poet's questions concerning the origin of Stella's beauty:

> Whence hast thou ivory, rubies, pearl and gold
> To show her skin, lips, teeth and head so well?
> 'Fool,' answers he; 'no Ind's such treasures hold,
> But from thy heart ...

Cf. also Barnes, *P&P* 48, a blazon in which the lady's body parts are compared to gold, pearls, and gemstones.

6 *golden parts*] *M* has the variant "pearles & stones," and the *T* reading seems like an instance of authorial revision and improvement because it adds another allusion to Penelope's famous blond hair, described for instance in Sidney, *A&S* 103.

9 *This wished voyage*] The poet's verse is compared to a ship, so the metaphorical voyage could be the circulation of his poems.

13–14 The final "beare" eliminates the idea of the symbiotic relationship between the poet's verse and the lady's beauty; the third person -s might have been lost to preserve the rhyme with "apeare." However imperfect, the *T* readings seem to be an improvement on the *M* text: line 13 is more grammatically consistent with "doe" in 14, and the repetition of "my verse" is eliminated.

## [36] *Heralds in armes doe three perfections coate*

This is the second sonnet in praise of Penelope Rich; see [35]. Given that it is absent from the two early manuscript collections, *M* and *H*, and from *D92*, its inclusion in *D94* indicates that the text derives from a later authorial collection which underwent further transmission, causing significant differences between the manuscript (*T*, *E*) and printed versions. The poet describes the lady's beauty in a blazon using terms from heraldry. Heraldry was present everywhere at the Elizabethan court and, when its conventions were employed in literature, the educated audience would be expected to understand (see Michael Leslie, "Heraldry," in *The Spenser Encyclopedia*, ed. Albert C. Hamilton [Toronto, 1990], 353–355).

1 *coate*] The spelling "quote" in *D94* has been annotated because it destroys the antanaclasis.

1 *doe three*] The unique variant in *E* omits the auxiliary and adds "rare" premodifying "perfections," thus replacing an empty function word with a lexical word.

3 *three*] *E* reads "things," which causes a repetition of the same word within the line and must be an error.

4 *be of note*] The variant "be a note" in *D94*, *E*, and *A* is not necessarily an error according to the *OED* (s.v. note, n.² 3.c): "An objective or visible sign which serves to identify or distinguish some person or thing." The preceding "honour" would postmodify "note."

5 *rich*] A pun on Penelope's married name (see notes to [35] above).

7 *Lordlye*] An allusion to Robert Rich, third Baron Rich, Penelope's husband. They got married in 1581.

9–12 The description of the coat of arms echoes Sidney, *A&S* 13, in which Cupid wins a match between gods because he is wearing Stella's face on his shield: "Cupid then smiles, for on his crest there lies / Stella's fair hair, her face he makes his shield, / Where roses gules are borne in silver field" (9–11).

10 *Two stars*] The lady's eyes. The metaphor was conventional enough, but Constable is fonder of sun-related imagery and here he is echoing Sidney, who

refers to Stella's eyes as stars throughout his sequence (see for instance Sidney, *A&S* 26 and 48).

**10** *waves of gold*] Her blond hair. See notes to [35] above.

**11** *the coate ... declare*] The *T* reading is better than *D94*'s "might by the starres appeare," which adds more grammatical words and creates a repetition "appeare"/ "appeareth" (lines 11 and 14).

**14** *in his armes*] A double meaning is intended: the part of the body and the coat of arms.

**14** *beares*] Williams, *Edition* (2: 102) suggests that the variant "weareth" in *D94* is a "crudely sexual pun drawing on the phrase 'to win and wear' a woman" (cf. *OED*, s.v. wear, v.¹ 8.b) which is uncharacteristic of Constable's style and must be considered an editorial change.

[37] *When murdring hands, to quench the thirst of tyrannie*

This is the third alexandrine in the *T* sequence. Whereas line 4 is a perfect iambic hexameter, the sonnet is rife with metrical irregularity concerning stressed feet and the placement of the caesura, of which line 2 is perhaps the best example.

This is the second sonnet addressed to Louise de Coligny (1555–1620), a French Huguenot noblewoman who was the widow of William the Silent, prince of Orange; see [30]. The sonnet alludes to the murders of Louise's father, Admiral Gaspard de Coligny, and her first husband, Charles de Téligny, which signalled the start of the St Bartholomew's Day Massacre in August 1572, and that of William, assassinated in July 1584.

The dating of this sonnet is problematic, although the poet's diehard Protestant stance marks it as an early work. Grundy (237) reads the allusions in line 2 as referring to Louise's father and first husband only, and she dates the sonnet sometime before the death of William of Orange in July 1584. However, I agree with Williams (*Edition*, 2: 102) that line 2 includes a reference to the Prince's murder. Constable must have heard and read accounts of the Massacre; Sidney, Walsingham and Jean Hotman had witnessed it in Paris, and it was also vividly narrated in print.

*the princesse of Orange*] Louise married William of Orange in 1583, and he was assassinated only a year later. She became dowager princess of Orange.

**1** The poet's allusion to those responsible for the deaths is vague enough to encompass Catherine de Medici and the Guise family in France, traditionally accused of instigating the Paris events, and Philip II of Spain, at whose request Balthasar Gérard murdered William the Silent. Catholicism and tyranny appear as inextricably linked.

2 *The worlds most worthye*] William the Silent.

2 *thy spouse*] This is ambiguous; it either clarifies the reference to William or alludes to Louise's first husband, Charles de Téligny.

2 *father*] Admiral Gaspard de Coligny.

5–8 On the paradoxical coexistence of fire and water, see sonnets [4] and [58]. Both elements are usually associated with the poet as a sorrowful lover, but here they are combined in the weeping lady's eyes.

11–12 *thyne eyes ... desire*] Cf. Daniel, *Delia* 22.2: "These tears, which heate of sacred flame distils." Cf. [23], dedicated to the queen: "Thine eye hath made a thousand eyes to weepe" (12).

14 *thy foes*] It is implied that Louise's enemies are also the poet's.

## [38] *True worthie dame, if I thee chieftayne call*

This is the second sonnet to the countess of Shrewsbury, but unlike in sonnet [31] the identity of the addressee is not entirely clear. The title was held by Elizabeth Talbot, "Bess of Hardwick" (ca. 1527–1608), who became dowager countess in late 1590 when the title passed to her daughter Mary Talbot (née Cavendish), wife to Gilbert Talbot. The military conceit in the sonnet, especially the emphasis on the lady being a figure of authority, seems more suitable to address Bess, a powerful matriarch. However, addressing two different ladies under the same title within the same sequence would be odd for a poet who was preoccupied with rank, so Mary Talbot could be the addressee. The poet's confession that he is in love with a lady from the countess's household or family further complicates the circumstances of the sonnet's composition.

*his deare ... government*] Probably Grace Pierrepont, daughter to Mary Talbot's sister Frances; see sonnet [1]. Commentators have mentioned Arbella Stuart, who was both her grandmother's and her aunt's ward (see Grundy, 237; Williams, *Edition*, 2: 102); however, other sonnets in the sequence, especially [63], make it clear that Arbella was a potential patroness but not the poet's mistress.

1–2 *chieftayne ... host*] The countess is compared to a general, and her army is made of the young ladies living on her estate, associated with the goddess of love because of their beauty.

10 *I doe appeale*] An explicit statement of the poet's reason for writing, which explains his efforts to praise the countess in the first two quatrains.

11–12 *A warrioure ... tooke*] The poet refers to himself as the lady's prisoner in sonnets [41] and [50]. The motif of war and conquest is found in contemporary sequences; see notes to [13]. Edmund Spenser depicts his mistress as a "cru-ell warriour" (Spenser, *Amoretti* 11.3). In Sidney, *A&S* 36, Astrophil laments that he has been conquered by Stella's beauty and voice and cannot escape:

> Stella, whence doth this new assault arise,
> A conquered, yelden, ransacked heart to win?
> Whereto long since, through my long battered eyes,
> Whole armies of thy beauties entered in (1–4)

**13** *youre heart*] Possibly a scribal error, as a third person pronoun would make more sense. If the pronoun is correct, the poet is pinning all his faith on being able to move the countess so that she will endorse his courtship.

**13–14** The countess is addressed as a potential agent of mediation on the poet's behalf. If she is indeed Mary Talbot, a veiled allusion to the Catholic belief in the Virgin as intercessor could be intended.

**14** *grace*] Mercy or favour, and also a possible allusion to the lady's name, as in sonnet [1]. This word is charged with different meanings in the sequence.

## [39] *Ladie whome by reporte I only knowe*

This sonnet is dedicated to Mary Herbert (1561–1621), countess of Pembroke from 1577, and must have been written after Constable heard news of the death of her brother Sir Philip Sidney. Although he had never met Mary in person, he followed the ongoing trend among poets of seeking her patronage both through written dedications and funeral sonnets in the memory of her brother. The poet's praise largely rests on comparison with her brother. Mary is one of the female dedicatees within the Sidney-Essex circle whose patronage Constable sought.

**1** *by reporte ... knowe*] Mary spent most of the year 1588 at Wilton House and did not return to London until November, so even if Constable had been in and out of court that year the two would not have met. She was at the centre of a thriving literary coterie, and written praise of her abounds; Hannay has pointed out that she "was viewed as the heir of Sidney's muse, as writer or as patron" only after her return to London (see Margaret P. Hannay, *Philip's Phoenix: Mary Sidney, Countess of Pembroke* [Oxford, 1990], 60). Mary's work "A Dialogue between Two Shepherds" ended up sharing print space with two of Constable's sonnets in *PR1* (1602).

**4** *his sister ... so*] Mary's portrayal as Sidney's sister has been discussed by Suzanne Trill as "double-edged." The countess "demonstrates the historical prejudices which consistently define women by reference to male relatives" (see Trill,

"Spectres and Sisters: Mary Sidney and the 'Perennial Puzzle' of Renaissance Women's Writing," in *Renaissance Configurations: Voices/Bodies/Spaces, 1580–1690*, ed. Gordon McMullan [Basingstoke, 2001], 191–211, at 195, 206).

**5** *million tongues reporte*] Nicholas Breton, Edmund Spenser, and Samuel Daniel were some of the many writers who addressed Mary Herbert in writing and dedicated works to her.

**8** *others*] A reference to his mistress, the sight of whom brings him suffering, may be intended.

**9** *in one place*] In the countess.

**10** *dazle eye*] Cf. the description of Stella's eyes in Sidney, *A&S* 7: "Lest, if no veil those brave gleams did disguise, / They, sun-like, should more dazle than delight?" (7–8).

**10** *feed love*] The nourishment motif is conventional, although the most common collocation in contemporary poems is "feed hope." In Spenser, *Amoretti* 88, the poet recalls the image of his absent mistress "and thereon feed my love-affamisht hart" (12).

**10** *ravish witte*] She also has an effect on others' minds. Cf. Sidney, *A&S* 80.2: "Since best wits think it wit thee to admire." See also sonnet [57].

**11** *princely grace*] An allusion to her nobility and her moral excellence; "grace" is probably used in the sense of virtue, regarded as divine in origin (*OED* n. 1.d), but it may also convey the sense of "favour" (n. 3.a), which she could bestow due to her status as a patroness.

**12** Elizabeth Hodgson reads this line as a "reversal of the mourner/mourned paradigm" because her mind is not said to be "similar to her brother's mind" but "to her brother himself" (see Hodgson, *Grief and Women Writers in the English Renaissance* [New York, 2015], 33). Nevertheless, "brother" could also be an unmarked possessive form, considering the use of "his" in line 14. Other contemporaries draw parallels between brother and sister. See for instance Barnes, *P&P*, "To the Most Vertuous Learned and bewtifull Lady Marie Countesse of Penbrooke," in which the poet envisions her place of eternal rest: "After thy mortall pilgrimage dispatch'te, / Unto those Planettes where thou shal't have place / With thy late sainted brother to give light" (8–10).

**13–14** He refers to his own poetry in honour of Sidney (see [52] to [54]). These lines round off a sonnet that may be read as Constable's act of self-presentation as a fellow poet and Sidney's literary inheritor (see Hodgson, *Grief and Women Writers*, 32).

[40] *Sweetest of Ladies, if thy pleasure be*

This sonnet is dedicated to Frances Walsingham, daughter to Elizabeth's spymaster Sir Francis Walsingham, who first employed Constable. Frances became Sir Philip Sidney's widow at his death in 1586 and married Robert Devereux, earl of Essex, before or in 1590. The body of the sonnet, with its call for revenge against Sidney's killers, must have been written before her second marriage; after it, Duncan-Jones observes, it did not make sense to portray her in mourning for her first husband (see Katherine Duncan-Jones, "Astrophel," in *The Spenser Encyclopedia*, ed. Albert C. Hamilton [Toronto, 1990], 75). The heading would have been added later, when she was countess of Essex, at the time when the sonnet was included in the sequence that has survived in *T*. Another poet, Edmund Spenser, dedicated *Astrophel*, an elegy on Sidney, to Frances; it was published in 1595 but had probably been composed a few years earlier (ibid.). The figure of Frances as other than a daughter and wife has only started to be studied by scholars, as Grace Ioppolo points out (see "Those Essex Girls: The Lives and Letters of Lettice Knollys, Penelope Rich, Dorothy Perrott Percy, and Frances Walsingham," in *The Ashgate Research Companion to the Sidneys, 1500–1700*, ed. Margaret P. Hannay et al. [Farnham, 2015], 1: 77–92, at 12).

2 *To murther hearts*] See notes to sonnet [10], "murders guilte." Cf. also Drayton, *Idea* 2.1–2: "My hart was slaine, and none but you and I, / who should I thinke the murther should comit?"

3–4 The catastrophic, dual effect of the lady's gaze on allies and foes alike is also depicted in one of Constable's sonnets to the queen; see [23].

3 *on Spaine*] Because Sidney was injured at the Battle of Zutphen (22 September 1586), in which English troops fought on the side of the Dutch revolting against Spanish rule. He died a few weeks later. Printed elegies on Sidney such as George Whetstone's *Sir Phillip Sidney, his honorable life* (London, 1587) are laden with anti-Spanish sentiment; the Spanish rule of the Low Countries is portrayed as tyrannical and as having the potential to threaten England.

6 *theyre owne ill*] This emendation, introduced by Grundy (155), avoids repetition of "will" and fits the logic of the poet's argument better.

6–8 Wishing for the lady to go to Spain entails that an enemy nation would be blessed by her presence and England deprived of it.

9 *thus doe I*] The poet has made such a wish.

10 *the new-found world*] The American territories claimed by Spain.

12–14 Williams identifies Sidney as "his sun" and "Frances's eye" as his heaven (Williams, *Edition*, 2: 104), but this is unclear. The conduplicatio has the rhetorical effect of emphasising the loss that English subjects would incur were Frances to go abroad.

[41] *Since onlye I, sweet Ladie, ye beheld*

This sonnet survives only in *T* and is the only one dedicated to a "Ladie Clinton." The identity of this lady has generated some confusion. Williams, *Edition* (2: 104) makes a case for her being Elizabeth Fiennes de Clinton, countess of Lincoln, better known as Surrey's "Fair Geraldine." She was one of the beauties of her age and a lady-in-waiting to the queen (see Susan Bridgen, "Clinton, Elizabeth Fiennes de [1528?–1589]," *ODNB*, https://doi-org/10.1093/ref:odnb/9549). However, this sonnet includes a reference to Constable's later love (possibly Grace) and has survived only in the later sequence; in addition, the headings in *T* were probably added in late 1590 or early 1591 (see p. 46), when the much older lady was dead. This lady must then be Elizabeth Clinton (née Knevitt) (1574?–1630?), daughter to Sir Henry Knyvet (or Knevitt), who was a soldier and member of Parliament. She married Thomas Clinton in 1584, and there is evidence that Thomas's grandfather Edward Clinton, first earl of Lincoln, and Constable's father Sir Robert were on good terms. Elizabeth would have been twelve years younger than Constable, but the age difference did not stop him from writing to Arbella Stuart, and Lady Clinton is not identified as the poet's mistress in any case. Elizabeth is best known for publishing a treatise on breastfeeding titled *The countesse of Lincolnes nurserie* in 1622. The sonnet is linked to [19] in that both are built around the idea of prefiguration.

1 *Since*] Grundy emends to "Once," which is more coherent with "Yet then" in the next line because the reference is to a fateful encounter.

4 *a shorte tyme*] The circumstances in which Constable may have seen this lady are unknown.

7 *youre ... shin'd*] When he first saw her.

8 *hold*] *T* has the past tense "held" due to a scribal slip which may have been caused by the same verb occurring at the end of line 4. The rhyme with "foretold" is broken.

6–8 See [38] for a similar image. An indirect source may be Desportes, who frequently complains about his metaphorical imprisonment. Cf. Desportes, *Diane* 1: 6.7–8.

9–11 The lady's beauty has an effect on her immediate surroundings, such that another woman will undergo a sort of contagion and become beautiful herself. Grundy (238) mentions the Neoplatonic idea of "the love of men for particular objects" being "due to the sweetness of God," which derives from Marsilio Ficino's commentary on Plato's *Symposium*.

11 *my deare*] Park, *THM* (508) and Hazlitt (44) alter the sense of the line by inserting commas, as if Lady Clinton were addressed as his beloved. However, his "deare" must be his later love, possibly Grace; see sonnets [1] and [63].

[42] *Fayre by inheritance, whome borne we see*

This sonnet survives in three manuscript collections and the two *Dianas* and provides invaluable information about transmission. Its occasional nature and the circumstances explained in the heading help date the sequence as it appears in *M* to late 1588. Constable was unfortunate in his choice of dedicatee because Lady Rich's baby died shortly after, and he felt compelled to justify the failure of his prophecy with another sonnet, [55].

*A calculation ... wonder*] See p. 88 for a full discussion of the variations to the heading in different sources in relation to changing social circumstances.

*borne ... wonder*] Penelope Rich's daughter was christened on 26 November 1588, and probably named Elizabeth after the queen, who stood godmother; the baby died shortly after (see Sally Varlow, *The Lady Penelope: The Lost Tale of Love and Politics in the Court of Elizabeth I* [London, 2007], 107). Around Europe it was widely believed that 1588 would be a year of upheaval; some astrologers had connected it with the end of the world. William Eamon quotes a prediction by German astronomer Regiomontanus (see Eamon, "Astrology and Society," in *A Companion to Astrology in the Renaissance*, ed. Brendan M. Dooley [Leiden, 2014], 181–182):

> The Eighty-Eight a famous year appears,
> Which brings distress more fatal than of old.
> If not in this year all the wicked world
> Do fall, and land with sea to nothing come;
> Yet Empires must be topsy-turvy hurled
> And extreme grief shall be the common sum.

The second edition of Raphael Holinshed's *Chronicles* echoes the widespread popular concern with predictions for this year, and almanac makers were explicitly "forbidden to allude to the prophecy" (see Garrett Mattingly, *The Armada* [New York, 2005], 185).

1 *Fayre by inheritance*] Because her mother is a beauty.

2–3 *the day ... sway*] She was born on a Friday, associated with Venus.

3 *planet*] The omission of this word in *H* produces a metrically faulty line.

4 In *M* this line reads "to thee the heavens this destenye decree," and there are variations upon this version in *H*, *D92*, and *D94*. The revision in *T* must be authorial in that it turns a very specific allusion to the baby girl's future into a more general prediction, which makes sense considering that the baby had died by the time the later sequence was put together and it would have been tactless to leave it as it was.

5–8 Cf. sonnet 7 in William Alexander's *Aurora* (London, 1604), in which the poet uses very similar imagery when describing the lady's eyes:

> Eye-ravish'd I go gazing on their rayes,
> Whilst they enrich'd with many princely prayes,
> Ore hosts of hearts triumphing still retire:
> Those planets when they shine in their owne kinds,
> Do boast t'orethrow whole monarchies of minds. (10–14)

Grundy (239) compares the final lines in Fletcher's sonnet on the daughters of a lady, in which he seems to be borrowing from Constable; see Fletcher, *Licia*, "A sonnet made upon the two Twinnes, daughters of the Ladie Mollineux, both passing like, and exceeding faire": "Both conquering Queenes, & both deserve a crowne. / My thoughts presage, which tyme to come shall trie: / That thousands conquerd, for their love shall die" (12–14).

9–11 An allusion to Alexander the Great, who as a young man reportedly complained that his father Philip would leave no territories for him to conquer and gain fame (see Plutarch, *The Life of Alexander*, in *Lives*, trans. Bernadotte Perrin [Cambridge, MA, 1914–1926], 7: 235). Cf. Henry Lok's rendering of the same allusion in his commendatory sonnet to King James printed in *PE*:

> If he with teares his sorrowes did bewray,
> To see his Father Phillip conquer all,
> And that more Worlds behinde there did not stay,
> Which for reward of his deserts might fall (5–8)

12–13 These lines display an unusual agreement between the versions in *T* and *M* against *H* and the *Dianas*; the *Y* archetype may have contained the alterations, which do not affect meaning.

14 *do*] The *M* variant has been chosen on the grounds of grammatical agreement.

## [43] *If Michaell the archpainter now did live*

This occasional sonnet is dedicated to Nicholas Hilliard (1547?–1619), the famous miniature painter. He was the royal limner and painted Queen Elizabeth and members of the court, including personages from the Leicester-Sidney circle such as Lettice Knollys, countess of Leicester, and Mary Herbert, countess of Pembroke. The portrait of Penelope Rich alluded to in the sonnet has apparently not survived, although the blond noblewoman in a miniature dated c.1590, held in the Royal Collection (RCIN 420020), is thought to be her.

*a picture ... Rich*] The circumstances of this portrait's production are connected with Constable's role in a 1589 intrigue which sent him to Scotland bearing letters, gifts, and portraits of noble ladies seeking the future king's friendship. A letter from William Cecil's spy in Edinburgh, Thomas Fowler, reports that "young Constable ... brought with him Rialta's picture," Rialta being Lady Rich's codename (HMC *Salisbury*, 3: 438). A letter by Penelope to her friend Jeanne Hotman mentions her wish to have a portrait by Hilliard sent to the French ambassador, which has led Margetts to suggest that two miniatures of her might have existed (see Michele Margetts, "Lady Penelope Rich: Hilliard's Lost Miniatures and a Surviving Portrait," *The Burlington Magazine* 130, no. 1027 [1988]: 758–61, at 759). It is perhaps no coincidence that one of Hilliard's daughters, born in 1586, was named Penelope (see Mary Edmon, "Hilliard, Nicholas (1547?–1619)," *ODNB*, https://doi-org/10.1093/ref:odnb/13320).

1 *Michaell*] Michelangelo Buonarroti (1475–1564), the famous Italian Renaissance artist.

1 *archpainter*] A pun on the name of Michael the archangel and Michelangelo, suggesting that the latter was the best painter of all.

4 *Raphaells*] Raffaello Sanzio (1483–1520), the famous Italian Renaissance painter. Raphael is also the name of an archangel. In the preface to his translation of Giovanni Paolo Lomazzo's tract on the arts, Richard Haydock states that "Hilliards hand" could be compared "with the milde spirit of the late worldes-wonder Raphaell Urbine; for ... his perfection in ingenuous Illuminating or Limming, the perfection of Painting, is (if I can judge) so extraordinarie ..." (Lomazzo, *A tracte containing the artes of curious paintinge carvinge & buildinge*, trans. Richard Haydock [Oxford, 1598], n.p.).

5–6 *in secreat ... confesse*] The image is of private confession made to a priest: in a private, or secret, setting, Michelangelo's judgement would differ from his public statement, imagined in lines 1–4. This is intended to voice the poet's own opinion. Constable is embedding a discussion of the secret art of miniature painting or limning, as opposed to more public forms of art, in an occasional sonnet which – much like a miniature – was instrumental in aristocratic social exchange. On the connection between both forms of artistic expression and their negotiation of the public and the private, see for instance Patricia Fumerton, "'Secret' Arts: Elizabethan Miniatures and Sonnets," *Representations* 15 (1986): 57–97.

7 *give to ... light*] Cf. Hilliard's own description of the art of limning (see Nicholas Hilliard, *The Arte of Limning*, ed. T.G.S. Cain and R.K.R. Thornton [Ashington, 1992], 44):

[Limning] excelleth all other painting whatsoever, in sundry points, in giving the true lustre to pearl and precious stone, and worketh the metals gold or silver with themselves which so enricheth and innobleth the work that it seemeth to be the thing itself, even the work of God and not of man.

On Hilliard's innovative techniques to depict precious metals, pearls and stones, see Fumerton, "'Secret' Arts," 67.

8 *youre*] Hilliard's.

8 An allusion to the Renaissance notion of the mimetic relationship between art and nature: Hilliard's skill with precious materials yields a work of art that rivals nature. The competition between art and nature as responsible for the lady's beauty is also seen in the beginning of Spenser, *Amoretti* 21: "Was it the worke of Nature or of Art? / Which tempred so the feature of her face?" (1–2).

10 *my Ladie*] Lady Rich.

11 *often sprinckling*] An indication that the lady may have sat for Hilliard more than once, and that the portraits were miniature portraits.

11 *black sparckling eyes*] Cf. Watson, *Hekatompathia* 7.3: "Her sparkling eies in heav'n a place deserve." Penelope's famous black eyes are eternized in Sidney, *A&S* 7, which also bears a painting allusion:

> When Nature made her chief work, Stella's eyes,
> In colour black why wrapped she beams so bright?
> Would she in beamy black, like painter wise,
> Frame daintiest lustre, mixed of shades and light? (1–4)

12 The line is incomplete with no signs of erasure. Park, *THM* (509) supplies "art you gave" to finish the line; Gray (lx) suggests "form you gave." Their emendations are conjectural; the idea must be that painting Lady Rich's jewellike eyes has boosted Hilliard's skill in depicting precious gems and pearls.

14 *rich*] A pun on Penelope's married name, which at the same time serves to praise the lifelike quality of Hilliard's "stones and pearles" and the beauty of the sitter. Similar wordplay is found in [35], [36], and [45].

[44] *Now, now I love indeed and suffer more*

This sonnet, which survives only in *T*, offers evidence that this manuscript contains a later sequence and that Constable wrote to more than one mistress, in that the poet compares his new, passionate love to a former one that caused him considerably less suffering.

4 Love's arrows had not truly wounded him before but they have now. Cf. Barnes, P&P 40.14–15, in which the poet describes the moment when he was wounded by Love: "And with thine ever-wounding golden arrow, / First pricked my soul, then pierced my body's marrow!"

6–7 *how ... oute?*] Tears and blood are equated as the poet being internally wounded by love results in visible weeping. Early modern assumptions about the body, perceived as leaky and excreting moisture, must be borne in mind. Prins translates some lines from Ficino's commentary on *Timaeus* explaining that sweat and tears were a means for the body to purify itself of an excess of phlegm (see Jacomien Prins, "The Music of the Pulse in Marsilio Ficino's *Timaeus* Commentary," in *Blood, Sweat, and Tears: The Changing Concepts of Physiology from Antiquity into Early Modern Europe*, ed. Manfred Hortsmanshoff et al. [Leiden, 2012], 393–413, at 406).

8 *smoke*] The lover's sighs.

9–11 Green wood is moist and must be dried before it can burn into a bright fire. Borrowing from Italian sources, the poet in Scève, *Délie* 334, compares himself to green wood in that he is made to burn, cry, and complain, much like green wood releases moisture while drying up and burning. In Ronsard, *Helene* 2.1.5–6, green wood is said to burn with more difficulty than dry (see Pierre de Ronsard, *The Labyrinth of Love*, trans. Henry Weinfield [Anderson, SC, 2021], 142). See also Churchyard's "Of a disdainfull persone" (Thomas Churchyard, *A pleasaunte laborinth called Churchyardes chance* [London, 1580], fol. 25v): "The greene wood smoks, awaie with sweate: / And warms them not, that laies it on" (15–16). The idea that the lover only feels passionate love later in life is found in Spenser, *Amoretti* 6.5–8:

> The durefull Oake, whose sap is not yet dride,
> is long ere it conceive the kindling fyre:
> but when it once doth burne, it doth divide
> great heat, and makes his flames to heaven aspire

A similar idea appears in book 2 of Philip Sidney's *Old Arcadia*, with Basilius defending his old-age passion (ed. Robertson, 95): "Old wood inflamed doth yield the bravest fire, / When younger doth in smoke his virtue spend" (3–4).

12 *it*] The poet's heart, described as made of dry wood and therefore easy to kindle.

[45] *Wonder it is and pitie tis that she*

This sonnet and [46], which survive in the Y-derived witnesses and T, form a narrative unit built on the same anacreontic conceit, Cupid as a beggar boy hoping for the lady's charity. Their connection is reinforced by their arrangement in the manuscripts: [45] and [46] are correlative in *T*, *H*, and *D94*, which means that they were together in the lost archetypes.

    **2–3** These lines echo sonnet [35].5: "No treasure, they would say, is rich but she." The pun on Penelope Rich's name indicates that she is the addressee of [45] and [46].

    **5** Constable adds a twist to the anacreontic conceit of Cupid looking for shelter and begging the poet-lover to let him in. Cf. *Anacreontea* 33 (see *Elegy and Iambus, Being the Remains of All the Greek Elegiac and Iambic Poets from Callinus to Crates*, ed. John M. Edmonds [London, 1931], 2: 63):

> Says Love, ('twas he) "Pray let
> Me in, nor send his ways
> A babe forlorn that strays
> This night so dark and wet."

This scene was rendered in English, for instance in a poem within Robert Greene's *Orpharion* (London, 1599), 45:

> Cupid abroade was lated in the night,
> his winges were wet with ranging in the raine,
> Harbour he sought, to mee hee tooke his flight,
> to dry his plumes I heard the boy complaine.
> I opte the doore, and graunted his desire

Cf. also Sidney, *A&S* 65, "Love, by sure proof I may call thee unkind."

    **6** This line is metrically faulty in *H* due to the omission of "that."

    **7** *I*] The use of the first-person pronoun is unique to *T*; "he" would be consistent with the third-person references to Love, but "I" is not necessarily an error.

    **8** For the idea of beauty being Cupid's food, cf. Desportes, *Diane* 1: 37. One of George Buchanan's epigrams, entitled "Amor," renders similar questions in Latin (see *Georgii Buchanani Scoti poemata* [London, 1716], 432): "Quae nutrix? Primo flore juventa decens. / Quo nutrit victu? Illecebris, vultuque venusto."

    **9** *yonge orphans*] Although the other witnesses agree on the variant "poor orphans," none seems preferable because both are consistent with the image of love as a beggar boy.

    **14** *more heate*] The heat linked to the fire of love.

[46] *Pittye refusing my poore love to feed*

See notes to [45], to which this sonnet is thematically linked. Following on the anacreontic conceit of Cupid (Love) as a beggar boy, the poet now asks for a kiss from the lady's lips.

**1** A reference to lines 6–7 in [45], in which love is shown no pity and thus has to feed on beauty only.

**3** *mouth ... beautie*] This line is echoed in Griffin, *Fidessa* 9: the poet says that his love, heart, hope, and constancy "all lye crying at the doore of Beautie" (6). In Sidney, *A&S* 9.5–6, Stella's mouth is also metaphorically referred to as a door: "The door, by which sometimes comes forth her grace, / Red porphyr is ... ."

**3–4** On the lady's refusal to grant her favour as an act of charity, cf. Sidney, *A&S* 47.7–8: "... though daily help I crave, / May get no alms, but scorn of beggary?"

**4** This line is metrically sound only if the omission of "thence," shared by the other witnesses, is a scribal error.

**6** *cherrie-tree*] The lady's lips. Cf. Campion's song "There is a garden in her face," in which the lady's face is described as a garden and her lips as cherries that may not be touched without her permission (see Thomas Campion, *The third and fourth booke of ayres* [London, 1617], sig. H2r): "There Cherries grow which none may buy, / Till Cherry ripe themselves doe cry" (5–6). See also Sidney, *A&S* 82.5–8:

> Sweet garden nymph, which keeps the cherry tree,
> Whose fruit doth far th'Hesperian taste surpass;
> Most sweet-fair, most fair-sweet, do not, alas,
> From coming near those cherries banish me.

**7–8** These lines are spoken by the poet's personified love (Cupid).

**8** *need*] The *T* reading, "meed," is an obvious scribal error.

**8** The word order in *T* and that shared by the other sources seem equally sound.

**9** *But ... eate?*] Presumably the lady's reply.

**10** *a goddesse son*] Cupid is the son of Venus.

**12** *need ... pine*] "Pine" is here used in the sense of "starve," but it plays on another meaning, "to suffer" (*OED* v.2): Cupid starves and the poet suffers.

**13** *the sweet ... tree*] A kiss. Cf. Desportes, *Diverses amours* 4.1–2.

**14** *give food*] Cf. Sidney, *A&S* 71, in which the poet attempts to rise from contemplation of Stella's beauty to virtue Neoplatonically but in the last line fails to leave earthly desire behind: "But ah, desire still cries: 'Give me some food.'"

[47] *If that one care had oure two hearts possest*

This sonnet survives only in *T*.
    **1** *that one care*] The poet's lovesickness.
    **2** The line is too short, and one word is missing after "once." Editors after Park, *THM* (511), supply the verb "felt," but their emendation is conjectural because the erased word is illegible.
    **4** *rigor*] Severity, in the sense of Desportes's "rigueur"; cf. for instance *Diane* 2: 69.
    **5–8** Constable may have had in mind Sidney, *A&S* 87, in which Astrophil and Stella part; she is said to cry and sympathise with his suffering:

> Alas, I found that she with me did smart,
> I saw that tears did in her eyes appear;
> I saw that sighs her sweetest lips did part,
> And her sad words my sadded sense did hear. (5–8)

In contrast, the addressee in Constable's sonnet remains unmoved, and her sympathy is imagined through an enumeration of physical symptoms.
    **8** *thy heart ... breast*] Love was often depicted as an exchanging or sharing of hearts; here some kind of union could occur if the lady empathized with the lover.
    **9** *other cares*] The lady's unidentified troubles; what causes her grief.
    **12** The poet plays upon the convention of the lover wounded by the lady's beauty or Cupid's darts and steers away from it to present a lover wounded by the lady's own suffering instead.
    **12–14** These lines recall the famous sonnet in book 3 of Sidney's *Old Arcadia* (ed. Robertson, 190), "My true love hath my heart, and I have his," and the identical rhyme can hardly be coincidental: "My heart was wounded, with his wounded heart, / From as from me on him his hurt did light, / So still methought in me his hurt did smart" (10–12). Other contemporary sonnets contain an appeal for the lady's pity. Cf. Daniel, *Delia* 10.14: "And let her pitty if she cannot love me," or Astrophil's impassioned plea in the last line of Sidney, *A&S* 45: "I am not I, pity the tale of me." See also *A&S* 44.3–5: "Such smart may pity claim of any hart; / Her heart (sweet heart) is of no tiger's kind: / And yet she hears, yet I no pity find."

[48] *Uncivill sicknesse, hast thow no regard*

The position of this sonnet in *T*, following a complaint on the lady's melancholy, number [47], makes sense in that both sonnets are about the lover's willingness to share her psychological or physical suffering. The lady's sickness is a common conceit in Italian, French, and English poetry. One of the closest parallels is Thomas Lodge, *Phillis* (London, 1593), 7.3–4: "Ambitious sicknes, what doth thee so harden, / Oh spare and plague thou me for hir offences." The poet in Desportes, *Cleonice*, "Stances," goes further and asks for his lady's life to be prolonged by having days deducted from his own (see Desportes, *Œuvres*, 208).

3–4 *in that ... dar'd*] For the idea that love touches parts of the lady's body freely but does not dare enter her heart, cf. *TF* 22.13–14: "... t'everie part, / Had free accesse but durst not touch her hart."

6 Although he suffers, sickness is too cruel a means of vengeance, so he does not wish it upon the lady.

8 *thoughts*] This reading seems preferable to the variant "wrongs" shared by the other witnesses, which must be an error of repetition. The personification of the poet's thoughts makes more sense.

11 *suffer payne*] Emotional and physical suffering are equated here.

13 *rewarded*] The variant "revenged" in *H*, *D92*, and *D94* seems inconsistent with "crave rewarde" in line 8.

14 *more*] *D94* reads "poore," a unique error which destroys the emphasis on adding to the poet's already grievous suffering.

[49] *Deare, though from me youre gratiouse lookes depart*

This sonnet is unique to *T* and has a remarkably personal tone through references to the lady's inconstancy and her love interest.

1 *gratiouse lookes*] Probably a pun on Grace, the name of Constable's later mistress, as in sonnets [1] and [63].

2–3 *that comfort ... receave*] Her company, which he deserved and enjoyed.

4 According to the widespread "cruel fair" motif, the lady delights in the lover's suffering. Cf. Drayton, *Ideas mirrour* 40.1–2: "O thou unkindest fayre, most fayrest shee, / In thine eyes tryumph murthering my poore hart."

5 *they ... heart*] The lady's current lover.

9–11 According to rural wisdom, birds sing when there is bad weather but it is about to change for the better, but not when the opposite is true.

12–14 He who enjoys the lady's company is compared to a bird that remains silent in good weather, fearful that his luck will end. The poet, in contrast, is hopeful and continues to sing despite his sorrow.

[50] *If ever any justlye might complayne*

This sonnet follows on from the disenchantment of [49] but paints a picture of continued loyalty in the face of adversity. Departing from the traditional conceit of the lady as the tyrant or torturer and the lover as the patient martyr, steadfastness under duress is emphasised. This choice of imagery has heavy Catholic undertones.

Cf. Drayton, *Ideas mirrour* 15, which offers a more conventional reversal of the conceit, envisioning the lady as imprisoned in his heart and unsettlingly leading to her metaphorical execution:

> My hart shall be the prison for my fayre,
> Ile fetter her in chaines of purest love,
> ...................................
> Ile binde her then with my torne-tressed haire,
> And racke her with a thousand holy wishes,
> Then on a place prepared for her there,
> Ile execute her with a thousand kisses. (5–6, 13–16)

3 *Change*] The poetic mistress is portrayed as fickle. Cf. [49].8: "Which like unto the weather changing art."

9–11 Those imprisoned for religious reasons were expected to renounce their faith and thus "wrong" God's name; comparing himself to a tortured man, the poet refuses to turn on the lady. These lines evoke both the Petrarchan idea of the religion of love and the state punishment given to Catholics under the rule of Elizabeth I. In his 1591 *De sanctorum martyrum cruciatibus*, Antonio Gallonio identifies the rack as a form of torture employed by "the Heretics of this present time in England" in order to "harass withal the Catholics they have cast into prison" and describes it as "a sort of torture wherein, after first stretching a man out on his back and binding his hands and feet joint by joint, they do little by little draw taut the ropes wherewith he is bound by certain wheels contrived to this end, till all his limbs be dislocated" (see Antonio Gallonio, *Tortures and Torments of the Christian Martyrs*, trans. Alfred R. Allinson [London, 1903], 69–70).

11 *be rackt*] Previous editors have inserted "were" or "be" before "rackt." An intransitive form of "rack" existed (see *OED* v.¹ 1.b) but the metre of the line is irregular in *T*. "Be" is supplied here because the error was probably caused by eyeskip: "he" and "be," which must have been contiguous in the copy text, would have looked very similar, and the scribe omitted the latter.

14 *dye*] The *T* reading "denye" has been amended; it must be a scribal error due to the similarity in spelling, the scribe's misinterpretation of the sense of the

sonnet – aggravated by the fact that this word appears in line 6 – or both. "Denye" destroys the meaning of the sonnet, since the point is that the poet refuses to retract his praise of the lady.

[51] *Sweete soule, which now with heavenly songs dost tell*

This sonnet is dedicated to Vittoria Colonna in *T* but is the second of "Foure Sonnets written by Henrie Constable to Sir Phillip Sidneys soule" prefacing the 1595 edition of Sidney's *An Apologie for Poetrie*. James Roberts was the editor both of this work and of *D94* and must have had access to a copy of the Z archetype of Constable's sonnets, $Z_1$. Roberts saw the connection between this sonnet and [52] and printed them on the same page of *AP*, even though the emphasis on the divine nature of the poet's works is much greater in the sonnet to Colonna and Sidney could hardly have been identified as an author of religious poetry by the general reading public at the time.

*Marquesse of Piscats*] Vittoria Colonna, marchesana di Pescara (1490–1547), an Italian noblewoman and writer. See sonnet [33].

*endued ... testefie*] Colonna was celebrated as the prominent female cultural icon of her age, especially after the first print publication of her *Rime* in 1538. Much of her poetry was written after the death of her husband, and her works turned increasingly spiritual in nature. Her reputation was sanctioned by her high social status, her development of existent literary models, and the traditionally female virtues – chastity and decorum – she exemplified (see Virginia Cox, "Women Writers and the Canon in Sixteenth-Century Italy: The Case of Vittoria Colonna," in *Strong Voices, Weak History: Early Women Writers and Canons in England, France, and Italy*, ed. Pamela J. Benson and Victoria Kirkham [Ann Arbor, 2005], 14–31). Colonna is also considered a supporter of religious reformation in Italy. Constable must have encountered and read her poetry in the original Italian.

1–4 Cf. sonnet [52].1–4. Both Colonna and Sidney are envisioned in heaven, singing songs in praise of God.

3 *thy skilfull Muse*] Her literary talent, particularly as a lyrical poet.

5–8 The emphasis shifts to Colonna's talent for religious poetry as manifested during her lifetime.

6 *fayre ... rayes*] A conventional allusion to the lady's beauty, also possibly encompassing her moral virtues. The line is too short in *T* due to scribal omission of a foot, so the *AP* variant is probably correct.

12 Praise for Colonna should be universal among poets, as indeed it was:

Michelangelo, Bembo, and Tasso were some of the poet-friends or admirers who wrote to her.

**13–14** These lines point to Constable's purported reason for writing in Colonna's memory: the effect on literary reputation goes both ways; her name endures as she is mentioned in other poets' works, and at the same time mentions of her give prestige and, potentially, fame to other poets.

### [52] *Give pardon, blessed soule, to my bold cryes*

This is the first of the three sonnets in memory of Sir Philip Sidney (1554–1586) preserved in *T*, and it also opens the prefatory matter to *AP* (see notes to [51]). Sidney died from a battle wound in the Low Countries on 17 October 1586, and his death triggered the publication of volumes of elegies at Cambridge and Oxford, and numerous dedications by individual friends and authors.

Among Constable's sonnets to Sidney, this is probably the least conventional and most personal in tone, in that it hints at their acquaintance: the poet apologizes for not mourning his death or writing to him before and expresses feelings of shock and grief. It is perhaps closest to some sections in "Amoris lachrymae," the elegy written by Nicholas Breton and published in the miscellany *Brittons bowre of delights* (London, 1591), sigs. A1r–B2v. Both seem to share what Falco has termed, when commenting on Breton's poem, a "grandiose evocation of the speaker's predicament" (see Raphael Falco, *Conceived Presences: Literary Genealogy in Renaissance England* [Amherst, 1994], 82).

**1** *blessed soule*] Sidney, addressed as a disembodied entity after his death.

**2** *importune*] The *T* reading, an adjective, seems preferable to the past tense verb in *AP*, "importund," which could be an error. This word must be qualifying "cryes" (1).

**3** *thow*] The repetition of "now" in *T* is an obvious scribal slip.

**5** *deare*] *AP* has the variant "sweet," and both seem equally appropriate.

**5** *slow cryes*] There is an error of repetition in *T* ("bold cryes"), so the *AP* reading, "slow cries," seems preferable. Grundy (167) borrows Gray's emendation "slow eyes" (lxxviii), which seems semantically coherent with "saw" (line 6) and the image of tears (7–8), but has no textual basis.

**6–8** Constable and Sidney were both in the Low Countries and may have met at some point before the knight's demise, but the reference here is probably to having seen Sidney's dead body and not having mourned him overtly.

**7–8** The use of "sacrifice" has religious connotations: the poet's tears are imagined as an offering in a transaction with a divine agent, a canonized Sidney.

9-10 These lines have greatly confused commentators, who tend to date the sonnet between Sidney's death and his London funeral in February 1587. John finds it "strange" that Constable did not know of Sidney's death (Lisle Cecil John, *The Elizabethan Sonnet Sequences: Studies in Conventional Conceits* [New York, 1966], 215-216). Grundy supposes that Constable could have been abroad at the time (242). However, considering the universal mourning elicited by Sidney's death and Constable's connections to the Walsingham-Leicester circle, this seems implausible. I interpret "know" in the archaic sense of "acknowledge" (*OED* v. 4.a) because the emphasis here is on the poet's public display of emotion or response in writing and this does not contradict the statement that he did in fact "sustayne" private grief (line 10). The marked shift from Sidney's eternal glory in heaven towards the speaker's own sorrow is accentuated and resembles Breton's in "Amoris lachrymae":

> I live, oh live, alas, I live indeede,
> But such a life was never such a death.
> While fainting heart is but constrainde to feede,
> Upon the care of a consuming breath:
> O my sweete Muse, that knowest howe I am vexed,
> Paint but one passion how I am perplexed. (139-144)

11 This sentence evokes Seneca's *Phaedra* 607: "Curae leves loquuntur, ingentes stupent" (light griefs speak, huge griefs are silent); see Lucius Annaeus Seneca, *Phaedra*, ed. Michael Coffey (Cambridge, 1990), 66.

11-12 The poet claims that he was struck dumb by Sidney's death and it was shock that prevented him from reacting and numbed his pain.

13-14 His excuse for his belatedness in mourning Sidney – and lack of writing in his praise – is far from unique and may be understood as an attempt to time his endeavours to please potential patrons from the Sidney-Essex circle. Falco notes that authors were forced to provide similar excuses because their delays in paying homage to Sidney "seem to have stirred a fair amount of contemporary comment" (*Conceived Presences*, 73 n37). Edmund Spenser's nine-year delay before his publication of *Astrophel* (1595) is well-known (see Duncan-Jones, "Astrophel," 75). George Whetstone fends off accusations made by friends and justifies his delay in writing in Sidney's memory: "Through zeale proceeded my slowness in writing, which cannot come too late, when good Sir Phillip Sidney liveth ever" (see Whetstone, *Sir Phillip Sidney*, sig. A4v). Another acquaintance, Thomas Moffet, admits that he had been "ashamed ... to have been seen tearless" at the time when everyone else was crying; he adds that Sidney's closest associates delayed the publication of "their expressions of sorrow" for fear that they might "wound rather than honor him" (see Thomas Moffet, *Nobilis: Or a View of the Life and Death of a Sidney and Lessus lugubris*, ed. Virgil B. Hetzel and Hoyt H. Hudson [San Marino, 1940], 69–70). Immense private grief is mentioned as the reason for the Oxford collection of elegies appearing one year after his death. See William Gager's address to Leicester in his *Exequiae illustrissimi equitis, D. Philippi Sidnaei* [Oxford, 1587], 2; see also G.W. Pigman, *Grief and English Renaissance Elegy* [Cambridge, 1985], 57).

**14** Cf. the last line in an acrostic poem printed in *Brittons bowre of delights* (sig. D2v): "Yet let me weepe when all the world is done." Considering that Constable's sonnet would have been circulating before its inclusion in Z, from which T derives, it is hard to say whose borrowing this is.


[53] *Great Alexander then did well declare*

This is the second of the three sonnets in memory of Sir Philip Sidney in *T*; see notes to [52]. It is the last in *AP*, and the only one included in *E*. The text is remarkably stable, as collation shows.

**1** *Great Alexander*] Alexander the Great (356–323 BC), the Macedonian ruler who became a legendary hero. Both Alexander and Sir Philip died at the age of thirty-two, and they are sometimes compared in contemporary elegies on Sidney. Cf. the beginning of George Whetstone's "Of the life, death, and Noble vertues of the most Adventurous Knight Sir Phillip Sydney" in Whetstone, *Sir Phillip Sidney*, sig. B1r:

> Alexander the chiefe of Royall Peeres,
> (Who won one World, and wisht another rise.
> That he too worlds, or one might conquer twise)
> In prime of youth, in Envies bane did light:
> Yet lives through fame, in spight of every spight. (3–7)

**2** *his united kingdomes*] Alexander's empire, which had territories stretching across three continents.

**3–4** Alexander's generals and friends, the Diadochi, fought for the control of his empire after his death, and there eventually emerged four large separate kingdoms: Macedon, Egypt, Syria, and Anatolia. One of Alexander's associates, alluding to the immense power bestowed on his generals, complained, "O, King ... now thou hast made many Alexanders" (see Plutarch, *Life of Alexander*, in *Lives*, trans. Perrin, 7: 343).

**6** *knight*] The poet's concern with rank, apparent throughout the sequence, helps strengthen the connection with past military leaders.

**7** *no mortall wight*] Parker (155) draws a connection between this line and Sidney, *A&S* 97, in which Diana's allies, the stars, shoot arrows of chastity: "... those starry nymphs, whose chase / From heavenly standing hits each mortal wight" (3–4).

**7–8** Alexander is admired for his martial skills, which Sidney shares, but in Sidney's case they are not even his most outstanding virtues. With this statement, the poet detracts from the tradition that immediately enshrined Sidney as a militant Protestant leader and aligns himself with the admirers who exalted him as a humanist, a writer, and a patron of learning.

**9** *of Macedon ... king*] Antigonus I (382–301 BC) became king of Macedon in 306 BC.

**10** *sate ... throne*] Ptolemy I (ca. 367–ca. 283 BC) became satrap of Egypt after Alexander's death, and pharaoh around 305 BC.

**12** *courteouse*] Many authors emphasise the qualities that made Sidney a courtier in the manner described in Castiglione's *Book of the Courtier*. Cf. Nicholas Breton's description in "Amoris lachrymae" (Breton, *Brittons bowre*, sig. A1v):

> Comely of shape, and of a manly face,
> Noble in birth, and of a princely minde,
> Kinde in effect and of a courtly grace.
> Courteous to all, and carefull of the kinde:
> Valure and Vertue, Learning, Bountie, Love,
> These were the parts that did his honour prove. (49–54)

**12** *liberall*] Sidney's generosity and, in particular, his patronage of the arts, was often recalled, especially in the hope that potential patrons would follow his example. In his dedication to the earl of Essex, Phillips describes Sidney as generous and kind (John Phillips, *The life and death of Sir Phillip Sidney* [London, 1587], 2):

> This most worthy Knight ... so behaved himself that for the exercise of perfect pietie, he was honoured and highly esteemed of all men, to the poore he was mercifull, to the learned liberall, to Sutors a great comfort, to the fatherlesse favourable, to the widdowes, helpfull, and to saye the truth, his hande, his heart, and purse, was always ready to support the distressed ... .

**13** Other fellow writers enumerated Sidney's virtues in the same vein. In an elegy printed in the miscellany *The phoenix nest*, he is described as "A spotlesse friend, a matchles man, whose vertue ever shinde, / Declaring in his thoughts, his life, and that he writ, / Highest conceits, longest foresights, and deepest works of wit" (14–16) (see *The phoenix nest* [London, 1593], sig. C2r).

**14** This line illustrates what Baker-Smith has called Sidney's "Scipionic resolution of conflicting talents," which is the "dominant" theme in the elegies (see Dominic Baker-Smith, "'Great Expectation': Sidney's Death and the Poets," in *Sir Philip Sidney: 1586 and the Creation of a Legend*, ed. Dominic Baker-Smith et al. [Leiden, 1986], 83–103, at 97).

## [54] *Even as when great mens heyres cannot agree*

This is the fourth and last alexandrine sonnet in the sequence. It concludes the triad dedicated to Sir Philip Sidney in *T* and it comes third in *AP*; see notes to [52]. The poet presents a metaphorical dispute between Sidney's personified virtues, all of which claim the deceased knight for themselves; there is an emphasis on universal collective mourning and Sidney's everlasting fame.

**1–6** These lines have been read as evidence that "poets could not agree on what Sidney represented" (see Gavin Alexander, *Writing after Sidney: The Literary Response to Sir Philip Sidney, 1586–1640* [Oxford, 2006], 193). Other poems honouring Sidney display the same anxiety and a similar "partition" conceit. Sometimes it is the Greek gods and muses that fight over him, as in a sonnet by Sir Arthur Gorges (*Poems*, 118):

> Mars and the Muses weare att mortall stryfe
> which of them had in Sydney grettest parte
> the one layde clayme unto his valyaunt harte
> The other to his mynde in knowledge ryfe (1–4)

The balance between martial and literary skills is emphasised in Whetstone, *Sir Phillip Sidney*, sig. B1v: "About his Healme, a Lawrell wreath is brayde, / And by his Swoord a Silver penne is layd, / And either saide, that he their glory was" (32–34). Different nations and heaven itself enter the dispute in Sidney's epitaph, and the metaphorical dismemberment renders him a universal figure (see John Eliot, *Ortho-epia Gallica* [London, 1593], 163):

> England, Netherland, the Heavens, and the Arts,
> The Souldiors, and the World, have made six parts
> Of the noble Sydney: for none will suppose,
> That a small heape of stones can Sydney enclose.

His body hath England, for she it bred,
Netherland his blood, in her defence shed:
The Heavens have his soule, the Arts have his fame,
All Souldiors the greefe, the World his good name.

**2** *part of thee*] This line is one foot too short in *T*, probably due to a scribal omission. The *AP* reading must be correct.

**2** Cf. Sidney, *A&S* 52, in which Stella is the object of a similar dispute: "A strife is grown between virtue and love, / While each pretends that Stella must be his" (1–2).

**5** *Invention*] The implication is that Constable was familiar with Sidney's literary production, unlike others who praised Sidney shortly after his death (see William A. Ringler, "The Myth and the Man," in *Sir Philip Sidney: 1586 and the Creation of a Legend*, ed. Dominic Baker-Smith et al. [Leiden, 1986], 3–15, at 11). "Invention" was associated with poetry – see for instance Sidney, *A&S* 1 – which hints at Constable's having read Sidney's sonnets as they circulated in manuscript before their publication. He went to great lengths to present himself as an insider of the Sidney circle.

**8** The focus shifts to Sidney's friends and mourners, who are deprived of him. In his translation of Guillaume de Saluste Du Bartas's "Babylone," Joshua Sylvester inserts a reference to "World-mourn'd Sidney" (*Bartas: His devine weekes and workes translated*, trans. Joshua Sylvester [London, 1605], 433). Whetstone rightly prophesied, "His losse will make his goodnes best knowne" (*Sir Phillip Sidney*, sig. A3v). Buxton mentions "the unparalleled magnificence of his funeral in St. Paul's" and "the endless lamentation for him throughout the civilized word" (John Buxton, *Sir Philip Sidney and the English Renaissance* [Basingstoke, 1987], 171).

**10** *thy soule gaineth*] Because Sidney's soul is immortal and has gone to heaven.

**11** *two lives*] Eternal life and fame. Cf. the last line in "The Life, Death, and Funerals, of Sir Philip Sidney knight" (John Phillips, *Life and death of Sidney*, n.p.): "My bodie earth, my soule the heavens hath wonne."

**14** These are the "two lives" mentioned in line 11. Day concludes his elegy by alluding to Sidney's immortal life and everlasting fame as well, although he makes explicit mention of his patronage (Angel Day, *Upon the life and death of the most worthy, and thrise renowmed knight, Sir Phillip Sidney* [London, 1586?], sig. B2v):

Can Sidneis name whose soule doth live in blisse,
Obscured lie. Whose bountie so did binde,

The heartes of all, to whom he was so kinde.
Nay Fame gainsaies (who rightly guerdons all)
That ere his deedes from minde of man should fall.

[55] *He that by skill of stars doth fates foretell*

This sonnet is linked with that on the birth of Penelope Rich's daughter; however, whereas [42] circulated extensively from 1588, this is preserved only in T. It offers an awkward explanation for the baby's demise despite the poet's own prophecy that she would grow to be beautiful like her mother.

*death ... daughter*] Robert and Penelope Rich's daughter Elizabeth was christened on 26 November 1588, with Queen Elizabeth, represented by one of her ladies, standing godmother. She must have died shortly after. See Sally Varlow, *The Lady Penelope: The Lost Tale of Love and Politics in the Court of Elizabeth I* (London, 2007), 107. Considering that Penelope had a total of nine children who survived infancy, four by Lord Rich and five by Charles Blount, Constable made an infelicitous choice of dedicatee.

*the former ... nativitye*] See sonnet [42].

1 *skill of stars*] A reference to astrology but also possibly a pun on Penelope's literary name, Stella. In Sidney, *A&S* 73.5, Astrophil calls her "my Star."

1–4 The poet's self-representation as a prophet is rooted in a tradition going back to the Augustan age, in which the word *vates*, which originally meant "soothsayer," was extended to include "poet." If his reasoning is sound, the poet argues, a prognostication is well-made even though bad luck causes events to take a turn for the worse.

5 *Phoenix*] A mythical bird that burnt itself and was reborn out of the ashes. See notes to sonnet [5].

7–8 According to literary tradition, there can only be one Phoenix alive at any given time. Cf. Drayton, *Ideas mirrour* 6.1, "In one whole world is but one Phoenix found." The same idea was later employed by Allyne in a poem to Prince Charles (Robert Allyne, *Funerall elegies upon ... Prince Henry* [London, 1613], sig. B3v). The poet argues that only one brother could survive; thus Prince Henry, the eldest, sacrificed himself for Charles's sake:

Admired Phoenix, springing up apace,
From th'ashes of another Phoenix bones,
Which (too too courteous) yeelded thee his place,
Least earth were burden'd with two birds at once

9–12 Blinded Death is assimilated to Cupid, who is also represented as blindfold, and shoots arrows. The imagery comes from Alciato's emblem "De morte et amore," bearing a story about Cupid and Death travelling together and mistakenly swapping arrows, which results in them shooting the wrong victim (see Andrea Alciato, *Emblematum liber* [Augsburg, 1531], sigs. D3v–D4r). In Thomas Wyatt's sonnet "The enemy of life, decayer of all kind," the poet recounts how death shoots at him and causes Cupid's original dart to go deeper into his heart (see Wyatt, *Collected Poems*, 54).

14 *good ill hap*] Because misfortune has enabled Penelope's survival.

[56] *Much sorrowe in it selfe my love doth move*

This sonnet, which survives in multiple sources, is a conventional love complaint.

3 *where*] The *T* reading is syntactically more coherent with the intended meaning of "misse" than the variant "whom."

4 *this last griefe*] His "follie," i.e, his unrequited love (3).

5 For the paradoxical connection between joy and pain, cf. Sidney, *A&S* 57.14, in which Astrophil says that Stella "so sweets my pains, that my pains me rejoice."

7–8 These lines are imagined as spoken by his lady. Petrarchan mistresses in English poetry are often described as smiling at the lover's suffering; see for instance sonnet 3 in William Percy's *Sonnets to the fairest Coelia* ([London, 1594], sig. A4r): "Ay me, ah no, teares, words, throbs all in vaine, / She scornes my dole, and smileth at my paine" (13–14).

13 In *T* the possessives "my" and "youre" are switched and must be considered errors because they contradict the meaning constructed throughout the sonnet: it is the lady's will, and not the poet's folly, that is to blame for his hopeless love. The readings in *H*, *D92*, and *D94* are correct.

14 Cf. Petrarch, *Rime* 224.14: "vostro, Donna, 'l peccato et mio fia 'l danno." This line was frequently adapted by English sonneteers; cf. Thomas Wyatt's "How oft have I, my dear and cruel foe" (Wyatt, *Collected Poems*, 28): "So shall it be great hurt unto us twain, / And yours the loss, and mine the deadly pain" (13–14). Daniel, *Delia* 15.14 provides a closer parallel: "The fault is hers, though mine the hurt must bee."

## [57] *Needs I must leave and yet needs must I love*

This sonnet survives only in *T* and *D94*, which means it is a later work. The variant readings in both texts indicate that they derive from different copies of the lost archetype Z. The content of the sonnet, with its pledge of eternal love, points at the poet's departure, perhaps his imminent exile. Cf. Sidney, *A&S* song 11, which presents the theme of absence and the impossibility of forgetting in a similar light:

> 'Well, in absence this will die:
> Leave to see, and leave to wonder.'
> Absence sure will help, if I
> Can learn, how myself to sunder
> From what in my heart doth lie. (11–15)

**2** *paynt ... woe*] An allusion to his hopeless writing of poetry. The *T* reading "paynt" seems preferable to the *D94* variant "tell" because it adds a connotation of falseness that is present in other contemporary works; see for instance Drayton, *Idea* 42.6–7: "They say (as Poets doe) I use to faine, / And in bare words paint out my passions paine." Cf. also Sidney, *A&S* 93.3: "What ink is black enough to paint my woe?"

**6** This whole line is missing in *T* and must be reconstructed using *D94*.

**10** *grace*] Probably a pun on Grace, the name of Constable's later mistress, as in sonnets [1] and [63].

**11** *prayse thee*] The reading "prayse beautie" in *T* is an obvious error of repetition that renders the line meaningless, as both halves of the line would contradict each other.

**12** In Sidney, *A&S* 35.13–14, praise itself is elevated whenever Stella is commended: "Not thou by praise, but praise in thee is raised; / It is a praise to praise, when thou art praised."

## [58] *My reason, absent, did myne eyes require*

This sonnet survives in most witnesses and evidences different stages of revision, especially when contrasting *M* and *T*. It is connected with sonnet [60] in that the poet blames his eyes for his misfortune.

As noted by Scott, *Sonnets* (315), this sonnet could have been inspired by Desportes, *Diane* 2: 47. Sonnets 19 and 20 in *TF* are similar in that the poet's heart and eyes blame each other for his falling in love, although there is no final judgement. See also Barnfield, *Cynthia* 1, which may have been inspired by Constable's sonnet and presents a trial scene in which conscience and reason refuse to condemn the (male) beloved as a thief because he has stolen the poet's heart with the consent of the poet's eyes. Although different in its development, the conceit of a strife between the poet's eyes and heart is found in Shakespeare, *Sonnets* 46, "Mine eye and heart are at a mortal war."

1 *My reason*] The possessive is omitted in *M* and the line is one syllable too short. This was probably a scribal error that is fixed in the other witnesses.

3 *neare ... should*] An alternative word order is shared by the other witnesses against *T*; neither order seems superior.

4–6 The poet's eyes are compared to guards who accept bribery, and stand accused of letting love into his heart. Cf. *TF* 20.5–6: "Hart said that love did enter at the eies, / And from the eies descended to the hart."

5 *hopes guifts*] The unique variant in *M*, "ritch hope," contains a pun on Penelope Rich's name; similar puns are found in [35], [36], and [45], as noted above. Its deletion as the sonnet made it to the next stage of transmission could be due to cautiousness on Constable's part.

7–8 Cf. *TF* 20.9: "Hart said eies tears might soone have quencht that flame." There is a similar image in Craig, *Amorose Songes*, "Idea after long sicknes, becommeth weil," although it is the lady who is asked to quench the poet's fire: "Weepe thou for me, thy teares may quench my fire" (12).

8 *Which ... quencht*] The line is significantly improved in *H*, *D92*, and *D94* compared to *M*. Not only does it avoid the "thoghe" anaphora (7–8), but the meaning is also altered. In *M* the poet states that his eyes could have used the water available (tears) to mitigate the fire of love, although quenching it would have been impossible anyway. In the other witnesses quenching the fire was a possibility, so greater emphasis is placed on his eyes' guilt.

9–10 Cf. Barnfield, *Cynthia* 1.9: "Conscience the Judge, twelve Reasons are the Jurie."

12 *wished*] The unique variant "wicked" in *M* makes no sense and must be a scribal error due to similar spelling.

13–14 In *TF* 19.1–3, the poet's eyes are sentenced to weep: "My Hart impos'd this penance on mine eies, / (Eies the first causers of my harts lamenting): / That they should weepe till love and fancie dies." Constable takes this image further in that weeping entails death by drowning. This line is imitated in Barnfield, *Cynthia* 1.13: "Your Doome is this: in teares still to be drowned."

[59] *Each day new proofes of new dispaire I find*

This is no doubt a later sonnet and survives in *T* and *D94*. It is hopeless, almost despairing in tone, as the poet contemplates going away in order to mitigate his suffering, which is described through images of torture and execution that connect it to sonnet [50]. It may well be read in the context of Constable's conversion, which would endanger his life and made him resort to self-exile.

Although not quite as dark in tone, the image of the melancholy lover as a prisoner pining in the absence of the lady is also found in Spenser, *Amoretti* 52.5–8:

> So doe I now my selfe a prisoner yeeld,
> to sorrow and to solitary paine:
> from presence of my dearest deare exylde
> longwhile alone in languor to remaine.

See also Griffin, *Fidessa* 5 and 6, revolving around the themes of trial and imprisonment.

6 *I*] The variant "it" in *D94* also makes sense in that it refers to "my minde" (5).

7 *which by the judge*] The order is transposed in *D94*, and the awkward result ("the which by judge") may be a compositor's error.

8 *lesse feare*] The variant in *D94*, "more ease," has an uncertain origin but cannot be entirely ruled out as an error because the meaning of the line is similar. Williams argues that the *T* reading is better because "the physical pain of self-blinding could hardly produce 'ease'" (Williams, *Edition*, 2: 117).

9 *in skarlet clad*] Judges wore scarlet gowns.

9–10 Cf. Sidney, *A&S* 73.11, in which Stella's lips are compared to "those scarlet judges, threatening bloody pain."

11 *the hangman ... me*] The image of the cruel hangman may derive from Philippe Desportes's "bourreau cruel," found for instance in Desportes, *Hippolyte*, "Chanson," line 82 (*Œuvres*, 136). Spierenburg discusses the social stigma and horror associated with hangmen: "The hangman's touch was considered as a penalty in itself.... In popular tales this touch emerges as the most dreadful of all for the condemned" (Peter Spierenburg, *The Spectacle of Suffering: Executions and the Evolution of Repression* [Cambridge, 1984], 19).

12–14 As if he were a long-time prisoner, the poet's life is full of so much suffering – a kind of metaphorical death – that actual death seems to be the only possible release. A similar death wish is expressed by other contemporaries; see for instance Watson, *Hekatompathia* 50.11: "O gentle Death let heere my dayes have ende."

EXPLANATORY NOTES • 319

[60] *Myne eye with all the deadlie sinnes is fraught*

This is a sonnet with a fascinating history of transmission that resulted in its inclusion in *M*, *H*, *T*, the printed *Dianas*, and *PR* (see figure 4 on p. 80). The lines listing the deadly sins are numbered in all versions but *M* and *H*. The *M* text is so different that it has not been collated and instead is edited and discussed as [60b].

The sonnet bears a thematic connection with [58] in that the poet continues to blame his eyes for his misfortune, this time describing their misdeeds through an enumeration of the seven deadly sins, which are said to have rightfully incurred the lady-goddess's wrath and led to the lover's damnation. Barnabe Barnes imitates this sonnet in Barnes, *P&P* 97, in which the seven sins are related to an excess of love. An early source for this conceit is the sequence of seven sonnets on individual deadly sins by Italian fourteenth-century poet Fazio degli Uberti (see Giosuè Carducci, ed., *Rime di M. Cino da Pistoia e d'altri del secolo XIV* [Florence, 1862], 308–313).

2 *it ... hye*] Because the lady is a quasi-divine being in the sonnet tradition, whereas the lover is lowly in comparison.

3–4 The metaphor of the eyes as inept watchmen is at the core of the conceit in sonnet [58]. Cf. Desportes, *Cleonice*, "Chanson" (*Œuvres*, 201), in which the poet accuses his eyes of betraying the door to his heart.

7–8 Wrath is not mentioned by name but murder is envisioned as a manifestation of it.

8 *consent gave*] This variant, shared by all the other sources, seems preferable to "was accessarie" in *T*, which seems semantically cohesive with the murder motif but creates a metrically corrupted line.

9–10 The poet in Spenser, *Amoretti* 35, also associates covetousness with the eyes: "My hungry eyes through greedy covetize, / still to behold the object of their paine" (1–2).

10 *gold*] A conventional metaphor for the lady's hair, but an allusion to Penelope Rich may be intended, as in other sonnets in the sequence; see for instance [35] and [36].

11–12 The order of these lines in *T* is the same as in the other manuscripts, *M* and *H*. The inversion in the printed texts, which affects the rhyme pattern, has no authority and can be considered an error; it first occurred in *D92* and is characteristic of that branch of transmission. Williams, *Edition* (2: 118) notes that "building up to unchastity is more dramatic than following an accusation of unchastity with one of gluttony," and I agree that the *T* order has greater authority and seems preferable.

11 *with teares drunke*] In the third dialogue of Petrarch's *Secret*, Augustine

admonishes Francescus for his profane love of Laura and describes the symptoms of love melancholy: "You felt a morbid pleasure in feeding on tears and sighs" (*Petrarch's Secret or the Soul's Conflict with Passion*, ed. William H. Draper [London, 1911], 133).

14 The fire of love is a torment that is nevertheless pleasant and being in love a kind of hell for the damned lover. The omission of "sweet" in *H* detracts from the oxymoron and would render the line too short, but the spelling of "damned" indicates that it was meant to be pronounced as two syllables.

### [60b] *Myne eye with all the deadly sinns is fraught*

This is the text of sonnet [60] as it survives in *M*, descended from the earliest authorial archetype, *X*. Features such as the proliferation of grammatical function words, enjambment, and awkward syntax render it imperfect when compared with later, revised versions. See pp. 78–81 for an account of its transmission as a case study that enables reconstruction of the stemma of Constable's secular sonnets.

10 *ritche treasure*] An allusion to Penelope Rich; similar puns are found in [35], [36], and [45]. Its deletion as the sonnet made it to the next stage of transmission mirrors that in sonnet [58] and could be due to cautiousness on Constable's part.

11–12 The order of the two final sins, gluttony and lust, in *M* must be authorial, as opposed to that in the printed witnesses.

12 *how ... thou art*] the sudden shift to a second-person pronoun creates some confusion, and the line risks being misinterpreted as an accusation against the lady instead of his eyes. Unlike in [60], the accusation of unchastity is not explained.

### [61] *If true love might true loves reward obtayne*

This sonnet develops what Lisle Cecil John has called "the mirror conceit" (John, *Elizabethan Sonnet Sequences*, 124): the poet is aware of the hopelessness of his love, but writes verse only so that the lady can look at herself in it and rejoice in her beauty, to which the lover's suffering and devotion testify. This conceit and the painting image link it to sonnet [4], and both form a thematic cluster in D92.

1 This line translates Petrarch, *Rime* 334.1: "S'onesto amor po meritar mercede."

**4** *lov'd*] All the other witnesses agree on the variant "sigh'd," but the change might be a later revision.

**6** *paint*] The choice of this verb adds a connotation of artificiality. See notes to sonnet [57].

**7–8** Grundy (245) finds a similar rendering of the mirror conceit in Desportes, *Diane* 1: 25. Cf. also the second dedicatory sonnet in Drayton, *Ideas mirrour*, in which his book of verse is referred to as "his mirror of Ideas praise." In the opening sonnet in Barnes, *P&P*, the poet describes his verse as a "true-speaking Glasse" where the lady may behold her "beauties Graces" (1–2). See notes to sonnet [4] for other parallels.

**8** *sight*] D94 bears the unique variant "praise," which destroys semantic cohesion with "glasses" and must have been introduced by the printer.

**12–14** Cf. Barnes, *P&P* 1.9–11: "But in this mirrhor equally compare, / Thy match-lesse beauty, with mine endlesse griefe: / There like thy selfe, none can be found so faire."

**14** This line conveys the imagined words of the lady at the reading of his poetry. It is written in a purer italic script for the sake of emphasis in the manuscript.

## [62] *Sometymes in verse I prays'd, sometymes I sigh'd*

The position, heading, and content of this sonnet mark it as the conclusion to the sequence in *T*, linked with the prose statement immediately below. It is also the final sonnet in *D94*.

**1** *sometymes I*] The D94 variant "somtime in verse I" is either an error of repetition or an attempt to create parallelism, resulting in an overlong line.

**3–4** The poet's resolution to keep his love hidden from the world recalls the argument between Astrophil and his wit in Sidney, *A&S* 34, in which the latter asks: "Art not ashamed to publish thy disease?" (5). Cf. also Lodge, *Phillis* 10.14: "So lovers must keepe secret what they feele."

**4** *unseene … night*] Cf. Barnes, *P&P* 100.3: "Complaining mine hid flames, and secret smartes." Constable makes use of the image of burning to refer to love throughout the sequence; see for instance sonnet [44].3: "Great flames they be which but small sparkles were."

**6** *follies*] This word binds introductory sonnet [1] and the conclusion together; it refers to the poet's past foolishness: his hopeless earthly love and, in particular, his written expression of it. Another meaning of "folly", "lewdness, wantonness" (*OED* n.¹ 3.a), may also be implied.

7 *flame*] *D94* reads "fire," which could be a printer's slip since it is repeated in the next line. "Fire" nevertheless fits the sense.

7–8 *flame ... light*] The Christian tradition associates the torments of hell with flames; that said, hell has also been interpreted to be a dark place based on Job 10:22 and Matthew 8:12.

9 *more paine lesse follie*] The line is too long in *T* ("more follie lesse follie") and its meaning is unclear unless the poet is establishing a contrast between private "follie" (his continuing love) and public "follie" (the act of publicizing it in verse). The reading "more paine more folly" in *D94* makes little sense, too. I agree with Williams, *Edition* (2: 120) that the "correct reading" for this line must be a combination of the *T* reading and the *D94* variant.

10 There are other contemporary poems in which the speaker seeks forgiveness for the follies of his youth; see for instance Hunnis's "A Lamentation touching the follies and vanities of our youth" (in William Hunnis, *Seven sobs of a sorrowfull soule for sinne* [London, 1583], 65), which is set to music: "So Lord with mercie doo forgive, / the follies of my youth" (23–24). Cf. also the last item under the general heading "Poems and sonets of sundrie other Noblemen and Gentlemen" in Newman's pirated edition of Philip Sidney's poetry (*Syr P.S. His Astrophel and Stella*, 80), which begins: "If flouds of teares could clense my follies past, / And smokes of sighs might sacrifice for sin" (1–2).

9–10 These lines, and not the final two, are indented in *T* to signpost the odd position of the couplet. Only one other sonnet, [21], shows this arrangement.

9–14 The different order of these lines in *D94* makes it worthwhile to transcribe them in full:

> For if one never lov'd like mee, then why
> skillesse blames hee the thing hee doth not know?
> and hee that so hath lov'd should favour show,
> for hee hath beene a foole as well as I.
> Thus shall hence-forth more paine more folly have
> And folly past, may justly pardon crave.

The move from the poet's wish for forgiveness to the reason why he may arouse some sympathy in the reader is smoother in *T*. The positioning of the couplet at the end in *D94* creates an awkward transition between lines 12 and 13. The rearrangement must have been the printer's doing, in an attempt to use the couplet as a conclusion and have the sonnet end with the apology.

11 *none ... mee*] This echoes the last line in sonnet [61].

12 *Still*] The strange *D94* variant "skillesse" must be an error.

*When I had ended ...*

This short statement in prose, combined with the introductory "The order of the booke," provides evidence that the arrangement of the sequence in *T* is authorial and was the product of meticulous planning. Constable's renunciation of secular love and love poetry is at the same time self-disparaging and melancholy.

*climatericall number 63*] Sixty-three had numerological significance "as the chief climacteric age, a critical stage of development for body and soul alike" (Alastair Fowler, *Triumphal Forms: Structural Patterns in Elizabethan Poetry* [Cambridge, 1970], 176). It was the product of number seven, symbolizing the body, multiplied by number nine, symbolizing the mind. Fowler notes that it was used by Constable and other contemporaries to organize their verse: in Sidney, *A&S*, there is a long single unit of sixty-three sonnets before the first song; and Drayton, *Idea*, has sixty-three sonnets in the 1619 edition of his *Poems* (Fowler, *Triumphal Forms*, 176). Constable is the only one who explicitly mentions the number's climacteric significance. Two sonnets of the original sequence of 63 are now lost due to a missing leaf; see p. 47.

*employe ... bitter*] He will continue writing, but not amatory verse. In his "Elegie sur les Dernieres Amours de Monsieur Desportes," Bertaut says that the poet recounted "ses douces amertumes" (his sweet bitterness) (Desportes, *Œuvres*, 227). In Watson, *Hekatompathia* 94.17–18, the speaker also renounces earthly love: "And since the heav'ns my freedome nowe restore, / Hence foorth Ile live at ease, and love no more." Cf. Barnes, *Divine Centurie* 1.1: "No more lewde laies of Lighter loves I sing." A similar renunciation is included in Spenser, *FH*, "A Hymne of Heavenly Love":

> Many lewd layes (ah woe is me the more)
> In praise of that mad fit, which fooles call love,
> ............................
> But all those follies now I do reprove,
> And turned have the tenor of my string,
> The heavenly prayses of true love to sing. (8–9, 12–14)

[63] *My Mistrisse worth gave wings unto my Muse*

Although last in the sequence, this sonnet is not its conclusion, but an addendum meant to rededicate the whole collection of verse to Lady Arbella Stuart. It is the third of three sonnets addressed to her; see [33] and [34]. Its appearance in *T* only and the reference to "his Grace" in the heading link it with sonnet [1]. Both must have been added by Constable as he rearranged his verse for circulation or presentation.

*divine protection*] The poet also refers to Arbella's divinity in sonnet [33]. When addressing a potential candidate for the throne, the word acquires a new layer of meaning besides the conventional Petrarchan one and resonates with the belief in the divine right of kings.

*his Graces honoure*] Probably Grace Pierrepont, addressed in sonnet [1] and alluded to through frequent puns on her name.

*his Muses aeternitye*] The everlasting fame of his verse.

1–2 The use of the past tense makes it clear that the sonnets were written before their rearrangement in this sequence and added to the fame of his mistress.

1 *wings*] In sonnet [27], dedicated to King James, the king's muse is also described as winged. Cf. Desportes, *Cleonice* 26.4, in which the poet says he is transported on the wings of his beloved.

5 *this booke ... peruse*] A presentation copy containing this sequence, which either was never produced or has been lost. Book giving was a popular form of social transaction; see Jason Scott-Warren, *Sir John Harington and the Book as Gift* (Oxford, 2001).

6–7 *Abroad ... flight*] Williams, *Edition* (2: 121) notes that this alludes to Constable anticipating "wider readership of this sequence from this point of manuscript publication." Although the sense of the word "abroad" seems to be "in public, so as to be widely known" (*OED* adv. 2), the sense of going out of one's own country (*OED* 4.a) may be implied, given that Constable was in the process of religious conversion and probably contemplating exile at the time. This is consistent with his need for a "protectoure" (8), and with the bird imagery employed by a friend of Constable's in a sonnet "upon occasion of leaving his countrye," which follows the sequence in *T* (fol. 44r): "Englands sweete nightingale, what frights thee so / As over sea to make thee take thy flight?" (1–2). See appendix A and notes.

9 *I ... vow*] He might have sworn allegiance to Arbella, which is surprising in light of his dedications and embassies to King James.

9 *she ... right*] Because Grace and Arbella were first cousins; Arbella was daughter to Elizabeth Cavendish and Grace to Elizabeth's sister Frances.

10 A word seems to be missing in this line, and the metre is irregular. Park, *THM* (517), Hazlitt (46), and Grundy (179) add the conjectural emendation "wing" after "Phoenix." This is also suggested by Gray (lxxxii).

10 *Phoenix*] See notes to sonnet [5]. Aemilia Lanyer uses the same metaphor

in her sonnet "To the Ladie Arabella," which prefaces her 1611 book of poetry (*The Poems of Aemilia Lanyer: Salve Deus Rex Judæorum*, ed. Susanne Woods [New York, 1993], 17): "Rare Phoenix, whose faire feathers are your owne, / With which you flie, and are so much admired" (3–4).

11 *carrion beakes*] The beaks of carrion birds, the poet's enemies who might speak ill of him and his mistress. "Carrion" has disturbing undertones that point at some unspoken deadly peril to the poet.

13–14 The ideal scenario the poet envisages is one where his social or political and romantic ambitions come together and are fulfilled, but his tone is one of wistful longing: "there" refers to a place that might not exist after all.

## [64] *My hope laye gasping on his dying bedd*

This is the first of two sonnets that survive only in *M*, a fact which points to an early date of composition. The reason why it was not included in later collections remains a mystery; the sonnet could have been intended for circulation among a very restricted group of friends privy to the circumstances of its composition, or else it could have been later discarded for fear of offending the lady in question. It is the only sonnet by Constable containing a reference to the lady's actual, instead of imagined, speaking, although her words remain unrecorded.

1 *his*] Referring to his personified hope.

2 *a word*] Perhaps "no," as in [59], and in Sidney, *A&S* 63.

5–8 See sonnet [20] for a similar appeal to the lady to show her divine powers by bestowing favour on the poet.

10 *live as better noe*] His life will be a sort of living death.

11–12 Cf. Spenser, *Amoretti* 43.1–2, in which the poet is afraid of angering the lady more by speaking: "Shall I then silent be or shall I speake? / And if I speake, her wrath renew I shall."

13 In sonnet [4], it is the poet's and the lady's eyes that conspire: "Myne eye thus helpes thyne eye to worke my smarte" (8).

## [65] *In Edenn grew many a pleasant springe*

This sonnet dedicated to the countesses of Cumberland and Warwick is the second that survives only in *M*. Its position immediately after sonnet [32b] would have made the identity of the addressees clear. Both are among Constable's earliest dedicatory sonnets. On its addressees and context, see notes to [32] and

[32b]. Here the two sisters are compared to two biblical trees in an allegory that emphasises their beauty, virtue and fruitfulness. Considering that Lady Anne Russell, countess of Warwick, had no children by her husband Ambrose Dudley and was widowed in 1590, the sonnet might have seemed tactless in retrospect and been excluded from the later collection.

*in imitation ... significations*] The reference is to Petrarch, *Rime* 18, in which two words, "parte" and "luce," are rhymed throughout the octave, and the two tercets repeat "morte," "desio," and "sole." Here the poet imitates this technique in the first eight lines only, playing on "spring" and homophones of "two."

1–2 *In Edenn ... trees*] The biblical Garden of Eden could stand for the Elizabethan court here. Cf. Genesis 2:9: "And out of the ground made the Lord God to grow every tree that is pleasant to the sight, and good for food." This verse had been rendered into poetry by Hunnis years earlier, in a work dedicated to the earl of Leicester, Lady Anne's brother-in-law (William Hunnis, *A hyve full of hunnye contayning the firste booke of Moses, called Genesis* [London, 1578], sig. A3v):

> And from the Earth, God made to springe
> all fruictfull Trees, so plaste:
> As both might well the Eye delight,
> and please the mouthe in taste.

2 *two*] The two trees singled out in Genesis are the tree of life and the tree of knowledge of good and evil (Gen. 2:9).

3–4 Both ladies had considerable influence; Lady Anne was Gentlewoman of the Privy Chamber and Lady Margaret was a literary patroness (see Hammer, *Polarisation of Elizabethan Politics*, 284; and Lewalski, *Writing Women*, 138).

6 *heate & moysture*] Referring to the sun and rain of spring. According to humoral physiology, heat and moisture were associated with life, as they were thought to lessen as the individual aged and became colder and drier. Women's bodies were also thought to be moister than men's. Dutch physician Levinus Lemnius expresses views that were popular at the time (*The touchstone of complexions*, trans. Thomas Newton [London, 1576], fol. 7v):

> Vitall moysture is the nourishmente and matter of naturall heate, whereupon it woorketh, and by the benefite therof is maintayned and preserved. With this Humour or vitall moysture, is naturall heate fed and cheerished, and from the same receyveth continuall mayntenaunce, and from it participateth vitall power, whereby all Creatures do live.

8 *did runn ... spring*] Cf. Genesis 2:10: "And a river went out of Eden to water

the garden; and from thence it was parted, and became into four heads." Cf. also Hunnis, *A hyve*, sig. A3v:

> From went a Ryver foorth
> to moyst this Garden than,
> Which afterward, devided was
> and in foure heades became.

12 *rivers fowr*] The four rivers named in Genesis: Pison, Gihon, Hiddekel (Tigris), and Euphrates (Gen. 2:11–14).

13 *virtues fower*] The four cardinal virtues, first outlined by Plato in book 4 of the *Republic*: prudence, fortitude, temperance, and justice.

12–13 The association between the four rivers of paradise and the four cardinal virtues dates back to Philo of Alexandria, who in *Legum allegoriae* 1.19 discusses "the largest river, of which the four are effluxes" as "generic virtue" or "goodness." From it spring "prudence, self-mastery, courage, justice." (See *Philo*, trans. F.H. Colson, G.H. Whitaker, J.W. Earp, and Ralph Marcus [Cambridge, MA, 1981], 1: 189). Cf. Sir William Leighton's later rendering of the same motif (*Vertue triumphant, or A lively description of the foure vertues cardinall* [London, 1603], sig. B2v):

> Next, wise men do these Cardinalls compare
> To the foure Rivers pure of Paradise
> Which water that faire garden Eden rare,
> The place of all delights and high devise.
> For as they moisten earth in every place,
> So those bedew the soule of man with grace.

14 Other references to the lady's presence as figuratively blessing or having some effect on her surroundings are found in sonnets [16] and [41].

[66] *Sever'd from sweete Content, my lives sole light*

This sonnet is found only in *D92* and serves as a preface to the collection in it. Grundy rather incongruously printed it first in her edition (Grundy, 109), a position in which it appears to be introducing the *T* sequence. Commentators have puzzled over the circumstances of this sonnet's composition, and some have read it as evidence of Constable's involvement in the publication of *Diana* (see p. 57). The poem reads well as a farewell gift and is thus linked to sonnet [1] and its prefatory role. It can also be understood as a renunciation of Constable's secular poetry, as the poet acknowledges that he has abandoned his sonnets. In this sense, the sonnet is similar to the prose conclusion to the *T* collection.

**1** The lady is often portrayed in Constable's poetry as a source of light; see for instance [11].4, or the allusion to her "eybeames" in [16]. Cf. Sidney, *A&S* 91.1–4:

> Stella, while now, by honour's cruel might,
> I am from you, light of my life, misled,
> And that fair you, my sun, thus overspread
> With absence' veil, I live in sorrow's night.

**2** *Banisht*] Cf. [58].12, in which the poet's eyes are sentenced to "banishment" from "wished sight." Sidney employs this word to refer to involuntary absence, brought about by the lady's wishes, as in Sidney, *A&S* 72.13–14: "But thou, desire, because thou would'st have all, / Now banish art ... ."

**2** *by over-weening wit*] By writing of his love too much, causing her annoyance. Cf. [57].2: "In vayne my witte doth paynt in verse my woe."

**4** Other than his writing poetry, no other cause of offence is mentioned, and the meaning of "fault" remains vague.

**6** Cf. Shakespeare, *Sonnets* 74.5–6, in which the poet imagines his beloved reading his sonnet: "When thou reviewest this, thou dost review / The very part was consecrate to thee."

**6** *these Sonnets*] Note that the term "sonnet" is not used by the poet himself anywhere else.

**6** *pictures of thy praise*] Constable's and Sidney's sonnets share a concern with writing as a form of painting or representation; see sonnet [57].2 and Sidney, *A&S* 70.10–11: "... my pen the best it may / Shall paint out joy, though but in black and white."

**8** *thy worth ... delight*] "Worth" may simply refer to the lady's excellence and virtue, which motivates Constable's writing, as in [63].1: "My Mistrisse worth gave wings unto my Muse." But it could also denote possessions or property (*OED* n.[1] 5), so the implication may be that the lady was unattainable due to her much higher social status.

**9** The poet has consciously given up his amatory poetry. This statement is linked with Richard Smith's description of the sonnets having been "left as Orphans" in his preface to *D92* (sig. A4r); see p. 58.

**10** The sonnets have been doubly rejected: first by the lady and, secondly, by the poet himself after coming to his senses.

**11** *blacke teares*] The words, made of black ink. Ink and tears are often connected in poetry, the former's blackness adding a connotation of sadness or mourning. Cf. Sidney, *A&S* 6.10, with a reference to "tears" that "pour out his [the lover's] ink," and 93.3: "What ink is black enough to paint my woe?" Cf. also Craig, *Amorose Songes*, "His Reconciliation to Lithocardia after absence": "Take then my faultles Sheet, / bedewd with mourning Inke" (21–22). A more complex rendering of this metaphor is found in sonnet [85].9–10: "My yncke even weepes, & teares with mourning blacke / made Incke againe ... ."

11 Spenser, *Amoretti* 1.6–7 offers a close parallel, also envisioning the poetic mistress as the reader: "Those lamping eyes will deigne sometimes to look / and reade the sorrowes of my dying spright."

13 *Fates*] The three Greek deities that controlled the lifespan of human beings and influenced human destiny.

13 *though ... repine*] An allusion to his bad fortune.

13–14 The lady should take pleasure in being immortalized in verse that at the same time attests to her divinity. The immortality-through-poetry motif is found in contemporary English sonnets; see for instance Spenser, *Amoretti* 75.11–12: "My verse your vertues rare shall eternize, / and in the hevens wryte your glorious name."

## Commentary on the *Spiritual Sonnets*

[67] *Greate god, within whose simple essence wee*

This is the opening sonnet in both *BE* and *HA* and the first in the triad to the Holy Trinity. The poet summarises Trinitarian doctrine as expressed in the Christian creeds, Augustine, and Aquinas. A major theme in the sequence – the poet's spiritual renewal – and the meditation-prayer structure are introduced. The language of secular love is borrowed but transformed to refer to the divine.

1–2 The reference is to the idea of divine simplicity, according to which God is simple as opposed to composite beings. He is not made of different attributes but identified with them. Cf. Augustine, *City of God* 11.10: "It is the things that are originally and truly divine that are called simple, because in them there is no difference between quality and substance... ." Augustine quotes Exodus 3:14, "I am that I am" (12.2). The poet invokes the concept of the aseity of God, his independent self-existence. On the idea that God is both essence and existence, see Aquinas, *ST* 1.3.4.

3 *doste*] The *HA* reading "dydd'st" seems superior in light of the use of the past "tooke" in line 4.

3–4 He refers to God the Son; see [68]. The thought of the Father, reflecting upon himself, generated a perfect image of himself, God the Son. In Colossians 1:15, St Paul says of God the Son that he is "the image of the invisible God, the firstborn of every creature." On the generation of the Word (Son) and his nature, see Aquinas, *ST* 1.27.2 and 1.35.2. Grundy (248) mentions Bellarmine's *Christian Doctrine*, in which he uses the analogy of the mirror: "God beholding himselfe, with the eye of understanding, in the glasse of his Divinitie, doth produce an Image most like unto him selfe" (Robert Bellarmine, *An ample declaration of the Christian doctrine*, trans. Richard Hadock [Douai, 1604], 21). In Spenser, *FH*, "A Hymne of Heavenly Love," the poet refers to God as "that high eternall powre" and recounts the begetting of the Son in similar terms: "It lov'd it selfe, because it selfe was faire; / (For faire is lov'd;) and of it selfe begot / Like to it selfe his eldest sonne and heire" (29–31).

5 *this god thus borne*] God the Son.

5–8 The language of love is employed by Augustine to refer to the Holy Spirit; Ayres summarizes it thus: "From eternity the Spirit comes to be the one who is common to Father and Son, who is the love of both by being 'of' and 'from' both." See Lewis Ayres, "Augustine on the Trinity," in *The Oxford Handbook of the Trinity*, ed. Gilles Emery and Matthew Levering [Oxford, 2011], 123–137, at 130). See Augustine, *The Trinity* 15.27. On the idea of spiration that underlies the breath metaphor, see Aquinas, *ST* 1.36.3. Cf. Spenser, *FH*, "A Hymne of Heavenly Love," in which the Spirit is portrayed as deriving from Father and Son, as the latter two

> ... raignd, before all time prescribed,
> In endlesse glorie and immortall might,
> Together with that third from them derived,
> Most wise, most holy, most almightie Spright (36–39)

8 *one spright*] The Holy Spirit.

8 *equall Deitie*] The notion of equality of the three persons was explicitly stated in the Athanasian Creed: "Sed Patris, et Filii, et Spiritus Sancti una est divinitas, aequalis gloria, coeterna maiestas." On the Trinity, Aquinas writes of three persons but one essence (Aquinas, *ST* 1.39.2).

10 *wil'st*] Miola transcribes "whilst," but this spelling is not recorded in *OED* (Robert Miola, *Early Modern Catholicism: An Anthology of Primary Sources* [Oxford, 2007], 190). It is most probably a second person form of "will."

11 The knowledge the poet is asking for originates in God, so he is essentially asking for an act of revelation that will help transform his life. Napier paraphrases Revelation 4:1 thus: "[T]he door of heavenly knowledge was opened unto me, and first, I was called, as by the mightie and fearfull trumpet of Gods Spirit, to

arise from earthly cares, & affections, to high & heavenlie contemplations ..." (John Napier, *A plaine discovery of the whole Revelation of Saint John* [London, 1593], 99).

11 *engrave*] The choice of verb conveys a sense of permanence: it will be no transitory knowledge.

12 *thy sonnes true ymage*] For Aquinas, the word "image" includes "the idea of similitude" (Aquinas, *ST* 1.35.1 co.). A "true image" would be something that bears perfect similitude to another thing. The concepts of *imago Dei* and *imitatio Christi* seem to combine here.

13 These sighs are rooted in the love of God, and granted by him through the envisioned act of revelation; they contrast with and replace former sighs caused by earthly love, as described for instance in [11].14, "sighes of my breast," or [2].3, "To thee my sighes in verse I sacrifice."

14 Cf. 1 Corinthians 6:19: "What? know ye not that your body is the temple of the Holy Ghost which is in you, which ye have of God, and ye are not your own?" Cf. Donne, *HS* 11.3–4: "How God the Spirit, by angels waited on / In Heav'n, doth make his temple in thy breast." Cf. also Barnes, *Divine Centurie*, 4.9–10: "O let my soule (thy Temple) be perfum'de / With sacred incense of thy vertuous grace."

## [68] *Younge Prince of heaven, begotten of that Kinge*

This is the second sonnet to the Holy Trinity. When addressing God the Son, Christ, the emphasis is on rank even as the poet meditates on his Nativity as an event that unites people of all social strata.

1 *Younge*] Probably an authorial improvement on the *HA* reading "Greate," meant to avoid the repetition of the same word as in [67] at the beginning of the sonnet. It would have stood out on the page because the first word in each sonnet is penned in large Gothic script in *BE*.

1 *begotten*] Christ is often referred to as God's only begotten son. The Nicene Creed includes the affirmation that the Son is "begotten, not made" and "of the same substance (consubstantial) with the Father."

1–2 *that Kinge ... make*] God the Father, creator of the world.

2 *which*] The scribe of *BE* consistently favours the use of this relative pronoun instead of "who" with a human antecedent.

3 An allusion to the Incarnation. The Nicene Creed says that Christ "came down from heaven, and by the Holy Spirit was incarnate of the Virgin Mary." Thus the poet emphasises Christ's humanity together with his divinity.

**4** The ancestry of Jesus Christ, tracing back to King David and beyond, is described in Matthew 1:1–17. See also Luke 1:26–27, 1:32, and 3:23–38. Commentators have noted that both the Virgin and her husband Joseph would have been descendants of David.

**5** *thie ... singe*] Luke mentions the angels' song and praise of God at the Nativity (2:13–14).

**6** An allusion to the adoration of the newborn Jesus Christ by the shepherds (Luke 2:8–20). They were often presented playing music in art and drama, and pipes are mentioned in an ancient carol (see Edith Rickert, ed., *Ancient English Christmas Carols* [London, 1910], 99):

> Down from heaven, from heaven so high,
> Of angels there came a great company,
> With mirth and joy and great solemnity,
> They sang terly terlow;
> So merrily the shepherds their pipes gan blow.

**7–8** Matthew mentions the "wise men from the East" who went to see the baby Jesus and brought him gifts (2:1–11). No Father of the Church states that the magi were kings. However, some prophets had foretold the visit of rich men from the East (Isaiah 60.3–6; Psalm 72:10–11), and the identification of the magi with Eastern kings was engraved in the collective imagination, especially from the sixth century. In Western tradition, the names of the magi are Melchior, Caspar, and Balthazar, and they brought gold, frankincense, and myrrh as gifts.

**9–10** The angels stand for the spiritual, heavenly nobility. Shepherds and kings are earthly: they represent the humble/poor and a higher, wealthy social rank respectively. The three groups – angels, shepherds, and kings – are nevertheless united in their praise of the newborn Christ.

**13** *from princelie race*] From the lineage of King David.

**13–14** *by povertie ... humilitye*] In the later middle ages, for "proponents of an exalted doctrine of Mary she also served, with her Son, as the supreme example of total poverty" (Jaroslav Pelikan, *Reformation of Church and Dogma (1300–1700)* [Chicago, 1984], 42). See for instance mentions of her humility and poverty in St Bonaventure, *The Life of Christ* (trans. W.H. Hutchings [London, 1888], 10–11, and 18).

[69] *Eternall sprite, which arte in heaven, the love*

This sonnet on the Holy Ghost concludes the triad to the Holy Trinity.

**1** *Eternall sprite*] The Holy Ghost or Holy Spirit.

**1 *which ... heaven*]** This follows the initial apostrophe, "Our Father," in the Lord's Prayer.

**1–2 *the love ... kisse*]** The process of the passing of breath or *spiration* between Father and Son becomes a kiss. Kuchar points to the Trinitarian iconographic representation of the "Throne of Grace," dating back to the twelfth century, in which "the Holy Spirit passes as a dove between the mouths of the Father and the Son." He offers a summary of the symbolic meanings of kissing in devotional culture and stresses Constable's "Bernardian eroticism" (Gary Kuchar, "Henry Constable and the Question of Catholic Poetics: Affective Piety and Erotic Identification in the Spirituall Sonnettes," *Philological Quarterly* 85 [2006]: 69–90, at 84–85; see also Nicolas Perella, *The Kiss: Sacred and Profane* [Berkeley, 1969], 52–57). Cf. the eighth sermon in Bernard of Clairvaux, *On the Song of Songs I*, trans. Kilian Walsh (Kalamazoo, 1976), 46:

> If, as is properly understood, the Father is he who kisses, the Son he who is kissed, then it cannot be wrong to see in the kiss the Holy Spirit, for he is the imperturbable peace of the Father and the Son, their unshakable bond, their undivided love, their indivisible unity.

Wickes, *Sonnets* (35) compares the initial invocation in Torquato Tasso's *Il Monte Oliveto* (see *Opere minori in versi*, ed. Angelo Solerti [Bologna, 1891], 1: 341): "Santo Spirto divin, Spirto fecondo, / E del Padre e del Figlio eterno amore [Sainted holy Spirit, fruitful Spirit, and eternal love of the Father and the Son]."

**4 *lovinge dove*]** The Holy Ghost is represented as a dove; the iconography is based on the narration of the Baptism of Jesus Christ (Matthew 3:16–17). The turtle dove was traditionally viewed as a symbol of love and faithfulness.

**5–8** A reference to Pentecost, when, fifty days after the Resurrection, the apostles received the Holy Spirit under the appearance of tongues of fire resting on their heads: "And they were all filled with the Holy Ghost, and began to speak with other tongues, as the Spirit gave them utterance" (Acts 2:1–4).

**6 *than*]** Neither this reading nor *HA* "thow" brings about disagreement with the verb; the omitted subject is still implied in *BE*.

**6 *his*]** His apostles.

**7–8** So that the apostles, through voicing their faith, might move others to convert.

**9 *True god of love*]** In opposition to Cupid, the god of earthly love, who also has wings but is here considered a false god. Cf. *The English Poems of George Herbert*, ed. Helen Wilcox (Cambridge, 2007), 1.8–9, in which Herbert complains to God about the preeminence of secular love in poetry: "... Cannot thy Dove / Out-strip their Cupid easily in flight?" See also 1 John 4:8: "He that loveth not knoweth not God; for God is love."

**9** *true love*] The love for God, far superior to profane love. The plural "loves" in *BE* destroys grammatical agreement and must be a scribal slip.

**10** *thy winges and fyre*] The wings of the dove and the tongues of fire at Pentecost.

**11** *my soule a spirit is*] In the sense that it is incorporeal. See Aquinas, *ST* 1.75.2.

**11–12** *with thy ... desire*] In Goscelin of Saint-Bertin's *Life of Edith*, the mystical experiences of the Anglo-Saxon saint are described in terms of flying: "She hastened towards him with her entire affection and, taking to herself the wings of a dove, she ardently desired to fly to his sanctifying embraces ..." (see Stephanie Hollis et al., eds., *Writing the Wilton Women: Goscelin's Legend of Edith and Liber confortatorius* [Turnhout, 2004], 33). The idea of the poet-believer flying upwards and leaving earthly suffering behind is also found in religious sonneteers; see for instance Barnes, *Divine Centurie*, 70.1–3: "Unto my spirite lend an Angels wing, / By which it might mount to that place of rest, / Where Paradice may mee releeve opprest."

**12** *like an Anngell*] Because both the human soul and angels share a spiritual nature.

**13** *a harte enflam'd*] With the love of God. Cf. the Spanish mystic St John of the Cross's poem "The Living Flame of Love" ("Llama de amor viva," in *Poesía* [Córdoba, 2003], 23): "¡Oh, llama de amor viva, / que tiernamente hieres / de mi alma en el más profundo centro! [O living flame of love / that tenderly wounds / my soul in its deepest center!]."

**13–14** Cf. Vittoria Colonna's sonnet 19 (*Sonnets for Michelangelo: A Bilingual Edition*, ed. and trans. Abigail Brundin [Chicago, 2005], 70), which refers to grace as a fire inflaming the poet's heart and capable of making her fly up towards God.

**14** The poet's wish to rise to the presence of God and join his court supersedes earlier desires to serve earthly kings. Fraeters notes that some "mystic visionaries are also transported during their ecstasy to ... the choirs of the highest angelic triad, where the contemplative angels – thrones, cherubim, and seraphim – enjoy the endless vision of God's countenance" (Veerle Fraeters, "Visio/Vision," in *The Cambridge Companion to Christian Mysticism*, ed. Patricia Z. Beckman and Amy M. Hollywood [Cambridge, 2012], 178–188, at 186). According to a tradition dating back to Dionysius the Pseudo-Areopagite (late fifth/early sixth century) the seraphim are the closest to God. In Isaiah 6:1–2 they are described as God's immediate attendants, hovering above his throne.

EXPLANATORY NOTES · 335

[70] *When thee, o holy sacrificed Lambe*

This reflection on the Eucharist structurally and logically follows the triad on the Trinity by emphasizing a direct relationship between God and the poet-believer through the act of Communion.

*the blessed Sacrament*] The Blessed Sacrament of the Altar, or the Eucharist, whose meaning was contested during and after the Reformation. As a Catholic convert, Constable embraced the belief that "the body, blood, soul, and divinity of Jesus Christ were really, truly, and substantially present in the Eucharist" (Trent Pomplun, "Catholic Sacramental Theology in the Baroque Age," in *The Oxford Handbook of Early Modern Theology, 1600–1800*, ed. Ulrich L. Lehner et al. [New York, 2016], 135–149, at 140–141). In print, this term survives only in one heading to a poem by a contemporary: Robert Southwell's "In Paschal feast, the end of ancient rite" is titled *A poeme declaring the real presence of Christ in the blessed sacrament of the aultar* and printed on its own (Douai, 1606).

1–2 *thee ... see*] The poet sees Christ in the bread and wine, thus asserting his belief in the Real Presence.

1 *sacrificed*] In 1562, the Council of Trent promulgated that "if anyone says that in the mass a true and real sacrifice is not offered to God ... let him be anathema" (Council of Trent, session 22, in *The Canons and Decrees of the Council of Trent*, trans. H.J. Schroeder [Rockford, 1978], 149).

1 *Lambe*] The Paschal lamb of the Israelites prefigured Christ. St John the Baptist calls Christ "the Lamb of God, which taketh away the sin of the world" (John 1:29).

2 *in severed signes*] In the separate signs of bread and wine, transubstantiated into Christ's body and blood, respectively. Grundy (249) suggests that "severed" carries a suggestion of "the action of the sacrificial slaying, and the appearance of the slain body."

2 *white and liquide*] The whiteness of the bread and the liquid state of the wine are the external accidents that remain the same, even as their substance changes.

3–4 In the poet's mind, the contemplation of bread and wine conjures the image of Christ's pale body after he shed his blood on the cross and redeemed mankind. This association emphasises the Catholic belief that "the sacrifice of the Mass was in no way independent of the single sacrifice on Calvary" (Pomplun, "Catholic Sacramental Theology," 142).

6 *vayled in white*] The colour of the bread, transformed into Christ's pale corpse.

7 *thy Syndon*] Christ's body was wrapped "in a clean linen cloth" (Matt. 27:59).

9 *Intomb'd in me*] The reading in *BE* is a semantic improvement on *HA* "Buryed," as it is more cohesive with the identification of the poet's body with a funerary monument. Hillman reflects that "Christ's offering of himself as bread, to be incorporated physically into the bodies of the believers, is the central symbol in Christianity of the mutuality of access to the interior of the body of the other" (David Hillman, "Visceral Knowledge: Shakespeare, Skepticism, and the Interior of the Early Modern Body," in *The Body in Parts: Fantasies of Corporeality in Early Modern Europe*, ed. David Hillman and Carla Mazzio [New York, 1997], 81–106, at 85).

9 *unto my soul appeare*] An address to God to manifest himself and, through the act of consumption/embodiment, reach the poet's soul.

10 This line refers to the poet's miserable state on earth and seems to look back on the idea of "banishment" in sonnet [58].12. Cf. his wish to be "in thy sight" in sonnet [69].14. The *BE* reading improves on *HA* in terms of metre.

11 *our fore fathers ... were*] The patriarchs of the Old Testament were believed to have resided in the *limbus patrum* until Christ descended to hell and opened the gates so that they could go to heaven with him. This belief evolved out of a reading of 1 Peter 3:19. Both limbo and the Harrowing of Hell are described in the apocryphal Gospel of Nicodemus and became part of the medieval imagination (see J.K. Elliott, "The 'Apocryphal' New Testament," in *The New Cambridge History of the Bible*, vol. 1: *From the Beginnings to 600*, ed. James Carleton Paget and Joachim Schaper [Cambridge, 2013], 455–478, at 465).

12–14 On the spiritual effects of the Eucharist on the communicant, Aquinas writes that "by this sacrament grace receives increase, and the spiritual life is perfected, so that man may stand perfect in himself by union with God" (Aquinas, *ST* 3.79.1 ad 1).

12 *didst give them light*] God's agency in the poet's conversion is emphasised.

13 *purgyng fire*] Limbo is here associated with purgatory, the place where souls were purified of their sins before entering heaven; purgatory was a controversial Catholic belief rejected by Protestants.

14 *the flames of bad desire*] Profane love. This wish supersedes Constable's earlier wish that the metaphorical flames of love in his heart be quenched with his tears; see sonnet [4]. God's grace alone can inspire the poet to mend his ways.

[71] *In that, Oh Queene of Queens, thy birth was free*

This is the first sonnet to the Virgin Mary, and it stands alone as compared to those organized into a triad, [79] to [81]. It was misattributed to John Donne in numerous verse miscellanies and collections of Donne's poetry and made it into his collected *Poems* in print. The version included in the 1635 edition is collated in the textual apparatus as representative of the misattributed tradition. Eckhardt provides a discussion of the recontextualization and misattribution of this sonnet – which continued until the late nineteenth century (see Joshua Eckhardt, "Publication," in *A Handbook of English Renaissance Literary Studies*, ed. John Lee [Hoboken, 2017], 295–307).

1 *Queene of Queens*] The *Salve Regina* was one of the popular medieval hymns addressing Mary as Queen of Heaven. The iconography of Mary enthroned in heaven and wearing a crown dates back to the sixth century; it was first found in a painting in Santa Maria Antiqua, a church in the Roman Forum (see Susan Haskins, *Mary Magdalen: Myth and Metaphor* [London, 1993], 19). Mary was traditionally associated with the "woman clothed with the sun, and the moon under her feet, and upon her head a crown of twelve stars" described in Revelation 12:1. Pelikan notes that "the portrayal of 'the coronation of the Virgin,' which became a standard part of the iconography of Mary during the twelfth century, regularly depicted her as sitting at Christ's right hand" (Jaroslav Pelikan, *The Growth of Medieval Theology (600–1300)* [Chicago, 1978], 168). In her commentary on this sonnet, Grindlay states that with this address "Constable is affirming her rightful place in heaven as man's mediatrix," mediating between Christ and mankind (Grindlay, *Queen of Heaven*, 142).

1–2 *thy birth ... bereave*] The dogma of the immaculate conception of the Virgin – the idea that Mary alone was free from original sin at birth – was not proclaimed until 1854. Although it is not explicitly mentioned in the Gospels, its origin dates back to the early church. The thirteenth-century Franciscan theologian Duns Scotus had brought forth arguments in defence of this idea, and at the time Constable was writing it was widely accepted among the Catholic populace. Among theologians, it was a highly controversial topic from the twelfth century onwards, and by the early seventeenth century, although for different reasons, it still was so. See an overview in Marina Warner, *Alone of All Her Sex: The Myth and Cult of the Virgin Mary* (Oxford, 2013), 241–260. The Council of Trent explicitly exempted Mary from original sin (see sessions 5 and 6, in *Canons and Decrees*, 23, 45). Jesuits were amongst the most militant proponents of the doctrine.

**2** *guilt*] In *DP* this word is substituted with the much more ambiguous reading "that," thus erasing the problematic allusion to the immaculate conception and making the sonnet more palatable to the general English reader.

**3** Augustine developed the idea of original sin and believed that it was transmitted during the sexual intercourse that led to conception.

**4** *his sole-borne daughter*] Mary had been elected as God's "beloved daughter from the beginning of time and predestined ... to be the mother of his only-begotten son" (Warner, *Alone of All Her Sex*, 242).

**5** *thy birthes nobilitie*] Mary was thought to have descended from King David's lineage.

**6** *his spirit*] The Holy Ghost.

**6** *thy spowse*] *DP* contains the variant "his," which destroys the link between Mary and the Holy Ghost and must be an error.

**7** A reference to the Incarnation. The Nicene Creed says that Christ "came down from heaven, and by the Holy Spirit was incarnate of the Virgin Mary."

**8** Mary is related to all three persons of the Trinity: Father, Son, and Holy Ghost.

**9–10** There is a change of addressee in these lines; the poet turns from the Virgin to earthly queens. For a discussion of Constable's rejection of earthly female rulers in favour of the Virgin, see pp. 122–123.

**10** *worldly*] *DP* reads "earthly," which could be an error of repetition of the word immediately above on the page.

**11–12** Cf. for example the terms in which John White, bishop of Winchester, praised queen Mary I at her funeral: "She was a king's daughter, she was a king's sister, she was a king's wife" (see John Strype, ed., *Ecclesiastical Memorials Relating Chiefly to Religion, and Its Reformation* [Oxford, 1816], 7: 408). McLaren comments that "for White and for many others, the formative power of these interpenetrating regalities cancelled out some of the debilities that were deemed to attach to women by nature – debilities that made them ill suited to rule" (Anne McLaren, "Memorializing Mary and Elizabeth," in *Tudor Queenship: The Reigns of Mary and Elizabeth*, ed. Alice Hunt and Anna Whitelock [Basingstoke, 2010], 11–27, at 16).

**13–14** Cf. Petrarch, *Rime* 366, "Vergine bella, che di sol vestita": "Tre dolci et cari nomi ài in te raccolti, / madre, figliuola et sposa" (Three sweet and cherished names you have collected: / mother, daughter, and bride) (46–47).

## [72] *When as the Prince of Anngelles, puft with pryde*

This sonnet to the archangel Michael is placed after that to the Virgin Mary following the order in the Confiteor. Drawing on the biblical tradition and probably inspired by artistic representations of the archangel as a warrior, the poet muses on Michael's military exploits and the defeat of the devil at the hands of the church. Cf. Barnes, *Divine Centurie* 47.8–11, in which Michael is a leader and defender in the battle for the poet's soul:

> What Champion Michaell my soule to defend,
> Will lend his puissant and victorious crosse,
> To conquere that olde Serpent, which assayles
> My feeble soule entombde in earthly drosse?

*St Michaell the Arkcaungell*] Michael is mentioned both in the Old and the New Testament. In Daniel 10:13 and 12:1 he is described as a prince of heaven; he also disputes with the devil over the body of Moses (Jude 1:9), and he is the past (and future) leader of the heavenly army that defeats the devil (as a "dragon" or "serpent"), who then falls with his angels (Revelation 12:7–9). He features in the apocryphal tradition and was "early regarded in the Church as the helper of Christian armies against the heathen, and as a protector of individual Christians against the devil" (Frank L. Cross and Elizabeth A. Livingstone, eds., *The Oxford Dictionary of the Christian Church* [New York, 1997], 1082). He is also thought to lead human souls to judgement after death. In art he is represented fighting or vanquishing the devil, often wearing armour.

1–2 Lucifer, who led the rebellion of a group of angels against heaven. Quoting St Augustine and Isaiah 14:13–14, Aquinas writes that he "sinned by seeking to be as God" (Aquinas, *ST* 1.63.3 co.) and that "the sin of the highest angel was the cause of the others sinning" (Aquinas, *ST* 1.63.8 co.).

1 *pryde*] Identified as the primal sin that originated all others.

3 *chose*] The *HA* variant "choose" is inconsistent with the past verb forms used throughout the sonnet.

5 *the Anngells ... side*] Lucifer's angels.

6 Cf. Isaiah 14:12: "How art thou fallen from heaven, O Lucifer, son of the morning! how art thou cut down to the ground, which didst weaken the nations!"

6 *in battell vanquisht*] The order of these words in *BE*, as compared to *HA*, creates a more regular iambic pentameter.

7 *the pride of heaven*] Lucifer was traditionally thought to have been the best of the angels; his name means "light bearer."

**7** *the drake of hell*] Cf. [77].10. Allusions to and artistic representations of the devil as a serpent or dragon are common.

**8** He was confined in hell, the "bottomless pit" (Revelation 20:3), described by Matthew as the "everlasting fire, prepared for the devill and his angels," where sinners are sent (Matt. 25:41). Cf. Robert Southwell's poem "The prodigall chylds soule wracke" (Southwell, *Collected Poems*, 39):

> Where cheyn'd in synn I lay in thrall
> Next to the dungeon of despaire
> Till mercy raysd me from my fall,
> And grace my ruines did repaire. (57–60)

**9–10** The Devil is locked and sealed in hell by an angel for a thousand years according to Revelation 20. When the thousand years are over, he will break loose and create confusion and war on earth, but heaven will defeat him again. The poet may be suggesting that the Catholic Church is "God's Church," which is assailed by the reformed but will win the fight.

**11–14** Michael is presented as a knight or *miles christianus* who embodies chivalric virtues. He has won the battle against the forces of hell, he is devoted to the Virgin, and he has defeated a monster, the devil.

## [73] *As Anne, longe barren, mother did become*

This sonnet develops an analogy between John the Baptist and the Old Testament prophet Samuel, which departs from the more common typological analysis of John as the new Elijah (see for instance Matthew 11:14). A second parallel is established between David and Jesus as royal figures anointed or baptised by a prophet and shepherds who tend to their flocks.

*St John Baptiste*] The son of Elizabeth, a cousin of the Virgin Mary's; he is considered the forerunner of Christ.

**1–2** Hannah, the mother of the prophet Samuel, was childless until she prayed to God for a son (1 Samuel 1:5–11). Samuel was the last judge and led the transition to a monarchy, inaugurated with Saul and David. Hannah is named "Anne" in the sonnet perhaps due to confusion with St Anne, mother to the Virgin Mary, whose name was also Hannah in Hebrew.

**3–4** John was the last prophet before Jesus. John's mother, Elizabeth, was childless and advanced in years (Luke 1:7). Both men are related by their prophetic role and their near miraculous births.

**5** *His ... spake*] Hannah spoke to God without making a sound (1 Sam. 1:13).

5–6 *thy father ... fore tell*] St John's father, Zechariah, was dumb throughout his wife's pregnancy because he had doubted God's word conveyed through the angel Gabriel; he recovered speech after the birth of his son and praised God (Luke 1:20–22, 1:64).

7 Probably an allusion to the Witch of Endor's invoking of the dead Samuel at Saul's request; Samuel foretold Saul's downfall (1 Sam. 28). He is said to be "in hell" based on the belief that souls did not go to heaven before the coming of Jesus Christ.

8 John was a prophet even in his mother's womb; he leapt with joy when the pregnant Mary visited Elizabeth (Luke 1:41–44).

9–10 King David, born a shepherd, was chosen by God to rule Israel and anointed by Samuel (1 Sam. 16:11–13).

11 *that highe ... make*] God.

12 *a holier liquor*] The water of baptism, which Jesus received from John.

13–14 Cf. Ezekiel 34:23: "And I will set up one shepherd over them, and he shall feed them, even my servant David; he shall feed them, and he shall be their shepherd."

[74] *He that for feare his Maister did deny*

The poet meditates on St Peter and St Paul as founders of the Catholic Church, celebrating their martyrdom and the establishment of the papacy in Rome.

1 *Maister*] Jesus.

1–2 Peter's denial of Jesus is narrated in all four gospels (Matthew 26:69–75, Mark 14:66–72, Luke 22:56–62, and John 18:16–27). The first person who recognised Peter is said to be a maid in all accounts.

3 *mightiest ... earth*] Nero was emperor of Rome from AD 54 to 68, in a century when the Roman Empire increasingly dominated Europe, North Africa, and the Near East.

3–4 The First Epistle of Clement is the earliest document suggesting that Peter was martyred under Nero. The apocryphal Acts of Peter (second century) describe his crucifixion, which was not exactly like Christ's because he asked to be crucified head down.

5 Paul was a Roman citizen from a Jewish family, and he himself admitted in his epistles that he had persecuted the early Christians (see for instance Galatians 1:13). Zeal was the personality trait traditionally associated with Paul; he refers to it in Philippians 3:6.

6 Paul witnessed and consented to the martyrdom of St Stephen (ca. AD 5–

ca. 34), considered the first martyr, who was stoned to death (Acts 7:59–60 and 8:1).

7 On the road to Damascus, Paul received a message from God and was temporarily blinded (Acts 3:9). The poet, however, considers that Paul was blind before he realised his error and converted, not after.

8 *the chieffe Apostle*] St Peter.

8 The First Epistle of Clement suggests that Paul was martyred. St Jerome writes that "he then, in the fourteenth year of Nero on the same day with Peter, was beheaded at Rome for Christ's sake and was buried in the Ostian way" (Jerome, *On Illustrious Men*, trans. Thomas P. Halton [Washington, DC, 1999], 13). The tomb of Peter is traditionally thought to be under the altar of St Peter's Basilica in Rome. For an overview of theories and written accounts concerning the relationship between Peter, Paul, and the city of Rome, see Roger Collins, *Keepers of the Keys of Heaven: A History of the Papacy* (New York, 2009), 6–10.

11 *the fatal ... founde*] Rome, founded by twins Romulus and Remus according to myth.

12 *Hebrue fisshers Chayre*] The chair of St Peter, or Holy See. Peter had been a fisherman before he met Jesus. He became the first Bishop of Rome.

13 *the Latyne ... throne*] Possibly an allusion to Romulus, who was raised a shepherd and became the first king of Rome after its foundation. He "was regarded as the founder of Rome, and notably the founder of sovereign power, of *imperium*" (John Scheid, "Cults, Myths, and Politics at the Beginning of the Empire," in *Roman Religion*, ed. Clifford Ando [Edinburgh, 2003], 117–138, at 133). See William H.C. Frend, "The Origins of the Papacy: c.33–440," in *The Papacy*, ed. Michael Walsh (London, 1997), 24–41.

14 *since*] The choice of this word signalling a starting point for the temporal and spiritual authority of the pope paints a picture of uncontested authority from the times of St Peter, disregarding conflict within the early church.

14 *the world ... one*] This is an explicit acknowledgment of the temporal and spiritual authority of the pope, which was a point of contention between Catholic and reformed churches.


[75] *For few nightes sollace in delitious bedd*

This is the first sonnet to St Mary Magdalene and it stands alone, as compared to those organized into a triad, [82] to [84]. Inspired by medieval legends and the contemporary literature of tears, the poet meditates on Mary's sinful past and present glory, and makes a wish to identify with her and abandon sin in order to merit eternal life.

*To St Mary Maudlyn*] Mary Magdalene, the biblical woman who was freed "of seven devils" by Jesus (Luke 8:2), was present at the Crucifixion (Mark 15:40, Matt. 27:55-56, John 19:25), found his tomb empty (Matt. 28:1-10, Mark 16:1-11, Luke 24:10, John 20:1-2), and was the first witness of the Resurrection (Mark 16:9, John 20:14-18). In the Western tradition, her legend arose from a conflation of this figure and different biblical women, and she was identified with the "sinner" in Luke 7:37-50 and largely portrayed as a repentant prostitute. Constable's treatment of the Magdalene owes much to medieval legends that were absorbed into the influential *Golden Legend* by Jacobus de Voragine (ca. 1260).

1-2 In *GL*, Mary Magdalene's noble birth and sinful youth are emphasised: "For so much as she shone in beauty greatly, and in riches, so much the more she submitted her body to delight, and therefore she ... was called customably a sinner" (4: 74).

3-4 In one of the multiple vignettes conforming the Magdalene's life in *GL*, she went to France, where she retired to a cave in the wilderness ("a right sharp desert") for thirty years to live a life of penance and contemplation (4: 82). Late medieval artistic representations of her as a penitent portray her naked, sometimes covered in hair, whereas in the Renaissance she became a beautiful Christian equivalent of Venus, as in Correggio's and Titian's paintings (see Joana Antunes, "The Late-Medieval Mary Magdalene: Sacredness, Otherness, and Wildness," in *Mary Magdalene in Medieval Culture: Conflicting Roles*, ed. Peter V. Loewen and Robin Waugh [New York, 2014], 116-139; and Michael Haag, *The Quest for Mary Magdalene* [London, 2016], 263-281).

4 *teares of grieffe*] Tears shed for her past sins. The tears shed by the repentant sinner were the focus of a literary tradition revolving around St Peter and Mary Magdalene in the European Counter-Reformation. Olson states that "the Magdalene's tears ... were used as an instrument to draw sympathizers who would identify with her as a repentant sinner, grieve over their own sins and seek penance" (Vibeke Olson, "'Woman, Why Weepest Thou?' Mary Magdalene, the Virgin Mary and the Transformative Power of Holy Tears in Late Medieval Devotional Painting," in *Mary Magdalene: Iconographic Studies from the Middle Ages to the Baroque*, ed. Michelle Erhardt and Amy M. Morris [Leiden, 2012], 361-382, at 369).

5-6 Her penance was successful, and eternal life in heaven is her reward. This made her a "figure for emulation by Early Modern English Catholics" (see Gary Kuchar, "Gender and Recusant Melancholia in Robert Southwell's Mary Magdalene's Funeral Tears," in *Catholic Culture in Early Modern England*, ed. Robert Corthell et al. [Notre Dame, 2007], 135-157, at 139).

**8** *a sea of pleasure*] Her boundless joy in paradise is contrasted with the "few nights sollace" at the beginning of the sonnet.

**9–11** Contemplation of the Magdalene's tears should remind the poet that he must resist the temptation to deviate from the right path and indulge in pleasures of the flesh, as he would then have to atone for his sins.

**12** *vertues roughe beginning*] Probably referring to penance and its three stages – contrition, confession, and satisfaction/penance – which cleanse the soul from sin and are the first step to lead a virtuous life, according to Catholic belief. These were described by the Council of Trent in 1551, which declared "contrition ... a true and beneficial sorrow" (see session 14, in *Canons and Decrees*, 90–99, 102).

**14** Giving up sin is a worthwhile effort because it will earn him eternal life.

## [76] *Because thou was the Daughter of A kinge*

This sonnet illustrates the influence of medieval hagiography on Constable's religious poetry, and his personal preference for female saints as the subjects of meditation. It seems more impersonal than the rest in the sense that the reflection on the saint's life is not followed by a petition for help or intercession, the only references to the poetic "I" being related to the purifying influence that writing on such a worthy subject has on his own verse.

*St Katheren*] St Catherine of Alexandria, one of the virgin martyrs traditionally included in the group of the Fourteen Holy Helpers, who suffered during the persecutions of the fourth century. Her cult started around the ninth century and became widespread throughout the middle ages. She was portrayed as the mystical bride of Christ; she was associated with wisdom and became the patron of students and philosophers among others. In art she often appears with a wheel, an instrument of torture constructed for her martyrdom and destroyed by angels. Constable is obviously familiar with medieval legends about her life, particularly GL.

**1** *Daughter of A kinge*] According to GL, she was the daughter of King Costus of Cyprus, and inherited the throne at fourteen (7: 3–4). Other versions of her story merely emphasised her noble birth.

**2–3** Catherine's beauty and wisdom are described at length in her legend: "She was so fair of visage and so well formed in her members that all the people enjoyed in her beauty" (*GL*, 7: 3). She was educated and clever and refuted the arguments of fifty pagan philosophers sent by emperor Maxentius to discuss reli-

EXPLANATORY NOTES • 345

gion with her and make her apostatise (7: 19–20). Here she appears to be replacing the female paragons of virtue and wisdom who were the addressees of Constable's dedicatory sonnets, specifically Arbella Stuart.

4 The image of the poet's winged muse also appears in the secular sonnets; see [27], [63].

5–7 *these graces ... deserv'd*] Her beauty was embellished by divine grace, which has given her eternal glory. Similar play on the word "grace" pervades the secular sonnets; see for instance [1].

7 *have*] The singular "haith" in *HA* destroys concord with "these graces."

7–8 *my muse ... singe*] Cf. [26].13–14 and [27].10–11, in which the same image of writing with a feather taken from an angel's wing is used in the portrayal of King James as a writer of religious poetry.

10 Catherine becomes for the poet a true *donna angelicata*. In *GL*, her purity and chastity despite being a princess with "riches, convenable opportunity, flowering youth, freedom without constraint, and sovereign beauty" that might have tempted another are emphasised (7: 29).

11 Her eloquence was a godsent gift; she employed it to convert others to the Christian religion (*GL*, 7: 29).

12–13 Martyrs were believed to receive a crown in Heaven. Revelation 2:10 is often quoted: "Fear none of those things which thou shalt suffer ... be thou faithful unto death, and I will give thee a crown of life." Martyrdom is first presented in the sequence as the soul's release from its bodily prison, which is immediately followed by glorification.

14 When Catherine was beheaded, legend says that "angels took the body and bare it unto the Mount of Sinai, more than twenty journeys from thence, and buried it there honourably" (*GL*, 7: 25).

[77] *Fayre Amazon of heaven, which took'st in hande*

This sonnet, like [76], contains a meditation on one of the most popular female saints in the late middle ages.

*St Margarett*] St Margaret of Antioch, also known as St Marina in the Eastern tradition. Like St Catherine, she was one of the virgin martyrs included in the list of the Fourteen Holy Helpers and her legend, which first appeared in writing in the late eighth century, sets her life during the persecutions of the fourth century. She is often portrayed with a dragon – the devil that she defeated – and her cult as the patron saint of pregnancy and labour was widespread in late medieval Europe. For a thorough account of the textual traditions of her legend, see Juliana Dresvina, *A Maid with a Dragon: The Cult of St Margaret of Antioch in Medieval England* (Oxford, 2016), 13–144.

1–2 Margaret is presented as a female counterpart to male warriors in the Christian tradition, St Michael and St George.

1 *Amazon of heaven*] Margaret is associated with the warrior women of Greek mythology, but the phrase makes it clear that she fights in God's name. Wickes notes that this is "a transformation no doubt of the Petrarchists' *bella guerriera*" (Wickes, *Sonnets*, 38).

2 *St Michaell*] An archangel and military leader in heaven; see notes to [72].

2 *St George*] The patron saint of England, whose legend dates back to the fourth century. His depiction as a dragon-slaying soldier-saint gained impetus after the Crusades. In medieval texts and art, he became an embodiment of chivalric values and martial prowess. On the development of his cult, see Samantha Riches, *St George: Hero, Martyr and Myth* (Sutton, 2000), 1–35.

3 *a Tyranttes ... hate*] Olybrius, a Roman provost, was besotted with Margaret and asked her to renounce her religion and marry him; she refused and he subjected her to gruesome tortures and eventually had her beheaded (see *GL*, 4: 67–70).

4 *lilly faith*] Cf. Song of Solomon 2:1: "I am the rose of Sharon, and the lily of the valleys," which is said by the bride. The lily is associated with the poetic mistress's fair skin in profane poetry, and with purity and innocence in the Christian tradition.

4 *retaynd in bande*] In *GL*, Margaret is imprisoned twice, and her encounter with the devil takes place on the second day (4: 67–69).

5–8 Margaret's feat in defeating the dragon-devil is all the more impressive because she had no help and was unmounted and unarmed, unlike St Michael and St George. Interestingly, her being female is not listed as a disadvantage.

6 *like ... hoste*] Cf. Revelation 12:7: "And there was war in heaven: Michael and his angels fought against the dragon ... ." In art, Michael is often portrayed alone vanquishing the dragon, but he is sometimes accompanied by other angels, as in a 1498 woodcut by Albrecht Dürer. See sonnet [72].

6–7 *that ... Celebrate*] St George is represented as a fully armoured knight on horseback, charging at the dragon with a sword or lance.

8 The *GL* recounts two different versions of Margaret's encounter with the dragon. In the one that the author lends credibility to, "a horrible dragon" appeared and "assailed her, and would have devoured her, but she made the sign of the cross, and anon he vanished away" (4: 68). The more fanciful version has Margaret being swallowed by the dragon and breaking free from its belly (4: 68–69).

9–10 The poet envisions his soul as trapped in his body and in danger of being swallowed by the devil. The notion of the soul imprisoned in the body dates back to Plato, *Republic* 10.611, in which the immortal soul is said to be "marred by communion with the body and other miseries" (trans. Paul Shorey [Cambridge, MA, 1937–1942], 2: 481). The gaping dragon metaphor alludes to the desires of the flesh to which his body is prone, and which endanger his soul's afterlife.

12 The idea that Margaret triumphed because of her virginity recurs in Old English accounts of her legend, as Hill has noted. See Carole Hill, "'Here be Dragons': The Cult of St Margaret of Antioch and Strategies for Survival," in *Art, Faith and Place in East Anglia: From Prehistory to the Present*, ed. T.A. Heslop et al. [Woodbridge, 2010], 105–116, at 107):

> The devil or dragon she has to overcome is her vulnerability to her own normal sexual impulses, perceived as threatening and dangerous to a vowed virginity ... spiritual deliverance comes through sexual integrity and from this follows a certain empowerment of the female flesh.

14 Kuchar analyses this line, especially the choice of wording in "passe for," as the poet's desire to enact the "performance of Margaret's heroic virginity." He adds that the sonnet is characterised by "Constable's theatrical sense of devotion as a performance, an act carried out so far that it becomes a reality for the devotee" ("Henry Constable," 76). Although not a virgin himself, the poet longs for a chaster life and spiritual renewal and expresses his desire in terms of "transgendered identification" with a virgin saint (ibid., 86), hoping that emulation will result in real transformation.

[78] *This day, oh blessed virgine, is the daye*

This is the first of the four sonnets that only survive in BE and has therefore been unnoticed by critics. It is very personal and sombre in tone; the poet draws on the Christian idea of life as a vale of tears and longs for release from his physical body.

*St Collett*] Nichol Boylet, known as Colette of Corbie (1381–1447), a French abbess who, after reportedly receiving some divine visions, undertook the reform of the Clares, an order of nuns, in an attempt to restore absolute poverty. She founded the order of Colettine Poor Clares. She was a tireless traveller and multiple miracles were ascribed to her, some of them associated with pregnant women and childbirth. An account of Colette's life was written by her confessor, Pierre de Vaux, in Middle French and later translated into Latin (see Pierre de

Vaux, *Vie de soeur Colette*, trans. Elisabeth Lopez [Saint-Etienne, 1994]). Constable's choice of addressee may be informed by something other than a date. See Nancy B. Warren, *Women of God and Arms: Female Spirituality and Political Conflict, 1380–1600* (Philadelphia, 2005), 13:

> Colette ... was a profoundly political saint. As a monastic reformer who needed papal authorization for her efforts, Colette was enmeshed in the struggles instantiated by the rivalries of two, and for a time three, popes. These rivalries intersected with international political conflicts ... ."

*the day ... nativitye*] St Colette's feast is on 6 March. This heading provides the only record of Constable's birthdate.

1–4 This beginning bears an uncanny similarity to that of a sonnet headed "To St Luke," attributed to Sir Toby Matthew, preserved only in manuscript; it is printed in Anthony G. Petti, "Unknown sonnets by Sir Toby Matthew," *Recusant History* 9 (1967): 123–158, at 145:

> When thou by glorious death didst first beginne
> to make thie soule, shake of her shirt of Clay
> mine was infusd, and on the selfe same day
> bound prentice to the bankrout trade of sinne (1–4)

Both poets muse on their birthday, which is at the same time a happy and a sorrowful date: happy because it was the day the saint died and his or her soul went to heaven, and sorrowful because an unhappy man was born. Sir Toby outright identifies himself as a sinner, whereas Constable seems to be suffering through a time of illness and contemplating his possible death.

5 If he gets to live longer, considering that his life is imperfect because he is too attached to worldly passions.

9–12 The physical pain of birth is linked to the suffering that the poet must undergo in order to leave behind his body, which, as in sonnet [77], he considers to be a prison of the soul. The focus on pain is not coincidental given that Colette's life was reported to be full of physical suffering, much of which she "considered a gift from God meant to bring her closer to perfection." Accounts of her life describe creaking sinews, bleeding, and ecstatic raptures among other visible signs (see Esther Cohen, *The Modulated Scream: Pain in Late Medieval Culture* [Chicago, 2000], 123–124). Additionally, the emphasis on pain may be read as an allusion to the self-mortification of ascetic practices during the stage of purification of the soul.

12 A first stage in the abandonment of his body is letting go of his appetites and leading a purer life so that he may merit God's grace.

13–14 The second stage is physical pain leading to death, through which he will leave his body behind and go to heaven with Colette and the other saints.

## [79] *Soveraigne of Queens, yf vayne ambition move*

This sonnet opens the triad dedicated to the Virgin Mary; the three sonnets are given individual headings in *HA* and grouped together under one heading in *BE*. This sonnet is thematically linked to [71] and [80] in that the poet elevates Mary above earthly queens.

3 *blessed Maryes*] An allusion to the three women named Mary present at the Crucifixion. In Mark 15:40 they are identified as "Mary Magdalene, and Mary the mother of James the less and of Joses, and Salome." "Mary the mother of James," *Maria Jacobi* in the Vulgate, is also mentioned in Matthew 27:56, Mark 6:3 and 16:1, and Luke 24:10. The allusion was noted in Alison Shell, "'I write of tears, and blud': Henry Constable on Mary Stuart" (presentation, The Renaissance Society of America Annual Meeting, Boston, 31 March 2016). I am grateful to her for the transcript of this paper.

1 *Soveraigne of Queens*] Cf. [71].1, in which the Virgin is addressed as "Queene of Queens." In both cases she is envisioned in her iconographic representation as Queen of Heaven and given preeminence over mortal female rulers.

2 *grace*] Favour, here implicitly contrasted with divine grace.

3 *thy sonne ... place*] Christ in heaven, which is compared to a prince's court.

4 *servants*] The saints, considered as "members of the Church triumphant, namely, those who, by grace, overcame temptation and ... now rejoice to see God face to face in heaven" (Neil J. Roy, "Saints," in *The Cambridge Dictionary of Christian Theology*, ed. Ian McFarland et al. [Cambridge, 2011], 455–457, at 455).

4 *servants ... above*] Members of the lowest social class in heaven are still higher in status than earthly monarchs.

5–6 *yf alluring ... sighs*] On the motif of the lover's sighs, caused by unrequited love, see for instance [2] and [11].

6–7 *thy lovely ... deface*] Mary replaces the beloved in the latter's role as *donna angelicata*. Cf. [3].10 in which the poet's mistress is said to have "An Angells face." She is supremely beautiful.

8 *zeraphins*] Seraphim, the highest class of angels; see note to [69].14.

9 *by ambition ... be*] Given the elevated nature of this ambition – his hope to merit divine grace through the Virgin's intercession – it renders him suitably humble and fit to be a servant.

10 *the highest kinge*] God.

11 *serve all his*] Become a servant to the saints in heaven, i.e., become a member of the heavenly court.

12 *chaste desires*] The love derived from contemplation of the Virgin is divine love. However, this phrase is often found in secular love poetry. Under the influence of Petrarchism and Neoplatonism, "chaste and adoring devotion to a beautiful mistress" was seen as "spiritually ennobling" (Helen Hackett, *Virgin Mother, Maiden Queen: Elizabeth I and the Cult of the Virgin Mary* [Basingstoke, 1995], 17). Ficino finds the origin of love in sight, and describes the lover's response, which can be either an ignoble "desire for physical embrace" or "a chaste desire for the heavenly beauty," which is the mark of the "most wise of all." He then traces the origin of this second type of love to God (see Marsilio Ficino, *Commentary on Plato's Symposium*, trans. Sears Reynolds Jayne [Columbia, 1944], 198). Cf. also Drayton, *Ideas mirrour* 1.12–14: "... thy sacred name, / Which name my Muse to highest heaven shal raise, / By chast desire, true love, and vertues praise."

13 *fairest Queene ... me*] The birth of love is conventionally located in the lady's eyes, from which Cupid's shafts are shot; here it is the Virgin's gaze that engenders heavenly love.

13 *from her throne*] The iconography of Mary as Queen of Heaven is closely related to belief in her assumption to heaven in body and soul, after which she is portrayed sitting on a throne next to her Son. Cf. Verstegan's poem "Conteyning the coronation of our blessed Lady" (Richard Verstegan, *Odes in imitation of the seaven penitential psalmes* [Antwerp, 1601], 40): "And that eternal ever three in one, / There crowned her the highest heavens Queene, / Where angels yeilded honor to her throne" (5–7).

13–14 Grindlay remarks that with this couplet the poet "counters Protestant representations of Mary as a humble handmaid via descriptions of the Virgin as both active and empowered." She is "an awe-inspiring figure who shows justifiable anger at the speaker for seeking earthly love" (Grindlay, *Queen of Heaven*, 144).

14 *Jelous*] What would be a negative trait in a worldly mistress is here a divine attribute. The term "jealous" is used to refer to God in biblical language in the sense of "having a love which will tolerate no unfaithfulness or defection in the beloved object" (*OED* adj. 4.c).

[80] *Whie should I any love, oh Queene, but thee?*

This is the second sonnet in the triad dedicated to the Virgin Mary and is thematically linked to [71] and [79]. Mary is presented as the only queen worth honouring; she replaces prospective patrons from the past in that her potential reward is unmatched.

1 Cf. the first line of [24], one of Constable's sonnets to Queen Elizabeth: "Most sacred prince, why should I thee thus prayse." Whereas in [24] the poet wonders why he should love her in particular, in this sonnet the implied answer to his rhetorical question is that he ought to honour and love the Virgin alone as his sovereign. On her iconography as Queen of Heaven, see [71].1 and [79].1.

2 *a thanckfull love*] The poet self-consciously employs the term "love" as a word articulating what Marotti has called "the realities of suit, service, and recompense" (Arthur Marotti, "'Love is Not Love': Elizabethan Sonnet Sequences and the Social Order," *English Literary History* 49 (1982): 396–428, at 398). This is the sense in which Constable and his fellow courtier-poets often used it in their quest for patronage or office.

3–4 These lines recount the "favour past" (2) that the poet received from Mary: she is the mother of God and therefore to be thanked for bearing and nursing him, and she has helped the poet during difficult times.

3 These images combined evoke late medieval representations of the *Vierge ouvrante* (or "Shrine Madonna"), statues which represented Mary nursing baby Jesus on the outside, and could be opened to reveal the Trinity contained in her womb (see Barbara Newman, *God and the Goddesses: Vision, Poetry, and Belief in the Middle Ages* [Philadelphia, 2003], 269–270). Allusions to her conception and breastfeeding emphasised the mystery of the Incarnation, and "milk symbolized the full humanity of Jesus" (Warner, *Alone of All Her Sex*, 197). Grindlay discusses this line as the poet's engagement with the *Virgo lactans* iconography, the Virgin as a source of nourishment (*Queen of Heaven*, 149).

3 *my saviour*] Christ.

5 *wourthe*] This is a quality constantly emphasised in Constable's secular poetry addressed to noblewomen. Cf. the reference to the countess of Shrewsbury's "high worth" in [31].8, or the epithet "worthy" describing Vittoria Colonna in [33].1.

6 *all*] Everyone else.

6 *in all perfections*] The second "all" in the line is missing in *HA*. Grundy (190), who uses *HA* as copy text, supplies "thy," borrowing the emendation in Hazlitt (58).

**7 *hoope of future meede*]** This is certainly the major motivation behind most of Constable's dedicatory sonnets.

**10 *dothe not satisfie*]** Praise of earthly ladies has remained unrewarded and desires of the flesh unfulfilled.

**11 *one*]** HA has the reading "all," but "one" need not be an error if the reference is to the one, true Christian joy as opposed to mundane happiness.

**12 *delightes*]** A common term in mystical accounts, describing a high degree of happiness or pleasure found in the contemplation of the divine. Aquinas states that "the delight thereof surpasses all human delight, both because spiritual delight is greater than carnal pleasure ... and because the love whereby God is loved out of charity surpasses all love" (Aquinas, *ST* 2-2.180.7 co.).

## [81] *Sweete Queene, althoughe thy beauty rayse up me*

This is the third and final sonnet to the Virgin and, as in [71], [79], and [80], the poet addresses Mary as Queen of Heaven and imagines her as mediatrix to his ascent and perfect union with God.

**1–2** An allusion to the Neoplatonic idea that contemplation of female beauty elevates the spirit of the beholder to desire and experience heavenly things, as articulated by Baldassare Castiglione and Agnolo Firenzuola, among others.

**4 *whick tooke ... thee*]** Christ was incarnated of God the Holy Ghost and the Virgin Mary.

**5** Although the Virgin is beautiful, her beauty is but a manifestation of the boundless beauty of God. In Dante, *Paradiso* 32, gazing at the Virgin's beauty is the necessary last step in preparation for the contemplation of the eternal light of God. Grindlay has emphasised that the poet makes it clear that "the Virgin is not at the pinnacle of heaven," and has offered parallels by contemporary writers who envision a theocentric heaven with God as only ruler and the Virgin as mediatrix (Grindlay, *Queen of Heaven*, 145–148).

**6–8** A prefiguration of the beatific vision. God's deity and beauty are envisioned as beams of light, as in *Paradiso* 33.82–84 (Dante Alighieri, *The Divine Comedy of Dante Alighieri: Paradiso*, ed. and trans. Allen Mandelbaum [New York, 1986], 301): "O grace abounding, through which I presumed / to set my eyes on the Eternal Light / so long that I spent all my sight on it!" Cf. also Spenser, *FH*, "A Hymne of Heavenly Beautie": "And looke at last up to that soveraine light, / From whose pure beams al perfect beauty springs / That kindleth love in every godly spright" (295–297).

**9** *my love of pleasure*] Some self-criticism regarding his former, sinful life is implicit here.

**9–14** The imagined encounter of the poet's perfected, spotless soul and God is that portrayed in St Bernard's sermons on the Song of Songs. Bernard anticipates the perfect union of bride (the soul) and bridegroom (God) in heaven, which will be superior to that obtained in contemplation, in sermon 52: "What do you think she will receive there, when now she is favored with an intimacy so great as to feel herself embraced by the arms of God, cherished on the breast of God ... " (*On the Song of Songs III*, trans. Irene M. Edmonds and Kilian Walsh [Kalamazoo, 1979], 51).

**10** *beauty self*] Divine beauty, which most perfectly embodies the notion of beauty.

**10** *sweetnes*] The variant "pleasure" in *HA* could have been caused by eye-skip, the scribe copying the word from the previous line.

**11** *enamo'rd soule*] The poet's personified soul is portrayed as female and identified as the bridegroom in the Song of Songs.

**11** *embrace and kisse*] Erotic imagery is here used to describe the moment of mystical union or spiritual marriage.

**12** *still*] Both this word and the *HA* variant, "shall," seem to fit the line.

**12–14** Delight is conceived as a spiritual experience that has an effect on the physical body.

[82] *Blessed offender, which thy self haste tri'd*

This sonnet opens a triad to St Mary Magdalene: the three sonnets are given the same individual heading in *HA* and grouped together under one heading in *BE*. In an extended address to the saint, the poet asks for a fellow penitent's sympathy and inspiration to abandon sin so that he, through penance, may reach heaven.

*To the Blessed ... Mawdlyn*] On Mary Magdalene, see notes to [75].

*Blessed offender*] The oxymoron emphasises that the Magdalene is both a former sinner and a saint. "Blessed offender" is a translation of *beata peccatrix*, a common title given to her in the medieval world. Past sin and contrition were deemed essential in her process of spiritual union with Christ.

**1–2** *thy self ... saincte*] Because she has been both.

**3** This is a reversal of the typical appeal of preachers to believers, an example of which is cited by Jansen: "When regarding Mary Magdalen we see her anxious, sorrowful and tearful, we too should be anxious, sorrowful and tearful along with her. If indeed you are a sinner, she gives you an example of weeping so that you will weep with her" (Katherine L. Jansen, *The Making of the Magdalen: Preaching and Popular Devotion in the Later Middle Ages* [Princeton, 2001], 205). Here the poet is asking the Magdalene to cry with him, as he is shedding tears of grief.

4 The line in *HA* is different and alludes to the Magdalene crying next to Christ's empty tomb (John 20:11). In *BE* the poet shifts the focus towards himself and Christ's salvation of mankind, asking for the saint's sympathy. Revision may be authorial, a commonplace image in literature replaced with a more personal, prayerlike petition.

4 *thy Maister*] Christ. The term alludes to John 20:16, where Mary calls Jesus "rabboni" (master) when she recognizes him after the Resurrection.

6 *former passions*] *HA* has the variant "fyrst desires." Both fit the line metrically and semantically, so this seems an instance of revision.

6 *feaver*] Early modern humoral conceptions of the body associated "fiery passion" with "a hot, moist sanguine stage." In literature, desire is frequently expressed in terms of heat and burning (see Lesel Dawson, *Lovesickness and Gender in Early Modern English Literature* [Oxford, 2008], 20–21). Cf. for example [8].11: "in me doth burne a fire."

6 *fainte*] Ambiguous; it may refer either to the poet's soul (5) or the Magdalene's "former passions" (6).

7–8 *that love ... pearse my side*] An allusion to the Holy Lance, the spear with which a Roman soldier pierced Christ's side after he was dead (John 19:34). Cf. Donne, *HS* 7.1–3, in which the poet uses the same image to refer to punishment: "Spit in my face, you Jews, and pierce my side; / Buffet and scoff, scourge and crucify me: / For I have sinned ... ." St Augustine was also conventionally represented as a heart pierced by arrows, based on his well-known statement, "With the arrows of your charity you had pierced our hearts" (*Confessions* 9.2:3, trans. Maria Boulding [New York, 1997], 233). Constable may be revising sonnet [7], in which (profane) love pierces the side of the lady's picture painted on the poet's heart. He uses the verb "taynt" to refer to the effect of earthly love on the heart in [7].9, and divine love on the Magdalene's.

9–10 *no foolishe ... Lampe*] An allusion to the parable of the ten virgins (Matt. 25:1–13), in which ten bridesmaids await the arrival of the groom for the wedding feast, but five (the foolish) run out of oil for their lamps and are absent at the moment of his coming. This parable has been interpreted in eschatological terms as the readiness or unreadiness of humans to receive God when he comes, and the resulting admission or exclusion from his kingdom.

**10 mawdlin**] The alternate spelling in *HA*, "Magdalen," is a substantive variant because it disrupts the metre of the line, adding one extra syllable. The metre in *BE* has been improved.

**10 a mawdlin ... boxe**] The Magdalene was traditionally identified as the unnamed "sinner" in Luke who brought an "alabaster box of ointment" into the pharisee's house, washed Jesus's feet with her tears, dried them with her hair, and anointed them (Luke 7:37–38). This identification resulted in her iconographic portrayal as a woman with long, loose hair holding an ointment box.

**11 oyle of grace**] Divine love and repentance will earn the poet admission to the kingdom of heaven; his female soul is identified with the Magdalene, bearing divine grace instead of ointment. The Council of Trent held that "the beginning of ... justification must proceed from the predisposing grace of God" and requires the believer's cooperation as he or she turns more and more to God (see session 6, in *Canons and Decrees*, 31–32). The poet may also be referring to grace as the state that his soul will return to after his sins have been cleansed.

**12–14** Possibly another reference to the parable of the ten virgins. The poet identifies with one of the wise women who were ready for the bridegroom's coming. Augustine identifies the virgins as the church as a whole and warns believers (*Sermons*, trans. Edmund Hill [New York, 1990], 476):

> Keep awake in your heart, awake in faith, awake in hope ... ; and when you fall asleep in the body, the time will come for you to rise. When you have risen, get your lamps ready ... . Then may that bridegroom be embraced by spiritual arms, may he lead you then into his home where you need never sleep, where your lamp can never go out.

The reference could also be to Luke 12:35–36, in which Jesus says to the disciples that they should be like slaves who are ready and with their "lights burning," waiting for their master to come home.

**14 in my spowses pallace**] Heaven. The soul is the bride and God is the groom in the Song of Songs, as portrayed in St Bernard's sermons. The symbolic marriage is the perfect mystical union of both.

[83] *Suche as, retir'd from sight of men like thee*

This is the second sonnet in the triad dedicated to St Mary Magdalene; see [82] and [84]. The poet meditates on the saint's legendary hermitage and his own sinful, solitary state, and prays for spiritual purification.

**1–4** Repentant sinners hope to merit eternal life and start their penance by retiring into a contemplative life in isolation. On the Magdalene spending thirty years in the wilderness, see notes to [75].3–4. Haskins notes that "many sinners, on seeing images of Mary Magdalen ... , according to the painter and critic Gian Paolo Lomazzo, were inspired to leave the delights of the world and to follow 'the harshness of solitude'" (*Mary Magdalen*, 260). Cf. Vittoria Colonna's sonnet on the Magdalene (*Sonnets for Michelangelo*, 76), which begins with a similar depiction of the eremitic saint who has left behind worldly passions:

> I seem to see a woman of passion and spirit,
> far from the errant crowd in her lonely dwelling
> and joyous in turning away from
> all the things rejected by her one true lover (26.1–4)

**3** *desarttes*] In *GL* the cave where the Magdalene lived was in the mountains and she had "no comfort of running water, ne solace of trees, ne of herbs" (7: 83). The image of the desert also reminds the reader of other hermit-saints such as St John the Baptist and St Jerome.

**4** *doe Angelles see*] Angels lifted Mary up to hear their song every day, and fed her (*GL*, 7: 83).

**6** *she*] The poet's soul, envisioned as a female penitent.

**6** *laments*] The reading in HA fits the metre better. The extra syllable in BE could be a scribal error.

**7** *findes*] The scribal slip in BE disrupts grammatical agreement with "she."

**8** *they ... me*] Not referring to "brutall passions," but to those related to divine grace, sent from above as a gift.

**11** *retyred*] The poet's isolation is metaphorical as he engages in meditation, but also very real, considering that he was living in exile.

**12** *change the ... love*] From profane or worldly love to love of God only.

**13–14** In his *Amoris divini emblemata* (1615), Otto Vaenius introduced an emblem of divine love ("Divini amoris") represented by a child with no blindfold, giving "the profane love emblems a religious twist ... to emphasise the continuum of love from the earthly to its most spiritual equivalent" (Els Stronks, "*Amor Dei* in Emblems for Dutch Youth," in *Ut pictura amor: The Reflexive Imagery of Love in Artistic Theory and Practice 1500–1700*, ed. Walter S. Melion et al. [Leiden, 2017], 547–582, at 565).

[84] *Sweete sainct, thou better can'st declare to me*

This sonnet concludes the triad to St Mary Magdalene. Like [82] and [83], it reflects the poet's anxiety concerning his sinful past and his hope for purification and union with the divine; the focus here is on his immortal soul which, once cleansed and freed from the body, will rise up towards God and join him in mystical marriage. This is the last sonnet in the collection in HA and it is followed by a triple "Amen" in italic hand, which leaves no doubt that no more were copied into this manuscript.

1–4 The poet argues that the Magdalene, as a reformed female sinner who has experienced pleasure, is better suited for mystical union than a virgin or a man would have been. The poet espouses the medieval and early modern belief that "women derive greater delight in sexual activity than men" (Kuchar, "Henry Constable," 75).

5 The poet's personified soul is portrayed as female and identified as the bride in the Song of Songs. This was a general trend among writers on mysticism and religious literature; the soul is female regardless of the sex of the body, the speaker adopting "the position of the 'weaker' sex" before God (Helen Wilcox, "Sacred Desire, Forms of Belief: the Religious Sonnet in Early Modern Britain," in *The Cambridge Companion to the Sonnet*, ed. A.D. Cousins and Peter Howarth [Cambridge, 2011], 145–165, at 163).

7 *betrothed to ... above*] This betrothal is the prelude to the imagined mystical marriage.

9 The notion of the body as the garment of the soul was embedded in the Platonic tradition. In *The Handbook of the Christian Soldier*, Erasmus, developing Origen's idea, speaks of a tripartite human nature, made up of spirit (*spiritum*), soul (*animam*), and flesh (*carnem*), with the soul in a middle position and the spirit being the closest to the divine (see *Collected Works of Erasmus* [Toronto, 1974–], 66: 51–52).

11–14 The moment of death and final union with God is compared to a night of marital bliss; the poet's female soul will be free from its bodily prison and achieve eternal happiness through marriage with the divine. The affective, even erotic language used echoes that of St Bernard (see Bernard of Clairvaux, *On Loving God* 10.27, in *Selected Works*, trans. G. R. Evans [New York, 1987], 195):

> When will it [the soul] experience this kind of love, so that the mind, drunk with divine love and forgetting itself, making itself like a broken vessel (Ps. 30:13), throw itself wholly on God and, clinging to God (1 Cor. 6:17), become one with him in spirit ... ?

## [85] *I write of tears and blud at on time shedd*

This sonnet begins the triad dedicated to Mary, Queen of Scots, which is unique to *BE* and reflects on her death, burial, and ascension to heaven. Here her execution is described in vivid terms and the poet points an accusatory finger at the English government. There is an emphasis on the emotional response both of eyewitnesses and the poet himself.

**the Blessed ... Scotland**] Mary Stuart (1542–1587) was executed on 8 February 1587 on a charge of treason for plotting the assassination of Elizabeth. Whereas supporters of the queen and her government emphasised political motivations, Catholic counterpropagandists made use of eyewitness accounts to reshape her into a martyr who died for her religion only (James E. Phillips, *Images of a Queen: Mary Stuart in Sixteenth-Century Literature* [Berkeley, 1964], 166). Constable is clearly aligning himself with the latter group.

**1–2 tears and ... eyes**] The blood gushing from Mary's beheaded body and the tears shed by the audience. The grief felt by witnesses of the execution is dramatically emphasised in Catholic accounts such as Adam Blackwood's: "Her constancy was such, that all the attendants, even her enemies, were moved; and there were not but three or four people in the whole company who could hold back the tears that distilled from their eyes" (*Martyre de la Royne Descosse, Dovairiere de France* [Edinburgh, 1588], 412; my translation). Allusions to tears were common in accounts of martyrs' executions; cf. the beginning of an elegy on Edmund Campion printed in Thomas Alfield, *A true report of the death & martyrdome of M. Campion* (London, 1582), sig. F1v:

> What yron hart that wold not melt in gréefe?
> what steele or stone could kepe him dry from teares,
> to see a Campion haled like a théefe
> to end his life ... (1–4)

**3–4** The sacrificial lamb is a symbol of meekness and innocence inextricably linked to Christ, the Lamb of God, and the scaffold becomes the altar on which Mary responds to his sacrifice with her own.

**4** Cf. the allusion to Edmund Campion and his Jesuits in another elegy on his execution, "Why do I use my paper, inke and penne," attributed to Henry Walpole and printed in Alfield's volume (*True report*, sig. E3r): "And yet behold these lambes be drawen to dye" (61).

**6 so dere ... A price**] Because she is a queen, and unfit to die in such a place.

**7–8 words suffice ... spredd**] Accounts of Mary's execution inveighing against the English queen and government had been circulating throughout Europe; however, the poet states that nothing that might be written will be enough.

8 *Aucthors*] Because of the lack of a genitive apostrophe, this term can be understood as singular – referring to Elizabeth – or plural – to Walsingham, Cecil, and others in her council. The ambiguity may be intentional.

9–10 The poet joins in the collective mourning, and the ink used to write this elegy and his tears are made of the same black substance. See notes to [25].9–10 and [66].11 on the connection between tears and blood, and the metaphorical blackening of tears with mourning.

11 Compare this very explicit reference to Mary's beheading with the description in the expanded French translation of Robert Turner's Latin pamphlet *Maria Stuarta*: "The blood ran from the body and flowed in great streams, crying to God and to men for vengeance for such a cruel, such a barbaric, such a tyrannic carnage" (translated in John D. Staines, *The Tragic Histories of Mary Queen of Scots, 1560–1690: Rhetoric, Passions, and Political Literature* [Aldershot, 2009], 98).

14 *blushe for shame*] Mary's blood metaphorically becomes the blush on the cheeks of her murderers, their visible shame an involuntary confession of guilt. Cf. Donne, HS 2.11–12, in which the poet addresses his "black soul": "O make thy selfe with holy mourning black, / And red with blushing, as thou art with sin."


[86] *It is not pompe of solemne funerall*

This is the second sonnet on the death of Mary, Queen of Scots. Following up on [85], it continues the chronological and logical sequence by focusing on the indignity of her Protestant funeral and imagining an alternate ceremony in which the dead queen is honoured by natural elements. A sonnet by a young Maffeo Barberini, who would later be Pope Urban VIII, provides a close parallel. It is titled "De nece reginae Scotiae" and deserves to be quoted in full (Barberini, *Poemata* [Rome, 1638], 168):

> Te quamquam immeritam ferit, ô Regina, securis,
> Regalique tuum funus honore caret;
> Sorte tua gaude, mœrens neque Scotia ploret:
> En tibi pompa, tuas quae decet exequias.
> Nam tibi non paries atro velatur amictu,
> Sed terras circum nox tenebrosa tegit:
> Non tibi contextis lucent funalia lignis,
> Sed cæli stellæ: nænia tristis abest,
> Sed canit ad feretrum Superûm chorus aliger: & me,
> Cælesti incipiens voce, filere iubet.

Spanish poet Lope de Vega adapted this poem in his *Corona tragica: Vida y muerte de la serenissima reyna de Escocia Maria Stuarda* (Madrid, 1627), and dedicated this work to Pope Urban. Constable could have encountered Barberini's poem during his stay in Italy, well before its publication in 1620.

1–4 The strong terms in which the poet berates those responsible for Mary's death and his emphasis on her sanctity echo those in an epitaph which soon disappeared from her grave; this epitaph states that the queen was dead "by barbarous and tyrannous cruelty" and mentions the "wicked sentence" (see William Camden, *Annals, or, The historie of the most renowned and victorious princesse Elizabeth, late queen of England* [London, 1635], 344).

1 *pompe of solemne funerall*] Mary's burial and funeral were delayed for six months. She was interred by torchlight on the night of 30 July, and the official funeral was held the following day, using an empty coffin. See a full account in Jennifer Woodward, *The Theatre of Death: The Ritual Management of Royal Funerals in Renaissance England, 1570–1625* (Woodbridge, 1997), 74–86. Woodward notes that Mary's funeral was modest and "cheap" in comparison with that of personages such as Sir Philip Sidney or the third earl of Rutland; however, French accounts of it appear to have been meant to "make the occasion more royal than it actually was, perhaps as a propaganda exercise to satisfy those who felt Mary Queen of Scots deserved a full state funeral" (ibid., 80, 85). Constable may have been familiar with the French sources. In 1612, King James moved his mother's remains from Peterborough Cathedral to a sumptuous tomb in Westminster Abbey (see for instance John Guy, *Queen of Scots: The True Life of Mary Stuart* [New York, 2004], 489–490).

3 *bloddy sentence*] Parliament proclaimed the sentence of death on 4 December 1586 (Julian Goodare, "Mary Stewart (1542–1587)," *ODNB*, https://doi.org/10.1093/ref:odnb/18248).

5 *schism-rites*] The funeral was carried out according to Protestant rites, and various accounts report that her Scottish mourners were purposefully absent (Woodward, *Theatre of Death*, 82–83). Catholic propagandists frequently referred to the official Church of England and queen as heretics or schismatics; see for instance the reference to "the faynte harted and wavering Schismaticks" in Robert Southwell, *An epistle of comfort* (Paris [i.e., London], 1587), sig. Y4v.

6 *suche A Corpes*] The body of a Catholic martyr.

7–8 Mary was a masterpiece of nature, adding beauty to her other creations, and nature in turn used the elements to honour her at her death.

9 *the heavens the hearse*] The sky serves as a covered catafalque.

10–11 *night ... we see*] The darkness of night performs the role of the black drapes hung around the church at the funeral service (see Woodward, *Theatre of Death*, 28).

**12** *serve*] The word is written "seue" with a superscript epsilon-like symbol indicating an *r*, but "sever" makes little sense and must be an error of metathesis; *serve* yields a metrically sound line and fits better semantically.

**12** The poet probably has in mind a "hearse of wax," covered with candles and tapers as described in John G. Nichols, ed., *The Diary of Henry Machyn, Citizen and Merchant-Taylor of London, from A.D. 1550 to A.D. 1563* (New York, 1968), xxix, instead of a heraldic hearse bearing only armorial symbols. Woodward notes that after the Reformation candles disappeared because they were related to the Catholic belief in intercession (*Theatre of Death*, 49).

**13–14** The sonnet is presented here as a form of funeral song, albeit a mortal one, unsuitable to mourn the Catholic martyr-queen; therefore, the poet is compelled to stop singing (writing) as the angels take over. Cf. the end of Lope de Vega's sonnet (*Corona trágica*, ed. Christian Giaffreda [Florence, 2009], 277): "y en tu sepulcro ya los coros bellos / angélicos, con voces inmortales, / para que calle yo comienzan ellos [and in your sepulchre the beautiful angelic choirs, with immortal voices, start singing so that I may fall silent]" (12–14; my translation).

[87] *I doe the wronge, o Queene, in that I saye*

This sonnet concludes the triad to Mary, Queen of Scots, and also the sequence in *BE*; the lower half of the manuscript page is blank. It is a poetic portrayal of Mary Stuart's ascension to heaven as a crowned martyr.

**1–2** These lines are directly connected with the ending of [86] as a sort of recantation.

**3–4** The poet tacitly accepts the Catholic doctrines of intercession and purgatory, especially the belief that the dead need the prayers of the living to leave purgatory and move on to heaven; however, Mary Stuart was innocent and does not need such prayers or angelic songs.

**5–6** Even if Mary had not been completely innocent, her martyrdom would have atoned for any sin. A martyr's death purges sin, and blood is given the cleansing properties of the water of baptism, which washes away the original sin of infants.

**6–8** In *GL*, St Catherine addresses the fifty scholars she has converted to Christianity before their execution in similar terms: "Doubt ye nothing, for the effusion of your blood shall be reputed to you for baptism, and garnish you with the sign of the cross, and ye shall be crowned in heaven" (7: 21). Christian martyrs' conquest of death and heavenly reward set them apart from, and above, pagan heroes (see Carole Straw, "'A Very Special Death': Christian Martyrdom in its Classical Context," in Margaret Cormack, *Sacrificing the Self: Martyrdom and Religion* [New York, 2001], 39–57, at 39–41).

**8** Mary's glorious ascension to heaven is portrayed in other contemporary works such as Spanish Jesuit Pedro de Ribadeneyra's *Ecclesiastical history of the schism of the kingdom of England* (1588): "The saintly queen's spirit flew up to heaven, pure, clean, and washed with her blood, leaving her body, its companion, lying upon the floor, soaked in that same blood" (trans. Spencer J. Weinreich [Leiden, 2017], 533). Even better known is Southwell's poem "Decease release. *Dum morior orior*," in which the poet speaks in Mary's voice (*Collected Poems*, 42): "By death from prisoner to a prince enhaunc'd / From Crosse to Crowne from thrall to throne againe" (32–33).

**9–10** Constable uses similar royal imagery in his sonnets to God the Son and to the Virgin; see especially [68], [71], and [79].

**10–11** *by whose ... stande*] Saints are traditionally depicted as the divine equivalent of worldly courtiers, populating the area closest to God's throne – much like members of his "Privy Council." Cf. the portrayal of heaven in Barnes, *Divine Centurie*, 84, which offers a Protestant counterpart in which the "Saintes" are God's martyrs and the Virgin is not mentioned as queen.

**13** *purple roobe ... dide*] Christ wore a purple robe during the Passion, and it became a symbol of martyrdom because of its association with the colour of blood. Purple is also a royal colour; therefore, Mary Stuart's robe unites both meanings. It may be significant that, according to some accounts of her execution, Mary wore purple inner sleeves and a crimson petticoat made of velvet on the scaffold (see Rayne Allinson, "The Queen's Three Bodies: Gender, Criminality, and Sovereignty in the Execution of Mary, Queen of Scots," in *Practices of Gender in Late Medieval and Early Modern Europe*, ed. Megan Cassidy-Welch and Peter Sherlock [Turnhout, 2008], 99–116, at 106–107).

**14** *Crowne of glory*] The notion of the crown of martyrdom dates back to Eusebius's account of St Stephen, the Christian protomartyr, whose name – *Stephanos* – means "crown": "He was the first to receive the crown, corresponding to his name, which belongs to the martyrs of Christ, who are worthy of the meed of victory" (Eusebius, *The Church History* 2.1.2, trans. Arthur C. McGiffert [Buffalo, 1890], 104). In the Latin poem that accompanies an engraving of her execution, Richard Verstegan depicts Mary's triumphal entry into heaven and her "crown of blood" (*Theatrum crudelitatum haereticorum nostri temporis* [Antwerp, 1592], 85). Cf. the description of Campion's heavenly abode and martyr's crown in "Why do I use my paper, inke and penne" (Alfield, *True report*, sigs. E4v–E5r):

His prison now the citie of the king,
his racke and torture joyes and hevenly blisse,
for mens reproch with angels he doth sing
a sacred song which everlasting is
for shame but short and losse of small renowne,
he purchase hath an ever during crowne. (139–144)

# Bibliographical Description of Main Textual Sources

## Marsh's Library MS Z3.5.21 (*M*)

This is an octavo-size volume measuring 165 × 110 mm and containing miscellaneous Elizabethan verse and prose. It has been at the library since its foundation in 1707.[1] Two years earlier, Archbishop Narcissus Marsh had purchased the vast collection of Edward Stillingfleet, bishop of Worcester, after his death in 1699.[2] This miscellany may well have been among the manuscripts that Stillingfleet was known to possess.[3] Name inscriptions inside the covers can be read as traces of ownership.[4] "William Sheridan," written inside the rear cover, probably refers to the nonjuring bishop of Kilmore and Ardagh (1635–1711), who refused to take the oath to William and Mary and lived in London from 1691.[5] A single owner is probably all that separates Sheridan and the compilers of the manuscript. This owner may be the "Robert Thornton" whose name appears on the inside front cover.[6]

 1. One of the earliest catalogue entries is found in John R. Scott, *Catalogue of the Manuscripts Remaining in Marsh's Library, Dublin* (Dublin, 1913), 66. The description of the contents of *M* is very brief. The first publication on this miscellany was Edward Dowden, "An Elizabethan MS Collection: Henry Constable," *The Modern Quarterly of Language and Literature* 1 (1898): 3–4.
 2. Mirjam M. Foot, *The Decorated Bindings in Marsh's Library, Dublin* (Aldershot, 2004), 2. To these 10,000 volumes were added the archbishop's own books and those of John Stearne, bishop of Clogher (d. 1745) and Elias Bouhéreau, Marsh's first librarian.
 3. Scott, *Catalogue*, n.p.
 4. Marcy L. North, *The Anonymous Renaissance: Cultures of Discretion in Tudor-Stuart England* (Chicago, 2003), 164.
 5. See Richard Bagwell, "Sheridan, William (1635–1711)," in *ODNB*.
 6. This could be one of the Thorntons of East Newton, Yorkshire, of the same name. One Robert Thornton studied at Pembroke in Cambridge (BA 1602–1603), was a staunch royalist, and became rector of Birkin, Yorkshire. Alternatively, this may be Robert Thornton, Esq. (ca. 1573–1637), who was granted a crest to bear with his "old ancient arms" in 1612, and who married Dorothy, daughter of Thomas Metham, and later Elizabeth, daughter of Sir

The miscellany is bound in contemporary limp vellum, the covers now worn with age and detached from the paper leaves. It consists of 190 irregularly numbered leaves in eighteen complete gatherings and six damaged or incomplete ones. Every page has ruled margins that are sometimes ignored by copyists, which could indicate that the volume was prebound. The collection is the work of a heterogeneous group of at least six scribes, some of whom write in different secretary and italic scripts.[7] At times, one scribe will fill a blank left by another with text, which proves that the book must have passed from hand to hand, sometimes returning to previous contributors.[8]

Focusing on the section containing most of the English verse (fols. 1–34), there seem to be six distinct hands belonging to five copyists, here identified as scribes A to E.[9] The longest stint is that of scribe A at the beginning of the volume, with texts written in a florid secretary hand; scribe A may have started the collection when he obtained a considerable number of poems.[10] Scribe B is skilled and versatile: he copies a number of poems between folios 15 and 30 in a neat italic hand, but uses a secretary hand to copy the sonnets by Constable and other pieces.[11] He seems to be responsible for several prose texts later in the volume. The contributions of C, D, and E seem relatively smaller in comparison.

The fifteen sonnets by Constable are on folios 25 to 28 and were copied by scribe B, who writes a slightly cursive set Elizabethan secretary hand with only a few

---

Richard Darley. See Venn, 4: 232–233; John W. Clay, *Dugdale's Visitation of Yorkshire with Additions* (Exeter, 1899–1917), 2: 17–18; Alice Thornton, *The Autobiography of Mrs. Alice Thornton, of East Newton, Co. York* (Edinburgh, 1875), 359–360. Woudhuysen points at a possible connection between the Robert Thornton who owned *M* and Thomas Thornton from Christ Church, Oxford, who was Sir Philip Sidney's tutor; see Woudhuysen, *Circulation*, 262–263. In any case, it is uncertain whether this Robert Thornton had a hand in the compilation or his name is a mark of ownership.

7. The term "scribe" is here applied to amateur as well as professional copyists.

8. For instance, a blank on folio 3 was filled later by scribe D, interrupting scribe A's stint.

9. My assessment differs from that in earlier studies of this manuscript; see L.G. Black, "Studies in Some Related Manuscript Poetic Miscellanies of the 1580s" (PhD diss., Oxford University, 1970), 1: 64–68; George Martin, "Marsh's Library MS z3.5.21: An Edition of the English Poems" (master's thesis, University of Waterloo, 1971), 15. Martin's observation that there are three different hands but all are the work of the same scribe seems an attempt at oversimplification.

10. This collecting pattern is described by Marcy L. North, "Amateur Compilers, Scribal Labour, and the Contents of Early Modern Poetic Miscellanies," *English Manuscript Studies* 16 (2011): 82–111, at 96.

11. The summary of Constable's treatise is written in an italic hand other than that of scribe B on fols. 93v–109v.

italic letterforms (see plate 1). Scribe B uses abbreviations and brevigraphs throughout. Punctuation is somewhat irregular, with colons, commas, periods, and some question marks scattered throughout. The consistent quality of the handwriting and the colour of the ink reveal that all the sonnets were copied in one stint, which may indicate limited access to the source text – it was possibly borrowed from its owner.

The sonnets are unnumbered, and some of them bear an indented heading explaining the subject matter or occasion. The scribe has left some space between the constituent parts of the sonnet, usually between the two quatrains and before the last six lines, and has indented the last two lines, but his desire to leave no blanks is revealed in the lack of spacing between the sonnets and the fact that many have been split across two pages. In general, the scribe adjusts the size of the script to the space available and frames the sonnets within the ruled margins; however, in some instances he has to add a word that does not fit the line below it by using a square bracket.

*M* offers a carefully made copy of the source text, with few scribal corrections. There is the occasional error caused by eyeskip, for example on folio 25r, where the scribe copies down a word twice in the same line and crosses out the second. Another error has to do with the identical pronunciation of the words "not" and "naught," and is amended (fol. 25v). On folio 27r the secretary ampersand sign is amended into "as" using darker ink.

## The Arundel Harington MS (*H*)

The Harington manuscript has been the property of the dukes of Norfolk and preserved at Arundel Castle since at least 1862.[12] It is a folio volume measuring 204 × 309 mm and containing 324 Tudor poems. It is bound in nineteenth-century calf with gold filigrees, and only 145 of the original 228 leaves remain.[13] Foliation seems to have been added at the time of compilation, and the quality of the original paper is consistent. Each page is ruled with thirty-three horizontal lines in faded, red-brown ink, and four ruled margins frame the text. Among the various hands in which the contents are written, two predominate. The one that Hughey terms hand A is a regular secretary hand; the other is the hand of Sir John Harington (bap. 1560, d. 1612), a set secretary in which, for instance, his translation of *Orlando furioso* is also written.[14]

    12. For a complete account of the provenance of this manuscript, see Hughey, 1: 14–26.
    13. Ibid., 1:11.
    14. See London, British Library, Add MS 18920. Other samples of Harington's hand are listed in Hughey, 1: 12 n5.

The first two sonnets by Constable and four lines of the third (fol. 148r–v) are in Harington's hand (H1) (see plate 2).[15] From the fifth line an unidentified scribe takes over and copies the rest (fols. 148v–153r); his hand (H2) only occurs in the miscellany once. H1 is an upright set secretary written in very dark ink; most letters are penned separately and have a calligraphic quality that likens them to those of a professional scribe. The almost complete absence of abbreviations and the careful punctuation indicate that quality, and not speed, was Harington's main concern.

H2 is a slightly cursive secretary hand; there are more abbreviated forms, and punctuation virtually disappears. However, the scribe copies as carefully as Harington and there are no visible deletions or corrections in the text of any of the sonnets.

Sonnets 1 to 9 in *H* are numbered on the left margin, sometimes twice, and all have a similar mise-en-page, with two sonnets per page. The lines of the sonnets are written on the ruled horizontal lines of the page, although Harington sometimes writes a little below or above them. A number of lines, usually those beginning and ending quatrains and the final two, are indented. There is a separation of one ruled line between the sonnets on a page. Sonnets are given no individual headings, with the exception of that on the birth of Lady Rich's daughter (sonnet 42).

## National Art Library MS Dyce 44 (*T*)

The Todd MS has been part of the collections at the Victoria and Albert Museum since its last private owner, the literary scholar Alexander Dyce (1789–1869), died and bequeathed all of his 14,000 books and manuscripts to the institution.[16] Dyce was responsible for the rebinding, foliation, and a number of annotations throughout the manuscript, for instance signalling the places where leaves are missing. His flyleaf inscription gives some clues about provenance:

> This valuable MS. belonged formerly to Todd; and from it were published in Park's ed. of *The Harleian Miscellany** thirty-eight sonnets by Constable which do not appear in the printed copy. Todd received the MS. as a present from Alderman Bristow, who had been a bookseller at Canterbury, and who had bought it along with the library of a family in Kent. *Vol. IX.

---

15. These sonnets are numbered 2, 8, and 3 in this edition.
16. J.P. Hopson, "Dyce, Alexander (1798–1869)," in *ODNB*.

One owner may separate Todd and Dyce.[17] In 1851 the writer on music and antiquary Edward Frances Rimbault (1816–1876) transcribed a ballad from *T* in *A Little Book of Songs and Ballads*.[18] The heading reads "A May-Day Ballad. From a MS. volume of old Songs and Music, in the editor's library, dated 1630. It was formerly in the possession of the Rev. J.H. Todd." Henry John Todd (bap. 1763, d. 1845) was a clergyman and literary scholar. In his edition of *The Poetical Works of John Milton*, he offers a general "retrospect to the more distinguished Sonnet-writers" of England, where he devotes several pages to Constable and mentions his ownership of a "very curious volume, in manuscript, of several Sonnets, Satires, Epigrams, &c. written by different poets in the reign of Elizabeth I; among which are Constable's 'Sonets.'"[19] His own inscription, in a worn leaf pasted on the rear endpaper, gives further information: "Given to me By Mr. Bristow Nov. 19. 1800. Brought from Mr. Brockman's." While *T* was in Todd's custody, Thomas Park used it to copy thirty-eight previously unpublished sonnets by Constable and include them in his 1812 edition.

The next link in the chain is William Bristow (d. 1808), an alderman and bookseller in Canterbury, who may have given Todd the manuscript while the latter was living there.[20] The "Mr Brockman" from whose house the manuscript came must have been James Drake-Brockman (ca. 1763–1832), who held the Brockman family's estate at Beachborough, Newington-next-Hythe, in Kent.[21] Ownership can then be traced back through the holders of the Brockman estate down to the original compiler, probably Henry Brockman.[22]

The miscellany is a small octavo volume measuring 140 × 95 mm. It was probably bound after composition; the binding holes in the gutter may be a trace of the original binding. It was then rebound in nineteenth-century brown

---

17. This has not been noted by Claire B. Williams, who traces ownership directly from Todd to Dyce; see Williams, *Edition*, 1: 11. Her dissertation on this miscellany is an important undertaking, comprising a diplomatic edition with commentary.

18. Edward F. Rimbault, *A Little Book of Songs and Ballads, Gathered from Ancient Music Books, MS and Printed* (London, 1851), 144–145. Other seventeenth-century versions of the ballad differ greatly.

19. Henry J. Todd, ed., *The Poetical Works of John Milton* (London, 1801), 5: 442–443.

20. Sylvanus Urban, "Obituary," *The Gentleman's Magazine* 78 (1808): 851–862.

21. Drake-Brockman matriculated from St John's, Oxford, in 1807 and was sheriff of Kent in 1791; see Joseph Foster, *Alumni Oxonienses: The Members of the University of Oxford, 1715–1886* (Oxford, 1888), 1: 164; Edward Hasted, *The History and Topographical Survey of the Country of Kent* (Canterbury, 1797), 1: 213. On the Brockman family, see Williams, *Edition*, 1: 12–13. Williams drew her information from the "Brockman Family History" website, which is now unavailable.

22. On Henry Brockman, see p. 43.

morocco with marbled endpapers and gilt-tooled filigrees and ornaments. The pages were trimmed in this process, which would explain their unusually small size.[23] Of the seventeen quires, most are made of eight leaves but the first, sixth, seventh, ninth, eleventh, and twelfth are imperfect.[24] At least three leaves were missing before Alexander Dyce added the foliation, and the manuscript consists of 117 leaves now.[25] All the leaves are made of French pot paper.

Three different hands – A, B, and C – appear in the volume.[26] Hand A is that of the main compiler, and is responsible for 301 out of 308 texts, including Constable's sonnets. It is a neat, legible mixed italic hand with regular, carefully penned letters that tilt slightly backwards; it is the product of an amateur rather than a professional scribe (see plate 3).[27] Hand B copied only six poems; it is a less consistent italic hand with some secretary forms.[28] Hand C occurs only once, in a poem written from a woman's perspective; it is a mixed hand with noticeable secretary letterforms written with a thicker quill.[29] These hands engaged with the volume at different moments in time.[30]

The sonnets by Constable are on folios 12r to 43r. Together with the two sonnets dedicated to him, they occupy gatherings 3–7, and only share the last one with unrelated material, a long verse satire titled "Satira sacra" (fols. 46r–49v). However, three blank pages (fols. 44v–45v) separate it from the sonnets. The body of the text is written in the compiler's mixed italic hand; a purer italic script is employed once to emphasise the last line in sonnet 61 (fol. 42r). Headings are written in the usual script, and Arabic numerals are used. A small sham-

---

23. The average size of an octavo leaf from the early modern period is usually 155 to 205 mm in length and 100 to 115 mm in width; see Beal, *Dictionary*, 270.

24. My collation agrees with that in Joshua Eckhardt, *Manuscript Verse Collectors and the Politics of Anti-Courtly Love Poetry* (Oxford, 2009), 274.

25. Dyce indicates as much himself in annotations he made on folios 36v and 78v. A stub between leaves 74 and 75 reveals that a third leaf is missing.

26. My paleographical analysis essentially agrees with Williams's; see Williams, *Edition*, 1: 19–22.

27. See Claire B. Williams, "'This and the rest Maisters we all may mende': Reconstructing the Practices and Anxieties of a Manuscript Miscellany's Reader-Compiler," *Huntington Library Quarterly* 80 (2017): 277–292, at 283.

28. The six pieces occur between folios 90 and 115, that is, quite late in the volume. Williams considers them "later gap-filling additions." See Williams, *Edition*, 1: 19.

29. I differ with Williams on the identification of hand C as italic, which – together with the poem's subject matter – supports her notion that the scribe could have been a woman, or else a man displaying a humorous misogynistic attitude. See Williams, "Reconstructing the Practices," 290–291. The piece is found on fol. 91r.

30. One poem entered by hand B has topical allusions to the year 1622; the lone entry copied by hand C resists dating.

rock device is used to mark the start and the end of the sequence: it appears next to the authorial ascription "H.C. Sonets" and the heading to the dedicatory sonnet "To his Mistrisse" (1), and beside the heading to sonnet 63.[31]

The only abbreviations used are those for *which* and *with* and for titles and honorifics (for instance, Q stands for "Queen"). Deletions or corrections to the text in the same hand are rare; in a few cases the scribe inserts a missing letter (sonnets 30 and 47); he strikes a word at the beginning of sonnet 34 and replaces it with two after a slip. In sonnet 37 a word is deleted. All in all, the scribe did not write hurriedly and chose neatness over speed. Punctuation is generally sparse, but sonnets on folios 26v to 32v – except for 27r – are heavily punctuated in a darker ink, which indicates a later revision, possibly by another person.

The mise-en-page makes the sonnets stand out from other contents in *T*. There is one sonnet per page, with two pages (fols. 12r, 42v) bearing a sonnet accompanied by a short prose text, the introduction and the conclusion to the sequence, respectively. Headings are centred on the page; when they are longer than two lines, they adopt an inverted triangle shape. Extra spacing separates the two quatrains and the last six lines when the sonnet ends with a couplet, or the two quatrains and the tercets when the rhyme pattern is Italian. Couplets are marked through indentation. This "extravagant spacing" afforded to the sonnets is uncharacteristic of the scribe as seen elsewhere in the manuscript, and may either indicate the special importance given to Constable's works or, in Claire B. Williams' words, "a shortage of time in which to work out a more spatially efficient layout for the sonnets."[32] Both factors might have been at work: limited access to the copy text would have been the reason for copying all the sonnets in a single scribal stint, as revealed by the consistent quality of the handwriting and ink.[33]

Throughout the collection of sonnets there are marginal annotations and markings on the page in different unidentified hands. A later reader used a pencil to write one or more *X* marks next to some headings and lines. The pencil annotation "not printed np" appears in full next to the heading of the first sonnet, abbreviated to "np" throughout the rest of the collection. The sonnets may have been marked thus by Thomas Park as he was preparing his 1812 edition, but not all the sonnets he marked as unprinted were in fact so.[34] The same hand is

31. This device appears twice more in *T*, at the end and the beginning of two elegies, on folios 69v and 70r, respectively, and its use cannot be explained in a straightforward manner. See two possible, if implausible, explanations in Williams, *Edition*, 1: 21.

32. Williams, "Reconstructing the Practices," 284.

33. Williams estimates that the copying process would have taken "under seven and a half hours for a professional to copy" (ibid.).

34. Sonnets 4, 8, 10, 13, 15, 18, 22, 36, 42, 45, 46, and 48 were in the printed *Dianas*. Sonnets 27, 32, and 54 were printed in other sixteenth-century works.

responsible for one textual correction in the margin, the cryptic "[so] for? copy" next to sonnet 3 (fol. 13r), with a caret marking the place of insertion in the line. Other marginal corrections are made by an unknown annotator who writes the initials "P.C." next to each.[35] These initials do not correspond to any of Constable's known editors. Considering that they offer variant readings extracted from printed sources, they could stand for "printed collection." A note by Alexander Dyce under sonnet 50 (fol. 36v) reads, "After this, a leaf (containing two sonnets) is wanting." This means that the second leaf of the sixth gathering was missing at the time of rebinding.

## Edinburgh University Library H.-P. Coll. 401 (*E*)

This volume has been at Edinburgh University Library since literary scholar James Orchard Halliwell-Phillips (1820–1889) donated it together with the major part of his collection in 1872–1873.[36] Previous owners include Joseph Haslewood and a "Mr Thorpe" mentioned in provenance inscriptions; they were attracted by some "Shakespearean verses" found on folio 60v, which were in fact misattributed.[37] In his manuscripts catalogue for 1831, bookseller Thomas Thorpe (1791–1851) lists the contents and notes that the miscellany "appears to have been commenced about the beginning of the XVIIth century, and finished about 1625 or 1630."[38] The fact that eight sonnets by Constable are correctly indexed in both Thorpe's and Haslewood's lists makes it all the more surprising that they have passed unnoticed by all editors to date.[39] The manuscript was compiled by Richard Jackson and remained in the possession of the Jackson family, as it was part of the collection of Richard's son Leonard in 1726, as described on one of the end leaves.[40]

---

35. These appear in sonnets 17, 20, 22, 46, 51, and 57.
36. See "Collection of James O. Halliwell-Phillipps," Edinburgh University Library Special Collections, accessed 2 April 2023, https://archives.collections.ed.ac.uk/repositories/2/resources/323. A nineteenth-century transcription of the miscellany exists as Washington, DC, The Folger Shakespeare Library, Folger MS M.b.26.
37. The misattribution of "From the rich Lavinian shore" and "Give me a cup of rich Canary wine" owed much to John P. Collier, who in his reference to the manuscript stated that he "had little doubt" that the lines were "genuine." See *The History of English Dramatic Poetry to the Time of Shakespeare: And Annals of the Stage to the Restoration* (London, 1831), 3: 275–276 n.
38. Thomas Thorpe, *Catalogue of Manuscripts for Sale* (London, 1831), 111.
39. Ibid., 113.
40. On Jackson, see p. 49.

The manuscript is a quarto measuring 190 × 150 mm, and it was rebound in gilt-tooled nineteenth-century black leather. An inscription on the spine reads "Blooms and Blossoms" and "1588. MSS. 1662." It consists of 116 leaves bound in gatherings of eight pages which were interleaved during rebinding. Some original pages were left blank and are included in foliation. The volume is written almost completely in Jackson's cursive secretary hand. He entered items over a long period of time, and there are a variety of scribal stints, with new additions filling up blanks, sometimes vertically, creating a haphazard impression.

The text of Constable's sonnets shows some use of common scribal abbreviations and brevigraphs contributing to the economy of space. There are only two corrections, which indicates a degree of care and attention in the copying process. In sonnet 36, Jackson has deleted a single letter before "lillies" (12). In 30, the poet praises the princess of Orange's hand by saying that her hand is fair "in hope & hue"; the scribe began to write "virtue" but stopped midword, crossed it out and wrote "hue." Punctuation is sparse.

The mise-en-page of folios 105v and 106r is perhaps the most striking feature. Folio 105v is crammed with text; there are six sonnets together in two columns of three, and the top margin has been used to fit in the headings to the first and fourth.[41] Even the left margin has been invaded with the heading to the fifth sonnet. There are vertical and horizontal lines separating the two columns and the sonnets from each other, so they appear to be framed within a rectangle; internal divisions within the sonnets are also marked with horizontal strokes. Final couplets tend to be slightly indented for emphasis. Headings occupy one to three lines. The beginning of folio 106v is very similar, but much of the page was left blank after copying the last sonnet.

## Bodleian Library MS Ashmole 38 (*A*)

This miscellany is the latest containing some of Constable's sonnets and has been kept at the Bodleian. It is a composite volume of about 243 leaves, mostly in folio size with some quarto leaves, especially in the second half of the volume.[42] On the verso of the second, unnumbered, page there is an "Index of authors named, by

---

41. The scribe might have copied sonnets vertically – the way columns are filled in a modern word processor – or horizontally, but given that 15 and 16 tend to appear together and that folio 106v has only two sonnets, one below the other, I lean toward the former. Therefore, on fol. 105v the first and fourth sonnets are at the top of the page, followed by the second and fifth, and the third and sixth at the bottom.

42. It has been described in Eckhardt, *Manuscript Verse Collectors*, 214–217.

WHB. 4/6/31" containing authors and item numbers which must have been added later. This index omits authors whose names are not written above or below their poems.[43] Burghe's own mixed italic hand predominates throughout the volume. Constable's sonnets are on pages 52 to 55, arranged four per page, with the exception of page 55, which contains only two. On the first page, the size of the script varies and diminishes gradually; the scribe appears to have become more aware of spacing limitations as he progressed, and on the following pages the sonnets are roughly the same size. The sonnets are flush with the left margin, and in most cases the last six lines are indented. On some sections the ink has bled and the text can only be read with difficulty.

## Yale Beinecke MS 621 (*Bn*)

Steven W. May and William A. Ringler describe this volume as "a composite collection of prose tracts with Henry Constable's 'Sonnet to the Queen' on an odd leaf, f.14v."[44] It was bought "from Laurence Witten on the Edwin J. Beinecke Fund" in 1980.[45] Witten (1926–1995) was an American rare-book dealer and collector who purchased it at a sale in 1961. Before it travelled to the United States the book was in the collection of the Tollemache family of Helmingham Hall, Suffolk.[46]

The manuscript is folio sized and was rebound in brown sheepskin. The front and rear covers are unadorned, whereas the spine has gilt horizontal lines and lettering reading "Jenkinson Relation 1561" and "State Papers MS." Variations of the "Nicolas Lebe" watermark with a capital *b* and the name of the French papermaker occur throughout most of the volume; archives record samples of this watermark dated from the mid-1560s to the late 1580s.[47]

43. For instance, "Oh, my dearest, I shall grieve thee" (item 36) is a well-known poem by Thomas Carew, but, unlike other Carew poems, it is not indexed.
44. *Bn* is number EV2334 in Steven W. May and William A. Ringler, *Elizabethan Poetry: A Bibliography and First-Line Index of Elizabethan Verse, 1559–1603* (London, 2004), 1: 197.
45. See "Orbis: Yale University Library Catalog," Yale University, accessed 10 January 2023, https://orbis.library.yale.edu/vwebv/holdingsInfo?bibId=9612653.
46. The Tollemaches were interested in manuscripts and books, and had connections with the Sidney family; see Woudhuysen, *Circulation*, 320–324.
47. See Briquet 8077 and 8081. See also numbers 1065 and 1714 in the "The Gravell Watermark Archive," accessed 10 June 2022, https://www.gravell.org. Similar watermarks occur in manuscripts of works by Philip Sidney, Sir John Harington, and Edmund Campion, and official documents and letters by Lord Burghley, Sir Christopher Hatton, and members of the Bacon family. On the Lebe watermark's occurrence in one of the *Arcadia* manuscripts, see Woudhuysen, *Circulation*, 394.

Eight different hands (A–H) are found in the volume, of which only two, hand B and hand C, are of relevance here. The second item is a sonnet by Constable (fol. 14v), number 25 in the present edition, copied in a mixed italic hand (hand B); the same scribe is also responsible for the pagination and marginalia in the next item, a copy of Constable's treatise against William Allen's defence of the defection of Sir William Stanley (fols. 15r–43r).[48] The main body of this lengthy prose work is written in a set secretary hand (hand C), with headings and highlighted words in the text written in a straight humanist italic script. These two hands appear nowhere else in the volume. Corrections to the text of the treatise are in the secretary script consistently found in letters sent by Constable at the outset of his career, in the mid-1580s, and appear to be authorial. The scribe responsible for hand B might have been copying from an authorial text and even reproducing Constable's spelling habits, which can be gathered upon comparison of the handwriting in the sonnet and Constable's letters.[49] In the letters, Constable often drops the final *e* in "writ" or "lik," omits this vowel in "vertus," and writes "conceipt" in its double sense of "conceit" and "concept." The abbreviation $w^t$ for *with* in this sonnet is shared as well.[50]

In terms of its physical features, the sonnet is written on paper that is different from the rest in the miscellany. It measures 210 × 336 mm and it is thick with uneven edges that are slightly torn, which may indicate trimming. There is a large diagonal crease and the bottom corner is folded onto itself. The small, faint watermark resists identification. The recto is mostly blank, with fragments of two inscriptions reading "Turning to the lov," in an italic hand, and "to my l" in secretary. The text of the sonnet occupies most of the verso, written with thick penstrokes in brown ink (see plate 4). The mise-en-page suggests that this was supposed to be a clean copy of the sonnet. The script is large, there is wide spacing between the lines, and the beginning of the second and third quatrain and the whole final couplet are slightly indented. Nevertheless, there is no horizontal ruling and the lines tilt slightly upwards; some letterforms are more heavily inked due to irregular pressure, and there are two scribal corrections, two in

---

48. The layout, margins, horizontal ruling, and variety of scripts suggest that the copy of the treatise was meant to be a fair copy, but there were extensive deletions and corrections at some point.

49. There is a degree of similarity between a few letterforms and ligatures in hand B and Constable's own script as seen in his correspondence. However, the scattered coincidences are not nearly enough to establish the sonnet in *Bn* as a holograph, and this hypothesis has been dismissed.

50. Love states that "arguments from spelling ... have their utility for the period before about 1800 when spelling was still not fully standardised." See Harold Love, *Attributing Authorship: An Introduction* (Cambridge, 2002), 116.

lines 13 and 14 made at the time of copying, plus an insertion in line 7 which seems to have been added later in different ink. The text is punctuated throughout with commas and periods.

## The 1592 Diana (*D92*)

Two copies of this small quarto edition have been preserved. The first is at Corpus Christi College, Oxford.[51] It is bound with nine other printed works in a *Sammelband*.[52] The binding is seventeenth-century parchment over pasteboard.[53] A manuscript inscription on the first free endpaper indicates that the book was one of the 350 volumes bequeathed to the library in the will of Brian Twyne (1581–1644), an antiquary and former fellow of the college who became Keeper of the Archives. A contents list on the verso of the first free endpaper is probably in his hand.[54] The second copy, digitised in *EEBO*, has been at the Huntington Library since the sale of the Britwell Court collection in Buckinghamshire, assembled by Henry Miller (1789–1848). It had previously belonged to the collector Richard Heber (1773–1833).[55] A handwritten note on the front

  51. The reference is Oxford, Corpus Christi College, Library Rare Books Collection, delt.22.9.(5).
  52. Dane defines a *Sammelband* as "a physical, material volume consisting of two or more books deliberately bound together in an early binding," and provides a useful classification. The Corpus Christi College copy was possibly a deliberate compilation by its owner, type II in the classification made by Dane. See Joseph A. Dane, *What Is a Book?: The Study of Early Printed Books* (Notre Dame, IN, 2012), 171–178. Before *D92*, which is the fifth item, come three letters by Harvey and Spenser printed as *Three proper, and wittie, familiar letters* (London, 1580); *The whole .xii. bookes of the Æneidos of Virgill* (London, 1573); Samuel Daniel's *The first fowre bookes of the civile wars between the two houses of Lancaster and Yorke* (London, 1595); and Josuah Sylvester's *Lachrimae lachrimarum* (London, 1612). The four following items have to do with James I's accession. They are Samuel Rowlands's *Ave Caesar: God save the King* (London, 1603); Michael Drayton's poem *To the Majestie of King James* (London, 1603); *Elizaes losse, and King James his wel-come* (London, 1603). The last item is Rowlands' satire *The knave of clubbs* (London, 1611).
  53. See "SOLO: Search Oxford Libraries Online," University of Oxford, accessed 1 April 2023, https://solo-aleph.bodleian.ox.ac.uk/?func=direct&doc_number=011963663&format=999&local_base=HOL60.
  54. A.J. Hegarty, "Twyne, Brian (1581–1644)," in *ODNB*. One of the works in Twyne's *Sammelband*, the translation of Virgil's *Aeneid*, was completed by his father, Thomas Twyne.
  55. The book was sold on 1 April 1924 for £2,700; see Sydney R. Christie-Miller and Herbert Collmann, *The Britwell Handlist; or, Short-Title Catalogue of the Principal Volumes from the Time of Caxton to the Year 1800 Formerly in the Library of Britwell Court, Buckinghamshire* (London, 1933), 1: 225, v–vi.

endleaf reads "Heber IV." This volume was bound by C. Lewis in the nineteenth century.[56]

The book is made of four quarto gatherings bound together yielding a total of sixteen leaves (thirty-two pages). There is no pagination and collation can be described as follows: sig. A1r, three lines of ornaments and a large signature A in the lower half; sig. A1v, blank; sig. A2r, title page; sig. A2v, blank; sig. A3r, dedication sonnet "To his absent Diana"; sig. A3v, blank; sig. A4r, [type ornament] preface "To the Gentlemen Readers" [type ornament]; sig. A4v, blank; sigs. B1r–D2v, sonnets "Sonetto primo" to "Sonnetto vinti" [type ornaments]; sig. D3r, sonnet "A calculation upon the birth of an honourable Ladies daughter, borne in the yeare, 1588. & on a Friday." [type ornament]; sig. D3v, sonnet "Ultimo Sonnetto"; sig. D4r–v, blank. A loose catchword at the bottom of sig. D3v, "Blame," mirrors that on sig. B1v and is an error; it was cancelled with a slip of white paper in both copies, but only the Corpus Christi copy retains it. Collation of the two copies reveals no stop-press changes.

The contents of the volume are complete. The title page reads "DIANA. / The praises of his Mistres, / in certaine sweete Sonnets. / By H.C. / [publisher's device] / LONDON, / Printed by J. C. for Richard / Smith: and are to be sold at the / West doore of Paules. / 1592" (see plate 5). The round device shows the figure of time, a bearded, hoofed man with wings, bearing a scythe and hourglass, dragging a naked, crawling woman (a personification of truth) out of a cave. The motto "Tempore patet occulta veritas" (Time reveals all hidden truths) frames the emblem, and Richard Smith's initials "R.S." are at the bottom. Smith used variations of the same device in other contemporary works.[57]

Twenty-three sonnets are included in *D92*, printed one per page, with print ornaments of varying design at the bottom, under the catchword and signature. The body is in roman type with some words in italics. The address to the reader begins with a large woodcut *t*. Numerals are used throughout one sonnet (60). The headings, in Italian, are printed in italic type. As to the layout of the sonnets on the page, there is a hanging indent of all lines but 1, 5, and 9, and the last two lines are indented further to the right than the rest. In the Huntington copy, a

---

56. "Huntington Library Catalogue," Huntington Library, accessed 1 April 2023, https://catalog.huntington.org/record=b1498122. Lewis's name is not recorded in the volume.

57. This device is number 213 in McKerrow, who notes that it "probably passed to William Wood c.1598." See Ronald B. McKerrow, *Printers' and Publishers' Devices in England and Scotland, 1485–1640* (London, 1913), 122–123. Smith first used it in his 1575 edition of Boccaccio's *Il filocolo*. See Kirk Melnikoff, *Elizabethan Publishing and the Makings of Literary Culture* (Toronto, 2018), 105.

manicule was drawn by an early reader on the margins of sonnets "nono" (4), "undeci" (60), "dodeci" (58), and "decisette" (16) signalling their particular interest to the reader. In the Corpus Christi copy there are no such markings; the only manuscript annotation is found in the sonnet "To his absent Diana" (sig. A3r), where "banisht by over ..." has been replaced with "chased [?] by oue' ..." in line 2.

## The 1594 Diana (*D94a* and *D94b*)

*D94* is the siglum used in this volume to refer to two separate editions or impressions – as catalogued in the RSTC – of which the second is but a slightly altered reprinting of the first. Both can be described bibliographically as A2, B–E8, F6, each copy consuming five full sheets of paper. The earliest printing (*D94a*) is a heavily trimmed-down octavo volume and survives in a unique copy at the British Library, rebound in green gilt-tooled leather.[58] Its provenance cannot be traced beyond an eighteenth-century owner, Edmond Malone (1741–1812), and it came to the British Museum in 1869. The date in the imprint of the title page is lost. A later hand added the pencil inscription "1584" and another corrected it to "(1594)" on the verso of the front flyleaf. Signature F is from Singer's 1818 facsimile edition.[59] Singer used the Bodleian copy of *D94b* for his transcription, which means that there are two sonnets by Constable, numbers 62 (sig. F6r) and 42 (sig. F6v), of which we have no original *D94a* text. The title page of *D94a* (see plate 6) reads:

> DIANA. / OR, / The excellent conceitful Sonnets / of H. C. Augmented with divers / Quatorzains of honorable and / lerned personages. / Devided

---

58. RSTC 5638. The shelf mark is London, British Library, C.39.a.60. The pages measure only 75 x 117 mm. The English Short Title Catalogue erroneously lists the Bodleian library as containing a copy, but this is *D94b* (RSTC 5638.3). See "English Short Title Catalogue," British Library, accessed 21 February 2023, http://estc.bl.uk/S91499. The confusion might have arisen from the existence of a copy of Singer's 1818 facsimile edition at Queen's College Library.

59. Samuel Weller Singer was most likely responsible for the misdating of this edition that the later hand sought to correct by inserting "1594." Singer included the erroneous date "1584" on the title page of his facsimile in order to complete it. In 1802 Ritson gave the correct date, "1594," in the transcription of the title page, so it is possible that the book had not yet been trimmed at the time. See Joseph Ritson, *Bibliographia poetica* (London, 1802), 172. The misdating issue is discussed in some depth in Hassell B. Sledd, "The '1584' Publication of Henry Constable's *Diana Augmented*," *Studies in Bibliography* 23 (1970): 146–148.

into viii. Decads. / Vincitur a facibus, qui iacet ipse faces. / [publisher's device] / AT LONDON, / Printed by James Roberts for / Richard Smith.

The new Latin motto, in italics, is translated by Kirk Melnikoff as "They shall be overcome by burning, who lie down themselves at the flames of love."[60] The device is the same as in *D92*, bearing the motto "Tempore patet occulta veritas" and Smith's initials.

The second printing (henceforth *D94b*) is given the conjectural date 1595 in the STC, but there is no contemporary or modern evidence that supports it.[61] *D94b* survives in two copies, one in the Bodleian Library and another in the Huntington Library;[62] the latter is digitised in *EEBO*. The Bodleian copy is a *Sammelband* consisting of 1590s works, which Edmond Malone unbound and rebound in eighteenth-century goatskin.[63] The Bodleian copy can be described as follows: sig. A1r, title page; sig. A1v, blank; sig. A2r, [type ornament] preface "The Printer to the Reader"; sig. A2v, [type ornament] sonnet "UNTO HER MAJE- / sties sacred honorable / Maydes"; sig. B1r, [type ornament] "The first Decad. / SONNET 1" [type ornament]; [type ornament] sigs. B1v–F6r, decad 1.1–decad 8.5 [type ornament]; sig. F6v, [type ornament] sonnet "A calculation upon the birth ..." FINIS. [type ornament]. American collector and scholar A.S.W. Rosenbach collated and owned the second copy of *D94b* until 1922, when it was bought by the Huntington. This volume is bound in brown morocco signed by "Riviere & Son." It is imperfect in that the title page and leaves A2 and B2 were missing and replaced with facsimile reproductions of the BL *D94a*.

60. Melnikoff, *Elizabethan Publishing*, 129.
61. RSTC, 5638.3. The printed version of the RSTC notes that if inferred dates are given followed by a question mark "a range of two or three years on either side is generally indicated" (1: xxxviii). Williams refers to this edition as *95* in her collation; see Williams, *Edition*, 1: 63. Grundy treats it as a unit with the previous edition and refers to it as *94*, adding sigla to indicate the edition in which a variant is found when they differ; see Grundy, 105.
62. Shelf marks are Oxford, Bodleian Library, Malone 436, and San Marino, Huntington Library, 28501. The printed RSTC only listed the latter location (1: 253).
63. Following *Diana* are Samuel Daniel, *Delia and Rosamond Augmented. Cleopatra* (London, 1594); Richard Barnfield, *Cynthia* (London, 1595); Bartholomew Griffin, *Fidessa* (London, 1596); Richard Linche, *Diella* (London, 1596); and two works by Gervase Markham, *The poem of poems* (London, 1596), and *The most honorable tragedie of Sir Richard Grinvile, Knight* (London, 1595). Shakespeare's *Venus and Adonis* (London, 1596) was originally bound into the volume but was removed by Malone and is now at shelf mark Oxford, Bodleian Library, Arch. G d.44. See the provenance notes by Malone on the flyleaves of this volume and of *Venus and Adonis*; in the former, he explains that in the process of rebinding he moved "Constable's sonnets ... which originally did not stand in the front" to the beginning of the *Sammelband*.

Therefore, the *D94b* title page survives in the Bodleian copy only. This title page presents only one small but noticeable spelling variation as compared to *D94a*: it has "learned" instead of "lerned" before "personages." The names of printer and publisher are missing, together with the date, due to heavy trimming.[64]

*D94b* was set from a copy of *D94a*; it contains the same number of sonnets and differences affect accidentals, chiefly spelling: abbreviations, the use of ligatures, punctuation, and some typefaces. Significant new variants or errors beyond those in *D94a* are scarce; one example is line 12 in sonnet 4 (sig. B3r), which reads "frō thine eye" in *D94a* and "from thine eyes" in *D94b*. Differences are noted in the textual apparatus to this edition.

Every page in the edition contains a single sonnet framed by print ornaments at the top and the bottom. Headings are added in two levels and state the number of decade and the sonnet number with the word "sonnet" in capital letters followed by a Roman numeral. The address "The Printer to the Reader" begins with a woodcut initial. Concerning the body of the sonnets, it is printed in roman type with some words in italics. As to the layout of the sonnets on the page, there is a hanging indent of all lines but 1, 5, 9, 13, and 14, which makes the last two lines stand out whether they rhyme or not.

## BL MS Harley 7553 (*HA*)

The first reference to the miscellaneous *HA* as a bound volume is a 1759 catalogue entry in Latin: "Codex partim membranaceus et partim chartaceus in quarto, continens Theologica quaedam, viz. Oratiunculas, Homilias, et Poemata."[65] A later catalogue describes it as "a book of fragments."[66] There are no records on the provenance of individual items in the volume. The Harley collection was built upon that of antiquary Sir Simonds D'Ewes (1602–1650), purchased by Robert Harley in 1704. However, no reference to a book of religious poems or an uncatalogued poetic manuscript of any kind is found in Watson's comprehensive list and analysis of the original items in that collector's library, or in an edition of the records of manuscript purchases by Harley's library keeper, Humfrey Wanley.[67] The manuscript is also missing from Wanley's "Catalogus

---

64. As a result, the pages are even smaller than *D94a*; they measure 74 × 108 mm.
65. *Catalogue of the Harleian Collection of Manuscripts* (London, 1759–1763), 2: n.p.
66. *Catalogue of the Harleian Manuscripts in the British Museum* (London, 1808–1812), 3: 535. This entry provides a concise list of contents.
67. Andrew G. Watson, *The Library of Sir Simonds D'Ewes* (London, 1966); Cyril E. Wright and Ruth C. Wright, eds., *The Diary of Humfrey Wanley, 1715–1726* (London,

brevior."[68] Given the variety of people and places involved in the Harleys' acquisition of books, it is difficult to even make an educated guess as to when and where the manuscript of Constable's sonnets came to their collection, when exactly it was bound with the other items, or what criteria the original binders had in mind. Perhaps all the items were acquired at the same time from the same source, which means that the volume was already a composite when it became part of the British Museum collection in 1753.

The volume contains forty-two leaves and has been bound at least twice. The current brown morocco binding with gilt decorations and marbled endpapers dates from the late nineteenth century. As an inscription on the last page reveals, an unidentified archivist revised the volume in 1897 and crossed out the foliation numbers on the upper right corner, adding his own beside them. Each item was numbered to match the corresponding 1808 catalogue entry.

Seventeen sonnets by Constable occupy ten leaves bearing their own foliation from one to ten, written in the same hand as the text, next to the volume foliation, which indicates that they were originally a separate item. All the leaves were cut and pasted on paper stubs during rebinding with the exception of the sixth and seventh (fols. 36v–37r), a pair of conjugate leaves or bifolium. The first leaf is larger and made of different paper than the rest; it contains the title to the sequence only: "Spirituall Sonnettes / To the honour of God: and hys Sayntes. / by H: C." Its darker colour and worn condition indicate that this leaf and its conjugate – now missing – would have been the original paper binding. The original booklet would have been formed by five bifolia quired together, and the pages are smaller than quarto size, most likely due to trimming.[69] The sonnets are written on folios 32 to 40, which are in fair condition. The watermark on the first, fourth, and seventh leaves is a circle with a crossbow and possibly the initials *S* and *D*. Watermarks of this kind are of Venetian origin. One of the closest designs in Briquet is found on paper dating from 1592.[70]

---

1966). There is no mention of *HA* in Wright's list of known sources for the volumes in the Harley collection, either; see Cyril E. Wright, *Fontes Harleiani: A Study of the Sources of the Harleian Collection of Manuscripts Preserved in the Department of Manuscripts in the British Museum* (London, 1972). For an overview of the provenance of the Harley collection, see "Harley Manuscripts," *British Library*, accessed 1 April 2023, https://www.bl.uk/collection-guides/harley-manuscripts.

68. London, British Library, Add MS 45701–45707.

69. They measure 190 × 136 mm. The average size of a quarto leaf from the early modern period is usually 190 to 240 mm in length and 155 to 205 mm in width; see Beal, *Dictionary*, 327.

70. See Briquet 755.

Constable's sonnets are written one per page. The layout of the pages is very similar. There are ruled margins in light brown ink at the top and on the right and left sides, which appear to have been set down before copying. Headings to the sonnets are written in italic script in the same brown ink above the top margin. The body of the sonnets is written in darker ink and in a set Elizabethan secretary hand. The scribe uses abbreviations for *with* and *which* regularly, whereas others are found only occasionally. Punctuation is abundant, with commas, colons, question marks, and periods used throughout. The neat appearance of the sonnets and the care with which their text was transcribed reveals that they are the work of a skilled professional or amateur scribe intent on producing a fair copy. Some small deletions or ink blottings can be found on folios 34r, 35v, 36r, and 37v, but there are very few scribal emendations. One evidences a momentary lapse and is perhaps the most interesting: on the first line of the sonnet "To our blessed Lady" (fol. 38r, sonnet 80), the scribe skipped "O queene" and then realised his mistake and corrected it. All the lines are indented but for the first, fifth, ninth, and twelfth; this hanging indent is shared with *BE*. Every sonnet ends with a flourish in the shape of a swirl positioned right below the last word. After the last sonnet, "To St Mary Magdalen" (fol. 40r, sonnet 84), the word "Amen" is written three times in italic script, decorated with flourishes (see plate 7). This and the fact that the verso is blank mark the end of the collection.

## Berkeley Castle Select Books 85 (*BE*)

This manuscript of Constable's *SS*, containing twenty-one sonnets, four more than *HA*, has been held at Berkeley Castle, Gloucestershire, since the late eighteenth century, when it was brought with other items from collections at Cranford Manor, Middlesex.[71] This house belonged to the Berkeley family; it had been bought by the widowed Lady Elizabeth Berkeley, née Carey (1576–1635), in 1618. She was the daughter of Elizabeth, Lady Hunsdon, and followed in her footsteps as a literary patroness and the addressee of numerous written works. Elizabeth Carey married Sir Thomas Berkeley (1575–1611) in 1595.[72] It was her

71. I am grateful to the former archivist at Berkeley Castle, David J.H. Smith, for information concerning the muniments and the provenance of this manuscript.
72. Elaine V. Beilin, "Carey, Elizabeth, Lady Hunsdon [née Elizabeth Spencer; other married name Elizabeth Eure, Lady Eure] (1552–1618)," in *ODNB*. The Careys were Queen Elizabeth's kin because they were descended from Anne Boleyn's sister Mary, who married Sir William Carey. Sir Thomas's mother was Katherine Howard, daughter of Henry Howard, earl of Surrey, and sister of Thomas Howard, fourth duke of Norfolk, both of whom were exe-

collection that was found at Cranford, so the manuscript has been in the hands of the same family practically since its creation.[73]

The manuscript is in excellent condition. It is a single quire in quarto size, with four sheets of paper folded, nested inside one another, and sewn at the fold, so that eight leaves and sixteen pages result.[74] The paper is French pot from one stock; the watermark is a single-handled pot with five baubles, a small bunch of grapes, and a crescent on top. The original binding has been lost. The booklet was rebound with a bifolium of the same size in 1806 by William Shrapnell, who was organizing the collection at Berkeley at the time. On the first page of the new bifolium, he wrote a new title page: "Spiritual Sonnets / by Henry Constable Esqre. / Manuscript." Pagination was added in pencil in the twentieth century.

The first leaf of the manuscript, in the same handwriting as the contents, bears the original title page: "Certen Spirituall Sonnets / to the honner of God and his Sainctes: / withe / Nyne other directed by particuler / devotion to 3 blessed Maryes: / By Hen. Conestable, / Esquire." There follow twenty-one sonnets, arranged two per page, with the exception of the last one, alone on the upper half of page 13. Pages 14–16 are blank, which lends more weight to the hypothesis that the booklet was prepared to contain Constable's sonnets only.

The layout and text are clearly the work of a professional scribe. The sonnets are centred on the page, the lines straight despite the lack of visible ruling. As in *HA*, all are indented with the exception of lines 1, 5, 9, and 12. Three different scripts are employed: textura or gothic blackletter, italic, and secretary.[75] The title page is written in the first two. Blackletter is also used in the headings to the sonnets, alone or in combination with italic, and for the first word in each sonnet. The beginnings of lines 5, 9, and 12 in each sonnet are in italic. Most of the body is written in a set, upright Elizabethan secretary script, with some interspersed italic words – mostly proper names and titles. The use of abbreviations and macrons follows common scribal practice. Different spellings of the same

---

cuted for treason. His father, Henry, Lord Berkeley, was at odds with Queen Elizabeth for his legal disputes with a royal favourite, the earl of Leicester. See Mary Hill Cole, *The Portable Queen: Elizabeth I and the Politics of Ceremony* (Amherst, 1999), 149.

73. In 1618 Elizabeth Carey was reported to be living in Cranford "amongst her thousands of books." John Smyth, *The Berkeley Manuscripts: The Lives of the Berkeleys, Lords of the Honour, Castle, and Manor of Berkeley in the County of Gloucester from 1066 to 1618*, ed. Sir John Maclean (Gloucester, 1883), 2: 435.

74. Each page measures 210 × 155 mm, so it is a relatively small quarto. The average size of a quarto leaf from the early modern period is usually 190 to 240 mm in length and 155 to 205 mm in width; see Beal, *Dictionary*, 327.

75. On the use of blackletter and italic in early modern manuscripts, see Anthony G. Petti, *English Literary Hands from Chaucer to Dryden* (London, 1977), 15, 19.

word occur in the text. The word "king" is written with *i* and *y* in the same sonnet (73.9, 73.11); "deity" appears as "deitie" (67.8) and "deitye" (81.6, 84.8); the word "angel" and its derived forms show the same degree of variation: the scribe writes for instance "Anngells" (68.5), "Arkcaungell" (heading to 72), and "Angelles" (76.8).

Punctuation is scarce in the manuscript, the most common marks being the comma and the colon, the latter of which sometimes marks the end of a sonnet. Capitalisation is often used for proper names and titles, although in some instances it does not conform to present-day usage, such as the capital "A" used as an article in 76.1. There are no scribal deletions or corrections. Another, probably later, hand intervenes twice. In 79.5, a word is crossed out and rendered illegible, and the word "prooue" added above it. In 72.1, the word "Prince" presents a curious alteration in that an additional *p* has been added after the original above the line. As for other features of the page, in sonnet 68 a series of swung dashes separates the two quatrains, a unique occurrence in the manuscript.[76] A flourish made with the pen in the shape of a swirl appears on the bottom-right corner of most pages.

---

76. The scribe may have used this decoration to fill up a blank between lines that was wider than he intended. See Beal, *Dictionary*, 416.

APPENDIX A

# Two Anonymous Sonnets from *T* Dedicated to Constable

*Source: T, fols. 43v–44r.*

**To H.C. upon occasion of his two former Sonets to the K. of Scots.**

Sweet Muses son, Apollo's chief delight,
Whilst that thy pen the Angells quill doth prayse,
Thow mak'st thy Muse keeping with Angells flight
And Angells wing the wing of tyme doth rayse.

That he, which chang'd blind love for love of light     5
And left tymes wings behind and loves below,
Amazed stands to see so strange a sight,
That Angells wings nor tyme nor love outegoe.

The danger is least when the heate of sun
The Angells and the other wings shall trye,     10
A highest pitch both tyme and love be done
And only she find passage through the skie.
    Then rest thy Muse upon the Angells winge,
    Which both thy Muse and thee to heaven may bring.

## To H.C. upon occasion of leaving his countrye and sweetnesse of his verse

Englands sweete nightingale, what frights thee so
As over sea to make thee take thy flight?
And there to live with native countryes foe,
And there him with thy heavenly songs delight?

What did thy sister swallowe thee encite 5
With her for winters dread to flye away?
Whoe is it then hath wrought this other spite
That when as she returneth thow shouldst stay?

As soone as spring begins she cometh ay,
Returne with her and thow like tidings bring. 10
When once men see thee come, what will they say?
Loe now of English poesie comes the spring.
    Come, feare thow not the cage but loyall be,
    And ten to one thy soveraigne pardons thee.

7 **spite** regrettable matter, annoying affair (*OED* n. 4)
9 **ay** aye, always (*OED* adv. 1)

## Notes to Appendix A

The authorship of these sonnets is unknown. They must be the work of someone familiar with not only Constable's sonnets but also his personal circumstances. This person might have been the same who provided Henry Brockman, the *T* compiler, with a copy of the sonnets.

*To H.C. upon occasion of his two former Sonnets to the K. of Scots.*

The author borrows heavily from Constable's sonnets in order to divert Constable's praise of King James toward the poet himself and encourage him to write religious poetry.

    *K. of Scots*] King James VI of Scotland.

    *his two ... Scots*] Sonnets [26] and [27], in which Constable emphasises King James's role as a David-like poet-king with a focus on religion (see p. 278). Sonnet [27] was printed and rather well-known. However, [26] was not; the writer of this dedicatory piece must have read Constable's works in manuscript.

    1 *Apollo's chief delight*] A favourite of Apollo in his role as the god of poetry.

    2 *the Angells quill*] A metaphor for a pen devoted to the writing of religious verse. Cf. [26].13–14: "The pen wherewith thow dost so heavenly singe, / Made of a quill pluckt from an Angells winge."

    3–4 Cf. [27].10–11. Constable's muse soars by taking on divine qualities. Time is commonly represented as a winged man in emblem books; here it may be associated with fame.

    5–6 The wording is practically taken verbatim from [27].1, "blind love," and [27].11, "Tymes wings behinde, and Cupids wings below." "He" could refer to James, whom Constable praises for being devoted to religious matters. Alternatively, it might stand for any poet who experienced a shift from secular to sacred.

    7 *so strange a sight*] The one described through metaphors of ascent in lines 9–12.

    7–8 Neither the wings of time nor the wings of secular love can make the poet soar higher than celestial wings can. Cheney's notion of the "myth of the winged poet," which was used by poets "to communicate the workings and goals" of poetry is relevant here (see Patrick G. Cheney, *Spenser's Famous Flight: A Renaissance Idea of a Literary Career* [Toronto, 1993], 12).

    9 *the heate of sun*] Cf. [3].1–4, in which love is presented as an Icarus-like figure in danger of getting his wings melted by the sun.

    11 *A*] Probably a scribal error for "at."

11–12 At a certain height, love and time must stop, whereas divine inspiration (on "Angells winge") alone is able to soar further. The pronoun "she" was commonly used for birds and suits the avian motif here. These lines could also be read as a warning against poetic ambition.

13–14 Considering the constant allusions to the sonnet dedicated to James, the wish that Constable would devote himself to religious poetry could here go hand in hand with the advice that he try to remain in the king's good graces.

## To H.C. upon occasion of leaving his countrye and sweetnesse of his verse

The avian motif is used to a different end here. Constable's exile is described in terms of bird migration and, as such, is considered reversible. The author is optimistic that Constable could win back the queen's favour. This sonnet must be dated in the autumn of 1591.

3 *native countryes foe*] France, here seen as the enemy even though the journey that took Essex and his retinue there was royally endorsed (see p. 18).

4 *heavenly songs*] This should not be read as an allusion to Constable's *Spiritual Sonnets*; there is no evidence that they had already been written.

5 *thy sister swallowe*] Perhaps the earl of Essex, whose circle Constable had joined by 1589, and to whom the poet continued to reach out during the first years of his exile.

6 *her*] The female pronoun was commonly used for birds.

6 *for winters dread*] As in the case of the reference to "spring" below (9), the seasons here are not meant to be interpreted in biographical terms – the voyage took place in summer. They are consistent with migratory patterns.

8 *she returneth*] Essex made some trips back to England during his French campaign, and eventually returned in January 1592 (see Paul Hammer, "Devereux, Robert, second earl of Essex [1565–1601]," *ODNB*, https://doi.org/10.1093/ref:odnb/7565).

10 *like tidings*] The nature of the reports or intelligence alluded to here is unclear. The author could have been corresponding with Constable and acquainted with specific events.

13 *the cage*] Imprisonment, presumably because of his religion.

13 *loyall be*] Constable should profess loyalty to Queen Elizabeth; the need to conform to the state religion at least outwardly is hinted at.

14 This intriguing line points at a reasonably close acquaintance between Elizabeth and Constable, which seems consistent with Constable's own anxiety about the figure of the queen as evidenced in his sonnets.

APPENDIX B

# Arrangement of the Secular Sonnets in All Sources

| Edition | First line | T | M | H | D92 | D94 | E | A | Other |
|---|---|---|---|---|---|---|---|---|---|
| [1] | Grace, full of grace, though in these verses heere | [1] – 12r | | | | | | | |
| [2] | Resolvd to love, unworthie to obtayne | [2] 1.1.1 12v | | 1 148r | [2] B1r | [1] D1.1 B1r | | [3] 52 | |
| [3] | Fly lowe, deare Love; thy sun dost thow not see? | [3] 1.1.2 13r | | 3 148v | [6] B3r | [3] D1.3 B2r | | | |
| [4] | Thyne eye, the glasse where I behold my hearte | [4] 1.1.3 13v | | | [10] C1r | [5] D1.5 B3r | | [9] 54 | |
| [5] | Delight in youre bright eyes my death did breede | [5] 1.1.4 14r | | | | | | | |
| [6] | When youre perfections to my thoughts appeare | [6] 1.1.5 14v | [2] 25r | 9 150r | [20] D2r | [33] D4.3 D1r | | | |

| Edition | First line | T | M | H | D92 | D94 | E | A | Other |
|---|---|---|---|---|---|---|---|---|---|
| [7] | It may be Love doth not my death pretend | [7]<br>1.1.6<br>15r | | | | | | | |
| [8] | Blame not my hearte for flying up so high | [8]<br>1.1.7<br>15v | | [11]<br>150v | [3]<br>B1v | [12]<br>D2.2<br>B6v | | | |
| [9] | Eyes curiouse to behold what nature can create | [9]<br>1.2.1<br>16r | | 2<br>148r | [4]<br>B2r | [2]<br>D1.2<br>B1v | | [4]<br>52 | |
| [10] | Ladye in beautye and in favoure rare | [10]<br>1.2.2<br>16v | [3]<br>25r–v | [15]<br>151v | [11]<br>C1v | [14]<br>D2.4<br>B7v | | [6]<br>53 | |
| [11] | Ladie of Ladies, the delight alone | [11]<br>1.2.3<br>17r | | | | | | | |
| [12] | Not that thy hand is soft, is sweete, is white | [12]<br>1.2.4<br>17v | | | | | | | |
| [13] | Sweete Soveraigne, sith so many mynds remayne | [13]<br>1.2.5<br>18r | | | | [32]<br>D4.2<br>C8v | | | |
| [14] | When beautie to the world vouchsafes this blisse | [14]<br>1.2.6<br>18v | | | | | | | |

390 • APPENDIX B

| Edition | First line | T | M | H | D92 | D94 | E | A | Other |
|---|---|---|---|---|---|---|---|---|---|
| [15] | Falselye doth envie of youre prayses blame | [15] 1.2.7 19r | | 6 149r | [14] C3r | [7] D1.7 B4r | | | |
| [15b] | False the report, & unjust is the blame | | [8] 26v | | | | | | |
| [16] | My Ladies presence makes the roses red | [16] 1.3.1 19v | [13] 27v–28r | 8 149v | [18] D1r | [9] D1.9 B5r | [1] 105v | | |
| [17] | Sweet hand, the sweet (yet cruell) bowe thow art | [17] 1.3.2 20r | [12] 27v | [21] 153r | [21] D2v | [19] D2.9 C2r | [2] 105v | | |
| [18] | The fouler hydes, as closely as he may | [18] 1.3.3 20v | [11] 27v | [19] 152v | [19] D1v | [18] D2.8 C1v | | | |
| [19] | Miracle of the world, I never will denye | [19] 1.3.4 21r | | | | | | | |
| [20] | A friend of myne, moaning my helplesse love | [20] 1.3.5 21v | | 4 148v | [8] B4r | [4] D1.4 B2v | | [5] 53 | |

ARRANGEMENT OF THE SECULAR SONNETS • 391

| Edition | First line | T | M | H | D92 | D94 | E | A | Other |
|---|---|---|---|---|---|---|---|---|---|
| [21] | Fayre sun, if yow would have me prayse youre light | [21] 1.3.6 22r | | [20] 152v | [23] D3v | [20] D2.10 C2v | | | |
| [22] | The sun his journey ending in the west | [22] 1.3.7 22v | | [12] 150v | [5] B2v | [13] D2.3 B6v | | | |
| [23] | Not longe agoe in Poland traveiling | [23] 2.1.1 23r | | | | | | | |
| [24] | Most sacred prince, why should I thee thus prayse | [24] 2.1.2 23v | | | | | | | |
| [25] | The love wherewith youre vertues chayne my sprite | [25] 2.1.3 24r | [5] 26r | | | | | | Bn, 14v |
| [26] | Bloome of the rose, I hope those hands to kisse | [26] 2.1.4 24v | [10] 27r | | | | [4] 105v | | |
| [27] | When others hooded with blind love doe flye | [27] 2.1.5 25r | | | | | | | PE, n.p. OBL, 204r O91, 288 |
| [28] | If I durst sigh still as I had begun | [28] 2.1.6 25v | | | | | | | |

392 • APPENDIX B

| Edition | First line | T | M | H | D92 | D94 | E | A | Other |
|---|---|---|---|---|---|---|---|---|---|
| [29] | If I durst love as heertofore I have | [29] 2.1.7 26r | | | | | [5] 105v | | |
| [30] | If nature for her workes proud ever were | [30] 2.2.1 26v | | | | | [7] 106r | | |
| [31] | Playnlie I write because I will write true | [31] 2.2.2 27r | | | | | | | |
| [32] | Yow, sister Muses, doe not ye repine | [32] 2.2.3 27v | | | | | [8] 106r | [2] 52 | PR1 [1], L7r PR2 [2], 222 |
| [32b] | Yee, sister Muses, doe not ye repine | | [6] 26r | | | | | | |
| [33] | That worthie Marquesse, pride of Italie | [33] 2.2.4 28r | | | | | | | |
| [34] | Only hope of oure age, that vertues dead | [34] 2.2.5 28v | | | | | | | |

ARRANGEMENT OF THE SECULAR SONNETS · 393

| Edition | First line | T | M | H | D92 | D94 | E | A | Other |
|---|---|---|---|---|---|---|---|---|---|
| [35] | O, that my songe like to a ship might be | [35] 2.2.6 29r | [9] 27r | | | | | | |
| [36] | Heralds in armes doe three perfections coate | [36] 2.2.7 29v | | | | [10] D1.10 B5v | [3] 105v | [12] 54 | |
| [37] | When murdring hands, to quench the thirst of tyrannie | [37] 2.3.1 30r | | | | | | | |
| [38] | True worthie dame, if I thee chieftayne call | [38] 2.3.2 30v | | | | | | | |
| [39] | Ladie whome by reporte I only knowe | [39] 2.3.3 31r | | | | | | | |
| [40] | Sweetest of Ladies, if thy pleasure be | [40] 2.3.4 31v | | | | | | | |
| [41] | Since onlye I, sweet Ladie, ye beheld | [41] 2.3.5 32r | | | | | | | |
| [42] | Fayre by inheritance, whome borne we see | [42] 2.3.6 32v | [15] 28r–v | [10] 150r | [22] D3r | [76] F6v | | [1] 52 | |

## APPENDIX B

| Edition | First line | T | M | H | D92 | D94 | E | A | Other |
|---|---|---|---|---|---|---|---|---|---|
| [43] | If Michaell the archpainter now did live | [43] 2.3.7 33r | | | | | | | |
| [44] | Now, now I love indeed and suffer more | [44] 3.1.1 33v | | | | | | | |
| [45] | Wonder it is and pitie tis that she | [45] 3.1.2 34r | | [17] 152r | [15] C3v | [16] D2.6 B8v | | | |
| [46] | Pittye refusing my poore love to feed | [46] 3.1.3 34v | | [18] 152r | [17] C4v | [17] D2.7 C1r | | [7] 53 | |
| [47] | If that one care had oure two hearts possest | [47] 3.1.4 35r | | | | | | | |
| [48] | Uncivill sicknesse, hast thow no regard | [48] 3.1.5 35v | | [13] 151r | [7] B3v | [21] D3.1 C3r | | | |
| [49] | Deare, though from me youre gratiouse lookes depart | [49] 3.1.6 36r | | | | | | | |

ARRANGEMENT OF THE SECULAR SONNETS • 395

| Edition | First line | T | M | H | D92 | D94 | E | A | Other |
|---|---|---|---|---|---|---|---|---|---|
| [50] | If ever any justlye might complayne | [50] 3.1.7 36v | | | | | | | |
| [51] | Sweete soule, which now with heavenly songs dost tell | [51] 3.2.3 37r | | | | | | | AP [2], A3r |
| [52] | Give pardon, blessed soule, to my bold cryes | [52] 3.2.4 37v | | | | | | | AP [1], A3r |
| [53] | Great Alexander then did well declare | [53] 3.2.5 38r | | | | | [6] 105v | | AP [4], A3v |
| [54] | Even as when great mens heyres cannot agree | [54] 3.2.6 38v | | | | | | | AP [3], A3v |
| [55] | He that by skill of stars doth fates foretell | [55] 3.2.7 39r | | | | | | | |
| [56] | Much sorrowe in it selfe my love doth move | [56] 3.3.1 39v | | 7 148v | [16] C4r | [8] D1.8 B4v | | [10] 54 | |
| [57] | Needs I must leave and yet needs must I love | [57] 3.3.2 40r | | | | [31] D4.1 C8r | | [11] 54 | |

396 • APPENDIX B

| Edition | First line | T | M | H | D92 | D94 | E | A | Other |
|---|---|---|---|---|---|---|---|---|---|
| [58] | My reason, absent, did myne eyes require | [58] 3.3.3 40v | [14] 28r | [16] 151v | [13] C2v | [15] D2.5 B8r | | | |
| [59] | Each day new proofes of new dispaire I find | [59] 3.3.4 41r | | | | [36] D4.6 D2v | | [14] 55 | |
| [60] | Myne eye with all the deadlie sinnes is fraught | [60] 3.3.5 41v | | 5 149r | [12] C2r | [6] D1.6 B3v | | [8] 53 | PR1 [1], L6v PR2 [1], 211 |
| [60b] | Myne eye with all the deadly sinns is fraught | | [4] 25v | | | | | | |
| [61] | If true love might true loves reward obtayne | [61] 3.3.6 42r | | [14] 151r | [9] B4v | [11] D2.1 B6r | | [13] 55 | |
| [62] | Sometymes in verse I prays'd, sometymes I sigh'd | [62] 3.3.7 42v | | | | [75] D8.5 F6r | | | |
| [63] | My Mistrisse worth gave wings unto my Muse | [63] - 43r | | | | | | | |

ARRANGEMENT OF THE SECULAR SONNETS • 397

| Edition | First line | T | M | H | D92 | D94 | E | A | Other |
|---|---|---|---|---|---|---|---|---|---|
| [64] | My hope laye gasping on his dying bedd | | [1] 25r | | | | | | |
| [65] | In Edenn grew many a pleasant springe | | [7] 26v | | | | | | |
| [66] | Sever'd from sweete Content, my lives sole light | | | | [1] | | | | A3r |

APPENDIX C

# Headings and Arrangement of the *Spiritual Sonnets* in the Two Manuscripts

| Edition | BE | Page | Title | HA | Folio |
|---|---|---|---|---|---|
| | Certen Spirituall Sonnets / to the honner of God and his Sainctes: / withe / Nyne other directed by particuler / devotion to 3 blessed Maryes. / By Hen. Conestable, / Esquire | | | Spirituall Sonnettes / To the Honour of God: and hys Sayntes / by H.C. | |
| | Certayne spirituall sonnetts to the honour of god and his Sainctes | 2 | General heading | | |
| [67] | To God the Father | 3 | [1] | To God the Father | 32r |
| [68] | To god the Sonne | 3 | [2] | To God the Sonne | 32v |
| [69] | To God the holy Ghoste | 4 | [3] | To God the Holy-ghost | 33r |
| [70] | To the blessed Sacrament | 4 | [4] | To the blessed Sacrament | 33v |
| [71] | To our Ladye | 5 | [5] | To our blessed Lady | 34r |
| [72] | To St Michaell the Arkcaungell | 5 | [6] | To St Mychaell the Archangel | 34v |
| [73] | To St John Baptiste | 6 | [7] | To St John Baptist | 35r |
| [74] | To St Peter & St Paule | 6 | [8] | To St Peter *and* St Paul | 35v |
| [75] | To St Mary Maudlyn | 7 | [9] | To St Mary Magdalen | 36r |
| [76] | To St Katheren | 7 | [10] | To St Katharyne | 36v |
| [77] | To St Margarett | 8 | [11] | To St Margarett | 37r |
| [78] | To St Collett on the day of her feaste and his nativitye | 8 | | | |

| Edition | BE | Page | HA | Folio |
|---|---|---|---|---|
| | *Nyne other sonnettes directed by particuler Devotion unto 3 blessed Maryes* | 9 | | |
| | [Subheading to the three sonnets that follow] To the blessed Virgin Marye, mother of God | 9 | | |
| [79] | "Soveraigne of Queens …" | 9 | [12] | To our blessed Lady ("Sovereigne of Queenes …") | 37v |
| [80] | "Whie should I any love …" | 9 | [13] | To our blessed Lady ("Why should I any love …") | 38r |
| [81] | "Sweete Queene: althoughe …" | 10 | [14] | To our blessed Lady ("Sweete Queene: although …") | 38v |
| | [Subheading to the three sonnets that follow] To the Blessed sinner St Mary Mawdlyn | 10 | | |
| [82] | "Blessed offender …" | 10 | [15] | To St Mary Magdalen ("Blessed Offendour …") | 39r |
| [83] | "Suche as, retir'd …" | 11 | [16] | To St Mary Magdalen ("Such as retyr'd from sight …") | 39v |
| [84] | "Sweete sainct, thou better …" | 11 | [17] | To St Mary Magdalen ("Sweete Saynt: Thow better …") | 40r |
| | | | *Amen. Amen. Amen.* | 40r |
| | [Subheading to the 3 sonnets that follow] To the Blessed Martir Marye, Queene of Scotland | 12 | | |
| [85] | "I write of tears …" | 12 | | |
| [86] | "It is not pompe of solemne …" | 12 | | |
| [87] | "I doe the wronge …" | 13 | | |

# Bibliography

## Archival Sources

Arundel, Arundel Castle
    The Arundel Harington MS
Berkeley, Gloucs., Berkeley Castle
    GL 5/129
    Select Books 85
Cambridge, MA, Harvard University, Houghton Library
    MS Eng 966.5
    MS Eng 966.6
Dublin, Marsh's Library
    Marsh MS z3.5.21
Edinburgh, Edinburgh University Library
    MS H.-P. Coll. 401
Grantham, Belvoir Castle
    Belvoir MSS Additional 1
London, British Library
    Add MS 11402
    Add MS 12049
    Add MS 12225
    Add MS 15225
    Add MS 18920
    Add MS 24195
    Add MS 28635
    Add MS 42518
    Add MS 45701–45707
    C.39.a.60
    Harley MS 6953
    Harley MS 7392
    Harley MS 7553
    Stowe MS 147

London, Lambeth Palace
    MS 660
    MS 708
    MS 3203
    MS 3205
London, The National Art Library, V&A Museum
    MS Dyce 44
London, Westminster Diocesan Archive
    A4/34
Hatfield, Hatfield House Library
    CP 18/55
    CP 35/50
    CP 167/4
    CP 175/3
    CP 179/156
    CP 187/71
    CP 188/108
    CP 191/54
Kew, The National Archives
    SP 12/126
    SP 12/165
    SP 12/60
    SP 15/28/2
    SP 15/29
    SP 15/34
    SP 77/5
    SP 77/6
    SP 78/10
    SP 78/11
    SP 78/51
    SP 84/19
New Haven, Yale University, Beinecke Library
    MS 621
Oxford, Bodleian Library
    Arch. G d.44
    Malone 436
    MS Ashmole 38
    MS Rawl. Poet. 85
    MS Rawl. Poet. 148
    Tanner MS 169
Oxford, Corpus Christi College Library, Rare Books Collection
    delt.22.9.(5)

Rome, Archivum Venerabilis Collegii Anglorum
  liber 282
San Marino, Huntington Library
  28501
Vatican City, Archivio Segreto Vaticano
  Fondo Borghese, series III, 73
  Segretaria di Stato, Francia (Nunziatura di Francia), 47–49
Vatican City, Biblioteca Apostolica Vaticana
  MS Vat. lat. 6227
Washington, DC, The Folger Shakespeare Library
  Folger MS M.b.26.
  Folger MS V.a.249

## Primary Sources

Alabaster, William. *The Sonnets of William Alabaster.* Ed. George M. Story and Helen Gardner. Oxford: Oxford University Press, 1959.
—. *Unpublished Works by William Alabaster.* Ed. Dana Sutton. Salzburg: Institut für Anglistik und Amerikanistik, 1997.
Alciato, Andrea. *Emblematum liber.* Augsburg: Heinrich Steyner, 1531.
Alexander, William. *Aurora: Containing the first fancies of the authors youth.* London: Richard Field, 1604. RSTC 337.
Alfield, Thomas. *A true report of the death & martyrdome of M. Campion.* London: [Richard Rowlands or Richard Verstegan], 1582. RSTC 4537.
Alfonso X the Learned. *Cantigas de Santa Maria: An Anthology.* Ed. Stephen Parkinson. Cambridge: Modern Humanities Research Association, 2015.
Alighieri, Dante. *The Divine Comedy of Dante Alighieri: Paradiso.* Ed. and trans. Allen Mandelbaum. New York: Bantam Books, 1986.
—. *Dante's Vita Nuova.* Ed. Mark Musa. Bloomington, IN: Indiana University Press, 1973.
Allen, William. *A copie of a lettre written by an English Gentleman, out of the campe of the low contryes, unto the Reverend, Master Doctor Allain, towching the act of rendring the Towne of Deventer and other places, unto the Cathol. King and his answerre and resolution unto the same.* Antwerp: [no printer's name], 1587. RSTC 370.5.
Allyne, Robert. *Funerall elegies upon the most lamentable and untimely death of the thrice illustrious Prince Henry.* London: Thomas Purfoot, 1613. RSTC 384.
Aquinas, Thomas. *The Summa Theologiae of St. Thomas Aquinas.* Trans. Fathers of the English Dominican Province. London: Burns Oates & Washbourne, 1920. http://www.newadvent.org/summa/index.html.
Arber, Edward, ed. *An English Garner.* 8 vols. London: E. Arber, 1877–1897.

—. *A Transcript of the Registers of the Company of Stationers of London, 1554–1640, A.D.* 5 vols. New York: Peter Smith, 1950.

Ariosto, Ludovico. *Opere minori*. Ed. Cesare Segre. Milan: Ricciardi, 1954.

Augustine. *The City of God XI–XXII*. Trans. William Babcock. The Works of Saint Augustine: A Translation for the 21st Century I/7. New York: New City Press, 2013.

—. *The Confessions*. Trans. Maria Boulding. The Works of Saint Augustine: A Translation for the 21st Century I/1. New York: New City Press, 1997.

—. *Sermons*. Trans. Edmund Hill. The Works of Saint Augustine: A Translation for the 21st Century III/3. New York: New City Press, 1990.

—. *The Trinity*. Trans. Edmund Hill. The Works of Saint Augustine: A Translation for the 21st Century I/5. New York: New City Press, 1990.

Barberini, Maffeo [Pope Urban VIII]. *Poemata*. Rome: Francesco Zanetti, 1638.

Barbiche, Bernard, ed. *Correspondance du nonce en France Innocenzo Del Bufalo, évêque de Camerino, 1601–1604*. Rome: Presses de l'Université grégorienne, 1964.

Barnes, Barnabe. *A divine centurie of spirituall sonnets*. London: John Windet, 1595. RSTC 1467.

—. *Parthenophil and Parthenophe*. London: J. Wolfe, 1593. RSTC 1469.

Barnfield, Richard. *Cynthia: With certaine sonnets, and the legend of Cassandra*. London: Humfrey Lownes, 1595. RSTC 1484.

Bellarmine, Robert. *An ample declaration of the Christian doctrine*. Trans. Richard Hadock. Douai: English Secret Press, 1604. RSTC 1834.

Bernard of Clairvaux. *On The Song of Songs I*. Trans. Kilian J. Walsh. Kalamazoo, MI: Cistercian Publications, 1971.

—. *On The Song of Songs III*. Trans. Irene M. Edmonds and Kilian J. Walsh. Kalamazoo, MI: Cistercian Publications, 1979.

—. *Selected Works*. Trans. G.R. Evans. New York: Paulist Press, 1987.

Birch, Thomas, ed. *An Historical View of the Negotiations between the Courts of England, France and Brussels, from the Year 1592 to 1617*. London: A. Millar, 1749.

Bird, Samuel. *A friendlie communication or dialogue betweene Paule and Damas*. London: Thomas East, 1580. RSTC 3086.

Blackwood, Adam. *Martyre de la royne descosse, dovairiere de France*. Edinburgh: Jean Nafield, 1588. RSTC 3108.

Blair, Charles H. Hunter, ed. *Visitations of the North, Part 4: Visitations of Yorkshire and Northumberland*. Publications of the Surtees Society 146. Durham: Andrews, 1932.

Blok, P.J. *Correspondance inédite Robert Dudley, comte de Leycester, et de François et Jean Hotman*. Haarlem: Les heritiers Loosjes, 1911.

Bonaventure. *The Life of Christ*. Trans. W.H. Hutchings. London: Rivingtons, 1888.

Breton, Nicholas. *Brittons bowre of delights*. London: Richard Jones, 1591. RSTC 3633.

—. *The pilgrimage to paradise*. London: Joseph Barnes, 1592. RSTC 3683.

Buchanan, George. *Poemata in tres partes digesta*. London: Rob. Gosling, 1716.

*Calendar of Letters and State Papers Relating to English Affairs Preserved Principally in the*

Archives of Simancas. Ed. Martin A.S. Hume. 4 vols. London: Her Majesty's Stationery Office, 1892–1899.
Calendar of State Papers and Manuscripts Relating to English Affairs, Existing in the Archives and Collections of Venice, and in Other Libraries of Northern Italy. Ed. Rawdon Brown et al. 38 vols. in 40. London: Her Majesty's Stationery Office, 1864–1947.
Calendar of State Papers Domestic: Edward VI, Mary, Elizabeth, and James I. Ed. R. Lemon and Everett Green. 12 vols. London: Her Majesty's Stationery Office, 1856–1872.
Calendar of State Papers relating to Scotland and Mary Queen of Scots, 1547–1603. Ed. Joseph Bain et al. 13 vols. Edinburgh: Her Majesty's General Register House, 1898–1969.
Calvin, Jean. *Sermons of John Calvin*. London: John Day, 1560. RSTC 4450.
Camden, William. *Annales rerum anglicarum, et hibernicarum, regnante Elizabetha*. London: William Stansby, 1615. RSTC 4496.
—. *Annals, or, The historie of the most renowned and victorious princesse Elizabeth, late queen of England*. London: Thomas Harper, 1635. RSTC 4501.
Cameron, Annie I., ed. *The Warrender Papers*. 2 vols. Edinburgh: Edinburgh University Press, 1931–1932.
Campbell, Thomas, ed. *Specimens of the British Poets*. 7 vols. London: J. Murray, 1819.
Campion, Thomas. *The third and fourth booke of ayres*. London: Thomas Snodham, 1617. RSTC 4548.
Carducci, Giosuè, ed. *Rime di M. Cino da Pistoia e d'altri del secolo XIV*. Florence: G. Barbèra, 1862.
Castiglione, Baldassare. *The Book of the Courtier; from the Italian, done into English by Sir Thomas Hoby, anno 1561, with an introd. by Walter Raleigh*. Ed. W.E. Henley. London: Nutt, 1900.
Chapman, George. *The memorable maske of the two honorable houses or Innes of Court; the Middle Temple, and Lyncolns Inne*. London: George Eld, 1613. RSTC 4981.
—. *Ovids Banquet of Sence*. London: James Roberts, 1595. RSTC 4985.
Chaucer, Geoffrey. *The workes of our antient and lerned English poet, Geffrey Chaucer*. Ed. Thomas Speght. London: Adam Islip, 1598.
—. *The Works of Geoffrey Chaucer*. Ed. F.N. Robinson. Boston: Houghton Mifflin, 1957.
Church, Henry. *Miscellanea philo-theologica, or, God, & man*. London: J. Norton and J. Okes, 1637. RSTC 5217.
Church of England. *Articles: Whereupon it was agreed by the archbysshops, and bisshops in M.D.lxii*. London: Richard Jugge and John Cawood, 1563. RSTC 10038.3.
Churchyard, Thomas. *A pleasaunte laborinth called Churchyardes chance*. London: John Kyngston, 1580. RSTC 5250.
Colonna, Vittoria. *Sonnets for Michelangelo: A Bilingual Edition*. Ed. and trans. Abigail Brundin. Chicago: University of Chicago Press, 2005.
[Constable, Henry?]. *A discoverye of a counterfecte conference helde at a counterfecte place, by counterfecte travellers, for thadvancement of a counterfecte tytle, and invented, printed, and published by one (person) that dare not avowe his name*. [Paris?]: [no publisher's name,] 1600. RSTC 5638.5.

Constable, Henry. *The Catholike moderator: Or, a moderate examination of the doctrine of the Protestants.* Trans. W.W. London: Eliot's Court, 1623. RSTC 5636.2.

—. *Diana: The excellent conceitful sonnets of H.C. augmented with divers quatorzains of honorable and lerned personages.* London: James Roberts, [1594?]. RSTC 5638, 5638.3.

—. *Diana: Or, the excellent conceitful Sonnets of H. C. augmented with diuers quatorzains of honorable and lerned personages; Deuided into viij. decads.* Ed. Samuel W. Singer. London, 1818.

—. *Diana: Or, the excellent conceitful sonnets of H. C. supposed to have been printed either in 1592 or 1594.* Ed. Edward Littledale. London: G. Woodfall, 1818.

—. *Diana: The praises of his Mistres, in certaine sweete sonnets.* London: John Charlewood, 1592. RSTC 5637.

—. *Diana: The Sonnets and Other Poems of Henry Constable.* Ed. William C. Hazlitt. London: B.M. Pickering, 1859.

—. *Examen pacifique de la doctrine des Huguenots.* [London: J. Wolfe], 1589. RSTC 5638.7.

Cooke, John. *Greenes Tu quoque, or, The cittie gallant.* London, 1614. RSTC 5673.

Costanzo, Angelo di. *Le Rime.* Padua: Giuseppe Comino, 1750.

Council of Trent. *Canons and Decrees of the Council of Trent.* Trans. H. J. Schroeder. Rockford, IL: Tan Books and Publishers, 1978.

Craig, Alexander. *The amorose songes, sonets, and elegies.* London: William White, 1606. RSTC 5956.

Crow, Martha Foote, ed. *Elizabethan Sonnet-Cycles: Delia and Diana.* London: K. Paul, Trench, Trübner, 1986.

Daniel, Samuel. *Delia and Rosamond augmented. Cleopatra.* London: James Roberts and Edward Allde, 1594. RSTC 6243.4.

—. *The first fowre bookes of the civile wars between the two houses of Lancaster and Yorke.* London: P. Short, 1595. RSTC 6244.

Davison, Francis, ed. *A poetical rapsodie.* 2nd ed. London: Nicholas Okes, 1608. RSTC 6374.

—. *A poetical rapsody.* 1st ed. London: V. Simmes, 1602. RSTC 6373.

Day, Angel. *Upon the life and death of the most worthy, and thrise renowmed knight, Sir Phillip Sidney.* London: Robert Waldegrave, 1586? RSTC 6409.

Dekker, Thomas. *The magnificent entertainment given to King James.* London: Thomas Man the Younger, 1604. RSTC 6510.

Desportes, Phillipe. *Les premieres oeuvres.* Paris: Robert Le Mangnier, 1575.

—. *Œuvres de Philippe Desportes.* Ed. Alfred Michiels. Paris: Adolphe Delahays, 1858.

Digges, Leonard. *A prognostication everlasting of ryght good effecte.* London: Thomas Gemini, 1556. RSTC 435.39.

Donne, John. *The Complete Poems.* Ed. Robin Robbins. Edinburgh: Pearson, 2010.

—. *The Oxford Edition of the Sermons of John Donne.* Vol. 1. *Sermons Preached at the Jacobean Courts, 1615–19.* Ed. Peter McCullough. Oxford: Oxford University Press, 2015.

—. *Poems*. London: Miles Flesher, 1635. RSTC 7046.
—. *The Variorum Edition of the Poetry of John Donne*. 8 vols. in 11. Ed. Gary A. Stringer and Jeffrey S. Johnson. Bloomington, IN: Indiana University Press, 1995–.
Dousa, Janus, the Younger. *Poemata*. Ed. Gulielmo Rabo. Rotterdam: Adrianum van Dijk, 1704.
Drayton, Michael. *Englands heroicall epistles*. London: James Roberts, 1599. RSTC 7195.
—. *Ideas mirrour: Amours in quatorzains*. London: James Roberts, 1594. RSTC 7203.
—. *Poems: By Michaell Draiton Esquire*. London: Valentine Simmes, 1605. RSTC 7216.
—. *To the Majestie of King James*. London: James Roberts, 1603. RSTC 7231.
Drummond, William. *The Poetical Works of William Drummond of Hawthornden*. Ed. L.E. Kastner. 2 vols. Edinburgh: William Blackwood, 1913.
Du Bartas, Guillaume de Saluste. *Bartas: His devine weekes and workes translated*. Trans. Joshua Sylvester. London: Humfrey Lownes, 1605. RSTC 21649.
Du Bellay, Joachim. *L'Olive*. Ed. Ernesta Caldarini. Geneva: Droz, 1974.
—. *Les oeuvres*. Paris: Arnoul L'Angelier and Charles L'Angelier, 1552.
—. *Les Regrets et Autres Œuvres Poëtiques*. Ed. J. Jolliffe and M.A. Screech. Geneva: Droz, 1974.
Du Moulin, Pierre. "Autobiographie de Pierre Du Moulin, d'après le manuscrit autographe, 1564–1658." *Bulletin de la Société de l'histoire du protestantisme français* 7 (1858): 170–182.
Dyce, Alexander, ed. *Specimens of English Sonnets*. London: William Pickering, 1833.
Edmonds, John M., ed. *Elegy and Iambus, Being the Remains of all the Greek Elegiac and Iambic Poets from Callinus to Crates, Excepting the Choliambic Writers, With the Anacreontea*. 2 vols. London: Heinemann, 1931.
Edwards, Richard. *The paradyse of daynty devises*. London: R. Jones, 1576. RSTC 7516.
Eliot, John. *Ortho-epia Gallica*. London: Richard Field, 1593. RSTC 7574.
*Elizaes losse, and King James his wel-come*. London: T. Creede, 1603. RSTC 21496.5.
*England's Helicon*. London: James Roberts, 1600. RSTC 3191.
Erasmus, Desiderius. *Collected Works of Erasmus*. 86 vols. Toronto: University of Toronto Press, 1974–.
Eusebius. *The Church History*. Trans. Arthur Cushman McGiffert. In *Nicene and Post-Nicene Fathers*, 2nd ser., ed. Philip Schaff and Henry Wace, 1: vii–404. Buffalo, NY: Christian Literature Publishing, 1890.
Evans, Maurice, ed. *Elizabethan Sonnets*. London: Dent, 1977.
Ficino, Marsilio. *Commentary on Plato's Symposium*. Trans. Sears Reynolds Jayne. Columbia, MO: University of Missouri, 1944.
Fletcher, Giles. *Licia, or Poemes of love in honour of the admirable and singular vertues of his lady*. London: John Legat, 1593. RSTC 11055.
Fowler, William. *The Works of William Fowler*. Ed. Henry W. Meikle, James Craigie, and John Purves. 3 vols. Edinburgh: W. Blackwood, 1914–1940.
Fulke, William. *A goodly gallerye with a most pleasaunt prospect, into the garden of naturall contemplation*. London: William Griffith, 1563. RSTC 11435.

Gager, William. *Exequiae illustrissimi equitis, D. Philippi Sidnaei*. Oxford: Joseph Barnes, 1587. RSTC 22551.
Gallonio, Antonio. *Tortures and Torments of the Christian Martyrs*. Trans. Alfred R. Allinson. London: Fortune Press, 1903.
Gascoigne, George. *The Complete Works of George Gascoigne*. Ed. John W. Cunliffe. 2 vols. Cambridge: Cambridge University Press, 1910.
Gorges, Arthur. *The Poems of Sir Arthur Gorges*. Ed. Helen E. Sandison. Oxford: Clarendon Press, 1953.
Gray, John, ed. *The Poems & Sonnets of Henry Constable*. London: Ballantyne Press, 1897.
Greene, Robert. *Greenes Orpharion*. London: James Roberts, 1599. RSTC 12260.
Greville, Fulke. *Certaine learned and elegant workes of the Right Honorable Fulke Lord Brooke*. London: Elizabeth Purslowe, 1633. RSTC 12361.
Griffin, Bartholomew. *Fidessa, more chaste then kinde*. London: Joan Orwin, 1596. RSTC 12367.
Hakewill, George. *An Answere to a treatise written by Dr. Carier*. London: John Bill, 1616. RSTC 12610.
Hakluyt, Richard. *The principall navigations, voyages and discoveries of the English nation*. London: George Bishop and Ralph Newberie, 1589. RSTC 12625.
Harington, John. *The Epigrams of Sir John Harington*. Ed. Gerard Kilroy. Farnham: Ashgate, 2009.
—. *Orlando furioso in English heroical verse*. London: Richard Field, 1591. RSTC 746.
—. *A Tracte on the Succession to the Crown*. Ed. Clements R. Markham. London: Nichols and Sons, 1880.
Harvey, Gabriel, and Edmund Spenser. *Three proper, and wittie, familiar letters: Lately passed betvveene two universitie men; Touching the earthquake in Aprill last, and our English refourmed versifying*. London: H. Bynneman, 1580. RSTC 23095.
Haslewood, Joseph, ed. *Ancient Critical Essays upon English Poets and Poesy*. 2 vols. London: Robert Triphook, 1811–1815.Hasted, Edward. *The History and Topographical Survey of the Country of Kent*. 12 vols. Canterbury: W. Bristow, 1797–1801.
Herbert, George. *The English Poems of George Herbert*. Ed. Helen Wilcox. Cambridge: Cambridge University Press, 2007.
Hilliard, Nicholas. *The Arte of Limning*. Ed. T.G.S. Cain and R.K.R. Thornton. Ashington: Mid Northumberland Arts Group, 1992.
Historical Manuscripts Commission. *Calendar of the manuscripts of the Most Hon. the Marquis of Salisbury, K.G., preserved at Hatfield House, Hertfordshire*. 24 vols. London: His Majesty's Stationery Office, 1883–1976.
—. *Eleventh Report, Appendix, Part VII*. London: Her Majesty's Stationery Office, 1887.
—. *The Manuscripts of his Grace the Duke of Rutland, G.C.B., Preserved at Belvoir Castle*. 4 vols. London: His Majesty's Stationery Office, 1888–1905.
*An homelie of Mary Magdalene, declaring her fervent love and zele towards Christ*. London: Henry Sutton, 1555. RSTC 18848.

Howard, Henry. *A Critical Edition of the Complete Poems of Henry Howard, Earl of Surrey.* Ed. William McGaw. Lewiston: Edwin Mellen Press, 2012.

Hunnis, William. *A hyve full of hunnye contayning the firste booke of Moses, called Genesis.* London: Thomas Marsh, 1578. RSTC 13974.

—. *Seven sobs of a sorrowfull soule for sinne.* London: Henrie Denham, 1583. RSTC 13975.

Ignatius of Loyola. *The Spiritual Exercises and Selected Works.* Ed. George E. Ganss. New York: Paulist Press, 1991.

Jacobus de Voragine. *The Golden Legend or Lives of the Saints.* Trans. William Caxton. Ed. Frederick Startridge Ellis. 7 vols. London: J.M. Dent, 1900–1931.

James VI and I. *The essayes of a prentise, in the divine art of poesie.* Edinburgh: Thomas Vautroullier, 1584. RSTC 14373.

—. *His Majesties poeticall exercises at vacant houres.* Edinburgh: Robert Waldegrave, 1591. RSTC 14379.

—. *The Poems of James VI of Scotland.* Ed. James Craigie. 2 vols. Edinburgh: Blackwood, 1955.

Jerome. *On Illustrious Men.* Trans. Thomas P. Halton. Washington, DC: The Catholic University of America Press, 1999.

John of the Cross. *Poesía.* Córdoba: El Cid, 2003.

Jones, Emrys, ed. *The New Oxford Book of Sixteenth-Century Verse.* Oxford: Oxford University Press, 1991.

Jonson, Ben. *The Complete Poems.* Ed. George Parfitt. New Haven: Yale University Press, 1975.

—. *The Workes of Benjamin Jonson.* Vols. 2–3. London: John Beale et al., 1641. RSTC 14754.

Kramer, Heinrich. *The Malleus Maleficarum.* Trans. Christopher Mackway. Cambridge: Cambridge University Press, 2009.

Kyd, Thomas. *The Spanish Tragedy.* Ed. David Bevington. Manchester: Manchester University Press, 1996.

La Primaudaye, Pierre de. *The third volume of the French academie.* London: Eliot's Court, 1601. RSTC 15240.

Lanyer, Aemilia. *The Poems of Aemilia Lanyer: Salve Deus Rex Judæorum.* Ed. Susanne Woods. New York: Oxford University Press, 1993.

Lechmere, John. *The relection of a conference touching the real presence.* Douai: Laurence Kellam, 1635. RSTC 15351.3.

Lee, Sidney, ed. *Elizabethan Sonnets.* 2 vols. New York: Dutton, 1904.

Leighton, William. *Vertue triumphant, or A lively description of the foure vertues cardinall.* London: Melchisedech Bradwood, 1603. RSTC 15435.

Lemnius, Levinus. *The touchstone of complexions.* Trans. Thomas Newton. London: Thomas Marsh, 1576. RSTC 15456.

Linche, Richard. *Diella, certaine sonnets, adjoined to the amorous poeme of Dom Diego and Ginevra.* London: James Roberts, 1596. RSTC 17091.

Lincoln's Inn Society. *Records of the Honorable Society of Lincoln's Inn.* 2 vols. London: H.S. Cartwright, 1896.

[Ling, Nicholas]. *Politeuphuia, wits common wealth.* London: James Roberts, 1597. RSTC 15685.
Lodge, Edmund. *Illustrations of British History.* 3 vols. London: G. Nicol, 1791.
Lodge, Thomas. *Phillis: Honoured with pastorall sonnets, elegies, and amorous delights.* London: James Roberts, 1593. RSTC 16662.
Lomazzo, Giovanni Paolo. *A tracte containing the artes of curious paintinge carvinge & buildinge.* Trans. Richard Haydock. Oxford: Joseph Barnes, 1598. RSTC 16698.
Machyn, Henry. *The Diary of Henry Machyn, Citizen and Merchant-Taylor of London, from A.D. 1550 to A.D. 1563.* Ed. Nichols, John G. New York: AMS Press, 1968.
Malipiero, Girolamo. *Il Petrarca spirituale.* Venice: Francesco Marcolini da Forlì, 1536.
Markham, Gervase. *The most honorable tragedie of Sir Richard Grinvile, Knight.* London: James Roberts, 1595. RSTC 17385.
—. *The poem of poems: Or, Sions muse, contayning the divine song of King Salomon, devided into eight eclogues.* London: James Roberts, 1596. RSTC 17386.
Martz, Louis L., ed. *The Meditative Poem: An Anthology of Seventeenth-Century Verse.* New York: New York University Press, 1963.
Matthew, Toby. *A True Historical Relation of the Conversion of Sir Tobie Matthew to the Holy Catholic Faith.* Ed. A. H. Mathew. London: Burns & Oates, 1904.
Mayor, J.E.B., ed. *Early Statutes of the College of St. John the Evangelist.* Cambridge: Cambridge University Press, 1859.
Medici, Lorenzo de. *Poesie del magnifico Lorenzo De' Medici.* Bergamo: Pietro Lancellotti, 1763.
Millman, Jill Seal, and Gillian Wright, eds. *Early Modern Women's Manuscript Poetry.* Manchester: Manchester University Press, 2005.
Miola, Robert S., ed. *Early Modern Catholicism: An Anthology of Primary Sources.* Oxford: Oxford University Press, 2007.
Moffett, Thomas. *Nobilis: Or a View of the Life and Death of a Sidney and Lessus lugubris.* Ed. Virgil B. Heltzel and Hoyt H. Hudson. San Marino: Huntington Library, 1940.
Montgomerie, Alexander. *Poems.* Ed. David J. Parkinson. 2 vols. Edinburgh: The Scottish Text Society, 2000.
Napier, John. *A plaine discovery of the whole Revelation of Saint John.* London: Robert Waldegrave, 1593. RSTC 18354.
Nelson, Thomas. *A short discourse: Expressing the substaunce of all the late pretended treasons against the Queenes Majestie.* London: George Robinson, 1586. RSTC 18425.
Norbrook, David, and Henry R. Woudhuysen, eds. *The Penguin Book of Renaissance Verse: 1509–1659.* London: The Penguin Press, 1992.
Ovid. *Amores: Medicamina faciei femineae; Ars amatoria. Remedia amoris.* Ed. E. J. Kenney. Oxford: E Typographeo Clarendoniano, 1965.
—. *Heroides and Amores.* Trans. Grant Showerman. London: Heinemann, 1914.
Palgrave, Francis T., ed. *The Golden Treasury of the Best Songs and Lyrical Poems in the English Language.* Cambridge: Macmillan, 1861.
Park, Thomas, ed. *The Harleian Miscellany.* Vol. 9. London: White, Cochrane, Murray, and Harding, 1812.

—. *Heliconia: Comprising a Selection of English Poetry of the Elizabethan Age*. 3 vols. London: T. Davison, 1815.

Percy, William. *Sonnets to the fairest Coelia*. London: Adam Islip, 1594. RSTC 19618.

Perkins, William. *A discourse of the damned art of witchcraft*. Cambridge: Cantrel Legge, 1610. RSTC 19698.

Persius. *Juvenal and Persius, with an English Translation*. Trans. G.G. Ramsay. London: Heinemann, 1928.

[Persons, Robert?] *A conference about the next succession to the crowne of Ingland*. [Antwerp: A. Conincx], 1595. RSTC 19398.

Petowe, Henry. *The second part of Hero and Leander*. London: Thomas Purfoot, 1598. RSTC 19807.

Petrarca, Francesco. *The Canzoniere, or Rerum Vulgarium Fragmenta*. Trans. Mark Musa. Bloomington, IN: Indiana University Press, 1999.

—. *Petrarch's Secret or the Soul's Conflict with Passion*. Trans. William H. Draper. London: Chatto & Windus, 1911.

Phillips, Edward. *Theatrum poetarum, or A compleat collection of the poets, especially the most eminent, of all ages*. London: Charles Smith, 1675.

Phillips, John. *The life and death of Sir Phillip Sidney, late lord governour of Flushing*. London: Robert Waldegrave, 1587. RSTC 19871.

Philo. *Philo*. Trans. F.H. Colson, G.H. Whitaker, J.W. Earp, and Ralph Marcus. 12 vols. Loeb Classical Library. Cambridge, MA: Harvard University Press, 1968–1981.

*The phoenix nest*. London: John Jackson, 1593. RSTC 21516.

Plato. *The Republic*. Trans. Paul Shorey. 2 vols. Loeb Classical Library 237 and 276. Cambridge, MA: Harvard University Press, 1937–1942.

Pliny the Elder. *Natural History*. Trans. H. Rackham, W.H.S. Jones, and D.E. Eichholz. 10 vols. Loeb Classical Library. Cambridge, MA: Harvard University Press, 1938–1963.

Plutarch. *Lives*. Trans. Bernadotte Perrin. 11 vols. Loeb Classical Library. Cambridge, MA: Harvard University Press, 1914–1926.

"Poetical Rhapsody." *Verse Miscellanies Online*. University of Reading and University of Oxford. Accessed 11 June 2019. http://versemiscellaniesonline.bodleian.ox.ac.uk/texts/poetical-rhapsody.

Poliziano, Angelo Ambrogini. *Prose volgari inedite e poesie latine e greche*. Ed. Isidoro del Lungo. Florence: G. Barbéra, 1867.

Prescott-Innes, R., ed. *The Funeral of Mary, Queen of Scots: A Collection of Curious Tracts*. Edinburgh: E. & G. Goldsmith, 1890.

Raleigh, Walter. *The discoverie of the large, rich, and bewtiful empire of Guiana*. London: Robert Robinson, 1596. RSTC 20635.

*The Return from Parnassus, or the Scourge of Simony*. Ed. Oliphant Smeaton. London: J.M. Dent, 1905.

Ribadeneyra, Pedro de. *Ecclesiastical History of the Schism of the Kingdom of England*. Trans. Spencer J. Weinreich. Leiden: Brill, 2017.

Rickert, Edith, ed. *Ancient English Christmas Carols, 1400–1700*. New York: Duffield, 1910.
Rollins, Hyder E., ed. *A Poetical Rhapsody, 1602–1621*. 2 vols. Cambridge, MA: Harvard University Press, 1931–1932.
—. *Old English Ballads 1553–1625*. Cambridge: Cambridge University Press, 1920.
Ronsard, Pierre de. *The Labyrinth of Love*. Trans. Henry Weinfield. Anderson, SC: Parlor Press, 2021.
—. *Œuvres complètes*. Ed. Jean Céard, Daniel Ménager, and Michel Simonin. 2 vols. Paris: Gallimard, 1993–1994.
Rowlands, Samuel. *Ave Caesar: God save the King*. London: W. White, 1603. RSTC 21364.
—. *The knave of clubbs*. London: Edward Allde, 1609. RSTC 21387.
Ruscelli, Girolamo, ed. *I Fiori delle Rime de' Poeti illustri*. Venice: Marchiò Sessa, 1586.
Sander, Nicholas. *De visibili monarchia ecclesiae libri octo*. Louvain: Rutger Velpius, 1571.
Sawyer, Edmund, ed. *Memorials of Affairs of State in the Reigns of Q. Elizabeth and K. James I*. 3 vols. London: William Bowyer, 1725.
Scève, Maurice. *Délie: Object de plus haulte vertu*. Ed. Françoise Joukovsky. Paris: Dunod, 1996.
Seneca, Lucius Annaeus. *Phaedra*. Ed. Michael Coffey. Cambridge: Cambridge University Press, 1990.
—. *Seneca his tenne tragedies, translated into Englysh*. Trans. John Studley. London: Thomas Marsh, 1581. RSTC 22221.
Shakespeare, William. *The Oxford Shakespeare: The Complete Sonnets and Poems*. Ed. Colin Burrow. Oxford: Oxford University Press, 2002.
—. *The Oxford Shakespeare: The Complete Works*. Ed. Stanley Wells and Gary Taylor. New York: Oxford University Press, 1986.
—. *Shakespeare's Sonnets*. Ed. Katherine Duncan-Jones. London: Arden Shakespeare, 2010.
Sidney, Philip. *An apologie for poetrie*. London: James Roberts, 1595. RSTC 22534.
—. *The Countess of Pembroke's Arcadia (The New Arcadia)*. Ed. Victor Skretkowicz. Oxford: Clarendon Press, 1987.
—. *The Countess of Pembroke's Arcadia (The Old Arcadia)*. Ed. Jean Robertson. Oxford: Clarendon Press, 1973.
—. *The Major Works*. Ed. Katherine Duncan-Jones. New York: Oxford University Press, 2008.
—. *The Poems of Sir Philip Sidney*. Ed. William A. Ringler. Oxford: Clarendon Press, 1962.
—. *Syr P.S. His Astrophel and Stella*. London: John Charlewood, 1591. RSTC 22536.
Société des archives historiques, ed. "Lettre de Pierre Dumoulin au pasteur Bouchard, sieur Du Meuillet." *Archives historiques du déparement de la Gironde* 19 (1879): 535–539.
Southwell, Robert. *Collected Poems*. Ed. Peter Davidson and Anne Sweeney. Manchester: Carcanet, 2007.

—. *An epistle of comfort to the reverend priestes, & to the honorable, worshipful, & other of the laye sort restrayned in durance for the Catholicke fayth.* Paris [i.e., London: John Charlewood?], 1587. RSTC 22946.

—. *A poeme declaring the real presence of Christ in the blessed sacrament of the aultar.* Douai: Laurence Kellam, 1606. RSTC 14560.5.

—. *Saint Peters complaint with other poemes.* London: John Windet, 1595. RSTC 22957.

—. *St Peters complainte. Mary Magdal. teares. With other workes of the author.* London: W. Barrett, 1620. RSTC 22965.

Spenser, Edmund. *Amoretti and Epithalamion.* London: P. Short, 1595. RSTC 23076.

—. *Fowre hymnes.* London: Richard Field, 1596. RSTC 23086.

Steen, Sarah J., ed. *The Letters of Lady Arbella Stuart.* Oxford: Oxford University Press, 1994.

Strype, John, ed. *Ecclesiastical Memorials Relating Chiefly to Religion, and Its Reformation, under the Reigns of King Henry VIII, King Edward VI, and Queen Mary the First.* 7 vols. Oxford: Samuel Bagster, 1816.

Sylvester, Josuah. *Lachrimæ lachrimarum, or, The distillation of teares shede for the untymely death of the incomparable prince Panaretus.* London: Humphrey Lownes, 1612. RSTC 23577.

Tasso, Torquato. *Opere minori in versi.* Ed. Angelo Solerti. 3 vols. Bologna: Nicola Zanichelli, 1891–1895.

*Testamenta eboracensia: A Selection of Wills from the Registry at York.* Ed. James Raine and John William Clay. 6 vols. Surtees Society 4, 30, 45, 53, 79, and 106. London: J.B. Nichols, 1836–1902.

Thornton, Alice. *The Autobiography of Mrs. Alice Thornton, of East Newton, Co. York.* Surtees Society 62. Edinburgh: Andrews, 1875.

Tofte, Robert. *Laura: The toyes of a traveller.* London: Valentine Simmes, 1597. RSTC 24097.

Tottel, Richard, ed. *Songes and sonettes, written by the ryght honorable Lorde Henry Haward late Earle of Surrey, and others.* London: Richard Tottel, 1557. RSTC 13862.

Varchi, Benedetto. *The blazon of jealousie: A subject not written of by any heretofore.* Trans. Robert Tofte. London: Thomas Snodham, 1615. RSTC 24593.

Vega, Lope de. *Corona trágica: Vida y muerte de la serenísima reina de Escocia María Estuarda.* Ed. Christian Giaffreda. Florence: Alinea, 2009.

—. *Corona tragica: Vida y muerte de la serenissima reyna de Escocia Maria Stuarda.* Madrid: Viuda de Luis Sánchez, 1627.

Verstegan, Richard. *Odes in imitation of the seaven penitential psalmes.* Antwerp: A. Conincx, 1601. RSTC 21359.

—. *Theatrum crudelitatum haereticorum nostri temporis.* Antwerp: Adriaan Huberti, 1592.

Virgil. *The whole xii bookes of the Æneidos of Virgill.* Trans. Thomas Phaer and Thomas Twyne. London: Wyllyam How, 1573. RSTC 24801.

W., T. *The tears of fancie: Or, Love disdained.* London: J. Danter, 1593. RSTC 25122.

Watson, Thomas. *The hekatompathia or Passionate centurie of love.* London: John Wolfe, 1582. RSTC 25118a.
Wentworth, Peter. *A pithie exhortation to her Maiestie for establishing her successor to the crowne.* Edinburgh: Robert Waldegrave, 1598. RSTC 25245.
Whetstone, George. *The rocke of regard, divided into foure parts.* London: H. Middleton, 1576. RSTC 25348.
—. *Sir Phillip Sidney, his honorable life, his valiant death, and true vertues.* London: T. Orwin, 1587. RSTC 25349.
Whitney, Geffrey. *A choice of emblemes, and other devises, for the moste parte gathered out of sundrie writers, Englished and moralized.* Leiden: Francis Raphelengius, 1586. RSTC 25438.
Wright, Thomas. *The passions of the minde in generall.* London: Valentine Simmes [and Adam Islip], 1604. RSTC 26040.
Wyatt, Thomas. *Collected Poems.* Ed. Joost Daalder. London: Oxford University Press, 1975.

## Secondary Sources

Adlington, Hugh. "Chaplains to Embassies: Daniel Featley, Anti-Catholic Controversialist Abroad." In *Chaplains in Early Modern England: Patronage, Literature and Religion,* ed. Hugh Adlington, Tom Lockwood, and Gillian Wright, 83–102. Manchester: Manchester University Press, 2013.
Adolph, Anthony R.J.S. "Segar, Sir William (c. 1554–1633)." In *ODNB.* Oxford University Press, 2004; online ed., 2016. https://doi.org/10.1093/ref:odnb/25033.
Alexander, Gavin. *Writing after Sidney: The Literary Response to Sir Philip Sidney, 1586–1640.* Oxford: Oxford University Press, 2006.
Allinson, Rayne. "The Queen's Three Bodies: Gender, Criminality, and Sovereignty in the Execution of Mary, Queen of Scots." In *Practices of Gender in Late Medieval and Early Modern Europe,* ed. Megan Cassidy-Welch and Peter Sherlock, 99–116. Turnhout: Brepols, 2008.
Álvarez-Recio, Leticia. "Contemporary Visions of Mary Stuart's Execution: Saintliness and Vilification." In *The Rituals and Rhetoric of Queenship: Medieval to Early Modern,* ed. Liz Oakley-Brown and Louise J. Wilkinson, 209–221. Dublin: Four Courts Press, 2009.
Anderson, Randal L. "'The Merit of a Manuscript Poem': The Case for Bodleian MS Rawlison Poet. 85." In *Print, Manuscript & Performance,* ed. Bristol and Marotti, 127–171.
Antunes, Joana. "The Late-Medieval Mary Magdalene: Sacredness, Otherness, and Wildness." In *Mary Magdalene in Medieval Culture: Conflicted Roles,* ed. Peter Victor Loewen and Robin Waugh, 116–139. New York: Routledge, 2014.
Asch, Ronald G. *Sacral Kingship between Disenchantment and Re-Enchantment: The French and English Monarchies 1587–1688.* New York: Berghahn Books, 2014.

Ayres, Lewis. "Augustine on the Trinity." In *The Oxford Handbook of the Trinity*, ed. Gilles Emery and Matthew Levering, 123–137. Oxford: Oxford University Press, 2011.

Badir, Patricia. *The Maudlin Impression: English Literary Images of Mary Magdalene, 1550–1700*. Notre Dame, IN: University of Notre Dame Press, 2009.

Bagwell, Richard. "Sheridan, William (1635–1711)." In *ODNB*. Oxford University Press, 2004; online ed., 2004. https://doi.org/10.1093/ref:odnb/25373.

Baker-Smith, Dominic. "'Great Expectation': Sidney's Death and the Poets." In *Sir Philip Sidney*, ed. Baker-Smith et al., 83–100.

Baker-Smith, Dominic, J.A. van Dorsten, and Arthur F. Kinney, eds. *Sir Philip Sidney: 1586 and the Creation of a Legend*. Publications of the Sir Thomas Browne Institute, n.s., 9. Leiden: Leiden University Press, 1986.

Bates, Catherine. "Desire, Discontent, Parody: The Love Sonnet in Early Modern England." In *Companion to the Sonnet*, ed. Cousins and Howarth, 105–124.

—. *The Rhetoric of Courtship in Elizabethan Language and Literature*. Cambridge: Cambridge University Press, 1992.

Beal, Peter. *Catalogue of English Literary Manuscripts*. Arts and Humanities Research Council, 2005–2013. http://www.celm-ms.org.uk.

—. *A Dictionary of English Manuscript Terminology, 1450–2000*. Oxford: Oxford University Press, 2008.

—. *In Praise of Scribes: Manuscripts and Their Makers in Seventeenth-Century England*. Oxford: Oxford University Press, 1998.

—. *Index of English Literary Manuscripts, Vol. 1: 1450–1625*. 2 parts. London: Mansell, 1980.

Beckson, Karl. "Gray, John Henry (1866–1934)." In *ODNB*. Oxford University Press, 2004; online ed., 2007. https://doi.org/10.1093/ref:odnb/60499.

Bednarz, James P. "The Passionate Pilgrim and 'The Phoenix and Turtle.'" In *The Cambridge Companion to Shakespeare's Poetry*, ed. Patrick Cheney, 108–124. Cambridge: Cambridge University Press, 2007.

Beilin, Elaine V. "Carey, Elizabeth, Lady Hunsdon [née Elizabeth Spencer; other married name Elizabeth Eure, Lady Eure] (1552–1618)." In *ODNB*. Oxford University Press, 2004; online ed., 2011. https://doi.org/10.1093/ref:odnb/4641.

Bell, Ilona. *Elizabeth I: The Voice of a Monarch*. New York: Palgrave Macmillan, 2010.

—. *Elizabethan Women and the Poetry of Courtship*. Cambridge: Cambridge University Press, 1998.

Bergin, Joseph. "Smith, Richard (1567–1655)." In *ODNB*. Oxford University Press, 2004; online ed., 2004. https://doi.org/10.1093/ref:odnb/25886.

Bindley, James. *A Catalogue of the Curious and Extensive Library of the Late James Bindley, Esq. F.S.A.* 4 vols. London: Bulmer, 1818–1820.

Birch, Thomas. *Memoirs of the Reign of Queen Elizabeth, from the Year 1581 till her Death*. 2 vols. London: Andrew Millar, 1754.

Black, L.G. "Studies in Some Related Manuscript Poetic Miscellanies of the 1580s." 2 vols. PhD diss., Oxford University, 1970.

Black, William H. *A Descriptive, Analytical, and Critical Catalogue of the Manuscripts Bequeathed unto the University of Oxford by Elias Ashmole.* Oxford: Oxford University Press, 1845.
Bossy, John. "The Character of Elizabethan Catholicism." *Past and Present* 21 (1962): 39–59.
—. "A Propos of Henry Constable." *Recusant History* 6 (1962): 228–237.
Bridgen, Susan. "Clinton, Elizabeth Fiennes de (1528?–1589)." In *ODNB*. Oxford University Press, 2004; online ed., 2008. https://doi.org/10.1093/ref:odnb/9549.
Briquet, Charles-Moïse. *Les filigranes: Dictionnaire historique des marques du papier des leur apparition vers 1282 jusqu'en 1600, avec figures dans le texte et 16, 112 facsimilés de filigranes.* 2nd ed. 4 vols. Leipzig: Karl W. Hiersemann, 1923.
Bristol, Michael D., and Arthur F. Marotti, eds. *Print, Manuscript & Performance: The Changing Relations of the Media in Early Modern England.* Columbus: Ohio State University Press, 2000.
Brundin, Abigail. *Vittoria Colonna and the Spiritual Poetics of the Italian Reformation.* Aldershot: Ashgate, 2008.
Bryson, Alan, and Steven W. May, eds. *Verse Libel in Renaissance England and Scotland.* Oxford: Oxford University Press, 2016.
Budiansky, Stephen. *Her Majesty's Spymaster: Elizabeth I, Sir Francis Walsingham, and the Birth of Modern Espionage.* New York: Viking, 2005.
Buxton, John. *Sir Philip Sidney and the English Renaissance.* 3rd ed. London: Macmillan, 1987.
Bynum, Caroline Walker. "'… And Woman His Humanity': Female Imagery in the Religious Writing of the Later Middle Ages." In *Gender and Religion: On the Complexity of Symbols*, ed. Caroline Walker Bynum, Stevan Harrell, and Paula Richman, 257–288. Boston: Beacon Press, 1986.
Cain, Tom, and Ruth Connolly, eds. *The Complete Poetry of Robert Herrick.* 2 vols. Oxford: Oxford University Press, 2013.
Casanova, José. *Public Religions in the Modern World.* Chicago: University of Chicago Press, 1994.
*Catalogue of Additions to the Manuscripts in the British Museum, in the Years 1848–1853.* London: British Museum, 1868.
*Catalogue of the Harleian Collection of Manuscripts.* 2 vols. London: D. Leach, 1759–1763.
*Catalogue of the Harleian Manuscripts in the British Museum.* 4 vols. London: G. Eyre and A. Strahan, 1808–1812.
Cheney, Patrick G. *Spenser's Famous Flight: A Renaissance Idea of a Literary Career.* Toronto: University of Toronto Press, 1993.
Christie-Miller, Sydney R., and Herbert Collmann. *The Britwell Handlist; or, Short-Title Catalogue of the Principal Volumes from the time of Caxton to the Year 1800 Formerly in the Library of Britwell Court, Buckinghamshire.* 2 vols. London: Bernard Quaritch, 1933.
Clay, John W. *Dugdale's Visitation of Yorkshire with Additions.* 3 vols. Exeter: William Pollard, 1899–1917.

Clutterbuck, Charlotte. *Encounters with God in Medieval and Early Modern English Poetry.* London: Routledge, 2017.
Coatalen, Guillaume. "An English Translation of Desportes' Christian Sonnets Presented to John Scudamore by Edward Ski[...]." *The Review of English Studies* 65 (2014): 619–646.
Cohen, Esther. *The Modulated Scream: Pain in Late Medieval Culture.* Chicago: University of Chicago Press, 2010.
Cokayne, G.E., et al., eds. *The Complete Peerage of England, Scotland, Ireland, Great Britain and the United Kingdom, Extant, Extinct, or Dormant.* 2nd ed. 14 vols. London: The St Catherine Press, 1910–1998.
Cole, Mary Hill. *The Portable Queen: Elizabeth I and the Politics of Ceremony.* Amherst: University of Massachusetts Press, 1999.
Collier, John Payne. *The History of English Dramatic Poetry to the Time of Shakespeare: And Annals of the Stage to the Restoration.* 3 vols. London: John Murray, 1831.
Collins, Joseph B. *Christian Mysticism in the Elizabethan Age with Its Background in Mystical Methodology.* Baltimore: Johns Hopkins Press, 1940.
Collins, Roger. *Keepers of the Keys of Heaven: A History of the Papacy.* New York: Basic Books, 2009.
Considine, John. "Goodere, Sir Henry (bap. 1571, d. 1627)." In *ODNB.* Oxford University Press, 2004; online ed., 2008. https://doi.org/10.1093/ref:odnb/11003.
Copeland, Clare. "Sanctity." In *The Ashgate Research Companion to the Counter-Reformation,* ed. Alexandra Bamji, Geert H. Janssen, and Mary Laven, 225–241. Farnham: Ashgate, 2013.
Corthell, Ronald, Frances E. Dolan, Christopher Highley, and Arthur F. Marotti, eds. *Catholic Culture in Early Modern England.* Notre Dame, IN: University of Notre Dame Press, 2007.
Cousins, Anthony D. *The Catholic Religious Poets from Southwell to Crashaw: A Critical History.* London: Sheed & Ward, 1991.
Cousins, Anthony D., and Peter Howarth, eds. *The Cambridge Companion to the Sonnet.* Cambridge: Cambridge University Press, 2011.
Cox, Virginia. "The Exemplary Vittoria Colonna." In *A Companion To Vittoria Colonna,* ed. Abigail Brundin, Tatiana Crivelli, and Maria Serena Sapegno, 467–472. Leiden: Brill, 2016.
—. *Lyric Poetry by Women of the Italian Renaissance.* Baltimore: The Johns Hopkins University Press, 2013.
—. "Women Writers and the Canon in Sixteenth-Century Italy: The Case of Vittoria Colonna." In *Strong Voices, Weak History: Early Women Writers and Canons in England, France, and Italy,* ed. Pamela Joseph Benson and Victoria Kirkham, 14–31. Ann Arbor, MI: University of Michigan Press, 2005.
Cross, Frank L., and Elizabeth A. Livingstone, eds. *The Oxford Dictionary of the Christian Church.* 3rd ed. New York: Oxford University Press, 1997.
Cummings, Laurence. "John Finet's Miscellany." PhD diss., Washington University, 1960.

Dane, Joseph A. *What Is a Book?: The Study of Early Printed Books*. Notre Dame, IN: University of Notre Dame Press, 2012.
Davies, Myles. *Athenae britannicae, or, A critical history of the Oxford and Cambridge writers and writings*. 9 vols. London: n.p., 1716.
Dawson, Lesel. *Lovesickness and Gender in Early Modern English Literature*. Oxford: Oxford University Press, 2008.
Daybell, James. *The Material Letter in Early Modern England: Manuscript Letters and the Culture and Practices of Letter-Writing, 1512–1635*. Basingstoke: Palgrave Macmillan, 2012.
De Vaux, Pierre. *Vie de soeur Colette*. Trans. Elisabeth Lopez. Saint-Etienne: Publications de l'Université de Saint Etienne, 1994.
Doran, Susan, and Paulina Kewes, eds. *Doubtful and Dangerous: The Question of Succession in Late Elizabethan England*. Manchester: Manchester University Press, 2014.
Dowden, Edward. "An Elizabethan MS Collection: Henry Constable." *The Modern Quarterly of Language and Literature* 1 (1898): 3–4.
Dresvina, Juliana. *A Maid with a Dragon: The Cult of St Margaret of Antioch in Medieval England*. Oxford: Oxford University Press, 2016.
Dubrow, Heather. *Echoes of Desire: English Petrarchism and Its Counterdiscourses*. Ithaca: Cornell University Press, 1995.
Duncan-Jones, Katherine. "Astrophel." In *The Spenser Encyclopedia*, ed. Hamilton, 74–76.
———. *Sir Philip Sidney: Courtier Poet*. New Haven: Yale University Press, 1991.
Eamon, William. "Astrology and Society." In *A Companion to Astrology in the Renaissance*, ed. Brendan Maurice Dooley, 141–192. Leiden: Brill, 2014.
*Early English Books Online*. ProQuest. Accessed 17 February 2023. https://eebo.chadwyck.com/home.
Eckhardt, Joshua. *Manuscript Verse Collectors and the Politics of Anti-Courtly Love Poetry*. Oxford: Oxford University Press, 2009.
———. "Publication." In *A Handbook of English Renaissance Literary Studies*, ed. John Lee, 295–307. Hoboken, NJ: John Wiley & Sons, 2017.
Eckhardt, Joshua, and Daniel Starza Smith. *Manuscript Miscellanies in Early Modern England*. Farnham: Ashgate, 2014.
Edmon, Mary. "Hilliard, Nicholas (1547?–1619)." In *ODNB*. Oxford University Press, 2004; online ed., 2008. https://doi.org/10.1093/ref:odnb/13320.
Elliott, J.K. "The 'Apocryphal' New Testament." In *The New Cambridge History of the Bible*, vol. 1: *From the Beginnings to 600*, ed. James Carleton Paget and Joachim Schaper, 455–478. Cambridge: Cambridge University Press, 2013.
Engels, William. "Constable's Spirituall Sonnettes and the Three Spiritual Ways." *Medieval and Early Modern English Studies* 14 (2006): 407–430.
Erhardt, Michelle A., and Amy M. Morris, eds. *Mary Magdalene: Iconographic Studies from the Middle Ages to the Baroque*. Leiden: Brill, 2012.
Evans, R.H., ed. *Catalogue of the Curious and Valuable Library of the Late Joseph Haslewood*. London: Evans, 1833.

Ewen, Cecil L'Estrange. *Witchcraft and Demonianism.* London: Heath Cranton, 1933.
Falco, Raphael. *Conceived Presences: Literary Genealogy in Renaissance England.* Amherst: University of Massachusetts Press, 1994.
Fleissner, Robert F. *Resolved to Love: The 1592 Edition of Henry Constable's Diana, Critically Considered.* Salzburg: Institut für Anglistik und Amerikanistik, 1980.
Fleming, Morna R. "The *Amatoria* of James VI: Loving by the Reulis." In *Royal Subjects: Essays on the Writings of James VI and I,* ed. Daniel Fischlin and Mark Fortier, 124–148. Detroit: Wayne State University Press, 2002.
Foot, Mirjam M. *The Decorated Bindings in Marsh's Library, Dublin.* Aldershot: Ashgate, 2004.
Foster, Joseph. *Alumni Oxonienses: The Members of the University of Oxford, 1500–1714.* 4 vols. Oxford: James Parker, 1891–1892.
—. *Alumni Oxonienses: The Members of the University of Oxford, 1715–1886.* 4 vols in 2. Oxford: James Parker, 1888.
Fowler, Alastair. *Triumphal Forms: Structural Patterns in Elizabethan Poetry.* Cambridge: Cambridge University Press, 1970.
Fraeters, Veerle. "Visio/Vision." In *The Cambridge Companion to Christian Mysticism,* ed. Patricia Z. Beckman and Amy M. Hollywood, 178–188. Cambridge: Cambridge University Press, 2012.
Fraistat, Neil. *Poems in Their Place: The Intertextuality and Order of Poetic Collections.* Chapel Hill, NC: University of North Carolina Press, 1986.
Freedman, Sylvia. *Poor Penelope: Lady Penelope Rich, an Elizabethan Woman.* Abbotsbrook: Kensal Press, 1983.
Frend, William H.C. "The Origins of the Papacy: c. 33–440." In *The Papacy,* ed. Paul Johnson and Michael J. Walsh, 24–41. London: Weidenfeld & Nicolson, 1997.
Fumerton, Patricia. "'Secret' Arts: Elizabethan Miniatures and Sonnets." *Representations* 15 (1986): 57–97.
Gajda, Alexandra. *The Earl of Essex and Late Elizabethan Political Culture.* Oxford: Oxford University Press, 2012.
Gibbons, Katy. *English Catholic Exiles in Late Sixteenth-Century Paris.* Suffolk: Boydell & Brewer, 2011.
—. "'A Reserved Place'? English Catholic Exiles and Contested Space in Late-Sixteenth-Century Paris." *French Historical Studies* 32 (2009): 33–62.
Goldring, Elizabeth. "Talbot [née Hardwick], Elizabeth [Bess] [called Bess of Hardwick], countess of Shrewsbury." In *ODNB.* Oxford University Press, 2004; online ed., 2004. https://doi.org/10.1093/ref:odnb/26925.
Goodare, Julian. "Mary Stewart (1542–1587)." In *ODNB.* Oxford University Press, 2004; online ed., 2007. https://doi.org/10.1093/ref:odnb/18248.
Gordon, Donald J. "Chapman's Memorable Masque (1956)." In *The Renaissance Imagination: Essays and Lectures by D.J. Gordon,* ed. Stephen Orgel, 194–202. Berkeley: University of California Press, 1975.
Greetham, David C. *Textual Scholarship: An Introduction.* New York: Garland, 1992.

Grindlay, Lilla. *Queen of Heaven: The Assumption and Coronation of the Virgin in Early Modern English Writing.* Notre Dame, IN: University of Notre Dame Press, 2018.

Gristwood, Sarah. *Arbella: England's Lost Queen.* London: Bantam, 2003.

Grundy, Joan, ed. *The Poems of Henry Constable.* Liverpool: Liverpool University Press, 1960.

Guiney, Louise Imogen. *Recusant Poets.* Ed. Geoffrey Bliss and Louise Imogen Guiney. New York: Sheed & Ward, 1939.

Guy, John. *Queen of Scots: The True Life of Mary Stuart.* Boston: Houghton Mifflin, 2004.

Haag, Michael. *The Quest for Mary Magdalene.* London: Profile, 2016.

Hackett, Helen. "The Art of Blasphemy? Interfusions of the Erotic and the Sacred in the Poetry of Donne, Barnes, and Constable." *Renaissance and Reformation* 28, no. 3 (2004): 27–53.

—. *Virgin Mother, Maiden Queen: Elizabeth I and the Cult of the Virgin Mary.* Basingstoke: Macmillan, 1995.

Hamilton, Albert C., ed. *The Spenser Encyclopedia.* Toronto: University of Toronto Press, 1990.

Hammer, Paul E.J. "Devereux, Robert, second earl of Essex (1565–1601)." In *ODNB.* Oxford University Press, 2004; online ed., 2008. https://doi.org/10.1093/ref:odnb/7565.

—. *Elizabeth's Wars: War, Government, and Society in Tudor England, 1544–1604.* New York: Palgrave Macmillan, 2003.

—. "Manners, Roger, fifth earl of Rutland (1576–1612)." In *ODNB.* Oxford University Press, 2004; online ed., 2008. https://doi.org/10.1093/ref:odnb/17962.

—. *The Polarisation of Elizabethan Politics: The Political Career of Robert Devereux, 2nd Earl of Essex, 1585–1597.* Cambridge: Cambridge University Press, 1999.

—. "Standen, Sir Anthony (d. in or after 1615)." In *ODNB.* Oxford University Press, 2005; online ed., 2008. https://doi.org/10.1093/ref:odnb/39703.

Handover, P. M. *Arbella Stuart, Royal Lady of Hardwick and Cousin to King James.* London: Eyre & Spottiswoode, 1957.

Hannay, Margaret P. *Philip's Phoenix: Mary Sidney, Countess of Pembroke.* Oxford: Oxford University Press, 1990.

Haskins, Susan. *Mary Magdalen: Myth and Metaphor.* London: HarperCollins, 1993.

Hasler, P.W., ed. *The History of Parliament: The House of Commons 1558–1603.* 3 vols. London: H.M. Stationery Office, 1964. https://www.historyofparliamentonline.org/research/members/members-1558-1603.

Hawkins, Thomas. *The Origin of the English Drama.* Vol. 3. Oxford: Clarendon Press, 1773.

Haynes, Alan. *The White Bear: Robert Dudley, the Elizabethan Earl of Leicester.* London: P. Owen, 1987.

Hegarty, A.J. "Twyne, Brian (1581–1644)." In *ODNB.* Oxford University Press, 2004; online ed., 2004. https://doi.org/10.1093/ref:odnb/27924.

Henderson, Diana E. "The Sonnet, Subjectivity and Gender." In *Companion to the Sonnet,* ed. Cousins and Howarth, 46–65.

Hicks, Leo. "Sir Robert Cecil, Father Persons and the Succession 1600–1601." *Archivum historicum Societatis Iesu* 24 (1955): 95–139.

Hill, Carol. "'Here Be Dragons': The Cult of St Margaret of Antioch and Strategies for Survival." In *Art, Faith, and Place in East Anglia: From Prehistory to the Present*, ed. T.A. Heslop, Elizabeth Mellings, and Margit Thøfner, 105–116. Woodbridge: Boydell & Brewer, 2010.

Hill, William Speed, ed. *New Ways of Looking at Old Texts: Papers of the Renaissance English Text Society, 1985–1991*. Binghamton, N.Y.: Renaissance English Text Society, 1993.

Hillman, David. "Visceral Knowledge: Shakespeare, Skepticism, and the Interior of the Early Modern Body." In *The Body in Parts: Fantasies of Corporeality in Early Modern Europe*, ed. David Hillman and Carla Mazzio, 81–106. New York: Routledge, 1997.

Hobbs, Mary. *Early Seventeenth-Century Verse Miscellany Manuscripts*. Aldershot: Scholar Press, 1992.

Hodgson, Elizabeth. *Grief and Women Writers in the English Renaissance*. New York: Columbia University Press, 2015.

Hole, Christina. "Some Instances of Image-Magic in Great Britain." In *The Witch Figure: Folklore Essays by a Group of Scholars in England Honouring the 75th Birthday of Katharine M. Briggs*, ed. Venetia Newall, 80–94. London: Routledge, 1973.

—. *Witchcraft in England*. Totowa, NJ: Rowman and Littlefield, 1977.

Hollis, Stephanie, W.R. Barnes, Rebecca Hayward, Kathleen Loncar, and Michael Wright, eds. *Writing the Wilton Women: Goscelin's Legend of Edith and Liber Confortatorius*. Turnhout: Brepols, 2004.

Hopson, J. P. "Dyce, Alexander (1798–1869)." In *ODNB*. Oxford University Press, 2004; online ed., 2005. https://doi.org/10.1093/ref:odnb/8342.

Horrox, Rosemary. "Constable, Sir Marmaduke (1456/7?–1518)." In *ODNB*. Oxford University Press, 2004l online ed., 2004. https://doi.org/10.1093/ref:odnb/6108.

Houliston, Victor. *Catholic Resistance in Elizabethan England: Robert Persons's Jesuit Polemic, 1580–1610*. Aldershot: Ashgate, 2007.

Hughey, Ruth W., ed. *The Arundel Harington Manuscript of Tudor Poetry*. 2 vols. Columbus: Ohio State University Press, 1960.

Hughey, Ruth. "The Harington MS at Arundel Castle." *Library* 15 (1935): 388–444.

Hultgren, Arland J. *The Parables of Jesus: A Commentary*. Grand Rapids, MI: William B. Eerdmanns, 2000.

Hunter, Michael. "Ashmole, Elias (1617–1692)." In *ODNB*. Oxford University Press, 2004; online ed., 2006. https://doi.org/10.1093/ref:odnb/764.

—. *Editing Early Modern Texts: An Introduction to Principles and Practice*. Basingstoke: Palgrave Macmillan, 2007.

Ioppolo, Grace. "Those Essex Girls: The Lives and Letters of Lettice Knollys, Penelope Rich, Dorothy Perrott Percy, and Frances Walsingham." In *The Ashgate Research Companion to the Sidneys, 1500–1700*, ed. Margaret P. Hannay, Mary Ellen Lamb, and Michael G. Brennan, 1: 77–92. Farnham: Routledge, 2015.

Jackson, Ken, and Arthur F. Marotti. "The Turn to Religion in Early Modern English Studies." *Criticism* 46 (2004): 167–190.
Jansen, Katherine L. *The Making of the Magdalen: Preaching and Popular Devotion in the Later Middle Ages*. Princeton: Princeton University Press, 2001.
Janssen, Geert H. "The Exile Experience" In *The Ashgate Research Companion to the Counter-Reformation*. Ed. Alexandra Bamji, Geert H. Janssen, and Mary Laven, 73–90. Farnham: Ashgate, 2013.
John, Lisle Cecil. *The Elizabethan Sonnet Sequences: Studies in Conventional Conceits*. New York: Russell & Russell, 1966.
Kastner, L.E. "The Elizabethan Sonneteers and the French Poets." *The Modern Language Review* 3 (1908): 268–277.
Kawasaki, Toshihiko. "From Southwell to Donne." *Eibungaku kenkyū* 39 (1963): 11–31.
Kelly, L.G. "Yong, Bartholomew (bap. 1560, d. 1612)." In *ODNB*. Oxford University Press, 2004; online ed., 2004. https://doi.org/10.1093/ref:odnb/30257.
Kennedy, Judith M., ed. *A Critical Edition of Yong's Translation of George of Montemayor's Diana and Gil Polo's Enamoured Diana*. Oxford: Clarendon Press, 1968.
Kilroy, Gerard. *Edmund Campion: Memory and Transcription*. Aldershot: Ashgate, 2005.
Knight, Jeffrey Todd. *Bound to Read: Compilations, Collections, and the Making of Renaissance Literature*. Philadelphia: University of Pennsylvania Press, 2013.
Kristeva, Julia. "Stabat Mater." In *The Female Body in Western Culture: Contemporary Perspectives*, ed. Susan R. Suleiman, 99–118. Cambridge, MA: Harvard University Press, 1986.
Kuchar, Gary. *Divine Subjection: The Rhetoric of Sacramental Devotion in Early Modern England*. Pittsburgh: Duquesne University Press, 2005.
—. "Gender and Recusant Melancholia in Robert Southwell's *Mary Magdalene's Funeral Tears*." In *Catholic Culture in Early Modern England*, ed. Corthell et al., 135–157.
—. "Henry Constable and the Question of Catholic Poetics: Affective Piety and Erotic Identification in the Spirituall Sonnettes." *Philological Quarterly* 85 (2006): 69–90.
Laoutaris, Chris. "'Toucht with Bolt of Treason': The Earl of Essex and Lady Penelope Rich." In *Essex: The Cultural Impact of an Elizabethan Courtier*. Ed. Annaliese F. Connolly and Lisa Hopkins, 201–236. Manchester: Manchester University Press, 2013.
Lee, Sidney. "Constable, Henry (1562–1613), poet." In *The Dictionary of National Biography*, ed. Leslie Smith, 12: 34–35. London: Smith and Elder, 1887.
—. *A Life of William Shakespeare*. London: Macmillan, 1901.
Leslie, Michael. "Heraldry." In *The Spenser Encyclopedia*, ed. Hamilton, 353–355.
Lewalski, Barbara Kiefer. *Writing Women in Jacobean England*. Cambridge, MA: Harvard University Press, 1993.
Loffman, Claire: *see under* Williams, Claire B.
Love, Harold. *Attributing Authorship: An Introduction*. Cambridge: Cambridge University Press, 2002.
—. *Scribal Publication in Seventeenth-Century England*. Oxford: Clarendon Press, 1993.

Love, Harold, and Arthur F. Marotti. "Manuscript Transmission and Circulation." In *The Cambridge History of Early Modern English Literature*, ed. David Loewenstein and Janel M. Mueller, 55–80. Cambridge: Cambridge University Press, 2003.

Luria, Keith P. "The Power of Conscience? Coexistence and Confessional Boundary Building in Early-Modern France." In *Living with Religious Diversity in Early-Modern Europe*, ed. C. Scott Dixon, Dagmar Freist, and Mark Greengrass, 109–125. Farnham: Ashgate, 2009.

Lyall, Roderick J. "Stella's Other Astrophel: Henry Constable's Diana and the Politics of Elizabethan Courtiership." In *Gloriana's Rule: Literature, Religion, and Power in the Age of Elizabeth*, ed. Rui Carvalho Homem and Fátima Vieira, 187–205. Porto: Editora da Universidade do Porto, 2006.

—. "'Thrie Truer Hairts': Alexander Montgomerie, Henry Constable, Henry Keir and Cultural Politics in Renaissance Britain." *The Innes Review* 54 (2003): 186–215.

Manning, Roger B. *An Apprenticeship in Arms: The Origins of the British Army 1585–1702*. Oxford: Oxford University Press, 2006.

Margetts, Michele. "Lady Penelope Rich: Hilliard's Lost Miniatures and a Surviving Portrait." *The Burlington Magazine* 130 (1988): 758–761.

Marotti, Arthur. "'Love is Not Love': Elizabethan Sonnet Sequences and the Social Order." *English Literary History* 49 (1982): 396–428.

—. "Malleable and Fixed Texts: Manuscript and Printed Miscellanies and the Transmission of Lyric Poetry in the English Renaissance." In *New Ways*, ed. Hill, 159–174.

—. "Manuscript, Print, and the English Renaissance Lyric." In *New Ways*, ed. Hill, 209–222.

—. *Manuscript, Print, and the English Renaissance Lyric*. Ithaca, NY: Cornell University Press, 1995.

—. "Manuscript, Print, and the Social History of the Lyric." In *The Cambridge Companion to English Poetry, Donne to Marvell*, ed. Thomas N. Corns, 52–79. Cambridge: Cambridge University Press, 1993.

—. "Manuscript Transmission and the Catholic Martyrdom Account in Early Modern England." In *Print, Manuscript & Performance*, ed. Bristol and Marotti, 172–199.

—. "Patronage, Poetry, and Print." *The Yearbook of English Studies* 21 (1991): 1–26.

—. *Religious Ideology and Cultural Fantasy: Catholic and Anti-Catholic Discourses in Early Modern England*. Notre Dame, IN: University of Notre Dame Press, 2005.

—. "The Transmission of Lyric Poetry and the Institutionalizing of Literature in the English Renaissance." In *Contending Kingdoms: Historical, Psychological, and Feminist Approaches to the Literature of Sixteenth-Century England and France*, ed. Marie-Rose Logan and Peter L. Rudnytsky, 21–41. Detroit: Wayne State University Press, 1991.

Marron, Stephen. "The Second Benedictine Mission to England." *Douai Magazine* 2, no. 3 (1923): 157–165.

Martin, George. "Marsh's Library MS z3.5.21: An Edition of the English Poems." Master's thesis, University of Waterloo, 1971.

Martin, Patrick H. *Elizabethan Espionage: Plotters and Spies in the Struggle between Catholicism and the Crown*. Jefferson, NC: McFarland & Company, 2016.
Martz, Louis L. *The Poetry of Meditation: A Study in English Religious Literature of the Seventeenth Century*. New Haven: Yale University Press, 1962.
Mattingly, Garrett. *The Armada*. New York: First Mariner Books, 2005.
May, Steven W. "Anne Lock and Thomas Norton's *Meditation of a Penitent Sinner*." *Modern Philology* 114 (2017): 793–819.
—. *The Elizabethan Courtier Poets: The Poems and Their Contexts*. Columbia, MO: University of Missouri Press, 1991.
—. "Henry Stanford's 'God Knows What.'" *English Manuscript Studies* 16 (2011): 70–82.
—. "The Poems of Edward DeVere, Seventeenth Earl of Oxford and of Robert Devereux, Second Earl of Essex." *Studies in Philology* 77, no. 5 (1980): 1–132.
—. "Stanford, Henry (c. 1552–1616)." In *ODNB*. Oxford University Press, 2004; online ed., 2008. https://doi.org/10.1093/ref:odnb/39706.
May, Steven W., and William A. Ringler. *Elizabethan Poetry: A Bibliography and First-Line Index of Elizabethan Verse, 1559–1603*. 3 vols. London: Thoemmes Continuum, 2004.
Mazzaro, Jerome. "Recusant Sincerity: Henry Constable at Spiritual Sonnets." *Essays in Literature* 17 (1990): 147–159.
McCoog, Thomas M. *And Touching our Society: Fashioning Jesuit Identity in Elizabethan England*. Toronto: Pontifical Institute of Mediaeval Studies, 2013.
McDermott, Roger N. "Neville, Charles, sixth earl of Westmorland (1542/3–1601)." In *ODNB*. Oxford University Press, 2004; online ed., 2008. https://doi.org/10.1093/ref:odnb/19924.
McKenzie, D.F. *Bibliography and the Sociology of Texts*. Cambridge: Cambridge University Press, 1999.
McKerrow, Ronald B. *Printers' and Publishers' Devices in England and Scotland, 1485–1640*. London: Bibliographical Society, 1913.
McLaren, Anne. "Memorializing Mary and Elizabeth." In *Tudor Queenship: The Reigns of Mary and Elizabeth*, ed. Alice Hunt and Anna Whitelock, 11–27. Basingstoke: Palgrave Macmillan, 2010.
Meij, Johannes van der. "Pierre du Moulin in Leiden, 1592–1598." *Lias* 14 (1987): 15–40.
Melnikoff, Kirk. *Elizabethan Publishing and the Makings of Literary Culture*. Toronto: University of Toronto Press, 2018.
Meyjes, G.H.M. Posthumus. *Jean Hotman's English Connection*. Amsterdam: Koninklijke Nederlandse Akademie van Wetenschappen, 1990.
—. "Protestant Irenicism in the Sixteenth and Seventeenth Centuries." In *The End of Strife: Papers Selected from the Proceedings of the Colloquium of the Commission internationale d'histoire ecclésiastique comparée Held at the University of Durham, 2 to 9 September 1981*, ed. D.M. Loades, 77–93. Edinburgh: T. & T. Clark, 1984.
Monta, Susannah Brietz. *Martyrdom and Literature in Early Modern England*. Cambridge: Cambridge University Press, 2005.

Morgan, Victor. *A History of the University of Cambridge, Vol. 2: 1546–1750.* Cambridge: Cambridge University Press, 2004.
Morris, Brian, and Eleanor Withington, eds. *Poems of John Cleveland.* Oxford: Clarendon Press, 1967.
Muir, Kenneth. "The Order of Constable's Sonnets." *Notes and Queries* 199 (1954): 424–425.
Murray, Molly. "'Now I ame a Catholique': William Alabaster and the Early Modern Catholic Conversion Narrative." In *Catholic Culture in Early Modern England,* ed. Corthell et al., 189–215.
—. *The Poetics of Conversion in Early Modern English Literature: Verse and Change from Donne to Dryden.* Cambridge: Cambridge University Press, 2009.
Nash, Jerry C. "The Fury of the Pen: Crenne, the Bible, and Letter Writing." In *Women Writers in Pre-Revolutionary France: Strategies of Emancipation,* ed. Colette H. Winn and Donna Kuizenga, 207–226. New York: Garland Publishing, 1997.
Newman, Barbara. *God and the Goddesses: Vision, Poetry, and Belief in the Middle Ages.* Philadelphia: University of Pennsylvania Press, 2003.
Newman, Christine. "Constable, Sir Robert (1478?–1537), rebel." In *ODNB.* Oxford University Press, 2004; online ed., 2004. https://doi.org/10.1093/ref:odnb/6110.
Nichols, John. *The Progresses, Processions, and Magnificent Festivities of King James the First, His Royal Consort, Family, and Court.* 4 vols. London: J.B. Nichols, 1828.
Norrington, Ruth. *In the Shadow of the Throne: The Lady Arbella Stuart.* London: Peter Owen, 2002.
North, Marcy L. "Amateur Compilers, Scribal Labour, and the Contents of Early Modern Poetic Miscellanies." *English Manuscript Studies* 16 (2011): 82–111.
—. *The Anonymous Renaissance: Cultures of Discretion in Tudor-Stuart England.* Chicago: University of Chicago Press, 2003.
—. "Household Scribes and the Production of Literary Manuscripts in Early Modern England." *Journal of Early Modern Studies* 4 (2015): 133–157.
—. "Ignoto in the Age of Print: The Manipulation of Anonymity in Early Modern England." *Studies in Philology* 91, no. 4 (1994): 390–416.
—. "Twice the Effort: Tracing the Practices of Stuart Verse Collectors through Their Redundant Entries." *Huntington Library Quarterly* 77 (2014): 257–285.
Olson, Vibeke. "'Woman, Why Weepest Thou?' Mary Magdalene, the Virgin Mary, and the Transformative Power of Holy Tears in Late Medieval Devotional Painting." In *Mary Magdalene: Iconographic Studies from the Middle Ages to the Baroque,* ed. Michelle Erhardt and Amy M. Morris, 361–382. Leiden: Brill, 2012.
Parker, Tom W.N. *Proportional Form in the Sonnets of the Sidney Circle: Loving in Truth.* Oxford: Clarendon Press, 1998.
Patterson, W.B. *King James VI and I and the Reunion of Christendom.* Cambridge: Cambridge University Press, 1997.
Pebworth, Ted-Larry. "Manuscript Transmission and the Selection of Copy-Text in Renaissance Coterie Poetry." *Text* 7 (1994): 243–261.

Pebworth, Ted-Larry, and Ernest W. Sullivan. "Rational Presentation of Multiple Textual Traditions." *The Papers of the Bibliographical Society of America* 83 (1989): 43–60.

Peile, John. *Biographical register of Christ's College, 1505–1905: And of the Earlier Foundation, God's House, 1448–1505; Vol 1., 1448–1665*. Cambridge: Cambridge University Press, 1910.

Pelikan, Jaroslav. *The Growth of Medieval Theology (600–1300)*. The Christian Tradition: History of the Development of Doctrine 3. Chicago: University of Chicago Press, 1978.

—. *Reformation of Church and Dogma (1300–1700)*. The Christian Tradition: History of the Development of Doctrine 4. Chicago: University of Chicago Press, 1984.

Perella, Nicolas. *The Kiss: Sacred and Profane*. Berkeley: University of California Press, 1969.

Pérez-Jáuregui, María Jesús. "Burning the Heretic: Conscientious Revision in Henry Constable's 'Falslie Doth Enuie of Youre Praises Blame.'" *English Studies* 93 (2012): 897–910.

—. "A Queen in A 'Purple Robe': Henry Constable's Poetic Tribute to Mary, Queen of Scots." *Studies in Philology* 113, no. 3 (2016): 577–594.

Petti, Anthony G. *English Literary Hands from Chaucer to Dryden*. London: Arnold, 1977.

—. "Unknown sonnets by Sir Toby Matthew." *Recusant History* 9 (1967): 123–158.

Phillips, James Emerson. *Images of a Queen: Mary Stuart in Sixteenth-Century Literature*. Berkeley: University of California Press, 1964.

Pigman, G.W. *Grief and English Renaissance Elegy*. Cambridge: Cambridge University Press, 1985.

Plett, Heinrich F. *Rhetoric and Renaissance Culture*. Berlin: Walter de Gruyter, 2004.

Polster, Kristen K. "The Fifth Humor: Ink, Texts, and the Early Modern Body." PhD diss., University of North Texas, 2012.

Pomplun, Trent. "Catholic Sacramental Theology in the Baroque Age." In *The Oxford Handbook of Early Modern Theology, 1600–1800*, ed. Ulrich L. Lehner, Richard A. Muller, and A.G. Roeber, 135–149. New York: Oxford University Press, 2016.

Prins, Jacomien. "The Music of the Pulse in Marsilio Ficino's Timaeus Commentary." In *Blood, Sweat, and Tears: The Changing Concepts of Physiology from Antiquity into Early Modern Europe*, ed. H.F.J. Horstmanshoff, Helen King, and Claus Zittel, 393–413. Leiden: Brill, 2012.

Questier, Michael C. "Catholic Loyalism in Early Stuart England." *The English Historical Review* 123 (2008): 1132–1165.

—. *Catholicism and Community in Early Modern England: Politics, Aristocratic Patronage and Religion, c. 1550–1640*. Cambridge: Cambridge University Press, 2006.

—. *Conversion, Politics, and Religion in England, 1580–1625*. Cambridge: Cambridge University Press, 1996.

—. "Elizabeth and the Catholics." In *Catholics and the "Protestant Nation": Religious Politics and Identity in Early Modern England*, ed. Ethan H. Shagan, 69–94. Manchester: Manchester University Press, 2005.

Rambuss, Richard. *Closet Devotions.* Durham, NC: Duke University Press, 1998.
Reid-Baxter, Jamie. "Scotland Will Be the Ending of All Empires." In *Kings, Lords and Men in Scotland and Britain, 1300–1625,* ed. Steve Boardman and Julian Goodare, 320–340. Edinburgh: Edinburgh University Press, 2014.
Rex, Richard. "The Sixteenth Century." In *St John's College, Cambridge: A History,* ed. Peter Linehan, 5–93. Woodbridge: Boydell Press, 2011.
Riches, Samantha. *St George: Hero, Martyr and Myth.* Sutton: Stroud, 2000.
Rickard, Jane. *Authorship and Authority: The Writings of James VI and I.* Manchester: Manchester University Press, 2007.
Riehl, Anna. "'Shine Like an Angel with Thy Starry Crown': Queen Elizabeth the Angelic." In *Queens and Power in Medieval and Early Modern England,* ed. Carole Levin and Robert Bucholz, 158–186. Lincoln, NE: University of Nebraska Press, 2009.
Rimbault, Edward F. *A Little Book of Songs and Ballads, Gathered from Ancient Music Books, MS and Printed.* London: J.R. Smith, 1851.
Ringler, William A. "The Myth and the Man." In *Sir Philip Sidney,* ed. Baker-Smith et al., 3–15.
Ritson, Joseph. *Bibliographia poetica: A catalogue of Engleish poets, of the twelfth, thirteenth, fourteenth, fifteenth, and sixteenth, centurys, with a short account of their works.* London: G. and W. Nicol, 1802.
Rivers, Isabel. *Classical and Christian Ideas in English Renaissance Poetry: A Student's Guide.* London: Routledge, 1994.
Rodda, Joshua. *Public Religious Disputation in England, 1558–1626.* London: Routledge, 2016.
Rogers, David. "'The Catholic Moderator': A French Reply to Bellarmine and Its English Author, Henry Constable." *Recusant History* 5 (1960): 224–235.
Rollins, Hyder E. "England's Helicon and Henry Chettle." *The Times Literary Supplement,* no. 1548 (1931): 749.
Rouget, François. "Philippe Desportes et la logique des recueils poétiques." *Réforme, Humanisme, Renaissance* 62 (2006): 97–108.
Rowe, Katherine. *Dead Hands: Fictions of Agency, Renaissance to Modern.* Stanford: Stanford University Press, 1999.
Rowse, Alfred L. *Eminent Elizabethans.* London: Macmillan, 1983.
Roy, Neil J. "Saints." In *The Cambridge Dictionary of Christian Theology,* ed. Ian McFarland, David Fergusson, Karen Kilby, and Iain R. Torrance, 455–457. Cambridge: Cambridge University Press, 2011.
Saenger, Michael Bird. "Did Sidney Revise *Astrophil and Stella*?" *Studies in Philology* 96, no. 4 (1999): 417–438.
Saunders, J.W. "The Stigma of Print: A Note on the Social Bases of Tudor Poetry." *Essays in Criticism* 1 (1951): 139–164.
Saward, John, John Morrill, and Michael Tomko, eds. *Firmly I Believe and Truly: The Spiritual Tradition of Catholic England.* Oxford: Oxford University Press, 2011.

Scarry, Elaine. *Naming Thy Name: Cross Talk in Shakespeare's Sonnets.* New York: Farrar, Straus, and Giroux, 2016.
Scheid, John. "Cults, Myths, and Politics at the Beginning of the Empire." In *Roman Religion*, ed. Clifford Ando, 117–138. Edinburgh: Edinburgh University Press, 2003.
Schoenfeldt, Michael C. "The Poetry of Supplication: Toward a Cultural Poetics of the Religious Lyric." In *New Perspectives on the Seventeenth-Century English Religious Lyric*, ed. John R. Roberts, 75–104. Columbia, MO: University of Missouri Press, 1994.
Scott, Janet G. *Les sonnets élisabéthains: Les sources et l'apport personnel.* Paris: Honoré Champion, 1929.
Scott, John R. *Catalogue of the Manuscripts Remaining in Marsh's Library, Dublin.* Dublin: A. Thom, 1913.
Scott-Warren, Jason. *Sir John Harington and the Book as Gift.* Oxford: Oxford University Press, 2001.
Serjeantson, Deirdre. "English Bards and Scotch Poetics: Scotland's Literary Influence and Sixteenth-Century English Religious Verse." In *Literature and the Scottish Reformation*, ed. Crawford Gribben and David G. Mullan, 161–190. Farnham: Ashgate, 2009.
Sharpe, Kevin. *Selling the Tudor Monarchy: Authority and Image in Sixteenth-Century England.* New Haven: Yale University Press, 2009.
Shell, Alison. *Catholicism, Controversy, and the English Literary Imagination, 1558–1660.* Cambridge: Cambridge University Press, 1999.
———. "'I write of tears, and blud': Henry Constable on Mary Stuart." Paper presented at the Annual Meeting of the Renaissance Society of America, Boston, 31 March 2016.
*A Short-Title Catalogue of Books Printed in England, Scotland, & Ireland and of English Books Printed Abroad 1475–1640.* Compiled by A.W. Pollard and G.R. Redgrave. 2nd ed. Revised by W.A. Jackson, F.S. Ferguson, and Katharine F. Pantzer. 3 vols. London: Bibliographical Society, 1976–1991.
Sledd, Hassell B. "The '1584' Publication of Henry Constable's *Diana Augmented.*" *Studies in Bibliography* 23 (1970): 146–148.
Smith, Daniel Starza. *John Donne and the Conway Papers: Patronage and Manuscript Circulation in the Early Seventeenth Century.* Oxford: Oxford University Press, 2014.
Smith, David Baird. "Jean De Villiers Hotman." *Scottish Historical Review* 14 (1917): 147–166.
Smyth, John. *The Berkeley Manuscripts: The Lives of the Berkeleys, Lords of the Honour, Castle, and Manor of Berkeley in the County of Gloucester from 1066 to 1618.* Ed. Sir John MacLean. 3 vols. Gloucester: John Bellows, 1883–1885.
Somos, Mark. *Secularisation and the Leiden Circle.* Leiden: Brill, 2011.
Spierenburg, Pieter. *The Spectacle of Suffering: Executions and the Evolution of Repression. From a Preindustrial Metropolis to the European Experience.* Cambridge: Cambridge University Press, 1984.
Spiller, Michael R.G. *The Development of the Sonnet: An Introduction.* London: Routledge, 1992.

—. *The Sonnet Sequence: A Study of Its Strategies.* Farmington Hills, MI: Twayne Publishers, 1997.
Staines, John D. *The Tragic Histories of Mary Queen of Scots, 1560–1690: Rhetoric, Passions, and Political Literature.* Aldershot: Ashgate, 2009.
Starner, Janet Wright. "'Jacke on Both Sides': Appropriating Equivocation." In *Anonymity in Early Modern England: What's in a Name?*, ed. Janet Wright Starner and Barbara Howard Traister, 43–80. Farnham: Ashgate, 2011.
Stillman, Robert E. *Christian Identity, Piety, and Politics in Early Modern England.* Notre Dame, IN: University of Notre Dame Press, 2021.
Stockard, Emily E. "Constable, Henry." In *The Encyclopedia of English Renaissance Literature*, ed. Garrett A. Sullivan and Alan Stewart, 1: 209–210. Chichester: Wiley-Blackwell, 2012.
—. "Henry Constable, English Poet (1562–1613)." In *Sixteenth-Century British Non-dramatic Writers, Second Series*, ed. David A. Richardson, 45–52. Detroit: Gale Research, 1994.
Stoye, J.W. "An Early Letter from John Chamberlain." *The English Historical Review* 62 (1947): 522–532.
Straw, Carole. "'A Very Special Death': Christian Martyrdom in its Classical Context." In *Sacrificing the Self: Martyrdom and Religion*, ed. Margaret Cormack, 39–57. New York: Oxford University Press, 2002.
Stringer, Gary. "Some Sacred and Profane Con-Texts of John Donne's 'Batter my hart'." In *Sacred and Profane: Secular and Devotional Interplay in Early Modern British Literature*, ed. Helen Wilcox, Richard Todd, and Alasdair A. MacDonald, 173–183. Amsterdam: VU University Press, 1996.
Stronks, Els. "Amor Dei in Emblems for Dutch Youth." In *Ut Pictura Amor: The Reflexive Imagery of Love in Artistic Theory and Practice, 1500–1700*, ed. Walter S. Melion, Joanna Woodall, and Michael Zell, 547–572. Leiden: Brill, 2017.
Sullivan, Ceri. 2013 "Constable, Henry (1562–1613), polemicist and poet." In *ODNB*. Oxford University Press, 2004; online ed., 2013. https://doi.org/10.1093/ref:odnb/6103.
Sutherland, Nicola M. *Henry IV of France and the Politics of Religion: 1572–1596.* Bristol: Elm Bank, 2002.
Teulet, Alexandre, ed. *Relations politiques de la France et de l'Espagne avec l'Ecosse au XVIe siècle.* 5 vols. Paris: Veuve Jules Renouard, 1862.
Thomas, Vivian, and Nick Faircloth. *Shakespeare's Plants and Gardens: A Dictionary.* London: Bloomsbury, 2014.
Thorpe, Thomas. *Catalogue of Manuscripts for Sale.* London: Thomas Thorpe, 1831.
Todd, Henry J., ed. *The Poetical Works of John Milton.* 6 vols. London: J. Johnson, 1801.
Trill, Suzanne. "Spectres and Sisters: Mary Sidney and the 'Perennial Puzzle' of Renaissance Women's Writing." In *Renaissance Configurations: Voices/Bodies/Spaces, 1580–1690*, ed. Gordon McMullan, 191–211. Basingstoke: Palgrave, 2001.
Tutino, Stefania. *Law and Conscience: Catholicism in Early Modern England, 1570–1625.* Hampshire: Ashgate, 2007.

Urban, Sylvanus. "Obituary." *The Gentleman's Magazine* 78 (1808): 851–862.
Van Dorsten, Jan. "The Final Year." In *Sir Philip Sidney*, ed. Baker-Smith et al., 16–24. Leiden: Leiden University Press, 1986.
———. *Poets, Patrons, and Professors: Sir Philip Sidney, Daniel Rogers, and the Leiden Humanists*. Publications of the Sir Thomas Browne Institute, Leiden, gen. ser., 2. Leiden: Sir Thomas Browne Institute at the University Press, 1962.
Varlow, Sally. *The Lady Penelope: The Lost Tale of Love and Politics in the Court of Elizabeth I*. London: André Deutsch, 2007.
Venn, John, and J.A. Venn. *Alumni Cantabrigienses: A Biographical List of All Known Students, Graduates and Holders of Office at the University of Cambridge, from the Earliest Times to 1900*. 2 parts in 10 vols. Cambridge: Cambridge University Press, 1922–1954.
Villeponteaux, Mary. *The Queen's Mercy: Gender and Judgment in Representations of Elizabeth I*. New York: Palgrave Macmillan, 2014.
Wagner, Bernard M. "New Poems by Sir Edward Dyer." *The Review of English Studies* 11 (1935): 466–471.
Wagstaffe, Sally Anne. "Forms and Methods of Religious Controversy in Paris: With Special Reference to Pierre du Moulin and his Catholic Opponents." PhD diss., Durham University, 1990.
Warner, Marina. *Alone of All Her Sex: The Myth and Cult of the Virgin Mary*. 2nd ed. Oxford: Oxford University Press, 2013.
Warren, Nancy Bradley. *Women of God and Arms: Female Spirituality and Political Conflict, 1380–1600*. Philadelphia: University of Pennsylvania Press, 2005.
Warton, Thomas. *The History of English Poetry, from the Close of the Eleventh to the Commencement of the Eighteenth Century*. 4 vols. London: J. Dodsley et al., 1774–1781.
Watson, Andrew G. *The Library of Sir Simonds D'Ewes*. London: British Museum, 1966.
Wickes, George. "Henry Constable: Courtier Poet." In *Renaissance Papers: A Selection of Papers Presented at the Renaissance Meeting in the Southeastern States*, 102–107. Columbia, SC: University of South Carolina Press, 1956.
———. "Henry Constable, Poet and Courtier, 1562–1613." *Biographical Studies* 2 (1954): 272–300.
———. "Henry Constable's Spiritual Sonnets." *Month* 18 (1957): 30–40.
Wiggins, Martin, and Catherine Richardson, eds. *British Drama 1533–1642: A Catalogue*. 9 vols. Oxford: Oxford University Press, 2012–.
Wilcox, Helen. "Sacred Desire, Forms of Belief: The Religious Sonnet in Early Modern Britain." In *Companion to the Sonnet*, ed. Cousins and Howarth, 145–165.
Williams, Claire B. "An Edition of National Art Library (Great Britain) MS Dyce 44." 2 vols. PhD diss., University of Sheffield, 2012.
———. "'This and the rest Maisters we all may mende': Reconstructing the Practices and Anxieties of a Manuscript Miscellany's Reader-Compiler." *Huntington Library Quarterly* 80 (2017): 277–292.
Williamson, Elizabeth. *The Materiality of Religion in Early Modern English Drama*. Farnham: Ashgate, 2009.

Willmott, Robert A. *Lives of Sacred Poets*. London: J.W. Parker, 1834.
Wimsatt, James I. "St. Bernard, the Canticle of Canticles, and Mystical Poetry." In *An Introduction to the Medieval Mystics*, ed. Paul E. Szarmach, 77–96. Albany, NY: State University of New York Press, 1984.
Wood, Anthony à. *Athenae oxonienses*. 2 vols. London: T. Combe, 1691–1692.
Woodward, Jennifer. *The Theatre of Death: The Ritual Management of Royal Funerals in Renaissance England, 1570–1625*. Woodbridge: Boydell Press, 1997.
Woolgar, Christopher. "What Makes Things Holy? The Senses and Material Culture in the Later Middle Ages." In *Sensing the Sacred in Medieval and Early Modern Culture*, ed. Robin Macdonald, Emilie K.M. Murphy, and Elizabeth L. Swann, 60–78. London: Routledge, 2018.
Woudhuysen, Henry R. "Sidney, Sir Philip (1554–1586)." In *ODNB*. Oxford University Press, 2004; online ed. 2014. https://doi.org/10.1093/ref:odnb/25522.
—. *Sir Philip Sidney and the Circulation of Manuscripts, 1558–1640*. Oxford: Clarendon Press, 1996.
Wright, Cyril E. *Fontes Harleiani: A Study of the Sources of the Harleian Collection of Manuscripts Preserved in the Department of Manuscripts in the British Museum*. London: British Museum, 1972.
Wright, Cyril E., and Ruth C. Wright, eds. *The Diary of Humfrey Wanley, 1715–1726*. 2 vols. London: Bibliographical Society, 1966.

# Index of Manuscripts

Arundel, Arundel Castle
    The Arundel Harington MS: 9, 39–42, 140–141, 147–154 *passim*, 248–325 *passim*, 366–367
Berkeley, Gloucs., Berkeley Castle
    GL 5/19: 98 n15
    Select Books 85: 92, 94–98, 135, 141, 147–154 *passim*, 329–363 *passim*, 381–383
Cambridge, MA, Harvard University, Houghton Library
    MS Eng 966.5: 103 n22
    MS Eng 966.6: 103 n23
Dublin, Marsh's Library
    Marsh MS Z3.5.21: 5 n27, 34–38, 47, 138, 140–141, 147–154 *passim*, 224, 248–327 *passim*, 364–366
Edinburgh, Edinburgh University Library
    MS H.-P. Coll. 401: 49–52, 141, 147–154 *passim*, 248–325 *passim*, 371–372
Grantham, Belvoir Castle
    Belvoir MSS Additional 1: 30 n159
Hatfield, Hatfield House Library
    CP 18/55: 10 n49
    CP 35/50: 21 n104
    CP 167/4: 11 n54
    CP 175/3: 21 n105
    CP 179/156: 20 n98
    CP 187/71: 26 n139
    CP 188/108: 97
    CP 191/54: 29 n155

Kew, The National Archives
    SP 12/60: 3 n9
    SP 12/126: 3 n9
    SP 12/165: 3 n7
    SP 15/28/2: 4 n20
    SP 15/29: 4 n19
    SP 15/34: 26 n134
    SP 77/5: 22 n109
    SP 77/6: 24 n120
    SP 78/10: 4 n17
    SP 78/11: 4 n19
    SP 78/51: 27 n144, 28 n150
    SP 84/19: 5 n24, 5 n25, 8 n39
London, British Library
    Add MS 11402: 30 n160
    Add MS 12049: 41 n32
    Add MS 12225: 28 n146
    Add MS 15225: 110 n26
    Add MS 18920: 53, 366 n14
    Add MS 24195: 281
    Add MS 28635: 140 n50
    Add MS 42518: 132 n3
    Add MS 45701–45707: 380 n68
    Harley MS 6953: 31 n163
    Harley MS 7392: 34
    Harley MS 7553: 20 n95, 92–94, 135, 137, 140–141, 147–154 *passim*, 329–357 *passim*, 379–380
    Stowe MS: 52 n72
London, Lambeth Palace
    MS 660: 22 n107
    MS 708: 29 n152

MS 3203: 29 n157
MS 3205: 29 n154
London, The National Art Library, V&A Museum
 MS Dyce 44: 19, 43–49, 63, 134, 136–137, 140–143, 145–146, 147–154 *passim*, 248–325 *passim*, 367–371
London, Westminster Diocesan Archive
 A4/34: 31 n164
New Haven, Yale University, Beinecke Library
 MS 621: 6, 33, 35, 52–53, 75, 82–83, 99, 128 n96, 141, 147–154 *passim*, 276–278, 373–374
Oxford, Bodleian Library
 MS Ashmole 38: 54–56, 140–141, 372–373
 MS Rawl. Poet. 85: 34
 MS Rawl. Poet. 148: 43 n45
 Tanner MS 169: 4 n21
Rome, Archivum Venerabilis Collegii Anglorum
 liber 282: 315
Vatican City, Archivio Segreto Vaticano
 Fondo Borghese, III, 73: 15 n70, 23 n117
 Segretaria di Stato, Francia, 47–49: 25 n125, 27 n141, 27 n142, 27 n145, 28 n147, 28 n148, 97 n11
Vatican City, Biblioteca Apostolica Vaticana
 MS Vat. lat. 6227: 26 n133
Washington, DC, The Folger Shakespeare Library
 Folger MS M.b.26.: 371 n36
 Folger MS V.a.249: 41 n32

# Index of First Lines with Regularized Spelling

| | |
|---|---|
| A friend of mine, moaning my helpless love | 178 |
| As Anne, long barren, mother did become | 233 |
| Because thou was the daughter of a king | 236 |
| Blame not my heart for flying up so high | 165 |
| Blessed offender, which thy self hast tried | 242 |
| Bloom of the rose, I hope those hands to kiss | 184 |
| Dear, though from me your gracious looks depart | 208 |
| Delight in your bright eyes my death did breed | 162 |
| Each day new proofs of new despair I find | 218 |
| Eternal sprite, which art in heaven, the love | 229 |
| Even as when great mens' heirs cannot agree | 213 |
| Eyes curious to behold what nature can create | 166 |
| Fair Amazon of heaven, which tookst in hand | 237 |
| Fair by inheritance, whom born we see | 201 |
| Fair sun, if you would have me praise your light | 179 |
| False the report, & unjust is the blame | 173 |
| Falsely doth envy of your praises blame | 172 |
| Fly low, dear Love; thy sun dost thou not see? | 160 |
| For few nights' solace in delitious bed | 235 |
| Give pardon, blessed soule, to my bold cries | 211 |
| Grace, full of grace, though in these verses here | 157 |
| Great Alexander then did well declare | 212 |
| Great god, within whose simple essence we | 227 |
| He that by skill of stars doth fates foretell | 214 |
| He that for fear his Master did deny | 234 |
| Heralds in armes do three perfections coat | 195 |
| I do thee wrong, oh Queen, in that I say | 247 |
| I write of tears and blood at one time shed | 245 |
| If ever any justly might complain | 209 |
| If I durst love as heretofore I have | 187 |
| If I durst sigh still as I had begun | 186 |
| If Michael the archpainter now did live | 202 |

## Index of First Lines

| | |
|---|---|
| If nature for her works proud ever were | 188 |
| If that one care had our two hearts possest | 206 |
| If true love might true loves' reward obtain | 221 |
| In Eden grew many a pleasant spring | 225 |
| In that, oh Queen of Queens, thy birth was free | 231 |
| It is not pomp of solemn funeral | 246 |
| It may be Love doth not my death pretend | 164 |
| Lady in beauty and in favour rare | 167 |
| Lady of Ladies, the delight alone | 168 |
| Lady whom by report I only know | 198 |
| Mine eye with all the deadly sins is fraught | 219 |
| Mine eye with all the deadly sins is fraught | 220 |
| Miracle of the world, I never will deny | 177 |
| Most sacred prince, why should I thee thus praise | 182 |
| Much sorrow in it self my love doth move | 215 |
| My hope lay gasping on his dying bed | 224 |
| My Ladies presence makes the roses red | 174 |
| My Mistrisse worth gave wings unto my Muse | 223 |
| My reason, absent, did mine eyes require | 217 |
| Needs I must leave and yet needs must I love | 216 |
| Not long ago in Poland travelling | 181 |
| Not that thy hand is soft, is sweet, is white | 169 |
| Now, now I love indeed and suffer more | 203 |
| O, that my song like to a ship might be | 194 |
| Only hope of our age, that virtues dead | 193 |
| Pity refusing my poor love to feed | 205 |
| Plainly I write because I will write true | 189 |
| Resolved to love, unworthy to obtain | 159 |
| Severed from sweet content, my life's sole light | 226 |
| Since only I, sweet Lady, ye beheld | 200 |
| Sometimes in verse I praised, sometimes I sighed | 222 |
| Sovereign of Queens, if vain ambition move | 239 |
| Such as, retired from sight of men like thee | 243 |
| Sweet hand, the sweet (yet cruel) bow thou art | 175 |
| Sweet Queen, although thy beauty raise up me | 241 |
| Sweet saint, thou better canst declare to me | 244 |
| Sweet soul, which now with heavenly songs dost tell | 210 |
| Sweet Sovereign, sith so many minds remain | 170 |
| Sweetest of Ladies, if thy pleasure be | 199 |
| That worthy Marquise, pride of Italy | 192 |
| The fowler hides, as closely as he may | 176 |
| The love wherewith your virtues chain my sprite | 183 |

| | |
|---|---|
| The sun his journey ending in the west | 180 |
| Thine eye, the glass where I behold my heart | 161 |
| This day, oh blessed virgin, is the day | 238 |
| True worthy dame, if I thee chieftain call | 197 |
| Uncivil sickness, hast thou no regard | 207 |
| When as the Prince of Angels, puffed with pride | 232 |
| When beauty to the world vouchsafes this bliss | 171 |
| When murdering hands, to quench the thirst of tyranny | 196 |
| When others hooded with blind love do fly | 185 |
| When thee, oh holy sacrificed Lamb | 230 |
| When your perfections to my thoughts appear | 163 |
| Why should I any love, oh Queen, but thee? | 240 |
| Wonder it is and pity tis that she | 204 |
| Ye, sister Muses, do not ye repine | 191 |
| You, sister Muses, do not ye repine | 190 |
| Young Prince of heaven, begotten of that King | 228 |

# General Index

Achelly, Thomas 133
Achilles 273
Acquaviva, Claudio, SJ 6
Acts of Peter (apocryphal) 341
Aeneas 61
Alabaster, William 15, 102, 113, 118 n63
Alciato, Andrea 315
Aldobrandini, Pietro, cardinal 14–15, 23, 27 n141, 27 n142, 27 n145, 28 n147
Alexander, William 298
Alexander the Great 201, 212, 298, 310–311
Alfield, Thomas 358, 362
Alfonso X the Learned 260
Alighieri, Dante 111, 352
Allen, William, cardinal 6–7, 35, 52, 276–277, 374
Allyne, Robert 314
Amalteo, Atilio, apostolic nuncio 14–15, 23
Amazons 346
angels 95, 122, 132, 160, 168, 184, 210, 228–229, 232, 236, 239, 243, 246–247, 250, 268, 276, 280, 331–332, 334, 339–340, 344–346, 349–350, 356, 361, 363, 383–384
Anne, saint 340
Anne of Denmark, queen consort of James VI and I 10–11, 22, 27, 97–98, 102, 186, 281–282
anonymity 34–35, 43, 54 n81, 58, 132

anti-Catholicism 34, 50, 53, 78, 93 n3
Apollo 132, 187, 281–283, 384, 386
Arber, Edward 56 n86, 60 n99, 60 n100, 65 n118, 137–138
archangels 232, 339, 383. *See also* Gabriel; Michael; Raphael
Archpriest (Appellant) Controversy 22
Ariosto, Ludovico 39 n28, 269
Articles of Religion 24, 276
Arundel Castle, Arundel 141, 366. *See also* Index of Manuscripts
Arundell, Sir Charles 4
Augustine, saint 17, 319, 329–330, 338–339, 354–355

Bacon, Anthony 21–22, 134
Bacon, Francis 50, 53 n73
Bagshaw, Christopher 22
Baily, John 68
Bancroft, Richard, archbishop of Canterbury 29 n157
baptism 247, 333, 341, 361
Barberini, Maffeo: *see* Urban VIII
Barnes, Barnabe 107, 113, 319; *A divine centurie of spirituall sonnets* 114, 280, 323, 331, 334, 339, 362; *Parthenophil and Parthenophe* 286, 289, 294, 301, 319, 321
Barnfield, Richard 317, 378 n63
Baroque, artistic 20
Bartas, Guillaume de Salluste Du 112, 280, 313

Bastard, Thomas 43
Baynam, Sir Edward 29
Beal, Peter 32 n1, 39 n24, 39 n27, 54 n77, 71 n144, 149 n8, 151 n15, 369 n23, 380 n69, 382 n74, 383 n76
Beaumont, Francis 54
Bedell, William, bishop of Kilmore 93 n3
Beinecke Library, Yale University, New Haven: *see* Index of Manuscripts
Bellarmine, Robert, cardinal 12 n57, 12 n60, 330
Bellay, Joachim Du 64, 111–112, 250, 269
Benedictines, in England 25
Berkeley, Elizabeth 97–98, 102, 381–382
Berkeley, Henry, 7th Baron Berkeley 382
Berkeley, Sir Thomas 97, 381
Berkeley, Thomas, 5th Baron Berkeley 1 n2
Berkeley, Thomas, 6th Baron Berkeley 1 n2
Berkeley Castle, Gloucestershire 92–93, 98 n14, 381–382. *See also* Index of Manuscripts
Berkeley family 1, 98, 381
Bernard, saint 117, 333, 353, 355, 357
Bible: King James 263; perfect or sacred numbers in 96 n8
—, books of: apocrypha 336, 339, 341; 1 Corinthians 331, 357; 1 John 333; 1 Peter 336; 1 Samuel 340–341; 2 Corinthians 271; Acts of the Apostles 333, 342; Colossians 330; Daniel 262; Exodus 329; Ezekiel 277, 341; Genesis 326–327; Isaiah 271, 332, 334, 339; Job 276, 322; John 333, 335, 341, 343, 354; Jude 339; Luke 118 n63, 262–263, 332, 340–341, 343, 349, 355; Mark 261, 341, 343, 349; Matthew 276, 332–333, 336, 340–341, 343, 349, 354; Philippians 341; Psalms 93, 277, 279, 332; Revelation 128, 276, 330, 337, 339–340, 345–346; Romans 94 n6; Song of Songs 117, 135, 333, 353, 355, 357
—, persons and places in: *see* angels; Anne; Calvary; Christ, Jesus; David; Devil; Eden, Garden of; Elijah; Elizabeth; Gethsemane; Hannah; heaven; hell; Jairus's daughter; James the Less; John the Baptist; John the Evangelist; Joseph; Lazarus; Mary, Blessed Virgin; Mary Magdalene; Mary, mother of James; Paul; Peter; purgatory; Samuel; Saul
Bird, Samuel 280
bishops and archbishops 22, 25–26, 29, 44, 338, 364. *See also* Bancroft, Richard; Bedell, William; Fletcher, Richard; Marsh, Narcissus; Stearne, John; White, John
Blackwood, Adam 358
Bochart, Rene 18 n89, 19 n90
Bodleian Library, Oxford 372, 377–378. *See also* Index of Manuscripts
Bolton, Edmund 133, 135, 140–141, 147
Bonaventure, saint 332
books, printed: binding 375 n52, 377–378; format 59, 65, 67, 69, 375–377; revision of texts in 68, 78, 86; title pages 12, 58, 60, 136, 148, 376–379
Borromeo, Frederic, cardinal 25
Bourbon, Catherine de, princess of Navarre 9
Breton, Nicholas 44 n46, 61, 113, 294, 308–309, 311
brevigraphs 151, 366, 372. *See also* abbreviations *under* manuscripts, scribal practices in
Bristow, Richard 23
Bristow, William 368
British Library, London: *see* Index of Manuscripts
Brockman, Henry 43–44, 48–49, 368, 386; as scribe 85 n153

Bucer, Martin 13
Buchanan, George 278, 302
Buckley, Thomas 34
Bufalo, Innocenzo del, apostolic nuncio 26–28
Burghe, Nicholas 54–56, 76 n148, 87, 133, 373

Caen 12
Calvary 335
Cambridge, university: Christ's College 49; Clare College 43; Corpus Christi College 36; Pembroke College 49 n64, 364 n6; Queen's College 36 n19, 377 n58; St John's College 3, 34–36, 133, 368 n21; Sidney Sussex College 34 n9
Camden, William 360
Campbell, Thomas 136
Campion, Edmund 14 n67, 358, 362, 373 n47
Campion, Thomas 303
Carew, Thomas 50, 54, 373 n43
Carey, Elizabeth: see Berkeley, Elizabeth
Carey, Sir William 381 n72
Carier, Benjamin 16, 30
Carleton, Dudley, viscount 29 n155
Carr, Robert 44
Casaubon, Isaac 13
Castiglione, Baldassare 260, 268, 311, 352
Catherine of Alexandria, saint 96, 116, 128 n95, 344–345, 361
Catholics and Catholicism 4, 6, 12–31, 34 n9, 46, 52, 93, 97–98, 101–103, 105, 110, 113, 120, 124, 126–127, 129–130, 132, 138–139, 144, 147 n2, 248, 256, 276, 284–285, 291 n1, 306, 335, 358, 360; beliefs 13, 17, 27, 104, 109, 122, 126–130, 264, 293, 335–337, 341, 344, 350, 361; poetry by 102, 110 n26, 112–113, 144; propaganda 13 n63, 93, 127, 358, 360. See also anti-Catholicism; church: Catholic; intercession; recusants

Cavendish, Charles 288
Cavendish, Elizabeth 324
Cavendish, Frances 16, 248, 324
Cavendish, Grace 17 n79
Cavendish, Sir Henry 7 n33, 17 n79
Cavendish, Mary: see Talbot, Mary
Cavendish, Sir William 7 n33
Cayet, Pierre, theologian 26
Cecil, Sir Robert 20 n96, 23, 26, 28–29, 52–53, 97
Cecil, William, Lord Burghley 3, 5, 8, 10–11, 288, 299, 359, 373 n47
Cecilia, saint 268
*CELM* (online *Catalogue of English Literary Manuscripts*) 34 n11, 50 n67, 52 n71, 53 n73, 92, 103 n22, 145
Chamberlain, John 8
Charles I, king of England 50, 314
Charles de Lorraine, 4th duke of Guise 27 n144
Charlewood, John 56, 59–60
chastity 18, 57, 119, 123 n78, 237, 239, 256, 265, 307, 311, 345, 347, 350
Chaucer, Geoffrey 132 n3, 252
Chettle, Henry 136, 139, 147
Christ, Jesus 129 n99, 242, 244, 330, 354, 362; ancestry 332; Ascension 229; Baptism 333, 341; burial 230, 336; coming of 271, 341; coming of the Magi 332; Crucifixion 268, 341; Harrowing of Hell 336; Incarnation 103, 331, 338, 352; as inspiration 104, 113; and Mary Magdalene 100, 118 n63, 353–354; millennial reign of 262; miracles 261; mystical marriage to 117, 344; nativity 104, 332; nursing of 123; Passion 253, 362; prayers to 331; prefigured 335; as prince of heaven 95, 100, 124, 228, 331, 337, 349; real presence in the Eucharist 30, 100, 129, 335–336; salvation through sacrifice of 100, 253, 335, 351, 354. See also Mary Magdalene

church 13, 15–16, 129, 232, 234, 332, 339, 349, 355; Catholic 13, 20, 27, 126 n89, 129, 284, 340–341; early 337, 342; of England 276, 360; Protestant 13, 123 n80
Church, Henry 258
Churchyard, Thomas 39, 301
Clement VIII, pope 13, 22–23, 25, 27
Cleves, Catherine of, duchess of Guise 24
Clifford, Margaret, countess of Cumberland 10, 37, 47, 81, 87, 190, 285, 325–326
Clinton, Edward, 1st earl of Lincoln 296
Clinton, Edward Fiennes de, earl of Lincoln 3 n9
Clinton, Elizabeth 200, 296
Clinton, Thomas 296
Colette of Corbie, saint 96, 118, 148, 347–349
Coligny, Gaspard de, seigneur de Châtillon 291–292
Coligny, Louise de, princess of Orange 5, 8, 52, 89, 188, 196, 283, 291–292, 372
collation, textual 44 n47, 70–71, 85–86, 99, 101, 135, 141, 143, 145, 149, 152–154, 254, 310, 369 n24, 376, 378 n61; in the edition of the poems 159–161, 163–165, 167, 170–180, 183–185, 187–188, 190, 194–195, 201, 204–205, 207, 210–222, 227–237, 239–244
Collège Mignon, Paris 20, 22
Collier, John Payne 371 n37
Colonna, Vittoria 47 n58, 67, 108, 111, 124, 192, 210, 287, 307–308, 334, 351, 356
Constable, Henry: anonymous sonnets to 19, 45, 48, 111 n27, 132, 324, 384–387; anti-Jesuit stance 22–23, 25; appearance 26; birthdate 3, 348; Catholic agent in England 27–28; Catholic connections 1, 19–20, 22–26, 28–29, 31; Catholic loyalism 21, 135; conversion 13 n63, 14–19, 46–47, 50, 78, 102, 105, 111, 121, 126–128, 139–140, 275, 284, 318, 324, 336; criticism and appraisal 105, 114, 118 n62, 130–146; death 30–31; debates on religion 24, 26, 28, 30; Dutch connections 5–6, 8, 14, 90–91; early career 3–14, 19, 97, 139, 274, 374; early Protestantism 4, 6, 12, 22, 111 n30, 120, 264; education 3, 36, 48; at the English court 7–9, 11–12, 27, 144, 285, 309; exile 18–26, 30, 48, 50, 57–58, 62–63, 93, 97, 102, 106, 110–111, 119, 124–125, 130, 132, 134, 140, 148, 230, 316, 318, 324, 356, 387; family 1–3, 7 n33, 9–10, 17, 19, 24, 26, 28–30, 36 n17, 102; French connections 12, 18 n89, 22–24, 26, 29; imprisonment and banishment 28–30; and King James 3–4, 9–11, 22–29, 37–38, 45–46, 51, 53, 108, 124, 127, 132, 134, 137, 278–283, 287–288, 324, 386; modern editions of his works 134, 136, 138, 145; patronage 9, 11, 16, 32, 46, 68, 105–106, 108, 115–116, 120, 124, 130, 140, 285, 288–289, 292–294, 309, 311, 326, 351, 381; and Queen Elizabeth I 6–7, 14, 18, 37–38, 45, 48, 52–53, 116, 120–125, 127, 181–183, 274–278, 283, 288, 292, 295, 351, 373, 387; reputation among contemporaries 5, 97, 131–134, 144, 279; return to England 27; in Rome 19–20; and Scottish poets 4, 11; and the Sidney-Essex circle 7, 9–10, 21–22, 40, 46, 90 n163, 116, 283–287, 289–295, 297–300, 387; and Sir Philip Sidney 7–9, 40, 46, 51, 62, 67, 107, 116, 133, 140, 199, 211–213, 294, 307–314, 328; and the Walsingham-Leicester circle 4–5, 7–8, 139, 278, 309
—, works: affective or erotic language and imagery in 105, 109, 114, 117, 123–124, 135, 170, 227, 241, 262, 273,

Constable, Henry, works – *continued*
333, 353, 357; arrangement of sonnets 33, 37, 41, 45, 49, 51, 55, 60, 65, 93–94, 96, 99, 130, 137, 148–149, 249, 272, 302, 323–324; canon of his poetry 37, 40, 51, 94, 135, 142, 147–148; circulation of works in manuscript 5–6, 8–9, 19, 32–56 *passim*, 61, 68–92 *passim*, 94, 98, 103, 105, 148 n7, 150, 251, 278, 289, 324–325; compilers of manuscripts with works by 6 n28, 33, 40, 43–45, 47–49, 52, 54, 69, 76, 87, 104, 142, 146, 364, 368–369, 386; dating of sonnets 20, 34 n10, 40, 46, 76, 93, 101–102, 120, 146, 255–256, 274, 276, 281, 291; headings and titles 4–6, 9, 19, 25, 33, 35, 37–38, 40, 45–53, 55–57, 59–60, 65–69, 87–90, 93–94, 96, 103, 108–109, 112, 125, 137–138, 148–150, 153, 157–249 *passim*, 252–254, 264, 270, 274, 276, 278, 284–285, 295–297, 321, 324, 348–349, 353, 366–367, 369–370, 376, 379–383; identity of Diana in 9, 57, 138, 289; involvement in publication of his sonnets 32, 57–59, 67; lost authorial manuscripts (archetypes) 33, 40–41, 47, 49, 52–53, 59, 65–68, 70–71, 75–91, 94, 97–99, 101–102, 149–152, 249, 262, 265, 276, 290, 298, 302, 307, 316, 320, 374; lost works 4, 22, 47–48; manuscripts 32–56, 70–104, 145, 374; misattributed works 12, 62, 102–104, 133, 136–138, 140, 147–148, 150 n12, 337; printed editions 56–68, 70–91; recantation of secular poetry 17, 46–47, 58, 61, 106, 109, 111, 115, 117, 122–123, 132, 248, 321, 323, 327, 331, 333–334, 338, 352, 361; rededication 47, 67, 116 n53, 248, 323; revision of texts 68, 70–71, 75–79, 81, 83, 85, 88, 90 n159, 99–101, 110 n24, 144, 146, 149, 258, 263–264, 271, 277, 286, 289, 297, 316, 321, 331, 354, 374; set to music 68; translations into other languages 5, 12 n59, 33, 69, 90–91, 140, 251, 256, 276. *See also* manuscript circulation

—, individual works: *A Commentarie or explication of a letter written by Cardinal Allen* 5–7, 16, 35, 37, 52–53, 120 n67, 128, 276, 374; a defamatory libel against Spain and the Jesuits 25–26; 1592 *Diana* 19, 40–42, 48, 50–51, 56–61, 63, 65, 70–90 *passim*, 130–131, 135 n19, 140–141, 143, 150, 226, 327–329, 375–377; 1594 *Diana* (*Augmented Diana*) 19, 51, 55, 59–66, 70–90, 109 n19, 134–138, 141–142, 148, 377–378; 1598 *Diana* (non-extant) 60, 65; *A discoverye of a counterfecte conference* 25; *Examen pacifique de la doctrine des Huguenots* (*The Catholike moderator*) 12–13, 16, 22 n107, 78, 120 n70, 128, 140, 276; occasional sonnets 45–47, 56, 87–89, 108, 158, 174–175, 177–178, 183, 186–187, 196–197, 199, 202, 270–271, 281, 286, 297–299, 366; secular sonnets (amatory and dedicatory) 4–6, 12, 32–91, 94, 97, 99, 105–111, 114, 119, 120–128 *passim*, 130–154 *passim*, 157–226 (texts), 248–329, 345, 352, 364–381; sonnet in Harington's *Orlando furioso* 53, 67, 76, 279; sonnet in King James's *His Majesties poeticall exercises* 66, 76, 85, 132, 135, 279–280; sonnets in Sidney's *An apologie for poetrie* 51, 62, 65, 67, 76, 85–86, 133, 135, 137, 140, 307–314; sonnets in *A poetical rapsody* 51, 55, 67–68, 76, 81, 87, 140, 285–286; *Spiritual Sonnets* 20, 27, 48, 92–106, 111–130, 135–146 *passim*, 148, 150, 227–247 (texts), 249, 274, 285, 329–363, 379–383, 387. *See also* Index of Manuscripts: Arundel,

Arundel Castle, The Arundel Harington MS; Berkeley, Gloucs., Berkeley Castle, Select Books 85; Dublin, Marsh's Library, Marsh MS Z3.5.21; Edinburgh, Edinburgh University Library, MS H.-P. Coll. 401; London, British Library, Add MS 18920; London, British Library, Harley MS 7553; London, The National Art Library, V&A Museum, MS Dyce 44; New Haven, Yale University, Beinecke Library, MS 621; Oxford, Bodleian Library, MS Ashmole 38
Constable, John 36 n17, 133
Constable, Sir Marmaduke, of Everingham 1
Constable, Sir Marmaduke, of Flamborough 1
Constable, Sir Robert, of Everingham 1
Constable, Sir Robert, of Flamborough 1
Constable, Sir Robert, of Newark-on-Trent 1, 3–5, 7 n33, 9, 296
controversy, religious 14–15, 22 n112, 25–26, 30, 120 n70, 140
conversion, religious 17–18, 22 n108, 25, 30, 102, 111, 117 n57, 138, 333, 342, 345, 361. *See also* conversion *under* Constable, Henry
Cooke, Henry 148 n5
Cooke, John 252
Cope, Sir Walter 29 n155
copy texts 41, 53, 65, 86, 88, 97, 142–143, 145, 149 n10, 150 n13, 351, 370; in this edition 49, 70, 148–152, 162, 181–182, 188, 193, 196, 199–200, 202, 206, 209, 219–221, 224, 228, 239, 246, 306
correspondence 3, 5, 9–11, 14, 19–24, 26–29, 52, 98 n14, 134–135, 139, 145, 278, 288, 299, 374–375
Council of Trent (1545–1563) 126 n89, 129–130, 335, 337, 344, 355

Counter-Reformation 93 n4, 112 n33, 114, 118, 141, 343
Cousins, Anthony D. 113 n40, 117 n57, 129 n99, 144
Craig, Alexander 265, 289, 317, 329
Crow, Martha Foote 62 n111, 137–138, 262
Cupid 108, 185, 203, 236, 243, 255–256, 262, 269, 290, 301–304, 315, 333, 350, 386

Dabridgecourt, Christiana 3
Daniel, Samuel 8, 39, 44, 56 n84, 60, 131–132, 136, 143, 255, 294; *Civil Wars* 375 n52; *Delia* 56 n84, 105, 137, 249–250, 252, 267, 269–270, 274, 292, 304, 315, 378 n63
David, biblical figure 124, 184, 228, 278, 332, 338, 340–341
Davies, Sir John 43
Davies, Myles 133
Davison, Francis 67, 87
Day, Angel 313
Dekker, Thomas 279
Denmark 11, 89, 186–187, 281–282
Desportes, Philippe 57, 65, 107, 112, 139, 272, 323; *Cleonice* 107 n7, 249, 254, 305, 319, 324; *Diane* 57, 107 n7, 257, 272, 296, 302, 304, 316, 321; *Diverses amours* 269, 303; *Hippolyte* 255, 318; *Premieres oeuvres* 107 n7, 112 n32; *Sonnets spirituels* 112
Deventer 6, 128 n96
Devereux, Frances, countess of Essex 46, 199, 295
Devereux, Robert, 2nd earl of Essex 9–10, 12–13, 16, 18–21, 23, 34 n10, 44 n46, 46, 116, 199, 285, 295, 311, 387
Devil (Lucifer, Satan) 96, 232, 339–340, 345–347
D'Ewes, Sir Simonds 379
Diana, mythological figure 281, 311

Digges, Leonard 257
Donne, John 54, 102–103, 106 n4, 115, 117 n59, 130, 152, 337; manuscript circulation 68, 70 n138, 148 n7; misattribution to 102–104, 150 n12, 337; religious poetry 103, 115, 331, 354, 359; secular poetry 43, 248, 255
Dorsten, Jan van 5 n24, 8 n37, 14, 90 n163
Douglas, Richard 11
Dousa, Janus, the Younger 90–91; translations of Constable 5, 90, 251, 256
Dowden, Edward 5 n27, 6, 138, 141 n60, 364
Dowland, John 43
Drake-Brockman, James 368
Drayton, Michael 56, 107; *Idea* 131, 295, 323; *Ideas mirrour* 250, 253, 261, 263, 305–306, 314, 321, 350; *To the Majestie of King James* 375 n52
Dudley, Ambrose, earl of Warwick 47, 326
Dudley, Robert, 1st earl of Leicester 5, 7–8, 10 n45, 13 n65, 16, 90, 116, 285, 310, 326, 382
Du Perron, Jacques Davy, cardinal 12, 22, 26, 30
Dyce, Alexander 136, 367–369, 371
Dyer, Sir Edward 34, 39, 133

Eden, Garden of 225, 325–327
Edinburgh University Library, Edinburgh: *see* Index of Manuscripts
Edith of Wilton, saint 334
Edmondes, Sir Thomas 23, 30 n161
Egypt 212, 311
Elijah, biblical figure 340
Eliot, John 312
Elizabeth, biblical figure 340–341
Elizabeth I, queen of England 3–4, 9–10, 97, 106 n2, 106 n6, 116, 120–125, 252, 275–276, 283, 285, 288, 297, 314, 350, 368, 382; and the Berkeleys 97, 381–382; conspiracies against 21, 24, 255, 358; court 126; foreign policy in the Low Countries 5–6, 276; harshness to Catholics 21, 23–24, 27, 52, 120, 124 n81, 129, 306; and Henri IV 18 n87, 23; imprisonment and execution of Mary, Queen of Scots 4, 35 n13, 125, 358–360; as Jezebel 275; portraits 287, 298; as Protestant queen 120, 123 n80; succession issue 10–11, 24–25, 122, 278, 287–288; as Virgin Queen 122–123; works dedicated to 4, 37–38, 45, 52–53, 120, 125, 260, 274–276, 351
*England's Helicon*, miscellany 136, 138–139, 147
English Civil War 54
Erasmus of Rotterdam 13, 357
errors 70–74, 101, 146; editorial principles regarding 152
—, in manuscript 49, 52, 56, 70, 77, 82–83, 99, 101, 104, 149–150, 250, 258, 272–273, 283, 293, 296, 315, 356, 366, 370, 386; of agreement 99–100, 334, 338, 356; misreading 99, 252, 254, 270, 273, 277, 306; omission 53, 79 n150, 100, 149, 250–251, 259, 265, 303, 306, 317; repetition 100, 104, 254, 270, 274, 290, 305, 308, 316, 321–322, 338, 366; in spelling 252, 269, 303, 317, 361
—, in printed books 53, 56, 84, 86, 256, 259, 305, 308, 318–319, 322, 376, 379
Eucharist 26, 30, 96, 128–129, 335–336. *See also* Christ, Jesus
Evans, Maurice 143
exiles, Catholic 18, 20–21, 24, 26. *See also* Constable, Henry: exile

Featly, Daniel 30 n161
Fernández de Córdoba, Antonio, duke of Sessa 24 n124
Fernández de Velasco, Juan, Constable of Castile 29 n154

*General Index* • 443

Ficino, Marsilio 296, 301, 350
First Epistle of Clement 341
Fleet Prison, London 29
Fleissner, Robert, editor of Constable 59, 70 n138, 77 n149, 143–144, 146, 149 n10
Fletcher, Giles 261, 273, 298
Fletcher, Richard, bishop of London 44
Flodden, Battle of 1
Flushing 8
Fowler, Thomas 10 n48, 11, 299
Fowler, William 66, 269
Foxe, John 264
France 4, 8, 18, 20, 22–24, 26, 28–30, 97, 130, 291 n1, 343, 387
Francis of Assisi, saint 175, 268
Fraunce, Abraham 36
Fulke, William 258

Gabriel, archangel 341
Gager, William 310
Gallonio, Antonio 306
Gascoigne, George 58, 274
George, saint 237, 346
Gethsemane 253
Gipps, Sir Richard 93 n3
God 6 n29, 14–15, 96, 112–113, 115, 120–129, 227 n1, 260, 262, 271, 275–278, 283–285, 288, 307, 326, 329–336, 338, 340–342, 346, 348–359, 362; aseity of 329; beauty of 352; as creator 300, 326; grace of 15, 17, 113, 119, 128, 130, 157, 231, 236, 238, 242–243, 248, 258, 327, 331, 334, 336, 340, 345, 348–349, 352, 355–356; mystical encounter with 117, 124, 244, 352–353, 355, 357; petitions to 114, 119, 127–129, 336; praise of 93–94, 227 n1, 307, 332, 380, 382; Throne of Grace 333; Word of 276
—, the Father 100, 128, 227, 331
—, the Holy Ghost 116–117, 229, 331–333, 338, 352

—, the Son: *see* Christ, Jesus
*Golden Legend*: *see* Jacobus de Voragine
Goodere, Sir Henry 29, 34–35, 43 n41
Gorges, Sir Arthur 7, 277, 312
Goscelin of Saint-Bertin 334
Gospel of Nicodemus (apocryphal) 336
grace 1, 16–17, 63, 104, 108 n16, 113, 119, 123, 128, 136, 157, 178, 197–198, 205, 216, 236, 238–239, 242–43, 248–249, 258, 275, 293–294, 296, 303, 305, 311, 316, 321, 324, 327, 334, 336, 340, 345, 348–349, 355. *See also* God: grace of
Gray, John Henry, editor of Constable 138, 262, 300, 308, 324
Greene, Robert 302
Greville, Fulke, Lord Brooke 39
Grey, Arthur, 14th Baron Grey of Wilton 3
Griffin, Bartholomew 107, 252, 265, 269, 303, 318, 378 n63
Grillo, Angelo 112 n33
Grindlay, Lilla 121 n72, 122 n75, 123 n80, 145, 337, 350–352
Grundy, Joan, editor of Constable 5 n23, 5 n24, 5 n27, 7 n32, 12 n57, 12 n58, 17 n79, 25 n131, 46 n57, 57, 60, 62–63, 77 n149, 102 n16, 107 n7, 108 n14, 112 n33, 134 n14, 137 n33, 142, 148 n6, 253, 255, 262, 267–269, 272, 274, 291–292, 296, 298, 309, 321, 330, 335; assessment of the sonnets 62, 112 n33, 114, 141; contents of edition 77 n149, 141–143, 147 n2, 148 n4, 378 n61; emendations 259, 264, 280, 295–296, 308, 324, 351; shortcomings 12 n57, 108, 143 n69, 276, 327
Guiney, Louise Imogen 17 n79, 139–140
Guise family 20 n97, 26–27, 127 n91. *See also* Charles de Lorraine, 4th duke of Guise; Cleves, Catherine of, duchess of Guise; Henry I, 3rd duke of Guise
Gunpowder Plot 29, 50

## 444 · General Index

Hackett, Helen 106 n2, 109–110, 120 n66, 120 n69, 120 n70, 121 n72, 122 n75, 123 n78, 123 n79, 144, 350
Hakewill, George 30 n162
Hannah, biblical figure 340
Harington, Sir John 7, 12 n60, 14, 36 n18, 39–40, 50, 53, 288, 366, 373 n47; and Constable's works 3, 9, 13, 36, 39–41, 53, 79, 84, 88; scribal habits 39–40, 53, 68, 85, 366–367; works 9 n43, 13–14, 39, 43, 53, 67, 76, 279, 281, 284
Harvey, Gabriel 132, 375 n52
Haslewood, Joseph 133 n6, 147 n2, 371
Hatton, Sir Christopher 373 n47
Hawkins, Thomas 134
Haydock, Richard 299
Hazlitt, William C., editor of Constable 136–137, 296, 324, 351
heaven 63, 95, 119, 121–126, 132, 145 n82, 160, 165, 168, 189, 199, 201, 210, 213, 228–229, 232–235, 237, 240, 246–247, 249–250, 260, 267, 281, 284, 295, 297, 301, 307, 312–313, 331–333, 336–343, 345–346, 348–353, 355, 360–362, 384; ascension to 125–126, 350, 352, 358, 361–362; earth and 168, 190, 228, 233; eternal life in 119, 235, 238, 241, 243–244, 309, 343, 353, 355–356; war in 346
Heidelberg, Germany 4
hell 63, 114, 120, 182, 222, 232–233, 235, 237, 275–276, 320, 322, 336, 340–341
Henri III, king of France 13
Henri IV, king of France, formerly of Navarre 4, 9, 12–14, 18, 20 n97, 22–26, 29–30, 127 n91
Henry, prince of Wales 50, 314
Henry I, 3rd duke of Guise 47
Henry VII, king of England 1 n1
Henry VIII, king of England 1, 11 n50, 278

heraldry 31, 51, 147 n2, 195, 290, 361. *See also* sonnets, conceits and imagery: heraldry
Herbert, George 112, 115, 333
Herbert, Mary, countess of Pembroke 7, 67, 97, 198, 284, 293–294, 298
Herbert, William, earl of Pembroke 67
heretics 6 n29, 13–14, 22 n108, 31, 76, 110, 264, 277, 306, 360
Herrick, Robert 49 n64, 50 n66
Hilliard, Nicholas 10, 287, 298–300
Holinshed, Raphael 297
Holland, Hugh 258
Holy Lance 354
Hotman, Jean, Marquis de Villiers-St-Paul 8–11, 14, 90, 291
Hotman, Jeanne 10 n45, 299
Howard, Henry, earl of Surrey 39, 45, 148 n7, 381 n72
Howard, Katherine 381 n72
Howard, Thomas, duke of Norfolk 381 n72
Howard, Thomas, earl of Surrey 1 n1
Hudson, Thomas 279
Hughey, Ruth W., editor of the Arundel Harington MS 39 n23, 40 n30, 46 n57, 77 n149, 141, 143, 146, 149 n10, 266, 366 n12, 366 n14
Hunnis, William 34, 322, 326–327

Icarus 249–250
iconography 118 n63, 121–122, 333, 337, 349–351, 355
Inns of Court 43; Lincoln's Inn 3; Middle Temple 43
intercession, belief in 105, 113, 116, 122, 128–130, 344, 349, 361
irenicism (irenism) 13–14
Isabella Clara Eugenia, archduchess of Austria 25
Italy 4, 93, 101, 130, 181, 192, 270, 274, 287, 307, 360

Jackson, Leonard 371
Jackson, Richard 49–51, 371
Jacobus de Voragine: *Golden Legend* 343–346, 356, 361
Jairus's daughter, biblical figure 262
James VI and I, king of Scotland and England 4, 9–11, 16, 24–28, 44, 50, 52, 88–89, 91, 97, 108, 124–125, 127, 184, 251, 278–283, 287, 349, 386–387; literary coterie 46, 108, 127, 281; poetic works 43, 66, 108, 278–279; as poet-king 345, 386; religion 23, 25–28, 127; succession to the English throne 12, 25–26, 97, 124, 127; works by others to 108, 298, 375 n52
James the Less, saint 349
Jerome, saint 342, 356
Jesuits 6, 22–23, 25, 27, 50, 52, 130, 337, 358
John the Baptist, saint 94, 128 n94, 233, 335, 340–341, 356
John the Evangelist, saint 96, 331
Jonson, Benjamin 30 n161, 50, 54, 132, 278
Joseph, saint 332

Keir, Henry 4 n16, 90 n163
Kinwelmarsh, Francis 34
Knollys, Lettice, countess of Leicester 298
Knyvet, Sir Henry 296
Kuchar, Gary 114, 117 n55, 119 n64, 124 n81, 144–145, 333, 343, 357
Kyd, Thomas 273

Lanyer, Aemilia 324–325
Lazarus, biblical figure 262
Lechmere, John 30 n161
Lee, Sir Sidney 93 n4, 138–139, 267
Leiden 14, 90
Leighton, Sir William 327
letters: *see* correspondence

Liège, Belgium 30
limbo 99, 120 n70, 230, 336. *See also* purgatory
Linche, Richard 378 n63
Ling, Nicholas 273
Lipsius, Justus 14
L'Isle, Claude de 9
Livy 60
Lodge, Thomas 56, 305, 321
Lok, Anne 112–113
Lok, Henry 66, 113, 298
Lomazzo, Giovanni Paolo 299
London 12, 293, 364; letters sent from 27 n142, 27 n145, 28 n149, 28 n150, 29 n154; Tower of 28–29, 134
López de Gómara, Francisco 289
love: divine 17, 105, 116–117, 122, 227, 239, 244, 323, 331, 334, 350, 354–357; earthly 16, 45, 51, 63, 105–106, 109, 111–112, 115–118, 122–123, 129, 229–230, 238, 244, 248, 320–321, 323, 329, 331, 333, 336, 350, 354–357, 386
Love, Harold 32 n1, 33, 54 n79, 68, 151 n17, 374 n50
Low Countries 5, 12, 15, 24, 90, 276, 283–284, 295, 308, 312–313
loyalism, religious 21 n102
Lyall, Roderick J. 4 n16, 10 n48, 11 n55, 13 n63, 16–17, 41 n33, 88 n158

Macedon 212, 310–311
Malone, Edmond 377–378
Manners, Edward, 3rd earl of Rutland 360
Manners, Sir George, of Haddon Hall 17
Manners, John, 4th earl of Rutland 9
Manners, Katherine 1
Manners, Roger, 5th earl of Rutland 19, 26, 30, 36
Manners, Thomas, 1st earl of Rutland 1, 7 n33, 17, 24 n123

manuscript circulation 8–9, 19, 32, 34, 44 n47, 46–47, 53 n74, 57, 61, 68–69, 76 n148, 91–92, 94, 98, 103, 150, 251, 278, 289, 324–325

manuscripts: holographs (autograph manuscripts) 37, 53, 71, 96, 98 n15, 148–151, 374 n49; provenance 33, 93 n4, 97, 142, 366–367, 377, 379–381

—, physical features of: binding 6, 53, 94, 136, 365–369, 371–373, 380, 382; blanks 39–40, 45, 67, 361, 365–366, 369, 372, 374, 376, 378, 381–383; fair copy 37, 41 n36, 96–97, 99, 102, 374, 381; foliation or pagination 366–367, 369, 372, 374, 376, 380, 382; format 34, 41 n36, 43, 52, 92, 94, 364, 368–369, 372, 379–380, 382; layout (mise-en-page) 141, 143, 145, 151, 365–367, 370, 372–374, 376, 379, 381–382; marginalia 132, 154, 371, 374, 376; scripts (hands) 93–94, 98 n15, 100, 151, 221, 254, 321, 331, 357, 365–367, 369–370, 372–374, 381–382; watermarks 93, 373–374, 380, 382

—, scribal practices in: abbreviations 87, 142, 145, 150–151, 153–154, 366–367, 370, 372, 374, 379, 381–382; annotations and inscriptions 62, 364, 367, 369–371, 375, 377; conscious revision 70–71, 77 n149, 81, 104, 146, 254, 370; punctuation 142, 151, 254, 268, 366–367, 370, 372, 379, 381, 383; spelling 70, 79, 83, 90, 99–100, 135, 138, 141–142, 144–145, 151 n16, 153–154, 250, 273, 278, 287, 290, 306, 317, 320, 330, 355, 374 n50, 379, 382; stints 50, 365 n8, 372

Margaret, saint 96, 113, 116, 119, 237, 345–347

Markham, John 133

Marotti, Arthur F. 10, 17 n84, 18 n86, 32–34, 39 n26, 54–55, 59 n95, 61 n107, 69 n132, 70 n138, 87 n155, 108 n17, 110 n26, 113 n40, 115 n52, 144 n77, 149 n8, 351

Marriot, John 103

Marsh, Narcissus, archbishop of Dublin 364

Marsh's Library, Dublin 5, 34, 48, 364. *See also* Index of Manuscripts

Marston, John 43 n41

martyrs 76, 96, 110, 116, 125–128, 234, 236, 245, 247, 264, 285, 306, 341–342, 344–346, 358, 360–362

Mary, Blessed Virgin 94 n7, 96, 103–104, 118–124, 127–128, 130, 189, 231, 239, 248, 260, 284, 332, 338, 340; beauty of 117 n55, 350, 352; biblical episodes 341; in courtly love 123 n78, 350; Hail Mary 248; immaculate conception 103–104, 122, 126, 130, 231, 337; lineage 332, 338; as mediatrix 122–123, 293, 337, 352; as Queen of Heaven 121–123, 145 n82, 231, 239–240, 247, 284, 337, 349–352; sonnets to 93–94, 102–103, 115, 125, 145, 228, 231, 239–241, 337, 339, 349–352, 362, 381; as Virgo Lactans 123 n80, 351

Mary, mother of James, biblical figure 349

Mary I, queen of England 78, 110, 121, 264, 285, 338

Mary Magdalene, saint 92 n1, 96, 100, 118–119, 125–126, 136, 235, 242, 337, 342–344, 349, 353–357, 381

Mary Stuart, queen of Scots 48, 121, 125–127, 358–361; funeral 126 n87, 360; as martyr 125–126, 358, 361–362; sonnets to 98, 121, 125–126, 128 n95, 148, 285, 359–361; trial and execution 125, 358–360, 362; works about 4, 35, 359–360, 362

Matthew, Sir Tobie 17, 29, 113, 348

May, Steven W. 7–8, 44 n46, 52 n71, 98 n13, 98 n14, 112 n36, 144 n76, 373

Medici, Catherine de 291 n1
Medici, Girolamo Casio de 112 n33
Medici, Lorenzo de 267
meditation 118–119, 329, 344; poetry of 118 n62
metaphysical poetry 114, 117 n59
Michael, archangel 94, 96, 101, 116, 128 n94, 130 n101, 237, 299, 339–340, 346
Middleburgh 8
miscellanies: manuscript 32–36, 39–40, 43, 48–50, 52–54, 69, 76 n148, 87, 94, 98 n14, 102, 133, 138, 141–142, 145–146, 337, 364–365, 367–368, 371–372, 374; printed 34 n10, 45, 67–68, 87, 135 n20, 140, 285, 308, 311
misprints 84, 270–271. *See also* errors, in printed books
Moffet, Thomas 309–310
Molin, Nicolo, ambassador 28 n149
Montemayor, George de 57
Montgomerie, Alexander 4, 90–91, 250–252, 283
Morpheus 289
Moulin, Pierre du 18–19, 26, 36
mourning 8, 116, 208, 245–247, 294–295, 308–309, 312, 329, 359–360
Mozzarello, Giovanni 268
Muses 63, 81, 87, 112, 132, 160, 185, 190–191, 210, 223, 236, 250, 269, 280, 284–287, 307, 309, 312, 323–324, 328, 345, 350, 384
mysticism 113–114, 117, 124, 334, 352–353, 355, 357
mythology, classical 288, 346. *See also* Achilles; Aeneas; Amazons; Apollo; Cupid; Diana; Icarus; Morpheus; Muses; Orpheus; Romulus; Thetis; Venus

Napier, John 331
Nashe, Thomas 43–44, 48 n61

National Art Library, V&A Museum, London: *see* Index of Manuscripts
Nelson, Thomas 275
Neoplatonism 116, 258, 273, 296, 350, 352
Nero 341
Netherlands: *see* Low Countries
Neville, Charles, earl of Westmorland 24
Newman, Thomas, printer 56 n84, 58–59, 69, 255, 322
Norris, Sir John 5 n24, 41 n32
Norton, Thomas 112 n36
Nottinghamshire 3, 31; Worksop 29 n157

Olney, Henry, printer 65, 67
Orpheus 262
Overbury, Sir Thomas 44
Ovid 41, 249, 266
Oxford, university: Christ Church College 365; Corpus Christi College 375–377

Paget, Charles 4, 25 n131
Palgrave, Francis T. 136
Palmer, John 36
papacy 20 n97, 128–129, 341. *See also* popes
Paris 4, 12, 14, 20, 22–25, 30, 102, 291; letters sent from 15 n70, 26 n139, 27 n141, 28 n147, 29 n155
Park, Thomas, editor of Constable 138, 143; *Harleian Miscellany* 47, 134–135, 137, 148 n5, 296, 300, 304, 324, 367–368, 370; *Heliconia* 92, 103 n21, 135
Parker, Tom W.N. 41, 45 n53, 58, 91 n165, 131–132, 253, 260, 262, 311
Parliament of England 20, 27, 360
Parry, Sir Thomas 28 n150
Paul, saint 94, 96, 114, 128 n94, 330, 341–342
Paulet, William 43
Peck, John 49

448 · *General Index*

Peck, William 49 n64
Peerson, Martin 68
penance 100, 118–119, 129, 235, 343–344, 353, 356
Percy, Henry, 4th earl of Northumberland 1 n1
Percy, William 315
Perkins, William 255
Persons, Robert, SJ 22 n111, 23–26
Peter, saint 94, 96, 114, 128 n94, 234, 341–343
Peterborough Cathedral 360
Petowe, Henry 267
Petrarch 33, 107, 123 n77, 132, 177, 225, 258–260, 263, 265, 268–271, 315, 319–320, 326, 338; love for Laura 177, 252, 271; Rime (*Il Canzoniere*) 111, 177, 252–253, 268, 270; turn to religion 111, 123, 320
Petrarchan sonnets 57, 64
Petrarchism 43, 45, 57, 61, 64, 105, 268, 274, 278, 283, 285–286, 306, 315, 324, 346, 350
Philip II, king of Spain 6 n29, 21, 291 n1
Philip III, king of Spain 25
Phillips, Edward 133
Phillips, John 311, 313
Phoebus: *see* Apollo
Pierrepont, Grace 16, 47, 63, 248, 292, 324
Pierrepont, Sir Henry 17
Pilgrimage of Grace 1
Plato 296, 327, 347
Poland 4, 181, 274
Poliziano, Angelo Ambrogini 267
popes 23–25, 27, 348; temporal authority of 128–129, 342
Posonby, William, printer 67
prayer 114, 119, 127–129, 333, 361
Protestants and Protestantism 3–4, 6, 12–15, 17–18, 23, 30, 36–37, 53, 78, 102, 104, 109, 120–121, 123, 125, 128–130, 268, 271, 274–275, 284–285, 336, 350, 359–360, 362
purgatory 120, 182, 276, 336, 361
Puritans 14 n67, 30, 34, 45, 262

Quarles, Francis 50
Questier, Michael C. 15, 17–18, 21 n102, 22 n112, 26 n137, 102

Rainolds, William 15
Raleigh, Sir Walter 7, 34, 39, 43, 50, 54, 64 n116, 260, 288
Raphael, archangel 299
Raphael, painter 299
recusants 26, 129. *See also* Catholics and Catholicism
Reformation, Protestant 4, 109–111, 128, 145, 261, 284, 307, 332, 335, 338, 342, 361
Reshoulde, James 34–35
*Return from Parnassus, The*, anonymous play 133–134
Ribadeneyra, Pedro de, SJ 362
Rich, Penelope 7, 9–10, 27, 44, 51, 56 n83, 62, 71 n146, 88, 97, 194–195, 202, 289, 300, 314–315; courtly intrigues 10–11, 299; daughter 35, 37–38, 46, 55, 59, 65, 88, 143 n70, 201, 297, 314, 367; portraits 10, 287, 298–299; sonnets to 7, 9, 38, 40, 57–58, 79, 88, 138, 159, 195, 248, 252, 254, 259, 289–290, 300, 302, 314, 317, 319–320
Rich, Robert, Baron Rich 10, 290, 314
Richard III, king of England 1 n1
Ricketts, Charles 138
Rimbault, Edward Frances 368
Roberts, James, printer 60, 62, 65, 67, 307, 378
Rollins, Hyder 68, 87 n157, 110 n26, 139, 147 n1
Rome 15, 19–21, 23–25, 27 n141, 60,

129, 341–342; St Peter's Basilica 342; Venerable English College 20
Romulus 342
Ronsard, Pierre de 132, 250, 265, 267, 270, 301
Rouen 18 n87, 22 n107
Rowlands, Samuel 375 n52
Russell, Anne, countess of Warwick 10, 37, 47, 81, 87, 190, 285, 325–326
Rutland, earls of 1, 3–4, 7 n33, 9, 16–17, 19, 24 n123, 26, 30, 36, 360. *See also* Manners, Edward; Manners, John; Manners, Roger; Manners, Thomas

sacraments: *see* baptism; Eucharist; penance
St Bartholomew's Day Massacre 291
saints 94, 96, 114, 116, 118, 124–126, 128, 130, 261, 268, 344–345, 349–350, 356, 362. *See also* Anne; Augustine; Bernard; Bonaventure; Catherine of Alexandria; Cecilia; Colette of Corbie; Edith of Wilton; Francis of Assisi; George; James the Less; Jerome; John the Baptist; John the Evangelist; Joseph; Margaret; Mary, Blessed Virgin; Mary Magdalene; Paul; Peter; Stephen
salvation 15, 17, 23, 105–106, 115, 128–130
Samuel, biblical figure 340–341
Sander, Nicholas 129
Saul, biblical figure 341
Scots language 91, 251, 278
Scott, Janet 62 n111, 107 n7, 139, 255, 257, 269, 316
scribes 34, 36–37, 39–40, 49, 69, 71, 81, 83–88, 93–94, 96, 99–101, 150–153, 254, 268, 272, 306, 331, 353, 365–367, 369–370, 372–374, 381–383. *See also* manuscripts, scribal practices in
secular love: *see* love: earthly

Segar, Sir William 28
Seneca, Lucius Annaeus 263, 309
seraphim 229, 239, 334, 349. *See also* angels
Shakespeare, William 131–132; *Hamlet* 132 n3; *The Rape of Lucrece* 266; *Richard II* 274; *Romeo and Juliet* 255, 261, 268; Sonnets 44, 139, 251, 261, 263, 265, 270, 272–273, 317, 328, 371; *Titus Andronicus* 263; *The Two Gentlemen of Verona* 268; *Venus and Adonis* 266, 378 n63
Shakespearean sonnet 64, 107
Shell, Alison 21 n102, 112 n34, 121–122, 126, 144, 284–285, 349
Sheridan, William 364
Sidney, Mary: *see* Herbert, Mary
Sidney, Sir Philip 3, 16, 40, 46, 57 n88, 67, 69 n136, 90 n163, 107, 131–132, 143, 278, 283, 289, 291, 293, 295, 298, 307–308, 360, 365, 373 n47; circulation of works 8, 34, 39–40, 62, 69–70; death 7–8, 37, 40, 46, 144, 293, 295, 308–309, 312–313; elegies on 7–8, 51, 61 n107, 295, 308–313; family 7–8, 16, 293, 373 n46; religion 14
—, works: *An apologie for poetrie* 67, 85, 307; *Arcadia* 52 n70, 262, 266, 301, 304; *Astrophil and Stella* 8–9, 33, 40, 44, 56, 58–61, 69, 105, 107, 109 n18, 114, 249–250, 252, 255, 259–260, 264, 267, 269, 271–275, 289–291, 293–294, 300, 302–304, 311, 313–316, 318, 321–323, 325, 328–329; *Certain Sonnets* 44, 61, 112, 137–138, 148
Sidney, Robert 7
Silingardi, Gasparo, apostolic nuncio 24–25
Simmes, Valentine, printer 68
sin 79, 104, 119–120, 126, 130, 173, 182, 189, 219, 242–244, 247, 275, 277, 285, 319, 322, 335–339, 343–344, 353, 355, 359, 361

Singer, Samuel Weller, editor of Constable 135–136, 377
Smith, Richard, Catholic priest 30 n161
Smith, Richard, publisher 58–62, 65, 328, 376, 378
sonnet form 103, 105–130
sonnets: alexandrine 86, 107, 114, 258, 270, 291, 312; metre 107, 114; religious 103, 105–106, 111–115, 117–118, 130, 142, 144, 147 n2, 150. *See also* Constable, Henry, individual works: *Spiritual Sonnets*
—, conceits and imagery 105, 139; anacreontic 42, 204–205, 301, 303; ascent 117, 160, 165, 185, 229, 236, 241, 258, 280, 352; astrology 109, 201, 214, 297, 314; birds 176, 185, 208, 214, 223, 229, 269–270, 305, 314, 325, 333; blazon 166, 169, 174, 188, 195, 265–266, 290; blood 162–163, 174, 183, 189, 196, 224, 230, 245–247, 253, 266, 277, 285, 301, 335, 359–362; blushing 171, 174, 263, 265–266, 359; breast 261, 304; charity 204–205, 302–303; concerned friend 107, 178, 271; crown and sceptre 184, 188–189, 231, 236, 247, 278, 362; cruel fair 120, 182, 208, 215, 275, 305, 315; deadly sins 38, 78, 108, 160, 171–174, 182–183, 219–220, 232, 263–264, 275, 277, 319–320, 339; death 163, 167, 169–170, 175, 199, 209, 211–214, 217–218, 224, 295, 306, 309, 315, 318; desert 235, 243, 343, 356; dove 229, 333; dragon 116, 232, 237, 339–340, 345–347; exile 217–218, 226, 318, 328, 336; eyes 159–162, 165–166, 170, 172, 174, 179, 181–182, 186, 188–191, 197–199, 202, 217–220, 235, 240, 242, 245, 249, 251–252, 258–259, 267, 274–275, 282, 286, 294–295, 300, 317, 319–320; fame 162, 172–173, 179, 181, 185, 190, 193–194, 198, 203, 210, 213, 223, 225, 293, 307–308, 312–313, 324; fire 38, 77, 157, 160–162, 165, 173, 182, 187, 189, 196, 203, 217, 219–220, 222, 229–230, 235, 250, 252–253, 258, 264, 275, 285, 292, 301, 317, 320–322, 334, 336; flight 160, 165, 176, 185, 223, 229, 249, 256, 270, 281, 324, 334; folly 111, 157, 215–216, 222, 248, 321–322; garden 38, 88, 174, 225, 265, 267, 326; gold 38, 79, 163, 170, 176, 194–195, 219, 254, 269, 289, 291, 319; hands 166, 169, 174–176, 184, 188, 193, 196–197, 236, 247, 259, 261, 288; heart 159, 163, 165, 172–174, 178, 187–188, 196–197, 200–201, 203, 206, 208–209, 213, 216–217, 219–220, 222, 235, 239, 241–243, 251, 255–257, 264 265, 293, 301, 304–305, 317, 319, 336, 354; heraldry 51, 195, 290; hunting 38, 109, 176, 269; ice 187; images, miracles, and relics 109–110, 164, 169, 175, 177, 227, 256, 261, 268, 271, 331; immortality 109, 160, 179, 192, 213, 313, 329; imprisonment 170, 176, 197, 200, 209, 230, 232, 237, 269, 292, 296, 306, 340, 347; ink 183, 226, 245, 277, 328, 359; jewels 202, 300; lady as a goddess or saint 42, 76, 79, 109–110, 160, 165, 169, 171, 175, 177–179, 188, 190–192, 219–220, 223 n1, 226, 250, 258, 270, 272, 278, 283, 285–286, 288, 292, 319, 324–325, 329; lady as a queen 170, 188–189, 201, 262, 283, 288, 298; lamb 230, 233, 245, 335, 341; lips 166, 169, 174, 188, 202, 205, 218, 259, 261, 271, 303, 318; mirror 161, 221, 320–321; murder 161, 167, 170, 196, 199, 201, 217, 219–220, 224, 230, 251, 295, 319; navigation 109, 163, 186, 194, 253, 289; night 165, 179–180, 182, 209, 219, 222, 244, 246, 272–273, 360; painting 161, 191, 202,

216, 221, 226, 252, 256, 287, 298, 321, 328; pelican 162, 253; Phoenix 162, 214, 223, 252–253, 314, 324; punishment or execution 38, 42, 76–77, 110–111, 120, 173, 183, 189, 209, 217–220, 232, 246, 264, 277, 285, 306, 317–319, 340, 360–361; revenge 178, 196, 199, 207, 295, 305; sacrifice 159, 184, 186, 211, 230, 245, 282, 308, 335; sea 181, 186–187, 235, 281; sickness 207, 224, 305; sighs 100, 116, 159, 168, 179, 186, 203, 222, 227, 239, 249, 261, 272, 281–282, 301, 320, 322, 331, 349; singing and music 168–169, 177, 184, 194, 210–211, 228, 236, 246–247, 261, 279, 307, 332, 361; star 171, 190–191, 195, 214, 246, 263, 286, 290, 314; storm 159, 249; sun 42, 77, 116, 165, 171–172, 174, 177, 179–180, 182, 186, 199–200, 249, 257, 263, 267, 271–272, 282–283; tears 95, 116, 120, 161, 174, 181, 186, 196, 201, 203, 206, 211, 217, 219–220, 226, 235, 242, 245, 252, 267, 274, 281, 292, 301, 304, 308–309, 317, 320, 328–329, 343, 358–359; throne 124, 184, 234, 239, 247, 279, 311, 342, 350; tomb 230, 236, 246, 336, 345, 359; tongue 172–173, 181, 190, 193, 198, 213, 224, 294; torments 110, 120, 175, 182, 187, 203, 207, 209, 215, 218, 268, 276, 285, 300, 305–306, 315, 320, 322; virginity 237, 242, 347, 355, 357; virtues 174, 183, 190, 193, 212–213, 235, 287, 311–312, 327, 344; warfare and conquest 197, 201, 232, 237, 292, 298, 339, 346; witchcraft 84, 110, 164, 254–256, 341; writing 108–109, 157, 159, 166, 172–173, 177, 179, 183–184, 186, 192–194, 210, 216, 221–223, 226, 236, 246, 259, 263–264, 270, 276–281, 287–289, 307, 320–321, 329, 359, 361. *See also* angels; Cupid; God; heaven; love; martyrs; Muses; sin

sonnet sequences 46 n55, 60, 69, 262, 268; collections qualifying as 33, 37, 45, 60, 92, 94, 144, 359; Constable's 33, 38, 40–41, 46–48, 57, 67, 78–79, 86, 88 n158, 94, 96, 98, 102, 105, 109, 111, 114, 116–117, 119, 121, 125–130, 132, 135, 137 n33, 143 n70, 148–150, 248–363 *passim*, 370, 380; by other poets 40 n31, 107 n7, 112, 114; popularity of 60, 62. *See also* Constable, Henry, individual works: secular sonnets; Constable, Henry, individual works: *Spiritual Sonnets*
Southwell, Robert, SJ 6, 112–113, 118 n63, 253, 335, 340, 360, 362
Spain 29, 52, 199, 295; English symphatisers of 24, 26; financial support of English Catholics 24; in the Low Countries 6, 283
Speght, Thomas 132
Spencer, Elizabeth, Baroness Hunsdon 381
Spenser, Edmund 8, 39, 56, 67, 131–132, 375 n52; *Amoretti* 262, 264–265, 268–269, 272, 282, 293–294, 300–301, 318–319, 325, 329; "Astrophel" 295, 309; *Fowre Hymnes* 323, 330, 352
Spenserian sonnet 64
Stafford, Sir Edward 4
Stafford, Joyce 4 n17
Staffordshire 1 n1
Standen, Sir Anthony 28
Stanford, Henry 98
Stanley, Sir William 6–7, 35, 52, 128 n96, 276, 374
Stationers' Register 12, 56, 59–60, 65, 67
Stearne, John, bishop of Clogher 364
stemmata, textual 49, 75–86, 142, 146, 149, 152, 320
Stephen, saint 341, 362
Stillingfleet, Edward 364

Stuart, Arbella 10–11, 16, 47, 116, 138, 193, 223, 287–288, 292, 296, 323–324, 345
Sylvester, Josuah 313, 375 n52
Symonds, Jean 23

Talbot, Elizabeth, countess of Shrewsbury (Bess of Hardwick) 7 n33, 292
Talbot, Frances 292
Talbot, George, earl of Shrewsbury 7 n33
Talbot, Gilbert, earl of Shrewsbury 7 n33, 10, 28–29, 46, 284, 292
Talbot, Grace 7 n33, 17 n79
Talbot, Mary, countess of Shrewsbury 7 n33, 10–11, 17, 29, 46, 121, 284–285, 287, 292–293
Talbot-Cavendish family 7, 10, 17, 248
Tasso, Torquato 112 n33, 308, 333
Taylor, John 43
tears: literature of 118, 342–343, 354, 358–359; vale of 118, 347
Téligny, Charles de 291–292
Thetis 180, 273
Thomas Aquinas 329–331, 334, 336, 339, 352
Thornton, Robert 364–365
Thornton, Thomas 365
Thorpe, Thomas 371
Throckmorton, Thomas 1, 4, 276
Todd, Henry John 134, 367–368
Todd MS: *see* Index of Manuscripts: London, The National Art Library, V&A Museum, MS Dyce 44
Tofte, Robert 62, 280
toleration, of religion 13, 21–23, 26, 124
Tollemache, Sir Lionel, 1st Baronet of Helmingham 52
Tottel, Richard 45 n54
Treaty of London (1604) 29 n154
triads, sonnets organised in 96, 122, 125–126, 312, 329, 332, 335, 337, 342, 349, 351, 353, 355, 357–358, 361
Trinity, Holy 93–94, 96, 117, 122, 124 n81, 231, 329–333, 335, 338, 351. *See also* Christ, Jesus; God, the Father; God, the Holy Ghost
Triphook, Robert 135 n22
Tudor, Margaret 11 n50, 278
Turner, Robert, Catholic priest 359
Twyne, Brian 375
Twyne, Thomas 375 n54
Tyrrell, Anthony 18 n88, 19 n90

Urban VIII, pope 359–360

Varchi, Benedetto 62 n110
variants 37, 49, 68–71, 76–77, 81, 83, 85–86, 99–100, 104, 142–144, 149 n11, 152–154, 250–252, 254–257, 262, 267–271, 273, 277, 280, 282–283, 286, 289–291, 298, 302, 305, 308, 315 316, 318–319, 321–322, 338–339, 353–354, 371, 378–379; accidental 70, 99, 143, 149–151, 379; authorial 86, 99, 282, 320; verbal (substantive) 70–71, 84, 99, 101, 149, 153–154. *See also* Constable, Henry, works: revision of texts; errors; manuscripts, scribal practices in
Vavasour, Anne 34 n10
Venus 112, 171, 197, 263, 297, 303, 343
Vere, Edward de, 17th earl of Oxford 34, 39, 44
Verstegan, Richard 350, 362

Walpole, Henry 358
Walsingham, Frances 46, 295
Walsingham, Sir Francis 3–4, 16, 52, 274, 291, 295, 359
Warton, Thomas 134, 147 n1
Watson, Andrew G. 379
Watson, Thomas 132, 272, 281, 300, 318, 323
Wentworth, Peter 35 n14
Westminster Abbey, London 360
Whetstone, George 295, 309–310, 312–313

White, John, bishop of Winchester 338
Whitney, Geffrey 253
Wickes, George 140, 146; on Constable's biography 3 n6, 3 n9, 11–12, 15 n70, 20 n94, 22 n106, 23 n114, 24 n121, 31 n164; on Constable's works 5 n23, 13 n63, 22 n107, 45–46, 58, 62, 93 n4, 112 n33, 114–115, 140, 148 n4, 148 n6, 333, 346
Wilcox, Helen 102 n17, 106 n4, 112–113, 130, 145, 333, 357
Williams (now Loffman), Claire B., editor of the Todd MS 145; on the compilation 43–45, 49, 81, 146 n87, 368–370; on Constable 48 n60, 57 n87, 71–72, 77 n149, 146, 149 n10, 261, 269, 271, 291–292, 295–296, 318–319, 322, 324, 378 n61
Williams, Sir Roger 18
William the Silent, prince of Orange 283, 291
Willmott, Robert A. 136
Wilton, Edward 20 n98

Windsor Castle, Windsor 97
witchcraft 84, 109–110, 164, 254–256
Wither, George 50
Wolfe, John, printer 12
Wood, Anthony à 133
Wood, William, publisher 60, 65, 376 n57
worldly love: *see* love: earthly
Woudhuysen, Henry R. 8, 32 n1, 34 n8, 39 n25, 40 n29, 40 n31, 52 n70, 61–62, 67 n123, 69 n133, 76 n148, 144 n76, 144 n78, 365, 373 n46, 373 n47
Wright, Thomas 258
Wroth, Mary 254
Wyatt, Sir Thomas 39, 45, 253, 315

Yong, Bartholomew 57
York, Rowland 6, 35
Yorkshire 1, 3 n10, 36 n17, 364–365

Zutphen 6, 8 n37, 295